Social Psychology

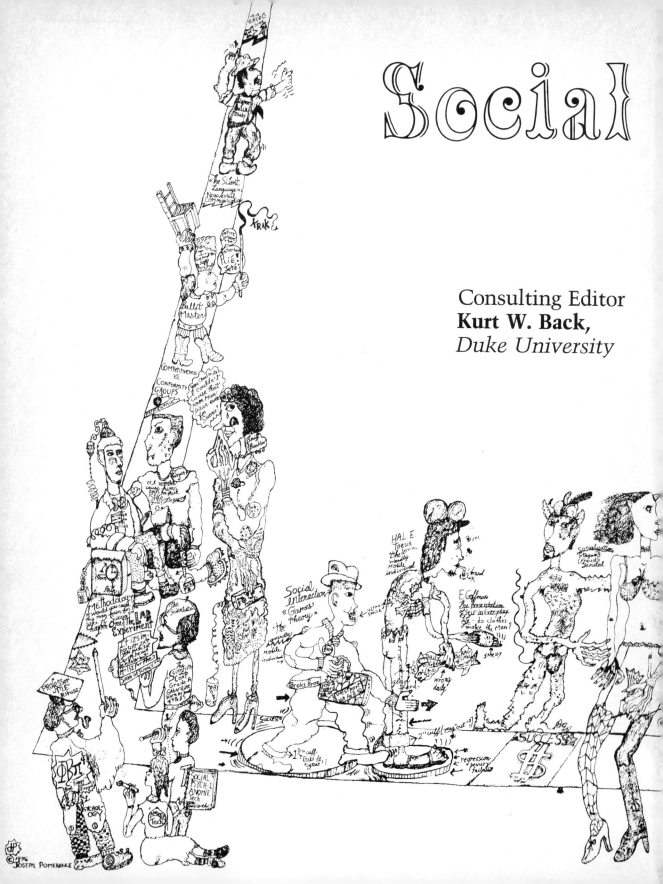

Social

Consulting Editor
Kurt W. Back,
Duke University

Psychology

The editors would like to thank all those
who contributed to the making of this book:

Stephen L. Klineberg, *Rice University,*
  for chapter 2 on socialization;

George L. Maddox, *Duke University,* and
Linda Breytspraak, *Duke University,*
  for feature material on adult socialization
  in chapter 2 on socialization;

William A. Gamson, *University of Michigan,*
  for chapter 3 on social interaction;

Robert A. Scott, *Princeton University,*
  for chapter 6 on deviance;

Lester W. Milbrath, *State University of New York at Buffalo,*
  for feature material on the way people relate to politics
  in chapter 7 on attitudes;

Joshua A. Fishman, *Yeshiva University,*
  for material on the sociology of language,
  in chapter 9 on language and communication;

Kenneth J. Gergen, *Swarthmore College,*
  for chapter 10 on perception;

Daniel Katz, *University of Michigan,*
  for material on power
  in chapter 11 on motives;

David C. Glass, *University of Texas,* and
Karen M. Smith, *University of Illinois,*
  for chapter 12 on stress.

John Wiley & Sons, Inc.
New York ● London ● Sydney ● Toronto

A LEOGRYPH BOOK

Project editor	Rodie Siegler
Editors	Ruth Zaslavsky
	Daniel Liberatore
Design	Sheila Lynch
Production	Eileen Max
Composition	David E. Seham Associates, Inc.
Illustrations	Joseph Pomerance
Photography by	Mark Sherman

Library of Congress Catalog main entry:
HM 251. S6715   301.1   76-30835
ISBN: 0-471-03983-7

Printed in the United States of America.

10 9 8 7 6 5 4 3 2 1

Contents

Preface

Purpose

This book is designed for the introductory course in social psychology at the college level. The aim of the book is to give the student a comprehensive overview of the core concepts of the discipline within the context of one or more relevant theories. These concepts include attitudes and attitude change, and the topics centering around the subject of groups—social interaction and group cohesion. Social interaction, for example, is discussed from the point of view of Goffman's self-presentation perspective, Homans's social exchange theory, the T-group perspective, and ethnomethodology. Thus, rather than presenting a number of theories irrespective of subject matter, the book has viewed social psychological concepts from a variety of theoretical perspectives.

In addition, a number of well-known social psychologists have contributed material on research topics in which they have special expertise: for example, David Glass on stress associated with heart disease as well as stress caused by

noise and other environmental pollutants; Joshua Fishman on the usage of language by different groups in the same political territory; and Stephen Klineberg on socialization.

Social psychology has had traditional concerns dating from its inception as a discipline. However, as the interests of particular researchers have broadened, new subject areas have been included in the field. In this text we have included a number of areas not usually approached from a social psychological orientation. Deviance, for example, has been presented in the labeling perspective, as an example of the interaction between the dominant society and an individual. The stress effects of the social and physical environment on the individual is another area. Language and nonverbal communication—the manner in which members of a social group share the means of communication—is still another example in which the perspective of the individual in the social context is applied outside of traditional social psychological concerns. The purpose of this book, then, is to present to students not only the customary topics but also some unusual subject matter studied by social psychologists that incorporates and illuminates the social psychological perspective.

Organization of the book

The book is composed of twelve chapters organized roughly from the individual to the group, to communication and movement within groups. The first chapter maps out the territory of the discipline, examines the research methods of the social sciences and social psychology in particular, and explores some of the ethical implications of research using human subjects.

Chapter 2 discusses human development from four theoretical perspectives, with an introductory section that examines the relationship of innate and acquired behavior. Chapter 3 offers four theoretical views of social interaction. Chapter 4 is an examination of group cohesion and group structure.

In chapter 5 the influence of group members on the individual is discussed, including the nature of mobs and mob behavior. The individual who is labeled deviant by the officials charged with social control is examined in chapter 6, as well as the consequences of labeling for such individuals.

Chapters 7 and 8 are concerned with attitudes and attitude change, the development of attitudes, especially those prejudicial to another group, and the processes by which an individual's attitudes change or are changed by others.

Language and communication are discussed in chapter 9, including nonverbal communication and the development of language. In chapter 10 the perception of self from outside cues is examined, as well as the ambiguity involved in the perception of others from insufficient evidence.

Chapter 11 is concerned with motives—the impulses that activate the behavior of individuals. These include aggression, affiliation, attraction, altruism, and power. The last chapter is concerned with stress caused both by living in society and by uncontrollable noxious elements in the environment.

Outstanding features

Readability. An introductory textbook carries the burden of conveying not only the important theoretical concepts in a discipline and the research studies that support these concepts, but the unique orientation of practicing members of that discipline. Social psychology is not merely an organized collection of studies, theories, and concepts, but more important, a particular way of viewing reality. In order to communicate the social psychological perspective to the introductory student, a text must be readable and logical as well. This book has been written with care to interest and inform the student. The organization of each chapter is designed to impart to the student a sense of what a researcher thinks and does in his work. The studies are presented in a fashion to highlight the scientific logic which motivated the investigator. Difficult concepts are explained and illustrated with examples from the literature and from life.

Box features. Each chapter includes page-length features in which an example of a concept presented in the chapter is developed more fully. In some cases a literary example is used; sometimes the relevant research is described in greater detail; or an event from contemporary life is introduced. For example, one box feature raises the issue of brainwashing in the Patricia Hearst case to illustrate the extremes of attitude change.

Summaries and bibliographies. At the end of each chapter there is a summary containing a synopsis of the major topics presented. This is then followed by a bibliography listing references cited in the chapter. The bibliographic style prescribed by the American Psychological Association has been used throughout.

Endmatter. The book contains a glossary of the important terms and concepts introduced in the text. Each term or concept is presented, as far as possible, in a slightly different manner from that of its original appearance. This offers the student another opportunity to absorb the meaning and context of some of the more difficult terms.

A full index containing both authors and concepts follows the glossary.

Social Psychology

Social Psychology Today

People need other people—to learn from them, to hurt them, to help them, to dominate them, and just to be with them. Thus, a basic dimension of social interaction is movement toward and away from other people. In many respects this movement toward and away from others can be considered the core assumption of social psychology. People and animals need other people and animals, and as a consequence, it is of little value to examine the behavior of a single organism in isolation. On those occasions when social psychologists do look at the behavior of individual organisms, the presence of others is generally assumed. This presence operates by means of psychological processes such as memory and symbolization, and social products such as norms, attitudes, and language. Gordon Allport says that:

With few exceptions, social psychologists regard their discipline as *an attempt to understand and explain how the thought, feeling, and behavior of individuals are influenced by the actual, imagined, or implied presence of other human beings.* The term "implied presence" refers to the many activities the individual carries out because of his position (role) in a complex social structure and his membership in a cultural group (1968, p. 3).

In this first chapter we shall not only describe the subject matter of social psychology but outline the different research methods that social scientists, and social psychologists in particular, use to study this subject matter. The

methodology of social psychology is not only a way of doing but a way of thinking. Therefore, we shall outline the logic of social research as well as the particular strategies employed.

2 What Is Social Psychology?

Otto Klineberg in a 1940 textbook defined social psychology as "the scientific study of the behavior of the individual related to other individuals. It is concerned with the individual in a group situation." This is a serviceable definition. It describes a boundary around the subject, marks it off from other material, and places a few items in the field thus delineated, such as "individuals" and "groups." However, for those who are not familiar with the territory, such a definition does not map out the landscape. It would not, for example, allow us to identify a topic as social psychological even if we were acquainted with many of the particulars.

The subject matter of a science can often be better approached by learning what questions are asked by those in the field. What are the areas that appear problematical and what areas are taken for granted and accepted without questioning? A classic problem that has interested social psychologists is racial discrimination and racial prejudice.

Let us start our discussion by asking how people who have not been trained in social psychology regard racial prejudice. The layman, the man or woman in the street, would regard racial prejudice as deplorable. Generally speaking, few Americans are willing to condemn any group outright. Americans were shocked and horrified by the concentration camps of Nazi Germany and fought in a world war to prevent the Germans from imposing their discriminatory practices on other nations. However, even at the time the Nazis were rounding up Jews and gypsies, confining them in camps, and then exterminating them in gas ovens, Americans were lynching blacks, placing quotas on the college admission of Jews, and treating American Indians as conquered peoples by confiscating their lands and denying them full citizenship. After war was declared on Japan and Germany, Americans themselves rounded up American citizens of Japanese ancestry, placed them in camps, and confiscated their property.

Questions asked in the social sciences

What kinds of questions do members of various disciplines in the social sciences ask in regard to such contradictions? A social historian investigating prejudice in America might start by examining the origins of prejudice against various ethnic groups. He might document the arrival of the millions of immigrants in the late nineteenth and early twentieth centuries and describe the living conditions of the immigrants in the unfamiliar urban environment. He might show how each group in turn was described as ignorant, dirty, and prone to drunkenness, and how each provided the labor for the dirty work of building the new nation. For example, the Irish and the Chinese laid track for the railroads to the Pacific, the Italians built roads and buildings, the Jews sewed clothes and established the garment industry.

A political historian studying American history might investigate prejudice against blacks by delving into the causes of the Civil War. He might ask questions about slavery, in which one group was under the complete control of another. He might look for the political consequences which stemmed from the right of individuals descended from Europeans to own the descendants of people from Africa. Black historians have been interested in raising questions concerning the willingness of blacks to endure their condition. Did the slaves not revolt? How were revolts put down or prevented? Under what conditions did the slaves live? What were their skills and what were their contributions to the country to which they had been brought against their will? Other American historians, interested in the conquest of the west, have asked what the effect of an unsettled territory was on a developing nation, labeling and documenting the wars with the indigenous population as a part of the trek west.

While historians inquire about the kinds of different groups that live in the United States, how they get here, and what has been their fate in the new land, political scientists ask about the relative power of the different groups. How do different groups exercise their right to vote? What power does this give them in respect to others? Is power held by the few, or do the many different ethnic, racial, as well as all kinds of interest groups, enter into a competition for power in which no group can attain any large degree of control over any other? Another kind of social scientist—the political economist—might ask, who profits when there is enmity between groups? Does the fanning of racial prejudice between different groups mask some of the more serious questions of economic control?

An anthropologist would look at racial prejudice from still another perspective. Anthropologists have been particularly interested in small-scale societies, the very groups that have become the targets of racial discrimination as industrialized nations have taken over the territories occupied by these societies. The culture of these groups, the manner in which they live, relate to each other, and make their living has been the classic concern of anthropologists. In doing this work, most anthropologists have had a larger purpose in mind; they have wanted to make clear to the members of industrialized societies the nature of these peoples—how they differ and how they are similar—in order to increase among so-called civilized people the tolerance for racial and cultural differences. Anthropologists have, in fact, documented intolerance for other people's differences among most of the peoples of the world.

As we close in on psychology and sociology, we are getting nearer to the concerns of social psychology. Psychology is the study of individual behavior. Thus, psychologists ask the question, how do prejudice and discrimination affect an individual who is a member of a target group? How does such a person feel about himself and about other members of his own group? Psychologists have documented self-hate and shame as well as fierce pride and a strong sense of group identity. Psychoanalysts have studied the dreams of minority-group members in order to discover the effect of racial prejudice on an individual.

Sociologists have studied discrimination itself, inquiring into its relevance. In perhaps the best-known of all studies on discrimination, a team of sociologists under the direction of the Swedish scholar Gunnar Myrdal (1942) studied discrimination against black Americans in social institutions in American society—education, employment, housing, medical care, and so forth. In every case they documented the inferior treatment received by the black, compared to his white counterpart.

Questions asked in social psychology

For social psychologists, racial prejudice has been a classic concern. What kinds of questions do they ask? Social psychologists are interested primarily in the prejudiced person. What makes one person a bearer of prejudice and another either friendly or neutral? How does an individual learn prejudice? Is racial prejudice a singular attitude or do we find a constellation of attitudes which mark the prejudiced person? Do prejudiced people hate only one group or does their prejudice extend to most target groups?

Social psychologists are interested in the process by which a person can be brought to change his attitudes toward others. What kinds of messages and what characteristics of a communicator are most likely to change attitudes? Under what circumstances are people more easily influenced? What are the characteristics of people who can be more easily persuaded? Is a person who works and lives with prejudiced people more likely to be prejudiced? Does contact with the targets of prejudice increase the original prejudice or decrease it? Under what conditions does it do so?

In short, the social psychologist looks at the individual as he affects, and is affected by, the members of society with whom he interacts. He examines that area in which the individual and the group intersect. In a culture like that of the United States in which the individual is regarded as unique, free, a creature of his own making, responsible for his own fate, the social psychologist takes a closer look. He makes observations concerning one individual's perception of another person. And then he studies the process by which one's perceptions of another's reactions to him affect the way the perceiver views himself. In short, social psychologists study the ways in which an individual is not unique and free, but molded and shaped by the people around him.

Social psychologists also study the social influences that bring about attitude change. One early researcher, for example, studied the political attitudes of Bennington College students who entered the school sharing the conservative attitudes of their parents. When the students graduated four years later, many had rejected the political attitudes of their parents and had adopted the liberal ideas prevalent at Bennington (Newcomb, 1943). Another famous experiment offers an explanation of why people seek one another out in moments of stress or fear (Schachter, 1959). In a third study, a researcher demonstrates that the unanimous opinion of members of a group may force a subject to make a response that belies the evidence of his own senses (Asch, 1951). Although social psychologists may work with rats and even cockroaches (Zajonc, Heingartner, and Herman, 1969), the relevance of research in social psychology always points to human behavior, and especially the behavior of individuals in relation to other people, whether they are in groups or alone.

Thus, the vantage point of the social psychologist is different from that of the historian, the political scientist, the anthropologist, the psychologist, and the sociologist. Yet, all of these disciplines are not mutually exclusive, just as the natual sciences are not self-contained, closed systems. Social psychology, sociology, anthropology, and the rest are, after all, social sciences which share a common interest—the individual and his society. It should not be surprising, then, that there are areas of overlap. Indeed, a certain amount of borrowing—of ideas, of methodologies—is constantly going on among them. One noted social psychologist, Muzafer Sherif, makes this point quite well:

What is relevant in a social situation is not solely a social-psychological problem. There are components in a social situation . . . whose study requires more than the social psychologist's wares. Such components include institutionalized power differentials among participants, role expectations, culturally defined systems of exchange, technological facilities, value orientations, and normative regulation of the interaction process. In other words, any social situation includes components that are subject matters for social scientists—sociologists, political scientists, anthropologists, etc. If we are to grasp the nature and the scope of factors in social situations, we have to borrow from these related social sciences (1970, pp. 146–147).

Scientific Method in Social Psychology

How does the social psychologist go about the study of "the behavior of the individual in a group situation"? In many ways, the average woman or man interacting, manipulating, perceiving, and planning future activities in a world full of people must function as a social psychologist. She observes, makes hypotheses, and builds theories. She bases her own behavior on her predictions of the behaviors of others. Built into her predictions are common sense, folk wisdom, and perhaps some of the findings that have filtered down into the nonscientific world from the research activities of the behavioral scientists. On what basis can we assert that the findings and predictions of the social psychologist have a greater chance of coming closer to the truth than those of the average person?

The bases of knowledge

Charles Peirce, the American philosopher, said there were four methods of knowing. The first is the method of authority; the fact that a respected source asserts a proposition to be true is cause enough to believe it to be true. Today there are many authorities and few wise men. One can believe in the Bible, or the Encyclopedia Britannica, the Chief Justice of the Supreme Court, a Nobel Prize winner, or one's father. But whom do we consult to find out which authorities to trust?

Peirce's second method of knowing is the method of tenacity: explanations of phenomena that have been believed for a long time acquire authority by means of their longevity. Many people believe that rural areas are places of innocence and purity and cities are sources of sin and corruption, beliefs that go back to the time of the first cities in history. How much truth is there in such propositions? Does the tenacity of an idea constitute a proof of its value?

Third, an *a priori* proposition is believed to be true: that is, a proposition that is self-evident is true. For example, any system of thought must be based on primary propositions that are assumed to be true as a starting point for the system. Such propositions in social psychology as that a human being is a social animal, that a human being has psychological needs would be *a priori* propositions. And finally, of course, the methods of science constitute a means of knowing.

Today scientific method is held in such high repute that to say a proposition is scientific is to convey a strong sense of authority—an authority more powerful for most people in industrialized societies than the church or the government. However, the basis for trust in the findings of science rests not on science as a source of authority but on the methods of scientific research. These alone form the basis for belief in the assertions put forth in the name of science.

Scientific method rests on reasoning and on the objectivity of its practitioners. Robert Merton (1973) sees science as an institution with the goal of extending that area of human knowledge which has been certified by the best efforts of scientists to be true. Supporting science is a set of norms—moral imperatives—adhered to by all scientists: "The mores of science . . . are bind- ing [on a scientist] not only because they are procedurally efficient, but be- cause they are right and good" (p. 268). Thus, science can be regarded as a self-correcting institution maintained by its members according to an ethos internalized by each scientist. The ethos of modern science, according to Mer- ton, comprises four elements: universalism, communism, disinterestedness, and organized skepticism. Each contributes to the objective stance of the sci- entist.

Universalism.   Universalism is a scientific norm which admits the contribu- tions of any scientist regardless of his or her nationality, race, or creed. The institution of science is democratic. When, in Germany under the Nazis, many scientists, because of their "racial" origin, were denied the right to pursue their careers, the norm of universalism was violated. For Germany the result was the loss of many of the leading scientists of the day, and the decline of science in Germany. For the rest of the scientific world, this Nazi policy served to reinforce the belief that "science must not suffer itself to become the hand- maiden of theology, economy, or state" (Merton, 1973, p. 260).

Communism.   The second integral element of the scientific ethos is com- munism: the common ownership of scientific findings. Scientific knowledge is held to be the product of social collaboration and thus is assigned to the community. The personal incentive for the scientist is restricted to being the first to discover or publish a scientific truth; he may not gain any direct mate- rial benefit as a result of his findings. This norm, therefore, insures control over a wide range of self-aggrandizing motives on the part of individual scien- tists.

   Disinterestedness makes possible the virtual absence of fraud in the scien- tific enterprise. Merton is quick to point out that the honesty of scientists cannot be attributed to a greater moral integrity on the part of scientists over nonscientists. Built into the scientific method are checks by scientific peers. Thus, peer criticism prevents a faulty idea or a spurious conclusion from cir- culating as a scientific truth. Indeed, the proliferation of scientific journals and the seemingly obscure jargon from which no scientific enterprise seems free are integral to the system whereby fellow scientists criticize published work. Such work is subject to the test of respect or neglect. Respected work becomes the basis for future lines of inquiry, finds a place in textbooks and lectures, and becomes a part of a discipline. It is for this reason that science must be public. Scientists in every area must be free to publish and to have access to the work of their colleagues in order to evaluate and criticize theory and research in their own areas of expertise.

Organized skepticism. Merton says that "the scientific investigator does not preserve the cleavage between the sacred and the profane" (p. 277). The scientist, in his attitude toward reality, must follow logic and the facts, no matter into what preserves of received knowledge they lead him. Conflict with other institutions may well result, but the norm of organized skepticism must be allowed to prevail.

In addition to Merton's account of the ethos of scientific inquiry, which insures objectivity on the part of the scientist, there is the special problem of objectivity in the social sciences. The objects of study in the social sciences are individuals and groups as they exist in an ongoing society. Thus, a social scientist is not only an investigator but part of the subject matter being investigated. As such, he cannot maintain the objective stance, for example, of a physicist vis-à-vis atoms or molecules. He brings to his research all of the biases and predispositions of any human being toward human behavior, and there is literally no way of his shedding his conceptual outlook, which contains these biases. One way, of course, to avoid bias is to hire a social scientist from another country to study a particularly sensitive national problem. This was done in the case of the Swedish economist, Gunnar Myrdal, who was asked to study the race issue in the United States just before World War II. Myrdal (1944) was sensitive to the problem of bias. He wrote:

> Scientific facts do not exist *per se*, waiting for scientists to discover them. . . . A scientific fact is a construction abstracted out of a complex and interwoven reality by means of arbitrary definitions and classifications. The processes of selecting a problem and a basic hypothesis, of limiting the scope of study, of defining and classifying data . . . involve a choice on the part of the investigator. The choice is made from an indefinite number of possibilities (1944, p. 1057).

Underlying every choice made are the biases and preconceptions of the investigator. There is no way out of this dilemma. Merton's concept of organized skepticism is an aid, however. The wary reader of published research, in addition to carefully scrutinizing a fellow scientist's methodology, may well ask why his colleague chose to study a particular problem, who is paying for the research, and whether the issues raised benefit one group in the society over another.

Thus we can see that science itself is in part a social psychological process. At the heart of the process is the individual scientist or small group of scientists interacting with colleagues in the attempt to add to and redefine the state of knowledge within their discipline. Indeed, many of the concepts of the scientific enterprise, such as free discussion, motivation, and the acceptance and transmission of facts and theory, are social psychological questions as well.

DEPROGRAMMING ULTRAVIOLENCE

"How about this new like treatment that gets you out of prison in no time at all and makes sure that you never get back in again?" a somewhat chastened but overly innocent Alex asks in Anthony Burgess's futuristic novel, *A Clockwork Orange* (1963). At fifteen, Alex is the leader of a teenage gang whose specialty is violent crime. Or, as Alex and his cohorts refer to it, "a bit of the old ultraviolence." Alex, who lives at home with his unsuspecting parents, spends the afternoons lying in bed, listening to Beethoven's Ninth Symphony, and fantasizing about the crimes he will commit and the ways in which he will torture his victims. His pleasures, whether they are intellectual, aesthetic, or sensual, are created by inflicting pain on others. In the evening Alex meets his buddies and they roam the streets searching for victims. One night, after a bout of exceptional violence, Alex is caught.

Faced with a lengthy prison term, Alex chooses the alternative of receiving treatment in an untried rehabilitation program. Then the mind scientists take over his life. He is taken to a hospital, dressed in stylish pajamas, injected with a mysterious substance after each meal, and told he will see films. He believes he has the system beat until he is strapped into a dentistlike chair. Electrodes are attached to his head to measure his response, and his eyelids are stretched upward and prevented from closing.

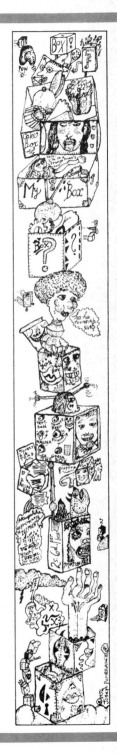

The room is darkened and the show begins. Alex is forced to watch movie after movie depicting the most outrageous acts of violence perpetrated by one group of human beings on another. Murders, mutilations, and deaths are shown on a wide screen accompanied by stirring classical music which resembles Alex's own bedroom fantasies. After hours of this treatment, a strange thing happens. At one time, Alex would have derived the greatest pleasure—in fact, would have been titillated to the extremes of ecstasy—by seeing Nazis mow down defenseless victims or watching groups of men repeatedly rape women. But now he feels unbearably nauseated.

"It was horrible," he says. "I don't understand. I never used to feel sick before. I used to feel like the very opposite."

"What is happening to you now is what should happen to any normal healthy human organism contemplating the actions of the forces of evil, the workings of the principle of destruction. You are being made sane, you are being made healthy," his doctor answers as Alex is strapped into his chair for his twice-daily dose of violence.

In time, Alex is "cured," but there are strange and unexpected side effects. He is not only allergic to violence; he is repelled by all the other elements that found their way into the films, such as music. Beethoven and Schoenberg, for example, make him deathly sick. Critics of Alex's rehabilitation say he has become a man without choice for whom "music and the sexual act, literature and art are a source not of pleasure but of pain." Finally, no longer able to bear his new personality, Alex commits a final act of violence—he leaps out a window to his death.

The moral of the tale for social psychologists is that the involuntary behavior modification fictionalized by Burgess has become a reality in prisons all over the world. Like the atomic scientists, social psychologists may have unbottled a genie.

The language of the social sciences

Social scientists are frequently criticized for their jargon; that is, their talk and their writing seem to be peppered with unfamiliar words, or familiar words used in unfamiliar ways. For the introductory student in social psychology, the first task is to try to understand how such words as socialization, interaction, conditioning, affiliation, cognition, affect, are used by those in the field. Such words are concepts and are ways of perceiving phenomena. Bernard S. Phillips (1966) points to three main elements in the language of scientific inquiry: concepts, propositions, and theories. We shall also discuss variables and hypotheses.

Concepts, propositions, and variables. A *concept* refers to a group of phenomena which are in some way alike. Racial prejudice is a concept that abstracts a common element, from such phenomena as denying a minority-group member a job to asserting that you would disown your sister if she married a Puerto Rican. That element is the attribution of an inferior status to a person because of his membership in a racial or ethnic group.

A *proposition* is a statement containing one or more concepts. It refers to observable phenomena and is testable. "Unemployment among young black men is twice that of their white counterparts" is such a proposition. Another might be, "Affiliation is greater among firstborn children." These statements qualify as propositions because they contain variables. A *variable* is a concept defined in such a way that greater or lesser amounts can be observed and measured; thus it becomes possible to test the proposition. "Unemployment among black men" is a variable. And, in fact, the Bureau of Labor Statistics regularly measures the number of unemployed black men as well as white men and reports these statistics by age groupings.

Affiliation is a more difficult concept to measure and convert to a variable. For example, when S. Schachter (1959) set up his series of experiments to study affiliation, he devised a description of an experimental situation that was somewhat threatening to his subjects and then asked them if they would prefer to sit in a room with some other people or wait alone until the experiment was set up. Those who chose to wait with others he defined as affiliative. Thus, affiliation becomes a variable by means of an *operational definition:* a definition derived from the results of a specific study or series of studies. Since it is not possible to study concepts such as affiliation, racial prejudice, or stress directly, "the investigator must devise some operations that will produce data he is satisfied to accept as an indicator of his concept" (Selltiz, Jahoda, Deutsch, and Cook, 1959, p. 43).

In many cases an operational definition may seem inadequate to the task of representing a concept. This is a matter for the judgment of critics. Often the satisfactory measurement and general acceptance of the meaning of a concept require not only a series of studies by one investigator but years of research by many different social scientists. *Attitude,* for example, a concept that was first defined and measured in the 1920s, is such a concept. Much like the concept of gravity in the physical sciences, we cannot point to it, see it, or touch it. Therefore, we must infer its influence by measuring properties which indicate its presence.

Hypotheses. When social scientists test a proposition, it is called a *hypothesis.* A hypothesis is a well-informed guess as to the nature of the phenomena being studied. A hypothesis may concern the characteristics of only one variable. For example, Type A individuals are competitive, over-achieving, and time-conscious. Or a hypothesis may attempt to show the relationship between two variables: for example, Type A individuals are more prone to heart disease than other people. The one-variable hypothesis is descriptive of the variable and is concerned with the frequency or characteristics of that variable. A two-variable hypothesis shows the relationship between the variables. This relationship may be one of correlation, as that between Type A individuals and heart disease, or it may predict that one variable is the cause of, or determines, the other. In the latter case, the hypothesis is called a hypothesis of *causal relationship:* for example, the unanimous opinion of three or more people as to the relative lengths of two lines will cause a group of subjects to conform in their answers one-third of the time. In this example, the variable "unanimous opinion" is the cause of "conforming answers." In effect, a hypothesis is a formal statement of the question the research is designed to answer.

In a hypothesis of causal relationships, the convention is to call the causal variable the *independent* variable and the result the *dependent* variable. Thus, in the above example, "unanimous opinion" is the independent variable and "conforming answers" is the dependent variable. In an experiment, the independent variable is manipulated and the dependent variable is a test of whether the manipulation changed the natural course of events. Consider, for example, the hypothesis, "Loud, uncontrollable bursts of noise lessen the ability of subjects to work steadily at unsolvable puzzles." The "loud, uncontrollable bursts of noise" is the independent variable; the "ability to work unsolvable puzzles" is the dependent variable. Phillips (1966) calls the independent variable the *presumed cause* and the dependent variable the *presumed effect*.

A *theory* is a set of systematically interrelated propositions (Zetterberg, 1963). It is the loftiest conceptual framework in a science, controlling, as it does, the direction of research. But more than that, a theory is an attempt to make sense out of many disparate research findings (Kaplan, 1964). A good theory should have explanatory power for many seemingly unrelated proofs of cause-and-effect relationships. Evolutionary theory in biology is an excellent example. It gives order, understanding, and an explanation for hundreds of separate observations. Unfortunately, there are no theories in social psychology as powerful as the theory of evolution.

Kenneth Gergen has suggested that perhaps the reason theories have not been developed in social psychology is that the item under analysis, the behavior of human beings, is not controlled by unchanging, constant properties. Gravity does not change, nor do the atomic properties of water. But as social conditions change, people change with them. Attitudes change, the characteristics of human relationships change, goals and goal-related behavior change. As a result, Gergen suggests that the explanations, observations, and causal relationships found by social psychologists today may in truth be but historical descriptions of human behavior in our own historical period.

Correlational and causal inferences

Selltiz and her colleagues wrote that "research always starts from a question of some sort," and that the questions must be answered by observations or experimentation in the world of reality (Selltiz et al., 1959). In the social sciences the answers may be in the form of a correlation found between two or more variables. A *correlation* exists between two variables when their values vary together; that is, the variations in one match the variations in the other. In a positive relationship, the values increase or decrease together. Or the variables may be inversely related: as the values of one variable increase, the values of the other decrease.

The inference of a *causal relationship* is a more powerful relationship between two variables than correlation. Indeed, there may be a correlation between two variables but no inference of causality. in the example of Type A individuals and proneness to heart disease, we may find a correlation between these two variables. However, the behavior of Type A individuals may be caused by a factor which also causes these people to have heart disease—in other words, an *antecedent variable*. In inferring causality, science relies on logic. Logic provides a causal explanation with the qualities of reason and plausibility. John Stuart Mill set forth four canons of relationships among variables which show the logic required for a causal analysis:

1. *The canon of agreement.* If a series of cases in which a certain set of phenomena occurs have only one thing in common, then that one thing must be regarded as a cause of the phenomena. For example, if we were to find that Type A individuals always developed heart disease, then we could say that their behavior might be a cause of their proneness to heart disease.

The problem for the researcher would be to show that his cases of Type A individuals had nothing in common with each other except their behavior.

2. *The canon of differences.* If a certain phenomenon to be explained is present in some of the cases and absent in others and there is only one thing that is different between the cases in which the phenomenon is present and those in which it is not present, that one thing must be the cause. Thus, for example, according to the canon of differences, one would have to show that a random sample of Type B individuals did not develop heart disease and that a sample of Type A individuals, similar to Type B individuals in every respect except their behavior, developed heart disease. Heart disease would be the phenomenon to be explained. The looked-for difference would be Type A behavior. Thus, Type A behavior becomes the cause of heart disease.

3. *The canon of concomitant variation.* This is essentially the same as correlation. However, to show causality, the researcher would have to show that the independent variable came first in time, and that there was no antecedent variable affecting both of the variables in question.

4. *The method of residues.* If a certain amount of the phenomenon to be explained is known to be caused by certain things, then what is left over, the residue, is caused by something else. According to the logic of the method of residues, the researcher might show that a certain amount of heart disease is due to overweight, another amount might be explained by old age, a third amount by stress-inducing life events. But these three factors are not sufficient to explain the incidence of heart disease. The residue might be explained by Type A behavior.

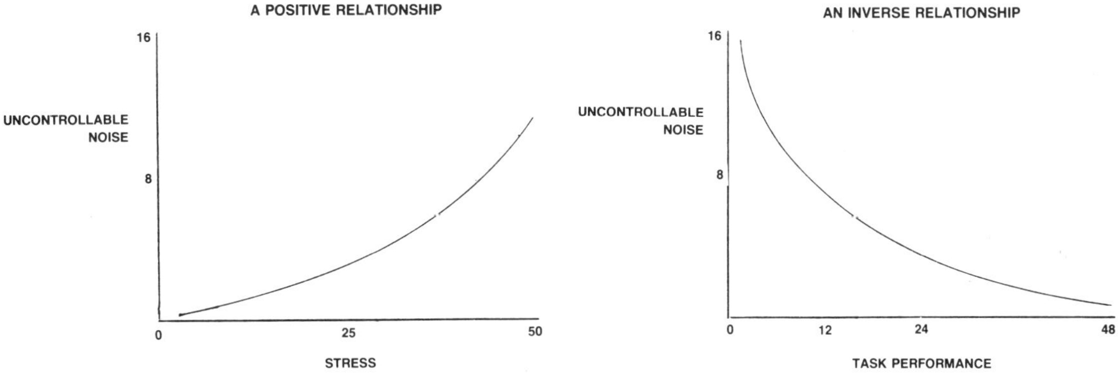

Figures 1–1 and 1–2.   In a positive relationship the curve rises from left to right: as one variable (stress) increases, the other variable (uncontrollable noise) increases. A curve indicating an inverse relationship falls from left to right. As one variable increases, the other decreases.

The logic of explanations that involve two variables is part of the conceptual equipment of most people educated in the Western tradition. We are trained to look for similarities or differences in analogous situations. Indeed, the anomaly, or the exceptional case, often leads to fresh insights. Do we find, for example, that as women fight their way into the higher echelons of management they, too, begin to succumb to heart disease to the same degree as their male counterparts? If we look at professions which require extreme competitiveness for success, such as professional tennis, hockey, and basketball, do we find a higher incidence of heart disease? Type A includes an extreme awareness of time. Do we find that people whose work puts them in a race against time, such as workers on piece rates or workers on a speeded-up assembly line, are more prone to heart disease?

Causality is a tricky matter. Again, no single study can possibly constitute proof of a causal relationship. Rather, many studies over time from many different sources lend credibility to propositions of cause-and-effect relationships.

Validity, reliability, and bias

Although few students trained in social psychology will ever actually do research, they nevertheless have a very real responsibility. They must provide the evaluation of the research of others. As Webb and his colleagues wrote, "Backstopping the individual scientist is the critical reaction of his fellow scientists" (Webb, Campbell, Schwartz, and Sechrest, 1966). In developing the habit of skepticism necessary for creative criticism, the principles involved in validity and reliability are important. Findings can be said to have *validity* if the researcher has actually measured what he has claimed to have measured, and has found what he has claimed to have found. In other words, are the findings true or are they spurious? And if the research were to be repeated and the findings were similar to those of the original study, the research is said to have *reliability*.

Several years ago there was a movie in which a newspaperman had discovered a small midwestern town whose population exactly mirrored the population of the United States as a whole—there were the same percentages of Republicans, Democrats, professionals, office workers, factory workers, as in the country as a whole. By asking the people in that town their opinions on various issues, the reporter was able to predict accurately how people all over the country felt. Everything went well until the people in the town became aware that he was using their opinions to make his predictions. They then no longer reported what they really thought, but rather, what they thought the newspaperman wanted to hear.

The reporter's polling suffered from what Selltiz and her colleagues (1959) have termed the "guinea pig effect," and what Campbell (1957) has called the "reactive effect of measurement." It is a problem of *bias,* similar to the problem faced by the social scientist when he asks questions of subjects. Bias can creep into any measuring instrument. Answers might vary considerably if, for example, the interviewer wore a lapel pin that said FBI, NBC, or Foundation for Equal Rights for Women.

Webb and his colleagues suggest that *role selection* is another source of bias:

Another way in which the respondent's awareness of the research process produces differential reaction involves not so much inaccuracy, defense, or dishonesty, but rather a specialized selection from among the many "true" selves or "proper" behaviors available in any respondent (Webb et al., 1966, p. 16).

It is generally assumed that a subject will behave under the conditions being studied in an experiment in the same fashion as he would upon encountering those conditions in his own life. But Webb and his colleagues point out that no person acts the same way in all circumstances. People behave differently in different roles. Moreover, being a subject in an experiment or a survey is in itself a special role which some subjects have encountered previously and which other subjects must learn. The role of subject may bias the subject and cause him to behave differently than he would in real life.

In addition to any bias introduced by the subject, the researcher himself may introduce bias. Several studies have shown that the expectations of the experimenter can affect the outcome (Rosenthal, 1966). It has been shown that if a teacher is told in advance that certain students are bright and others dull, those students identified as being bright will, in fact, do better even though they had not previously differed in intelligence from those who were labeled dull. The teacher's expectations influence her interactions with her students, creating a self-fulfilling prophecy. She tends to notice and approve the "bright" student when he gives a correct response, and to ignore the mistakes. With the dull student there is surprise at a correct response. This same effect held when researchers were told in an animal learning experiment that one group of rats was bright and another dull. The "bright" rats did better.

In concluding this discussion of scientific method, it must be emphasized that although we talk of science in the singular, it is not a thing of itself. It is an accumulation of the work of hundreds of thousands of human beings who follow the scientific method, who communicate with each other, who accumulate concepts, hypotheses, and theories over time, who reassess and change theories, and who maintain an attitude of skepticism. The words of Abraham Kaplan, who was interested in the philosophy of the behavioral sciences, are especially pertinent in this regard:

Science is a cooperative enterprise; every scientist is deeply dependent on his colleagues for criticism or corroboration of his findings. Moreover, science is a cumulative enterprise; the scientist builds on what others have established, and contributes, in turn, a basis for still further construction. All this interdependence requires that scientists understand one another with as little uncertainty of meaning as can be. The communication of scientific ideas is not a matter merely of the sociology of science, but is intrinsic to its logic; as in art, the idea is nothing till it has found expression (1964, p. 269).

16

Strategies for Gathering Data

Let us assume that an investigator has chosen a topic for a research project. Topics are chosen for a variety of reasons: a topic may have some deep-seated personal significance for the researcher; it may carry more prestige than others; it may represent a line of inquiry for which funds are readily available; or it may have a practical application. However, before a researcher recruits subjects for an experiment or writes a questionnaire, he needs to formulate his problem in terms of a hypothesis, using specific concepts which, in turn, can be operationally defined as variables.

The formulation of a hypothesis directs the inquiry toward certain specific facts. For the most part, facts are not just lying around waiting for a researcher to gather them up. Facts must be transformed into data; that is, they are of no value unless they conform to the definitions of the variables being measured. This requires a good deal of ingenuity. Situations need to be devised, or questions must be asked, or settings must be created or discovered so that behavior will yield data that can be measured. Thus we speak of *research strategies*— strategies for making the world display facts that suit our scientific purposes.

Unobtrusive measures. The strategy of the use of *unobtrusive measures* is to collect data without disturbing the natural situation in any way, to obtain measures that "do not require the cooperation of a respondent and that do not themselves contaminate the response" (Webb et al., 1966, p. 2). Unobtrusive measures might be used to corroborate the findings of survey or experimental work, to supplement and cross-validate the more conventional measures. The following unobtrusive measures were suggested by Webb and his associates:

The degree of fear induced by a ghost-story-telling can be measured by noting the shrinking diameter of a circle of seated children.

The role of interaction in managerial recruitment is shown by the overrepresentation of baseball managers who were infielders or catchers (high-interaction positions) during their playing days.

Library withdrawals were used to demonstrate the effect of the introduction of television into a community. Fiction titles dropped, nonfiction titles remained unaffected (Webb et al., 1966, p. 2).

Unobtrusive measures require detective work on the part of the researcher. Just as Sherlock Holmes scrutinized boots, fingernails, and worn bits of carpet for clues, the unobtrusive investigator seeks measures of social behavior that already exist in a setting and that betray an activity, an attitude, or an interest. One researcher, for example, measured the wear and tear on different pages of the *International Encyclopedia of the Social Sciences* to determine the degree to which different sections were read. "In some cases of very heavy use . . . 'dirt had noticeably changed the color of the page so that [some articles] are immediately distinguishable from the rest of the volume'" (Mosteller, 1955, quoted in Webb et al., 1966). Suits of armor and other antique articles of clothing are clues to the size of people in other times. W. L. Warner (1959) found the social structure of Yankee City mirrored in its graveyards. The male head of the family was often buried in the middle of a family plot, his gravestone larger than that of the females. Measures which depend on physical traces of human behavior are particularly useful at the outset of a study, or to corroborate measurements taken by a more active interference on the part of the investigator. They can seldom be used as sole evidence.

In addition to physical clues, there are archives with data which can be converted for use by the social scientist. Emile Durkheim's classic study of suicide relied on archival data. Suicide, he theorized, was inversely related to

*Native Americans
have been victims
of racial prejudice
since the first white man
set foot on American soil.
Social psychologists are
concerned with the nature
of prejudice;
anthropologists,
with the victims.*

COURTESY OF THE
AMERICAN MUSEUM OF
NATURAL HISTORY.

the degree of integration of a society. He used nationality, religion, age, sex, and marital status as social indicators for degrees of integration and related them to suicide rates—all of which data he found in the public record.

The federal government collects and publishes a great deal of statistical information. Summaries of the periodic census of agriculture, business, labor, health, and foreign trade, as well as actuarial figures concerning birth, marriage, and death, are contained in the *Statistical Abstract of the United States*, and in *Historical Statistics of the United States, Colonial Period to 1957*. Much of the above material concerning individuals is kept according to census tract and offers a unit of analysis suitable for community studies, or at the very least, for compiling descriptive statistics about a neighborhood under study.

Another, and probably the most important source of data is data collected by the survey method. A researcher may collect far more data in a survey than is used in his analysis. This data may be processed onto computer tape and may be used for purposes of comparison, for establishing trends, or for the development of new hypotheses. Universities and other research institutions have developed archives for survey research. One such research institution is the

Anthropologists use photographs as data. Does a study of this picture raise any questions?

Roper Public Opinion Research Center at Williams College, which has collected data from over forty research organizations.

Caveats, however, are in order for data collected for other purposes. The definitions of categories used in the collection of actuarial statistics may not coincide with those used by the social psychologist. "Household," "unemployment," and various categories of criminal offenses are precisely defined by government statisticians. The researcher is thus limited to the concepts developed by someone else. Furthermore, the original informants may have had good reason to either minimize or maximize their answers, depending upon the question. As Selltiz and her colleagues (1959) point out, individual income-tax declarations tend to be an underestimate, whereas the listing of expense-account items will represent an overestimate. Statistics concerning illegitimacy may be less accurate than those on marriages, births, and deaths. Accurate divorce rates are notoriously difficult to estimate because people do not necessarily divorce in the same state in which they are married, and many people obtain divorces out of the country.

Survey research

One method available to the behavioral scientist is to ask people questions. When answers from a large number of subjects are collected, they constitute the data for the method that is called *survey research*. This method is used extensively by the television networks and by public opinion organizations such as the Gallup Poll and the Harris Poll. With the use of computer techniques, for example, election results can be predicted with a high degree of accuracy on the basis of very little information. For many years the use of computer techniques was the principal tool of sociologists who studied such phenomena as patterns in voting preferences, the causes of intensive participation in union politics, and racial prejudice in housing projects.

In order to be able to generalize the results of a survey to a larger group than those units actually questioned, the survey researcher draws a random sample from his *population*—that is, the entire group under study. If every member of a population has an equal chance to be chosen as a unit of the sample, then the researcher is not open to the criticism that his results reflect the behavior of only the particular people he questioned; he can claim that his sample is representative of the entire group. Suppose, for example, that you wanted to study the effect of television violence on young children. You might decide that ten-year-olds would make an ideal target population. Rather than question your own ten-year-old, his friends, and the children in his fifth-grade class, you might get the names of all 10,000 fifth-graders in a given city or state. To draw a random sample, you might put all their names in a box, shake them up, and draw out 500 names. This would assure each child an equal chance of being chosen. You would then be able to generalize your findings to the total population of 10,000 fifth-grade students.

In a survey, the data consist of the answers that subjects give to questions. The questions may be asked directly by an interviewer, or a questionnaire may be administered to the subjects. In either case, questionnaires are carefully constructed to tap the sought-for variables. Surveys are seldom used in social psychology. They are often massive affairs and require large sums of money. They do not lend themselves to the more subtle relationships between individuals or between an individual and a group. They are, however, well suited to quantitative analysis, especially of variables that are relatively easy to measure: hospital visits, unemployment, census data, voting preferences. Nevertheless, social psychologists have measured the incidence of mental illness as well as heroin use in a population by means of survey techniques and have found relationships between these dependent variables and the independent variables of age, sex, and socioeconomic status.

In survey research the data consist of answers to questions.

Observation

In contrast to survey research, which can require hundreds of thousands of dollars, squads of interviewers, pretests of questionnaires, coding of answers, and the extensive use of the computer, observational studies often require a single individual armed with only a notebook and a pencil. *Observation* is the traditional research method of anthropologists in the field who carefully note and describe the daily activities of people in small-scale societies. The anthropologist must have the cooperation of informants—others native to the society being observed—in order to learn the language, to discover such variables as family and status relationships, and to interpret her observations. The anthropologist also uses the camera and the tape recorder. Notes must be systematic so that the data are accessible months or even years later.

The techniques of the anthropologist have been utilized by sociologists (Whyte, 1943; Liebow, 1967; Sudnow, 1967). Often a researcher will observe interactions in a particular setting before embarking on a survey or an experiment, in order to clarify his concepts and formulate useful hypotheses. The researcher may participate as a member of the group being studied, living with members, eating, playing, and interacting with them. In the most famous of all *participant-observer* studies, the researcher W. F. Whyte studied a street-corner gang of Italian-American adolescents in Boston in the late 1930s. His subjects knew that Whyte was a young social scientist and was observing them for scientific purposes. In fact, the gang leader, who acted as Whyte's informant, offered insights of his own to Whyte's study.

In another study, the researcher Julius A. Roth had contracted tuberculosis and was hospitalized for a considerable period of time. Roth utilized the time to study the social structure of the hospital, the medical personnel, and the patients. He focused his analysis on the passage of time in the hospital setting. In his study (1963), Roth did not make an effort to disclose his dual role as patient and observer. Since his research goals were impersonal and abstract, it is highly unlikely that he would have been able to affect any of the behavior he observed in terms of the concepts he was employing.

In a participant-observation study by three well-known social psychologists, the situation did not allow for full disclosure by the researchers. In 1956 Leon Festinger and two of his associates heard of a small religious group that called themselves "The Seekers." One of their members had made a prediction that on a specific day, floods would bring about the end of the world. The three social psychologists wanted to see what would happen when the end of the world, which they did not think was at hand, failed to come as predicted. In an appendix to their account of this group, the authors explained the manner in which they used the participant-observer method. Five trained observers sought access to this somewhat clandestine group, became members, and continued to make observations, take notes, and report to the researchers. The researchers, too, showed themselves to the leaders and made an avowal of interest in the group, in the occult, flying saucers, and other such matters that were of importance to the Seekers.

Since the group, for the most part, consisted of only about ten people, the presence of five participant observers who were, so to speak, only watching could scarcely have failed to influence the members. Indeed, the authors admit that this was so, particularly in the case of the ruses that the observers used to gain credibility with the other members, such as inventing dreams and proclaiming their interest. In fact, each new person was seen by the leader as an emissary sent by the Creator. Nevertheless, the authors maintained that their central hypothesis—that the faith of the group as a whole would be strengthened by the failure of the prophecy—was unaffected by the participation of the observers (Festinger, Riecken, and Schachter, 1956). The ethics of such ruses and cover stories in research will be discussed in a later section in this chapter.

The experimental method

The *controlled experiment*, the principal research design used in social psychology, is employed primarily to show causal relationships between two or more variables. It is the concept of *control* that makes the experimental method different from either the survey or the observational method. The controlled experiment is similar to an experiment in the natural sciences. The experimenter measures a substance as precisely as possible, does something to the substance, and measures it again. Any difference found in the substance after the second measurement can be attributed to the treatment, sometimes called *intervention* or *manipulation*—what the experimenter did to the substance. In the chemistry laboratory, control is achieved by careful avoidance of any contamination by the outside environment. Pure substances are used so that it is not possible to attribute the change to anything but the intervention of the experimenter. In social psychology, both validity and reliability are attained by the use of three important features built into the design of the controlled experiment: experimental and control groups; pretests/posttests; and randomization.

Pretest/posttest. In an experiment in which a researcher is interested in the deleterious effects of environmental stress, for example, he may use sudden, loud noises as the independent variable, and the level of performance on a specific task as the dependent variable. If he sets a group of subjects to work on a given task, introduces sudden and loud noise periodically into the experimental situation, and then measures their performance, against what can he compare the scores? He will have made a record only of how well a group can perform under certain supposedly unfavorable circumstances. However, if he measures their performance first and then measures their performance after they receive the treatment—the loud noises—he can attribute the cause of a poorer performance of the task to the treatment conditions—the loud noises. Without a pretest as well as a posttest, there is no basis for comparison of the scores.

There are those who might object, and rightly so, that the subjects might be bored, tired, or hungry, and for any one of these reasons, performed less ably the second time. Or perhaps, like the subjects in the Western Electric study (Roethlisberger and Dickson, 1939), their performance continued to improve no matter how unfavorable the working conditions; or that the subjects were sophomores who had been promised class credit for offering themselves as subjects and so were determined to do as well as they possibly could regardless of the conditions. In order to avoid these confounding factors, two groups of subjects are needed for a controlled experiment.

THE CONTROLLED EXPERIMENT

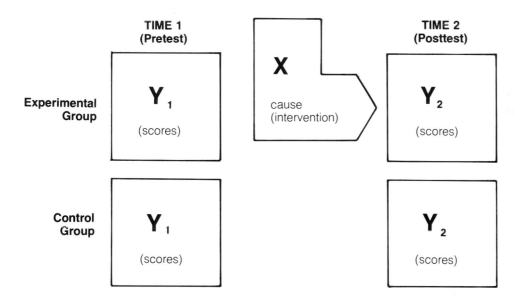

Figure 1–3. *With the addition of random assignment of subjects to groups, the investigator gains control over his experiment. X represents the independent variable; Y represents the dependent variable.*

Experimental and control groups.   Subjects who receive the treatment are called *experimental subjects.* All experimental subjects are said to belong to the *experimental group.* The *control group* consists of subjects who do not receive the treatment. In an experiment in which the effects of environmental stress are being studied, for example, members of both groups will be asked to perform a task. In an experiment the treatment may be administered to the subjects individually or as a group. (The subjects do not constitute a group in the sociological sense of the word.) When the members of the experimental group are performing the task, they will be subjected to sudden bursts of loud noises. The control group will perform the same task under all the same circumstances, except that they will not receive the treatment of the sudden loud noises.

What does this procedure accomplish toward establishing the validity of a causal relationship? It provides the control group as a valid basis of comparison. We can point to the control group and say that their scores on the performance task are higher; therefore, the independent variable, the sudden bursts of loud noises (the treatment), caused the poorer performance by the experimental subjects. The conditions were the same for all; the only difference was the experimental treatment. However, the skeptical critic may still object. How do we know, he may say, that the members of the experimental group are not in some way used to loud noises? Perhaps they live in a dorm next to an elevated railway or next to the music department, and are used to sudden bursts of loud noises, or for some other reason are disposed, as a group, toward lower scores. Again, there is an answer.

Randomization.   With the addition of randomization, the design of the controlled experiment is complete. *Randomization* uses *chance* to determine the assignment of subjects to either the experimental or the control group. This means that each subject must have an equal chance of being assigned to one or the other group. When this is accomplished, there is the assurance that no systematic error due to the possession of any special attributes or characteristics of the subject of one group or the other can be introduced into the findings.

Thus, controls are built right into a controlled experiment in the social sciences. The experimenter controls the independent variable. He does not have to seek out instances of environmental stress, for example, to measure its effect. He does not have to search for people who live in noisy places and then compare their school records or performance at work with those of people who live in quiet places.

Jones and Gerard (1967) find two major reasons why the controlled experiment is the most useful design for showing cause-and-effect relationships:

First of all, the ability to control—to provide for the absence or presence of critical antecedent conditions—implies that experiments can reproduce a particular cause-effect sequence . . . Events that occur naturally, without human intervention, are much less apt to recur in the same form or in the same context. [And secondly] if our observations are at the mercy of naturally occurring events in the environment, it is almost always the case that these events are imbedded in complexes of other events . . . so that we cannot with confidence attribute the observed effect to one rather than the other (1967, p. 39).

On the other hand, the technique of the controlled experiment forces the investigator to isolate in an artificial fashion only a few variables. The controlled experiment is designed to produce an effect, not to study the conditions under which such an effect might take place. Furthermore, many so-called experiments really demonstrate only that the influence of a condition in nature can be produced in the laboratory. Ideally, generalizations based on laboratory findings should be tested in a field situation, and this is rarely done. Thus, there is no single strategy that solves all research problems. We must then admire all the more those classic studies—and we will encounter many of them in this book—that have elegantly and parsimoniously revealed clues to the workings of the human mind and heart.

Ethics: The Human Use of Human Beings

It is obvious from the above discussion that the design of a valid experiment in social psychology is a complex enterprise that requires considerable ingenuity on the part of the investigator. But the experiment does not end with a good design. Having solved the creative problems, the investigator must now put the design into practice, a process which raises a whole new group of problems. Foremost among these is devising a way to use human subjects as humanely as possible. In other words, the investigator must resolve a number of ethical issues, including the use of deception, the invasion of people's privacy, and the subjection of individuals to humiliation, pain, or other stresses.

Experimental deception

Perhaps more than any other discipline, social psychology must resort to deceiving subjects. One of the most outspoken critics of this practice is Herbert Kelman. Kelman (1967) points out that the underlying assumption of the use of deception is easy to understand: that is, if the subject is aware of the conditions of the experiment, and of the phenomena under investigation, then the outcome of the experiment might be so biased that no valid conclusion could be drawn from it. In other words, a human subject must be kept as naive as possible about the experiment so that he will respond spontaneously and naturally, as he would in a real-life situation.

For example, Solomon Asch (1951) devised a classic experiment which studied individual conformity to group pressure. In this study, a group of individuals is presented with a number of vertical lines and asked to choose those that are equal in length. In ordinary situations, the task would be simple because the lengths of the lines are, in most cases, unambiguous. However, in the experimental situation, one of the individuals is naive and the rest of the group have been instructed beforehand to make deliberately incorrect choices about the lengths of the lines presented to them. The object of the experiment is to discover whether the group's incorrect consensus can pressure the naive subject into denying the evidence of his senses and choosing the same lines that the group has chosen—that is, the wrong lines.

Obviously, in such a situation, the subject must be naive; if he knew that the other group members were providing incorrect responses in order to pressure him to do the same, he would not yield to the pressure and the researchers would have no experiment. In order to allay the subject's suspicion, the researcher must often resort to the use of a cover story. In the above study, for example, Asch told the subjects that they were participating in a study of visual perception. Thus, the use of deception is an important part of the experiment.

A number of social psychologists, as well as other social scientists, view the practice of experimental deception critically. The work of Stanley Milgram is a case in point. In a number of experiments (1963, 1965), Milgram told subjects that they were taking part in a learning study. They were then instructed to administer increasingly powerful electric shocks to another individual. The victim, a confederate of the researcher, was not really being shocked. The experiment was set up to study obedience, in a situation in which following orders meant harming an innocent person whom the subject did not know. It is possible that some of those who obeyed orders and shocked the victims later experienced remorse and lowered self-esteem as a result of their actions.

In many a social psychological experiment, behavior is judged in light of the contribution that the findings will make to science. Some investigators feel that the potential contribution to social psychological knowledge can, in the long run, benefit the entire human race. Thus, for these scientists, the contribution to knowledge outweighs any psychological damage that may be done to the individual.

Moreover, there is another facet of this problem which must be explored. Human beings are used in other experimental situations in everyday life, but the experimenters are not criticized for their actions. For example, any therapy offered to an individual by a physician is really an experiment. If a physician discovers that a patient has cancer, the physician may recommend surgery. If this treatment fails to arrest the disease, the physician may try radiation therapy or chemotherapy. In general, people do not object to being manipulated in this manner as long as it is not done systematically in the name of science, but in the name of therapy.

Furthermore, many political actions are little more than badly designed social experiments without the consent of the public. Examples of such political experiments include negative income tax, the busing of children to achieve racially integrated schools, and censorship. Thus, experimental safeguards are necessary against extremes, but the experiments themselves must be viewed in terms of what is habitually done in society.

What kinds of experimental safeguards have been designed by social psychologists? The American Psychological Association has published a guide to experimental situations entitled *Ethical Principles in the Conduct of Research with Human Participants* (1973). The guide lists a number of ethical principles to which investigators should adhere. Among the principles are the following:

Ethical practice requires the investigator to inform the participant of all features of the research that reasonably might be expected to influence willingness to participate and to explain all other aspects of the research about which the participant inquires. . . .

Openness and honesty are essential characteristics of the relationship between

Follow-up Questionnaire in Milgram's Obedience Study

During the Experiment	Defiant Subjects	Obedient Subjects	All Subjects
1. I fully believed the learner was getting painful shocks.	62.5%	47.9%	56.1%
2. Although I had some doubts, I believed the learner was *probably* getting the shocks.	22.6%	25.9%	24.0%
3. I just wasn't sure whether the learner was getting the shocks or not.	6.0%	6.2%	6.1%
4. Although I had some doubts, I thought the learner was probably not getting the shocks.	7.6%	16.2%	11.4%
5. I was certain the learner was not getting shocks.	1.4%	3.8%	2.4%

Figure 1–4. In a study much criticized for deceptive manipulation of subjects, those subjects who obeyed were more suspicious. The defiant subjects believed in the reality of the experimental situation to a greater degree.

SOURCE: Adapted from Milgram, S. Interpreting obedience: Error and evidence. A reply to Orne and Holland. In A. G. Miller (Ed.), *The social psychology of psychological research.* New York: Free Press, 1972. P. 141.

investigator and research participant. When the methodological requirements of a study necessitate concealment or deception, the investigator is required to ensure the participant's understanding of the reasons for this action and to restore the quality of the relationship with the investigator.

Ethically acceptable research begins with the establishment of a clear and fair agreement between the investigator and the research participant that clarifies the responsibilities of each (pp. 1–2).

Role-playing

There are those, however, who feel that guidelines are not enough. Kelman, in particular, has gone a step further, stating that psychologists should abandon the use of deception entirely and seek out alternative experimental techniques that would assure the validity of the experimental outcome and assure that the subjects are treated as humanely as possible. One of these alternative techniques is *role-playing*, in which the experimenter describes a situation to the subject and then asks him how he would respond if actually in that situation. Thus, the subject is informed of the nature of the experiment and instructed to behave as if he were really in a certain situation.

However, as Miller (1972) and Freedman (1969) point out, this technique has a number of limitations. In a summary article on role-playing, Miller points out that there is a positive attraction to the use of the technique in social psychological experiments for two reasons. First, role-playing involves a more ethical and dignified atmosphere: in the experimenter–subject relationship, honesty and collaboration replace the rigid, impersonal scientist–object situation that typically prevails in the laboratory. Moreover, the technique obviates suspicion, recalcitrance, and apprehension on the part of the subject. However, citing the works of those who have tried to substitute role-playing for deception (for example, Greenberg, 1967), Miller states that the success of such studies is generally limited. Miller concludes his review as follows:

In conclusion, the prospects for role-playing as an alternative to deception are very poor. There are serious shortcomings at both the empirical and epistemological level. People may or may not be able to role-play in a form similar to their actual behavior (1972, p. 634).

Freedman (1969) notes a further limitation of the role-playing technique. It is doubtful, he says, that responses given by a subject reflect how he would behave in real situations. The subject is merely guessing or offering an opinion, a situation which represents a return to prescientific days when intuition and consensus were valued in place of actual data. In Freedman's words:

The argument comes down to the simple truth that data from role-playing studies consist of what some group of subjects guesses would be their reaction to a particular stimulus. The subjects are giving their estimates, their intuitions, their insights and introspections about themselves or others. If we are studying the myths and values of a society, these data would be useful. If we want to know how people actually behave, they are, at best, suggestive. If we are interested in their behavior (other than guessing behavior), we must ordinarily use the experimental method (1969, p. 111).

Furthermore, the use of the role-playing technique does not always eliminate the ethical problem that the subject's self-esteem may be adversely affected. In an experiment by Philip Zimbardo and his colleagues (1973), for example, college students were asked to take the roles of prisoners and guards in a simulated prison environment. As the experiment progressed, the students acting as guards became so sadistic toward the students acting as prisoners that the experiment had to be discontinued. It is highly probable that both prisoners and guards suffered some psychological damage as a result of this experiment.

The experimenter in a white coat manipulating dials is the stereotype of the scientist. This social psychologist is collecting data by means of a chart recorder.

Other ethical problems

In some experiments, individuals are subjected to physical and mental stress. Thus, subjects may be deprived of food, sleep, or water; they may be subjected to loud noises or electric shocks; they may be exposed to temperature extremes; or they may be asked to eat unpleasant-tasting substances.

According to the guidelines of the American Psychological Association (APA), when physical discomfort is judged necessary in order to study some important problem, the researcher must take all precautions to assure that the discomfort is kept at a minimum. Thus, the APA (1973, p. 2) has published the following principle:

The ethical investigator protects participants from physical and mental discomfort, harm, and danger. If the risk of such consequences exists, the investigator is required to inform the participant of that fact, secure consent before proceeding, and take all possible measures to minimize distress. A research procedure may not be used if it is likely to cause serious and lasting harm to participants.

The investigator should, for example, be aware of all possible dangers involved in the proceedings he is using. He should warn the subjects that they may experience some pain and give them the option of withdrawing or terminating the experiment whenever they choose. Moreover, the experiments should have built-in safety precautions, such as checking and pretesting equipment, screening staff and subjects alike, and formulating emergency plans to deal with accidents.

In some studies, says the APA, the variable being tested is psychological stress. In such an experiment, the subject's fear and anxiety are aroused in order that the investigator can examine conflict or frustration. In other studies, the subject is given an opportunity to lie, cheat, or steal in order to arouse his sense of guilt. In still others, he is exposed to scenes depicting human suffering.

Is there any way to avoid, eliminate, or minimize such situations? Sometimes anxiety or stress can be studied in naturally occurring conditions rather than experimentally established laboratory conditions. Thus, anxiety can be investigated by interviewing students before and after an important examination, or by studying patients sitting in a dentist's waiting room. Another way is to control the variable being studied (for example, anxiety or self-esteem), so that it has a favorable rather than a detrimental effect on the individual. Thus, the experimenter can create conditions that lower rather than raise the subject's anxiety, or increase rather than decrease his self-esteem.

The final major ethical problem facing the experimental social psychologist is that of the invasion of the subject's privacy. The APA rule for this subject states:

Information obtained about the research participants during the course of an investigation is confidential. When the possibility exists that others may obtain

EXPERIMENTING WITH OBEDIENCE

During the Nuremberg War Trials after World War II, most of the former Nazi leaders insisted that they had committed atrocious crimes because they were "only following orders." In recent times, adviser to former President Nixon, John Ehrlichman, and army Lieutenant William Calley, pleaded the same defense when accused of criminal acts. If you were in the shoes of these men—if you were instructed to harm an innocent person whom you did not even know—how would you behave? Would you go against your moral precepts and obey the instructions? Or would you refuse to hurt the other person? In an experiment conducted in 1960, psychologist Stanley Milgram found that all of his subjects obediently followed his instructions to administer ostensibly painful electric shocks to another person. Indeed, despite the agonizing "cries" of the victim, twenty-six of the forty subjects delivered the most powerful shock possible, simply because they had been instructed to do so by the experimenter.

In Milgram's experiment, volunteer subjects were told that they were participating in a study testing the effect of punishment on memory. They were then asked to give increasingly powerful electric shocks to a third person who was hidden from view in another room. The subjects were told that regardless of what happened in the course of the experiment, they would receive payment.

Then the experiment began. The subjects were introduced to an instrument panel designed to simulate an electric shock generator. The instrument clearly showed gradations in the severity of shocks, ranging from "Slight Shock" (15 volts) to "Danger: Severe Shock" (45 volts).

The victim was actually an accomplice to the experiment and was not, in fact, being shocked. He remained silent until the subject pressed Shock Level 300. Then the victim began to cry out and to pound on the wall of the room in which he was confined. Previously, the subjects had been told that the electric current produced pain but no permanent tissue damage. When they heard the pounding, most subjects asked for guidance. They wanted to know whether to continue with the experiment and whether it was necessary to hurt the victim. The experimenter politely but firmly asked the subjects to continue. After the 315 shock level, the victim was silent and his answers no longer appeared. Almost all the subjects were distressed. Most sweated, trembled, stuttered, bit their lips, or groaned. A few were convulsed by fits of hysterical laughter. One man broke out in such uncontrollable laughter that the experiment had to be halted.

After the experiment, Milgram explained the study; he introduced each subject to the victim and pointed out that the victim was only pretending to be shocked. The subjects tried to convince the researcher that they were not sadistic people, but were merely trying to cooperate with the experiment. The few who had laughed confessed that they had not done so out of enjoyment, but because they were terribly upset with what they were doing.

There is no doubt that Milgram's experiment made a significant contribution to our understanding of obedience. However, many investigators—both inside and outside the field of social psychology—have taken issue with the ethics of the experiment. Milgram's methods have highlighted an issue that is far from settled—the manipulation of human beings in the laboratory.

access to such information, ethical research practice requires that this possibility, together with the plans for protecting confidentiality, be explained to the participants as a part of the procedure for obtaining informed consent.

The investigators must keep confidential anything revealed about particular subjects during the course of the experiment. Thus, religious preferences, racial prejudices, sexual practices, and personal attributes such as intelligence, honesty, or courage should not be divulged to others without the subject's permission. Furthermore, the subject's anonymity must be insured. In publishing results of the study, "attempts should be made to disguise the individuals and dissociate sensitive material from individuals to the extent that this can be done without jeopardizing the research" (APA, 1973, p. 95).

Finally, the experimenter has an obligation to try to remove any guilt or shame feelings that the experiment may have instilled in the subject. Thus, the APA rule states:

After the data are collected, ethical practice requires the investigator to provide the participant with a full clarification of the nature of the study and to remove any misconceptions that may have arisen. Where scientific or humane values justify delaying or withholding information, the investigator acquires a special responsibility to assure that there are no damaging consequences for the participant.

Jones and Gerard (1967) have amplified this point, stating that the researcher has an obligation to debrief the subjects at the end of the experiment. During this period, the experimenter explains to the subjects the nature of the study, and if necessary, attempts to allay any feeling of guilt or lowered self-esteem that the experience may have engendered in the subject. Finally, the experimenter should communicate to each participant a summary of the experiment's results. In this way, the subjects (who are usually students) not only gain firsthand knowledge and experience about experimental procedure, but also learn how their participation has contributed to the understanding of human behavior.

Summary

Social psychology may be defined as an attempt to understand and explain how the thought, feeling, and behavior of individuals are influenced by the actual, imagined, or implied presence of other human beings. Social psychology differs from other social sciences not only in its methodology—how it goes about studying its subject—but in the questions it asks. Regarding racial prejudice, for example, a social psychologist is interested primarily in the prejudiced individual: the investigator seeks to determine how the biased person affects, and is affected by, the members of the society with whom he interacts.

The social psychologist studies the behavior of individuals in a group situation by using the scientific method, which rests on reasoning and on the objectivity of its practitioners. There are a number of concepts in the language of scientific inquiry which bear explaining. A proposition, for example, is a statement containing one or more generalizations about some phenomenon. Propositions contain variables: that is, concepts defined in such a way that greater or lesser amounts can be observed and measured. To test a proposition, the investigator formulates a hypothesis, a well-informed guess as to the nature of the phenomenon being studied. A hypothesis may contain one variable, or it may attempt to show the relationship between two variables. In a hypothesis of causal relationship, the causal variable is known as the independent variable, and the result is called the dependent variable.

A theory is a set of systematically interrelated propositions that tries to make sense out of many disparate research findings. Two key principles of social psychological research that affect all theories are validity and reliability. Findings have validity if the researcher has actually measured what he claimed to have measured. If the research is repeated and the findings are similar to those of the original study, the research has reliability.

A social psychologist can use a number of research strategies to gather his data. The strategy of the use of unobtrusive measures, for example, is to collect data without disturbing the natural situation in any way. Using the survey method, the researcher questions people directly. Or the investigator may observe his subjects, recording their activities with pen and paper, tape recorder, or camera. Finally, there is the principal research method used in social psychology, the controlled experiment, in which the investigator measures some phenomenon, does something to it, and measures it again. Three important elements of the contolled experiment are the pretest/posttest procedures; the use of the experimental and the control group; and the use of randomization in assigning subjects to groups.

In social psychology, human beings are used extensively as subjects in experiments. In conducting his experiment, the social psychologist must exercise great care in the use of his human subjects. He must perform his experiments with humans according to the ethical principles established by the American Psychological Association (APA). Thus, if he resorts to deception in the experiment, the researcher must debrief his subjects afterwards to make sure that they understand the reasons for his actions. The investigator must safeguard the subjects' privacy by keeping confidential any personal information obtained during the research. Finally, says the APA, the social psychologist must attempt to minimize or eliminate humiliation, pain, and other stress.

Bibliography

ALLPORT, G. W. The historical background of modern social psychology. In G. Lindzey and E. Aronson (Eds.), *The handbook of social psychology.* Vol. 1. Reading, Mass.: Addison-Wesley, 1968.

AMERICAN PSYCHOLOGICAL ASSOCIATION. *Ethical principles in the conduct of research with human participants.* Washington, D.C.: American Psychological Association, 1973.

ASCH, S. E. Effects of group pressure upon the modification and distortion of judgment. In H. Guetzkow (Ed.), *Groups, leadership, and men.* Pittsburgh: Carnegie Press, 1951.

BRAMEL, D. A dissonance theory approach to defensive projection. *Journal of Abnormal and Social Psychology,* 1962, **64,** 121–129.

BRAMEL, D. Selection of a target for defensive projection. *Journal of Abnormal and Social Psychology,* 1963, **66,** 318–324.

BURGESS, A. *A clockwork orange.* New York: W. W. Norton, 1963.

CAMPBELL, D. T. Factors relevant to the validity of experiments in social settings. *Psychological Bulletin,* 1957, **54,** 297–312.

FESTINGER, L., RIECKEN, W. W., AND SCHACHTER, S. *When prophecy fails.* Minneapolis: University of Minnesota Press, 1956.

FREEDMAN, J. Role playing: Psychology by consensus. *Journal of Personality and Social Psychology,* 1969, **13,** 107–114.

GREENBERG, M. S. Role playing: An alternative to deception? *Journal of Personality and Social Psychology,* 1967, **7,** 152–157.

HANEY, C., BANKS, C., AND ZIMBARDO, P. Interpersonal dynamics in a simulated prison. *International Journal of Crime and Penology,* 1973, **1,** 69–97.

JONES, E. E., AND GERARD, H. B. *Foundations of social psychology.* New York: John Wiley and Sons, 1967.

KAPLAN, A. *The conduct of inquiry: Methodology for behavioral science.* Scranton, Pa.: Chandler Publishing, 1964.

KELMAN, H. C. Human use of human subjects: The problem of deception in social psychological experiments. *Psychological Bulletin,* 1967, **67,** 1–11.

KLINEBERG, O. *Social psychology.* New York: Henry Holt, 1940.

LIEBOW, E. *Tally's corner: A study of Negro streetcorner men.* Boston: Little, Brown, 1967.

MERTON, R. K. *The sociology of science: Theoretical and empirical investigations.* (Edited and with an introduction by N. W. Storer.) Chicago: University of Chicago Press, 1973.

MILGRAM, S. Behavioral study of obedience. *Journal of Abnormal and Social Psychology,* 1963, **67,** 371–378.

MILGRAM, S. Some conditions of obedience and disobedience to authority. *Human Relations,* 1965, **18,** 57–76.

MILGRAM, S. Interpreting obedience: Error and evidence. A reply to Orne and Holland. In A. G. Miller (Ed.), *The social psychology of psychological research*. New York: Free Press, 1972.

MILLER, A. G. Role playing: An alternative to deception. *American Psychologist*, 1972, **27**, 623–636.

MYRDAL, G. *An American dilemma.* Vol. 2. *The Negro social structure.* New York: Harper and Row, 1944.

NEWCOMB, T. M. *Personality and social change.* New York: Dryden Press, 1943.

PHILLIPS, B. S. *Social research: Strategy and tactics.* New York: Macmillan, 1966.

ROETHLISBERGER, F. J., AND DICKSON, W. J. *Management and the worker.* Cambridge, Mass.: Harvard University Press, 1939.

ROSENTHAL, R. *Experimenter effects in behavioral research.* New York: Appleton-Century-Crofts, 1966.

ROTH, J. A. *Timetables.* Indianapolis: Bobbs-Merrill, 1963.

SCHACHTER, S. *The psychology of affiliation.* Stanford, Calif.: Stanford University Press, 1959.

SELLTIZ, C., JAHODA, M., DEUTSCH, M., AND COOK, S. W. *Research methods in social relations.* (Rev. ed.) New York: Holt, Rinehart and Winston, 1959.

SHERIF, M. On the relevance of social psychology. *American Psychologist*, February 1970, **25**(2), 144–156.

SUDNOW, D. *Passing on: The social organization of dying.* Englewood Cliffs, N.J.: Prentice-Hall, 1967.

WARNER, W. L. *The living and the dead.* New Haven, Conn.: Yale University Press, 1959.

WEBB, E. J., CAMPBELL, D. T., SCHWARTZ, R. D., AND SECHREST, L. *Unobtrusive measures: Nonreactive research in the social sciences.* Chicago: Rand McNally, 1966.

WHYTE, W. F. *Street corner society.* Chicago: University of Chicago Press, 1943.

ZAJONC, R. B., HEINGARTNER, A., AND HERMAN, E. M. Social enhancement and impairment of performance in the cockroach. *Journal of Personality and Social Psychology*, **13**(2), 83–92.

ZETTERBERG, H. L. *On theory and verification in sociology.* Totowa, N.J.: Bedminster Press, 1963.

2

Socialization

Every newborn infant threatens the social order. Its biological potentialities are so broad and so indeterminate that no society ever leaves it free to grow into adulthood undirected. During the long years of its immaturity, impulses and capacities are channeled into relatively narrow patterns of behavior, motive, belief, and attitude. We shall seek in this chapter to uncover the major processes of learning and development that appear to underlie that transformation and to account for the way a growing person gradually becomes capable of functioning within the system of interlocking roles and reciprocal expectations that defines the social order of his society.

The crucial place of socialization in the development of human beings and the distinctive quality of man's social life can be grasped only when viewed within the context of the whole evolutionary process. It used to be stated with some assurance that all other animals are governed by instinct and react blindly to their environment in preprogrammed predictability. Humans, in contrast, were thought to be free from such instinctual forces and to enter

37

the world as blank slates fully open to the arbitrary writings of experience, uniquely endowed with consciousness, rationality, and a free will. We now know that the true picture is far more complex and much more interesting.

38 The Nature of the Species

Every animal species, including *Homo sapiens*, evolved over millennia to fit a particular ecological niche. Its characteristics can be understood only in the light of its evolutionary history and its current environment. Ethologists have shown, moreover, that it is not only in physical traits that one animal species is different from another. Complex patterns of behavior also appear to have been built in over the course of evolution. Stickleback fish engage in elaborate courting rituals, pregnant rats build nests to house their young, and baby goslings follow their mothers—all in characteristic ways that are predictable simply from knowing that we are dealing with a representative of a particular species reared in its ordinary habitat. Evolved behavior patterns of this sort are not innate, in the sense that they will automatically unfold as the animal matures. Research has shown that nearly every form of behavior is modifiable through experience and learning.

A pregnant rat, for example, builds a nest by gathering strips of paper or other material, and when her pups are born she retrieves them by carefully picking them up in her mouth and carrying them back to the nest. Nest-building and retrieving both occur in all normal rats; they occur in rats which have been raised in total isolation, and which have had no prior opportunity to observe another female caring for her young; and they occur with no evidence of practice, since both are performed perfectly by a rat the very first time she is pregnant and gives birth. Clearly these appear to be fine examples of evolved behavior patterns that are innate in the rat species, transmitted directly through the genes with no need for special learning experiences.

In this case, however, as in so many others, an interpretation based purely on genetic determinants turns out to be inadequate. Daniel Lehrman (1961) described a study by B. F. Riess in which isolated rats were raised in an environment that prevented them from manipulating or carrying any objects. When these rats became pregnant, they did not build normal nests nor retrieve their young normally. They scattered the nesting material all over the cage. They carried their pups from one spot to another, often injuring them in the process, and never managed to collect them at a nest-place. It appears, therefore, that the maternal behavior of nest-building and retrieving, while characteristic of the rat species, is neither innate nor specifically learned. It emerges only in certain situations, and only through continual experience with manipulating objects. What makes this behavior species-predictable is that the experiences upon which it depends may be expected to occur under the normal conditions of a rat's environment, and the rat is biologically prepared to learn with great ease what rats do when giving birth.

And so it is with most species-predictable behaviors. We have learned that the behavior is dependent for its emergence on continual interactions between the organism's biological heredity and the environment in which it develops. Learning, in most cases, does not seem to be simply "added on" to what is given in biology. Rather, the forces of heredity and the experiences acquired in the environment interpenetrate in a lifelong process of interaction to actualize the biological potential. Theodosius Dobzhansky (1950, p. 88) stated it well: "Heredity is not a status but a process. What is inherited is not a 'trait' but a capacity to develop certain traits under certain conditions. Heredity begins at conception and ends at death."

Phylogenetic continuities

Still, the important fact remains that the farther one descends the animal scale, from man through the primates to lower mammals and beyond, the more rigid and fully predictable is the animal's response to the stimuli it meets in its environment. A squirrel that encounters its first nut on a tile floor, for example, will immediately run through its instinctive burying program. It scratches at the tiles as though it were digging, bears down on the nut with its nose as if to push it into the floor, and completes the sequence with covering movements in the air—all of which leaves the nut as fully exposed as before (Hess, 1962). It is as if the squirrel's brain in this instance were operating as a telephone switchboard whose sole function is to connect incoming sensory messages to preprogrammed motor responses. The animal appears on the scene with a complex and coordinated series of seemingly fixed actions, the nut acts as a releaser, and the burying program unfolds in an automatic sequence at the first sight of an appropriate nut.

Fixed action patterns of this sort become increasingly rare as one ascends the animal scale. In higher organisms, communication appears to go on within the brain as well as into and out of it (Hebb, 1966). Neural connections now increasingly occur over association areas, collections of neural cells that are not given over to receiving incoming stimuli or coordinating outgoing responses, but are available instead for registering the learning of complex behaviors and for representing the goals to be achieved through that activity. Behavior derives increasingly from mediating processes in the brain itself rather than as a direct reaction to immediate stimulation. A period of delay now intervenes between stimulus and response, and the eventual behavior is no longer predictable simply from the nature of the stimulus input and knowledge of the physiological state of the organism. It is this progressive phylogenetic increase in the proportion of the brain composed of association areas that underlies the striking evolutionary shift from primarily reflexive to primarily purposeful modes of communication.

Lower animals coordinate their behaviors through reflexive and automatic responses to such stimuli as a scent, touch, or sound given off by a fellow member of the species. The complex coordination of behavior in an ant or bee colony is a good example of this kind of communication, as is the elaborate courting behavior of the male stickleback fish so admirably described by Niko Tinbergen (1952). Higher animals, in contrast, are able to direct their behaviors in terms of the goals they seek to achieve.

When a dog barks to be let out of the house or a chimpanzee begs its neighbor for a share of the food, the communication is unmistakably governed by the intent to achieve a particular behavioral effect in another. Hebb and Thompson (1968) describe an intriguing example of such a purposeful behavior in captive chimpanzees. When they see a visitor arrive on the scene, these charming creatures have often been observed to slip quietly over to the faucet, fill their mouths, and wait serenely at the front of the cage with no sign of hostility until the visitor is within range, at which point he is suddenly drenched with water. Even without the symbolic potentialities of human language, chimpanzees are able to anticipate a goal and to plan a series of complex actions.

Higher animals are able to generate mental images of objects or events that are no longer or not yet present in their immediate sensory environment. They are capable of conceptual thought, and these images can serve to guide their actions. But there is no evidence as yet to suggest that chimpanzees or any other infrahuman animals have developed a way of dispassionately communicating their thoughts to others, of discussing their plans for the future or reminiscing about a past event. For this to occur, they would have to be able to use an externalized conventional code of symbols, a code that each animal not only can respond to itself but can communicate to another who will respond to it in at least a roughly similar way. As Hallowell (1955, p. 8) expressed it, "By means of a drawing, vocalization, or perhaps even by gestures, I can make *you* acquainted with *my* dream. Consequently, in the case of man, extrinsic symbolic systems ... made it possible for groups of human beings to share a common meaningful world."

When a chimpanzee begs for food or asks a friend for a grooming, it is engaging in symbolic actions, making gestures that stand for the act or feeling that it seeks to communicate. The whole process is made up of a single isolated gesture, usually closely connected with emotional display and without the arbitrary character of the signs and symbols of human speech. This is as far as the chimpanzee's capacities normally go, but a normal achievement rarely reflects the full range of an organism's potentialities.

Several years ago, Allen and Beatrice Gardner (1969) launched an extraordinary series of studies with the help of an unusual chimpanzee named Washoe. As a result of their work, later replicated and extended by many others, we now know that the language gap between man and ape is not as large as once was assumed. Washoe was able to learn a wide range of symbolic gestures taken from the American Sign Language that the deaf use. Using her hands, she was able to name objects and combine signs in various ways, and thus to communicate her wants and feelings to her human companions. She could do so, however, only after intensive and prolonged training.

In sharp contrast, language acquisition on the part of human children is practically impossible to prevent, save through environmental aberrations so drastic that the child has little chance to survive at all. The human infant shows from the first that he is built to speak. He responds to vocalizations, he babbles early, and he learns to speak easily, with no one having to teach him through specific training. The capacity and motivation for language are so much a part of the human organism that they develop even under the most unfavorable conditions of neurological impairment. A congenitally deaf child, for example, never hears a spoken word; he rarely babbles in infancy; he usually fails to develop intelligible speech. Yet he learns, with incomparably greater ease than Washoe, to communicate in sign language and in writing. There must have been forces in the evolution of the human species that made the propensity and drive for language essential to the survival of our hominid ancestors.

Language as such is not innately given in human biology, just as the nest-building behavior of the female rat will not automatically emerge in the course of maturation. The rat does, however, have an innate predisposition to acquire easily the skills of manipulating and collecting objects and to combine these skills into nest-building and retrieving when the time comes to nurture her pups. A human child's propensity for language is equally characteristic of our species. In apes and humans, as Louis Breger (1974, p. 24) has shown, "instinctual patterns are less fixed, take longer to develop, and are more variable in final outcome than those of other animals. They are, nonetheless, there. . . . Our evolution has left us with instinctual predispositions to act and react in those areas centrally related to our survival."

Human evolution

The special evolution of the human brain created one of those rare quantum leaps in species development. We are the pioneers in a very recent and entirely new form of evolution. All other species evolve primarily by way of the blind forces of mutation and natural selection. The invention of language, and the transmission of cultural traditions that language makes possible, created in human evolution a process akin to the inheritance of acquired characteristics, and they have transformed man's way of life over the past 4,000 years more than biological evolution has in fifty times as long an interval. It is now clear, moreover, that the emergence of culture preceded, and indeed made possible, the biological evolution of our distinctively human characteristics.

The enlarged human brain not only required a larger skull; it also demanded the birth of the fetus at a much earlier stage in its development. Whereas the brain of a newborn chimpanzee has already reached 60 percent of its eventual adult size, only 22 percent of the brain growth in humans occurs before birth. Not until the end of its fourth year does the child's brain reach even 80 percent of its adult size. This far longer period of biological immaturity demanded a more complex set of child-caring skills. Such skills could only have been developed after the emergence of a rudimentary social system marked by the sexual division of labor and a stable family structure that freed the mother or another specialist in child care to concentrate on protecting the helpless and slowly maturing infants. A complex social life based on collective hunting and food-sharing, in turn, required a more complex system of symbolic communication. The fossil evidence clearly suggests that it was only after the development of these elementary forms of cultural activity that much of what is distinctively human began its slow evolution. The human brain, from the immediate point of view, makes language and the transmission of culture possible. But, as Sherwood Washburn (1959) has shown, "from the long-term evolutionary point of view, it is culture which creates the human brain."

Man's central nervous system gradually developed over the span of some one million years in large part through interaction with a cultural environment. As a result, that neurological system has now become incapable of directing our behavior or of organizing our experience without the guidance provided by the accumulated fund of cultural symbols.

We are born in utter helplessness, the most immature and inadequate infant animals in existence. We have no preprogrammed modes of response to our environment beyond a handful of simple reflexes, and no capacity to satisfy our own needs or to survive at all without the prolonged and intimate ministrations of nurturant adults. Our survival came to depend primarily on educability, on the capacity to modify behavior tendencies under the influence of experience, foresight, and reasoning. Thus the inventions of language and culture replaced biological heredity as the most important determining agents in human behavior. It is this replacement that most clearly differentiates humans as a species from all other animals and that creates the conditions for the fundamental shaping of individual personality and behavior by social experience. How that shaping occurs and by what processes, we shall seek to understand in the pages that follow.

FACTORS CRITICAL TO CHILD DEVELOPMENT

In an effort to isolate the factors critical to the healthy development of infants, René A. Spitz (1946) studied 164 children under four different conditions. The children were selected from four different environments. The first group consisted of the children of urban professionals. The second group came from a small fishing village where nutrition, housing, and medical care were scarcely adequate. In the third category were the children of young women imprisoned in a penal institution. Children in the fourth group were foundling babies in Latin America abandoned by their mothers.

Spitz graded the babies on a development quotient based on the development of perception, body mastery, social relations, and so on. Although the foundling babies' average scores were almost as high as those of the middle-class babies during the first four months, by the end of the first year the scores of the foundlings was twenty-nine points lower than those of the lowest-scoring village children.

What had caused the startling regression in the foundling babies? Spitz compared conditions in the foundling home and in the penal institution and discovered that, in the main, the foundling babies were more likely to be breast-fed, but only for three months, and were visited more often by doctors. However, all of the foundling babies were confined to their cubicles until they were fifteen to eighteen months old, and half of them were located in a dimly lit area. The infants in the nursery of the penal institution, by contrast, remained in well-lit cubicles for the first six months of life. Most nursery children had several toys, but none of the foundling babies had any. In the nursery, the babies were able to look out of their cubicles into a pleasingly painted corridor in which there were always mothers or nurses. But in the foundling home, the children faced a bleak corridor, deserted except at feeding time, when six or seven nurses appeared.

Most important, in the foundling home, bed sheets were hung over the foot and sides of the bed, obscuring the children's field of vision. Try as they might, the babies were unable to see anything but the ceiling. They lay on their backs all day and never learned to sit up. In time, their bodies wore hollows in their mattresses, preventing them from raising themselves even if they had wanted to. Thus, although the physical care of the foundling babies, with frequent doctor visits and proper food, was adequate, the emotional and cognitive deprivation of these babies was similar to that of feral children—children who, for one reason or another manage to grow up without human contact.

At the end of two years, the researchers retested the foundling-home children. They discovered that 37 percent of the children had died. All the survivors were severely retarded in their development. Most could not walk unassisted, and some were incapable of any locomotion; the majority were only partially toilet-trained and only a few could speak several words.

The researchers concluded that without adequate stimulation, both environmental and social, a baby's development will deteriorate. Deprived of intimate contact with people and of challenges from the environment, the babies' resistance to disease was lowered and they developed physically at a slower rate. Thus, babies, in order even to survive, need stimulation, attention, feedback—all of which, according to Spitz, are provided most adequately by a mother.

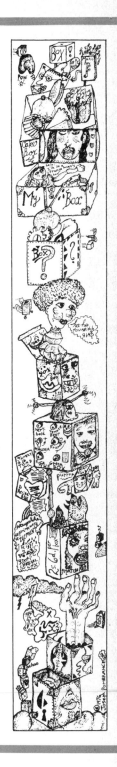

During the long years of its immaturity, a child experiences an extraordinarily broad set of complex events. We need the guidance of theory before we can begin to know what to look at and what types of experience are likely to be most important in their impact on the growing person. The scientific study of the socialization process has been dominated by four conceptual approaches in particular. Each emerged out of a separate theoretical tradition and developed largely in isolation from the others. Each sensitizes us to a different aspect of the complex interaction between a growing child and his changing encounters with the people and ideas that become significant in his life. In its selectivity and in the underlying assumptions to which it is wedded, each also distorts some part of the complex reality with which it deals.

An illustrative episode

We begin our conceptual journey with a simple behavioral episode, a few moments abstracted from the many years of social interaction that separate infancy from maturity. In the course of their classic study of child-rearing patterns among Boston mothers, Sears, Maccoby, and Levin (1957, pp. 365–366) caught this glimpse of a little girl emerging out of infancy and into a world

*An automatic sequence
of burying
may be triggered
when a squirrel
first encounters a nut.*

composed of rewards and punishments, or symbols and meanings, of physical objects that call for exploration and mastery, and of cultural restraints that shape a personality capable of self-control:

Martha's parents brought her along one Sunday afternoon when they came for a visit. She was seventeen months old, full of curiosity and mischief. While we had coffee and cookies, she thirstily drank down a glass of milk, ate half a cookie, and began an eager exploration of her surroundings. Toddling most of the time, crawling occasionally, she left trails of crumbs and tipped over cups wherever she went. One of the floor lamps fascinated her especially. It was tall and straight, made of a single, glossy round of wood, just the right size for Martha to get a good grip on. When she stood up against it, clutching happily, the lamp teetered and swayed in what was obviously an entrancing fancy for Martha.

Twice her father had to put down his cup and lean across the room to prevent a crash. Twice he said, clearly and distinctly, "Now Martha, don't touch." Each time he took her by the hand and led her over to some toys. These distracted her only briefly.

After the second interruption, Martha began a general exploration of the room again. Now she went a little more slowly, and several times glanced at her father. As she came closer to the lamp, however, she stopped looking his way and her movements were all oriented toward the lamp. Deliberately she stepped toward it, came within a couple of feet of it, and lifted her arm partly, a little jerkedly, and then said sharply, commandingly, "Don't touch."

There was an instant of struggling silence; then she turned and stumbled across the room, flopped down on the floor, and started laughing excitedly. Her father, laughing with her and obviously adoring, reached out and hugged and snuggled her for minutes (Sears et al., 1957).

What is really going on in this interaction among father, daughter, and lamp? What does it reflect about the essential forces that comprise the socialization process? What are its crucial features in terms of their impact on the way this little girl is learning to function in her society? Four quite different answers emerge from the relevant literature.

Psychoanalytic Perspectives: Freud and Erikson

The objective study of socialization was given its initial impetus by the work of Sigmund Freud. He was the pioneer, the first to attempt a comprehensive theory of human personality, to claim that there was order in the manifold processes of development, and to point to the key dimensions that he saw as defining the central problems of socialization in early childhood.

Psychosexual modalities

It was Freud's belief, later elaborated by Erik Erikson (1950), that children grow psychologically according to a biological plan, as their instinctual drives propel them forward to meet the environment on terms that change as they mature. A child is born as an undifferentiated mass of physiological urges and simple reflexes, his actions motivated only by a blind seeking of immediate relief from uncomfortable states of bodily tension. His initial interactions with his surroundings occur via the mouth, and the oral gratifications he obtains in sucking and then in biting soon permeate all his experiences. He incorporates not only food, but sights and sounds as well, and he grows by absorption, acquiring, through the quality of the nurturance that he receives, his first sense of the trustworthiness of the world that surrounds him.

As physiological maturation proceeds, this passive stage of oral dependency is thought to evolve into a period of active exploration that brings a new kind of confrontation with the environment. Anal muscles increasingly come under voluntary control, and whether or not his culture dictates that toilet training should now begin, the alternating modes of retention and elimination, of holding on and letting go, come to dominate the child's encounters with his environment.

A psychoanalyst would have little difficulty recognizing in the episode of father and child described above a clear expression of the anal mode of relating to one's surroundings. Martha begins by thirstily drinking a glass of milk and eating half a cookie, but there are no signs of lingering over such oral gratifications, no compulsive sucking, no passive absorption of the surrounding scene. Instead, she actively explores her new environment, and she does so in a distinctly anal way, by alternately holding on and letting go—first with regard to the lamp itself, then in her interactions with her father as well. The oscillating pattern of approach and retreat, first stubborn and disobedient, then suddenly obeying with joyous release, would appear unmistakably to the psychoanalyst as a reflection of the anal stage that she has entered and as a projection of her own internal processes onto the external environment.

Developmental crises

Considerations such as these suggest further that this may be but one episode in a broader confrontation focused at this stage on the issue of autonomy and self-control (Erikson, 1950), part of a sequence of decisive encounters that are precipitated both by a child's changing capacities and a society's changing demands. Martha has reached a stage of physical maturity where she can now begin to seek increasing independence from her parents' enveloping control, to experience herself as a separate and autonomous being. Her parents' tolerant firmness in the face of these halting efforts at independence may enhance her sense of self-control. If, on the other hand, they insist on maintaining too much control themselves or make demands that are beyond her capacities,

Martha might well emerge from such encounters with an overwhelming sense of her own smallness and inadequacy, with lasting feelings of shame in herself and of doubt in her capacity to control the potential anarchy of her impulses.

The psychoanalytic perspective leads us to view the socialization process as a continuing series of critical encounters between a person's growing capacities and society's changing pressures. The growing child confronts the socializing efforts of an ever-widening circle of significant others. As the child matures within his family and then moves into the wider community of school and peers, he faces further crises in connection with such issues as competence, identity, and intimacy (Erikson, 1950, 1959). From such encounters, lasting qualities are thought to emerge that comprise essential aspects of the individual's personality. Freud himself believed that what happens from birth to the age of five or six becomes relatively fixed, primarily because these early experiences are absorbed unconsciously for the most part, and are not readily available to the conscious mind. Thus, they remain uninfluenced by the more rational and cognitive learning of later years. In Freud's view, it was the very young child, not the adolescent or even the school-ager, who was the "father of the man" he would become.

The place of emotion

Above all, a psychoanalyst would draw our attention to the emotional intensity that permeates this simple moment of interaction between Martha and her father—the "struggling silence" as she approached the lamp that final time, the "excited laughter" that accompanied her successful efforts at self-control. What this suggests is that the real drama in this episode is no longer between the child and her father. Its locus is now within Martha herself, in an internal conflict between reciprocally propelling and restraining forces. The external world comes to be represented internally as socialization proceeds, and that internalization occurs with considerable emotional intensity.

Martha was not simply imitating her father when she said to herself, "Don't touch." Something much more sweeping and powerful was occurring. She had stopped looking in his direction as she approached the lamp that final time. She looked at herself for guidance, and the command she followed was her own. It is as if a part of her father had now become a part of her, establishing an internal agency of self-control and self-instruction, perhaps the beginnings of the superego. In its emphasis on the process of *identification* as a phenomenon of far greater scope and power than simple imitation, psychoanalysis stresses the emotional quality of the relations that develop within the family and that establish the conditions that will motivate a child to take on spontaneously the socialized behaviors his parents represent.

Conceptual limitations

In spite of their unquestionable insights, psychoanalytic conceptions no longer dominate the study of socialization. There were many efforts to test the hypothesis that an adult's personality is shaped decisively in his initial experiences at the breast or on the toilet. This early research was focused on specific infant care practices, and it yielded at best only vague and inconsistent correlations with personality attributes in adulthood. Researchers in this tradition now concentrate, instead, on the overall emotional tone of parent–child relationships, and they have sought to measure such broad and ambiguous variables of family interaction as warmth, permissiveness, hostility, or rejection. Here, too, the research results have remained inconclusive and difficult to replicate.

The overwhelming emphasis on mother–child interactions that still persists in socialization studies is also due, at least in part, to Freudian influences. There would seem to be little question that the family is indeed of prime importance in the socialization process. It forms the context in which a child first encounters such pervasive experiences as sexuality, inferiority, authority, and support. It is also there in the family that he first experiences the role differentiations that underlie all organized social life, in the distinctions his parents and siblings make on the basis of age, sex, and generation (Parsons and Bales, 1955).

But parents are no longer the unchallenged influence they once might have been. Increasingly, in modern societies, schools, peers, and the mass media have broadened the socialization process, and the accelerating pace of change itself may have diminished the relative power and influence of childhood experiences by calling for continual transformations of the personality and behavior styles first acquired in family interactions. Psychoanalytic theory provides few reliable guidelines for assessing the impact of these other socializing forces.

The scientific study of socialization calls for the empirical verification of testable hypotheses, and in this regard psychoanalytic theory seems particularly inadequate. For the followers of Freud, the central phenomena of personality development occur inside the person, in the form of desires, fantasies, feelings, and internal conflicts. These are virtually impossible to observe and measure. The theoretical conceptions of the Freudians are so rich, and there are so many ways by which overt behaviors can be linked to unconscious motivations, that it is difficult to conceive of any empirical findings that the theory could not explain. Almost any childhood record, it would seem, can be made compatible with almost any outcome in adulthood. Clearly, as social scientists we shall have to add to the sensitive poetry of psychoanalysis the more rigorous and testable propositions that derive from other perspectives.

Learning Theory: Behaviorism

The revolution in psychology wrought by behaviorism (Watson, 1925) may have carried us too far in the opposite direction. If fantasies, desires, and emotions are inherently private and unobservable, then a scientific psychology, it was argued, should deliberately ignore them and confine its attention exclusively to overt behavior—to actions that can be observed and measured. It should seek to establish empirical laws that govern the relationship between observable behavior and the external, equally observable consequences that follow upon it. Such a scientific approach assumes that the concepts and principles that apply to lower animals in laboratory experiments can account for human behavior as well. Socialization, in this view, refers to the changes in behavior that result directly from experience.

Environmental determinism

If you place a rat in an empty cage, it will usually engage in basically random movements, much as Martha might appear to do in this episode as she explores her surroundings. If the cage is rigged in such a way that a food pellet discharges when a bar is pressed, the rat will eventually press it by accident and then more consistently as each response is followed by reinforcement. Similarly, in Martha's random movements around the room, nothing noteworthy happens until she touches the lamp and her father suddenly pays attention. No wonder she returns to the lamp a second time. No organism responsive to physical contact and human interaction would fail to do so.

Her father's second intervention, however, was somewhat less friendly. There was surely more brusqueness in his manner, more anger in his voice, and these responses now counterbalanced his nurturant attentions. The ambivalence in her father's interventions is precisely reflected in Martha's oscillating behavior of approaching, hesitating, and retreating in the presence of the lamp. To see in this behavior an expression of internal forces that represent the anal stage of development is to substitute mystical, mentalistic fictions for observable relations between stimuli and responses. Martha is confronting a classic approach–avoidance conflict in this episode, not unlike what a rat would exhibit if an electric shock were suddenly administered along with the food pellet every time it pressed the bar.

The conflict created by this confusion of positive and negative payoffs is resolved when Martha echoes her father's words, in a generalized imitative response that has undoubtedly been rewarded before. The unambiguous smiles and hugs of approval that she now receives will further strengthen the imitative tendencies she exhibits here. What purpose, a behaviorist would ask, is served by assuming that Martha is in the throes of some decisive emotional encounter with her father or within herself? What evidence is there to justify seeing in this episode the emergence of some internal moral agency, created through a mysterious process of identification with the parental figure?

Complex behaviors, according to the behaviorist perspective, are acquired by individuals as a direct function of the forces applied to them by the socializing agents in their environment. The behaviorists see no fundamental differences in this regard among children, adolescents, or adults. The differences reside only in societal expectations, in the behaviors that are considered appropriate at successive ages, and hence in the external reinforcements that accompany

*Parents rely heavily
on learning theory:
the carrot
or the stick.*

them. There are no inner laws of development here, nor is there a biological plan that establishes distinct stages according to age and that dictates sequential changes in psychological structures within the child himself. There is only a continual process of feedback between behavior and its consequences. All children learn from their environment in identical ways, but what they learn and when they learn it will be as variable as the cultural forms that human beings have invented. As B. F. Skinner (1971, p. 83) wrote in *Beyond Freedom and Dignity*, "It is the contingencies we arrange, rather than the unfolding of some predetermined pattern, which are responsible for the changes observed."

Why do boys usually develop the attitudes and behaviors that in Western eyes are appropriate for males and different from those that girls acquire? Surely not because of some inevitable biological determinism of the "anatomy-is-destiny" school, as psychoanalysts have suggested. Perhaps sex roles develop in part by imitation of same-sexed older models or through the symbolic messages carried in children's readers and media broadcasts. But primarily, according to the hypothesis of learning theory, boys and girls behave in a manner appropriate to their sex because American parents, teachers and peers presumably have tended to discourage expressions of aggression and achievement more consistently in girls than in boys, and they have discouraged passivity, dependency and expressions of fear more consistently in boys than they have in girls. Social roles are expressed in, and perpetuated by means of differential contingencies and histories of reinforcement.

Whether all behavior is viewed as determined by such reinforcement histories (Skinner, 1971), or whether an emphasis is also placed on the role of imitation and observational learning (Bandura and Walters, 1963), the process of socialization is assumed to be an exclusive function of the external forces that are applied to the child. There is in this view no internal structuring, no personality as that term is usually understood, that must be taken into account in an effort to explain the maintenance or change in any pattern of behavior. If a child acts in some objectionable way, the responsibility lies with the environmental contingencies that continue to reinforce that behavior, and it is the environment, not some attribute of the individual, that must be changed.

By directing our attention to the environmental forces responsible for the maintenance and change of behavior, the perspective of learning theory has helped to clarify the importance of social structures and role expectations in instructing children to conform to cultural definitions of acceptable behavior and in changing their responses when those expectations are altered. By focusing on the relationship between environmental antecedents and behavioral consequences, the propositions of learning theory lend themselves directly to the experimental method and to the canons of scientific clarity and rigor.

Shortcomings: The human dimension. If, indeed, a child becomes what he is purely as a function of environmental pressures, the process of socialization is, in essence, transformed into an engineering problem. The behavioral scientist has only to manipulate the environmental conditions and he can produce in any child whatever results he deems desirable. The object of these attentions, the developing human being, is treated as an essentially passive and malleable recipient of external influences that shape and then sustain certain habits of response, in a one-way process of manipulation. Some crucial dimensions of human experience seem to be missing from this analysis.

An overly narrow focus on what is readily observable in a laboratory situation may have obscured the qualities that make human behavior and social interaction different, not only in degree but in kind, from what can be found in the behavior of other animals. The experimental paradigm that informs the perspective of learning theory may be adequate to investigate the effects of specific situational variables on specific behavior systems—the reduction in the duration and frequency of temper tantrums, for example, when parents are carefully instructed in how to avoid reinforcing them in any way—but it has come to seem impoverished when applied to the complex relationships in which children actually develop.

Socialization takes place within structures of reciprocal interactions, and the child is an active participant, stimulating and reinforcing parental behaviors as well as being influenced by them. Constitutional variations in temperament, energy level, stature, or body build elicit different responses from socializing agents (Bell, 1968). And surely, parents cannot be construed as abstract dispensers of consistent child-rearing practices in accordance with known principles of behavior modification. Their responses to their children are affected by situational strains and conflicting pressures, by their own anxieties and insecurities. A child's dependence, after all, is only half of the context of human relatedness and need that defines the socialization process.

Human interactions entail mutual coordinations of behavior and complementary expectations. Learning a role means much more than the simple stamping in of acceptable behaviors. It involves the symbolic and reflective learning of a relationship, and parents as well as children are socialized through the interactions that express their interdependency. Human beings must ultimately be studied within the unique context of their full humanity.

Symbolic Interaction

The special capacity for language not only differentiates humans from other species, but confers a distinctive quality on the relationship of a human being to his environment. The symbolic interactionist sees the world as essentially comprising not objective physical stimuli but subjective and symbolic meanings that are constructed and maintained in social interactions. In this perspective, the heart of the socialization process is the transformation of a newborn infant whose modes of responding to the environment resemble those of other animals, into a social actor whose responses are now unique to human beings. It means that a child learns to participate in the creation and perpetuation of the elaborated systems of meanings and relationships that comprise the culture and social structure of the society to which he belongs. And it is a learning process that can occur only through symbolic communication.

An infant engages solely in nonsymbolic interactions, responding, for the most part, immediately and unreflectively to its own physiological urges and its parents' actions. During the second year of life, however, a different level of interaction begins to emerge, in which the child responds to her parents on the basis of her interpretations of her parents' actions. At seventeen months of age, Martha is in the process of making this transition.

The development of the self

The first time her father led her away from the lamp to safer toys, Martha seems to have reacted to his actions and words as if they were only physical gestures, with no broader meaning beyond that interaction itself. She responded in complementary and nonreflective ways, moving where her father led her and looking at the objects to which her attention was directed. When her father left her perceptual field to join the others, she was again free to follow her impulses, and they led her to the lamp again.

The second intervention clearly brought something new, but its novelty lay less in the physical changes in her father's gestures than in the meanings that Martha now seemed to attribute to them. She was beginning at this point to recognize that her father's actions meant something more than the physical gestures themselves; behind them lay inner attitudes of anger and impatience, an intention to carry out more drastic measures, and the possibility of a negative evaluation of herself. As George Herbert Mead (1934), one of the originators of this perspective, would have put it, a "conversation of gestures" is changing in this episode into interaction by way of "significant symbols." The vehicle for this decisive transformation is the acquisition of language, the process by which it occurs is role-taking, and its central consequence is the eventual emergence of a coherent conception of self.

When Martha said to herself, "Don't touch," she was not just imitating sounds she had heard before. She was actively pretending to be her father at the same time that she consciously remained herself, imaginatively reenacting both parts of the preceding interactions in which she had participated. For perhaps the first time, she was now beginning to view herself from her father's perspective, to evaluate and control her own behavior by imagining the way others in her surroundings evaluate her. Thus a spanking may hurt far more than the physical pain it engenders, for it also carries the threat of abandonment, disapproval, and humiliation. The influence on human beings of the rewards and punishments they experience can be understood only in the light of the symbolic meanings that they attach to them.

Mead pointed out that it is by means of taking the role of a significant other, such as a parent, that a child gradually comes to be able to view herself as an object of her own activities. She can then represent to herself what she wishes to communicate to others; to conceive and respond to herself in the ways that significant others do. In this manner, she can learn to anticipate and evaluate the reactions of her parents and others before actually carrying out a contemplated course of action. In all these respects, the experiencing of the self is an inherently social phenomenon, since it is only by recognizing how significant others experience us that we can fully experience ourselves.

The process by which the self develops begins when a young child plays at the roles of specific others, pretending to be his mother, his schoolteacher, the policeman, or an older brother, acting toward himself as he has seen these others act. It progresses to gamelike activities, as the growing child now comes to view his own behavior within the framework of the groups in which he

When a child experiences the humanity of another he becomes more human.

participates, in terms of which his own actions have particular meaning. The final development occurs in adolescence when he fashions a conception of the abstract community, of what Mead called the *generalized other*. He has grown, in other words, from a conception of "what Mommy expects of me" to "what the team or the family expects," and finally to "what one is expected to do"—that one being himself as part of the whole society insofar as he understands it. Once a conception of the generalized other is established, a person can construct a self-image characterized by a degree of unity, coherence and stability that was lacking in his earlier identifications with specific people. Berger and Luckmann (1966, p. 126) put it this way: "Primary socialization ends when the concept of the generalized other (and all that goes with it) has been established in the consciousness of the individual. At this point he is an effective member of society and in subjective possession of a self and a world." (See the discussion of social order in chapter 6.)

The acquisition of language, the development of role-playing, and the emergence of the self combine to create a social actor, a person who guides his own actions by taking into account the meanings, values and identities that he shares with others in his culture. These, in turn, inform his interpretations of himself and his social world. He has become capable of participating in the ongoing process of collective life, in which individuals fit their lines of action to one another by mutually taking each other's roles, and where words and meanings are the foundation of social cohesion and of social conflict (Blumer, 1969).

Socialization and self-direction

The symbolic interaction perspective offers a view of the socialization process that differs in important respects from the other approaches we have examined. If we accept its premises, we can no longer view the child as a passive reactor to physical stimuli or emotional impulse. A child is not a wordless organism whose unsuitable responses are automatically extinguished and more appropriate ones shaped and sustained by purely external contingent reinforcements. Nor can we be satisfied with a view of socialization that places the crucial events wholly inside the child himself, abstracted from his ongoing interactions with others. We observe instead a reflective creature, sensitive to symbolic meanings, who fashions his conceptions of his own identity out of the social relationships in which he is embedded. A social actor, guided by his self-conceptions, imaginatively constructs his actions on the basis of the meanings that objects and events come to have for him. Let us reexamine, in this light, the process of sex-role learning that results in psychological differences between boys and girls.

In a survey of all the available evidence, Maccoby and Jacklin (1974) concluded that this process cannot be adequately explained in terms of the differential shaping of boy-like and girl-like behavior by socialization agents. Parents, the data reveal, generally treat a child of their own in terms of their knowledge of his or her individual characteristics, with little reference to sex-role stereotypes, and their values concerning how the two sexes ought to behave are remarkably similar. Children seem to adopt sex-typed patterns of play and interests for which they have never been directly rewarded, and they avoid sex-inappropriate activities for which they have never been punished. Socialization, at least in terms of sex-role learning, appears to be far more self-directed than learning theory would allow. Nor does the psychoanalytic concept of identification with the same-sex parent appear to be adequate to explain the evidence. According to Freudian views, a child learns the details of a sex role by imitation of that adult model; and he will do so whether or not external reinforcements are administered, because, by virtue of identification, he is internally motivated to take on the attributes of his same-sex parent. But the sex-typed behavior of children generally shows little resemblance to that of adult models. Boys generally select all-male play groups though they rarely observe their fathers avoiding the company of females, and girls play hopscotch and jacks though such games are never engaged in by their mothers.

Processes of direct reinforcement and simple imitation are clearly involved in sex-role learning, but they are not sufficient to account for the developmental changes that occur. The symbolic interaction perspective would emphasize, instead, the active role of self-conceptions. In the early development of the self-image, a child recognizes his own sex-identity, and he elaborates an increasingly complex conception of "masculinity" and "femininity" as he organizes information about sex-role behavior from a wide variety of cultural sources—from the games and toys available to him, from movies and televi-

Figure 2–1. Verbal ability is thought to be largely a product of socialization. As this table shows, females, from ages 3 to 17, consistently score higher on verbal tests measuring a range of aptitudes. The superiority of females in such skills is one of the few generalizations to emerge from the study of sex differences. The one interesting exception in the table, the English boys, reflects the fact that British culture places heavy emphasis on verbal skills in males.

SEX DIFFERENCES IN VERBAL ABILITY

| Study | Age | Mean scores | | Sex scoring higher |
		Boys	Girls	
Shipman (1971) (U.S.A.):	3–4	25.9	26.8	F
Stanford Research Institute (1972) (U.S.A.):				
Reading	5	32.57	36.15	F
	7	55.01	62.09	F
Language	5	12.09	12.53	F
	7	18.36	19.69	F
Gates (1961) (U.S.A.):				
Reading speed	7	7.37	8.43	F
Vocabulary	7	9.41	11.26	F
Comprehension	7	7.05	8.66	F
Reading speed	10	19.63	20.94	F
Vocabulary	10	26.36	28.16	F
Comprehension	10	22.60	23.64	F
Reading speed	13	20.07	21.49	F
Vocabulary	13	37.15	39.60	F
Comprehension	13	30.49	31.33	F
Brimer (1969) (England):	8	17.60	15.98	M
	9	22.36	19.34	M
	10	26.80	23.60	M
	11	29.20	26.88	M
Svensson (1971) (Sweden):				
School I–1961	13	87.54	89.61	F
School II–1961	13	88.69	90.18	F
School I–1966	13	114.58	123.32	F
School II–1966	13	54.61	58.36	F
Droege (1967) (U.S.A.):				
General aptitude test				
battery	14	93.20	95.55	F
	15	96.60	100.03	F
	16	98.70	102.93	F
	17	100.19	103.38	F

SOURCE: Adapted from Maccoby, E. E., and Jacklin, C. N. *The psychology of sex differences.* Stanford, Calif.: Stanford University Press, 1974. Table 3–4.

sion, advertisements and children's readers, teachers' expectations, and peer-group interactions. As they grow older and for reasons not yet well understood, children will differ in the degree to which their conceptions of "masculinity" or "femininity" become central to their self-definitions. Only for some will such conceptions come to serve as consistent bases for the self-monitoring of activities, interests, and personal attributes. The evidence reviewed by Maccoby and Jacklin revealed very few clear and consistent differences between men and women over the wide range of psychological variables that have been studied. It seems likely, however, as the authors suggest (1974, p. 360), that if the subjects in these studies had been more carefully selected to include only those women who considered it important to be feminine and those men for whom masculinity was central to their self-concept, the chances are that greater sex differences would have been reported, and the results would have been much more consistent than they were found to be. From the perspective of symbolic interaction theory, we cannot understand behavior simply by studying external environmental forces; we must seek to see the world and its influences from the point of view of the subjects themselves.

Researchers in this tradition reject experimental designs that make it impossible to take into account a person's active role in selecting, interpreting and ordering the influences of his social world, and they are unlikely to be much interested in efforts to uncover the unconscious dynamics of his mental life. Instead, we are likely to find them in homes, schools, and playgrounds, carefully observing the construction of mutually dependent social interactions, and conceiving of children as psychological and social beings in their own right, rather than merely as incomplete or deficient adults (Dreitzel, 1973).

There is still more to human development, however, than we have seen from these three perspectives. We have come to recognize that, in some very important respects, childhood is more distinctive than most of us had thought. A person's ways of knowing and understanding the world change as he matures, and those cognitive transformations profoundly affect his experience of the external events that are likely to be important in the socialization process.

The Cognitive–Developmental Perspective

Our fourth conception of the socialization process derives from the monumental work of Jean Piaget. His careful observations of infants, children, and adolescents in their active constructions of progressively more adequate conceptions of reality have transformed our understanding of the nature of child development. All biological organisms construct and maintain themselves through active processes of interchange with their environment. Human beings develop psychologically as well as physiologically through this same process of adaptation, assimilating a new experience into preexisting cognitive structures and simultaneously accommodating those structures to fit the novel contours of that experience. "Intelligent activity," as John Flavell (1963, p. 17) has shown in his presentation of Piaget's theory, "is always an active, organized process of assimilating the new to the old and of accommodating the old to the new." The process begins in the first months of life.

PIAGET'S TEST FOR THE CONSERVATION OF LIQUIDS

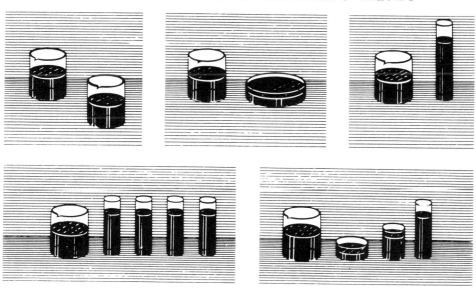

Figure 2–2. Piaget used glasses of different shapes to study the way the preoperational child deals with the concept of conservation. For example, in the drawing in the upper right, the two glasses have the same capacity. But if the contents of the short, wide glass are poured into the tall, narrow one, the preoperational child will say that the taller glass contains more liquid than the short one. He is not capable of understanding that the amount of liquid in each is the same regardless of the container's shape.

SOURCE: Inhelder, B. Criteria of the stages of mental development. In J. M. Tanner and B. Inhelder (Eds.), *Discussions on child development: A consideration of the biological, psychological, and cultural approaches to the understanding of human development and behavior.* Vol. 1 of the Proceedings of the First Meeting of the World Health Organization Study Group on the Psychological Development of the Child, Geneva, 1953. New York: International Universities Press, 1953. Pp. 75–96.

The development of intelligence

The newborn infant, as we have already seen from other perspectives, has no internal devices for mentally representing objects or events that are not immediately present in his perceptual field. His responses to stimuli, originally reflexive and immediate, gradually become purposeful and directed. He comes to fashion for himself the concept of objects as permanent, independent entities. As he begins his second year of life, he can be observed exploring the contours of his environment, modifying what he does to the objects he encounters in order to observe the effects of his actions.

This period of *sensorimotor* development draws to a close as the child ac-

PIAGET'S TEST FOR THE CONSERVATION OF SURFACE

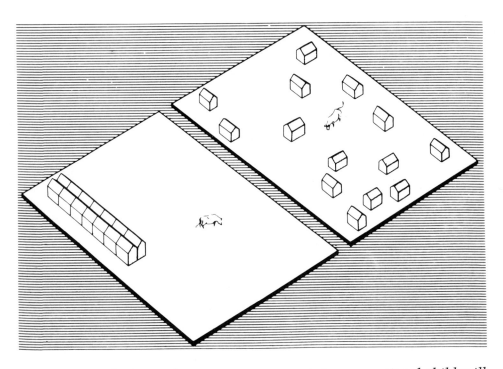

Figure 2–3. *Which cow has more grass to eat? A preoperational child will answer that the cow on the field at the left has more grass. The arrangement of the houses on the fields leads the youngster to believe that the field on the right is smaller than that on the left. In reality, the fields are equal in size, and each one contains the same number of houses.*

SOURCE: See Figure 2–2.

quires the ability to imagine the effect of his actions mentally without having to carry them out. He has reached the level of development attained at a somewhat earlier age by an infant chimpanzee. In human beings the sensorimotor stage marks only the first step in a long process of learning to deal with symbols and to manipulate representations of actions and events. Cognitive activities of thinking and reasoning gradually develop into coordinated systems of mental operations that are progressively freed from the concrete realities of action and perception, to become by adolescence the abstract and logical operations of adult intelligence.

When Martha began that "eager exploration of her surroundings," there was much more at stake than the diffuse expression of instinctual impulses, and hers were not just random movements awaiting external reinforcements. It was an active, purposeful exploration, a motivated curiosity and a seeking of novelty, that led to her discovery of the lamp. And it was her fascination with the effects that she could have on the lamp, with her ability to make it "teeter and sway" by her own actions, that led her to return to it despite her father's repeated commands to leave it alone. These were sensorimotor actions directed to physical objects, but when she approached the lamp that final time there was evidence of a higher level of cognitive development. She stopped to reflect. Looking at the lamp, she carried out mentally her previous actions of reaching and touching, and without a glance at her father, she imitated his words and actions on the basis of the images she carried within herself. With this ability to internalize actions and to represent mentally perceptual events, the sensorimotor period is over, and Martha shows in this episode that she has entered the period of *preoperational thought*.

At first, such mental images will mirror the sensorimotor actions of the previous stage, as the child simply runs off in his mind the actions he once had to carry out overtly. Language now develops rapidly, and in his first fumbling attempts to come to grips with the new world of symbols, he assimilates experience to his own actions and viewpoint. The three- or four-year-old child is convinced, for example, that the moon follows him at night and that the sun was made to keep him warm. He believes that anything that moves is alive, that the names of things are inherent in the things themselves, that his dreams and thoughts are real events that others can see as well as he, and that he gets more orangeade when he pours it from a short, wide glass into a taller, thinner one. Such ways of thinking inexorably create discrepancies for the child in his interactions with his environment, and as he attempts to come to grips with them, he gradually arrives at a reorganization of his cognitive processes.

The preoperational child, for example, generally deals with the environment in terms of before-the-eye reality. In the prototypical Piagetian experiment, a child is shown two beakers of identical shape and size. The examiner fills the first, then the child pours water into the second until he is sure that both contain exactly the same amount of liquid. While the child watches, the contents of the second beaker are poured into a third one, a beaker taller and thinner than the other two. The examiner might then ask, "Is there the same amount of water in these two glasses, or is there more in this one, or less?" The average four- or five-year-old is likely to answer that the third beaker now contains more water than the first. The higher level of the liquid in the thinner beaker is simply too powerful a stimulus for him to deny.

After further experiences of this sort and with increasing age, a child will come to realize spontaneously that the greater height in that third beaker is compensated by its smaller width. His attention shifts to the transformations involved instead of the perceptual appearances alone. This redirection of thought readily leads to the recognition that transformations can be reversed: the water from the taller, thinner beaker can be poured back into the original wider one, and its height will now be the same as it was before. The specific problem at hand becomes simply one particular instance in a whole system of potential transformations and compensations: every increase in height brings an exactly compensating decrease in width, and no matter what the shape of the second beaker, the water can be poured back into the first and its original shape restored.

For a child aged seven or eight who has reached the period of *concrete operations*, the conservation of liquid across transformations in the shape of its containers is no longer a perceptual problem. It has become a logical necessity that derives from an organized and coherent self-regulating system of cognitive operations. There is now a definable structure to the child's way of thinking about events, one that is likely to be manifested throughout the whole range of reasoning and intelligent activity that he exhibits. Consider, for example, the development of moral judgments.

Moral development

As Piaget (1932) has shown, four- and five-year-old children tend to judge that a boy who breaks twelve cups through an unavoidable accident is more to blame than one who breaks a single cup while trying to steal some jam. Why? Because it is worse to break twelve cups than one cup. The preoperational child, we have seen, can deal only with before-the-eye reality. In this analogous realm, he judges moral conduct in terms of the immediate physical consequences of the act. Only later, as his intelligence develops into the structures of concrete operations, will he move toward moral judgments based upon the less visible intentions that lie behind an action.

The development of intentionality in moral reasoning seems particularly difficult to attribute to specific learning experiences. We have little reliable information concerning changes in parental treatment as a child grows older, but it would appear to be extremely unlikely that most parents consistently punish their children according to the consequences of their actions at age five, and then shift to discipline consistently based on intentions at age seven or eight. Yet most American children tend to make this particular transition in their judgments of behavior during that period. Nor does the concept of selective reinforcement seem sufficient by itself to explain why the timing of this development tends to be correlated with tested intelligence; nor why age

PIAGET'S TEST FOR NUMERICAL CORRESPONDENCE

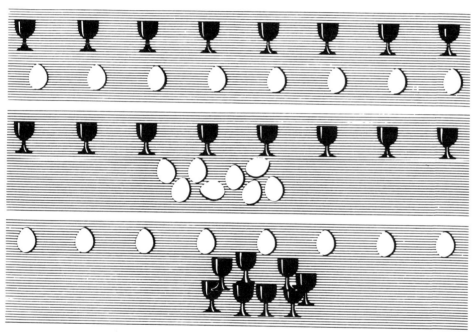

Figure 2–4. The average four- or five-year-old cannot handle the concept of one-to-one correspondence between physical objects. In each of the drawings shown here, there are eight eggs and eight egg cups. A child examining the top drawing could easily see that the number of cups equals the number of eggs because there is a one-to-one correspondence between the objects. In the middle drawing, however, the child would estimate that there are more egg cups than eggs because the eggs are concentrated in a small space. For the same reason, the preoperational child viewing the bottom drawing would estimate that there are more eggs than egg cups.

SOURCE: See Figure 2–2.

trends in this direction have been found among children in every culture, social class, sex group, and subculture in which such investigations have been carried out (Kohlberg, 1969, p. 374).

With the consolidation of concrete operations, the child has achieved a coherent and unified structure of interrelated mental processes by which he can deal logically and consistently with present events. But the eight- or nine-year-old is not yet readily able to apply this same logic to purely verbal propositions, to deal with possibilities that are not directly before him or that he has not already experienced. A further transformation and reintegration of cognitive structures occur at ages eleven or twelve, when the final transition to *formal operations* generally begins. "The most prominent feature of formal thought," as Inhelder and Piaget (1958, p. 252) have shown, "is that it no longer deals with objects directly but with verbal elements."

Adolescence

With the development of formal operations, the adolescent need no longer confine his logical processes to the real and the present. He can think about his own thoughts and manipulate images and propositions whose only reality is in the words he says to himself. When confronted with a conceptual or empirical problem, he can generate the full range of alternative explanations that might obtain in the situation. He can consider logically and consistently what would follow from each hypothesis if it were true, and he can then direct his actions and observations by possibilities that exist only in thought. Flavell (1963, p. 223) summarized this development: "The child deals largely with the present, with the here and the now; the adolescent extends his conceptual range to the hypothetical, the future, and the spatially remote."

The consolidation of formal operations is clearly a prerequisite for the emergence of an abstract conception of the "generalized other" and for a unified self-image based upon it—the achievements of adolescence that symbolic interactions have emphasized. It should now be evident as well that the identity crisis that psychoanalysts also attribute to adolescence simply could not occur to an average eight- or nine-year-old child. With only concrete operations to mediate his conceptions of reality, a preadolescent is unable to deal logically with the abstract "if–then" propositions that inform his anticipations of adulthood, and his images of that future remain open to the projection of unrealistic wish-fulfilling fantasies (Klineberg, 1967; Cottle and Klineberg, 1974). "The capacity for formal operations," Erikson (1962) has written, "forms not a contrast but a complement to the need of the young person to develop a sense of identity, for, from all possible and imaginable relations, he must make a series of ever-narrowing selections of personal, occupational, sexual, and ideological commitments." The average nine-year-old would be unable to deal with such issues, even if pressures from parents, teachers, and peers were prematurely to demand it. "The social role of the adolescent," Roger Brown (1965, p. 232) observed, "requires him to deal in possibilities, to entertain alternatives and envision consequences. Formally operational intelligence enables him to do so."

Cognitive development, in this conception, is neither a simple mirror image of external experiences nor a mere unfolding of responses in a predetermined maturational sequence. It involves, as Piaget (1970, p. 703) expressed it, "a set of structures progressively constructed by continuous interaction between the subject and the external world." An enriched educational environment may well accelerate the development we have described, but the sequence of stages appears to be invariable, and the changes they involve are not simple acts that can be readily taught, but complex patterns of thinking and reasoning that a child seems to arrive at spontaneously through the force of his own logic. Specific external influences can only affect a child's development, Piaget writes (1970, p. 721), "if he is capable of assimilating them, and he can do this only if he already possesses the adequate instruments or structures."

More generally, Piaget's work has made it clear that the socialization process cannot be understood as the simple transmission of norms and values from one generation to the next. The child himself is an active processor of his society's moral rules, and he will understand and interpret those rules in different ways as his conceptions of reality change with the form of his intelligence. If the child's cognitive structures, his modes of processing information and of drawing connections among events, do indeed undergo such fundamental transformations in the course of development, then the same parental demands, the same learning experiences will have different effects as a function of his psychological processes at the time. A child's changing cognitive characteristics will mediate and transform those very events that comprise the socialization process itself.

The Changing Experience of Childhood

The study of early socialization has long comprised one of the most active areas of research and theory in the behavioral sciences. In our effort to present a comprehensive overview, we have taken a broad theoretical approach, ignoring for the most part the more specific controversies and the legion of small-scale empirical studies that relate to them. The four conceptual perspectives we have examined reflect different basic assumptions about the nature of the child himself and of the ways individuals and their societies interrelate. Is the growing person essentially a passive reactor to external influences, his behavior patterns shaped and structured by the contingencies of reinforcement he encounters in his environment? Or does the child himself play an active role in his own socialization, influencing his social milieu as well as being influenced by it, selecting and transforming the impact of external events? If the latter, are those internal and directing forces primarily emotional and based upon biologically predetermined maturational sequences? Or are they primarily conceptual and cognitive, their order a function of broadening social experience and of a growing mastery of symbols and higher-order abstractions?

The position one takes with regard to such issues will shape the pattern of questions one asks about the socialization process and the research methods by which one approaches them. We have as yet no single theory that satisfactorily encompasses all aspects of personality development and social learning, but a general shift in emphasis has occurred in recent years. The more deterministic models of psychoanalysis and behaviorism, once supremely dominant in socialization research, are now declining in influence. In their place, we find a more complex conception of the child as social actor, engaged in the early stages of a lifelong process of symbolic and reflective learning within a cultural context that extends far beyond the confines of parents or family—a child who, as he matures, comes increasingly to monitor his own socialization, selecting role models and interpreting the events he experiences in terms of his developing self-conceptions and his changing cognitive constructions of reality.

The traditional conception of socialization has emphasized the training function of child-rearing, the responsibility of parents and schools to guide the child into proper paths, to teach him to conform to the norms of his society. It is reflected in the psychoanalyst's emphasis on the channeling of impulses and the behaviorist's preoccupation with the shaping of behavior through contingencies of external reinforcement. But it is a conception that would appear to be appropriate for an age that has now passed into history.

At the risk of oversimplifying a complex and multifaceted process, it might be suggested that before industrialization transformed the societies of the Western world, most individuals had little awareness of alternatives to their own particular way of life. Social change was generally slow and easily integrated into existing structures, so that it rarely disrupted the sense of participation in a timeless and predictable social order. Child-rearing was then a more communal responsibility, and growing up was a continuous and integral experience, as a child in his widening web of social contacts met others who would reinforce and confirm the earlier learning he acquired in interaction with his parents. In such relatively stable and homogeneous societies, the

SOCIALIZATION IN THE MIDDLE AND LATE YEARS

Socialization has not ordinarily been conceived as a lifelong process. Theorists have, until recently, focused on development in childhood and adolescence. As a result, most developmental theorists believe that a commitment to conforming behavior and a self-identity emerge in childhood and are validated as adolescents are integrated into adult life. But current investigators of adult socialization challenge the assumption that commitments, conforming behavior, and self-identity are stable in the adult years. George Maddox and Linda Breytspraak (1974) have reviewed the issues in adult socialization. The perspective which emerges emphasizes a number of factors that affect development in later years.

Among the most important of these factors are the individual's physical and social environments. Socialization in the middle and late years and its consequences for the self involve a transaction between the person and the environment. Not only are persons in a continual state of development and change, but so is the environment. Both can be thought of as having a past, present, and future. Their continual interaction with each other makes it impossible to conceive of either as ever remaining static.

As Maddox and Breytspraak point out, a key element mediating the response of the individual to the environment is the access of individuals variously placed in a society to the resources and opportunities for personal development and self-fulfillment that are potentially available. The inability to pursue these lead to deviant, unconventional behavior and alienation. The focus on differential access to the opportunities necessary to achieve personal fulfillment are a function of age, sex, ethnicity, and social class.

Indeed, these factors are the most commonly used explanatory variables in behavioral and personality research. Social class is a good indicator of differential access to the important social rewards of prestige and power. Predictably, lower socioeconomic status has been found to be a correlate of self-regard. Self-disparagement is a commonly reported consequence of the familial and interpersonal experiences indicated by lower socioeconomic status. The effect of such experiences increases the probability of self-disparagement, as well as of maladaptive responses to stress in the middle and later years.

A study by Kutner and his associates (1956) supports this conclusion. After noting that social status is significantly related to health, marital status, employment, and self-concept among persons sixty-five years of age and older, Kutner's evidence suggests not only that higher social status and a positive self-concept predict high morale among the aged, but also that social status mediates the negative impact of declining health and loss of social roles on morale.

Although most investigators agree that the environment is an important factor in the development of the individual in middle and later years, they would also agree that it is not the only one. Other factors include such personal characteristics as the identity of the self, the structure and functioning of the ego, and social competence. However, there is much disagreement about various aspects of each of these three factors. Moreover, as Maddox and Breytspraak point out, many comments about development in the middle and late years have run considerably ahead of the evidence.

future was a known continuum stretching indefinitely ahead, and a child could see in his parents and grandparents a sure and unquestioned image of himself grown older. It was here that the experience of childhood most readily fit the traditional conceptions of socialization, for there were known and stable social roles for children to fit into after appropriate training, and there was a continuity between early socialization and the demands of adulthood that could insure the smooth transmission of that culture to succeeding generations.

In the highly modernized and rapidly changing societies of today, the process of socialization has become far more complex and problematical. Parents are no longer sure enough of the staying power of their own ways of behaving to try forcefully to instill them in their children, and adolescents turn increasingly to their peers for sources of identity and interpretations of the world they are entering. Growing children are no longer exposed to a stable, consistent pattern of social expectations and cultural values, and the broadening context of socialization now includes parents as only one of the many and conflicting influences that a child confronts.

*In adolescence
it's what your friends
think that counts.*

Above all, the accelerating speed of social change and the growing recognition that current patterns may threaten man's very survival on this planet have underscored the dilemma of educating children for an unknown future (Levy, 1972). As Kenneth Keniston (1971, p. 73) has written, "If growing up were merely a matter of becoming 'socialized,' that is, of learning how to 'fit into' society, it is hard to see how anyone could grow up at all in modern America, for the society into which young people will someday 'fit' remains to be developed or even imagined."

It has become more difficult to draw a sharp distinction between primary and secondary socialization—between the early learning in childhood when basic values, motives, and personality styles were thought to be established, and the later learning of adulthood that was assumed to be confined to the acquisition of specific role-related skills (Brim and Wheeler, 1966). Adult roles today have become far more fluid than this suggests. Major life options remain open throughout adulthood, as problems of choice and freedom, of commitment and meaning, now dominate the relationship between the individual and society. In the behavioral sciences, such central theoretical constructs as socialization, personality, character and identity—once clearly structured with predictable continuities—now refer, in a way that may be unique in history, to lifelong, open-ended and self-directed processes. The changes in assumptions and emphasis that we have seen in the study of socialization reflect these new realities.

Summary

Each new person that is born has the potentiality to become a member of any society on earth. Socialization is the process by which a child responds to the efforts of the older members of her own society to learn their ways. It can be seen as a process which restricts a child's behavior, attitudes, motives, and values, until she conforms to the prevailing social order.

Human babies, however, are not the only newborns who undergo the socialization process. The different species of the animal world have each evolved a complex pattern of behavior which their young must learn and experience. Animal behavior, as ethologists have discovered, is not determined solely by the inheritance of a syndrome of behavioral traits. Heredity endows the organism not with an inherited behavior but with a capacity to develop certain behavior under certain conditions. "Heredity begins at conception and ends at death."

Social psychologists have developed several different perspectives to explain the way a child learns to function in her society. The first is the psychoanalytic interpretation by Freud and its modification by Erikson. Freud divides the child development process into several stages. The oral stage features incorporation of food, and sights and sounds as well. The child is taking in the world. Freud's next stage is the anal stage, interpreted by Erikson as a learning to alternately hold on and let go. Erikson interprets the development from one stage to the next as a confrontation in a series of crises, each of which must be mastered in the process of reaching maturity. The principal shortcoming of the psychoanalytical perspective lies in the impossibility, because of its subjectivity, to verify empirically any of its propositions.

Learning theory, or behaviorism, on the other hand, has been criticized for its concern with only what can be observed and its denial of subjective phenomena. According to the behaviorists, inner laws of development and biological stages do not exist, since they cannot be observed and measured. Behaviorists view socialization as a continuous process of feedback between behavior and its consequences. All children learn from their environment in identical ways; children differ because each child's environment differs from the next. The shortcoming of the behaviorist perspective lies in its omission of the active participation of the child. Each child brings something of his own to the process that is unique, as does each parent. Socialization is an interaction between human beings, not a manipulation of human engineering.

According to the perspective of symbolic interaction, socialization is a learning process that takes place through symbolic communication. The importance of behavior lies not in the objective, observable behavior itself, but in the meaning it has both for the actor and those he comes in contact with. Each individual makes an interpretation of his own behavior and the behavior of others through a continuous process of action, interaction, and reaction. One reacts to the meaning of an act to both oneself and the one who performs the act, rather than to the act itself. Thus, the symbolic interactionist is interested in the world from the point of view of the subjects of his study—how they select, interpret, and order the influences of their social world.

The cognitive–developmental perspective derives from the work of Piaget, who is concerned with the psychological, as well as the physical, adaptation of children to their environment. Important in this adaptation are the processes of assimilating new experience and accommodating to the old. Piaget's interest is in the development of intelligence, the cognitive activities of thinking and reasoning. Piaget sees the child as gradually becoming freed of the necessity to root his thought in the concrete realities of action and perception, and by adolescence, capable of abstract and logical reasoning. This perspective is, like the psychoanalytic perspective, one in which development is conceptualized in stages. A child's moral development parallels his intellectual development, and between the ages of five and eight he makes the shift in attribution of blame and guilt from accidental actions to intentional ones. Piaget's work has made it clear that socialization does not consist merely in transmitting norms and values from one generation to the next, but that the child, too, is an active processor of his society's moral rules.

Socialization does not come to an abrupt halt upon physical maturity. An individual experiences a lifelong process of symbolic and reflective learning within a cultural context that extends far beyond parents and family. In the rapidly changing societies of today's world, major life options remain open throughout adulthood. Socialization is no longer confined to childhood but becomes an open-ended, self-directed process.

Bibliography

BANDURA, A., AND WALTERS, R. H. *Social learning and personality development.* New York: Holt, Rinehart and Winston, 1963.

BELL, R. Q. A reinterpretation of the direction of effects in studies of socialization. *Psychological Review,* 1968, **74,** 81–95.

BERGER, P. L., AND LUCKMANN, T. *The social construction of reality.* Garden City, N.Y.: Doubleday, 1966.

BLUMER, H. *Symbolic interactionism: Perspective and method.* Englewood Cliffs, N.J.: Prentice-Hall, 1969.

BREGER, L. *From instinct to identity: The development of personality.* Englewood Cliffs, N.J.: Prentice-Hall, 1974.

BRIM, O. G., JR., AND WHEELER, S. *Socialization after childhood: Two essays.* New York: John Wiley, 1966.

BROWN, R. *Social Psychology.* New York: Free Press, 1965.

COTTLE, T. J., AND KLINEBERG, S. L. *The present of things future: Explorations of time in human experience.* New York: Free Press, 1974.

DOBZHANSKY, T. The genetic nature of differences among men. In S. Persons (Ed.), *Evolutionary thought in America.* New Haven: Yale University Press, 1950.

DREITZEL, H. B (Ed.) *Recent sociology No. 5: Childhood and socialization.* New York: Macmillan, 1973.

ERIKSON, E. H. *Childhood and society.* New York: W. W. Norton, 1950.

ERIKSON, E. H. Identity and the life cycle: Selected papers. *Psychological Issues,* 1959, **1** (Whole No. 1).

ERIKSON, E. H. Youth: Fidelity and diversity. *Daedalus,* 1962, **91,** 5–27.

FLAVELL, J. H. *The developmental psychology of Jean Piaget.* New York: D. Van Nostrand, 1963.

GARDNER, R. A., AND GARDNER, B. T. Teaching sign language to a chimpanzee. *Science,* August 15, 1969, **165,** 664–672.

HALLOWELL, A. I. *Culture and experience.* Philadelphia: University of Pennsylvania Press, 1955.

HEBB, D. O. *A textbook of psychology.* (2nd ed.) Philadelphia: W. B. Saunders, 1966.

HEBB, D. O., AND THOMPSON, W. R. The social significance of animal studies. In G. Lindzey and E. Aronson (Eds.), *The handbook of social psychology.* (2nd ed.) Vol. 2. Reading, Pa.: Addison-Wesley, 1968.

HESS, E. H. Ethology: An approach toward the complete analysis of behavior. In R. Brown et al. (Eds.), *New directions in psychology.* New York: Holt, Rinehart and Winston, 1962.

INHELDER, B. Criteria of the stages of mental development. In J. M. Tanner and B. Inhelder (Eds.), *Discussions on child development: A consideration of the biological, psychological, and cultural approaches to the understanding of human development and behavior.* Vol. 1 of the Proceedings of the First Meeting of the World Health Organization Study Group on the Psychological Development of the Child, Geneva, 1953. New York: International Universities Press, 1953.

INHELDER, B., AND PIAGET, J. *The growth of logical thinking from childhood to adolescence.* (A. Parsons and S. Milgram, trans.) New York: Basic Books, 1958.

KENISTON, K. *Youth and dissent: The rise of a new opposition.* New York: Harcourt Brace Jovanovich, 1971.

KLINEBERG, S. L. Changes in outlook on the future between childhood and adolescence. *Journal of Personality and Social Psychology,* 1967, **7,** 185–193.

KOHLBERG, L. Stage and sequence: The cognitive–developmental approach to socialization. In D. Goslin (Ed.), *Handbook of socialization theory and research.* Chicago: Rand McNally, 1969.

KUTNER, B., FANSHEL, D., TOGO, A., AND LANGNER, T. *Five hundred over sixty.* New York: Russell Sage Foundation, 1956.

LEHRMAN, D. S. Problems raised by instinct theories. In R. C. Birney and R. C. Teevan (Eds.), *Instinct: An enduring problem in psychology.* New York: D. Van Nostrand, 1961.

LEVY, M. J., JR. *Modernization: Latecomers and survivors.* New York: Basic Books, 1972.

MACCOBY, E. E., AND JACKLIN, C. N. *The psychology of sex differences.* Stanford, Calif.: Stanford University Press, 1974.

MADDOX, G. L., AND BREYTSPRAAK, L. M. The self and its development: Socialization in the middle and late years. Unpublished manuscript, 1974.

MEAD, G. H. *Mind, self, and society: From the standpoint of a social behaviorist.* Chicago: University of Chicago Press, 1934.

PARSONS, T., AND BALES, R. F. *Family, socialization and interaction process.* New York: Free Press, 1955.

PIAGET, J. *The moral judgment of the child.* New York: Harcourt Brace Jovanovich, 1932.

PIAGET, J. Piaget's theory. In P. H. Mussen (Ed.), *Carmichael's manual of child psychology.* (3rd ed.) New York: John Wiley, 1970.

SEARS, R. R., MACCOBY, E. E., AND LEVIN, H. *Patterns of child rearing.* New York: Harper and Row, 1957.

SKINNER, B. F. *Beyond freedom and dignity.* New York: Vintage, 1971.

SPITZ, R. A. Hospitalism. In R. S. Eissler, A. Freud, H. Hartmann, and M. Kris (Eds.), *The psychoanalytic study of the child.* Vols. 1 and 2. New York: International Universities Press, 1946.

TINBERGEN, N. The curious behavior of the stickleback. *Scientific American,* December 1952, **187,** 22–26.

WASHBURN, S. L. Speculations on the interrelations of the history of tools and biological evolution. In J. N. Spuhler (Ed.), *The evolution of man's capacity for culture.* Detroit: Wayne State University Press, 1959.

WATSON, J. B. *Behaviorism.* New York: W. W. Norton, 1925.

3

Social Interaction

Most of us fill our lives with a series of smoothly managed social interactions. We move from situation to situation, talking to complete strangers at one point and to close friends at another. The substance of our interaction varies radically from one context to the next and, frequently, within a single context. For the most part, we are able to manage this *tour de force* without any conscious thought as we easily shift our demeanor and behavior, tailoring them to each different situation.

Of course, sometimes we stumble. We become embarrassed or embarrass others, we feel uncertain about the appropriateness of our responses, or the interaction falters in a bog of mutual resentment. But despite these occasional failures, we do pretty well most of the time—so well that we tend to take our success for granted. One need only witness the awkwardness of young children interacting with strangers to recognize that the skill we take for granted was learned, frequently with difficulty, over a considerable number of years.

This fact leads us quite logically to the question, what is the nature of social interaction? What happens when two or more individuals encounter one another in a social situation? The answer to this question depends upon the extent to which the responses of one or all parties are conditioned by what the

75

other parties do or say. In other words, how contingent are the acts or words of one party on another? For example, is the response of one participant in an interaction contingent on the action of another? Is each participant equal in his power to influence the direction of the interaction? Or does one person control the situation? How might an exchange of pleasantries be categorized within this context?

The Process of Interaction

Social situations vary in the extent to which the responses of one or all parties are contingent, or dependent, on what the other parties say or do. The term *interaction* implies contingency, and we are loath to use it when such contingency is obviously not present. We hesitate to say that two babies are "interacting" when they happen to be playing next to each other, each listening to his own drummer and responding to the other only in the minimal way necessary for coexistence.

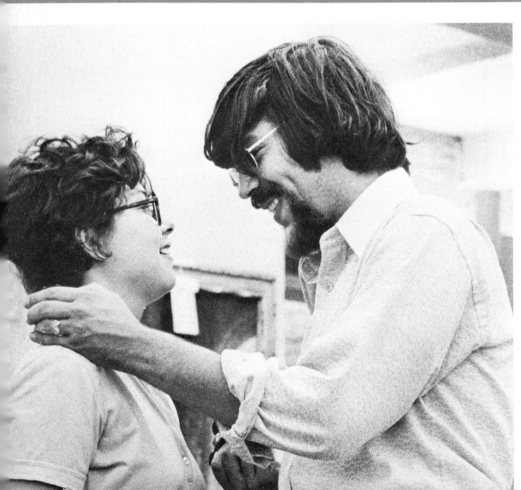

*Mutual
contingency*

Using the idea of contingency as a starting point, Jones and Thibaut (1958) and Jones and Gerard (1967) make several distinctions that help us to analyze what is going on when two or more people are engaged in any interaction situation. These investigators assume two basic determinants of any person's behavior in an interaction situation—the plans he brings into the situation, and the actions of others toward him in the situation. The term *plans* refers to the goals and motives with which one enters an interaction situation, the beliefs and cognitions about how these goals can be achieved, and the pattern of attitudes and expectations about the situation and the others with whom one is interacting.

In order for an investigator to determine how the responses of one party are contingent upon the actions or words of the other party in any social situation, he might begin by asking three questions: (1) To what degree are the individual's responses determined by his own plans? (2) To what degree are they contingent on the responses of others? (3) To what degree are they based on a genuine combination of the two? Furthermore, the answers to these questions may be different for different people—some may be responding to others even though these others are following their own plans in a noncontingent fashion. In the light of these considerations, let us see how the idea of contingency works by examining four different kinds of contingency: pseudocontingency, asymmetrical contingency, reactive contingency, and mutual contingency.

Pseudocontingency

The *pseudocontingency* situation is characterized by each participant reacting primarily to his own plans; his responses are minimally contingent on the responses of others. The prefix "pseudo" is well chosen, since typically, in such situations, there is an appearance of response to others. Consider, for example, the following case: A conference of social psychologists is being held on "New Directions in Social Psychology." The chairman of the meeting makes some initial remarks on the topic and then opens the floor to discussion. A lengthy two-hour discussion follows in which many speakers comment several different times. A mischievous researcher later takes the transcript of the conference and divides it up into units consisting of a set of uninterrupted remarks by a participant. After removing all identification of speakers, these units are rearranged into nine random sequences. Readers who have not attended the conference are given a set of ten transcripts, including the one that actually took place and the nine that were randomly constructed. Each reader is asked to pick out the "correct" transcript—that is, the one that actually occurred. The readers are unable to identify the correct transcript with better than chance frequency. Later, when these readers are asked to pair remarks, by putting one unit together with the one that immediately followed it, they tend to match a given individual's later remarks with his own earlier remarks rather than selecting the other person's remarks that actually followed.

Conferences such as the above frequently provide good examples of pseudocontingency although it may be difficult to detect. The norms of social interaction require the appearance of genuine contingency. Thus, one introduces his remarks by such phrases as, "Apropos of Tom's point, it's interesting that...," or "I don't agree with the point that George made earlier because I feel that...." These ritual linkages help to create the illusion that the speaker's remarks are contingent on the discussion rather than the very same ones he has made in the last six similar conferences.

To be sure, there is some degree of contingency in such interactions. One does not speak while someone else is talking, and is tactful in finding an appropriate opening to insert one's remarks. Interaction has its traffic rules that must be obeyed. But the contingency in such a response is minimal, since the content bears little relation to the remarks of previous speakers.

Pseudocontingency is implied in a variety of pejorative remarks about common interaction situations. "They were talking past each other," or "Neither heard a word the other said," we might say of a discussion in which each person seems so intent on making his point that his responses are largely noncontingent. Or a bargaining session in which each side rigidly repeats a fixed position may be described as a "ritual" rather than a genuine negotiation with give and take. Participants in a pseudocontingent interaction are sometimes characterized as "wooden and mechanical" and as "actors playing out their parts" to distinguish such interaction from the more spontaneous kind in which one is responding in important ways to what others are doing and saying.

Before we dismiss such pseudocontingent interaction merely as an undesirable mode of behavior of some self-centered exhibitionists, we should consider two important special cases having no connotations of social undesirability. The first of these special cases is social ritual. A wedding, for example, is a pseudocontingent interaction. The bride and groom say "I do" at the preappointed time, while others in the ceremony carry out their parts on cue. Besides these formal and institutionalized rituals, there are informal ritual elements in many social situations. These informal rituals have important functions in smoothing social interaction. For example, when two strangers meet and begin talking of the weather, they are engaging in a form of pseudocontingent interaction that enables the speakers to establish sufficient bonds to move on later to authentic contingent interaction. Leavetakings and welcomings are filled with a variety of harmless but useful ritual elements that help to handle some of the interaction problems that such occasions produce.

The second special case of pseudocontingent interaction involves some aspects of role behavior. A *role* may be defined as a set of expectations about the ways in which the occupant of a given social position ought to behave. These role prescriptions may be divided into three categories: *required* behavior, *permitted* behavior, and *prohibited* behavior. The required part may be small in many cases, allowing frequent opportunities for individuals to function in different ways. A good many role-connected interactions, therefore, have important elements of contingency in response. However, to the extent that participants in an interaction are engaging in behavior required of their roles, the interaction is pseudocontingent. The interaction between a judge and a defense attorney in a routine case provides an example.

Asymmetrical contingency

In *asymmetrical contingency*, some people base their behavior on the responses of others, but these others are responding largely to their own plans in a noncontingent fashion. This is well illustrated in the following case:

A personnel interviewer is talking to a job applicant. The personnel interviewer has a standard list of topics that he covers with any applicant. For the applicant, the job interview is a new experience, and he does not know precisely what questions to expect.

The personnel interviewer is asking a series of planned questions that are standard for the situation. The applicant's responses, on the other hand, are a reaction to the questions and cues he receives from the interviewer. To the extent that the interviewer actually reacts to the applicant, joking or initiating interaction not required by his role, the interaction approaches mutual contingency.

Reactive contingency

Reactive contingency is the opposite of asymmetrical contingency. It is, in a sense, the pure contingency case in which the plans one brings into a situation are ignored and one responds only to what others are saying or doing. The best examples of this are panics, as in the following situation:

Spectators watching a soccer game are carrying on an argument about the relative merits of two players. Push leads to shove, and a general melee develops in which people find themselves wrestling with others without regard to, or knowledge of, the opinions of the two players.

To distinguish this situation from the mutual contingency case, one must go beyond the fact that people are reacting to each other. As Jones and Gerard (1967, pp. 511–512) note, it "has often been stressed that interaction involves a mutual responsiveness, in which each person's responses become stimuli for the other; the fact that interaction also involves a persistence of self-regulated ongoing responses has been less clearly emphasized."

80 Mutual contingency

This final case is the full-fledged social interaction situation in which the participants are responding in important ways to others, but are doing so in the light of their own plans. Distinguishing this type of interaction situation from that of relative contingency helps to emphasize both the influence of one's own plans and the responsiveness to others. It is hardly necessary to cite examples of *mutual contingency*. Most of our continuing and important relationships are of this type.

The rest of this chapter will explore the interaction processes that we normally take for granted. Thus, we are in the unusual position of having a full supply of answers where there are no questions. But it is through the creation of questions that our basic purpose will be served; our intention is to force the recognition that many aspects of social interaction are problematic and require

The presentation of self of most used-car salesmen has become a caricature of the self-seeking, aggressive personality.

explanation. Our principal questions are, what order or pattern is there in the myriad daily social interactions that fill our waking hours? How is this order maintained, what causes it to break down, and how is it reestablished? What insights can we gain about what is going on in these interactions from various ways of describing and analyzing them?

In trying to answer these questions, four orientations to social interaction will be described. The word "orientation" rather than "theory" is used deliberately, because the views presented are intellectual perspectives concerning interaction rather than a series of related and testable propositions about it. In some cases, testable propositions can be and have been derived from the general orientation and it is possible to make judgments about whether these specific propositions are right or accurate. But each of the orientations is in some sense "right"—that is, social interaction can be described in its terms. However, each of the four orientations is not addressed to exactly the same phenomenon. Social interaction is a broad concept and each perspective focuses on particular aspects, ignoring others. The meaningful question is not whether a given view is correct, but whether it is useful. One should ask of any particular orientation whether it helps us to understand something important that is going on among people. What kinds of interaction processes does it especially illuminate and what are its limitations? With these considerations in mind, then, let us consider the four orientations in turn.

Goffman: Self-presentation

The first of the four orientations to social interaction is one studied extensively by Erving Goffman and others: *self-presentation*. For Goffman (1959), the crux of any social interaction is what the participants are saying about themselves through the things they do and say. Each person is faced with the problems of presenting himself to others. The presentation will emphasize some of one's many attributes and will hide others. In a variety of ways—some of them unconscious—a person will attempt to control the impression of himself that others develop. Thus, an individual may impress others as being sophisticated or naive, imaginative or dull, aggressive or docile—or any of a number of other behavioral alternatives. For this reason, says Goffman, the analyst of social interaction should turn his attention to the techniques people employ to create and manage the impressions they make on others, and should observe carefully the conditions under which one or another technique is effective.

Not surprisingly, the self-presentation perspective places strong emphasis on self-presentation as a means of social influence. Goffman makes this argument quite explicit. Moreover, he grants that an individual may have diverse goals in an interaction situation. For example, the person may want other people to treat him with great respect, or to think that he respects them. Alternatively, he may want others to know how he actually thinks about them, or he may wish others to think that he has formed no definite impression of them. On the other hand,

he may wish to ensure sufficient harmony so that the interaction can be sustained, or to defraud, get rid of, confuse, mislead, antagonize, or insult them. Regardless of the particular objective which the individual has in mind and of his motive for having this objective, it will be in his interest to control the conduct of the others, especially their responsive treatment of him. This control is achieved largely by influencing the definition of the situation which the others come to formulate, and he can influence this definition by expressing himself in such a way as to give them the kind of impression that will lead them to act voluntarily in accordance with his own plan. Thus, when an individual appears in the presence of others, there will usually be some reason for him to mobilize his activity so that it will convey an impression to others which it is in his interests to convey (Goffman, 1959).

Given this argument, it is not surprising that interactions in Goffman's world are surrounded by an aura of calculation. This effect is increased by his use of the theatrical analogy and imagery. Participants in social interaction are engaged in *performances*, which can be evaluated, as an actor's can, in terms of technical excellence or sloppiness in producing intended effects. Carried to its extreme, this view places much emphasis on the ritual elements of an interaction. Each performer is intent on successfully maintaining his part and each helps the others to do the same.

However, the theatrical analogy is not exactly accurate. A better analogy than the well-rehearsed play is the improvised skit. Performers in ordinary interaction have not read the script in advance and, consequently, things can unexpectedly disrupt the definition of self that is being projected, causing the interaction to come to a bumbling halt.

Fortunately for all of us, we develop skills that help to avoid disruptions or to minimize them and restore order when they occur. Goffman distinguishes *defensive* and *protective* practices (1955). When an individual employs tactics to prevent his own presentations from being discredited, he is employing defensive practices; when he exercises tact to save the definition of the situation presented by another, he is employing protective practices.

For example, a person is acting defensively when he avoids subjects or activities which would convey an impression not in line with the one he is promoting. When such moments occur, the person will change the subject of conversation or suggest another type of activity. He will attempt to do this as calmly as possible, without showing feeling, until he redefines the situation in accordance with the self he wishes to present. The individual will appear to be extremely modest and diffident, or even playful, in regard to his self. In this manner, he manipulates the situation so that his self will not be "discredited by exposure, personal failure, or the unanticipated acts of others."

Similar observations can be made about protective practices. The individual appears to be extremely polite, extending to the other participants in the interaction all the ritual civilities due them. He is very discreet, not mentioning details that might negatively affect the claims of the others. His words will be full of indirection, ambiguity—even deception—so that they might not offend the dignity of the others. If he does try to belittle the others, he will do so jokingly. In this way, the other participants can save face by responding as good sports who are confident enough people to put aside for the moment their usual high standards of dignity and honor.

This perspective is in full panoply when self-presentation has an ulterior motive going beyond the mere maintenance of smooth social relations. For those who intuitively or consciously understand the secrets of impression

Strategy in the game of tennis is not restricted to the court. The ability to psych out an opponent is as valuable as the big serve.

management, self-presentation can be used in the active service of social influence. This can be illustrated by a discussion of the fascinating and somewhat mysterious topics of embarrassment and ingratiation.

84 Manipulation by embarrassment

Embarrassment is a pervasive and unpleasant state that we have all experienced. Since we can recognize its onset and sense the conditions likely to produce it, we tend to act in ways that will avoid this experience; therein lies its potential for social influence. Modigliani (1966) has suggested different ways in which the manipulation of the embarrassment potential in a situation will lead another to act in desired ways. One technique is to encourage the other person to present a self that can be maintained or restored only if he engages in certain desired behavior. In Stephen Potter's delightful examples of gamesmanship, the expert gamesman exploits the other's claims to sportsmanship and fair play. These gambits would be ineffective against one who made no claims to such attributes. But by subtly creating a situation in which the opponent's very act of winning can be viewed as ungenerous and unfair, Potter's expert gamesman makes losing the only path for the other to avoid embarrassment. This is the basic art of "winning without actually cheating."

A more aggressive tactic is to create an embarrassing scene that can be terminated only by the other person acceding to one's desires. Imagine, for example, a black couple attempting to register at a hotel whose management maintains a discriminatory attitude toward blacks and other minorities. The room clerk or manager, intent on maintaining a public image of composure and graceful service, may very well feel that yielding involves less inconvenience and unpleasantness than continuing the embarrassing scene. In general, the more defensive and insecure one is about having his projected self accepted by others, the more easily he can be embarrassed and, hence, the more easily he can be manipulated in this manner.

The above gambits exploit people's tendencies to employ defensive measures to maintain their presented self, or self-image, and, thus, to avoid embarrassment. It is also possible to exploit protective measures. If a person is interacting with tactful, considerate, and sensitive individuals, he can take advantage of their kindness in the following manner: First, he indicates by his demeanor that he is quite insecure about the self he is presenting and is easily embarrassed. Then, he places the other in a position where, if the other fails to act in the desired manner, he will apparently discredit, discompose, and embarrass this unfortunate and vulnerable person. Modigliani suggests "a youthful and shy Girl Scout dispensing cookies" or "a somewhat inept, mildly deformed Fuller Brush man with a slight speech impediment" as examples. If, furthermore, the Fuller Brush man "can manage to put himself further out on a limb by gaining

HOW TO PSYCH OUT YOUR OPPONENT

"I am the greatest. I am the champ. Foreman will fall in five, and that's no jive." These words, which might have been uttered by champion boxer Muhammad Ali, are more than mere braggadocio. They are meant to instill fear in the heart of his opponent. Ali is the master of a practice that is probably as old as the human race. Some call it "psyching out the opponent." Stephen Potter (1948) calls it *The Theory and Practice of Gamesmanship, or the Art of Winning Games without Actually Cheating.*

Potter's book is probably the best attempt to explain the art of psychological one-upmanship. The book was intended as a tongue-in-cheek guide to playing games, particularly tennis, by learning how to gain a psychological advantage over an opponent. But the maneuvers and tactics described by Potter—the ploys of getting a person to feel ill at ease or inferior—are applicable in any number of personal interactions on or off the courts.

The success of Potter's method depends on getting an opponent to undercut his own sense of confidence. Potter shows how everyday situations can be manipulated to your own advantage. Even sharing a friendly beer can be the prelude to establishing supremacy. Potter calls this phase "drinkmanship."

Once the opponent is unsettled, an experienced gamesman can use half a dozen or more techniques to keep his opponent at a disadvantage. He may, for example, make a drawn-out process of tying his shoelace, after the opponent at squash or lawn tennis had served two or three aces running. Or he may engage in the extended nose-blow, with subsequent mopping up not only of the nose and the rest of the face, but of imaginary sweat from the forehead as well.

After the game is underway, the player following the rules of gamesmanship will be sure to chip away at his opponent's weaknesses. Oeing shrewd, however, a crafty gamesman will never openly admit that his opponent has any weaknesses at all. Instead, if the partner requires minutes of concentration before each shot, then the gamesman should play nonchalantly. He might even whistle if he thinks that might upset his opponent. If the partner asks for advice, then the gamesman should give it freely but praise his partner's strong points in a way that makes them seem like faults. The course Potter recommends is praise, followed by dissection and discussion of the play. He ends by leaving a trace of doubt. In this way, the opponent will be left with the impression that he is playing with a superior partner.

Conversely, knowing when and how to "psych up" an opponent is often the key to success. Coaches who drive their teams to a frantic pitch in the locker room know that their players will go out on the field convinced that they are invincible.

In common with many other gamespeople, Potter was a master amateur psychologist. He claims he was always able to beat a friend who was better than himself if he reminded his partner of something that made him feel guilty. Then, there is the ploy of diversionary conversation. Potter would try to unearth any of his opponent's problems—for example, the possible loss of a job—that might affect his opponent's playing ability. Using all of these tactics, Potter was able to boast that he had built up a reputation as a formidable chess player without ever actually winning a game.

entrance and unpacking his entire display case, he is virtually assured of some kind of sale" unless his victim is oblivious to the embarrassment caused by discrediting others in social interaction (Modigliani, 1966, p. 51).

86 The ingratiation ploy

Another example of impression management in the service of social influence is that of *ingratiation*. "The term 'ingratiation,' " Edward Jones writes (1964, p. 11), "refers to a class of strategic behaviors illicitly designed to influence a particular other person concerning the attractiveness of one's personal qualities." In short, it is a means of currying favor. The potential for ingratiation is often present in social interaction because of the difficulty of knowing accurately how others view us. This difficulty stems from two sources. We have the potentially incompatible desires to learn objectively about ourselves and to be judged favorably as well. Thus, says Jones, in the desire to be judged favorably, a person will present an appealing and charming self to those he wishes to impress. In extreme cases, however, such a ploy can lead to failure to build a solid self-identity because such an individual is always artfully changing his self in his attempts to curry the favors of others.

The ingratiation ploy cuts two ways. The same things that make an ingratiator seek to appear attractive to another also make the others seek to appear attractive to the ingratiator. But this practice can be deceptive, because being attractive also means being agreeable. One can hardly hope, then, to receive an accurate picture of his true self from the communications he receives from others. These observations have led Jones to the conclusion, "Perhaps one of the poorest ways to find out what others think of us is to ask them. . . . Ingratiation and the related activities of face-work generate a considerable amount of mischievous noise which masks and distorts feelings and judgments as they are conveyed across the interpersonal chasm" (Jones, 1964, pp. 19 and 33).

Jones has conducted a series of experiments amply demonstrating Goffman's observation that one can be taken in by one's own performance. Since we rarely know exactly where we stand on most evaluative dimensions, distortion is always possible. The distortion is fed by one's own vanity, the desire to think the most of oneself. Thus, when an individual receives approval, his vanity is served in that it causes him to think that others have seen and admired his true self. Vanity is also at work when a person receives disapproval, preventing him from believing that his true character has been seen and correctly appraised.

There is, then, a cooperative relationship between the ingratiator and the person he is trying to impress. The target person is loath to believe that such favorable feedback about himself is hypocritical and the ingratiator does not want to admit to himself that he is insecure or has ulterior motives. Thus, both the ingratiator and the target individual want to believe that the latter is a superior person. The ingratiator's compliments are misinterpreted by both parties as true appraisals. In sum, the study of ingratiation suggests an amoral moral: flattery may get you somewhere.

The Machiavellian connection

It is a very short jump from the ingratiator to the operator who tries to turn every social interaction to his advantage. Nearly all of us are familiar with this type of person: he talks you into lending him your last dollar, your term paper, your car, and even, if you happen to be the appropriate sex, your body. The prototype of this kind of individual has been suggested by Niccolo Machiavelli (1469–1527), the Italian statesman and writer. Machiavelli's book, *The Prince*, instructed aspiring politicians how to be successful by putting power and the manipulation of others before morality and ethics. Thus, the term "Machiavellian" refers to anyone who attempts to reach his goals by manipulating others.

Using Machiavelli's work for their starting point, Richard Christie and Florence Geis (1970) rewrote a number of the Italian's aphorisms in modern English. They revised half of these so that they stated the exact opposite of what Machiavelli originally intended. The statements were then presented to a large and varied sample of subjects—1,196 undergraduate students from three departments of three different universities. The subjects were instructed to agree or disagree with such statements as "Anyone who completely trusts anyone else is asking for trouble," and "Most people are basically good and kind."

Students who consistently agreed with statements like the first but disagreed with statements like the second were rated as Machiavellian. Conversely, subjects who disagreed with the first type of statement but agreed with the second type were considered non-Machiavellian.

The next part of the experiment involved placing the subjects in situations which would actually bring out their manipulative personalities. In laboratory studies, it was found that those who responded to the questions in a Machiavellian manner were Machiavellian in their actions as well. Thus, these individuals tended to be more scheming and manipulative than the non-Machiavellians. Christie and Geis designed a game which tested the cunning and ruthlessness of the players. Appropriately enough, the game was called the "con game" because it involved three players who were given a sum of money to divide—but they were to divide it only two ways. Thus, one of the players, the most un-Machiavellian of the three—would end up with nothing.

Here's how the game worked. The three players—call them Tom, Dick, and

Harry—were given ten dollars to split between any two of them. A typical transaction might begin with Tom agreeing with Dick to split the money fifty-fifty. Harry, not wanting to be left out, makes Tom a better offer: Tom could have six dollars and Harry would settle for four. Dick responds to this by offering Harry six dollars while he would take only four. Tom then presents Harry with an even better deal, and the bargaining continues till the two best Machiavellians split the money between them. The investigators found that those who ended up with the most money tended to have high scores on the

---

A TEST FOR MACHIAVELLIANISM

Do you strongly agree *(5 points)*, agree *(4 points)*, feel neutral *(3 points)*, disagree *(2 points)*, or strongly disagree *(1 point)*?

		5	4	3	2	1
1.	The best way to handle people is to tell them what they want to hear.	—	—	—	—	—
2.	Anyone who completely trusts anyone else is asking for trouble.	—	—	—	—	—
3.	It is safest to assume that all people have a vicious streak and it will come out when they are given a chance.	—	—	—	—	—
4.	Never tell anyone the real reason you did something unless it is useful to do so.	—	—	—	—	—
5.	It is wise to flatter important people.	—	—	—	—	—
6.	Barnum was very wrong when he said there's a sucker born every minute.	—	—	—	—	—
7.	Most men forget more easily the death of their father than the loss of their property.	—	—	—	—	—
8.	Generally speaking, men won't work hard unless they're forced to do so.	—	—	—	—	—
9.	The biggest difference between most criminals and other people is that criminals are stupid enough to get caught.	—	—	—	—	—

Figure 3–1. Do you have a Machiavellian personality? Mark your agreement or disagreement with the items and add up your score. A score of from 35 to 45 points would indicate full-blown Machiavellianism. A score of from 9 to 18 would reveal a person low in Machiavellian tendencies.

SOURCE: Adapted from Christie, R., and Geis, F. *Studies in Machiavellianism.* New York: Academic Press, 1970. Pp. 17–18.

Machiavellian questionnaire. The losers, by contrast, had lower scores on the written part of the experiment.

Christie and Geis also found that the Machiavellian personality exists in all walks of life. For example, they found no positive correlations between Machiavellians and political ideology, social class, ethnic group, or geographical region. Furthermore, the Machiavellians were more apt to be successful in the highly competitive American society, even to the extent of doing better in school.

Homans: Social Exchange

An emphasis on calculation is shared by this second perspective on social interaction, *social exchange*. What is being calculated is somewhat different, however. There is profit, say the supporters of this view, in regarding social interaction as a kind of economic transaction. Thus, George C. Homans (1958, pp. 13–14) suggests that "social behavior is an exchange of goods, material goods but also nonmaterial ones such as the symbols of approval or prestige."

This view of social interaction has an appealing common-sense quality about it. It seems quite natural to speak of the "give and take" in social relationships and to consider some relationships "bad bargains." "Men have always explained their behavior," Homans argues, "by pointing to what it gets them and what it costs them" (1961, p. 13). No matter how we feel about reducing human relationships to the commonalities of the marketplace with its haggling and bargaining, we recognize much that is familiar in the proposition that social exchange governs much of our daily activities. We deal, however, in "commodities" that are emotional or intellectual rather than material. Two lovers, for example, forge covenants in which affection, support, and physical satisfaction are mutually exchanged. If one of the parties fails to fulfill his or her obligations by withholding any or all of these, the relationship may be terminated by the other.

Exchange theory draws its inspiration in part from the idea of an economic transaction and in part from the animal studies of the behavioral psychologists. But some theorists believe that the link with behavioral psychology is a weak one. Deutsch and Krauss (1965, p. 116), for example, feel that "the only link between Homans [that is, social exchange theory] and behavioristic psychology is the psychological hedonism which underlies both the law of effect and the doctrine of economic man." The law of effect was first stated by E. L. Thorndike more than seventy years ago, as "pleasure stamps in; pain stamps out." The same hedonistic idea—that we always act to achieve maximum pleasure and to avoid pain at all costs—remains with us today under the rubric of stimulus–response in reinforcement theory, discussed in chapter 2. In economic terms, pleasure is the equivalent of reward; pain, the equivalent of cost. Thus, exchange theory rests on the central idea that social relationships involve a calculus of rewards and costs for the participants.

90 The utility of exchange theory

What kinds of observations about social interaction can be developed from rewards and costs as a central idea? Homans (1958) suggests several. For example, if an individual gives much to others in interactions, he tries to get much from them in return. Thus, one seeks to balance the books. In dealings with others, the things gained from a relationship may be rewards, whereas the things given may be costs. Not surprisingly, one tends to maximize profits, which can be calculated by subtracting the cost from the reward. Furthermore, the individual, in his attempt to increase profits, tries to make sure that no one else in the social interaction reaps more rewards than he does.

Some of these observations say less than they first appear to because of a hidden circularity. For example, Homans makes the following argument (1961, p. 61): "We define psychic profit as reward less cost, and we argue that no exchange continues unless both parties are making a profit." It is impossible to suggest how one might disprove this proposition because there is no way of defining rewards and costs independently of the behavior they are being invoked to explain. To be more specific, the expenditure of time and money might normally be thought of as a cost. However, consider the case of the average parents who spend many thousands of dollars and uncounted hours raising children in the face of an uncertain payoff. According to exchange theory, where is the profit? The sacrifice of time and money must be regarded as a pleasure for the mother and father. For most parents it is difficult to tally the rewards at the end of any particular day. It is even more difficult when the house is finally empty of offspring, to balance the newly found freedom from the responsibility for children against so many years of child care. An exchange theorist might say the exchange is an indirect one—the care of a new generation is in payment for the care expended by the generation before, each generation, in turn, repaying their parents by bringing up the next generation.

In sum, the exchange orientation can tell us nothing about the validity of the proposition that a voluntary relationship will be discontinued unless both parties are making a profit. Of course, there are those men or women who find no rewards in parenting and do abandon their families. However, if we are willing to assume that the basic exchange proposition is true, we can then make inferences about what people find costly and what they find rewarding from observing social interactions.

One of the most fruitful derivations of Homans's use of the exchange perspective is his development of the concept of *distributive justice*. Homans argues that there exists a pervasive norm governing social exchange: people will expect their rewards to be proportional to their costs and investments. If they bring the same investments to an exchange, and their costs are equal, they will expect a profit equally. If one man brings more into the exchange and hence has more at stake, he will be entitled to a larger share of the rewards, reflecting his greater investment. We bring these notions of fair exchange and reciprocity to our daily social transactions, and we are indignant and angry if they are violated to our disadvantage and guilty or sheepish if we get more than we think we deserve.

There is a good deal of explanatory power in this basically simple idea. For instance, the distributive justice argument is useful in generating quite unexpected propositions about who will join with whom in coalition situations. Imagine the following case: Successive balloting at a presidential nominating convention has reduced the list of candidates to three: Candidate A who controls 48 percent of the vote, Candidate B who controls 30 percent, and Candidate C who controls 22 percent. Each of the three has absolute control over the votes of his supporters and a simple majority is needed for nomination. Obviously, some coalition must emerge, but who will join with whom?

If a norm of distributive justice prevails, the answer is that Candidate B and C will join. "The existence of this norm works against coalitions which are larger than necessary. If a player gets from a coalition his parity price, i.e., an amount proportional to his resources, he gets the most by maximizing the ratio of his resources to the total resources of the coalition. Since his initial resources are the same regardless of which coalition he joins, the lower the total resources, the greater will be his share" (Gamson, 1964, p. 88). Thus, distributive justice suggests that that coalition will form which is the smallest among those that are sufficient to win. In this case, Candidates B and C, with 52 percent of the vote between them, form the smallest winning coalition. Each has chosen a coalition that will give him the largest share and still be part of a winning combination. If there were four candidates with 34 percent, 24 percent, 24 percent, and 18 percent, respectively, the predicted winning coalition, by the same reasoning, would be the one between the strongest and the weakest (34 percent and 18 percent). This argument can be applied to coalition situations with any number of participants and any distribution of initial votes or resources. Not surprisingly, the concept of distributive justice has little or no meaning for the Machiavellian: he or she does not believe in it. In the example above, if Candidate C were a Machiavellian, he would demand complete equality with whomever he joins—whether it be Candidate A or B

Threat and cooperation

One way to get one's partner to cooperate and to accede to one's wishes is by the use of threat—that is, to express an intention of doing something detrimental to the interests of the other actor in a particular social situation. Suppose, for example, a young man invites a young lady (who is visiting from out of town) to his apartment for the night with the purpose of seducing her. He may be surprised when she accepts his invitation. But he may be even more surprised when she rejects his advances. Faced with this situation, the young man might sulk and give up. But if he is without scruples, he may threaten the woman, telling her that he intends to spread the word that she is perverted in her sexual tastes. This, of course, is known in legal circles as blackmail and/or rape and is punishable by the courts.

Sometimes the threat works and the young lady, not wishing her name to be dragged through the mud, so to speak, will yield to the man's advances. Often, however, the ruse fails: the person threatened becomes even more adamant in his or her refusal. An excellent example of this situation is seen in an experiment designed in 1960 by Morton Deutsch and Robert Krauss.

In this study, two female subjects were told to pretend that each was the president of a trucking firm with the job of transporting goods overland. As Figure 3–2 indicates, one subject headed the Acme company, the other the Bolt firm. Each of the two was to move her truck from "start" to "destination" as quickly as possible. For every trip completed, each earned an imaginary 60 cents, minus the operating expenses, which amounted to one cent a second. So, if it took 40 seconds to move the truck from start to finish, the player's profit would be 60 cents, 40 cents, or 20 cents. Speed, in other words, was of the essence.

Each competitor had a choice of two routes: a short, direct route and a long, circuitous one. Since the profits were figured on the basis of time required to get from start to destination, it was logical that the short route would be the obvious choice of both contestants. However, there was a catch: the short route included a narrow road which would accommodate only one truck at a time. Since both players could not simultaneously use the short route and make a profit, some kind of cooperative bargaining was called for. In order to maximize their profits, each player decided to take turns in using the short route, and things ran quite smoothly, each player making a tiny profit.

In the next part of the experiment, however, the subjects did not fare nearly so well as far as cooperation and profits were concerned. The investigators introduced the element of bilateral threat in the form of two gates at either end of the short route; one gate was controlled by the president of Acme, the other by the president of Bolt. Each president could close her gate, thus preventing the other from reaching her destination. The object was to see whether the use of threat would increase or decrease profits for the players.

The investigators found that in the bilateral threat situation, both players constantly disagreed over who would take the shortest route and make the most profits. Thus, time and again, each prevented the other from moving her truck over the short route. Since both were forced to make frequent use of the long route, which was not affected by the gates, each lost substantially. The unilateral threat situation—in which Acme alone could control her gate—resulted in less heavy losses for her. However, it was not as profitable as the no-threat situation.

Is there a lesson here for the powerful who can use threat in attempts to bend

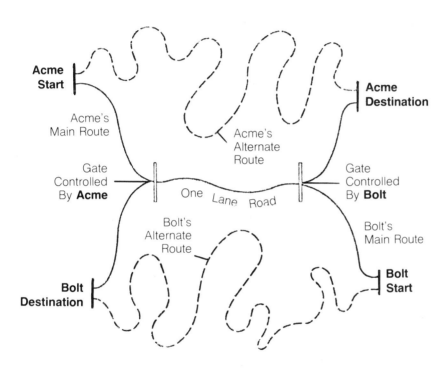

Figure 3–2. The Acme–Bolt trucking game, designed by Morton Deutsch and Robert Krauss (1960), explores how the use of threat hinders cooperation between two individuals. Using the road map shown here, each of the two players must move her truck from start to finish as quickly as possible to obtain the most profits. In the "no-threat" condition, the game runs smoothly as the two players cooperate to maximize their profits. But when either or both of them can threaten the other by closing her gate, disagreement rather than cooperation reigns, and both players lose time and money.

SOURCE: Deutsch, M., and Krauss, R. M. The effect of threat upon interpersonal bargaining. *Journal of Abnormal and Social Psychology*, 1960, **61**, 183.

others to their will? No one can say for sure. Another similar experiment conducted by Philip Gallo (1966), for example, showed that cooperation greatly increased in threat situations when the stakes were higher. In his experiment, Gallo substituted real money for the imaginary money used in the Deutsch and Krauss experiment. Does that mean, then, that people become increasingly cooperative as the value of profits rises?

Game theory

The mathematical theory of games of strategy has provided social psychologists with both insight and techniques for analyzing social interaction. The participant in social interaction depicted by game theory is essentially the same participant we have already met in exchange theory. He is a profit maximizer who aims at obtaining as many rewards as possible with the lowest costs possible. He is assumed to be dealing with other participants who have similar motivations.

The term "game" connotes a certain frivolity and casual involvement that frequently seem inappropriate or even offensive when applied to situations which may involve our most vital interests and values. The model of a game is, like the earlier model of an economic transaction, an analogy. In this instance, the analogy suggests that the participants in an interaction have certain resources available to them for achieving certain conscious goals or objectives within a set of rules specifying constraints and opportunities. The focus of analysis is on the skill with which the participants use their resources in competition with others or, in other words, how well they handle their strategic problems.

This perspective has contributed a number of helpful distinctions for analyzing interaction processes. Consider, for example, the difference between a game of chance and a mutually contingent interaction with a live, reacting opponent. The first kind, a "game against nature," presents its own kind of problems. A player may have to decide whether he should pursue a course with a small chance at a great payoff (a long shot) or, alternatively, one with a rather good chance at a modest payoff (a sure thing). An essential feature of his choice is that what he does will not alter the probability of his strategy leading to the desired outcome. Whether he chooses to bet on red or black in an honest game of roulette, the probability of either of these colors coming up will not change. The roulette wheel will neither thwart nor help him. As social psychologist William Gamson (1966, p. 147) notes, "Lady Luck may seem capricious at times, but her impersonality and indifference to efforts to charm her has been repeatedly demonstrated."

The situation changes fundamentally when we enter an interaction with a live adversary. Our strategic choices must now be based on the assumption that what our opponent does will depend in part on what he thinks or knows we will do. A new concern has emerged—we must consider our responses partly as communicative acts. To do so involves a kind of mental role-playing. One must ask himself, if I were he and saw myself making such moves, what would I make of them and how would I respond?

In many interactions, game theory makes an important distinction that helps us to characterize social relationships in terms of conflict. The basis for this distinction is the interaction among the rewards or payoffs to the different players. Thus, there can be a pure conflict game, a pure collaboration game, or a mixed-motive game. Let us consider these three kinds of situations.

The pure conflict game. In this type of game, the gains and losses of the players add up to zero, regardless of the outcome. For obvious reasons, this situation is also called a *zero-sum game*. Thus, in a zero-sum situation which involves two players, whatever one player wins, the other necessarily loses.

In this kind of game, there is no area of common interest among the participants, and strategies will be designed accordingly. In everyday life, this situation is virtually nonexistent. Outside of the parlor, there are few such games. Conflict in social life is typically mixed with some important elements of common interest. Even war is not a zero-sum game since there are some outcomes in which both parties may suffer severe losses. Negotiating over the price of a house, going out on a strike for higher wages, outmaneuvering a rival for a promotion, and demonstrating for the adoption of an open-housing ordinance are all non-zero-sum situations with important elements of common interest as well as conflict. As Thomas Schelling (1960, p. 83) points out, "These are the 'games' in which, though the element of conflict provides the dramatic interest, mutual dependence is part of the logical structure and demands some kind of collaboration or mutual accommodation—tacit if not explicit—even if only in the avoidance of mutual disaster."

The pure collaboration game. Schelling has suggested that zero-sum games serve as one limiting case in a theory of interdependent decision-making—the extreme of pure conflict. At the other extreme, we have the pure collaboration situation in which players win or lose together since they have identical interests with respect to all outcomes. In many cases of this type, coordination is complicated by communication difficulties. Under such conditions, some interesting strategic questions are involved and these have been exploited brilliantly by Schelling (1960). To illustrate the problem, imagine a man who loses his wife in a department store without any prior agreement on where they are to meet. What strategy should he use for finding her? The trick is to coordinate predictions about the other's behavior, "to identify the one course of action that their expectations of each other can converge on" (Schelling, 1960, p. 54).

Schelling has devised a series of problems in tacit coordination enabling individuals to test their skills in this art. The following examples, adapted from Schelling (1960, pp. 56–57), assume that no prior communication is allowed among the pairs of participants:

1. Name either heads or tails. If you and your partner name the same thing, you both win $1. Otherwise, you both get nothing.

2. Circle one of the numbers listed in the line below. You and your partner each win $1 if you succeed in circling the same number. Otherwise, you both get nothing.

7   18   13   261   99   50

3. Name an amount of money. If you and your partner name the same amount, you can have the amount you named up to a maximum of $1. Otherwise, you both get nothing.

4. The older of you has an income of $100 a month, and the younger has an income of $50. Together you must pay a tax of at least $15. Write down the amount of tax that you and your partner should pay. If your tax asessments for both parties agree, you will pay that tax. If you fail to write down the same set of figures, you will pay a tax of $15 each.

There are clearly better or worse answers to the above questions and a player's performance can be evaluated by how much he wins or loses compared to other players who have been confronted with the same task. The solutions embody certain strategic principles that can be applied to situations other than the artificial ones described above. A solution may depend more on imagination than logic; any solution is arbitrary in the sense that, if the same alternative also occurs to the other party as a solution, then it is a good one no matter how silly it may seem.

One major characteristic of solutions to tacit coordination problems is the prominence of the alternative. A husband and wife who vigorously argued about the merits of a particular painting might well find it the most suitable meeting spot if they accidentally became separated in an art museum because it is still very much on their minds. Besides conspicuousness of an alternative, uniqueness is an important and related principle of selection. If the husband and wife in the art museum had disagreed on several paintings but agreed on only one, the latter would be a less ambiguous alternative despite the fact that they had less dramatic discussion about it. In sum, pure coordination games, like pure conflict games, isolate a recognizable class of interaction situations with basically similar strategic problems.

The prisoner's dilemma: Mixed motives.   Between the limiting cases of pure conflict and pure coordination, there is a rich and varied assortment of mixed-motive situations involving both conflict and common interests. Some of these are essentially bargaining situations; a buyer and seller may share a strong desire to make an exchange, but they must balance this desire against the seller's additional objective of getting as much as possible and the buyer's conflicting objective of paying as little as possible. There are also many other mixed-motive situations in which the strategic problems are quite different from bargaining. The one most analyzed and subjected to experimental study is the prisoner's dilemma, named after the following anecdote used to illustrate it:

"Two prisoners charged with the same crime are held incommunicado. If both confess, both can be convicted. If neither confesses, neither can be convicted. However, if one confesses while the other holds out, the first not only goes scot free but gets a reward to boot while the second gets a more severe punishment than he would have gotten if both confessed. Should a rational prisoner confess or hold out under these circumstances?" (Rapoport, 1964, p. 290).

The dilemma is a real one with no easy resolution. Figure 3–3 depicts this situation schematically. If each pursues the reward, both suffer. If each is trustworthy, both gain. But the solution of not confessing is unstable because a temptation exists for both parties. If one is certain that the other will be trustworthy, then it pays for him to inform and gain the reward (considerations of morality aside). If, on the other hand, he is certain the other will not be trustworthy, then it still pays him to inform because if he alone is trustworthy, then his penalty will be more severe (five years instead of one). By such logic, both prisoners, unable to communicate, may be led to a solution in which both do worse than they would by remaining trustworthy.

The prisoner's dilemma offers possibilities to study, in a controlled and systematic way, a conflict situation which contains many of the basic elements of conflict in everyday life. The idea of a mixed-motive game may seem simple. Quite frequently, however, situations of this type are misconstrued as pure conflict or pure coordination games. The Soviet Union and the United States, for example, have clear areas of common interest, including the avoidance of nuclear war as an absolute minimum. Furthermore, both may realize their own goals better through trade relations which bolster both economies; both might find comfort in the containment of Chinese influence in Southeast Asia. On the other hand, there are conflicts of interest as well—each country wishes to maintain or extend its influence in some areas at the expense of the other.

As Gamson notes (1966, pp. 152–153), "This mixed-motive situation is sometimes treated as a pure conflict situation. Consider the following arguments: (1) 'The Soviet Union desires a leveling off of the arms race so it can divert resources to nonmilitary programs. It also desires increased trade with the Western nations as a way of bolstering its economy. Since the Soviet Union is our opponent, we should not aid it in these objectives.' (2) 'The Soviet Union

would like to see Candidate X elected President of the United States. Therefore, we should all vote for Candidate Y.' The validity of both of these arguments depends on the pure conflict assumption—only then does it follow that
benefit to an adversary is injurious to one's own cause. If we are locked in a
mortal struggle, then the actions which bolster the Soviet economy necessarily
injure us. But once we admit the existence of common interests, then simply
knowing how an action affects our opponent does not tell us how it affects us.

In sum, the existence of important elements of conflict in a situation does
not make it one of pure conflict; similarly, important elements of common

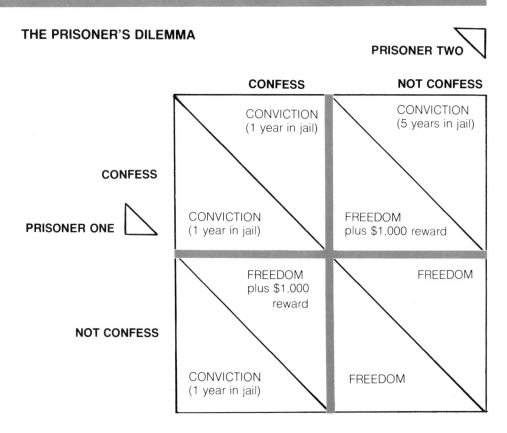

THE PRISONER'S DILEMMA

PRISONER TWO

	CONFESS	NOT CONFESS
CONFESS	CONVICTION (1 year in jail) / CONVICTION (1 year in jail)	CONVICTION (5 years in jail) / FREEDOM plus $1,000 reward
NOT CONFESS	FREEDOM plus $1,000 reward / CONVICTION (1 year in jail)	FREEDOM / FREEDOM

PRISONER ONE

*Figure 3–3.   The Prisoner's Dilemma is a good example of a mixed-motive
game. In the matrix shown here, each prisoner is accused of a crime, held
incommunicado, and faced with the dilemma of cooperating with his partner
or competing against him to obtain freedom. If both prisoners trust one
another and refuse to confess to the crime, they are released; if both confess,
they are convicted and receive light sentences. But if one prisoner is certain
that the other will be trustworthy, then it pays for him to turn state's evidence and confess, thus earning the reward and his freedom.*

interest do not necessarily define a situation as one of pure coordination. The classification of interdependent decision suggested by Schelling is a conceptual tool useful in avoiding such errors in the analysis of social interaction.

T-Groups

Exchange theory deals primarily with the communication of conscious meaning. Bargaining requires a clear perception on the part of those engaged in the transaction of values, means, and ends. In T-groups, on the other hand, the aim is to reveal to the participants patterns of behavior which they unconsciously have been following. There is an assumption that motivations and goals can be as unknown to individuals as strong emotions; that, in fact, these wellsprings of behavior can lead a person to behave in ways that are counterproductive as well as harmful, both to the individual and to the people with whom he interacts. Thus, according to the T-group perspective, there is, underlying the overt and apparently banal content of many of our ordinary interactions, a nether world of subtle and disguised communication, much of it so emotionally charged that it can be made explicit only with great difficulty, if at all. Freud and his successors in the development of psychoanalytic theory have concerned themselves with this nether world, and they provide much of the inspiration for those interested in this aspect of interaction today.

The distinctive focus of this perspective is, as Warren G. Bennis and his associates have put it, on "those interactional dimensions which contain an emotional base." The concern is with "that class of interactions where feelings are basic and pivotal in the interpersonal exchange" (Bennis et al., 1964, p. 16). These interpersonal feelings are regarded "as the basic, raw data of interpersonal relationships." Emotional feelings deeply embedded in the subconscious are not easily accessible either to the people who experience them or to observers. To gain access to the emotions that, in one way or another, underlie interpersonal relationships, psychologists working within this perspective have used techniques developed in the T-group. The T in T-group is short for training or sensitivity-training. T-groups are self-analytic groups. Members of T-groups focus on interpersonal relations and group process as they are manifested in the very group doing the analysis. The purpose of this analysis is to develop a greater sensitivity to the unconscious realm of subtle and disguised communication.

Such groups bear some similarity to therapy groups but their focus is more on understanding the immediate interaction experience rather than on producing some personality or behavioral change in the participants. Nor is there any implication that the interpersonal processes in T-groups reflect pathologies; on the contrary, they are utilized because they make the hidden content of normal interaction more accessible. T-groups, Philip Slater (1966, p. 1) argues, "may profitably be studied not only because of the involvement they arouse but also because the norms of such groups support the removal of certain inhibitions which characterize formal task groups and informal social groups in everyday life. While such norms do not eliminate the surface structures which are found in all naturally formed groups, they succeed in making underlying feelings more conspicuous."

If the objective of T-groups is to bring feelings to the surface, they seem to serve their purpose well. Any number of participants can testify to the intensity of the emotional encounters they produce. It is the deliberate refusal to follow the everyday norms of social interaction that causes T-groups to be more turbulent than natural groups. These norms exist to bring about calm and unruffled interaction by suppressing personal emotion. However, other norms arise as the group begins to interact. If the leader does not impose such rules on the group at the beginning, they will be automatically generated when the group discusses such matters as purpose and leadership. Typically, there might be rules such as what constitutes a fit topic for discussion, and what topics are "wasting the time of the group." For example, discussions of feelings aroused by the leader or other group members are encouraged; sports, the weather, child-raising are not allowed. Norms concerning status are suspended; everybody is regarded as equal, and furthermore, everybody must participate equally.

Inside a T-group

Indeed, this last question—that of leadership—can create quite a bit of turbulence in the typical T-group. Leadership can become the central issue, even replacing that for which the group was originally formed. The relationship between the members of the group and the leader (sometimes called a "trainer"), and the attendant issues of dependency and authority, can be seen by examining a transcript of a self-analytic group. The transcript is reported in Mann (1967, pp. 22–25). The excerpts are taken from a group that has been meeting for some weeks. It is now in its fourteenth session and the exchange below occurs in the middle of this session. In earlier meetings, the "group had . . . gone through a period of sustained and direct attack upon the leader and upon Harry, a group member many felt to be too scornful of them and too closely identified with the leader" (Mann, 1967, p. 10). The leader of the group, called here "Dr. Allen," is present during the discussion that follows, although he remains silent.

GINO (to Merv): One comment I'd like to make is that when you talk about Dr. Allen, you always put a little capsule on your right shoulder so as to shut him out. I have that feeling every time. . . .
MERV: That might be true.

* * * *

GINO: It's a very curious thing about sitting on the side. Most of you sit so that you can see the leader and avoid this influence.

FRANK: Do you observe this consistently, or are you just putting a couple of points in here?

GINO: I'm not trying to be disruptive.

MERV: Well, the reason—I have to be frank—is that I get the impression that he is sort of floating over me—I like to shut him off. Sometimes I—the idea that he's sitting there with sort of a smug attitude. It does bother me. I—

GINO: Smug attitude?

MERV: Not smug. I'm using that because I heard it used too many times, I suppose.

GINO: You're using that because you have a reason to. What I wanted to say was this. It's amazing, I see it sometimes, it's the blankest face I've ever seen at times. He won't take the smile off for ten minutes straight.

FRANK: That's a Mona Lisa look (laughter).

GINO: I think that it's an attempt to be ambiguous, so that we won't have guidance from his expression.

*   *   *   *

MERV: I don't think being sort of ambiguous is exactly what I mean. I mean a sort of all-pervading type of thing. In other words, I feel sometimes uncomfortable talking about Dr. Allen because of the fact that I see him in a position of power over me.

GINO: Dr. Allen?

MERV: I see him sort of like the analyst, sort of looking through me. He has got this power. He has more knowledge than I do and really knows what's going on in this group and sometimes I can feel the way Frank does.

*   *   *   *

In sensitivity-training groups the norms of everyday social interaction are suspended. Moreover, each group member is regarded as equal and each must participate equally in the group discussion.

JANICE: For me, the point is, is he a group member or is he not a group member? Do we talk *to* him or do we talk *about* him in the third person, or do we talk away from him?

* * * *

FRANK: I think you *have* to discuss him in the third person, for one reason because he doesn't talk back to you like other people in the group do. So you feel like he's *trying* to distance himself and—

HARRY: If you accuse him more directly, he'll answer, I'm sure.

FRANK: A couple of times he hasn't answered.

HARRY: Ask him a question about himself.

FRANK: About what?

HARRY: About himself.

FRANK: I know a couple of times I've asked him a question and he sat there and stared with this kind of look like "I'm not in here." And so then you have to talk about a person in the third person.

HARRY: Maybe he's saying about that, "I can't answer that question."

BOB: Maybe he's saying, "You're asking too much."

HARRY: It may be a question that it's better, perhaps, to talk it out among us.

FRANK: Well, anyway, there's some different relationship there. I think most people in this group feel that they could talk to any other person, person to person; with him, you have to use the long-distance operator.

JANICE: Maybe it's because we're sitting back here. But somehow, you're right, Harold, when I ask Dr. Allen a question, he usually answers, but I have the feeling that I have to shout, "Hello, down there." (laughter) (Mann, 1967).

The problem of describing feelings

Is it really possible to describe the feelings in such an interaction so that independent observers could agree on what is being expressed? Is it possible to study such feelings systematically, or should one leave this realm of interaction to poets and novelists? Suppose, for example, you were a psychologist studying the encounter-group phenomenon and you wished to learn how the group members and leader actually felt toward one another. How would you do this? The most logical starting point would be to record the words and actions of each member as he interacted with the leader. But there are problems with such an approach. To illustrate the problems involved, how should one characterize Harry's feelings toward the leader in the above interaction? Should one attend only to the relatively rare occasions when he speaks directly to the leader, or should one also include his defense of the leader, as when he argues above, "It may be a question that it's better, perhaps, to talk it out among us?" Furthermore, if Harry is attacked by other members when he implicitly or explicitly defends the leader, should such attacks be viewed, at least in part, as feelings expressed toward the leader?

A number of adventurous attempts have been made to tackle the formidable problem of measuring the subtle feelings in social interaction. One such attempt by Mann (1967) will be briefly presented to illustrate what can be done. Mann has set up a system which focuses on the feelings being expressed between the members and the leader in self-analytic groups. However, his system does not claim to deal with feelings in social interaction outside of T-groups, or even to deal with those feelings outside of the member–leader relationship that are being expressed in self-analytic groups. The most difficult problem in describing feelings is that a person may express his feelings symbolically as well as directly. To treat only the direct expressions would be to surrender from the outset all hope of understanding the world of implicit feelings. Mann tries to cope with this issue by describing each expression both in terms of the feeling it expresses and in terms of the level of inference employed by the observer.

Thus, for Mann, the two coordinates of any act are the *level of inference* and the *category* into which the act can be placed. The level of inference is so called because in most cases, the investigator must infer what is taking place, both manifestly and latently, between a leader and a particular group member.

Four levels of inference describing the leader–member interaction are established by Mann. The first level is the direct expression in which the member clearly identifies himself as the possessor of the feelings and names the leader as the target (e.g., "I feel uncomfortable talking about Dr. Allen because I see him in a position of power over me"). The second and third levels involve acts in which the leader is not clearly identified. For example, the object mentioned may be the group as a whole or some group member who seems, for the particular member in question, to stand for the leader (e.g., "I'm sick and tired of having Harry always interpreting what others are supposed to *really* mean"). Mann notes that, when inferring that such a statement expresses feelings about the leader, it is not assumed that it is not also directed at Harry. Nor would the statement be categorized as an expression of feeling toward the leader unless there was some indication that Harry stands for the leader in the mind of the attacking member. This might occur, for example, if the member had previously shown irritation at the leader's tendency to interpret remarks, and if this interpretive mode had been highlighted as one of the leader's prominent characteristics.

In the final level of inference, the group member appears in disguised or symbolic form but the leader may or may not be disguised. For example, the member may suggest that others in the group or outside of the group have certain feelings toward the leader. Previous remarks, the context of the present remarks, and the tone of the comments may enable the investigator to infer that the attributed feelings are a projection of the speaker's own feelings.

Having inferred the level of interaction that is taking place between the target member and the group leader, the investigator's next step is to place his inferences about the feelings expressed by the target member into categories. Mann has established sixteen categories. Some of these deal with the emotional response the member may have toward the leader. Included in these are hostile impulses, such as resisting the leader or withdrawing from the interaction to decrease its intensity. Others deal with positive and affectionate impulses, such as accepting the leader by agreeing with him, or approving of his behavior as he leads the group. Some categories deal with authority relations between the member and the leader: a group member who shows dependence, for example, responds to the leader's power by being deferential in his remarks and his actions. Finally, some categories indicate how the target member feels about himself vis-à-vis the leader. Among these categories are such ego states as anxiety, self-esteem, and depression.

How does one pinpoint and describe the feelings of the target member with this system? Take, for example, the category "identifying." What overt behavior might be coded as "identifying" behavior? Mann argues that an important expression of feeling between member and leader occurs when "one member takes the role of the leader in relation to another member, [or] when he responds to another member in a manner suggestive of the leader's style or usual message" (Mann, 1967, p. 49). "When a member interrupts the flow of conversation in the group to comment on the feelings being expressed . . . , we feel that a useful inference about his feelings may be that he has identified somewhat with the group leader" (Mann, 1967, p. 49).

As one can see, the inference process is a complex one and requires highly trained observers. The reliability of these judgments can be measured in a variety of ways. Mann reports very high agreement (93 percent to 98 percent) between two independent observers on whether any given act is relevant or not relevant to leader–member feelings. There is also better than 90 percent agreement between observers on which of the four levels of inference is involved. The rate of agreement on the proper content category for an act is not quite this high, but it is still very respectable and meets accepted standards in the field. These figures demonstrate that "one need not abandon all claims to reliability simply because one goes a bit beneath the surface to record interpersonal behavior at the feeling level and even at the level of symbolically expressed feelings" (Mann, 1967, p. 65).

Having reliably described and categorized the expressed feelings in social interaction, one can then go on to explore such things as individual differences and shifts in the feelings being expressed as a group develops. Happily, even disguised feelings are not completely inaccessible to observers and need not be ignored in the study of social interaction. Thus, the T-group becomes a device for raising the awareness of subconscious feelings and making them visible for an observer to record. The human potential movement has also used many of the T-group techniques for developing greater awareness on the part of the individual for therapy, personality change, and personal growth. (See the discussion of intensive groups in chapter 4.)

Ethnomethodology

Ethnomethodologists, like the observers of T-groups, are interested in hidden meanings. It might be said that the perspective of the ethnomethodologists is to view social intercourse as if one were a visitor from another world who knew nothing of humans or human society, in that the ethnomethodological perspective treats social interaction as fundamentally problematic. The remark at the beginning of this chapter, that the management of our daily interactions is a *tour de force*, is very much in this spirit. It is fitting to pay "to the most commonplace activities of daily life the attention usually accorded extraordinary events . . . to learn about them as phenomena in their own right" (Garfinkel, 1967, p.1). We are all lay social psychologists, planning and explaining our behavior to ourselves and to others in the process of managing our daily lives. However, we are not very self-conscious about it, and we take such production for granted. This fact makes life interesting for the ethnomethodologists, because it leaves them the task of discovering our management secrets even when we are unaware of them ourselves.

This aspect of ethnomethodology is illustrated in an experiment conducted by Garfinkel. He asked his students to report on conversations that they heard. The students were to write on one side of a page what was said by the participants in the conversation; on the other side, they were to jot down what the participants actually understood by their conversation. Here, from Garfinkel (1967, pp. 25–26), is an example of one conversation and the student's explanation of it:

Conversation	Interpretation
HUSBAND: Dana succeeded in putting a penny in a parking meter today without being picked up.	This afternoon as I was bringing Dana, our four-year-old son, home from the nursery school, he succeeded in reaching high enough to put a penny in a parking meter when we parked in a meter zone, whereas before he had always had to be picked up to reach that high.

WIFE:	Did you take him to the record store?	Since he put a penny in a meter that means that you stopped while he was with you. I know that you stopped at the record store either on the way to get him or on the way back. Was it on the way back, so that he was with you or did you stop there on the way to get him and somewhere else on the way back?
HUSBAND:	No, to the shoe repair shop.	No, I stopped at the record store on the way to get him and stopped at the shoe repair shop on the way home when he was with me.
WIFE:	What for?	I know of one reason why you might have stopped at the shoe repair shop. Why did you in fact?
HUSBAND:	I got some new shoe laces for my shoes.	As you will remember I broke a shoe lace on one of my brown oxfords the other day so I stopped to get some new laces.
WIFE:	Your loafers need new heels badly.	Something else you could have gotten that I was thinking of. You could have taken in your black loafers which need heels badly. You'd better get them taken care of pretty soon. (GARFINKEL, 1967)

The ethnomethodologist is interested in the understandings that make it possible for the *conversation* between husband and wife in the above example to take place without the necessity of supplying the *interpretation*.

The wrench in the works

Just as the T-group is used to make hidden meanings observable, the deliberate, almost mischievous use of trouble and disruption is often the tool of the ethnomethodologists to make visible the common cultural base, the unspoken meanings we all, in one cultural tradition, agree, to a greater or lesser extent, to live by. As Garfinkel (1967, p. 37) puts it, "Procedurally it is my preference to start with familiar scenes and ask what can be done to make trouble."

Alan Funt, with his candid camera idea, stumbled onto the same principle. An ethnomethodologist is an Alan Funt with a serious interest in learning something from people's attempts to restore interaction to its normal state following a puzzling disruption. Witness, for example, what happens when an ethnomethodology student carries out an assignment in which she has been asked to seek clarification of the meanings of commonplace remarks (Garfinkel, 1967, p. 43):

> On Friday night, my husband and I were watching television. My husband remarked that he was tired.
>
> WIFE: How are you tired? Physically, mentally, or just bored?
> HUSBAND: I don't know. I guess physically, mainly.
> WIFE: You mean that your muscles ache or your bones?
> HUSBAND: I guess so. Don't be so technical.
> *(After more watching.)*
> HUSBAND: All these old movies have the same kind of old iron bedstead in them.
> WIFE: What do you mean? Do you mean all old movies, or some of them, or just the ones you have seen?
> HUSBAND: What's the matter with you? You know what I mean.
> WIFE: I wish you would be more specific.
> HUSBAND: You know what I mean! Drop dead!

The husband is irritated with his wife because she is suddenly and inexplicably refusing to participate in the assumed consensus on which their interaction depends. As with all our communication, the husband says a tiny fraction of what he intends to communicate and assumes that his spouse will understand the balance. This works quite well most of the time because the assumption goes unchallenged even though we know, for example, that a child may understand only a fraction of it. It is very difficult, if not impossible, to continue interacting with someone like this wife who will not accept the assumed consensus. In this case, the reaction is indignation because the husband correctly interprets the wife's refusal as deliberate. If he thought it was not deliberate, he might call a psychiatrist instead of getting angry.

In an experiment by William Gamson with his social psychology students, the students were asked to create an interaction situation in which their behavior was "unaccountable." In other words, the students were asked to create a situation in which the other party is forced to recognize that the assumed consensus is lacking. The students are asked to enter a store, choose an inexpensive object, and offer more than the list price. It is important that they offer more rather than less because the latter behavior is definable without much difficulty as chiseling. But offering more is unaccountable, and it was predicted that it would be followed by alarm and strenuous efforts to render the behavior understandable.

Many students had difficulty with this assignment, but they also were quite inventive. One girl went into a local variety store where jelly beans, normally priced at 49 cents a pound, were on sale for 35 cents. She engaged the salesgirl in conversation about the various candies and finally asked for one-half pound of jelly beans. The salesgirl wrapped them and asked for 18 cents.

STUDENT: Oh, only 18 cents for all those jelly beans. There are so many of them. I think I will pay you 25 cents for them.

SALESGIRL: Yes, there are a lot and they are only 18 cents today on sale.

STUDENT: I know they are on sale but I want to pay 25 cents for them. They are worth at least that to me. I love jelly beans.

SALESGIRL: No, you see they are selling for 35 cents a pound today and you ordered one-half pound. Half of 35 cents is 18 cents.

STUDENT: (voice rising) I am perfectly capable of dividing 35 cents in half. That has nothing to do with it. It's just that I feel that they are worth more and I want to pay more for them.

SALESGIRL: (suddenly becoming quite animated) What's the matter with you? Are you crazy or something? Everything in this store is overpriced. Those jelly beans cost the store about 3 cents. Now do you want them or should I put them back?

At this point, the student became quite embarrassed, paid the 18 cents, and hurriedly left (private communication).

Several things are interesting about the above example. It is not surprising that the puzzled victim takes measures to normalize the interaction. She tends to assume that the student is confused or lacks information. Less obviously, she becomes acutely uncomfortable when this initial attempt to account for what is happening fails. The student also becomes extremely uncomfortable even though she knows what is going on. In a great many other cases, the students found themselves unconsciously rendering their behavior more accountable. Thus, the student above invented a passion for jelly beans. It is not just the target person but all participants in the interaction who experience the pressure to remove the threat to social interaction that is created by their mischief.

The reaction to someone who refuses to accept "what everyone knows" with all its attendant vagueness is not simply the reaction of one who has been inconvenienced. It is mildly annoying to be asked to define one's terms in an argument when one is using language with some self-consciousness and precision. It is downright threatening to be asked to do so when one is using language with typical imprecision, because one's terms may hide a good deal of confusion and ignorance.

It is sometimes easier, for example, for an instructor to teach graduate students than introductory students because graduate students allow the teacher to get by with certain terms. They are too sophisticated to question such "simple" words as "role" or "institution." The failure to accept the shared academic jargon would place them outside of the guild. They learn the rules for using such language and do not ask embarrassing and threatening questions that might uncover the thinness of the underlying professional consensus. Introductory students may be subject to many similar pressures, but they are not expected to share the same corpus of concepts. Consequently, they have the same dangerous quality as the child who is too young to know that certain family affairs are not fit topics for discussion with outsiders. Part of socialization is learning to keep one's mouth shut about such embarrassing matters as the emperor's new clothes.

The case of the imaginary consensus

Some of the ethnomethodologist's interaction gambits are designed to demonstrate the extent to which we construct our unspoken, shared meanings even when none exist. We operate *as if* we share an underlying consensus regardless of whether we actually do, and we interact in ways that avoid discovering whether this assumed consensus is false. Garfinkel recruited ten undergraduates "by telling them that research was being done in the Department of Psychiatry to explore alternative means to psychotherapy 'as a way of giving persons advice about their personal problems' " (Garfinkel, 1967, p. 79). Each subject was seen individually by a person represented as a student counselor in training. The subject was asked first to discuss the background of some problem that concerned him and then to address a series of questions to the counselor that could be answered by a "yes" or "no." The counselor heard the questions and gave the answers from an adjoining room by means of an intercom system. The subject was also asked to record his reactions between answers, but these reactions could not be heard by the counselor.

One subject was Jewish and had been dating a gentile girl. He felt that his father, though not outwardly opposed to this arrangement, was not too pleased with it. The young man wondered whether he should have a long talk with his father about the girl; if his father did not want him to date the girl, should he continue to do so, he asked the counselor. The young man seemed surprised when the counselor gave him an affirmative reply, and he wondered whether he should tell the girl about the problems he was having at home. Once again, he expressed surprise when the counselor said no. The young man went on in this vein, reacting to, and building on, the counselor's replies.

After the interview was over, the subject was asked to give his reactions to the counselor's advice. "The answers I received," he said, "I must say that the majority of them were answered perhaps in the same way that I would answer them to myself knowing the differences in types of people. . . . The conversation and the answers given, I believe, had a lot of meaning to me. I mean it was perhaps what I would have expected from someone who fully understood the situation. One or two of them did come as a surprise to me. . . . I feel that it had a lot of sense to me and made a lot of sense."

Actually, the subject in the above demonstration was receiving a preprogrammed, random sequence of "yes" and "no" answers that was in no way contingent on his questions. The subject assumed, of course, that he was in a mutually contingent interaction. The interesting point is the relative ease with which he was able to maintain this assumption regardless of the answers. This does not take place through some blind malleability or other-directedness on the part of the subject. He has his own opinions and is quite capable of disagreeing with the advice, but he finds it reasonable in its own terms. The counselor lacks information or perhaps is more objective, but nothing occurs to upset the assumption of an underlying consensus. This consensus, however, is entirely of the subject's construction.

No real consensus need exist, in this perspective, for people to interact smoothly so long as all parties assume consensus and do not act in ways that challenge it. This is characteristic of social interaction, and it is only when ethnomethodologists poke their fingers through the thin crust and we see the strenuous efforts to restore the assumed consensus that we can recognize the considerable management task involved.

Where are the four orientations most instructive and where do they add the least to our understanding? With the exception of T-group dynamics and, to a lesser extent, social exchange, they do not tell us much about more intimate forms of social interaction. Most of the orientations focus on well-ordered and institutionalized interaction. With the exception of game theory and T-group dynamics, their subject matter is behavior governed by well-established norms and expectations—for example, work associates engaging in some collective task.

Again with the exception of T-group dynamics, ambivalence is hardly recognized. The psychological animal of game theory or social exchange knows exactly what he wants and is not troubled by contradictory feelings as he searches for the best method of pursuing his interests. And the deliberate manager of impressions of the self-presentation perspective never seems to disgust himself as he performs the scenario he has worked out for himself.

Social exchange and game theory do have something to say about how the constraints of power, status, or other external inputs to an interaction situation influence the nature and course of the interaction. The other orientations deal with such matters obliquely and indirectly.

In sum, each of the four orientations has something useful to show us, and, taken together, they cover a considerable range. Social interaction is a rambling house with many wings and nooks. Some orientations, like social exchange, light up the main part of the house. Others figure the natural light is bright enough in the main house and concentrate on revealing the bedrooms and the dark wings where the servants live or the mad sister is kept hidden. And there are undoubtedly many dusty corners, untouched by any of the orientations, awaiting some new social psychologist to reveal their contents.

PATCHING THE SOCIAL FABRIC: THE FAMILY NETWORK

At the turn of the century, most people lived with others or in large extended families. But in contemporary urban America, more people live alone or with only one other person. When problems strike, they feel adrift, isolated, and often shamed into silence. To help cope with this problem, Ross Speck and Carolyn Attneave (1973) have suggested an idea which methodically reorganizes the bonds that once existed between people, but that today are ritualized or overlooked.

The idea is known as the family network, in which forty or fifty people who are aware of a person's problem are invited to gather together in someone's house. Over the course of five or six two-hour sessions, the group helps the individual or family face up to their hidden but unresolved conflicts. The two investigators got their idea from R. D. Laing, the noted British psychiatrist. Laing has suggested that no matter how isolated an individual appears to be, his psychological problems are often rooted in his relationships with those around him. A child may be schizophrenic, but regardless of psychiatry's attempt to help him, he may remain disturbed if his family is disturbed.

According to Speck and Attneave, "The social network is a relatively invisible, but at the same time a very real, structure in which an individual, nuclear family, or group is imbedded. There are malfunctioning social networks as well as malfunctioning families and individuals. The retribalization goal of social network intervention attempts to deal with the entire structure by rendering the network visible and viable, and by attempting to restore its function."

Thus, social network intervention seeks and triggers the forces of healing within the social fabric of people whom society views as pathological. When a family or individual asks for help, an "intervention team" (usually three people) begins by identifying and notifying members of the network. They may contact sisters and brothers, cousins, friends, business associates, neighbors, and peers. On an appointed day, all these people—some of whom may not have seen one another for years or may never have met—assemble to hear the family's problems and discuss what they can do to help.

In the case of a teenage boy with a drug habit, for example, the network organized itself into committees to help him find a job, an apartment, and ways out of his drug habit. First, the network members listened to an "inner circle" of the boy's peers discuss their experiments with drugs. Then an "outer circle," composed of members of the boy's parents' generation, was given the floor. As often occurs when different generations discuss an issue, there was disagreement over how to tackle the problem. The resulting conflict was the beginning of a dialogue that helped the boy and his family interact so that the other members present could serve as a reflecting audience. Soon the underlying family problems that contributed to the boy's drug habit were exposed.

Once set in motion, the network gains a momentum of its own. By showing people that others care in the ways in which an extended family or a tribe used to care, a network can help people realize things they would never acknowledge if left to themselves.

Summary

Every day, we enter into numerous social interactions, rarely stopping to analyze just what is happening between ourselves and others. But there are many aspects of social exchange that are problematic and require explanation. Thus, social psychologists try to find patterns in our daily social dealings. How are these patterns formed? How do they break down? How are they reestablished?

One begins to answer such questions by examining the process of social interaction itself. All social interactions vary in the degree to which the response of one party is contingent upon what the other parties say or do. Thus, whenever two or more people interact, there can be a state of pseudocontingency—each actor reacts to his own plans and ignores the acts and responses of the others. At the other extreme is mutual contingency, in which the participants respond to others, but in light of their own plans. Between these poles are intermediate states known as asymmetrical contingency and reactive contingency.

There are a number of theoretical perspectives that attempt to penetrate the kinds of processes that take place during interaction. Of these, four stand out as being particularly relevant. In self-presentation, developed by Goffman, the phenomena to be studied are the techniques people use, both consciously and unconsciously, to create and manage the impressions that they make on others. The second perspective, Homans's theory of social exchange, views social interaction as an economic transaction. In Homans's eyes, in one's dealings with others one tries to extract as many rewards as possible while maintaining the lowest possible cost.

A similar theory of social interaction is seen in game theory, in which the individual attempts to maximize profits by obtaining the greatest number of rewards at the least cost. For game theorists, the participants in a social interaction have certain resources available to them to achieve certain goals. They follow a set of rules which specify constraints and opportunities. The skill with which the game players use these rules is the focal point of this theory. Using the rules, participants may engage in a pure conflict game, a pure collaboration game, or a mixed-motive game.

The third orientation is that of the T-group, which aims to reveal to the participants the patterns of behavior that they unconsciously have been following. The fourth approach is that of ethnomethodology. Like the observers of the T-group, the ethnomethodologist wishes to ferret out the hidden meanings of social exchange. These researchers attempt to examine the most commonplace activities of daily life—buying candy in a store or borrowing a book from a library, for example—as if they were rare and extraordinary events.

Bibliography

BENNIS, W. G., SCHEIN, E. H., BERLEW, D. E., AND STEELE, F. I. *Interpersonal dynamics.* Homewood, Ill.: Dorsey Press, 1964.

CHRISTIE, R., AND GEIS, F. (Eds.) *Studies in Machiavellianism.* New York: Academic Press, 1970.

DEUTSCH, M., AND KRAUSS, R. M. The effect of threat upon interpersonal bargaining. *Journal of Abnormal and Social Psychology,* 1960, **61,** 181–189.

DEUTSCH, M., AND KRAUSS, R. M. *Theories in social psychology.* New York: Basic Books, 1965.

GALLO, P. S. Effects of increased incentives upon the use of threat in bargaining. *Journal of Personality and Social Psychology,* 1966, **4,** 14–20.

GAMSON, W. A. Experimental Studies of coalition formation. In L. Berkowitz (Ed.), *Advances in experimental social psychology.* Vol. 1. New York: Academic Press, 1964.

GAMSON, W. A. Game theory and administrative decision-making. In C. Press and A. Arian (Eds.), *Empathy and ideology.* Chicago: Rand McNally, 1966.

GARFINKEL, H. *Studies in ethnomethodology.* Englewood Cliffs, N.J.: Prentice-Hall, 1967.

GOFFMAN, E. On face-work: An analysis of ritual elements in social interaction. *Psychiatry,* August 1955, **18,** 213–231.

GOFFMAN, E. *The presentation of self in everyday life.* Garden City, N.Y.: Doubleday, Anchor, 1959.

HOMANS, G. C. Social behavior as exchange. *American Journal of Sociology,* May 1958, **63,** 597–606.

HOMANS, G. C. *Social behavior: Its elementary forms.* New York: Harcourt Brace Jovanovich, 1961.

JONES, E. E. *Ingratiation.* New York: Appleton-Century-Crofts, 1964.

JONES, E. E., AND GERARD, H. B. *Foundations of social psychology.* New York: John Wiley, 1967.

JONES, E. E., AND THIBAUT, J. W. Interaction goals as bases of inference in interpersonal perception. In R. Tagiuri and L. Petrullo (Eds.), *Person perception and interpersonal behavior.* Stanford: Stanford University Press, 1958.

MANN, R. D. *Interpersonal styles and group development.* New York: John Wiley, 1967.

MODIGLIANI, A. Embarrassment and social influence. Doctoral dissertation, University of Michigan, 1966.

POTTER, S. *The theory and practice of gamesmanship, or the art of winning games without actually cheating.* New York: Henry Holt, 1948.

RAPOPORT, A. *Strategy and conscience.* New York: Harper and Row, 1964.

SCHELLING, T. C. *The strategy of conflict.* Cambridge, Mass.: Harvard University Press, 1960.

SLATER, P. E. *Microcosm.* New York: John Wiley, 1966.

SPECK, R. V., AND ATTNEAVE, C. L. *Family networks.* New York: Pantheon Books, 1973.

4

Group Cohesion

Humans are among the most social of animals. Observation, as well as our own experience, confirms how widespread is the human tendency to congregate in groups. A college student, for example, could tick off any number of groups to which he belongs: student organizations, athletic teams, or fraternities. He would probably mention classes that he attends with other students, or a small core of friends with whom he spends much of his time. He would almost certainly mention his family and probably his religious, political, and ethnic affiliations as well. Other individuals, especially members of the middle class, would doubtless mention an equally varied number of organizations.

Groups, then, seem to form the cornerstone of our social life. But what exactly is a group? Do the individuals sitting in a waiting room at a bus station constitute a group? How about the audience at a ballet? Or a listing of unrelated people who happen to have the same first name? As with the central concepts in other disciplines, it is difficult to arrive at a single, all-inclusive definition of a group. Some investigators say that the key idea behind the group is that all of its members must relate to one another in an observable and significant way. Others say that it is the interaction among individuals that makes the aggregation a group. Many social scientists maintain that a set of people striving toward a common goal constitutes a group. Still others believe that the satisfaction derived by the members of a relationship qualifies the

115

members as a group. Finally, a growing number of investigators hold that the group is an amalgam of all of the above ideas—and more. Thus, any set of individuals that exhibits all or some of the following attributes constitutes a group: frequent interaction; awareness—both by group members and outsiders—of belonging to a group; a system of shared norms and interconnected roles; pressure from other members to conform to norms; a common goal; satisfaction derived from members in the relationship; a structure with communication networks and a leader; and a modification of the individual's behavior as a result of group membership.

Any assemblage of individuals which exhibits all or some of these characteristics certainly qualifies as a group. Most families, for example, fall into this category. At the other extreme is the set of people who interact with one another for a brief while to accomplish some objective. For example, imagine a subway or train station late at night with six individuals waiting for the train. The people do not know one another and are not interacting. Suddenly, one of the six—a young woman—loses her balance and falls off the platform onto the tracks. Immediately, two men rush forward to help her. A third grabs the signal lantern and waves it over the tracks, signalling the distant but fast-approaching train to stop. Another man rushes to the stationmaster's office to inform him of the accident. The sixth person, an elderly man, runs back and forth on the platform shouting for help. After a few moments, the woman is helped back onto the platform, shaken but unhurt. She thanks the five people, the train arrives, and all board it, ending the interaction. These six individuals exhibited only one of the defining characteristics of a group: they shared a common goal for a short period. They acted as a group only as long as was necessary. After the danger passed, they disbanded. In between the polar extremes of the tightly knit family and the temporary, short-lived group is a whole spectrum of groups which exhibit a few or many of the characteristics that set groups off from other social phenomena.

Despite the great variety in groups, they all share one characteristic: the cohesion or cement that holds them together and marks the division of their members from other groups. Indeed, cohesion may be considered the defining characteristic of groups. An investigation of cohesion, as well as its role in groups, will give us some insight into the fundamentals of social interaction.

The Nature of Cohesion

Group cohesion is, roughly, the feeling that keeps people together in one group, or rather, that which makes a member feel closer to some people than to others. A more formal definition has been given by Leon Festinger (1950): the resultant force that keeps members within a group. We can conceptualize forces of different strengths impelling people to stay within a group or to leave it. Consider, for example, a social club such as is found among many ethnic groups: Italian, or Lithuanian, or Polish. People leave the club for various reasons, including the cost of dues, the competing demands for resources and time, a change in the characteristics of the membership, such as age, or a change in the activities and goals of the club. Some forces for cohesion might include personal advantage derived from the club's activities, the symbolic importance of membership in an organization of compatriots in an alien land, and particularly, the comfort and support of people who share a common language and culture. The resultant force is the degree to which reasons to remain in the club outweigh those to stay out of it. We must look for the reasons members remain in the group in order to arrive at a way of measuring strength of cohesion.

Measures of group cohesion

One can use several different techniques to assess the existence and strength of group cohesion. The simplest and most commonly used way is to question the members directly. One might ask, for example: How much do you like this group? How much does it mean to you? How do you like the individual members in the group? Another way to achieve the same end is to ask members indirect questions, such as who their closest friends are. Based on the answers to such questions, one could then determine what proportion of friends falls into a specified group. Under special conditions we can also introduce certain behavioral measures. Among these are finding how much time members spend with their group, how much effort is required to make individuals leave the group, and whether they are willing to work for the group.

Another way is to measure the patterns of interaction within a group, to determine certain facts. For instance, does everyone talk to everyone else, or are some people excluded? In a larger group, one might try to discover if there are subgroups which can be identified by exclusive interaction or discussion.

Alternatively, one can consider the way people talk about a group, or act within a group. How often, for example, do they use the word "we" instead of "I," or do they talk about the group as a subordinate whole? Finally, more intricate techniques such as projective tests can be used. For example, an investigator might ask group members to look at a picture which shows several people engaged in conversation, and to make up a story about the picture. The extent to which the members see the protagonists in the picture interacting can be used as a measure of the group's cohesion. In general, all these indicators show the same situations as being either cohesive or noncohesive.

Which indicator a researcher would use depends on its availability in a particular situation. Moreover, several such indicators may be used for confirmation from different sources to increase the validity of measurement.

Sociometry. One method of measurement is fundamental to many of the approaches we have considered. It involves asking people how close they are to certain people in a group, as compared to other people outside the group. This approach has been called *sociometry* by its originator, Jacob Moreno (1934). Moreno sought to measure the forces of attraction and repulsion that bind and divide individuals within a group. Thus, investigators who use the technique of sociometry ask individual group members whom they would like to work with, vacation with, attend a party with, and so on. In one of the earliest investigations of this type, Moreno (1934) studied young girls who were detained in an institution for delinquents. He wanted to learn how the girls chose their cottage mates. To obtain this information, Moreno asked the girls such questions as "Whom would you like to sit next to in class?", "Whom would you invite to a party?", "Whom would you like to work with?". He plotted the responses of the girls in a figure known as a sociogram.

Figure 4–1 shows such a graphic representation of the feelings of group members. The direction of the arrows that connect the circles symbolizes the choosers and the chosen. Double arrows represent mutual choices. The internal cohesion of the group is symbolized by the number of interconnecting lines within the group. In addition, a sociogram can show not only different subgroups but group stratification as well. In Figure 4–1, for example, members of a group were asked whom they would like to be with most. Ed is the most popular member of the group, the star, because he was chosen by Myron, Joe, Frank, Cally, and Penelope. Poor Mary, by contrast, is the least popular: she has chosen no one and no one has chosen her. Al and Bob form a subgroup, a separate mutual attraction society, who like to spend time only with one another. Frank, Penelope, and Ed form another subgroup because they are mutually attracted to one another.

By examining sociograms such as this, investigators can learn much about group structure and dynamics. In addition to indicating group cohesion, sociograms reveal variation among individuals in their social interactions. The technique also pinpoints cliques which form along age, sex, or ethnic lines.

Such a device, then, is a most convenient way to assess the structure of groups as well as the position of individuals within a group. Moreno himself has identified a number of patterns and positions which may have great consequences for individuals. He found, for example, that he could predict how rumors and gossip would spread after plotting the choices among group members in sociograms. When one of the girls was caught stealing, only the other members of her immediate group knew about it the very next day. A week later, the gossip had traveled through social networks to other girls in the institution. Moreno has put the sociogram to another practical use. He reorganized groups along the lines of sociometric preferences. This, for the most part, increases the efficiency and the adjustment of all concerned.

Since Moreno's work, many investigators have used the sociogram for a variety of purposes. It has been employed to analyze clannishness, to uncover personality problems, and to study leadership in groups. The drawback of the visual format used in the sociometric test is that with a group of any size it becomes too complicated. In addition, propositions based on sociograms are necessarily impressionistic in nature. Fortunately, however, because of the relationships between algebraic and geometrical systems, graphs can now be analyzed by standard techniques in matrix algebra. In this way, sociometry has virtually become a part of higher mathematics (Lindzey and Byrne, 1968).

The entire mathematical superstructure, however, should not blind us to the fact that the same line may represent different questions and thus may have

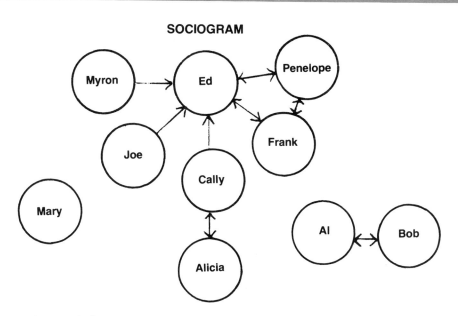

SOCIOGRAM

Figure 4–1. If this sociogram represented a work group, how would you describe the relationships within the group? Would your description change if you were told that the names represented children in a kindergarten class?

more than one meaning. In a play group, for example, findings may vary depending upon what activity the children are asked they would like to do with another person. If a child were asked with whom she would like to play softball, the choice might be different than if she were asked whom she would choose to help her with a poster for a crafts fair. Similarly, in the sociogram in Figure 4–1, the lines connecting the individuals might be entirely different if the members were asked whom they would like to lead them. Most of the arrows might point to Bob, Myron, or anyone else, rather than to Ed.

Moreno, who saw in sociometric tests a practical tool for restructuring groups (even the whole society), stressed the importance of which question was asked, and warned against overgeneralization from one question to another. On the other hand, if we want to distill a specific trait of groups, such as cohesion, from these questions, we must consider the questions as more or less equivalent, or as measures which, however imperfect, tap in an equal way the cohesion of groups.

One question may be as good as another, and if one person chooses another person in answer to three different questions, we may give the relationship a higher score than if he had made only one choice out of three. We must keep in mind, however, that this method is not always legitimate and that under some conditions one question may be of paramount importance and may negate the evidence of the other question. This difficulty in measurement reflects the fact that although we consider cohesion a force that can be measured, we must not forget the qualitative differences between groups.

Conditions of cohesion

Cohesion is a certain pattern of relationships: the denser the pattern and the stronger the relationships are, the more cohesion we expect within the group. Cohesion is also subjective: people know they belong to a group and value one group membership over other memberships and other features in their lives. Most people know that membership in their family, for example, means more to them than does membership in their trade union or professional organization. This knowledge has an emotional tone, which gives the meaning of group membership and cohesion a special character. In this way, group membership becomes part of the identity of the person. A man conceives of himself as a Rockefeller, or a Roman Catholic, or a Communist.

Cohesion can be created quickly and temporarily in a group, and this makes it possible to study experimentally the genesis of cohesion, as well as its influences and consequences. Conditions for cohesion can be created through instructions given to subjects in an experiment. As Back (1951) has shown, for instance, subjects may be told that they will like one another, or that they are similar to one another, and, to a great extent, they will act accordingly. Or one can promise a joint reward to make subjects interdependent. For the duration of the experiment and the conditions studied in it, the subjects will then form a cohesive group. This experimental manipulation indicates how cohesion can be aroused.

In one experiment by Thibaut (1950), he used groups of adolescents from settlement houses and camps. Each group was divided into two parts, depending on previous sociometric choices. The division was made so that each member had chosen as many people in his group as in the other one. During the session itself the subjects played games; however, one of the groups experienced most of the enjoyment of the games, while the other group did most of the menial work, such as holding the baskets for balls to be thrown into. The principal finding was that under all possible variations of this technique, as measured by subsequent sociometric tests, cohesion within the disadvantaged group increased, especially if the group had undergone some special experience, such as attempted rebellion.

In another study by Albert Myers (1962), it was learned that *threat* increases group cohesion. Myers formed a number of three-man rifle-shooting groups. Some of the groups competed against one another and some did not. Results showed that the teams that competed—and faced the possibility of losing to other teams—were more tightly knit than the teams that did not compete. Individuals in the competitive teams, for example, felt more attracted to their teammates than did those in noncompetitive teams. When asked to describe their feelings toward an absent team member—whether he was friendly or unfriendly, cooperative or uncooperative, capable or incompetent, for example—members of the competitive teams consistently reported positive feelings toward the absent member. And they did so even though the teammate's absence put them at a disadvantage in competition with other complete teams.

Thus, outside pressure or threat affects the development of group cohesion, even to the extent that it has been claimed that the existence of an outside enemy is a necessary condition for the creation and maintenance of a group. However, an enemy is not essential to a group. For instance, there may be differences in the extent to which individuals perceive a threat as dangerous (see chapter 12). In Schachter's study of affiliation (1959), he found that subjects who had undergone a threat of electric shock were more likely to choose to wait for the shock with other people, especially with people who had endured the same kind of threat. (Schachter's affiliation study is fully discussed in chapter 11.) Moreover, Schachter found that firstborn and only children, to a greater extent than others, reacted with the need for company in conditions of anxiety. This is true not only in experiments; it is known that firstborn and only children display such behavior in more often initiating and continuing psychotherapy, a situation in which they seek a person to help when they are anxious, i.e. feel threatened. Moreover, such individuals show a lower aptitude for becoming fighter pilots where danger and anxiety must be faced alone.

Cohesion can also be induced through positive action, by inducing people to like one another by special techniques, or by creating a warm atmosphere. Encounter groups, and other similar groups in which the formation of intimacy among strangers is important, use such strategies.

Consequences of cohesion

What are the consequences of heightened group cohesion? What rewards do people find in groups in addition to the overt reason they give for joining a group in the first place? Studies have attempted to analyze this feeling and to ascertain its components. One important component of cohesion has been called *deindividuation:* that is, feeling oneself to be, and looking on others, not as a particular, separate person, but as part of a group. A study by Festinger, Pepitone, and Newcomb (1952) found that during an animated discussion (corresponding to higher cohesion) people did not remember who said what as well as they did during a less animated discussion (corresponding to lower cohesion). This study is more fully discussed in chapter 5. Other studies of deindividuation, however, have produced conflicting results. The question of whether group membership enhances or diminishes responsibility, for example, is an intriguing question which is still unresolved.

One important aspect of deindividuation—perhaps the reason for its appeal to group members—is the fact that with deindividuation each person becomes predictable in his outlook and behavior. If we are sure that everyone will act only as a group member, we do not have to worry about individual idiosyncrasies. This predictability is best expressed in a tendency of group members to enforce uniform attitudes and behaviors. The effect of a cohesive group is to produce a pressure for uniformity and conformity to the group; this happens to such an extent that the degree of conformity can almost be used as a measure of cohesion.

Studies by Back (1951), which showed different ways of creating cohesion, indicated also that under those conditions where people were expected to like one another or were working for greater rewards, they influenced one another more. However, even this general principle must be approached with caution. Conformity is usually enforced only for issues of importance to the group. If members conform on important issues, there may be little pressure for them to conform on less important ones. In studies of elections, for instance, it has been shown that only when the election becomes an important issue in the group will membership in a political party become salient (Berelson, Lazarsfeld, and McPhee, 1954). Between elections, politics is not central, and topics and opinions diverge.

Four Group Models

We have identified a core of concepts and conditions common to situations of high cohesion. Different theorists have looked at group cohesion from different points of view, depending on which feature they consider to be most important and which examples of particular groups they had in mind when they formulated their theories. We have selected four different models of group cohesion which present contrasting patterns of attraction and aggression, of total involvement and instrumental action. These are cohesion in the family, the work group, the community, and the interest group.

Freud and the family

The family is one of the oldest and most persistent forms of human association. Considered as a group, the family has a number of distinct characteristics. Most significant among these are the biological basis of the association, the permanent affiliation of the members, its history of growth and aging, and the strong bond which binds the members of the family together. Family members are more clearly differentiated from each other than those of any other group. Their position is predetermined; they are dependent on each other, with all the emotional ties and problems that this may involve.

It seems an obvious choice, therefore, for some investigators to make the family a model of all group interaction. The theorist most identified with this approach is Freud. Freud expounded his views on the relation of psychoanalysis to social psychology primarily in two works: *Totem and Taboo* (1922) and *Group Psychology and Analysis of the Ego* (1949). In the first, Freud describes the family model in historical–genetic form. He postulates the original family as a horde consisting of the dominant male, his females, and his sons and daughters. Here he adopts the myth of the primordial horde originally proposed by Lang in 1905. Because the father prevents the sons from having access to the females, a power struggle occurs which results in the overthrow and killing of the father and the assumption of power by his sons. The group is then apparently transformed into one in which the brothers have joint power, kept together by guilt; this guilt is partly expiated through the totemic feast in which they eat (i.e., identify with) the father. However, the guilt can never be totally expunged. The emergence of religion and rituals (such as totemic feasts) is an example of efforts to atone for the primordial crime.

In the second volume, *Group Psychology and Analysis of the Ego*, Freud applies this model to modern social groups. He focuses on two large-scale organizations, the army and the church. In both groups he finds not only a strong dependence on, but also a resentment of, leadership. Members of each would like to eliminate and incorporate the leader, but the suppression of this inadmissible wish leads to an emotional reaction of strong positive attachment (cathexis) to the leader and the group he represents. Thus the group becomes a projection of an equivalent tension within the psyche of the individual: the struggle between the ego and the superego and their eventual integration into one functioning unit are equivalent to the relationship between the leader and the mass of followers. In effect, the superego is the internalized leader. Thus, Freud analogizes conflict within a group to conflict within the psyche: in his view, the same kinds of disturbances which lead to mental illness in the individual lead to social strife in the group.

Freud apparently did not intend his use of the metaphor of the primordial horde to be taken literally. In fact, in the second book he agreed with its

Like most other family groups, the members of this one from Brooklyn, New York, have strong bonds that link them together.

characterization as a "Just-So" story. But he did think that the processes he described are acted out in every individual, and that for every individual the basic constellation of the family will be carried over into other group relations. For example, Holmes (1967) discusses the same phenomenon in an interesting study in which he likens the participants in a university seminar to the primal horde.

Freud's exposition contains some important features of the family model. Prominent among these are strong emotional ties, based in part upon denial of any negative affect; a hierarchical structure; and relative independence from external influences. There is an intensity in the feelings between members of the group, not only the expressed feelings, but more especially half-hidden, not admitted, unconscious feelings. These produce ambivalence—simultaneous positive and negative feelings—among group members. Social psychologists who follow this approach concentrate on the dynamics of the group members, admit the existence of both affection and conflict within the group, and concentrate their attention on the dynamics within the group, not on its relation to other parts of society.

In addition to the family itself, some researchers (Slater, 1966) apply this model to therapy groups and some training groups which are similar to them. Thus, social psychologists who have dealt with groups of this kind have been hospitable to the family model and even to the metaphors of the Freudian approach.

As an example, Slater (1966) describes a seminar on social interaction that was conducted by using the group's own process as the main material for learning about group process in general. The nature of the group conforms rather closely to the family model. There is a natural division of power: the teacher, although he acts as a nondirective leader, has the power of grading the members, as well as the function of transmitting information and cultural standards to them. The strong emphasis on group interaction makes the emotional reactions more intense and isolates the group from the larger society—at least for the duration of the session.

Slater shows that in a therapy group conducted under these conditions, Freud's model is almost literally enacted. The class tries to eliminate the leader by attempting to exclude him in different ways. If the situation permits, they exclude him from the sessions for a while and then try to reorganize the group without him. This results in the assumption of more responsible positions by the different group members: instead of defining their positions in the seminar primarily in relationship to the leader (father) and thus assigning to him a position of extreme power, group members start working out relationships with each other and assume responsibility for group progress. After this sometimes painful readjustment, the leader can again be accepted in the group—as a part of the group—so to speak, digested. Even an actual meal frequently occurs; usually a student brings some food and drink as an excuse for a party. Slater shows how this sequence corresponds to the primordial crime and thus contends that Freud's theory describes observable group behavior. At least he shows how the ideas derived from Freud's theory offer an interpretation of the actions of certain types of groups.

The family model is also useful for understanding neurotic or otherwise inefficient behavior. Childhood is the time when many traits are acquired and fixed, and it might be useful, in treating difficulties in later life, to reenact behavior within the family in the therapy situation. This reenactment is, of course, what Freud noticed in neurotics; their behavior led him to recognize the importance of the family. Freud's model forms the basis for *transactional analysis*, as developed by Eric Berne (1961, 1964).

Berne, in *Games People Play* (1964), distinguishes three ego states which are based on the family. Each ego state is available to all of us at any given time. These states are: (1) the parental ego state, which is like that of parental figures; (2) the adult state, which objectively appraises reality; and (3) the child ego state which symbolizes relic states that were formed in early childhood. Interactions are not between one person and another, but between the ego state of one and the ego state of another. Berne feels that virtually all social transactions are games which are played between parent, adult, or child ego states for a variety of reasons: to avoid facing reality, to hide true motives, or to rationalize certain manners of behaving. For Berne, games are played to gain social advantage over others as well as to gain psychological advantage for oneself. In most of Berne's games, all participants win something and one rarely loses everything.

Consider, for example, the game Berne calls "Schlemiel." According to Leo Rosten, "schlemiel" is a Yiddish word meaning, roughly, "a clumsy, butter-fingered, all-thumbs, gauche type," or "a social misfit, congenitally malad-justed" (Rosten, 1968, pp. 348–349). There are two players in this game: Black, the host of a party, and White, a guest, who is the schlemiel. The game starts as White spills a drink on the evening gown of the hostess. Black, seeing this, is at first angry; then he realizes that if he shows his anger, White will win the game. So Black keeps his temper, thus thinking he has won. White then apologizes and Black forgives him, strengthening his belief that he has won.

But White is not quite finished in his destructiveness and quest for forgiveness. He burns a hole in the sofa with his cigarette, manages to put a chair leg through an expensive lace tablecloth, and spills gravy on the new Persian rug. The child in White is ecstatic because he is having such a good time damaging Black's property, for all of which he has been forgiven by Black. Black, meanwhile, has displayed an immense amount of self-control. In this way, both Black and White profit in this game. For this reason, Black is not at all eager to end the friendship.

The antithesis of the game—the point at which it would be stopped—can occur if Black refuses to forgive White. Thus, after White apologizes for spilling his drink on the hostess's gown, Black would not absolve him. Instead of saying "It's okay," for example, Black would say, "You can embarrass my wife and wreck my house, but don't apologize." In acting in this way, Black is transformed from the forgiving parent (to White's child) to an objective adult who assumes the blame for inviting White to his party. If Black were to take this course of action—become an anti-schlemiel, in effect—White's response might be one of rage. Thus, playing anti-schlemiel can make one an enemy, or, at the very least, the object of unpleasant verbal responses. Berne's analysis of this game is shown in Figure 4–2.

Berne's theory shows a limitation of the applicability of the family model: it is most suitable when the parent and child (as ego states) are present, and least suitable when adult interaction occurs. Correspondingly, it is applicable to therapy groups or other groups with a similar emotional impact, whereas it is weak in situations where adjustment to present external realities is

---

ANALYSIS OF A GAME

Thesis: I can be destructive and still get forgiveness.
Aim: Absolution.
Roles: *Aggressor*, Victim (Colloquially, Schlemiel and Schlemazl).
Dynamics: Anal aggression.
Examples (1) Messily destructive children.
           (2) Clumsy guest.
Social Paradigm: Adult-Adult.
   ADULT: "Since I'm polite, you have to be polite, too."
   ADULT: "That's fine. I forgive you."

Psychological Paradigm: Child-Parent.
   CHILD: "You have to forgive things which appear accidental."
   PARENT: "You are right. I have to show you what good manners are."

Moves: (1) Provocation-resentment.
        (2) Apology-forgiveness.

Advantages: (1) Internal Psychological pleasure of messing.
           (2) External Psychological—Avoids punishment.
           (3) Internal Social—"Schlemiel."
           (4) External Social—"Schlemiel."
           (5) Biological—provocative and gentle stroking.
           (6) Existential—I am blameless.

*Figure 4–2.
This is
Berne's analysis
of a transaction
between two people.
One is the victim;
the other the aggressor.
Berne calls the game
"Schlemiel"
to characterize the
behavior of the aggressor.*

SOURCE: Adapted from Berne, E. C. *Games people play.* New York: Grove Press, 1964.

paramount. Thus, the family model becomes especially valuable in dealing with emotional problems of group members. It is based on early experiences of the individual, if not of the human race, and its characteristics may become prominent under conditions of individual stress.

Homans and the work group

A contrasting approach uses a work group as a model—a group by means of which people can attain a specific goal. The work group differs from the family model in that individuals enter the group more or less voluntarily, and in that the focus is on goals, not on the emotions.

Among the theorists of group formation, Homans (1950, 1961) can be considered representative of those who assume this kind of group to be the basic form for all groups. Central to Homans's view is that groups are analyzed completely from the point of view of the individual member. An individual will enter a group if he feels that he will obtain rewards from his membership in it, and will leave it if he finds that he does not. Within the group itself, the chief rewards are derived from the actions of other members, and from any goals which are mediated through them. Because this is true for all members, the group takes on the appearance of a collection of self-contained individuals, each looking for maximum benefit. Group stability results when each person acts in a way which gives him considerable benefit and benefits other members as well. The process by which a group is established is a summation of individual learning experiences, or a game in which rules are developed for an equitable distribution of rewards. Thus, as we saw in chapter 3, Homans considers social behavior as an exchange.

Clearly, it is easier to obtain benefits for all members if some rewards are introduced from the outside than if the total "capital" of the group is fixed. Therefore, this model applies particularly well to a special-purpose group, such as a work group. Homans's favorite example is a study by Roethlisberger and Dickson (1946) of a group of workers wiring transformers in a Western Electric plant. Their job was to connect wires to banks of terminals that would be part of switches for central office telephone equipment. For this reason, the room was known as the bank-wiring room.

The interactions of fourteen employees who worked in the wiring room were studied by Homans. The fourteen included nine wiremen, whose task it was to connect the wires to the bank of terminals; three solderers, who soldered the connected wires in place; and two inspectors, who examined the completed work for defects. The group was observed intensively; the interplay of material rewards and social reinforcements in establishing patterns of behavior among members was amply documented. Also documented was the lighthearted, gamelike aspect of the situation.

A number of factors influenced the ways the group interacted with one another. Chief among these was the method by which they were paid, known as group piecework. According to this wage-incentive system, the amount received by each member of the group depended not only on his individual output, but on that of the group as well. For this reason, a good deal of attention was paid to one another's working practices, and a body of unstated norms emerged to govern interactions among members. As Homans (1950, p. 79) observes:

The men . . . adopted a definite code of good behavior, revealed by what the men
said and, in different degrees, by what they did. Even the men who did not live up
to the code knew what it was.

Among the articles of this code was one prohibiting "rate busting"; that is, turning out too much work. Another, by contrast, discouraged "chiseling," which meant turning out too little work. "Squealing," or telling the supervisor anything that would be detrimental to a co-worker, was forbidden. Further, the workers were banned from acting superior or officious toward their co-workers, even if one did have authority over others, as was the case with the supervisors. Each member was expected to observe the norms of this code, and these norms were enforced by the group in a number of ways, since the consensus was that they worked for the benefit of all the members. If one worker violated a norm, he was criticized, ostracized, or even physically reprimanded. A person who was producing more than his daily quota, for example, would be "binged," or struck strongly on the upper arm, by another.

The men also engaged in frequent games: shooting dice, betting on horses, playfully binging one another, and generally "horsing around." They formed cliques whose members interacted among themselves more than they did with others in the bank-wiring room. Thus, the relationships among the workers involved more than interacting for the purpose of getting the job done. Their informal social organization offered the men a high degree of personal satisfaction and diversion from the tedium of their jobs. The organization also affected their work output, both individually and as a group.

The relations of the group are similar to those in the family model, in that basic antagonisms are overcome to bring about the attraction between the members of the group. However, in the work group this process occurs without the strong ambivalent feelings of the family model and constitutes essentially a rational choice in which the gains outweigh the losses. It must not be thought, however, that this model does not take emotions into account. Feeling and sentiment are important, but are considered as a kind of reward which may occur because of association with another person. Thus, depending upon the amount and intensity of feelings so produced, some group interactions will have a higher positive value than the material gains alone would justify.

The characteristics of the work-group model follow from Homans's explanation of group membership and interactions from the motivations of the individual members. Group membership is seen as a means to an end, and thus the relationship of the group to its environment, including other competing groups, becomes important. Even within the group, cooperation is based on a compromise so that all members are satisfied to a certain degree; one could almost call cooperation the lesser evil, since the possibility of conflict is squarely faced. The relationships within the group will depend on which members have needs and which members have resources. These will determine the relative power positions, which may be equal or stratified. Finally, the group so described is likely to be a special-purpose group.

Lewin and community

Another principle of organization is spatial: people who live in close neighborhoods, as well as those who may be close together for only a short time, are by the nature of their connection thrown into frequent interaction. This kind of

All sports teams, such as this girls' basketball team, are highly cohesive groups.

association, which may lead to a feeling of identity, is called *community*. Its workings can be seen in purely spatial arrangements. But it can also be extended to groups whose members are close to each other in a metaphorical sense, in feeling close or having a common life.

The model of the community is best represented by the theories of Kurt Lewin (1951). His basic system, field theory, accepts only explanations based on contemporary conditions and does not include historical explanation, in contrast, for instance, to Freud. Thus, Lewin defines "a field at a given time" which includes at one point in time all factors which are influential in a person's action. He distinguishes two kinds of factors: *spatial*, which shows the relationship of conditions in the subjective environment, his *life space*, and *dynamic*, which shows *attraction* and *rejection* for the person.

The investigation of spatial relationships leads to a kind of geometrical representation, which Lewin called *topological psychology* (1947a). The purely spatial relationship of things in the psychological environment, whether they are objects, people, or even ideas, determines much of a person's actions. Thus, closeness and distance to others, the means of entering or leaving a group, can be represented by spatial relations or, as Lewin would put it, by regions within a field. This theory of a social field subdivided into regions can best be visualized in a physical community. Houses can be built to form neighborhoods, which have a definite meaning to their inhabitants and also to those of other neighborhoods. These spatial relations, almost by themselves, force the creation of a group. We can look at groups based on different criteria in the same way: ethnic and racial groups, clubs, and training groups can be visualized as if they were spatial communities in relation to other communities. These relations can be defined by the ease with which one can move from one to another.

The other aspect of the field is dynamic. One can visualize forces which push people in different directions, *driving forces*, or hinder them from moving, *restraining forces*. These forces will then define how a person does actually move within his life space. The definition of cohesion cited at the beginning of this chapter, the resultant force of staying within the group, is based on Lewinian theory. His model makes it possible to treat membership in groups as a given without justifying it through individual or biological considerations. It is especially adapted to situations where current group membership entails changes in behavior and belief.

Thus Lewin (1947b) could study the influence of group decisions, i.e., decisions taken in a group context, where the decision is made as part of the commitment to the group. He found that decisions to eat different kinds of food, such as dark bread or less preferred cuts of meat, were more likely to be acted on if made as group decisions than if made individually as the result of a lecture. Later research has refined these results by taking into consideration the kind of group and the kind of content of the decision. Another line of research shows the importance of purely spatial arrangements in group formation, in arranging seating patterns for newly formed groups as well as living arrangements in housing projects and neighborhoods (Cartwright and Zander, 1968).

The kind of group which emerges from this model is one which has meaning for the members and which is especially effective in producing an attitude change in members. The model thus examines the conditions under which members change and begin to exhibit attitudes and beliefs common to the group or to act in a similar way. The model is especially adapted to those groups which are created for the purpose of producing attitude or personality change: therapy groups, therapeutic communities, or the small groups assembled for controlled experiments. This is not surprising, because Lewin's main interest was in investigating conditions which could produce attitude and habit changes. Two features which we have noted in the previous models, the strong emotional, cathectic relations between the members and their individual motives, are given less importance in this model; the group by itself and the fact of membership in it are considered to be of overriding importance. This model can be applied especially to industrial, community, and training situations.

The characteristics of Lewin's model derive from the factors which hold a group together at any particular moment. There is an attempt to play down conflict within the group, either by rational discussion or by subdividing the group. In this and some related models, purely personal relationships are considered to be detrimental to the group (Bion, 1961). Rosabeth Kanter (1972), for example, found in her study of nineteenth-century communitarian societies that those communes, such as the Shakers, that eliminated family life were longer-lasting than those that permitted strong family bonds; family ties took precedence over allegiance to the group and membership splintered away. In his futuristic novel *1984*, the British author George Orwell envisions a society in which the individual's bonds to the community are much stronger than his bonds to his family, a manipulation designed to prevent allegiance to any competing group.

Differences in power within the group arise mainly from different functions to be performed within the group, whereas in Freud's formulation power derives from ascribed status, i.e., the father figure, and in Homans's formulation it derives from the resources to control other people's gratification. In Lewin's ideal group, power is related only to the function a person exerts in relation to the whole group. Schematically, any member could be put into any position, which, in fact, is done in experiments and in some applications of democracy, such as in classical Athens where offices were assigned by lot.

EST: TEARING APART AND REBUILDING THE PSYCHE

Experiencing an awakening or undergoing a "conversion" in an encounter group is a personal moment highly charged with conflicting emotions. Often the exact moment of conversion is hard to pinpoint because it is an outgrowth of accumulated events. The "high" of the experience is connected with the presence of others and the ways in which they express the changes that are happening to them. But most significant, and what makes the T-group or encounter group both elusive and attractive, is that graduates agree that something has happened but are at a loss to describe what.

The recent phenomenon known as EST (Erhard Seminars Training) is an example of a T-group experience that relies on the conversion of the group to support the conversion of individuals. Once people have suffered through four 15- to 18-hour sessions where they are denied cigarettes, food, drink, and bathroom privileges, they swear they have "gotten it."

What is EST and how does it work? Graduates are cautioned not to say too much lest Erhard Werner, founder and creator of EST, lose potential customers, whom he charges $250 each. But reporters and disillusioned graduates have described his techniques.

According to Mark Brewer (1975), the EST process incorporates the fundamentals of brainwashing, embroidered with the trappings and language of Eastern meditative religions, and packaged with the slick, salesmanlike style that appeals to Western minds. The main thrust of the "training" is to tear a person down, making the trainee realize the worthlessness of his life, and then rebuild his confidence and credit the change to EST.

The training is authoritative and exhausting, says Brewer. The trainees are asked to sit in straight-backed chairs arranged in three orderly rows. They must not talk, but if one wants to "share" a personal experience, he is to raise a hand and wait for permission to speak. After the trainee divulges his innermost feelings, the trainer begins to insult him. He tells the trainee that he has made a mess of his life, he calls him all kinds of derogatory names, and repeatedly reminds him how out of touch he is with himself and his life. Whenever a trainee attempts to share an experience, he is ripped apart by the trainer. For this, the trainer is applauded by the rest of the group.

On the second day, the trainees are asked to choose one big problem they would like solved. After nearly eight hours of coaching, repetition, meditation-directed instructions, the majority are on the floor writhing, sobbing, groaning, and claiming a "conversion." By breaking and then rebuilding its participants, EST convinces people to accept themselves as they are.

The trainees have been asked to suspend judgment until the end of the course, and since all have paid $250, most are willing to take a wait-and-see attitude. Typically, after the session, many state that the trainer bored, frustrated, or enraged them, but they were told that such feelings were normal. However, they were not prepared for the breaking process and when it occurred, they did not know what was happening to them. The sobbing, fainting, and moaning are reminiscent of revival meetings and, like the sinners of yesteryear, these new converts feel they have been saved.

Simmel and sociability

The three models of the family, the work group, and the community do not exhaust the different bases on which groups are formed. A residual category of groups can be formed for a variety of reasons, none of which corresponds to either a primordial or a practical condition of human life such as we have been able to identify in the first three types. In this residual category we can include social clubs, social gatherings, and any group of people who gather together to gossip and enjoy each other's company. Perhaps the best term to identify these groups is *sociability*, referring to a prevalent tendency of people to congregate with each other.

Sociability in its purer form has, strangely enough, not been studied very much by social psychologists; description of parties has been more the field of the novelist than the scientist. Probably the theorist whose thinking comes closest to taking sociability as a model is Simmel (Simmel, 1950; Coser, 1956). His work is distinguished by its emphasis on the general forms of social life, independent of content, and its acceptance of conflict as an important feature in insuring the viability of society. Thus, from the point of view of the whole of modern society, a multiplicity of free-forming and dissolving groups is a necessity to mediate sharp conflicts of diverging interests. Conflicts define the differences of groups from each other, giving them identity and cohesion. In addition, they bring individuals and groups into closer contact, forcing them to find a *modus vivendi* and thus establish the rules and forms of social life.

The importance of this model lies in the fact that it stresses the need for group formation as an end in itself, regardless of the ostensible reason for any particular group. It plays down the emotional involvements of the group members. Neither strong feelings within the individuals nor attachments between members of the group are given much place in the model. In fact, multiple memberships, what Simmel (1955) calls "the web of group affiliations," are a virtual necessity; together, the various groups effect a measure of social stability. Members will be only partially involved in each group. Relations within each will not take on overwhelming importance. However, life within the group—at a party, for example—is an aim in itself above and beyond any other aims which may be served. Thus, conflict is acceptable within and between groups: what is important is the manner by which this conflict is managed.

Simmel's model is important in that it draws attention to the existence of social behavior even in the absence of strong attractions or feelings between the group members. Contact among people, motivated by some common interest, point of view, lifestyle, or even conflict, will generate a viable pattern of social interaction and formation of groups. To be sure, in each of the other models social contact also leads to group formation, but there is always an additional condition or motivation which is the main basis of social cohesion.

Here, however, we look at a variety of social groups that have no overriding reason to exist and find that almost any original reason that brings people together will lead to similar kinds of interaction. These regularities may be evidence of a tendency or drive of sociability or gregariousness.

In effect, this model is defined mainly in a negative way. It describes those kinds of groups which do not derive from the family, the work group, or the community. It may also represent the fact that there is a basic tendency for sociability beyond the requirements of specific conditions.

Maintenance of Cohesion

The ways individuals interact within a group greatly affect group cohesion and functioning. Two of the most fundamental ways individuals can interact, both interpersonally and in a group, are by cooperating or competing with one another. The cohesion of the group depends, in large part, upon the ways in which the two forces are balanced against one another.

Competition and cooperation

What do we mean by these two concepts? George Homans (1961, p. 131) defines *cooperation* as occurring "when, by emitting activities to one another, or by emitting activities in concert to the environment, at least two men [*sic*] achieve a greater total reward than either could have achieved by working alone." It is easy to summon up examples of cooperative behavior. When two roommates who share an apartment agree to split the housekeeping tasks between them, for example, they are cooperating. The behavior of each benefits the other as well as himself.

Competition, by contrast, occurs when each participant "emits activity that, so far as it is rewarded, tends by that fact to deny reward to the other" (Homans, 1961, p. 131). Examples of competition are especially plentiful in the world of sports, where two individuals, or two groups of individuals, strive to reach a goal that denies any reward to their competitors. The trucking game, as described in chapter 3, would tend to show that most individuals would rather compete than cooperate in social interactions, even though cooperation usually results in greater gain to the participants.

Morton Deutsch (1968) has developed a theory which describes how cooperation and competition affect the functioning of small groups (that is, those in which members engage in face-to-face interaction). According to Deutsch, there are three psychological implications of cooperation. The first of these is *substitutability*, which means that the behavior of all the members involved in a cooperative venture is interchangeable. If one member has engaged in a certain action to achieve the goal, no other member need repeat the same action. For example, when a member of a pit crew changes a tire of his team's racing car, no other pit crewman need change the same tire. Second is *positive cathexis*, which means that if the behavior of one participant in a cooperative interaction moves the group closer to its objective, the *action* of that member will be accepted, liked, or rewarded by other participants. A home run by a baseball player, for example, gets him a handshake and pats on the back from his teammates. Deutsch's third psychological implication of cooperation is *positive inducibility*—if a member of a cooperative venture acts so that the group is brought closer to its objective, the other participants will accept any of his actions and this will induce them to support him.

In a competitive situation, by contrast, the psychological implications are the exact opposite. There will be no substitutability; similarly, positive cathexis and positive inducibility will be frowned upon rather than accepted by others; and the others will try to prevent rather than support those acts which move an individual closer to his objective.

Deutsch tested his theory on his students in a simple experiment. He told half of his classes that they would be graded on a cooperative basis: the grade of each student would be the same and it would depend upon how the class fared against other classes in a discussion of the same topic, human relations. Deutsch then told the other half of his classes that they would be graded on a competitive basis: contributions of each student to the discussion of the human relations problem would be ranked "so that the person who contributes most to the solution will receive a rank of 1, the one who contributes next most will receive a rank of 2, etc. . ." (1968, p. 469).

The results of the experiment are interesting. Individuals in the group who cooperated to achieve a solution to the problem were more highly coordinated than those in the competitive group. Moreover, the cooperative groups were more receptive to one another's ideas, were friendlier to one another, and learned one another's last names more quickly than did those in the competitive situation. Among individuals in the competitive classes, by contrast, there was less communication—statements had to be repeated frequently, and there was a good deal of misunderstanding. Moreover, individuals tended to be more aggressive toward one another, and members reported more anxiety than did those in the cooperative situation. Deutsch concluded his study with these words:

It seems that educators might well reexamine the assumptions underlying their common usage of a competitive grading system. One may well question whether a competitive grading system produces the kinds of interrelationships among students, the task-directedness, and personal security that are in keeping with sound educational objectives" (1968, p. 482).

The ballet company.   In some groups, competition among individuals must, of necessity, be keen. Yet, at the same time, the competing members must cooperate with one another if the group objective is to be reached. The success of the group is determined by how well these two forces are counterbalanced. An excellent example of the dynamics of such a balancing act is seen in a ballet company studied by Sondra Forsyth and Pauline Kolenda (1966).

In any ballet company, the investigators write, there is constant competition among the dancers:

Each class, rehearsal, and performance can be viewed as competition between the dancers for praise and recognition by the teacher and other dancers, and each performance as a competition for praise and recognition by critics and audience. Classes, rehearsals, and performances as competition, function also to establish rankings within the company hierarchy. Generally, competition tends to disrupt harmonious interpersonal relations" (1966, p. 123).

*In a dance company there is always a tension between cooperation and competition.
A company must dance as a unity, yet dancers are always in competition for parts.*

COURTESY OF
ALVIN AILEY AMERICAN
DANCE THEATER.

The strain of this competition is further heightened by the demand for co-operation. And this double strain typically lasts for long periods—four or five hours every day, possibly for years. How does this combination of individual competition and group cooperation operate in such a company? According to the investigators, there are three kinds of factors that keep a ballet company functioning: ". . . those that seem important in stimulating competition, those that appear to prevent the arousal or expression of resentment and jealousy and the outbreak of conflict, and those that contribute positively to the develop-ment of group solidarity or integration" (p. 143).

Competition is prevented from disrupting the group in a number of ways. First, the good of the company and the good of the performance are constantly cited by the teacher and students alike to prevent individuals from pursuing their own goals to the exclusion of those of the group. Then, too, the teacher goes out of her way to be fair in judging who the top students are. These standards of fairness are shared by students and teacher so there is seldom a question of disagreement from the other dancers when a student is judged excellent by the teacher and appropriately rewarded. Since each student is placed in a hierarchy, ranking limits the competition for roles among dancers to roles of the same or of slightly lower or higher status. Thus, each student is not in direct competition with all other dancers for the top roles. Moreover, the informal friendships and cliques that students form among themselves also help to prevent the disruptive effects of competition. If, by some chance, an undeserving dancer receives a high rank, for example, she may be ignored in the dressing room by other dancers, and the student who actually deserved the rank will receive affection and respect.

Finally, there are the judgments of the outside world. In most cases, a ballet teacher is like a dictator—her every command is obeyed unquestioningly. Furthermore, she constantly criticizes troupe members, and rarely praises them. She censures individuals for the slightest deviation from normal be-havior. She is able to be so dictatorial because she has led the company to successful performances in the past, and the students trust her methods, how-ever tyrannical they may seem. But if the critics and audience criticize the teacher for the performance of the company, the students will lose faith in her. If the critics point out, for example, that the ranking system is unjust, she must take steps to rectify this if she is to maintain order and discipline in her troupe. Finally, the troupe members share a common fate: the reputation of the entire company as it performs before an audience reflects on the reputation of each dancer. The company will fail if it is not constantly successful.

In the performance, write the authors, "self-orientation and collectivity-orientation coincide; the individual's self-interest is furthered by the success of the company" (p. 145). Thus, in a ballet company and similar groups where there is strong commitment, severe negative sanctions against aberrant behavior can be institutionalized and accepted by the group members. Furthermore, jealousy and conflict are avoided because the norms of the system are recognized and complied with by all. Finally, when members direct themselves to cooperation and collective behavior, their attention is correspondingly distracted from their own goals.

Group communication networks

Another important factor that affects group cohesion is the opportunity for communication among members. In some groups, communication is open-ended, so to speak: a member can approach and discuss personal or group matters with any other member. In other groups, by contrast, members must communicate to other members through channels. In the military, in a large university, or in a business organization, the people whom one can discuss problems with or bring ideas to are rigidly specified. In the army, for example, a private cannot drop uninvited into a general's office for a casual chat. Instead, he must have a good reason to see the superior officer. Then, he must go first to his sergeant, who may relay the issue to the company commander, who may relay it to his superior, and so on, up the chain of command. In such cases, it is not unusual for the private's message to be sidetracked so that it never reaches the general. The general, by contrast, can summon a private to his office at any time.

In large-scale organizations like the army, there are definite, well-established communication networks through which information flows from one individual to another. These networks may have the effect of limiting communication in different ways. The classic experiment in the analysis of communication networks was conducted by Leavitt (1951). Leavitt seated five subjects around a table. Each subject was separated from his neighbor by a slot through which he could pass notes. No verbal communication was permitted. Each slot could be opened or closed by the investigator in order to control the flow of information. Therefore, individuals could communicate with one another only when the slot between them was open. The subjects could use the open slots in any way they pleased, but they were not informed about the actual configuration of the network.

Leavitt created four network configurations. According to the degree to which they are centralized, these are the circle, the chain, the Y-pattern, and the wheel. In a circular network, each subject could pass or receive information to or from two others in the group. Clearly, such an arrangement makes for a decentralized group. The chain pattern is also relatively decentralized in that three members can communicate with two other members, but two people can communicate with only one other person.

The Y-pattern is somewhat centralized: the person in the middle of the Y can talk to three other people. However, the three isolated individuals at the terminals of the Y can communicate with only one other person. Finally, the wheel network produces a strongly centralized group. Each member can communicate only with a central individual: this person, in turn, is able to send notes to the other four subjects.

What have psychologists learned about communication, group structure, and cohesion from this simple experiment? First, they discovered that the shape of the network affects the productivity of the group. For example, the centralized groups (the wheel and the Y) were most efficient in channeling information among group members. Each group member in such configurations passes his information to the leader, who then disseminates it to all other members. By contrast, the decentralized groups (the circle and the chain) waste time because messages must pass back and forth through a greater number of channels. The centralized network, then, appears to be most efficient in processing information.

However, another investigator (Shaw, 1954) found this to be true only when the task was to solve simple problems. In more complicated problems, Shaw found, the decentralized network fared much better in terms of efficiency and productivity. Apparently, complex problems require much freer communication and more interaction among group members, and so are better solved by a decentralized structure.

The shape of the communication network also affects the morale of individual group members. It was found that the more open the channels of com-

COMMUNICATION PATTERNS

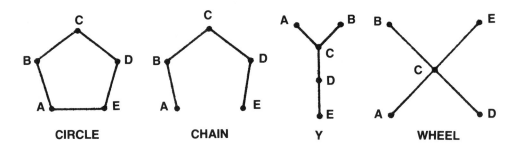

CIRCLE   CHAIN   Y   WHEEL

Figure 4–3.   A person can talk only to the people indicated by the black lines. Not only is productivity affected by communication patterns, but so, too, is the morale of group members.

SOURCE: Leavitt, H. J. Some effects of certain communication patterns on group performance. *Journal of Abnormal and Social Psychology*, 1951, **46**, 38–50.

munication, the happier were the group members. Satisfaction with group membership was higher, for example, among those who interacted in a decentralized network than among those who communicated through centralized networks. It seems that the opportunity to interact with others and to participate in group decisions brings greater satisfaction and greater cohesion. In addition, in the centralized network, those in the center (that is, those with access to the most people in the network) were happiest with that group structure, whereas those on the periphery suffered a decline in productivity because the dissatisfied members tended to work less efficiently.

The findings contain certain interesting contradictions, then. For example, the structure of the centralized group tends to increase efficiency, whereas member dissatisfaction with the arrangement tends to decrease it. Just the reverse, of course, is true for the decentralized group.

Other investigators believe that neither productivity nor morale is the important factor that needs to be studied to understand the functioning of communication networks. The crucial element, say these theorists, is organization—the relative ease or difficulty with which group members organize themselves around a task. It is quite easy, for example, for members to organize communication channels among themselves in the wheel structure because there is really only one logical, efficient arrangement possible. In the circle, on the other hand, members must take time to plot out the most efficient communication channel because there are so many options available.

One study which deals with the importance of organization to the communication network has been conducted by H. Guetzkow and H. Simon (1955). These investigators found that organization affected the performance of the network, no matter what its structure. They also established another kind of network similar to the circle—the all-channel group in which each member could communicate with all other members of the network. It was found that after a group worked out an efficient system of organization for itself, the circle and all-channel networks reached solutions to simple problems just as rapidly as highly organized wheel networks. However, the all-channel groups required considerable time—up to ten trials—before they arrived at their most efficient organization. And only a handful of the circle networks succeeded in efficiently organizing themselves in twenty trials, after which they improved slightly. Thus, over time, the differences in productivity among the different kinds of networks appear to decrease, if not disappear altogether.

Working in Groups

Good communication enables group members to work together more efficiently. Another important aspect of the study of group phenomena is the way members work together to achieve group goals. This discussion will focus on two aspects of work in groups: leadership, and how group members solve problems together.

Leadership

In most groups there is a leader, one individual who influences the behavior of the group members in important ways. The leader issues orders and directs the activity of the members, settles disputes, approves or disapproves of member behavior, attempts to maintain group esprit de corps, and represents the group in its dealings with the outside world.

The phenomenon of leadership is a complex one. It has been studied by many researchers from many points of view in an attempt to discover why some individuals become leaders and others do not. Early studies of leadership, for example, focused on the personal traits, or characteristics that leaders were supposed to possess in any situation. Known as the "great man" theory, this approach held that some individuals are born with charisma—the grace that induces others to follow them. This approach attempted to enumerate a number of *personal traits,* a catalogue of characteristics that might include everything from body build to intelligence to energy level. But researchers were unable to compile a list of the traits that were shared by all leaders and that unequivocally separated leaders from followers.

Investigators then focused on the *situation* as the important determinant of leadership. Supporters of this view held that leaders are made, not born. They arise whenever conditions are right and their appearance depends upon such variables as the nature of the group and its objectives, the personalities and abilities of individual group members, and the situation the group finds itself in at any given time. In short, the situational approach holds that anyone can become a leader if he happens to be in the right place at the right time.

This hypothesis found some support in a study conducted by Alex Bavelas, Albert Hastorf, Alan Gross, and W. Kite (1965). These investigators theorized that communication ability was the key to leadership; if an individual, even a shy one, can be persuaded to talk more than other members, he can rise to the top position in the group. The investigators divided their experiment into several parts. In the first part, they assembled college students who did not know one another. The subjects were divided into a number of four-man discussion groups. Each group was told that it was to discuss a particular human relations problem for ten minutes. The group would be observed by the experimenters through a one-way mirror, and they would measure each individual's contribution to the discussion.

In the second part of the experiment, the subjects were asked to complete questionnaires in which they were to indicate which group members possessed leadership ability, based on the previous discussion. Next, each group was again instructed to discuss another human relations problem. The subjects were told that they would receive immediate feedback on their contributions to the discussion. This was done by providing each subject with a panel containing a red and a green light. Each subject could see only his own light panel. The subjects were told that the green light would be activated by experimenters when a subject made a positive contribution toward the solution of the problem. The red light would flash when a subject's comment interfered with the discussion, preventing the group from coming to a solution. The lights, of course, served as positive or negative reinforcements to the subjects.

The investigators had selected from each group an individual who had talked least in the first discussion session, and who had received a low ranking in leadership on the questionnaires. During the discussion, this individual's green light was activated whenever he said anything. At the same time, the other members of the group were negatively reinforced—their red lights were activated—nearly every time they spoke. Thus, the quiet, low-ranking individual was encouraged to talk, whereas the other members were discouraged. Finally, the groups took part in a third discussion the same as the first, in that the members were not reinforced in any way.

The results of this study are interesting. They show that the least talkative, low-ranked individual actually did contribute more to the discussions because he was positively reinforced to do so. By contrast, the other members who had been negatively reinforced talked less. And the positively reinforced subject continued to do more talking in the third session, even though he was receiving no reinforcement. More surprising was the fact that group members changed their negative opinions about the target subject's leadership ability by giving him a very high leadership ranking at the end of the third discussion session.

Another indication of the relationship of verbal output to leadership is seen in an experiment conducted by Fred Strodtbeck, Rita Simon, and Charles Hawkins (1958). These investigators found that individuals of high status tended to contribute more to discussions than did those of low status. In this study, the three investigators arranged mock trials and selected juries from official jury pools. They found that individuals of high social status—professionals, managers, and the like—talked more and contributed more to the jury deliberations. Moreover, they were perceived by low-status individuals—workers, servants, clerks, and such—as being leaders. High-status individuals, for example, were selected as jury foremen more often than were those of low status.

The analysis of the communication aspect of leadership reveals yet another significant fact: a group can have two different leaders who exhibit different *types* of leadership behavior. That is, each plays a different kind of leadership role. According to Robert Bales (1970), the first type of leader tends to be considerate to group members. He is friendly, supportive, and encouraging. He frequently alleviates group tension with humorous remarks or jokes. He asks group members for their suggestions about how to proceed with the task at hand. In short, he is concerned with maintaining the morale of the group. Bales calls this type the *socioemotional* leader.

The other type of leader is more authoritarian and is interested only in getting a particular job done. He gives orders rather than asking for suggestions or opinions. This type of individual is known as the *task* leader. As Hollander (1958) points out, the task leader has a great deal of idiosyncracy credit—he is allowed, even expected, to deviate and to offer unusual approaches to problems.

Ronald Lippitt and Ralph White (1965) have looked at the phenomenon of leadership in terms of the *style* of leadership rather than the roles of leaders. In a classic experiment, these investigators attempted to contrast the effects of autocratic versus democratic styles of leadership on a group. The researchers assigned adult leaders to groups of ten-year-old boys who engaged in various hobbies. Each adult was instructed to behave in an authoritarian, democratic, or laissez faire fashion toward his group. The autocratic leader was highly authoritarian; he led the group with an iron fist, dictating policy and activities without asking the boys for their opinions or suggestions. Moreover, he did not personally participate in any of the activities. The style of the democratic leader was just the opposite: he encouraged discussion of policy and activities. He allowed the youngsters to choose their tasks as well as their workmates. Under the laissez faire leader, the group was completely unstructured. The boys were simply given their work materials and left on their own. In effect, the group was leaderless.

Lippitt and White found that the laissez faire groups fared worst in terms of productivity: both the quantity and the quality of their work were low. The autocratic groups produced the most work, but members seemed to be less motivated and more aggressive toward one another. Indeed, when the leader temporarily left the room, most boys stopped working. The spirit of the democratic group, by contrast, appeared to be quite high. Members tended to be more content with group membership and their role in it. They volunteered for work and continued working in the leader's absence. Finally, the quality of their work, in some cases, was superior to that of the other groups.

The Fiedler theory. Other important research that contrasts the styles of leadership has been conducted by Fred Fiedler (1964, 1967). Fiedler's research on leadership is quite extensive. It involves some thirty-five studies spanning twenty years and covering roughly 1,500 groups of all kinds. Fiedler's model attempts to determine how the leader's personality is related to the situation in which he finds himself. In some respects, then, the Fiedler theory represents a blending of the trait model with the situational model.

Fiedler calls his theory "the contingency model of leadership effectiveness." The theory starts with the hypothesis that there are two types of leaders: those concerned primarily with the people they are leading, and those concerned primarily with getting a specific job done. The former might be called people-oriented leaders, the latter, task-oriented leaders. Fiedler determined whether a leader was task-oriented or people-oriented by administering a personality test. On the test, leaders were asked to grade the most incompetent person they ever worked with in such qualities as friendliness, helpfulness, pleasantness, and so on. For obvious reasons, the test is known as the Least Preferred Co-worker (LPC) test. Fiedler found that some leaders were quite unsparing in their denigration of their least preferred co-worker, whereas others were a little more charitable. Fiedler hypothesized that an individual who had nothing good to say about an incompetent worker would not be concerned about the way his subordinates related to him. He would be interested only in completing the task at hand. "I'm not running a popularity contest," he might remark. Such a

This small centralized group is efficient in solving problems. Each group member passes his part of the solution to the leader, who then disseminates the information to other group members.

person, then, would tend to be authoritarian, even dictatorial; he would generate tension in the group by his uncompromising demands upon members. By contrast, the leader who sees the poorer co-worker in a favorable light tends to be more relaxed, friendlier, and more considerate toward his followers. Members seem to be less tense and more satisfied under this type of leader. Clearly, the former type of leader corresponds to Lippitt and White's authoritarian leader, whereas the latter is similar to their democratic leader.

Having determined leader personality, Fiedler's next step was to determine the circumstances under which each type would be most effective. In other words, in what kinds of situations are people-oriented leaders better than task-oriented individuals? Fiedler hypothesized that the answer to this question depended upon the degree to which the situation was favorable to the leader. Whether or not a situation favored a given leader depended upon three factors: (1) the leader's personal relations with the group (rated from good to bad); (2) the situation of the task which the group must engage in (from structured to unstructured); and (3) the leader's power (from high to low) over the group.

Thus, the most favorable situation for the leader is one in which his personal relations with the group are good, the task is highly structured (that is, it is quite clear to all), and the leader's power over the group is at its peak. Conversely, the most unfavorable situation for a leader is one in which his personal relations are bad, the task is unstructured, and his hold over the group is at a low point.

Fiedler believed that the task-oriented leader would perform best in a situation that favored leadership. Under conditions in which the task is structured, the leader wields full power and is supported by his subordinates. Group members obey the leader because his instructions facilitate accomplishing the job at hand. However, the task-oriented leader also outperforms his group-oriented counterpart under unfavorable circumstances. Apparently, in such a situation, conditions are so demoralizing to the group that the members perceive it most advantageous to follow the leader in getting the job over and done with.

Fiedler suggests that the people-oriented leader would be more effective in a situation that was only moderately favorable to him. For example, if he is in a position of power, the task is highly structured, but his personal relations with the group are not so good; the leader tries to improve group feelings toward him rather than concentrate on the task. By contrast, the task-oriented leader in a similar situation would concentrate only on the task, ignoring the ill feelings of his subordinates. The resulting poor group morale would adversely affect the accomplishment of the task.

Thus, the phenomenon of leadership is a complex one that involves the interaction of several factors. Some investigators (Blake and Mouton, 1964) disagree with Fiedler's model, stating that a good leader is concerned both with the feeling of his group members and the task at hand—not with one or the other. However, most investigators agree that, in spite of its limitations, Fiedler's model has shed considerable light on the subject of leadership.

Problem-solving in groups

Our society is heavily influenced by small groups. Every day, committees in government, business, education, and other fields make collective decisions that affect our welfare. Such groups would seem to be more productive than a lone individual working on the same problem. Group members working together can pool their resources and experience; offer alternative suggestions as to possibilities; and arrive at a consensus. It is quite impossible, for example, for a lone man to build, launch, and guide a spaceship to a landing on the moon, but a coordinated team of scientists, engineers, and technicians has carried out such a task successfully. But is the group actually more efficient in arriving at solutions to problems than an individual working alone? Can a ten-man team work more effectively at a particular problem than the same ten people working by themselves? This question has been extensively probed in recent years, and some of the results are quite interesting.

A classic experiment designed to test this proposition was conducted by D. W. Taylor, P. C. Berry, and C. H. Block (1958). These investigators set five-person groups to work on five problems, then assigned five individuals, working alone, to the same five problems. There was a time limit of twelve minutes per problem for both sets of subjects. In a sample problem, for example, the subjects were asked to offer ideas on how to convince European tourists to visit America, or to offer an overweight person advice on dieting. The subjects were instructed to suggest as many ideas as possible and to give their imaginations free play.

The results were tabulated in terms of the number and uniqueness of ideas presented by each set of subjects. Surprisingly, the people working on their own scored higher in both categories than did the individuals who pooled their resources. Indeed, the solitary individuals generated nearly twice as many ideas, in both categories, as did the groups; they produced an average of more than 68 different ideas, compared to 37.5 for the five-man groups. Similarly, the individuals working alone came up with an average of nearly 20 unique, or creative, ideas, whereas the people working in groups produced slightly fewer than 11 such ideas.

But how valid are these findings? Do solitary individuals actually offer more and better-quality solutions than groups attacking the same problem? If so, why are group efforts so prevalent in our society? As one might suspect, the study of Taylor and his colleagues has certain limitations. For one thing, the time during which the groups worked together was not considered. A group that has had time to assess its members' capabilities and to organize itself often does better than one that has not. For example, a study by D. Cohen, J. W. Whitmeyer, and W. H. Funk (1960) indicates that group productivity was increased when the members had worked with one another in the past and had developed some kind of organization.

This finding is related to another important variable omitted from the Taylor study: the personalities of the group members. Although the findings are not consistent in this area, some studies have shown that homogeneous groups (that is, groups whose members have the same or similar personalities) sometimes are more productive than heterogeneous groups. Thus, if all or most members of a group prefer to operate under democratic conditions, such a group may be more efficient than one in which some of the members prefer democratic procedures and some authoritarian rules. Since this variable was not controlled in Taylor's study, we do not know what effect it had on the outcome.

On the other hand, heterogeneity frequently increases group productivity because it offers more alternatives, less uniform prejudices, and more critical views. In a study by L. Hoffman and Norman Maier (1961), for example, it was found that heterogeneous groups often functioned more efficiently than their homogeneous counterparts on the same problem. After group heterogeneity and homogeneity had been determined on the basis of personality tests, the two kinds of groups were tested with a number of varied problems. In one problem, for example, the groups were to find the best way for a five-man team to cross a mined road. Hoffman and Maier found that the heterogeneous groups came up with higher-quality solutions than did the homogeneous groups. One reason for this, say the investigators, might be that the members of the heterogeneous groups are less apt to operate from the same assumptions and prejudices than are groups who have more or less the same outlook on certain matters. Interestingly enough, Hoffman and Maier also found that groups that were heterogeneous with respect to sex—that is, groups having male and female members—also did better than groups composed of all males.

Finally, the nature of the problems makes a difference when groups are being compared with individuals working alone. Thus, a problem that has only one solution will affect group performance, as will a problem to which there is no single correct answer. An algebra problem, for example, will be handled differently by a group than will a search for suggestions about how to merchandise and advertise a new automobile model. In a one-solution problem, the group may depend upon its most proficient member for the answer. If the resources of the most competent member outweigh those of solitary individuals working on the same problem, then the group may arrive at a solution faster and more

WHAT HOLDS COMMUNES TOGETHER?

Most nineteenth-century communes had utopian goals. They sought to build the best of all possible worlds, and formulated systems of beliefs and practices which induced individual members to foster group unity. Outstanding examples of this type of community include the Shaker communes and the Oneida commune, founded by John Noyes in New York State. As one would expect, some communes of the last century were more successful than others. Dozens of experiments, such as the famous Brook Farm, sprang up, enjoyed several years' popularity, then faded away. But the celibate Shakers, who believed in strict separation of the sexes, and the more life-loving Oneidans, who believed in "complex" marriages or "free sex," were two stable communities.

Why did these two communities, one celibate and the other sexually free, outlast all the rest? Sociologist Rosabeth Moss Kanter (1972) has explored the workings of a number of communes. She suggests three links that connect the individual to a social system: retention of members, group cohesiveness, and social control. The most successful communities devised different techniques to fulfill these requirements.

Communes attempt to influence the individual to become totally committed to the group. Instead of feeling that he or she owes personal loyalty to one group member, the individual is encouraged to feel a sense of belonging to the group as a whole. For example, one modern-day California commune of fifty members calls itself the "Lynch family," after its founder, David Lynch.

The Shakers and the Oneidans also encouraged members to feel that their new-found brotherhood was a replacement for their biological families. Members called each other "brother" or "sister." Both groups further distinguished between themselves and the outside world by following a shared set of beliefs and adhering to a special dress code. Some areas of Shaker communities were off-limits to visitors, and although the Oneida community welcomed visitors, they performed special cleaning "bees" to purify their buildings after the departure of guests. Such regulations increased the loyalty of members and encouraged group cohesiveness. But all these efforts would have been futile without definite methods of social control.

Kanter shows that successful communities have well-developed social practices governing the interaction of individuals which result in a high level of commitment. Thus, says Kanter, members retain commitment when they feel they are sacrificing something. The Shakers relinquished sex but replaced it with a feeling of comradeship. The Oneidans allowed sexual liaisons but frowned on monogamous couples.

Kanter found that communities fare best when there is no intermediate group between individuals and the larger community. If couples are permitted to form lasting attachments, they drain energy away from the community and toward individuals. Similarly, if members are allowed to communicate with their biological families, their allegiance to their new family is weakened. But both the Shakers and the Oneidans were successful because through different means—celibacy and mixed marriage—they separated individuals and welded members into a functioning whole.

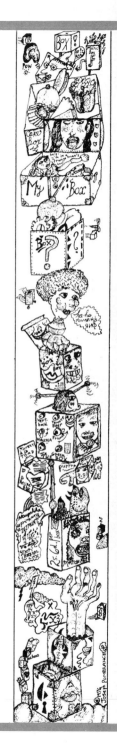

efficiently. The reverse, of course, is also true. If a solitary individual has more talents than all the members of the group, he may reach a solution faster.

Thibaut and Kelley (1969) hold that the group will arrive at a solution that is as acceptable as that of its most proficient member under two conditions. First, very few steps must be required for the solution. "The most competent member can solve the problem about as readily in the group setting as when he is alone. Its complexity is not such as to make his efforts highly vulnerable to distraction and interferences presented by the social situation" (Thibaut and Kelley, 1969, p. 65). Second, the most proficient member must, upon reaching the solution, be able to convince the other members of its correctness.

More complex problems—those whose solutions depend upon a number of steps—are better solved by groups than by individuals working on their own. In such groups, each member attacks a part of the problem, then confers with his or her colleagues to try to eliminate mistakes. An individual working alone on the same problem does not have this capability; he must perform all of the steps himself. Under these circumstances, the chances that errors may creep in are quite high.

Similarly, problems whose solutions require input from several separate disciplines are most effectively solved by groups. Librarians working on a problem involving solid geometry, quantum physics, and the geology of desert areas will not do nearly so well as a group of mathematicians working on the same problem. By the same token, the group of mathematicians will be far less efficient than a group which includes a mathematician, a physicist, and a geologist.

Thus, although there is evidence to the contrary, one cannot make the generalization that individual performance is more efficient than group performance in solving problems. Many factors must be considered—the nature of the task, the group makeup, the talents of the individuals, the time element, and more—before any judgment can be reached.

The risky shift.   An interesting aspect of decision-making in groups is the risk involved. Do groups, in general, tend to be more conservative in their decisions than individuals? It would seem, impressionistically, that groups would take fewer risks because group decisions by their nature seem to be compromises that leave little room for boldness or daring. A number of experiments, however, suggest that this is not so. Groups have a tendency to be willing to take greater risks than individuals in decision-making. In a study by Nathan Kogan and Michael Wallach (1967), for example, people, both as individuals and in groups, were presented with a number of situations about which they were asked to make decisions. The choices for the various situations involved elements of risk that ranged from high to low. Accordingly, the test is known as the Choice Dilemmas Questionnaire (CDQ). Figure 4–4 shows a typical situation from a CDQ devised by Kogan and Wallach (1967).

In the first part, after being presented with a number of situations similar to the one above, each subject was told to answer each problem on his own. The subjects were then convened in groups and told to come to a unanimous decision concerning the same situations. The results showed that the group decisions tended to be less conservative than the average of those made by individuals working privately. Appropriately enough, this phenomenon is known as the *risky shift.* Similar results have been obtained in other research (Dion et al., 1970; Zajonc et al., 1972). The subjects in these and other studies were varied: they included both sexes, many nationalities, and were from all walks of life. From such studies, investigators have concluded that decisions made by groups tend to be bolder than those made by individuals.

A typical situation from the Choice Dilemmas Questionnaire (CDQ)

Mr. A, an electrical engineer, who is married and has one child, has been working for a large electronics corporation since graduating from college 5 years ago. He is assured of a lifetime job with a modest, though adequate, salary, and liberal pension benefits upon retirement. On the other hand, it is very unlikely that his salary will increase much before he retires. While attending a convention, Mr. A is offered a job with a small, newly founded company which has a highly uncertain future. The new job would pay more to start and would offer the possibility of a share in the ownership if the company survived the competition of the larger firms.

Imagine that you are advising Mr. A. Listed below are several probabilities or odds of the new company's proving financially sound.

PLEASE CHECK THE *LOWEST* PROBABILITY THAT YOU WOULD CONSIDER ACCEPTABLE TO MAKE IT WORTHWHILE FOR MR. A TO TAKE THE NEW JOB.

—The chances are 1 in 10 that the company will prove financially sound.

—The chances are 3 in 10 that the company will prove financially sound.

—The chances are 5 in 10 that the company will prove financially sound.

—The chances are 7 in 10 that the company will prove financially sound.

—The chances are 9 in 10 that the company will prove financially sound.

—Place a check here if you think Mr. A should *not* take the new job no matter what the probabilities.

Figure 4–4. Which choice would you make?

SOURCE: Adapted from Kogan, N., and Wallach, M. A. Risk taking as a function of the situation, the person, and the group. In G. Mandler (Ed.), *New directions in psychology.* Vol. 3. Page 133. New York: Holt, Rinehart and Winston, 1967.

Why should this be so? A number of theories have been advanced to account for this phenomenon. Among the most important of these are those that emphasize the diffusion of responsibility and cultural values. Wallach, Kogan, and Bem (1964), for example, have suggested that groups tend to make riskier choices than individuals because the responsibility for the decision is spread out among the members. No single member, in other words, is obliged to assume the blame for a wrong decision; the group as a whole, then, can afford to be more innovative.

If this hypothesis is correct, then the risky shift must occur during group discussions. The best way to test it would be to determine if an individual would make a daring decision without taking part in group discussion. This is exactly what was done by H. Lamm (1967), and by A. Teger and D. Pruitt (1967). In Lamm's study, a number of subjects completed Choice Dilemmas Questionnaires. The same subjects then listened and watched through a one-way mirror as a group discussed the same situations presented in the questionnaire. As the subjects observed the discussion, they were instructed to make decisions on the situations being discussed. The results showed that after listening to a discussion, subjects generally made bolder decisions than they did on the questionnaires, even though they did not participate in the group. This study would tend to show that the diffusion-of-responsibility hypothesis does not explain the phenomenon of the risky shift.

Another hypothesis that offers an explanation of the risky shift has been proposed by Roger Brown (1965). This theory states that both risk-taking and caution in decision-making have cultural values. In other words, in some cultures, people admire risk-taking, whereas in others, caution in decision-making is the norm. In Western society, for example, films, plays, folktales, and other media frequently present the hero as a swashbuckling, devil-may-care individual whose daring behavior saves the day and gets him the heroine, great wealth, or some other culturally valued reward. Moreover, because of this romantic image, many Western individuals tend to think of themselves as bolder than others. However, during group discussions, such individuals discover that they are actually more conservative than others. To rectify this unflattering situation, then, they tend to make daring decisions in discussions.

Clark, Crockett, and Archer (1971) have tested this hypothesis by asking subjects to complete a CDQ. It was learned that individuals who had been shown to admire risky behavior became more daring during discussions than those who had indicated a low opinion of such behavior. Clark and his colleagues also showed that only those individuals who had indicated that they thought themselves more daring than fellow subjects actually suggested the boldest alternatives during group discussions.

Finally, the cultural value explanation is supported by research reported by Dean Pruitt (1971). According to this study, Ugandan subjects were asked to complete CDQ's. These non-Western subjects showed a great deal of caution in individual decision-making and remained cautious during group discussions. Furthermore, they did not think that their behavior was more bold or daring than that of fellow countrymen. It appears, then, that Ugandans do not value risky behavior as highly as they value caution.

Thus, according to the cultural value hypothesis, individuals who value risk will tend to be more daring in group discussions than will those who value caution. Recently, the entire risky shift phenomenon has come under fire. Some psychologists, for example, doubt that it has any validity outside of the laboratory. Thus, Cartwright (1973, p. 231) writes, "We still do not know how the risk-taking behavior of 'real life' groups compares with that of individuals." Although there are limitations to the concept of risk as a cultural value, and although some investigators disagree with all or parts of it, it seems to offer the best current explanation of the risky shift phenomenon.

Summary

The group is the bedrock of social life. There are many types of groups, but they all share one common ingredient—cohesion. Cohesion is the resultant force that keeps members within a group. The existence and strength of group cohesion can be determined in several ways. Among the most important of these is sociometry, which involves asking group members how close they are to other group members and to individuals outside the group.

Theorists are also interested in the origins of group cohesion—how it develops and what its consequences are. One important factor in the genesis of cohesion is the existence of outside threat, whereas an important consequence of cohesion is deindividuation.

Social psychologists have developed a number of models of group cohesion. Four of the most important of these models are the family, the work group, the community, and the interest group. The theorist most strongly identified with the family model is Freud. Among family members, strong cohesion factors include strong emotional ties, a hierarchical structure, and independence from external influence. Freud's model also forms the basis for Berne's theory of transactional analysis.

The second approach to the group is the work group, as analyzed by Homans, in which members seek to attain a specific objective. According to Homans, groups should be analyzed from the point of view of the individual member. Group stability results when each member acts in a way that nets him great benefit, and benefits the rest of the group as well.

Another theory of group cohesion sees groups as organized in space. Individuals who live close together in neighborhoods interact frequently, a phenomenon which can lead to a feeling of group identity, or community. The most outspoken proponent of this view is Lewin, who calls his approach to the group field theory. In Lewin's field there are two kinds of factors: spatial, which show the relationships of conditions in the group's environment, and dynamic, which show attraction and rejection for the individual in the field.

The fourth model of group cohesion is Simmel's theory of sociability. Sociability refers to the tendency of individuals to congregate with each other. Under this heading can be included clubs, council meetings, social gatherings, and so on.

Two ways in which cohesion is maintained within the group are cooperation and competition among group members. A third factor is the network for communication among members. In many groups, members can communicate with others only through specific channels, the nature of which can affect the morale and production of group members.

Another key aspect in the study of group phenomena is the way members work together to obtain objectives. Perhaps the two most important aspects of the process of working in the group are leadership and how members solve problems together. Leaders are thought to arise as a result of a combination of personality attributes and the nature of the situation in which the group finds itself. Investigators also have discovered that groups tend to take more risks in their decisions than do individuals working alone on the same problems.

Bibliography

BACK, K. W. Influence through social communication. *Journal of Abnormal and Social Psychology*, 1951, **46,** 9–23.

BALES, R. F. *Personality and interpersonal behavior.* New York: Holt, Rinehart and Winston, 1970.

BAVELAS, A., HASTORF, A., GROSS, A., AND KITE, W. Experiments on the alteration of group structure. *Journal of Experimental Social Psychology,* 1965, **1,** 55–70.

BERELSON, B., LAZARSFELD, P. F., AND McPHEE, W. *Voting: A study of opinion formation in a presidential campaign.* Chicago: University of Chicago Press, 1954.

BERNE, E. C. *Transactional analysis in psychotherapy.* New York: Grove Press, 1961.

BERNE, E. C. *Games people play.* New York: Grove Press, 1964.

BION, W. R. *Experiences in groups.* New York: Basic Books, 1961.

BLAKE, R., AND MOUTON, J. *The managerial grid: Key orientations for achieving production through people.* Houston: Gulf Publishing, 1964.

BREWER, M. We're gonna tear you down and put you back together. *Psychology Today,* August 1975, **8,** 39.

BROWN, R. *Social psychology.* New York: Free Press, 1965.

CARTWRIGHT, D. C. Determinants of scientific progress: The case of research on the risky shift. *American Psychologist,* 1973, **28,** 227–231.

CARTWRIGHT, D., AND ZANDER, A. (Eds.) *Group dynamics.* (3rd ed.) New York: Harper and Row, 1968.

CLARK, R. D., CROCKETT, W. H., AND ARCHER, F. L. Risk-as-value hypothesis: The relationship between perception of self, others, and the risky shift. *Journal of Personality and Social Psychology,* 1971, **20,** 425–429.

COHEN, D., WHITMEYER, J. W., AND FUNK, W. H. Effects of group cohesiveness and training upon creative thinking. *Journal of Applied Psychology,* 1960, **44,** 319–322.

COSER. L. *The functions of social conflict.* New York: Free Press, 1956.

DEUTSCH, M. The effects of cooperation and competition upon group process. In D. Cartwright and A. Zander (Eds.), *Group dynamics.* (3rd ed.) New York: Harper and Row, 1968.

DION, K. L., BARON, R. S., AND MILLER, N. Why do groups make riskier decisions than individuals? In L. Berkowitz (Ed.), *Advances in experimental social psychology.* Vol. 5. New York: Academic Press, 1970.

FESTINGER, L. Informal social communication. *Psychological Review,* 1950, **57,** 271–282.

FESTINGER, L., PEPITONE, A., AND NEWCOMB, T. M. Some consequences of de-individuation in a group. *Journal of Abnormal and Social Psychology,* 1952, **47,** 382–389.

FIEDLER, F. A contingency model of leadership effectiveness. In L. Berkowitz (Ed.), *Advances in experimental social psychology.* New York: Academic Press, 1964.

FIEDLER, F. *A theory of leadership effectiveness.* New York: McGraw-Hill, 1967.

FORSYTH, S., AND KOLENDA, P. Competition, cooperation, and group cohesion in the ballet company. *Psychiatry,* 1966, **29,** 123–145.

FREUD, S. *Totem and taboo.* London: Kegan Paul, 1922.

FREUD, S. *Group psychology and analysis of the ego.* London: Hogarth, 1949.

GUETZKOW, H., AND SIMON, H. The impact of certain communication nets upon organization and performance in task-oriented groups. *Management Science,* 1955, **1,** 233–250.

HOFFMAN, L., AND MAIER, N. Quality and acceptance of problem solutions by members of homogeneous and heterogeneous groups. *Journal of Abnormal and Social Psychology.* 1961, **62,** 401–407.

HOLLANDER, E. P. Conformity, status, and idiosyncracy credit. *Psychological Review*, 1958, **65**, 117–127.

HOLMES, R. The university seminar and the primal horde: A study of formal behavior. *British Journal of Sociology*, 1967, **18**, 135–150.

HOMANS, G. C. *The human group*. New York: Harcourt Brace Jovanovich, 1950.

HOMANS, G. C. *Social behavior: Its elementary forms*. New York: Harcourt Brace Jovanovich, 1961.

KANTER, R. M. *Commitment and community*. Cambridge, Mass.: Harvard University Press, 1972.

KELLEY, H. H., THIBAUT, J. W., RADLOFF, R., AND MUNDY, D. The development of cooperation in the "minimum social situation." *Psychological Monographs*, 1962, **76**(19), 1–19.

KOGAN, N., AND WALLACH, M. A. Risk-taking as a function of the situation, the person, and the group. In G. Mandler (Ed.), *New directions in psychology*. Vol. 3. New York: Holt, Rinehart and Winston, 1967.

LAMM, H. Will an observer advise higher risk-taking after hearing a discussion of the decision problem? *Journal of Personality and Social Psychology*, 1967, **6**, 467–471.

LANG, A. *The secret of the totem*. London: Longmans, Green, 1905.

LEAVITT, H. J. Some effects of certain communication patterns on group performance. *Journal of Abnormal and Social Psychology*, 1951, **46**, 38–50.

LEWIN, K. Frontiers in group dynamics. Concept, method and reality in social science: Social equilibria and social change. *Human Relations*, 1947, **1**, 5–41. (a)

LEWIN, K. Group decision and social change. In T. M. Newcomb and E. L. Hartley (Eds.), *Readings in social psychology*. New York: Holt, Rinehart and Winston, 1947. (b)

LEWIN, K. *Field theory in social science: Selected theoretical papers*. New York: Harper and Row, 1951.

LINDZEY, G., AND BYRNE, D. Measurement of social choice and interpersonal attractiveness. In G. Lindzey and E. Aronson (Eds.), *Handbook of social psychology*. (2nd ed.) Vol. 2. Reading, Mass.: Addison-Wesley, 1968.

LIPPITT, R., AND WHITE, R. An experimental study of group life. In H. Proshansky and B. Seidenberg (Eds.), *Basic studies in social psychology*. New York: Holt, Rinehart and Winston, 1965.

MORENO, J. *Who shall survive?* Washington, D.C.: Nervous and Mental Disease Publishing, 1934.

MYERS, A. Team competition, success, and adjustment of group members. *Journal of Abnormal and Social Psychology*, 1962, **65**, 25–32.

PRUITT, D. Choice shifts in group decision: An introductory review. *Journal of Personality and Social psychology*, 1971, **3**, 339–360.

ROETHLISBERGER, F., AND DICKSON, W. *Management and the worker*. Cambridge, Mass.: Harvard University Press, 1946.

ROSTEN, L. *The joys of Yiddish*. New York: McGraw-Hill, 1968.

SCHACHTER, S. *The psychology of affiliation.* Stanford, Calif.: Stanford University Press, 1959.

SHAW, M. E. Some effects of problem complexity upon problem-solution efficiency in different communication networks. *Journal of Experimental Psychology,* 1954, **48**, 211–217.

SIMMEL, G. *The sociology of Georg Simmel.* (K. H. Wolff, ed.) New York: Free Press, 1950.

SIMMEL, G. *Conflict and the web of group affiliations.* New York: Free Press, 1955.

SLATER, P. *Microcosm.* New York: John Wiley and Sons, 1966.

STRODTBECK, F., SIMON, R., AND HAWKINS, C. Social status in jury deliberations. In E. Maccoby et al. (Eds.), *Readings in social psychology.* New York: Holt, Rinehart and Winston, 1958.

TAYLOR, D. W., BERRY, P. C., AND BLOCK, C. H. Does group participation when using brainstorming facilitate or inhibit creative thinking? *Administrative Science Quarterly,* 1958, **2**, 23–47.

TEGER, A. I., AND PRUITT, D. G. Components of group risk-taking. *Journal of Experimental Social Psychology,* 1967, **3**, 189–205.

THIBAUT, J. W. An experimental study of the cohesiveness of underprivileged groups. *Human Relations,* 1950, **3**, 251–278.

THIBAUT, J. W., AND KELLEY, H. H. Group problem-solving. In G. Lindzey and E. Aronson (Eds.), *The handbook of social psychology.* (2nd ed.) Vol. 4. *Group psychology and phenomena of interaction.* Reading, Mass.: Addison-Wesley, 1969.

WALLACH, M. A., KOGAN, N., AND BEM, D. J. Diffusion of responsibility and level of risk-taking in groups. *Journal of Abnormal and Social Psychology,* 1964, **68**, 263–274.

ZAJONC, R. B., WOLOSIN, R. J., AND WOLOSIN, M. A. Group risk-taking under various group decision schemes. *Journal of Experimental Social Psychology,* 1972, **8**, 16–30.

5

Influence

The acts, beliefs, and feelings of others have a tremendous impact on our lives. As children, we consciously copy the behavior of the adults in our world. When we reach our teens, most of us go through a ritual of revolt, rejecting the values of the older generation. At the same time, however, the influence of our elders is replaced by the even stronger influence of our peers, so much so that the adolescent years have sometimes been referred to as the "years of conformity" rather than the "years of revolt." As adults striving to be independent, we are constantly influenced by the actions of others, even those who are total strangers to us.

This chapter will explore some of the nuances of social influence. It will examine the effects that the presence of others has on a person performing a task such as playing the guitar or learning a language. It will look at the ways in which a group can exert pressure on an individual to abandon the social constraints that normally control his behavior and to engage in acts he would never think of doing alone. The chapter will also discuss the phenomenon of collective behavior—how an unorganized collectivity of people can influence an individual's behavior. Finally, it will analyze the interesting and important

159

topic of conformity, in which the individual is pressured by the group to conform to its norms, even though to do so causes him to reject his own judgment.

160 Social Facilitation

If you have ever spoken or performed before an audience, you know how unnerving the experience can be. The presence of only two or three other friends can produce anxiety in a speaker or performer. Before performing, you may begin perspiring excessively. A lump may develop in the back of your throat. You may lose your appetite and have difficulty concentrating. Even professional public figures—entertainers, for example, who earn a living performing before audiences—admit to being tense and nervous both before and during a performance. However, for some individuals, such as professional athletes, an audience has been known to have the opposite effect: it may prove exhilarating and improve performance. The presence of an audience, then, often affects the way a given task is accomplished.

The presence of others

In the first quarter of this century, F. H. Allport (1920, 1924) found that individual performance of certain tasks was better in the presence of others who were performing the same task than when the tasks were carried out alone. Allport called this phenomenon *social facilitation*. In Allport's studies, the task performed by the subjects ranged from simple to complex. They included, for example, canceling vowels from words in newspapers, compiling word-association lists, and doing simple multiplication problems, as well as refuting involved philosophical arguments. In all the tasks except the last one, the presence of others affected performance positively. The work of other investigators (for example, Chen, 1937) showed that this phenomenon was not unique to humans. It was also true for ants, chickens, rats, green finches, and other animals. In both humans and lower animals, then, these researchers found evidence suggesting that the presence of others—either as mere spectators or as participants in the same chores—has the effect of improving the performance of a simple task.

But these findings were contradicted by the work of other researchers who found that an audience interfered with an individual's performance. Thus, Pessin (1933) showed that college students who were asked to learn nonsense syllables required more time to learn the syllables in front of an audience than when alone. Similarly, Husband (1931) found that an audience interferes with the learning of a finger maze. In contrast to the effect of social facilitation, then, this inhibiting effect may be called *social interference*.

These contradictory findings discouraged investigators from continuing research in this area until the mid-1960s, when Robert Zajonc proposed a theory that attempted to reconcile the contradictions. Zajonc based his hypothesis on the findings of psychologists who study the phenomenon of drive, or motivation, in humans and other animals. According to drive theorists, an increase in motivation induces an individual performing a simple task to give the most dominant, or well-learned, responses in her behavioral repertoire. But a person performing a complex task or learning a new one will not have an appropriate response available. Such responses must be mastered and added to her storehouse of habitual behavior.

Zajonc took this information and proposed that the physical presence of another individual increases motivation. Thus, says Zajonc, a person performing a task in the presence of others will be aroused; this arousal will facilitate the performance of simple tasks, and will hamper the performance of difficult or unfamiliar tasks.

Let us consider learning tasks as an example. When a person is new to a task, she has not yet learned to choose, from the myriad of possibilities, the one correct response. In such a situation, an audience will arouse her so that she gives incorrect responses most of the time. Thus, if a person is learning Greek, the guitar, or any other task of similar difficulty, her first responses are most likely to be incorrect. However, after a person has learned a skill—has become proficient in playing the guitar so that playing it properly has become a habit, for example—the correct responses become the dominant ones, and the presence of other people stimulates the emission of these strong responses. Zajonc summarizes his argument as follows:

[An] audience enhances the emission of dominant responses. If the dominant responses are the correct ones, as is the case upon achieving mastery, the presence of an audience will be of benefit to the individual. But if they are mostly wrong, as is the case in the early stages of learning, then these wrong responses will be enhanced in the presence of the audience, and the emission of correct responses will be postponed or prevented (p. 270).

In concluding his study, Zajonc says that social-facilitation effects also have a potential benefit for students:

If one were to draw one practical suggestion from . . . social-facilitation effects . . . he would advise the student to study all alone, preferably in an isolated cubicle, and to arrange to take his examinations in the company of many other students, on stage, and in the presence of a large audience. The results of his examination would be beyond his wildest expectations, provided, of course, he had learned his material quite thoroughly (p. 274).

Testing Zajonc's hypothesis. Several studies have attempted to test the social facilitation hypothesis. In a study by Ranier Martens (1969), for example, it
was found that the presence of an audience increases the perspiration produced
on the palms of a subject's hands. Martens's experiment is based on the observation that the amount of perspiration found on the palms of a person's hands
is a reliable physiological and objective measure of arousal, or anxiety. Accordingly, his experiment called for forty-eight subjects to perform a complex
motor task; half of the subjects learned the task alone, and half learned it in the
presence of a nonparticipating audience. The investigator took sweat prints of
the subjects' palms before and during their performance. The results showed
that the subjects performing before an audience had greater amounts of perspiration on their palms during performance than did those working alone. In
other words, the audience increased the arousal levels of these subjects. (See
chapter 12 for a discussion of the arousal of the sympathetic nervous system—
the GAS syndrome.)

Interestingly enough, Martens's finding also supported Zajonc's other
hypothesis, namely, that increased arousal due to the presence of others interferes with learning a difficult task. Martens found, for example, that the subjects who learned the task before an audience committed more errors than did
those working alone.

But an even more convincing confirmation of this aspect of the Zajonc
theory was produced by Cottrell, Rittle, and Wack (1967). In this study, students were given a list of word pairs (consisting of two-syllable adjectives) to
learn. Some of the pairs were easy to learn because their constituent words
were closely related or similar in meaning (for example, adept–skillful,
barren–fruitless). Others, by contrast, were not related and included such pairs
as arid–grouchy, and desert–leading.

To test the social facilitation hypothesis, the students first memorized the
word pairs alone, then in the presence of others. Zajonc's hypothesis was
supported in that the subjects learned easier pairs faster in the presence of
others than they did in private. In others words, the presence of the audience
enhanced performance on these easy tasks because it stimulated the dominant
responses, which were the correct ones. On the other hand, the subjects did
better alone than in the group condition when they attempted to learn the
difficult word pairs. In this latter situation, the presence of an audience ham-
pered performance by arousing the subjects, who then gave their less well
learned, but incorrect, responses.

Modification of Zajonc's theory. Zajonc's hypothesis states that it is the
mere presence of others that increases the individual's arousal level and hence
affects his performance of a task. But is this really true? Might there not be
other characteristics of the audience that bring about this effect? Some inves-

tigators believe that this indeed is the case (Cottrell, Wack, Sekerak, and Rittle, 1968).

Cottrell and his associates designed an experiment in which the subjects attempted to learn a task that consisted, first, in learning a number of nonsense words, then, in identifying as many of the words as possible as they were projected on a screen. The words were flashed so rapidly that they had the effect of being subliminal; that is, they were slightly below the subject's threshold of visual perception. The subjects were divided into three groups—each group was to learn the words under one of three different conditions.

In the first condition, the subjects performed the task by themselves. In the second, they performed it before an audience of two interested spectators who happened to be fellow students. In the third situation, they performed the task in the presence of two individuals who were blindfolded and so could not judge the subject's performance. Thus, the investigators were comparing how the

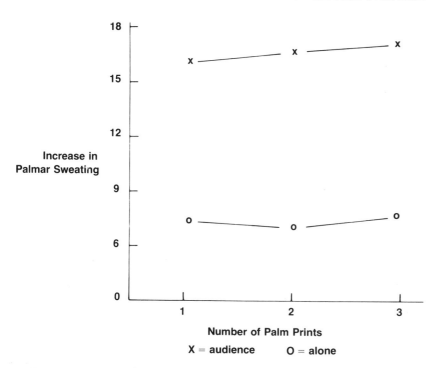

THE EFFECT OF AN AUDIENCE ON PERFORMANCE

X = audience   O = alone

Figure 5–1. Individuals performing a complex motor task in the presence of an audience showed greater palmar sweating than those who performed the same task alone.

SOURCE: Adapted from Martens, R. Palmar sweating and the presence of an audience. *Journal of Experimental Social Psychology,* 1969, **5,** 373.

subjects performed alone, before an interested audience, and in the company of those who were merely physically present.

The results of the experiment do not support Zajonc's argument that it is only the physical presence of others that affects one's motivation and performance. The investigators found that it is the presence of an interested audience that increases the tendency of the subject to perform better. The mere presence of an audience, by contrast, did not affect performance in a positive way. Indeed, the investigators found that there was no difference whatsoever between the trials in which the subject performed alone and those in which the blindfolded people were present.

The evaluation theory. If mere presence of an audience does not explain the effects of social facilitation, what does? A study by Martens and Landers suggests that it is the evaluative aspects of an audience that produce social facilitation or social interference. Thus, if an individual suspects that he is being evaluated by his audience—whether in terms of appearance, manners, intelligence, performance, or whatever—he will tend to be tense and aroused. Conversely, if the audience appears to be open and easy rather than judgmental, one tends to perform in a more relaxed manner (Martens and Landers, 1972).

In the Martens and Landers experiment, male undergraduate students were asked to perform a motor task that involved using two rods to guide a ball up an incline. The game is quite difficult and requires a certain amount of manual dexterity. As in the experiment by Cottrell and his colleagues (1968), the subjects were divided into three groups and each group performed the task under a different condition.

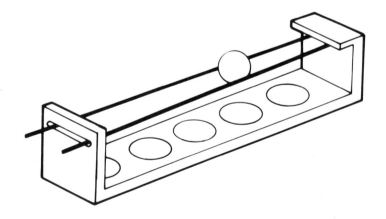

Figure 5–2. Martens and Landers used this device, known as "roll-up," in their social facilitation experiment. The subjects were to move the ball up the incline by manipulating the two rods on which the ball rests.

SOURCE: Martens, R., and Landers, D. Evaluation potential as a determinant of coaction effects. *Journal of Experimental Social Psychology,* 1972, **8**, 350.

In the first condition, each subject could see his score, as well as the performances and scores of the other subjects participating in the experiment. Appropriately enough, this condition was called the "direct-evaluation" condition. In the second situation, the "indirect-evaluation" condition, the subjects could not see one another perform, but they could see all the scores. Finally, in the "no-evaluation" condition, the subjects could see neither the performance nor the scores of the others.

Martens and Landers found that the "direct-evaluation treatment resulted in significantly poorer performances when compared to the no-evaluation treatment . . . and the indirect-evaluation treatment" (p. 353). In other words, when learning a difficult task, those subjects who were in the position of being evaluated by their fellows were so aroused that their dominant responses to the task were the incorrect ones. Those in the no-evaluation position, by contrast, were more relaxed and emitted the correct responses. Indeed, there was no difference at all in the performances of those in the indirect-evaluation and no-evaluation conditions.

Thus, this experiment provides evidence that Zajonc's hypothesis should be modified to reflect the fact that the effects of social facilitation depend upon the degree to which the subject perceives that his performance is being judged by others.

The role of evaluative self-awareness. Recently, researchers investigating the phenomenon of social facilitation have begun to focus on self-awareness as a key factor. For example, a study by Barry Liebling and Philip Shaver (1973) examined the role that *evaluation* and *self-awareness* played in task performance. The investigators point out that there is evidence indicating that highly anxious individuals do not do well on intellectual tasks because they divide their attention between the task and certain aspects of themselves. Thus, they are in a state of anxious self-attention, which means they are prone to "self-evaluation, self-depreciation, worrying about failure, and perception of [their] own disturbing and disruptive autonomous arousal" (p. 297). Subjects with little anxiety, on the other hand, devote all their attention to the task and so perform more proficiently.

It was also known that individuals who feel that they are being evaluated will be aroused to perform poorly. Liebling and Shaver formulated a new hypothesis: A person who is performing a task under conditions of high self-awareness and high evaluation will not do as well as one who is not so self-conscious or aware that she is being evaluated. The researchers thus had two variables to be tested: self-awareness and evaluation by others.

The next problem was how to test the two variables. Placing the subject in a condition in which she perceived that she was being evaluated was simple enough: all that was needed was to inform the individual that her performance would be judged and compared with those of others. To test the self-awareness variable, the experimenters placed a mirror in front of a subject so she could observe herself performing the tasks.

The study, which involved copying a passage of Swedish prose for five-minute intervals, was divided into three parts. In the first part, all the subjects (forty female undergraduate students) sat at desks and copied the same passage for five minutes. They were instructed to work as quickly and as accurately as possible. In the next part of the experiment, half of the subjects copied the same passage but sat facing a mirror in which they could view themselves. This was known as the "mirror condition." The other half copied the passage without the mirror (the "no-mirror condition").

In the third part of the study, the subjects were again split into two groups. Half of those in the mirror condition were told that their performance would be evaluated and would reflect their level of intelligence. The other half, by contrast, were told that their performance was not being evaluated. The same was done for those in the no-mirror condition. Thus, there were four condi-

*Does an audience
of one's teammates
help or hinder
athletic performance?*

tions being tested: mirror–high evaluation; mirror–low evaluation; no-mirror–high evaluation; no-mirror–low evaluation.

The results bore out the prediction of the researchers: Those who performed in a high-evaluation condition and in the presence of a mirror fared worse than those who performed in a low-evaluation condition with a mirror. Thus, those subjects who were being judged and who were aware of themselves as they copied the Swedish passage made more errors than those who were not being judged but who could see themselves performing the task. Liebling and Shaver concluded their study with the following observation:

The relevance of our analysis for research on social facilitation deserves a final comment. If social facilitation effects are mediated by objective self-awareness, we should find the same pattern of results obtained in the present study when Mirror and No-Mirror conditions are replaced by Audience and No Audience (Liebling and Shaver, p. 304).

Deindividuation

In the previous chapter we saw how a group can pressure individual members to behave in a manner in which they would not ordinarily behave when alone. Thus, the phenomenon of the risky shift establishes the principle that even conservative individuals make bolder decisions when they are part of a group than in private. Similarly, as we saw in our discussion of social facilitation, groups can affect one's motivation and task performance. Social psychologists have also concerned themselves with the common observation that within the protection of a group, members may violate the social norms they usually observe in social situations. Members of a basketball team, for example, might cry and embrace one another after winning a championship. Furthermore, some group members may do things they will be ashamed of later. A group of youths may attack an old, defenseless man or members of a theater crowd may trample others to death as they seek to escape a fire. This aspect of group behavior, in which the members lose their sense of individuality and become submerged in the group, is known as *deindividuation*.

Evidence for deindividuation

The phenomenon of deindividuation was first studied in 1952 by L. Festinger, A. Pepitone, and T. Newcomb. These investigators designed an experiment which tested two hypotheses: The phenomenon of deindividuation is accompanied by a reduction in the restraint of group members; and groups whose members have reduced their restraints are more attractive to members than those in which there is no deindividuation.

To test these propositions, the investigators first asked twenty-three groups of male undergraduate students to discuss a statement which proposed that most college students hated one or both parents. The investigators chose this topic because they felt that most individuals would exercise a good deal of restraint when it came to expressing hatred of their parents. During the discussion period, which lasted forty minutes, each student was identified by a tag on which his name had been prominently printed.

Festinger and his colleagues predicted that the more group members threw off restraints and criticized their parents, the more deindividuated would be their particular discussion group. The measure of deindividuation consisted of the degree to which members of a group failed to note the participation of other

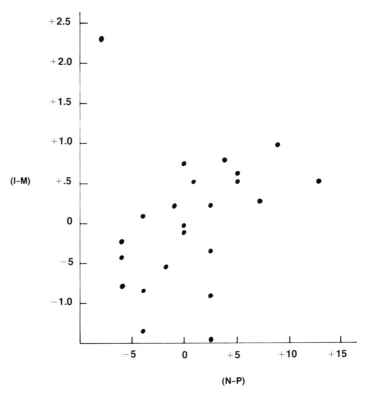

DEINDIVIDUATION IN A GROUP

Figure 5–3. Festinger and his colleagues found a fairly high correlation (.59) between the subjects' reduction in restraint (N–P) and their ability to identify who said what (I–M) during a discussion of parental attitudes.

SOURCE: Festinger, L., Pepitone, A., and Newcomb, T. Some consequences of deindividuation in a group. *Journal of Abnormal and Social Psychology,* 1952, **47**, 386.

members as individuals. In other words, deindividuation would have the effect of inducing members to become submerged in the group. To test this proposition, the researchers theorized that in the deindividuated group each student would be able to remember only what was said or done by the group as a whole. Individuals would not be able to remember who said what and when during the group discussions. The results showed that an increase in the expression of negative attitudes toward one's parents was accompanied by an increase in the inability of each member to identify which student had made which statements. Hence, attention was diverted from the individuals toward the group.

The investigators also found that those groups in which restraints had been reduced—that is, where deindividuation had occurred—were more attractive to members than those in which there was no deindividuation. This attractiveness was determined by asking the students to complete a questionnaire after their group discussion. The students were to indicate the degree to which they would like to return to the same group to discuss similar topics.

The Zimbardo study. The work of Festinger and his associates has been amplified and extended by Philip Zimbardo (1970). Zimbardo set out to discover how deindividuation resulted in the expression of such extremely negative behaviors as hostility and theft. He believed that deindividuation is "a process in which a series of antecedent social conditions [produces] . . . changes in perception of self and others and [results in] a lowered threshold of normally restrained behavior" (1970, p. 251).

To test his hypothesis, Zimbardo assembled a number of groups, each consisting of four female students. They were told that they were participating in a study of human empathy and that they were to administer electric shocks to a female student who was in the next room. Students could view the subject through a one-way mirror. The target subject was not actually being shocked; however, her cries, writhing, and grimacing apparently were real enough to convince her tormentors that their "shocks" were causing her great pain. Zimbardo set up his experiment so that each four-woman group was administering the shocks in either of two conditions. In the first condition, the girls were dressed in bulky laboratory coats with hoods that covered their faces. They were not introduced to one another, nor were they addressed by name when the experimenter explained the mechanics of the study to them. Moreover, the experiment was conducted in semidarkness. This situation, called the "deindividuation condition," clearly was intended to reduce individuality and responsibility.

In the other condition, by contrast, individuality was emphasized. The members of each four-woman group wore their own everyday clothes and received name tags. In giving them their instructions, the researchers politely addressed each student by name. The room was well lit so that group members could see one another. In this second situation, each subject's individuality was underscored. Zimbardo predicted that the students in the deindividuation situation would show less restraint against administering shocks than would those in the individuation situation. The results bore out his prediction. Members of deindividuated groups shocked their victims nearly twice as long as did members of individuated groups.

Zimbardo's experiment contained another interesting variable: the victim's personality. Prior to the actual administration of the shocks, each subject listened to a tape on which Zimbardo conducted a five-minute interview with one of two target persons with totally different personalities. One woman appeared to be very pleasant and altruistic, stating that she was teaching retarded children while helping her fiancé through medical school. The other woman was obnoxious, self-centered, and highly critical. She particularly loathed the Jewish students at the school, she said.

The results of this aspect of the experiment are quite revealing. They show, for example, that the groups in the depersonalized, deindividuated condition administered long shocks to either kind of person, whether pleasant or obnoxious. "These sweet, normally mild-mannered college girls," Zimbardo writes, "shocked another girl almost every time they had an opportunity to do so, sometimes for as long as they were allowed, and it did not matter whether or not that fellow student was a nice girl who didn't deserve to be hurt" (1970, p. 270). The subjects in the individuated condition, by contrast, were more discriminating. They varied the duration of their shocks according to the personality of the target subject. Thus, the pleasant, affable victim received shocks of shorter duration than did the "bitchy" woman.

From these studies and others, Zimbardo has hypothesized that the deindividuation phenomenon has two key characteristics. The first of these is the anonymity of group members. The individual acting as a member of a group is willing to violate group norms because he perceives that he is anonymous. In the experiment above, for example, the gowned and hooded students without name tags, operating in semidarkness, were anonymous. The same is true for members of the Ku Klux Klan, as well as for riot police who wear the same clothing, have the same weapons, and whose protective visors mask their faces and hence their individuality.

We have met the second feature of deindividuation—the diffusion of responsibility—in the previous chapter. When one is a member of a group, one tends to perceive that the responsibility for group actions is diffused, or spread out, among all the other members. No one member need bear the brunt of the blame for a group action. Indeed, members may even perceive their actions as acceptable or morally correct because the group as a whole participates. (In chapter 11, there is a discussion of nonintervention in an emergency situation if others are present and do not intervene.)

Zimbardo has noticed another aspect of deindividuation: once deindividuation has begun and has gathered momentum, it is difficult to reverse or to terminate. He cites the following account of the riot at the 1968 Democratic Convention in Chicago:

> The ones who actually got arrested seemed to have gotten caught up among the police, like a kind of human medicine ball, being shoved and knocked back and forth from one cop to the next with what was obviously *mounting* fury. And this was a phenomenon somewhat unexpected, which we were to observe consistently throughout the days of violence—that rage seemed to engender rage; the bloodier and more brutal the cops were, the more their fury increased (Zimbardo, 1969, p. 244).

Thus, it appears that the pathologically antisocial behavior exhibited by some groups is due, in part at least, to the process of deindividuation. Zimbardo feels that his findings are applicable to society in general, especially to large cities where residents are apt to develop feelings of anonymity. It may be,

This sixteen-year-old is on duty in Northern Ireland. Will his uniform and training as a British soldier overcome his moral restraints and permit him to injure or kill his fellow countrymen?

Zimbardo writes, that deindividuation is the phenomenon behind much of the social aggression—thefts, muggings, vandalism, and the like—that seems to prevail in large metropolitan areas.

172 Collective Behavior

Two automobiles collide at a busy intersection and immediately a ring of curious passersby surrounds the scene. In an urban ghetto area, a white policeman arrests a black man for drunken driving and a riot erupts as other blacks come to the man's aid. The fans at a rock concert begin to smash the seats, hurl bottles and debris, and physically attack one another.

Such events are examples of *collective behavior*, defined by Stanley Milgram and Hans Toch (1969, p. 507) as "group behavior which originates spontaneously, is relatively unorganized, fairly unpredictable and planless in its course of development, and which depends on interstimulation among participants." It also includes crazes, fads, mass hysteria, rebellions, and religious revivals.

Because of its very nature, collective behavior is difficult to analyze. It is not possible, for example, for an investigator to interrupt a member of a lynch mob and question him about his feelings and the reasons for his actions. Instead, a researcher must rely on the memories of individuals who have participated in or witnessed an event. By interviewing a number of people, the researcher may be able to tease out all the elements of the event. In most cases, however, it is not possible to reconstruct the event with any degree of accuracy, because the emotional turbulence of the incident often clouds the memory and judgment of a witness. Thus, most of what is known about collective behavior is based on theories rather than upon empirical data. Two concepts have been developed to explain the spontaneous nature of collective behavior: imitation and contagion.

Imitation and contagion

"Imitation is the sincerest form of flattery," says the old adage. Imitation is also an important aspect of social psychology because much social behavior is imitative. Early in life, for example, children learn to imitate their elders. As they mature, most of their behavior is influenced by the behavior of those around them. At public events, for example, we stand when we see others stand, applaud when others applaud, even yawn when others do so. We learn to imitate virtually all kinds of behavior—good, bad, and indifferent. We may be influenced to donate money to charity simply because others do so. Similarly, we may become prejudiced against other ethnic groups because our family and neighbors exhibit prejudiced behavior.

In the past, investigators such as Gabriel Tarde (1903) theorized that imitative behavior was innate, a part of our biological equipment. However, because of the work of N. E. Miller and J. Dollard (1941), Albert Bandura (1969), and others, this view has been replaced by the hypothesis that imitative behavior, like many other kinds of human behavior, is learned.

Contagion is mass imitation, the concept by which feelings or behavior spread from one participant in a crowd to another. In the words of sociologist H. Blumer (1946, p. 176), social contagion "attracts, and infects, individuals, many of whom originally are merely detached and indifferent spectators and bystanders. At first, people may be merely curious about the given behavior, or mildly interested in it. As they catch the spirit of excitement and become more attentive to the behavior, they become more inclined to engage in it."

As Melvin DeFleur, William D'Antonio, and Lois DeFleur (1971) point out, there are two kinds of contagion: emotional and behavioral contagion. *Emotional contagion* is said to unify the feelings of a crowd. It helps the individual to abandon the social norms that usually constrain his behavior so that his actions are motivated chiefly by his emotions. Emotional contagion is more likely to occur in situations in which participants share the same attitudes, beliefs, and values, facilitating the process of imitation among individuals. Thus young people attending a rock concert will tend to be more overcome by the performance than would an audience composed of older men and women. Similarly, the participants in the urban riots during the summer of 1967 tended to be young, male, and black (National Advisory Commission on Civil Disorders, 1968).

Emotional contagion is also increased when all the participants focus their attention on one particular person or object. For example, the members of an audience at a religious revival become transfixed by a powerful religious leader. All the participants react to his words simultaneously. As he makes point after point, the audience responds as one person. Under these conditions, an individual member is open to all kinds of emotional suggestions and he tends to behave in the same manner in which the people around him behave.

One of the most important mechanisms of emotional contagion is *circular reaction*, defined by Kurt and Gladys Lang (1961, p. 209) as "a process by which the emotions of others elicit the same emotions in oneself, which, in turn, intensify the emotions of others." For example, if one person is able to generate a wave of anger or fear throughout a crowd, the behavior of the crowd will reinforce his original emotions, and possibly provoke stronger outbursts in him. This strengthened feeling will then spread through the crowd, stimulating him to still stronger responses. In this way, the members of a crowd can mutually stimulate and reinforce one another's responses until they reach a fever pitch.

In *behavioral contagion*, actions spread from individual to individual. For example, a person who throws a bottle at the umpire in a baseball game may trigger a barrage of bottle-throwing by other fans. During a fire in a crowded theater, an individual who shoves others out of the way as he heads for the exit may set off a stampede in which many people are prevented from reaching the exit. Some investigators believe that behavioral contagion stems from the fact that individuals in stressful collective situations feel compelled to act but lack norms to guide their behavior. If one member of a crowd suddenly crashes through a police barricade and throws a rock, for example, his act can serve as a norm for others. This idea, known as the emergent norm theory, will be considered in detail later in this section.

The June bug.   In June, 1962, some fifty-nine women in a North Carolina textile factory reported being bitten by a "bug" that made them ill enough to stay home. Some of the victims were even hospitalized. Symptoms included nervousness, nausea, weakness, numbness, and insect bites. At first, ten women reported symptoms of the mysterious malady. Within a few days, it had spread to forty-nine others. The victims blamed the illness on a "bug" that was said to have come with a new shipment of fabric from England. Medical personnel and entomologists called in to investigate the incident examined the victims and the plant. They found nothing that could have caused the mysterious symptoms. Within eleven days, the symptoms vanished as suddenly as they had appeared, and all the women were back at their jobs. In the end, the medical authorities blamed the illness on anxiety and nervousness.

After the incident, two social psychologists, Kerckhoff and Back (1968), interviewed those who worked at the plant, both victims and nonvictims alike. They attributed the outbreak to *hysterical contagion*, which they define as "the dissemination of a set of symptoms among a population in a situation in which no manifest basis for the symptoms may be established" (p. 12). The investigators found two interesting patterns. First, the "bug" initially attacked social isolates, those who interacted only rarely with others in the plant and who had few friends among their co-workers. These individuals were "struck" first, say the investigators, because they had few social restraints or controls against aberrant behavior such as fainting. From the few friends of the isolates, the bug quickly spread to others. The investigators found that members of cliques all seemed to be affected at around the same time: when one member of a small circle of friends reported symptoms, others in the clique quickly followed suit.

The other interesting pattern involved stress and strain produced by the job. Only those who were under strain seemed to fall victim to the bug. Sources of strain included working overtime, and neglecting family responsibilities as a result of the overtime. By calling in sick for a day or two, these individuals could alleviate or postpone such strain. Thus, the June Bug gave them a good excuse to stay home.

These findings bear out those of others in several respects. First, they show that strain renders members of a collectivity very open to suggestion and to the acceptance of bizarre stories and rumors. Second, contagion spreads more rapidly among friends than among strangers. Finally, emotions or behavior quickly diffuse among those who share beliefs, attitudes, and values.

Theories of crowd behavior

The first serious attempt to understand the phenomenon of collective behavior was undertaken in 1895 by Gustave Le Bon. In his now classic work, *The Crowd*, Le Bon proposed that the crowd has a collective mind "which makes [the participants] feel, think, and act in a manner quite different from that in which each individual of them would feel, think, and act were he in a state of isolation" (p. 29). But, says Le Bon, this collective mind is quite retarded, preventing the crowd from accomplishing deeds that require intelligence. Indeed, crowds transform participants into barbarians who act only by instinct. As part of a crowd, the individual may behave like a beast, committing antisocial acts which he would never commit on his own.

The Lang approach. Kurt and Gladys Lang (1961) have proposed a theory which attempts to account for the development of a crowd. They enumerate five steps by which a collectivity is transformed into a crowd. These steps serve to define a crowd as well as to explain the mechanisms of crowd behavior.

In the first step, a number of people gather together and interact intensely. The key factor here is the number of people involved. The group must be at least hall-sized—too large for a room of ordinary size, yet small enough for intimate interaction. A small group—one of ten or twelve individuals, for example—does not constitute a crowd because the members are less likely to merge into the group and lose their identity. In larger gatherings, consisting of more than twenty individuals, the participants can become anonymous, in that the status and role of each are less perceptible. However, the group must not be so large that frequent and direct interaction cannot take place.

In Lang's second step in crowd formation, a crowd forms as a result of some extraordinary agitation. "An audience listening to a lecture on cybernetics might act out its fright in case of fire; it is not likely to mob the speaker just because it disagrees with what he is saying. [But a] parade crowd, given the proper musical and visual stimulation, could be aroused to some heights of patriotic ecstasy, thus transforming the nature of the interaction" (p. 119).

In the next step, the intensified feelings must culminate in a mood that is shared by all participants. The mood has the effect of dissolving ordinary social restraints. The Langs cite the example of people pressed together viewing a parade as it passes down a narrow street. Under certain conditions the people may stop viewing the parade and begin interacting violently with one another. Certain individuals may react to others who press close to them as they try to obtain a better view. The persons who are jostled or displaced may give the intruders a dirty look, then verbally accuse them. As the shoving and accusations continue, tension mounts, until it breaks out in anger.

In step four, the mood of the crowd is transformed into action as those involved begin to redefine the situation. To continue the above example, some members of the crowd are no longer watching the parade, but are arguing over who is pushing whom and who is at fault. This is the most important condition for the formation of a crowd. As the situation is redefined by the participants, the ordinary expectations of status and role are ignored. Participants become anonymous and need not be concerned about the judgment of others who do not share the crowd's mood. "Condemnation from nearby spectators is ineffective because it involves no loss of face, no expulsions, no demotions, no other kinds of sanctions" (Lang and Lang, 1961, p. 120). Indeed, the very passivity of the onlookers is interpreted as acquiescence and may even contribute to the feelings of invincible power that frequently develop in members of a crowd.

During the redefinition phase, participants often lose their ability to judge their own feelings and behavior. Why should this occur? The Langs say no one is really certain yet, but two factors may play key roles in this process. First, the participants may perceive that there are definite rewards for throwing off social restraints and behaving abnormally. Second, the individual who acts as part of a group can successfully evade the guilt for his abnormal behavior. For example, the person who hurls a bottle at the umpire in a baseball game reaps a kind of reward from this action: he indulges himself, he lets off steam, and he achieves a certain notoriety in the eyes of other spectators. Indeed, the crowd's failure to condemn the person's actions is interpreted as approval, and encourages further bizarre behavior on the part of both the bottle thrower and others. Individuals who see others behave abnormally may become convinced that they can behave in a similar manner without blame or guilt. As the Langs point out: "Thus, a college boy who ordinarily would not burglarize steals into the women's dormitory to carry off silk panties. Encouraged by his peers and 'brothers,' he enters the crowd spirit from which he had probably once considered himself immune. The risk of group punishment only serves to underline his belongingness, and the group action exempts him from personal guilt" (p. 121).

Finally, say the investigators, the redefinition of the situation results in the formation of a crowd in which many of those assembled respond in the same manner. Participants do not act as they would in their usual roles because they are joined to one another by deep emotional feelings. Some of an individual's usual control in social situations is abandoned and his inhibitions begin to disappear. The investigators make the analogy to a choir:

In every choir, people who are ordinarily self-conscious about their ability to carry a tune sing in full voice along with others. In the same way the mood shared in an aggressive, destructive, or orgiastic crowd seems to offer a milieu that protects individuals from self-consciousness and the pangs of anticipatory guilt (Lang and Lang, 1961, p. 121).

Emergent norm theory. A somewhat different approach to crowd behavior, known as the *emergent norm* theory, has been proposed by R. H. Turner, both by himself (1964) and, later, in collaboration with L. M. Killian (1972). According-ing to this view, a collectivity of people in an ambiguous situation is trans-formed into a crowd when they perceive the emergence of a norm to guide their behavior so that they behave more or less in unison. Thus, as we saw in a previous example, the people restrained by a police barricade did not know what to do until one of their number threw a rock. The restless, milling people then perceived that a norm had arisen to govern their actions—they, too,

The anti-Vietnam war movement was able to assemble demonstrations of over a quarter of a million people. Volunteers equipped with only armbands for identification, stationed along the parade routes, served as a self-policing force.

started hurling rocks and curses at the police. According to emergent norm theorists, once the norm is perceived, the participants feel pressure to observe it. Turner and Killian also hold that there is no such thing as homogeneity of crowd behavior—the crowd does not act in a uniform manner. Instead, only a few individuals engage in bizarre or antisocial activities. Most of the crowd members are merely curious and interested observers of the proceedings who, by their very passivity, support the actions of the active minority. Thus, say norm theorists, individuals in a crowd do not act because they are "infected" with contagious emotions or because they are merely imitating their neighbors. Rather, participants behave as they do because they perceive that their behavior is correct—that is, in accordance with a norm.

Although the emergent norm theory does much to focus on the actual mechanics of crowd behavior, it raises questions that must be answered before the explanation can be fully accepted. For example, what factors determine which norm will emerge? And why is the emergent norm always destructive? Furthermore, as Milgram and Toch (1969) point out, this interpretation of crowd behavior does not entirely do away with the concept of contagion, as it claims. It replaces the diffusion of emotions in a crowd with the diffusion of some cognitive factor—that is, with a common perception of a standard of conduct. But this standard is not perceived simultaneously by all participants. It must originate with one or two individuals. So, instead of a spreading of emotions, there is, according to norm theory, a spread of a cognitive factor.

Conformity

As we have seen, people influence in important ways those with whom they interact. The presence of others, for example, can hamper or facilitate an individual's performance of a task. Similarly, together with many strangers, an individual can be induced to throw off normal social constraints and engage in destructive or antisocial behavior. Even the actions of others may be imitated when an individual becomes part of an excited crowd. It should come as no surprise, then, that there is experimental data which show that an individual can be induced by others to disbelieve the evidence of his own senses. Indeed, the pressure to conform can force an individual to accept the judgment of the majority not only in ambiguous situations, but in circumstances so obvious that the error in judgment is absolutely unmistakable to any normal person.

The tendency to conform

The first significant study of conformity was conducted by Muzafer Sherif in 1935. Sherif was studying the ways in which individuals tend to create their own norms when none is present. To do this, he used an interesting perceptual

THE FUNERAL OF THE WORLD'S GREATEST LOVER

The third decade of this century was a prosperous time in America. It was also the heyday of heroes, an age of spectacle, an age when showmanship was king. All across the land, people hungered for any kind of public display. Many individuals, pursuing fame at any cost, tried to satisfy this hunger. Some daredevils dangled upside down from airplanes, while others walked tightropes stretched between high buildings. Gertrude Ederle had become the first woman to swim the English Channel and Harry Houdini thrilled crowds with his daring escapes. In 1927, perhaps the greatest hero of all—Charles Lindbergh—successfully completed the first solo airplane flight across the Atlantic. It was only fitting, then, that one of the most adored heroes—the great silent-film star Rudolph Valentino—should be venerated in death as he had been idolized in life.

Valentino's funeral was one colossal spectacle. The 31-year-old idol had died on August 23, 1926, when infection set in following surgery for a perforated ulcer and appendicitis. During the eight-day period of his hospitalization, the newspapers and radio kept the public abreast of the star's condition. Rumors were constantly circulating that Valentino was near death or dying. The hospital was besieged with telephone calls, flowers, and candy. Some well-wishers even sent "miracle" drugs and medical advice to the star's physicians. Then, when the end finally came, thousands of weeping mourners kept vigil outside the hospital. Inside, nurses and other hospital personnel wept hysterically.

The body was removed to a funeral parlor and placed on view in the late afternoon of August 24th. By that time, some 12,000 people had been patiently waiting for hours for a final glimpse of the star. Later in the evening, the crowd swelled to around 60,000. They stood in a line, in some places four abreast, that snaked around eleven city blocks.

As time wore on and patience grew thin, the mourners became unruly. The crowd overflowed into the six-lane street, disrupting traffic for hours. Several hundred policemen, including a troop of mounted police, repeatedly charged the throng in an attempt to contain it. Clothes were torn from bodies, and people were trampled with each charge of the horsemen. Some individuals were arrested for disorderly conduct. At least ten were cut by flying glass when the windows of the funeral parlor were broken as eager members of the crowd jostled one another to enter the place. A makeshift aid station, with a doctor and several nurses, was set up on the first floor of the funeral parlor to care for the injured. At midnight, when the undertaker closed his doors, a long line still waited to view the remains.

The scene was repeated at the funeral parlor the following day when the body was again placed on view. But this time, heavy wood planks were bolted across the front of the building to protect it from further damage. That night, it was estimated that some sixty to eighty thousand people had filed past the coffin. On September 3rd began the six-day train ride back to Hollywood for burial. At railway stations along the way, large crowds gathered for a glimpse of the train. In Chicago, when the coffin was transferred to another train, a number of people were injured when a throng that jammed the station's concourse got out of hand. On September 6th, the train finally reached the suburbs of Los Angeles where the actor's body was removed and buried the following day (Chaplin, 1959).

illusion known as the autokinetic phenomenon, in which a stationary point of light seen by an observer in a darkened room appears to move. The illusion of movement is created because of the lack of background to serve as an objective frame of reference. Sherif saw in this phenomenon an opportunity to examine the influence of others on an individual's performance of a task. He designed an experiment in which a subject was placed in a darkened room and asked to estimate how far the stationary light "moved." After trials with a number of subjects, results showed great variation in individual estimates. Some subjects, for example, thought the light moved only a few inches, whereas others saw the light moving as much as 20 or 30 feet.

But Sherif found that after a number of trials, the subjects began to establish standards of their own with which to compare their estimates. In the words of Sherif (p. 324), each subject establishes "a range and a point within that range which is peculiar to the individual." In the beginning trials, for example, the subject may report seeing the light move 20 inches, then 5 inches, then 15 inches. In succeeding trials, he begins to establish a definite range, reporting, perhaps, that the light appeared to move 15 inches, then 12 inches, then 14 inches. Thus, the range established in this case would be 12–15 inches.

In the next part of the experiment, Sherif placed three or four people in the same darkened room with the light. Each of these individuals had participated in the first part of the experiment and had established his or her own range. However, the range of each was different. The investigator found that when a small group consisting of two or three subjects was exposed to the same light point and instructed to announce their estimates individually, they began to influence one another. Thus, suppose that two subjects with privately established ranges of 5 to 8 inches and 18 to 25 inches, respectively, were placed in the same darkened room. After several trials, their opinions would begin to converge until they had established a common range of, say, 11 to 15 inches, although, of course, the pinpoint of light had never actually moved.

This experiment shows that an individual can, in an ambiguous situation, influence another person to conform. However, it does not show that the individual automatically and unthinkingly conforms to the behavior or words of another. Because the situation was not clear-cut, the subject was really only guessing—he had nothing objective on which to base his estimates. In effect, he was using the consistent estimates of the other individual as a guideline for his own estimates. In order to test a person's unthinking conformity to the judgments of others, someone would have to devise an experiment in which the situation was less ambiguous.

The Asch experiments. The social psychologist Solomon Asch (1951, 1955) did just that. In Asch's experiment, which is now recognized as a classic, seven male college students are seated around a conference table and are told that they are participating in an experiment in visual judgment. The experimenter instructs them that they will be shown a number of cards on which vertical lines appear. Their task is to judge the lengths of some of the lines. Thus, he shows them two white cards. On one card is a single vertical line which the experimenter calls the "standard." On the other card are three vertical lines, one of which is the same length as the standard line. The students are asked to choose the line on the second card that matches this standard.

The first two trials go smoothly. The subjects announce their judgments in the order in which they are seated around the table. The group unanimously chooses the same matching line each time. But on the third trial, one of the subjects—the person seated in the next to last chair—deviates from the others in his selection of the correct line. He appears to be surprised at the judgment of others. On the fourth trial, the same subject again disagrees with the other six, who are again unanimous. This further disturbs the deviate—he smiles embarrassedly or answers in a low voice.

However, the deviate is not aware of the fact that he is the only naive subject in the group. Before the start of the experiment, the other six had been instructed to give incorrect answers in most of the trials. (The first student in the group has a card which tells him when to answer incorrectly; the other five students simply follow his lead.) Thus, the target person is actually giving the correct answers; he is a minority of one who is caught between two countervailing forces: the evidence of his senses and the unanimous judgment of others in the group. His task is difficult because he must announce his judgment in public before a group of persons who unanimously disagree with him on a clear-cut issue. Moreover, they have publicly stated their disagreement, and they have done so before he announces his answer.

In order to eliminate any suspicion by the naive subject that the others are in collusion against him, the experimenter has instructed the other six subjects to give the correct answers on six of the eighteen trials. This means that on twelve trials, the subject is put in a position where he may be forced to doubt the evidence of his senses.

How do most subjects perform on this test? The results showed that most of the time subjects do not conform. About 67 percent of the judgments given by 123 subjects from three different colleges were not influenced by the judgments of the group. But a surprisingly high percentage of judgments—slightly more than 33 percent—were incorrect answers. In other words, the subjects yielded to group pressure by giving an incorrect answer in 33 percent of the trials. Asch points out that there were individual differences. About one-quarter of the subjects refused to conform; they disagreed with the majority on all twelve trials. Some individuals went with the majority most of the time.

The performances of individuals in this experiment tend to be highly consistent. Those who strike out on the path of independence do not, as a rule, succumb to the majority even over an extended series of trials, while those who choose the path of compliance are unable to free themselves as the ordeal is prolonged (Asch, 1955, p. 33).

The ethics of such an experiment have been highlighted in the novel *Kinflicks* by Lisa Alther. She dramatizes the reactions of an unsuspecting subject who is pressured to go against the evidence of her own senses:

The senior explained the rules. . . . After several practice runs, the experiment began in earnest. I was sitting on the far end and was always the last to express my judgment, but it really didn't matter because we all agreed anyway. Yes, yes, that card was shorter than the control. And that one was longer. And so on. I was becoming very impatient and irritable.

During the sixth round the atmosphere of bored agreement suddenly shifted, and I found the three others blandly agreeing that a card was shorter, which to me was obviously longer.

And again. "Longer," said the first girl. "Longer," agreed the second. "Longer," said Eddie with a yawn. "The *same*," I insisted staunchly.

And yet again. I kept glancing around furtively as the others perjured with indifference the testimony of their senses. Or at least of *my* senses.

"The same," said the first girl. "The same." "The same," agreed Eddie. "*Longer*," I mumbled belligerently. Damn! How could they call it the same, when it was so obviously longer?

"Shorter," said the first girl. "Shorter," said the second. "Shorter," said Eddie, stretching luxuriously. "The same?" I suggested uncertainly. It *couldn't* be short-er. Could it? The others glanced at me with surprise.

"Longer," said the first girl, about a card that to me was clearly shorter. "Longer," confirmed the second girl. "Longer," agreed Eddie. Unable to endure the social isolation any longer, I intentionally belied the verdict of my eyes and said casually, "Longer." It felt marvelous to be in step with the others. I breathed a deep sigh of relief.

"The same," said the first girl. "The same." "The same." "Shorter," I wailed pitifully. Was something wrong with my eyes? I squinted and then opened them as wide as possible, trying to rectify my apparently faulty vision. Then I stared so intently at the control card that my vision blanked out altogether and I couldn't see anything for a few seconds. Eddie and the first girl looked at me, then glanced at each other and shrugged.

After two dozen of these runs, in which they agreed and I differed, or in which they agreed and I pretended to agree, interspersed with runs in which we all genuinely *did* agree, I could no longer tell what was shorter or longer than what. I would see a card as shorter. The others would call it longer, and before my very eyes the card would quiver and expand until it did in fact look longer. Or it would waver playfully back and forth between long and short.

Soon I was feeling nauseated, and my eyes were burning. "The same," said the first girl, about a card that had originally looked longer to me. "The same," said the second. "The same," said Eddie. I widened and narrowed my eyes several times, as the size of the card fluctuated. Then I fell out of my chair and collapsed on the floor, sobbing.

Eddie knelt down and helped me up, saying, "Now, now Ginny. It's just an experiment. Where's your Spinozan detachment?"

I collapsed on her shoulder and wept while she patted my back consolingly. The senior running the test came up and said, "You really did quite well, Ginny. You stood up to the others sixty-five percent of the time. The average so far is forty-three percent."

"*What* average?" I asked between sobs, looking up.

"The average number of correct responses the subject gives in contradiction to the pretend subjects."

"*Pretend* subjects? You mean this whole thing was staged?" I turned on Eddie in a rage.

"We thought you'd figured it out by now," the senior said. "You mean you hadn't?"

I raised a fist to slug Eddie. She put an arm around me affectionately. I pulled away.

"I'm sorry, Ginny, but it had to be done," Eddie said.

"*Why* did it? You could have at least told me."

"If I'd told you, it wouldn't have worked, would it? And you *are* in search of Truth, aren't you? Or doesn't that extend to the truth about yourself?"

I stomped out of the lab, my vision so strained and blurred that I bumped into the door casing. Back on my hall, I went to the bathroom and threw up. Then I went to my room and drew the curtains and climbed in bed and pulled the covers over my head (Alther, 1976, pp. 223–225).

Alther's fictionalized portrayal of the Asch experiment vividly demonstrates the anguish a subject might experience. In all fairness to those who argue that deception is necessary, it must be noted that in the novel, the girls who ran the experiment did not conduct a responsible debriefing session (see chapter 1). In addition to raising the question of ethics in the use of human subjects, Alther shows two variations in conforming behavior. Ginny began by trusting her senses, but when she conformed to the group's opinion she felt a tremendous sense of relief. However, as the experiment proceeded, she began actually to see the lines as the others said they saw them.

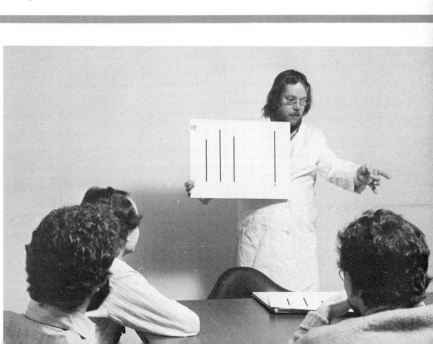

The experimenter waits for the answer from the subject. The confederates have all chosen the first line from the left. Will the subject conform?

Why people conform

Having discovered that individuals can be pressured into conforming with the group, the next logical question facing investigators was, why? Why do perfectly rational and intelligent individuals discard the evidence presented to them by their senses and agree with others whom they may not even know? Attempts to answer this question have led psychologists to focus on two primary factors. These are *informational* pressure and the *normative* pressure of the group.

We all know that we obtain much of our information about the world from others. Even much of the information we have about ourselves comes from others. If we lose our way while traveling through a strange town, we ask directions of a policeman or a resident of the town—someone we can trust to give us the information we need to get back on the right road. By and large, we follow the advice or copy the behavior of others because we feel that they have knowledge or information that will be helpful to us. And those that we feel we can trust as the most correct source of information are the ones we tend to imitate or believe.

The same mechanism appears to be at work in the experiments on conformity. One tends to trust the majority as a source of information and to doubt one's own judgment because he feels that the majority has a greater chance of being right. This is especially true in an ambiguous situation such as the Sherif experiment, in which one lacks a frame of reference on which to base a decision. Conformity to group thinking, then, depends upon the amount of confidence one has in the group as a source of information. It follows that the more one trusts the group, the more one's own confidence is weakened and the more likely one is to conform.

Another reason why the individual conforms to the group is that he does not want to be labeled as a deviant, an outcast. One believes as the group does because he fears that the group will in some way force him to think as they do. As we saw in chapter 4 in the Western Electric study, the group can physically punish a deviant to make him conform. At the other extreme, one might conform to group norms simply because of a reluctance to be conspicuous or to lose face.

Freedman and Doob (1968) designed an experiment in which one of a group of strangers was pointed out as deviant. They were not told the nature or degree of his deviancy—only that the individual was different in some way from the rest of the group. The experimenters then informed the group members that they were to select one of their number to participate in a learning experiment. Participation in the experiment was particularly undesirable because it required that the subject receive electric shocks if he answered certain questions incorrectly. Without fail, the group chose the individual who had been pointed out to them as a deviant to participate in the experiment.

Later in the same study, the group was asked to choose another of their number to take part in another learning experiment. However, the individual who was chosen to participate would be financially rewarded for his part in the study. The group was virtually unanimous in choosing someone other than the alleged deviant for this task. This experiment would tend to show that a group will punish deviancy if the members have the power to do so. The more power a group has to punish a deviant, the more pressure it can bring to bear on him to conform.

Group variables affecting conformity

The degree to which an individual trusts the group as a source of information, or the degree to which he dares to deviate from group norms, are dependent upon a number of factors. Chief among these are the characteristics of the group itself: group size, unanimity, cohesiveness, and status.

Group size. As Asch (1951, 1955) has pointed out, the size of the group is an important factor in compelling the individual to conform—but only up to a point. In a series of trials, Asch varied the size of the majority from one to fifteen individuals. When a subject, asked to match lines, was opposed by only one other individual, his opinion was virtually unaffected. When confronted with two others who opposed him, however, the individual's conformity greatly increased: he tended to yield to group pressure and to give the wrong answer nearly 14 percent of the time. When confronted with a majority of three others, the subject's errors climbed to slightly less than 32 percent. Beyond this point, however, the addition of more people to the opposition had little effect on conformity. A majority of seven, for example, led to conformity and incorrect answers in 37.1 percent of the trials, whereas a majority of fifteen actually led to a slight drop in conformity pressure, causing the individual to reply incorrectly 31.2 percent of the time. In other words, a majority of fifteen individuals yields about as much pressure to conform as a majority of three.

However, a later study showed that larger groups do elicit greater conformity from individuals than do smaller ones. Gerard, Wilhelmy, and Connolley (1968), for example, used a group of high school students in an Asch-like experiment. The investigators found that the subject was more likely to conform to the group opinion and to reply incorrectly when the unanimous majority included six or seven people than when it was composed of only three or four. Male subjects, for example, replied incorrectly in 30.1 percent of the trials when faced with a majority of seven individuals, compared to 24.1 percent incorrect replies when confronted with a majority of five others.

Group unanimity. A decrease in group unanimity adversely affects the group's power to enforce conformity. Asch (1951, 1955) demonstrated this by placing his subjects in two different situations. In each, the opposition was not unanimous. First, Asch set up his comparison of lines experiment so that one other individual supported the subject against the majority. Results showed that in this condition, the majority's influence on the subject was reduced by 75 percent: the subject committed only one-quarter the errors that he did when opposed by a unanimous majority. When questioned after the experiment, the subjects typically praised the persons who had supported them, stating that that person was very warm and had inspired confidence.

In the second condition, Asch tested the effect of the defection of the supporting partner to the side of the majority. In this experiment, the partner was instructed to support the subject in half of the trials. The support of the partner lessened the individual's tendency to conform. However, in the seventh trial, the partner joined the opposition, making it unanimous. Not surprisingly, this defection had the effect of restoring group conformity pressure to its full power. After the partner had joined the majority, the subject lost his independence and began to follow the group by answering incorrectly. Indeed, Asch observes, the submission of the subject to the majority "was just about as frequent as when the minority subject was opposed by a unanimous majority throughout" (1955, p. 6).

After the experiment, Asch questioned the subject to learn why the loss of support induced him to yield to group pressure. Most subjects replied that they felt they had been deserted by their partners. Asch then modified the procedure so that the partner would leave the room in the middle of the experiment, stating that he had an appointment with the dean. The results showed that the errors committed by the subject tended to rise after the partner left, but not as sharply as they did when the partner defected to the other side.

One might expect that the quality of the support might have some effect on the individual's ability to resist group conformity pressures. For example, if, during a seminar on English literature, one gets involved in an argument with the rest of the students, one might feel stronger and more confident if another seminar member rises to his support. But suppose the supporter was not one of the brighter students. Would this affect one's position, or one's estimation of his position? Common sense might dictate that such support would have little or no effect on the strength of one's position. However, an interesting study by Allen and Levine (1971) shows this not to be the case. These investigators set up an Asch-type experiment in which the subject was to receive support from another individual. However, the partner, who was wearing glasses with very thick lenses, made it clear to the subject that his vision was effective only for close distances. Thus, in an experiment in which visual acuity was extremely important, this partner might be more of a hindrance than a help. Nevertheless, results showed that the support of the individual with a visual problem somewhat lessened the group conformity pressure on the subject: he made more independent and correct responses than he did when faced with a totally unanimous group.

Group cohesion. If unanimity of a group can induce the subject to conform, it is logical to expect that strong group cohesion might have the same effect. Deutsch and Gerard (1955), for example, devised an Asch-like experiment which pitted five groups against one another. Each member of the group that made the least number of errors in the line comparison trials was to receive a pair of tickets to a play. The results show that individual members are more likely to yield to discrepant group pressure and to commit errors when they are working toward a goal than when they are not. Subjects tended to agree with group decisions because not doing so would mean losing the theater tickets. When questioned after the experiment, this was borne out. Some of the subjects, for example, reported feeling obligated to the group. Others felt that the group would somehow treat them as deviant if they did not go along with the majority, even though the subject perceived the group as being wrong.

Status. The status of majority members can also exert conformity pressure on an individual. If the majority members are of high status, for example, the group pressure to conform is likely to be more powerful than if the majority members are low-status individuals. E. P. Torrance (1955), for example, designed an experiment which tested the effects of status on group decision-making among three-man Air Force crews. The crews were composed of a pilot and a navigator, who were officers (with the pilot in command), and a gunner, who was an enlisted man.

It was found that the pilot's correct solution to a problem brought unanimous agreement from the other two. But when the pilot was wrong and the others disagreed with him, his status enabled him to pressure the others into accepting his answer. By contrast, if the gunner came up with the correct solution, the group accepted it only about 40 percent of the time. Indeed, in many cases when the gunner was right, the higher-status individuals were able to prevail upon him to change his mind. Apparently, the gunner's lower status detracted from his ability to persuade the others. Thus, the thinking of the high-status individual tended to induce group conformity, whereas that of the low-status person had little or no positive effect on conformity.

Characteristics of the situation

There are many variables present in the situation itself that may affect the degree to which the individual conforms to group pressure. Among these situational factors are the nature of the stimulus; whether one responds publicly or privately to the stimulus; the degree to which one is committed to his position; and the individual's perception of his own competence.

Nature of the stimulus.   The content of the stimulus that the individual must judge is quite important in the conformity situation. Is the stimulus ambiguous or clear-cut? Is the subject's task merely a perceptual one, or must he supply information or an opinion? Asch (1951) found that an ambiguous stimulus increases the likelihood that the individual will conform to the group. In his line comparison experiment, he found that the smaller the difference among the lengths of the lines being judged—that is, the closer the lines came to being the same size—the more likely was the individual to yield to group pressure and make incorrect choices.

In another study, Deutsch and Gerard (1955) found that the more a subject is obliged to rely on his memory when passing judgment, the more likely he is to conform to the group. These investigators designed an Asch-type experiment that consisted of two parts. In the first, the subject was presented with comparison lines and asked to make a judgment while the lines were still in view. In the second part, the experimenters showed the lines to the subject for a few seconds, removed them from view, then asked the subject for his opinion. Results showed that those subjects who had to rely on their memory tended to conform more than those who gave their responses while the stimulus was in front of them.

In one of the more important conformity experiments, Richard Crutchfield (1955) modified the Asch situation so that he could test five subjects simultaneously. Subjects were asked to give judgments on the lengths of lines, the areas of geometric figures, vocabulary items, the completion of number series, the opinions of other subjects, and one's own attitudes on certain issues. Crutchfield placed each of his five subjects (who were business and military men in executive positions) before an electrical console upon which the choices of all the subjects would be displayed. Each console was separated from the other by a partition, so the subjects could respond in private. The questions—all multiple choice—were projected on a screen at the front of the room, and each subject was to indicate his answer to each question by activating a switch on his console.

Each subject saw four lights go on, assumed he was looking at the choices of the others, and then made his own choice. In fact, the experimenter at a master panel rigged the lights in an approximation of the Asch study. As Crutchfield observes, "The entire situation is, in a word, contrived, and contrived so as to expose each individual to a standardized and prearranged series of group judgments. By this means, the simulated group judgments can be made to appear sensible and in agreement with the individual, or, at chosen critical points, in conflict with his judgments" (p. 192).

The results are revealing. In some cases the subjects took the typical Asch line comparison test. On this particular test, about 30 percent of the subjects bowed to group pressure and chose the incorrect lines. In another instance, the subjects were to indicate which of two figures (a star and a circle) was larger. Some 46 percent chose the incorrect figure. In the third series of tests, the subjects were to complete a numbers series; 30 percent conformed to group pressure by supplying incorrect answers. Finally, when asked to give an opinion on a statement such as "I believe we are made better by the trials and hardships of life," 31 percent went along with the majority in disagreeing with the statement. In all of these tests, the mean conformity score was 38 percent, very close to the conformity score in Asch's original experiment.

Anonymity. Crutchfield's device leads us into the next situational variable—whether a subject gives his judgment publicly, or privately and anonymously. Does a person conform to a greater extent if he must give his answer in front of the group? Does anonymity allay his fear of group retaliation for deviancy, and thus give him more independence? These questions were explored in an interesting study by Deutsch and Gerard (1955). These investigators administered Asch-like perception tests to subjects in both face-to-face and anonymous situations. In the latter, the subjects responded to stimuli from private booths. Results showed that those in the anonymous condition conformed less to group pressure than did those who gave their responses publicly: 25 percent of the responses made by those in private booths conformed to the group, compared to 30 percent for those in the face-to-face situation.

The idea that the pressure to conform to group standards is lessened in the anonymous situation raises another interesting question: Does the conforming subject really accept what the group believes, or is he merely going along with it in order to avoid being labeled a deviant? If, for example, he is merely complying to avoid retaliation, might he not follow his own judgment once group pressure is lifted?

A study to test this question was conducted by Herbert Menzel (1957). This investigator interviewed a number of physicians, asking them for their evaluations on the safety or usefulness of certain drugs that had been recently introduced. He found that many of the doctors favored using the drugs. Menzel then went to nearby pharmacies and examined the prescriptions written by the physicians for their patients. He learned that the physicians expressed attitudes publicly that were at variance with their private attitudes: although they expressed approval of certain of the drugs to the interviewer, they did not necessarily prescribe them for their patients.

Commitment. The above example prompts one to ask, what is the effect of the subject's commitment in the conformity situation? Will a person who is more committed to his position tend to conform less than one who is not? Asch found that individuals who are committed, that is, who start out by refusing to conform, continue to be independent throughout the procedure. "The most significant fact about them," Asch wrote in 1955, "was not absence of responsiveness but a capacity to recover from doubt and to reestablish their equilibrium." Thus, many of those who did not conform felt that they had to "call the play as they saw it."

Deutsch and Gerard (1955) tested commitment in an Asch-like experiment by placing individuals in four different conformity situations. In the first condition, there was no commitment at all: after viewing the comparison lines, the subjects did not announce their judgments until the majority had done so. Other individuals committed themselves privately—but minimally—by writing their answers on a "magic pad." (This is a children's toy that consists of a layer of graphite overlaid with a sheet of thin plastic. One writes on the plastic overlay with a sharp stylus, then erases the writing by lifting the overlay.) After writing their responses on the magic pad, the subjects listened as the others announced their answers. The subjects then publicly gave their responses, and erased the pad. In the third condition, the subjects wrote their answers on a piece of paper, but did not sign their names. Moreover, they had been informed beforehand that the papers would not be collected by the experimenter. In the final condition, the subjects wrote their responses on paper and signed their names, knowing that the responses would be collected. Thus, the experimenters were testing the degree of commitment. Commitment was nonexistent in the first condition, and increased in each successive situation.

Results showed that conformity to the group decreased as commitment increased. Nearly 25 percent of those who had made no commitment conformed to group pressure, whereas 16.3 percent of those who had used the magic pad (private but minimal commitment) conformed. The figures for the last two categories—those with the strongest degrees of commitment—are the same: only 5.7 percent of these individuals in both categories gave conforming responses. Thus, psychologists have shown, on the basis of evidence from these studies and others like them, that expressing one's opinion, either publicly or privately, induces an individual to stick to it.

Individual competence. Another important factor that can increase individual conformity to the group is the degree of competence or expertise in the subject. If an expert auto mechanic finds himself in disagreement with a group of automobile salesmen about some mechanical problem, for example, will he yield to the pressure by going against his own judgment and conforming to the group decision? Generally, individuals who feel they possess more expertise

ROACHES, TOO, GET AUDIENCE JITTERS

Performing before an audience can be a nerve-racking experience. Even seasoned professionals report having "butterflies" before they step on stage. At one time or another, all of us have felt uncomfortable while performing in public. On the other hand, it has been observed by both scientists and nonscientists that an audience often enhances a performance. Which is the case?

Recently, a trio of social psychologists investigated this phenomenon, using the lowly cockroach as a subject. In a series of experiments, Robert Zajonc, Alexander Heingartner, and Edward Herman (1969) showed that either outcome may result when an audience is present during an action. The determining variable turns out to be the familiarity of the action to the performer.

For the first set of experiments with the cockroaches, Zajonc and his colleagues constructed a straight runway bordered at one end by a floodlight and at the other end by a darkened safety area. Since cockroaches flee from light, the researchers wanted to observe how quickly the insects could reach safety. In the first condition, solitary cockroaches were placed on the straight runway, the floodlight was turned on, and the time it took the insects to find their way to safety was recorded. The researchers then repeated the experiment with the addition of "audience boxes" which housed the spectator cockroaches. When other roaches were present, the researchers discovered that in this first condition with the straight runway, the cockroaches found their way to safety more quickly. The explanation of the scientists for this phenomenon is that it is the instinct of cockroaches to run away from the light. The addition of spectator cockroaches aroused the subjects and elicited a dominant response—to run faster along a straight runway away from the light.

In the second set of experiments, solitary cockroaches were released into a course containing a maze with an L-shaped path to safety in order to offer a challenge and a complication to the cockroaches. They found that a cockroach traveling the course alone had no difficulty finding the darkened area. However, when spectator cockroaches were introduced, again the cockroach became aroused. But instead of being energized to increase his performance, the insect took longer to find his way to safety.

Why had the presence of other cockroaches aroused the subjects to improve their performance in the first set of experiments but retarded them in the second? Running in a straight line away from light is a dominant response for cockroaches, whereas running along an L-shaped course into a light to reach safety is a more complex task that requires learning.

The researchers offer the following explanation. In the straight-runway conditions, the appropriate response of the cockroach was elicited; the bright light "drove" the insect directly to the darkened place. This drive was energized by the social stimulation of the audience. In the second condition, the cockroaches had to face the light when they turned the corner to reach safety—an inappropriate response in which the insects had to learn to act contrary to their instincts. It is in this situation—a complex task that requires learning and concentration—that an audience causes performers to become distracted, jittery, nervous, and otherwise incapable of doing their best.

than others in a given situation tend to be more independent in their judgments.

Two studies in particular (Mausner, 1954; Snyder, Mischel, and Lott, 1960) have borne this out. Both of these studies have two parts. In the first part, the subject is given unique information, or somehow induced to perceive that he is more expert in some particular matter, than the other members of the group. In the second part, he is placed in the standard Asch-type situation in which the others disagree with him by giving incorrect replies to presented stimuli. The results of these studies confirm the observation of Jones and Gerard (1967) that the more competent the subject believes himself to be, the less he will conform to discrepant group pressure: "The greater the subject assumed ability relative to others, the greater his independence in the face of the discrepancy" (p. 401).

Characteristics of the individual

If both the group and the situation can influence conformity, it would seem logical to expect that certain individuals, by virtue of their psychological makeup, would be more prone to yield to group pressure than others. Although there is some evidence that individual personality is a factor in conformity, most psychologists feel that searching for personality characteristics that correlate with conformity is not very rewarding. As Hollander and Willis (1972, p. 444) point out:

It is increasingly clear that the search for sovereign attributes of a conforming personality has not been especially fruitful. True, for any particular situation individual differences are invariably observed, and these are often substantial, but it is also true that conformity in one situation is not generally a very reliable predictor of conformity in other situations.

Sometimes the absence of a relationship between two variables turns out to be informative. There are those who think, for example, that women are more suggestible than men, that young people, or for that matter, older people, are more easily influenced, or that whole groups of people, because of their racial, ethnic, or cultural characteristics, might be more prone to conformity. What does the evidence show?

Age differences. If conformity is learned, as some say it is, then it would seem that the tendency to conform to group pressure would increase as the individual grows older. Psychologists who hold this view point out that children of five or six years of age exhibit a great deal more independence than high school students who dress and behave like their peers. But other investigators say that independence increases with age: kindergarten children, for example, progress from a world in which all their ideas and values are taken from their caretakers to the world of adolescence which is characterized by revolt against the older generation. Later in life, independence is held up as a desirable goal and conformity is frowned upon.

Allen and Newtson (1972) studied the relationship between age and conformity and found no consistent pattern. These investigators selected a number of boys and girls who were attending the first to the tenth grades. The subjects were then given an Asch-type line comparison test. The investigators found that females tended to show more independence as they grew older, but the picture for boys was less clear. From first grade to ninth grade, boys showed a tendency toward independence. But from ninth to twelfth grades—the high school years—they tended to conform more. Thus, for the present we must say that there seems to be no evidence of a relationship between age and conformity.

Sexual differences.   The relationship between sexual differences and conformity shows no consistent pattern either. Do females always conform more than males? In the past, investigators believed this to be the case. They pointed out that women in our culture are encouraged to be docile and conforming, whereas men are encouraged to be aggressive and independent. In one study, Julian, Regula, and Hollander (1967) found that women conformed to group pressure in 28 percent of the trials, but men yielded only 15 percent of the time.

In recent years, however, investigators have begun to cast critical eyes on such findings. Sistrunk and McDavid (1971), for example, hypothesized that the type of materials used in testing sexual differences in conformity—that is, the content of the stimuli—might have something to do with past findings of a high rate of female conformity. These investigators examined the possibility that since males had devised and administered conformity tests in the past, male subjects might be more familiar with the items on the test than female subjects. In such cases, a male would be less likely to join the majority and agree to false statements. Sistrunk and McDavid predicted that statements that were neither meaningful nor interesting to women would lead women subjects to greater conformity than men, simply because of their unfamiliarity with the statements. Conversely, items that were more familiar and significant to women would produce greater independence in female subjects. This hypothesis should not be surprising: we have already seen how a subject's expertise with material significantly reduces his conformity.

The investigators devised a test which contained both male- and female-oriented material and asked a number of male and female subjects to pass judgment on them. The male-oriented material included items about politics, football, and automobiles, whereas the female-oriented materials contained items on child care, fashion, cooking, and the like. The test was then presented to 270 male and female high school and college students. Beside each item on the test, there appeared a number, purported to be the response of a majority of the subjects who had taken the test in the past. Conformity was determined by the degree to which the subject conformed with, or deviated from, the so-called majority response.

The results are revealing. They show that 34.15 percent of the males conformed on masculine-oriented items, whereas 43.05 percent of them conformed on feminine-oriented items. The males, in other words, tended to conform more on items with which they were unfamiliar, and to be more independent on items they presumably knew more about. The same was true for the females: nearly 43 percent of the women conformed on masculine items, compared to 34.55 percent for feminine items. On neutral items—that is, those that were not slanted toward either sex—conformity was about equal. Thus, the investigators conclude, there appears to be little or no difference in conformity between the sexes. On any given test, a person will show more independence on items about which he or she has a great knowledge.

Cultural differences.   A number of investigators have uncovered evidence indicating that the members of some nationalities tend to conform more than the members of others. Milgram (1961), for example, compared French and Norwegian university students by administering Crutchfield-type conformity tests. (This procedure, it will be remembered, asks the subjects to respond to a variety of stimuli, including perceptual, informational, and opinion-type stimuli.) Milgram found that the Norwegians appeared to be more conforming than the French. "No matter how the data are examined," he writes (1961, p. 50), "they point to a greater independence among the French than among the Norwegians." Investigators are not certain why this should be so. However, Milgram believes that part of the reason may be that French culture encourages independence and individuality, whereas Norwegian culture encourages allegiance to the group.

In a similar study by Frager (1970), American and Japanese students were compared for conformity. Frager found that the Japanese tended to be more independent than their American counterparts. He believes that contemporary Japanese youth tend to be nonconformists because they are rebelling against the westernization and modernization of their society, a process that has destroyed much of their cultural heritage. In another cross-cultural comparison, Bronfenbrenner (1970) found that Russian children are more apt to conform to social pressures than are American children.

How meaningful are these studies? Some psychologists believe that there are definite differences in conforming behavior among different nationalities.

Others, however, disagree and point to other explanations that may be just as valid in explaining relative cross-cultural conformity. Concerning Milgram's study, for example, Hollander and Willis (1972, p. 445) observe:

One very real possibility is that the French group was exhibiting substantially stronger anticonformity tendencies than the Norwegian group. If so, it could well be that the French subjects were at the same time *less conforming but more dependent*. While Norwegians felt less free to not conform, the French may have felt less free to conform. Or, if one may put it this way, the French may have been in some degree conforming to a norm of anticonformity.

Another interesting question that is raised by these studies of cultural differences is, is there a conforming personality? Do some people conform in every situation regardless of all the other variables? Most psychologists believe that such an entity does not exist. As Vernon Allen (1975, p. 3) states:

To conceptualize persons as being either conformers or independents (or nonconformers) is an egregious oversimplification that manifestly does violence to the available data. It is now abundantly clear that behavior under group pressure is the resultant of an interaction between dispositional and situational factors; a consistent personality syndrome characteristic of "conformers" and "nonconformers" has not been observed.

There are many students whose first reaction to conformity studies may be one of surprise, disbelief, or even indignation. How can a subject be so weak as to make a response she knows to be untrue? The lesson to be drawn from these conformity studies, however, is not to judge what seem to be the frailties of others, but to understand, especially since the findings have been replicated so many times, that out of one hundred responses, roughly one-third will conform to the majority opinion regardless of the known truth or falsity of the issue. That is the way people behave, at least at this time in history, in the Western world. The explanation for their behavior, or the light that such behavior throws on the human condition, is a matter for a social theorist or philosopher.

Summary

The behavior and attitudes of others influence virtually every aspect of our lives. One of the ways in which others can influence us is through social facilitation, in which the presence of other people affects an individual's performance of certain tasks. The reason for this, according to Zajonc, involves the fact that the presence of another person increases motivation. This, in turn, facilitates the performance of simple tasks but hinders the performance of more difficult tasks which involve learning.

Another way the group can influence individual behavior is through deindividuation, in which a group member loses his sense of individuality and becomes submerged in the group. Deindividuation often includes throwing off normal social restraints and engaging in extremely negative behavior, a phenomenon studied extensively by Zimbardo.

A related concept is collective behavior, group behavior which originates spontaneously, is unorganized, and is unpredictable. Theorists who have attempted to analyze collective behavior include Le Bon, who proposed that a crowd possesses a collective mind. Other theorists, such as Kurt and Gladys Lang, conceptualize five steps by which a collectivity is transformed into a crowd. Lastly, Turner and Killian postulate that crowds form when members perceive the emergence of some norm to guide their behavior.

Another interesting aspect of the influence of the group on the individual is conformity, by which a group member is induced to behave as other members behave, even though he perceives that their response to a stimulus is incorrect. The classic demonstration of conformity to group pressure was produced by Asch when he experimented with subjects' judgment of certain perceptual stimuli. In his research, Asch found that subjects rejected the evidence of their senses and yielded to group pressure 33 percent of the time. People conform because the group brings certain informational or normative pressures to bear on them.

There are many variables affecting conformity. Characteristics of the group itself influence conformity, as do characteristics of the situation and of the person who conforms. Among the group characteristics is that of group size—the minimum size necessary for conformity appears to be three individuals in addition to the subject. Other group characteristics include group unanimity (the less unanimous the group, the weaker its power to produce conformity); group cohesion (the stronger the cohesion, the higher its conformity pressure); and the status of the majority members (the higher their status, the more powerful will be group pressure to conform).

Among the situational factors that influence conformity is the nature of the stimulus. For example, the more ambiguous the stimulus, the more the individual tends to conform. Similarly, a person who responds in private and anonymously to the stimulus is less apt to yield to group pressure.

The variables of the individual include age, sex, and cultural differences. Although there is some evidence that individual psychological makeup is a variable in conformity, most investigators believe that the conforming personality as such does not exist.

Bibliography

ALLEN, V. L. Social support for nonconformity. In L. Berkowitz (Ed.), *Advances in experimental social psychology.* Vol. 8. New York: Academic Press, 1975.

ALLEN, V. L., AND LEVINE, J. M. Social support and conformity: The role of independent assessment of reality. *Journal of Experimental Social Psychology,* 1971, **7,** 48–58.

ALLEN, V. L., AND NEWTSON, D. Development of conformity and independence. *Journal of Personality and Social Psychology,* 1972, **22,** 18–30.

ALLPORT, F. H. The influence of the group upon association and thought. *Journal of Experimental Psychology,* 1920, **3,** 159–182.

ALLPORT, F. H. *Social psychology.* Boston: Houghton Mifflin, Riverside Editions, 1924.

ALTHER, L. *Kinflicks.* New York: Alfred A. Knopf, 1976.

ASCH, S. E. Effects of group pressure upon the modification and distortion of judgment. In H. Guetzkow (Ed.), *Groups, leadership, and men.* Pittsburgh: Carnegie, 1951.

ASCH, S. Opinions and social pressure. *Scientific American,* 1955, **93**(5), 31–35.

BANDURA, A. *Principles of behavior modification.* New York: Holt, Rinehart and Winston, 1969.

BLUMER, H. Collective behavior. (First published in 1939.) In A. M. Lee (Ed.), *New outline of the principles of sociology.* New York: Barnes and Noble, 1946.

BRONFENBRENNER, U. Reaction to social pressure from adults versus peers among Soviet day school and boarding school pupils in the perspective of an American sample. *Journal of Personality and Social Psychology,* 1970, **15,** 179–189.

CHAPLIN, J. P. *Rumor, fear and the madness of crowds.* New York: Ballantine Books, 1959.

CHEN, S. C. Social modification of the activity of ants in nest-building. *Physiological Zoology,* 1937, **10,** 420–436.

COTTRELL, N. B., RITTLE, R. H., AND WACK, D. L. Presence of an audience and list type (competitional or non-competitional) as joint determinants of performance in paired associates learning. *Journal of Personality,* 1967, **35,** 425–434.

COTTRELL, N. B., WACK, D. L., SEKERAK, G. J., AND RITTLE, R. H. Social facilitation of dominant responses by the presence of audience and the mere presence of others. *Journal of Personality and Social Psychology,* 1968, **9,** 245–250.

CRUTCHFIELD, R. A. Conformity and character. *American Psychologist,* 1955, **10,** 191–198.

DEFLEUR, M. L., D'ANTONIO, W. V., AND DEFLEUR, L. B. *Sociology: Man in society.* Glenview, Ill.: Scott, Foresman, 1971.

DEUTSCH, M., AND GERARD, H. B. A study of normative and informational social influences upon individual judgment. *Journal of Abnormal and Social Psychology,* 1955, **51,** 629–636.

FESTINGER, L., PEPITONE, A., AND NEWCOMB, T. Some consequences of de-individuation in a group. *Journal of Abnormal and Social Psychology,* 1952, **47,** 382–389.

FRAGER, R. Conformity and nonconformity in Japan. *Journal of Personality and Social Psychology,* 1970, **15,** 203–210.

FREEDMAN, J. L., AND DOOB, A. N. *Deviancy.* New York: Academic Press, 1968.

GERARD, H. B., WILHELMY, R. A., AND CONNOLLEY, E. S. Conformity and group size. *Journal of Personality and Social Psychology,* 1968, **8,** 79–82.

HOLLANDER, E. P., AND WILLIS, R. H. Some current issues in the psychology of conformity and nonconformity. In E. P. Hollander and R. G. Hunt (Eds.), *Classic contributions to social psychology.* New York: Oxford University Press, 1972.

HUSBAND, R. H. Analysis of methods in human maze-learning. *Journal of Genetic Psychology,* 1931, **39,** 258–277.

JONES, E. E., AND GERARD, H. R. *Foundations of social psychology.* New York: John Wiley and Sons, 1967.

JULIAN, J. W., REGULA, C. R., AND HOLLANDER, E. P. Effects of prior agreement from others on task confidence and conformity. Technical Report 9, ONR Contract 4679. Buffalo: State University of New York, 1967.

KERCKHOFF, A. C., AND BACK, K. W. *The June bug: A study of hysterical contagion.* New York: Appleton-Century-Crofts, 1968.

LANG, K., AND LANG, G. E. *Collective dynamics.* New York: Crowell, 1961.

LE BON, G. *The crowd.* London: Unwin, 1903.

LIEBLING, B. A., AND SHAVER, P. Evaluation, self-awareness, and task performance. *Journal of Experimental Social Psychology,* 1973, **9,** 297–306.

MARTENS, R. Palmar sweating and the presence of an audience. *Journal of Experimental Social Psychology,* 1969, **5,** 371–374.

MARTENS, R., AND LANDERS, D. M. Evaluation potential as a determinant of coaction effects. *Journal of Experimental Social Psychology,* 1972, **8,** 347–359.

MAUSNER, B. The effect of prior reinforcement on the interaction of observer pairs. *Journal of Abnormal and Social Psychology,* 1954, **49,** 65–68.

MENZEL, H. Public and private conformity under different conditions of acceptance in the group. *Journal of Abnormal and Social Psychology,* 1957, **55,** 398–401.

MILGRAM, S. Nationality and conformity. *Scientific American,* 1961, **205**(5), 45–51.

MILGRAM, S., AND TOCH, H. Collective behavior: Crowds and social movements. In G. Lindzey and E. Aronson (Eds.), *The handbook of social psychology.* Vol. 4. Reading, Mass.: Addison-Wesley, 1969.

MILLER, N. E., AND DOLLARD, J. *Social learning and imitation.* New Haven: Yale University Press, 1941.

NATIONAL ADVISORY COMMISSION ON CIVIL DISORDERS. *Report to the President.* New York: Bantam Books, 1968.

PESSIN, J. The comparative effects of social and mechanical stimulation in memorizing. *American Journal of Psychology,* 1933, **45,** 263–270.

SHERIF, M. A study of some social factors in perception. *Archives of Psychology, 1935,* **30**(187).

SISTRUNK, F., AND McDAVID, J. W. Sex variables in conforming behavior. *Journal of Personality and Social Psychology,* 1971, **17,** 200–207.

SNYDER, A., MISCHEL, W., AND LOTT, B. E. Value, information, and conformity behavior. *Journal of Personality,* 1960, **28,** 333–341.

TARDE, G. *The laws of imitation.* New York: Holt, 1903.

TORRANCE, E. P. Some consequences of power differences on decision-making in permanent and temporary three-man groups. In A. P. Hare, E. F. Borgatta, and R. F. Bales (Eds.), *Small groups: Studies in social interaction.* New York: Alfred A. Knopf, 1955.

TURNER, R. H. Collective behavior. In R. E. L. Faris (Ed.), *Handbook of modern sociology.* Chicago: Rand McNally, 1964.

TURNER, R. H., AND KILLIAN, L. M. *Collective behavior.* Englewood Cliffs, N.J.: Prentice-Hall, 1972.

ZAJONC, R. B. Social facilitation. *Science,* 1965, **149**(3681), 269–274.

ZAJONC, R. B., HEINGARTNER, A., AND HERMAN, E. M. Social enhancement and impairment of performance in the cockroach. *Journal of Personality and Social Psychology,* 1969, **13**(2), 83–92.

ZIMBARDO, P. The human choice: Individuation, reason, and order versus deindividuation, impulse, and chaos. In W. J. Arnold and D. Levine (Eds.), *Nebraska symposium on motivation, 1969.* Lincoln: University of Nebraska Press, 1970.

6

Deviance

Whores, freaks, muggers, imbeciles, thieves, junkies are all called hard names and all belong to the general class of deviants. There is only one other class of people: the normals. Some people may be found in between these two classes, but they are usually on their way out of one and into the other. Deviance is not so much what you do as something that is done to you. Included among the deviant are people with physical and mental disabilities, such as psychosis, blindness, or retardation, people who practice alternative lifestyles, particularly those that offend normal public opinion, and, of course, people found guilty of statutory crime. The modes of deviance are specific to the culture: what is deviant in one culture may be normal in another.

We must note, however, that studies of deviance, which engaged philosophers, social reformers, and penologists long before the social sciences became established, have not always taken the subject in just this light (Rothman, 1971). For example, much of the scientific work done on deviance in the early decades of this century assumed a different position—one that is now called the correctionalist perspective (Wheeler, 1966, 1967; Cohen, 1963,

201

1966). Only in recent years have investigators, influenced by Mead's theory of symbolic interaction (1934), begun to work from the currently prevalent view, known as the labeling perspective (Schur, 1971).

The Correctionalist Perspective

From the *correctionalist perspective*, deviance is thought of as behavior that violates the shared norms of a group. Thus the question for the investigator is: Why do some people violate these norms while others do not? In practice, of course, investigators concentrate on violators of the norms that are found in the form of legal statutes, not on those who outrage unwritten codes. Such other norm violators as people with physical or mental disabilities are assumed to be the proper subjects of other disciplines.

The correctionalists ask the question: Why do some people become deviants (law-breakers)? One answer given is that physical or constitutional factors predispose them to it (e.g., Hooten, 1939a, 1939b; Lombroso, 1918; Sheldon, Hartle, and McDermott, 1949). The deviant is born with instincts to behave in criminal or other antisocial ways. A possible example is the XYY chromosome in men, which has shown up with some frequency in violent criminals. In the general population the XYY chromosome is extremely rare.

Another answer is that deviant tendencies are the result of psychological processes (Bandura and Walters, 1959; Bowlby, 1946; Alexander and Staub, 1931; McCord and McCord, 1956, 1960; Redl and Wineman, 1957). People acquire the motivations to behave in deviant ways through early socialization resulting in fixations, ego and superego defects, or defense mechanisms, to mention only a few of what by now has become a very long list of reactions.

The biological answer and psychological answer both take the same approach. Some factor, whether biological or psychological, is hypothesized to be common among deviants of a particular type but rare among normals, or vice versa. Then a theory is propounded to explain why the presence or absence of this factor is related to the occurrence of deviant behavior. The aim of research is to determine the relative prevalence of the factor by comparing samples of deviants with comparable groups of normal subjects.

Other investigators—notably sociologists—have been inclined to locate the causes of deviance in social groups and social structures (Gibbs and Martin, 1964; Merton, 1968; Cohen, 1965; Cloward, 1959; Faris and Dunham, 1939; Sellin, 1938; Sutherland and Cressey, 1960). They show, for example, how society's opportunity structure generates a condition of anomie for those denied access to it. Cultural deprivation, rapid and uneven social change, and subcultural conflict have also been proposed as factors giving rise to deviance. Once again, the theory maintains that the condition in question affects different elements of the population differently, resulting in higher rates of deviant behavior in the affected groups than in others. The aim of research is to determine the rate of deviance within the affected groups and compare this with the rate for other similar groups in the population. Biological and psychological explanations are often wedded to these sociological theories to explain why only some but not all of the people belonging to the groups affected by the causal factor succumb to its adverse influence and become deviant.

Inadequacies of correctionalism

Before one can even ask how people become deviants one must know what the norms are, who the normals are, and who the deviants are. Investigators working from the correctionalist perspective simply assume they do know these things. Normal people are those who do not violate norms; deviants are those who do, and nothing more. How the normals react to the deviants has nothing to do with the initial identification because it obviously followed that identifi-

Five Modes of Individual Adaptation

Modes of Adaptation	Culture Goals	Institutionalized Means
I. Conformity	+	+
II. Innovation	+	−
III. Ritualism	−	+
IV. Retreatism	−	−
V. Rebellion	±	±

Figure 6–1. According to Robert Merton, an individual can adapt to his culture in any of the five ways shown here. The (+) signifies acceptance by the individual, the (−) indicates rejection, and the (±) signifies rejection of prevailing values and substitution of new ones. For example, individuals in the first category—the conformists—accept both cultural goals and the institutionalized means of reaching them. Merton sees modes II through V as deviant—a failure of the individual to accept both the cultural goals and the institutionalized means that prevail in a given group.

SOURCE: Adapted from Merton, R. K. *Social theory and social structure.* (Enlarged ed.) New York: Free Press, 1968. P. 194.

cation. "We are presented," Young observes (1974, p. 64), "with a 'taken-for-granted' world where social reaction against a particular individual or group is obvious . . . the workings of the state and its relationship to law and the judiciary are . . . left unexamined." That is, the treatment of deviants is thought to be no part of the problem of how people came to be deviants in the first place. From this perspective, however, it is difficult to explain the accounts of deviance offered by some deviants themselves:

> They don't become any less junkies, at all, for being in the place [USPHS hospital at Lexington, Kentucky]. . . . This identification of yourself as a junkie. After the first six, eight months that I was making it, I never said, "Well, I'm a junkie," as an excuse or anything. But now I say it constantly. I always refer to myself as a junkie, even when I'm not hooked or anything. And when you're introduced to somebody for the first time, the first thing you find out is whether he's a junkie or not (Hughes, 1971).

Another inadequacy of the correctionalist perspective stems from its assumption that the deviant individual is the pathological product of a failure of socialization. In a psychological theory, for example, deviance is viewed, to use Young's phrase (1974, p. 64), as "a formless face of the id bursting through a hernia in the superego." However, this way of explaining deviant behavior portrays it as somehow compelled and not the person's own choosing. It is described as being motivated by forces beyond the person's control, forces that propel him or her into pathological forms of behavior. Such explanations, Matza suggests, treat deviants like physical objects, not persons (1969).

All psychodynamic theories of deviance, and some biological ones as well, trace the roots of a person's motivation for deviant behavior to events occurring in the early months and years of life. (In fact, the causal factors in many biological theories predate the birth of the deviant individual.) The deviant disposition, once established, is ready to emerge full-blown as deviant behavior; situational factors do no more than trigger it. These theories obviously deny that the person's present circumstances have much effect on his or her deviant behavior—a denial that seems unrealistic, especially to the social psychologist, who makes present circumstances the main subject of his study.

The correctionalist perspective also has some noteworthy practical consequences. If, as the correctionalist assumes, situational factors arising in adult life serve only to release a preset deviant impulse, then the professional expert—the police officer, lawyer, judge, youth counselor, parole officer, social worker—can treat the problem only after it has appeared. To be sure, if the expert is incompetent or careless, she may aggravate the situation, but since the deviance precedes the intervention by the expert, her actions can obviously have nothing to do with the genesis of the deviant behavior.

It is becoming clear, however, to many observers that the expert helps to create and enforce the definitions of deviance. Lay people increasingly turn to experts to decide whether a given pattern of behavior is deviant or not, and their decisions have important consequences for the subsequent handling of the person whose behavior is in question.

Furthermore, if the deviant is loaded with irresistible forces, going through life like a bomb primed to explode, then the victim of a deviant act is never more than an innocent passerby, just the person who, as Young points out (1974, p. 66), "happens to be the first accidental social atom into which the deviant collides." Thus there is nothing rational in the deviant's choice of a mark, and no suggestion of conflict between the deviant and the victim is necessary to explain the deviant act.

From the correctionalist perspective, as we have noted, deviance arises from a personal quality that some people have and others do not, a quality that leads them to engage in behavior that violates the shared norms of a group. But years of study have not yielded any important evidence as to what, if anything, these qualities might be. "Investigators have studied the character of the deviant's background, the content of his dreams, the shape of his skull, the substance of his thoughts—yet none of this information has enabled us to draw a clear line between the kind of person who commits deviant acts and the kind of person who does not" (Erikson, 1966, p. 5).

The correctionalist perspective simply accepts as given the social norms that define deviance. Yet concepts of deviance vary from subculture to subculture within societies, and from one culture to another throughout the world (Scott, 1970). There are countries, for example, where one can drive one's car as fast as one pleases, and countries where speed is strictly limited; countries where it is prohibited to own a gun and countries where everyone has one. No one, as it happens, has succeeded in defining empirical properties which all deviant acts can be said to share—even with a given group. "Behavior which qualifies one man for prison may qualify another for sainthood, since the quality of the act itself depends so much on the circumstances under which it was performed and the temper of the audience which witnessed it" (Erikson, 1966, pp. 5–6).

The Labeling Perspective

One of the main features distinguishing the *labeling perspective* from the correctionalist is its recognition that "social groups create deviance by making the rules whose infractions constitute deviance, and by applying those rules to particular people and labeling them as outsiders" (Becker, 1963, p. 9). Deviance is no longer seen as a quality of an action or a feature of someone's behavior, but as a consequence of the application of rules and sanctions by other people. The deviant is merely a person to whom a label has been effectively applied. As Erikson puts it:

> The term "deviance" refers to conduct which the people of a group consider so dangerous or embarrassing or irritating that they bring special sanctions to bear against the person who exhibits it. Deviance is not a property inherent in any particular kind of behavior; it is a property conferred upon that behavior by the people who come into direct or indirect contact with it (Erikson, 1966, p. 6).

Whereas the correctionalists asked why some people are deviants, investigators who take the labeling approach ask how people confer the label of deviance on others. Thus the analysis shifts attention away from the recipient of the label and focuses instead on the process by which people decide that a certain pattern of behavior may or may not qualify for a label of deviance. Then, after this decision has been made, the investigator tries to analyze instances in which the labels have been applied.

Some consequences of the labeling perspective

One conclusion that has emerged from this effort is that, in many cases at least, labeling takes place through definite processes. As Back has noted, investigators do not claim that such processes always occur, or that they are of paramount importance, but only that they do happen (1975). Extensive studies of people on the way to becoming deviant will be necessary to determine the extent to which these processes operate in actual instances. We will discuss what has already been discovered about these processes in a later section of this chapter.

Another conclusion reached by investigators working from the labeling perspective is that deviant labels are conferred on persons for many different reasons. Some persons are labeled deviant for their beliefs, others for the manner in which they behave. Even a person's physical appearance may earn him a deviant label; and there are cases, such as illegitimacy, in which the label is conferred on children, not on account of their actions, ideas, or appearance, but only on account of the status into which they are born.

At the same time, deviant labels are conferred selectively. Knowing of one person who received a deviant label for a certain kind of behavior, a physical trait, or ascribed status does not enable us to conclude that all people performing the same act or having the same trait or status will also be labeled deviant. This point is illustrated by data from studies of mental illness (Scheff, 1966). One study of average people living in midtown Manhattan showed that 80 percent of those interviewed displayed at least one symptom of psychiatric illness. Nearly one-fourth of the respondents were judged to have impaired

WHO GETS LABELED?

Who gets arrested? And who is committed to mental institutions? There is an assumption casually made by most people that criminals are arrested and the insane are institutionalized. The labeling perspective challenges these assumptions. The following two studies illustrate an alternative viewpoint.

Irving Piliavin and Scott Briar (1964) studied "the conditions influencing, and consequences flowing from, police actions with juveniles" (p. 206). They found that various options were open to a policeman when he stopped a youth suspected of a crime or involved in a suspicious activity. He could release the boy, file a report, turn him over to a parent or guardian with an "official reprimand," summon him to juvenile court, or detain him in juvenile hall. The sociologists found that the course of action the police choose depends on the way they perceive a boy. If the boy is characterized by polite speech, neat clothing, and respect in addressing a police officer, the police act more leniently. On the other hand, uncooperative or hostile youths are labeled "toughs" or "punks" and are treated more harshly.

The sociologists also found that the police are more likely to stop youths who are black or who, because of their dress or actions, are perceived as criminally inclined. The single most important personal characteristic to the police who were observed in this study was the youth's demeanor: whether he was perceived as cooperative or uncooperative. Thus, the actions of a youth, criminal or otherwise, do not constitute the criterion for arrest, but rather his attitude. A boy who is properly polite, deferential, or perhaps even apologetic in the eyes of a policeman will probably be only reprimanded and released, whereas another boy, engaged in the same activity, who is fractious, obdurate, or who appears nonchalant is arrested.

Edwin Lemert (1967) makes a similar point concerning the so-called mentally ill: "It is the deviations of the psychotic person from customary role expectancies which increase his social visibility and put strains upon others that provide the impetus to insanity proceedings." Furthermore, the attitudes of the community toward mentally ill people, and even the community's relationship with the family of the disturbed person, will affect how a person is labeled.

Lemert cites the case of a retarded boy of a Polish family living in a town in the midwest where his family was never fully accepted. The boy was tolerated when he was younger, but when he reached maturity he became more willful. Egged on by a group of taunting boys, he threw stones through the window of an old man living alone. The boy was taken into custody and diagnosed as mildly schizophrenic. At about the same time, a woman with two daughters moved into the area and complained about this boy. The state, influenced by the fears of the woman and the community, institutionalized the boy. When the youth's father asked the governor to interfere, he, too, was considered demented. In this case, the community's distrust of the family and its dislike of the boy surfaced with the result that the youth was labeled mentally disturbed and locked away. Thus, according to the labeling perspective, it is not the actions of an individual which are the main criterion for his or her arrest or institutionalization, but the attitudes of those members of the community charged with maintaining social order.

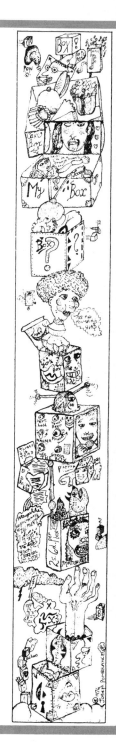

functioning because of mental illness (Srole et al., 1962). In another study, this one in a rural area, Leighton found that 57 percent of all respondents had some psychiatric disorder, and that nearly 20 percent of them could be classified as significantly impaired (1963). These data suggest that in any community there are many people whose behavior is quite bizarre—they hallucinate, have fits of rage, have visions, hear voices—and yet only a few of them are labeled mentally ill. Pasamanick's study in Baltimore provides further evidence of this (1961). He found that for every mental patient in a treatment facility there are nearly twenty mentally ill but untreated people in the community. Dividing his respondents into two groups, neurotics and psychotics, he found that one-half of the psychotics were not being treated. That is, Baltimore had as many untreated cases of psychosis as treated ones.

In view of these findings, the next questions for researchers are: How do some people escape being labeled as mentally ill or otherwise deviant? How do some people get the label? What is the meaning of the label to a person who is labeled? What is its meaning to a normal person?

Implications of the deviant label. When a person has been labeled deviant, other people usually draw inferences about him. Some, for example, may conclude that the person is morally inferior. As Goffman put it in his book *Stigma* (1963, p. 3), "he is reduced in our minds from a whole and usual person to a tainted, discounted one." The deviant or stigmatized person may not be considered altogether human; he may be held morally culpable for his situation or condition. The implications of such imputations are explained by Goffman (1963, p. 5) in the following way:

We exercise varieties of discrimination, through which we effectively, if often unthinkingly, reduce his life chances. We construct a stigma-theory, an ideology to explain his inferiority and account for the danger he represents, sometimes rationalizing an animosity based on other differences, such as those of social class. We tend to impute a wide range of imperfections on the basis of the original one, and at the same time to impute some desirable but undeserved attributes, often of a supernatural cast, such as a "sixth sense" or "understanding."

Deviant labels are *essentializing* labels: they make global statements about a person's entire character. To say that someone is mad or a criminal implies that he ought to be treated as if madness or criminality were his defining trait. The reasoning runs like this:

One will be identified as a deviant first, before other identifications are made. The question is raised: "What kind of person would break such an important rule?" and the answer is given: "One who is different from the rest of us, who cannot or will not act as a normal human being and therefore might break other important rules" (Becker, 1963, pp. 33–34).

People who have been labeled deviant are often regarded by others as dangerous—with justification, of course, in the case of murderers and violent mad people. But such fears are not always reserved for these cases. Most people stigmatized with the label of deviant are no more likely to harm anyone than a normal person, yet they are often treated as threatening, dangerous characters. Heretics whose ideas challenge our most basic values and ideas, freaks whose hair style, grooming, and manner of dress challenge conventional conceptions of propriety and respectability, and people with deformed bodies are all harmless, yet all bear the deviant label.

When someone is labeled deviant, he or she may be relegated to a *marginal status* in the group or community. As Erikson notes, the deviant is often demarcated from the rest of the community and moved to its *symbolic bound-*

CRIMINAL JUSTICE OFFICIALS' BELIEFS ABOUT THE RELATIONSHIP OF MARIHUANA USE TO AGGRESSIVE ACTS
(Figures in Percentages)

A. "Most aggressive acts or crimes of violence committed by persons who are known users of marihuana occur when the offender is under the influence of marihuana."

	Probably true	Probably not true	Not sure
Judges	17.3	44.2	29.5
Probation officers	14.5	60.0	21.8
Clinicians	6.1	76.5	13.0
Total	15.2	51.2	26.0

B. "When the offender is not under the influence of marihuana but is attempting to obtain marihuana or the money to buy it."

	Probably true	Probably not true	Not sure
Judges	35.6	30.6	25.0
Probation officers	27.3	44.5	21.8
Clinicians	20.0	60.9	15.7
Total	32.1	37.0	23.2

SOURCE: U.S. Commission on Marihuana and Drug Abuse. *Marihuana: A signal of misunderstanding.* The Technical Papers of the First Report of the National Commission on Marihuana and Drug Abuse. Vol. 1. Washington, D.C., March 1972. Page 434.

Figure 6–2. For many officials administering criminal justice, the label "marijuana user" becomes global. Marijuana users are seen as people who may be dangerous.

aries (1966, p. 11). He or she is often excluded from participating fully in a group's activities and denied freedoms that others have as a matter of right. He may be confined in an institution where he cannot engage in the everyday activities that normal people take for granted. The scope of this curtailment of freedoms and its consequences for the self-concept of the deviant individual have been described by Goffman in his essay on total institutions (1961). We should not suppose, by the way, that confinement in institutions and other forms of social isolation are limited to people who have violated statutes or behave in unpredictable or bizarre ways. Many people among the blind, the physically handicapped, the elderly, and the indigent are also subjected to social isolation, often in institutions (Scott, 1969; Barker et al., 1953).

The Labeling Process

How are labels of deviance conferred? From the correctionalist viewpoint, it seemed to be a simple matter of comparing the candidate's behavior with a norm; if the behavior deviated from the norm, the candidate was a deviant. We realize now, however, that it is not a simple matter at all. As noted before, labeling often takes place through a definite process. This process is one in which the meanings of the candidate's actions and personal characteristics are constructed through complicated negotiations between the candidate and those who respond to his actions and characteristics.

It is a complex process, filled with ambiguity. In a complicated, rapidly changing society such as ours, symbolic boundaries and shared definitions concerning reality are continuously shifting. Groups with quite different world-views and moral systems are frequently forced into contact with each other and come into conflict over their norms. As a result, much of the labeling that occurs, especially insofar as it involves heresy, arises out of the collective desire to clarify boundaries. Labeling is not the simple application of a well-ordered and unambiguous classification system.

Despite these complications and ambiguities, researchers have had some success in describing labeling processes. One of the most useful organizing principles for their descriptions has been Lemert's distinction between *primary* and *secondary deviance.*

Primary deviance, according to Lemert, can occur by means of a variety of social, cultural, psychological, or physiological factors, either by chance or because of a recurring set of circumstances. An individual may know that the act in question is recognized as socially undesirable and yet, in the case of primary deviance, there are only marginal implications for the person concerned. A young musician might sniff a little cocaine on a gig; a high school senior might "borrow" her friend's father's car for the evening; a young woman might accept money for sexual favors. The undesirable act might result in problems that are dealt with in an informal fashion without recourse to any of the social institutions set up to deal with deviance. "This is done either through normalization, in which the deviance is perceived as normal variation—a problem of everyday life—or through management and nominal controls which do not seriously impede basic accommodations people make to get along with each other" (Lemert, 1967, p. 40).

Secondary deviance includes the same types of attributes and actions—those associated with physical defects and incapacity, crime, drug addiction, and mental disorders—as primary deviance, but only when they belong to

a special class of socially defined responses which people make to problems created by the societal reactions to their deviance. These problems are essentially moral problems which revolve around stigmatization, punishment, signification, and social control. . . . They become central facts of existence for those experiencing them, altering psychic structure, producing specialized organizations of social roles and self-regarding attitudes. . . . The secondary deviant, as opposed to his actions, is a person whose life and identity are organized around the facts of deviance (Lemert, 1967, pp. 40–41).

Given this distinction, it obviously becomes important to ask under what circumstances individuals move from primary to secondary deviance. Scheff's study of mental illness provides one answer to this question: "The usual reaction to residual rule-breaking (that is, bizarre behavior) is denial, and in those cases most rule-breaking is transitory. . . . However, in a small proportion of cases the reaction goes the other way, exaggerating and at times distorting the extent and degree of the violation. . . . The societal reaction to rule-breaking is to seek out signs of abnormality in the deviant's history to show that he was always essentially a deviant" (1966, pp. 81–82).

Scheff concludes that "the labeling process is a crucial contingency in most careers of residual deviance" (1966, p. 83). In support of these assertions, he cites a study of combat neurosis by Glass (1953), who found that combat neuroses are often self-terminating if the soldier is kept with his unit and given only the most superficial medical attention. He also reports that the military experience with psychotherapy or neuropsychiatric casualties has been very disappointing. Apparently the soldier who has been removed from his unit to a hospital often goes on to become chronically impaired. Scheff interprets this study to mean that the soldier's deviance is made permanent by the labeling process that is implicit in his removal and hospitalization (1966).

Although most students of social deviance appreciate how important societal reactions are in the labeling process, there has been very little research on the subject. Little is known about why societal responses toward some deviations take the form of *denial* and *normalization* while in other cases deviations are recognized and responded to harshly. People's reactions toward anomalies in general, however, do seem to be influenced by the following factors:

First, people will probably be less tolerant of deviations that directly challenge core ideas and organizing principles of their world-view than of deviations that bear on more peripheral matters. For example, we may react strongly to people who hold extremely heretical ideas, but tend to be more tolerant of those whose behavior brings harm to people who have already been relegated to inferior statuses.

Second, the manner in which deviations occur also affects the reactions they evoke (Lemert, 1951). For example, prostitutes who charge high fees and live the kind of lifestyle that usually goes with a good income are seldom stigmatized, but those whose fees and income are low become the object of police roundups.

Third, the willingness of people to deny, ignore, or normalize deviations depends on how the deviation affects them personally. Many of us are prepared to overlook a colleague's drinking problem as long as she is sober on the job and does not cause us extra work. When her drinking begins to impair her usefulness as a co-worker, however, our willingness to overlook the problem is greatly reduced.

Fourth, societal reactions to deviance depend on the kind of anomaly that occurs. Certain forms of deviance are "normal" in the sense that they are familiar to nearly everyone. Crime, delinquency, alcoholism, and mental illness are traditional forms of deviance; we know what these problems are; society has evolved standard ways of responding to them. Other kinds of deviance, however, seem new at first. When confronted with them, we do not quite know how to respond. Men who wear their hair long are recent examples of such a deviation. When this style first appeared, it was greeted with a certain amount of amusement. After a few years, however, many seemed to become less willing to tolerate it. A general feeling began to arise among some segments of the society that "something ought to be done about these long-haired people." The problem was that it is not illegal for anyone to wear his hair long. The pressure to "do something" resulted in many phony raps, such as arrests and general police harassment based on the rigorous enforcement of technical local and city ordinances, health inspections, routine questioning, and frequent searches for drugs.

Who gets labeled?

Deviant labels are clear-cut sketches of social types, but the reality we impose them on is quite untidy. Many people who receive the label do not much resemble the sketch—no closer, at any rate, than many others who do not get the label. The studies of mental illness discussed earlier, for example, show that up to 80 percent of the people in any community have at least one major sympton of a mental disorder—yet few are labeled mentally ill. Kinsey's report on male sexual behavior estimates that nearly two-fifths of the white male population of the United States have had at least one overt homosexual experience to the point of orgasm (Kinsey et al., 1948) between adolescence and old age—yet few are labeled gay. Studies of crime show that a majority of people in our society have at one time or another engaged in some kind of illegal activity that could have earned them a heavy fine, a jail sentence, or both (Quinney, 1970, chap. 4), and research on blindness shows that there are only a small number of people in our society who are, in fact, blind, but large numbers whose vision is severely impaired but who nevertheless can see (Scott, 1969). There is presumptive evidence that some "hard-core" cases of deviance (people who are completely blind, professionally criminal, patently mad) escape any public signification, while many of the people who have been publicly identified as deviants resemble the ambiguous cases that have not (Scott, 1969, pp. 69–70; Pasamanick, 1961; Scheff, 1966, pp. 47–50; Quinney, 1970, pp. 151–172).

Being labeled for deviance is sometimes purely a matter of chance. This can happen, for example, as a result of community pressure on the police to demonstrate their effectiveness in dealing with crime. Many police departments provide themselves with a ready defense against sudden public outcries by routinely amassing evidence to show that they are dealing with various categories of crime (Matza, 1969, pp. 180–195). When the public becomes irate about muggings in the parks, the police can, with no extra effort, produce records showing the number of arrests for mugging in the past year. Of course, the police cannot arrest every mugger or realistically hope to prevent muggings altogether. Their goal must be the more modest one of creating the impression that they have the problem under control, which can be accomplished by apprehending and booking a certain number of people each month for this crime.

Some observers have suggested that labeling in the informal context of personal interactions is as much of a political process as the labeling that occurs in formal agencies of social control. For example, Thomas Szasz has suggested that current procedures for admitting persons to mental hospitals make it easy for acquaintances and relatives to get rid of a troublesome person simply by testifying that she is no longer in control of her actions. Szasz cites many cases in which the label of mental illness has been applied to people just because they have become troublesome (1961). Szasz's approach to informal interactions seems promising because it calls attention to the social and political contexts in which the meanings of primary deviance are constructed, thus avoiding the tendency to seek the source of deviance entirely in the individual. A character in Faulkner's *As I Lay Dying* (1946) put it this way:

> Sometimes I think it ain't none of us pure crazy and ain't none of us pure sane until the balance of us talks him that-a-way. It's like it ain't so much what a fellow does, but it's the way the majority of folks is looking at him when he does it.

A label's meaning to the normal

What do we know about the meaning of a deviant label to the normal person? First, the label is never conferred in generic form, simply as "deviant." Labels are always specific: "nut," "thief," "whore," "weirdo," "junkie." Investigators in social science may to some extent be able to examine deviance in general, but when labels are actually applied to people, they are clearly not equivalent or interchangeable. Different deviant labels apply to distinct different kinds of anomalies.

Second, we know that deviant labels are more than just names. They imply a great deal about the labeled person. Scheff (1966) has summarized studies dealing with the content of the label "madman," as revealed through the mass media and folklore of our culture:

> Persons who are mentally ill, even when they do not seem to be, are basically different. This is one theme, among others, which recurs in reference to mental illness in ordinary conversation. This theme, together with the "looks and acts different" theme, and the "incurable" theme, is probably part of a single larger pattern: These deviants, like other deviants, belong to a fundamentally different class of human beings, or perhaps even a different species (Scheff, 1966, p. 77).

Public stereotypes of the blind, according to Scott (1969),

> rest upon the implicit assumption that blind people possess personalities and psychologies that are different from those of ordinary people. It is supposed that the blind dwell in a world that is apart from and beyond the one ordinary men inhabit. This world, which is believed to be less gross and materialistic than our own, is said to be infused with a spirituality that gives its inhabitants a peculiar purity and innocence of mind. Those who live in the world of the blind are believed capable of experiencing unique inner feelings and rising to aesthetic heights that are beyond the abilities of all but the most unusual of sighted men. At the same time, this world is thought to be filled with melancholy; expressions of playfulness and humor are out of keeping. Such gloom is said to be cast upon the blind because of their need to settle some great inner conflict. The blind are assumed to be frustrated, cursing their darkness as they reflect back to the days when they could see. They are thought to be helpless, and their abilities are questioned at every turn. It is believed that there are few things a blind man can do for himself, and his mental void precludes any real intellectual development

and performance. Helplessness, dependency, melancholy, docility, gravity of inner thought, aestheticism—these are the things that common-sense views tell us to expect of the blind.

We can think of the stereotype as a putative identity that belongs to the person labeled deviant. If we examine stereotypes closely, we see that they comprise a kind of unwritten folk theory about the kind of person to whom they are applied: how he thinks, what his limitations are, how he is likely to behave, what he can and cannot do. Of course, all social labels, deviant and normal, impute an identity to the person to whom they are attached. Normal labels such as parent, lawyer, or army officer, however, seem to be less global than deviant ones. As noted earlier in this chapter, deviant labels tend to cover every aspect of the person's character. It is also quite possible that deviant labels distort reality more than normal ones do.

To what use do we put these putative identities? Perhaps the most important function they serve is to give us a blueprint of how we should behave when we interact with those we have labeled deviant; and it is in this way that the labels may become *self-fulfilling prophecies.* For example, when we label someone stupid we lower our expectations of the person's intellectual

These kids wear their label proudly.

capacities, perhaps allowing her no opportunity to learn the skills she would' need to repudiate our initial assumptions. Chevigny and Braverman have described a self-fulfilling prophecy that occurs with blind people. The assumption that a blind person is helpless leads sighted people to do everything for him, thus denying him all opportunity to learn how to function independently in everyday life (1950, chap. 1).

The putative identity that accompanies a deviant label is something the labeled person cannot ignore because other people will not let him. Scott recalls a blind man he interviewed. "He was a professor at a large city college; his work schedule required him to use public transportation frequently. He told me that when he traveled on buses or subways, people would sometimes drop coins in his lap or press money into his hand" (private correspondence). No matter what he does, the assumptions that lead people to such actions are things he simply cannot ignore; the identity is forced upon him by others.

Becoming a deviant:
The construction of a deviant identity

Under certain circumstances the putative identity accompanying a deviant label may become a personal identity for the labeled individual: the person may actually come to believe what other people are assuming about him or her. This is not hard to understand, since part of our self-image is based on our perception of the responses of others. "Each to each a looking glass is," and even our most private self-attitudes often reflect the attitudes of others. Deviance is not, therefore, something that a person *is,* but something he *becomes.* The role of nondeviants in the process is fundamental, for the process of becoming deviant resembles that of becoming a doctor: it is a career process in which some people drop out while others endure, in which personal identity is created and then changed as the person becomes involved in his career activities, and in which the granting of legitimacy to be a practitioner is primarily in the hands of other people. In short, deviance is a learned social role.

Primary deviance. David Matza's portrayal of this learning process starts with a subject who finds herself at what Matza calls the *invitational edge* of deviance (1969). Suppose the person has been offered a chance to take drugs, or finds herself in a situation in which she could engage in homosexual behavior. If she is willing to try, what exactly does that mean? Matza's interpretation is that she is prepared to experiment (1969, pp. 111–117). That is, in some hypothetical way she imagines herself personally engaging in the deviant behavior, as being the kind of a person who might do it.

In order for the process to go any further, the subject must make the transition from casual interest to actual practicing commitment. Matza emphasizes,

does and knows about drug users. Again the product of this process of reconsideration is action: either she goes on using drugs or she walks away from the situation.

Before examining secondary deviance let us pause to note three of Matza's key points. First, we must understand the process in light of the fact that the actor is a subject who constructs meanings himself, and in doing so is able to, and in fact does, exercise choice and will. The meanings he constructs are continually changing as he encounters new activities and events. Second, the development of a deviant identity is to be understood as a change in human consciousness. The end product is a subtle moving away from the person's prior reality to a different one in which experiences never previously known to him are now known firsthand, though his peers, parents, and friends may never have gone through them. Third, the process is a distinctly human one filled

PERCENT OF DRINKERS AMONG ADULTS* AND HEAVY DRINKERS AMONG ALL DRINKERS, BY OCCUPATION AND SEX**
U.S.A. 1964-1965

Men	Drinkers	Heavy Drinkers
Professionals	82%	18%
Businessmen	81%	30%
Semiprofessional, technical workers	76%	38%
Farm owners	60%	20%
Clerical workers	79%	30%
Sales persons	79%	27%
Craftsmen; foremen	77%	25%
Semi skilled workers	63%	36%
Service workers	86%	28%
Laborers	75%	27%

Women	Drinkers	Heavy Drinkers
Professionals	81%	6%
Businessmen	70%	9%
Semiprofessional, technical workers	80%	6%
Farm owners	26%	0%
Clerical workers	66%	8%
Sales persons	79%	1%
Craftsmen; foremen	56%	7%
Semi skilled workers	54%	11%
Service workers	48%	17%
Laborers	42%	9%

Percent 25 50 75 100

*Age 21 +   ** Occupation of Chief Family Breadwinner   ☐ Drinkers   ☐ Heavy Drinkers (of All Drinkers)

Figure 6–3. Drinking is not considered deviant by most Americans. Alcoholism is often regarded as an illness and alcoholics are seldom considered dangerous or different from anyone else. Yet from 10 to 20 million Americans are considered to have a "problem" with drinking.

SOURCE: U.S. Department of Health, Education, and Welfare. Health Services and Mental Health Administration/National Institute of Mental Health. National Institute on Alcohol Abuse and Alcoholism. *First special report to the U.S. Congress on alcohol and health.* Washington, D.C., December 1971. Page 28.

with the doubts, fears, and other feelings prominent in any human engagement. And finally, the process is an open one. It neither holds the person in its grasp nor unfolds without him. Throughout the formative process, the person may decide to continue the deviant activity or, after due consideration, discontinue it.

Secondary deviance. Secondary deviance begins when the person's participation in deviant activity has become a part of himself. The process of becoming a deviant continues in a direction influenced by the illegality or stigmatizing character of the deviant activity.

The term Matza uses to designate this influence on becoming a deviant is *signification.* The most potent and meaningful signification of deviance is "a specialized and protected function of the modern state. The main substance of that state function is the authorized ordaining of activities and persons as deviant, thus making them suitable objects for surveillance and control" (1969, p. 145). Signification poses a whole new set of problems for the person to consider as he proceeds through the open process of becoming a deviant.

Matza introduces this aspect of the deviant process with the seemingly obvious observation that most forms of deviant behavior are banned. But *ban* has a major consequence for the person who engages in deviant behavior. He is bedeviled by it.

Ban . . . virtually guarantees that further disaffiliation with convention will be a concomitant of affiliation with deviation; put slightly differently, that the scope or range of disaffiliation will . . . go beyond the amount implicit in the deviation itself. The logic of ban creates the strong possibility that the subject will become even more deviant in order to deviate. . . .

Ban hardly makes commitment to a deviant path inevitable; it only assures the compounding of deviation as long as the path is maintained. Such a consequence is neither surprising nor unintended. A main purpose of ban is to unify meaning and thus to minimize the possibility that, morally, the subject can have it both ways (1969, p. 148).

Perhaps the most elementary problem confronting the person is secrecy. There are several aspects to this problem, one of which is the person's sense of *transparency.* "Conscious of ban, and conscious that he has flaunted it, the subject becomes self-conscious," afraid that he can be seen through (Matza, 1969, pp. 150–151). The person who engages in deviant behavior must occasionally act as if he had done nothing out of the ordinary. This bedevils him because he must learn to cope with this problem of exposing himself through slips of the tongue and nonverbal gestures, or revealing to others that he possesses information he would not have if he were really innocent.

His fear of being transparent forces the person into a new perspective on ordinary conversations. When he finds himself in a conversation about the deviant activity, he must try to appear normal. As Matza suggests, one problem this raises is that he is something of an expert, and he may inadvertently "blow his cover" by succumbing to the desire to demonstrate superior knowledge. Moreover, the person must be alert throughout the conversation. He has to behave in a natural, casual way, reacting to things just as anybody else would. Thus he finds himself in the curious predicament of imitating himself as he thinks he ordinarily is. The person also tries to minimize the contribution he makes to the conversation, but in a way that will not arouse suspicion.

Matza suggests that in this state of mind the person will inevitably begin to hear himself and others in a somewhat altered way. Conversations take on ulterior meanings and the person acquires the rather peculiar perspective of the former insider who is now secretly an outsider who is trying to act as though he is still an insider. The person

has devoted psychic effort to keeping his secret. As a result, [he] has built the meaning of duplicity, enriched the meaning of being devious, temporarily established the feasibility of being opaque; finally, he has created some distance between himself and right-minded associates (Matza, 1969, p. 154).

The more serious consequences of illegal deviance are *intervention* and *correction.* The person now comes face to face with the duly appointed agents of

The drug subculture has become institutionalized. From the opium fields of Indochina and Turkey, the drug makes its way from connection to connection to the back alleys in America.

social control. He learns firsthand that there are people who make their living trying to prevent him from doing what he has been doing, people who make a career of stopping him, correcting him, rehabilitating him. They keep records on his life, develop theories about how he got to be that way. They can "summon or command his presence, move him against his will, set terms on which he may try to continue living in civil society" (Matza, 1969, p. 164).

And they seem to take what he did very seriously. He may see himself as a normal person who happens to have done something illegal, but they now call him a thief or a junkie. Thus, apprehension and the display of authority have the effect of leading him to wonder in his own mind if he is essentially what this one action signifies.

Matza concludes that the genuine confusion and ambiguities that arise throughout this process may finally be settled by one thing: Does he do the act again? If he does, it is subjectively interpreted as the outward expression of what the inner person really is. It is an action he creates, and on the face of it the essentializing process now becomes a part of him. If the person repeats the action again and again, he does so because he now regards himself as deviant, and so relates to the world in that fashion. The creation of a full-blown identity as deviant is now complete.

It is interesting to note the parallels between the phenomena of deviance and leadership. Early researchers investigating leadership, for example, believed that leaders were born. Later theorists held that individuals acquired leadership through social interaction. According to the labeling perspective, the act of being labeled a leader confers a quality of difference on the individual. In this sense a leader is perceived as deviant by others and, in turn, reacts to this new attitude toward himself. Harry Truman, Lyndon Johnson, and Gerald Ford are all examples of perfectly ordinary men who acquired charisma from the office. William Shakespeare, one of the most insightful students of human behavior, summed this up in his words from the play *Twelfth Night:* "Some men are born great, some achieve greatness, and some have greatness thrust upon them."

Deviant subcultures.   By choice as well as circumstance, doctors spend much of their time with other doctors, and mothers of young children with other mothers. Part of their sense of being a doctor or a mother is derived from their association with the group. The formation of a deviant identity may likewise be encouraged by membership in a deviant subculture, though not necessarily for every kind of deviance. Association with a deviant group is a practical necessity for some kinds of deviance, such as prostitution, gambling, confidence games, and political radicalism, whereas alcoholics, epileptics, and paupers can get drunk, have seizures, or be poor without the services of any specially organized group.

Whether a deviant has practical needs for specialized group participation is fairly easy to determine, but his expressive needs are a different matter. To say that the deviant needs subcultural definition seems most plausible, Lemert believes,

for certain kinds of criminals, such as con men, whose high degree of technical differentiation sets them apart from other criminals as well as from society. Prostitutes frequently experience conflicts about their identities, which appear to be most easily solved through relationships with pimps, or in some instances through homosexual relationships. Political radicals also seem to require association with like persons as audiences to validate the "ideological purity" important to differentiating or culturing their identities. However, at the other extreme are the mentally disordered who, outside of hospitals at least, tend to be threatened psychologically by the presence of others with a comparable stigma (1967, p. 47).

Criticisms of the labeling perspective

Although the labeling perspective has gained a following among American social scientists today as a way to approach problems of deviance and social control, it is not without its critics. Young (1974), Gibbs (1972), Gove (1970), and Back (1975) have all pointed out that the labeling perspective tends to deny

*The street peddler
pursues a deviant
business style. Some
of his merchandise has
"fallen off a truck";
some is honestly purchased.*

the importance of the deviant act, in some cases even to make it seem unreal. With mental patients, for example, the evidence does not support the contention that significant others are primarily responsible for labeling the behavior of their errant family members insane (Gove, 1970). There are problems, moreover, with the definition of deviance suggested by the labeling perspective. If an individual engages in behavior that violates the shared rules of a group and yet manages to conceal it, is he a deviant or not? (Gibbs, 1972, p. 42).

From the labeling perspective, deviants are often assumed to be open-minded, calm, rational individuals. Yet people often act irrationally. Young points out that people do in fact behave in ways that support the deterministic assumptions of the correctionalists and do opt for manifestly untenable solutions to their problems. There has also been a tendency to romanticize the deviant's lifestyle, thereby denying the possibility that he may be leading a way of life that is disorganized or pathological (Young, 1974, p. 73).

Another critic, Alvin Gouldner, contends that the labeling perspective consists of little more than an ideology about deviance that social scientists have devised to serve the interests of the ruling élite (1968).

Finally, there are those who complain that the labeling perspective, by its very nature, is inherently untestable and therefore of little value to the social scientist. However, the major advantage of this perspective is that in focusing on the interaction between society and those it labels deviant, it forces the student of behavior to consider the deviant as fully human, and like himself, responsible for his actions.

The Social Construction of Reality

We have seen how deviant labels are conferred on some individuals and how these labels become internalized as guides to behavior. But how did the labels get to be there in the first place?

Since deviance is a social label, the answer to this question may be found in the larger social order to which the label belongs. In their book *The Social Construction of Reality*, Berger and Luckmann (1966) offer a perspective of the social order derived from phenomenological philosophy that provides a basis for the explanation of the labeling perspective which follows. The *social order* is the all-embracing frame of reference in a society which its members know as reality. It is through this frame of reference that objects, persons, and events are identified, defined, arranged, and interpreted. We understand these meanings as "the way things are" (Berger and Luckmann, 1966).

Social institutions, taken as commonly accepted, established ways of doing things, arise from the human tendency to pattern. The child learns these patterns and experiences them as real. They confront her as things that are "out there"; she apprehends them as external and coercive because her efforts to modify them meet with the same resistance she encounters in dealing with the natural world. Thus, the institutional world is experienced as objective reality. It has a history that antedates the individual's birth and is not accessible to her biological recollection; it was there before she was born and will be there after her death.

Since she did not create it, however, its meaning must be interpreted to her in legitimizing formulas. If she asks why only the old men may perform the rain ceremony or only weapon makers may sleep with their maternal cousins, an elder will show her how the meanings of all the institutions in the society are integrated. "Reflective consciousness superimposes the quality of logic on the institutional order" (Berger and Luckmann, 1966, p. 64). It is also necessary for a society to develop mechanisms of social control to manage deviance from the institutionally programmed courses of action.

The social order

In some societies, including those in the Western tradition, all sectors of the social order are integrated into an all-encompassing moral framework called the *symbolic universe.* The symbolic universe confers a sense of rightness on the social order. We know the social order as a reality that is independent of ourselves and able to coerce us into acting and thinking in prescribed ways. But despite the sense of stability and certainty derived from this knowledge, it is still true that the social order imposes order on things that are by their own nature unstructured. "Order," writes Mary Douglas, "implies restriction: from all possible materials, a limited selection has been made and from all possible realities a limited set has been used" (Douglas, 1966, p. 94). The social order is an attempt to impose a sense of order on a reality that is chaotic. This basic chaos poses a grave threat to social order. Order connotes restriction, but disorder is virtually unlimited since its potential for patterning is infinite. As Berger and Luckmann put it:

All social reality is precarious. *All* societies are constructions in the face of chaos. The constant possibility of anomic terror is actualized whenever the legitimations that obscure the precariousness are threatened or collapse. The dread that accompanies the death of a king, especially if it occurs with sudden violence, expresses this terror. Over and beyond emotions of sympathy or pragmatic political concerns, the death of a king under such circumstances brings the terror of chaos to conscious proximity. The popular reaction to the assassination of President Kennedy is a potent illustration. It may readily be understood why such events have to be followed at once with the most solemn reaffirmations of the continuing reality of the sheltering symbols (Berger and Luckmann, 1966, pp. 103–104).

Among other things, the social order involves a system for classifying human existence. The viability of this system depends on its clarity; that is, people must conform in some reasonable degree to their categories. However, no classification system can allow for everything. There will always be some people who do not fit—not because of any fault of their own necessarily, but "because the act of classification involves imposing a sense of clear ordering on phenomena which by their nature are chaotic" (Douglas, 1966, p. 35).

A deviant, therefore, is an anomaly, a person who cannot be classified in the normal social order. Others detect in the person's behavior, appearance, or existence some significant transgression of the imposed boundaries of order in the symbolic universe. Once labeled a deviant, the person is more than just an offense against logic, however. Given the precariousness and sanctity of the system, the person is also in some sense an enemy of all others, a kind of sinner.

Probably the reason most people are so offended by graffiti is that it destroys their sense of the order of things.

The functions of deviance for society

According to some investigators, however, the deviant does indeed perform a valuable function for society (Durkheim, 1950; Dentler and Erikson, 1959; Coser, 1962). Kai Erikson argues that deviant behavior sharpens the symbolic boundary lines between the community and what lies beyond it. The function of deviance, he believes, is to keep these boundaries clearly demarcated, and to help to clarify them anew when they begin to be obscured. "Morality and immorality meet at the public scaffold, and it is during the meeting that the line between them is drawn" (1966, p. 12). He also contends that a community's symbolic boundaries can remain a meaningful point of reference for its members only as long as they are repeatedly tested by people on the fringes of the group and are repeatedly defended by those who represent the group's inner morality. For this reason he concludes that deviant behavior may be an important way of preserving group stability. Deviant forms of behaving, by marking the outer edges of group life, give the inner structure its special character and thus supply the framework within which the people of the group develop an orderly sense of their own cultural identity (Erikson, 1966, p. 13).

Controlling the deviant also provides visible evidence of the power and force of the social order against what Berger and Luckmann call the "night side" of human life, which lurks ominously "on the periphery of everyday consciousness."

Just because the "night side" has its own reality, often enough of a sinister kind, it is a constant threat to the taken-for-granted, matter-of-fact, "sane" reality of life in society. The thought keeps suggesting itself (the "insane" thought par excellence) that, perhaps, the bright reality of everyday life is but an illusion, to be swallowed up at any moment by the other, the "night-side" reality (Berger and Luckmann, 1966, p. 98).

To contain and control anomaly is, therefore, to master a very powerful force. It creates the illusion that the social order is awesome and potent.

Mechanisms of universe maintenance

No social order can survive unless its members develop mechanisms to deal with anomalies and to protect the symbolic universe against the surrounding chaos. One such mechanism is *misperception,* the tendency to misconstrue as normal and ordinary the phenomena that are in reality anomalous. Just because they are not perceived as anomalies, examples are difficult to find in everyday life. An example of how misperception operates under laboratory conditions has been provided in a study by Bruner and Postman on the perception of incongruity (1949). In this study, subjects were asked to identify after short exposure a series of playing cards. Most of the cards were normal, but some were anomalous. Kuhn has described the experiment and its results in these words:

After each exposure the subject was asked what he had seen, and the run was terminated by two successive correct identifications. Even on the shortest exposures many subjects identified most of the cards, and after a small increase all the subjects identified them all. For the normal cards these identifications were usually correct, but the anomalous cards were almost always identified, without apparent hesitation or puzzlement, as normal. The black four of hearts might, for example, be identified as the four of either spades or hearts. Without any awareness of trouble, it was immediately fitted to one of the conceptual categories prepared by prior experience (Kuhn, 1962, p. 63).

One of the findings of this study suggests that misperception will be effective as long as the anomalous event occurs only rarely. Kuhn goes on to say:

With a further increase of exposure to the anomalous cards, subjects did begin to hesitate and to display awareness of anomaly. Exposed, for example, to the red six of spades, some would say: "That's the six of spades, but there's something wrong with it—the black has a red border." Further increase of exposure resulted in still more hesitation and confusion until finally, and sometimes quite suddenly, most subjects would produce the correct identification without hesitation (1962, p. 63).

Another mechanism of universe maintenance is to *normalize* the anomalous event—to categorize it as something already known and understood within the existing system of meanings. An amusing example of this mechanism is provided by Tom Wolfe in his book about Ken Kesey and the Merry Pranksters. Wolfe describes Kesey and his group as they take a trip across America in a Day-Glo colored 1939 International Harvester school bus. The Pranksters had wired the bus for sound, with large speakers mounted on the roof and inside. He then describes a confrontation between the Pranksters, all of whom were on acid, and a cop who stopped the bus. He writes:

The cop yanked the bus over to the side and he starts going through a kind of traffic-safety inspection of the big gross bus. . . . Man, the license plate is on the wrong side, and there's no light over the license plate and this turn signal looks bad and how about the brakes, let's see that hand brake there. The cop is thoroughly befuddled now, angry, because Cassady's monologue had confused him [Cassady was the driver], for one thing, and what the hell are these . . . people doing. By this time everybody is off the bus rolling in the brown grass of the shoulder, laughing, giggling, yahooing, zonked to the skies on acid . . . and the cop, all he can see is a bunch of crazies in screaming orange and green costumes, masks, boys and girls, men and women, twelve or fourteen of them, laying in the grass and making hideously crazy sounds—Christ Almighty, why the hell does he have to contend with . . . so he wheels around and says, "What are you, uh—show people?" "That's right, officer," Kesey says, "we're show people. It's been a long

row to hoe, but that's the business." "Well," says the cop, "you fix up these things
and . . ." He starts backing off toward his car, cutting one last look at the crazies,
" . . . And watch it next time. . . ." And he guns off (Wolfe, 1968, pp. 70–71).

Third, a symbolic universe may be protected against the threat of deviance
through the mechanism of denial. People may persuade each other that something another person said or did in fact never happened. This mechanism is
probably effective only when the phenomenon in question is symbolic or behavioral and not physical.

No social order could survive if these were the only ways in which it could
protect itself against the threats posed by deviance. Each of these mechanisms
has major limitations. Misperception, denial, and normalization can have only
limited use in dealing with persistent phenomena such as madness, physical
impairment, homosexuality, or heresy. Sometimes, therefore, the society will
try to transform the anomalous event into a more normal one. An interesting
example of this mechanism is found in some research by Robert Edgerton on
hermaphroditism (Edgerton, 1964). In our society, one of the most rigidly defined boundary lines is the one differentiating men from women. Most of us
assume that this line is inherent in nature. The hermaphrodite or intersexed
person poses a special problem because "it" stands as glaring testimony to the
fact that the line between the sexes is not as inherently clear as we assume. We
regard intersexed people as freaks and insist that they assume either a male or a
female identity. As Edgerton says,

All concerned, from parents to physician, are enjoined to discover which of the
two natural sexes the intersexed person most appropriately is, and then to help
the ambiguous, incongruous and upsetting "it" to become at least a partially
acceptable "him" or "her" (Edgerton, 1964, p. 1290).

In this case the symbolic universe is preserved by surgically altering the anomaly so that it conforms to our cultural system for classifying the sexes. How we
respond to physical anomalies such as hermaphrodites depends, however, on
how the boundary lines are drawn in our culture. Edgerton shows, for example,
that the Navaho offer the hermaphrodite a high status in their community. An
intersexed person is believed to be a supernaturally designated custodian of
wealth, and the family that gives birth to such a child will have its future
wealth assured. Special care is taken of such children and they are accorded
unusual respect and reverence.

The same mechanism may also be employed when the deviance is behavioral. Then we call its application therapy. Commonly, therapy involves an
attempt by a professional to help the deviant gain greater insight into his
problems, either in order to prevent him from deviating too sharply from
normal patterns or to restore him to everyday life. As Berger and Luckmann

have suggested, therapy concerns itself with deviations from the commonly accepted definitions of reality. Therapy, they write,

must develop a conceptual machinery to account for such deviations and to maintain the realities thus challenged. This requires a body of knowledge that includes a theory of deviance, a diagnostic apparatus, and a conceptual system for the "cure of souls" (1966, p. 113).

Experience suggests that therapy may be successfully applied only in a limited number of cases. The various talk therapies seem to work for only certain types of people, and devices or surgical procedures to treat most cases of physical impairment have not yet been developed. It is, therefore, not possible to change each anomalous event to correspond more closely to the boundaries of the symbolic universe. Because a certain amount of anomaly is simply unchangeable, each social order must evolve ways of dealing with it. Berger and Luckmann suggest that this is accomplished by the mechanism of *nihilation*. "The conceptual operation here is rather simple. The threat to the social definitions of reality is neutralized by assigning an inferior ontological status, and thereby a not-to-be-taken-seriously cognitive status, to all definitions existing outside the symbolic universe" (Berger and Luckmann, 1966, pp. 114–115).

Almost always, the social order remains relatively intact in its contact with the deviant and it is the deviant who is changed. Occasionally, however, he may redefine the boundaries of the symbolic universe in a manner that renders him no longer anomalous. This relationship between deviance and social change has been widely discussed by sociologists, but it has not received the systematic attention it deserves. We need only look around us to see the crucial role that deviance plays in changing social order. The much-publicized counterculture of the 1960s, originally the exclusive domain of a small group of deviant students and intellectuals, has by now prompted the stable middle class to reexamine some of its most cherished values (Roszak, 1969). Similarly, opponents of the Vietnam war, who were initially but a small minority regarded as deviants and rebels by the majority, significantly altered that majority's opinion.

This analysis of the social order provides an explanation for deviant labels, why we confer them on people, and why they take the forms they do. It also explains why people may be labeled as deviant for reasons other than their behavior, and makes the imputation of moral inferiority that accompanies the label quite understandable. The reason that people who are labeled deviant may be thought dangerous and harmful also becomes apparent, for the deviant threatens the boundaries of our symbolic universe in ways far more serious than physical violence. Moreover, our discussion of the mechanisms of universe maintenance enables us to see why the deviant is relegated to a marginal status in the group and why things are done to him in order to get him to fit into our world.

230 Dealing with Deviance in Other Cultures

In our culture, whatever is done about deviance is done to the labeled individual, not to those doing the labeling. There seems to be implicit in this response an assumption that the causes of deviance reside with the labeled individual, and that a solution to the problems raised by deviance can be achieved by treating the deviator. But this approach is by no means universal. In certain African tribes, for example, the family is the basic focus of social control efforts, and in Polynesian cultures, the extended family and even the entire village become a focus of attention when people feel that something should be done about one member's deviant actions (Scott, 1976; Howard, 1970).

In our culture, again, people whom we label deviant often make us angry, and our anger can lead us to treat them in punitive ways. If it is a case of crime against property or persons, we may, of course, be justified in punishing deviants to the extent that they have harmed others, but the truth is that our anger is not reserved for murderers or thieves alone. The history of the treatment of people who are crippled, maimed, mentally ill, orphaned, or destitute is a story of sadism, brutality, and neglect.

These punitive tendencies are not universal. For example, among the Nuer in Africa and the Rotuma of Polynesia, primary emphasis is placed on maintaining harmonious social relationships with others. When an offense has been committed against someone, the offender may not be punished at all. Instead, he may be treated in ways that insure social harmony and allow the person to retain his normal status in the group (Scott, 1976; Howard, 1967).

Another striking feature of the actions taken against the deviant in our culture is that we spend much more effort drumming the person out of normal society than we do bringing him or her back into the fold. A provisional role, such as that of the student, for example, is terminated by a ceremony. In this way, an individual's movement out of the temporary role and back into the normal social routines is marked both for the person himself and the community to which he belongs. However, as Erikson (1966) has observed, the termination of the deviant role is seldom celebrated:

He is ushered into the deviant position by a decisive and often dramatic ceremony, yet is retired from it with scarcely a word of public notice. And as a result, the deviant often returns home with no proper license to resume a normal life in

PRISONERS AND GUARDS

Society traditionally has claimed that the "punishment should fit the crime," and that prisons are what they are—a collection of disorderly, hard-to-manage prisoners—because of the personalities of the inmates. Similarly, it has been assumed that if guards become heavy-handed or inhumane toward their charges, it is because the prisoners deserve that kind of treatment. Social psychologist Philip Zimbardo (1973) thought otherwise. He felt that the sociological roles of men in prison were a determining factor in inmate behavior. He simulated a prison environment and selected twenty-one male college student volunteers, who were randomly assigned to the roles of either prisoner or guard. None of the subjects had criminal records and all the subjects showed emotional stability.

The prisoners were required to wear uniforms with an identification number on the front and back. They were to stay in the "prison" for the duration of the experiment and were not allowed any personal belongings. The guards wore khaki-colored uniforms, reflecting sunglasses, and carried whistles and police night sticks.

Almost immediately, the experimenters were amazed at what they were recording by means of video tape and hidden microphones. Guards and prisoners were free to initiate any kind of interactions, but according to Zimbardo, "The nature of the encounters tended to be negative, hostile, affrontive, and dehumanizing." Prisoners immediately adopted very passive responses. The guards mainly issued commands, given in impersonal terms, which usually meant calling a prisoner by his number and often insulting him. They threatened the prisoners with physical violence (outlawed by the experiment) or swore at them.

Day by day, the guards began to escalate their harassment of the prisoners. The prisoners' response was to "behave less." According to Zimbardo, "The prisoners had begun to adopt and accept the guards' negative attitude toward them. . . . The typical prisoner syndrome was one of passivity, dependency, depression, helplessness, and self-deprecation." All of the prisoners felt that they were being subjected to unendurable stress. Indeed, after the sixth day, five of the ten prisoners asked to be dismissed from the experiment without pay because of extreme emotional upset—crying, anxiety, and psychosomatic rashes induced by stress. But the guards, who "enjoyed the extreme control and power which they exercised," did not want the experiment to end. Later, in a postexperimental session, one of the guards observed, "They [the prisoners] didn't see it as an experiment. It was real and they were fighting to keep their identity. But we were always there to show them who was boss."

Once placed in the role of guard, ordinary men were eager to "insult, threaten, humiliate, and dehumanize their peers," writes Zimbardo. He concluded that "Most dramatic and distressing to us was the observation of the ease with which sadistic behavior could be elicited in individuals who were not 'sadistic types,' and the frequency with which acute emotional breakdowns could occur in men selected precisely for their emotional stability" (Haney, Banks, and Zimbardo, 1973).

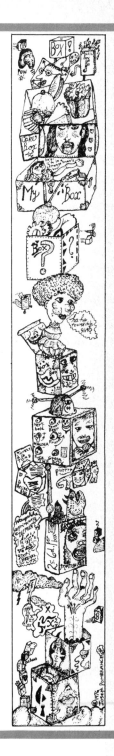

the community. Nothing has happened to cancel out the stigmas imposed upon him by earlier commitment ceremonies; nothing has happened to revoke the verdict or diagnosis pronounced upon him at that time. It should not be surprising, then, that the people of the community are apt to greet the returning deviant with a considerable degree of apprehension and distrust, for in a very real sense they are not at all sure who he is (Erikson, 1966, p. 16).

This point is supported by the observation of several students of social control agencies, that procedures for bringing individuals into these institutions are far more elaborate and codified than are the release procedures, and that many more people are employed to process the deviant into the agency than to bring him back out again (Scott, 1969, 1972).

Once again, this manner of treating the deviant is not universal. Because the maintenance of social harmony is a primary value in certain African tribes, a major effort is devoted to keeping the person in the group on terms that will minimize tensions among people. A case of murder in a small Nuer village provides an example (Scott, 1976). From the point of view of the villagers, the problem raised by this act was that the network of social relations between two families had been disturbed. The two families agreed upon a third party to adjudicate the case. The adjudicator's task was to reach a compromise that would reestablish and ideally even strengthen social relations between the families. After long deliberation, it was decided that the murderer's family would have to give a daughter in marriage to the other family. Because of the significance of marriage for family ties, this "penalty" had the effect of reinforcing the link between the two groups which had been ruptured by the murder. It was expected that the murderer would be rehabilitated by his own family, and only if that failed would some other, more formalized procedure then be used to deal with him.

The concern for harmony is reflected in the legal procedures followed in adjudicating such cases. Initially, blessings are pronounced in which all parties, including spectators, participate. The purpose of these blessings is to unite everyone in a common ceremony before the hearing begins. The words of the blessing emphasize the virtue of harmony and its importance for the well-being of the whole group. Litigants, spectators, and the adjudicator all sit mixed together, with none of the spatial separation that occurs in our courtrooms. Testimony and questioning are lively and uninhibited; anyone is free to participate. The mediator and the others present point out the faults committed by both parties, and after everyone has been heard, the mediator expresses the consensus of the group. The person held at fault formally apologizes to the others and as a gesture of sincerity, gives them a token gift. The wronged party then gives in return a smaller token gift in order to show good will and acceptance of the group decision.

Yet another feature of conferring a deviant label in our culture is that we often try to justify it by appealing to abstract principles or sets of rules that have presumably been violated by the deviator's actions, appearance, or beliefs. In the courtroom, for example, a judge applies a set of legal principles to the facts of the case so as to determine whether the person conforms to an abstract legal notion of what is criminal, insane, or heretical. We have on the books many crimes without victims, offenses that violate only abstract principles, not persons (Schur, 1965). Certain sexual practices, gambling, and using certain drugs are examples.

Among the Nuer, however, actions that violate abstract concepts of morality go unnoticed as long as they do not interfere with the network of social relations between families or with the fulfillment of needs considered essential to the society. Thus, nothing happens to the heretic. It is felt that the gods will deal with him; if they do nothing, it only proves that he was not a heretic in the first place.

The labeling perspective, a view that is ideologically in direct opposition to the prevalent correctionalist attitude toward the deviant, raises unsettling questions about people who have murdered, raped, or otherwise assaulted their fellow human beings. For those of us brought up to think according to the correctionalist perspective, it is very hard to neutralize the fear of falling victim to such a person if he is not dealt with by the existing institutions of criminal justice or by current medical practices.

It is for this purpose that a study of the manner in which deviance is handled in other societies becomes of interest. Since the methods of the correctionalists for dealing with deviants have not emptied the jails or the hospitals, perhaps there is something to be learned from alternative practices. This is not to say that such methods of dealing with deviance should be slavishly imitated, but that institutional arrangements of other societies very different from our own can serve to stimulate thought and discussion to the end of making our own institutions more workable both for the deviant and for the community.

Summary

According to the labeling perspective, deviance is not only what an individual does but something that is done to him. Deviant acts are culturally determined: a deviant act in one culture may not be so defined in another. The correctionalist perspective views deviance as behavior which violates shared norms, particularly legal norms. Correctionalists ask the question: in what way are law-breakers different from us? Explanations range from physical or constitutional factors to psychological and environmental factors. From the labeling perspective, the correctionalist view has a number of shortcomings. In the first place, correctionalists take norms for granted; they do not see them as problematic. Secondly, deviance is viewed as beyond the control of the individual, not something chosen or a part of a process. And finally, the professionals that society appoints to handle deviance, such as the police, the judges, the parole officers, are viewed as a part of the solution to deviance, not as a part of the problem.

The fundamental proposition of the labeling perspective is that social groups, by making rules, create deviance; the rules are applied to particular people who are then labeled as outsiders. The deviant is a person to whom a label has been effectively applied. The research question is, what is the process by which some people are able to label other people as deviant? After a person is labeled deviant, he becomes stigmatized and viewed as dangerous.

Lemert has distinguished between primary and secondary deviance, emphasizing process and the social psychology of the individual concerned. As society brands an individual as deviant, he comes to accept the label. To the nondeviant, the deviant are different from themselves in some basic way. Normals construct deviant stereotypes around such labels as the junkie, the prostitute, the madman, the criminal. A deviant may reinforce his deviant identity by membership in a deviant subculture. The labeling perspective has been criticized for denying the harm to others of antisocial behavior, for romanticizing deviance, and for being untestable by scientific method.

The philosophical basis for the labeling perspective lies in phenomenology. Berger and Luckmann say that we form our view of reality by means of the social order, the all-embracing frame of reference of the society to which we belong. The social order makes reality nonproblematic and offers explanations for the way things are. The symbolic universe is a term Berger and Luckmann use for the moral framework of the world as we experience it. It imposes a moral rightness on the social order. Any person or behavior that is perceived as inconsistent with the social order, then, becomes deviant. Deviance serves the function of marking the boundaries of permissible behavior as well as preserving group stability. The symbolic universe is maintained against anomalies by misperception, normalization, denial, transformation, and nihilation. Occasionally, however, the anomaly or deviance becomes the basis for a significant alteration of the social order.

In Western societies, by and large, the blame for deviance is placed on the labeled and not on the labeler. In certain smaller societies, social harmony is a more important consideration, and rather than cast out the deviant, the members seek to bring together the parties alienated by his behavior.

Bibliography

ALEXANDER, F., AND STAUB, H. *The criminal, the judge and the public.* New York: Macmillan, 1931.

BACK, K. Policy enthusiasm for untested theories and the role of quantitative evidence: Labeling and mental illness. In C. Schuessler and N. J. Demerath, III (Eds.), *Social policy and sociology.* New York: Academic Press, 1975.

BANDURA, A., AND WALTERS, R. *Adolescent aggression.* New York: Ronald Press, 1959.

BARKER, R. G., WRIGHT, B. A., MEYERSON, L., AND GONICK, M. R. *Adjustment to physical handicap and illness: A survey of the social psychology of physique and disability.* Revised Bulletin No. 55. New York: Social Science Research Council, 1953.

BECKER, H. S. *Outsiders.* New York: Free Press, 1963.

BERGER, P. L., AND LUCKMANN, T. *The social construction of reality.* Garden City, N.Y.: Doubleday, 1966.

BOWLBY, J. *Forty-five juvenile thieves.* London: Balliere, Tindall and Cox, 1946.

BRUNER, J. S., AND POSTMAN, L. On the perception of incongruity: A paradigm. *Journal of Personality,* 1949, **18,** 206–223.

CHEVIGNY, H., AND BRAVERMAN, S. *The adjustment of the blind.* New Haven, Conn.: Yale University Press, 1950.

CLOWARD, R. Illegitimate means, anomie and deviant behavior. *American Sociological Review,* 1959, **24,** 164–176.

COHEN, A. The study of social disorganization and deviant behavior. In R. K. Merton, L. Broom, and L. S. Cottrell, Jr. (Eds.), *Sociology today.* New York: Basic Books, 1963.

COHEN, A. The sociology of the deviant act: Anomie theory and beyond. *American Sociological Review,* 1965, **30**(1), 5–14.

COHEN, A. *Deviance and control.* Englewood Cliffs, N.J.: Prentice-Hall, 1966.

CONNOR, W. D. Deviance, control, and social policy in the U.S.S.R. Doctoral dissertation, Princeton University, 1969.

COSER, L. Some functions of deviant behavior and normative flexibility. *American Journal of Sociology,* September 1962, **67,** 172–181.

DENTLER, R., AND ERIKSON, K. T. The functions of deviance in groups. *Social Problems,* 1959, **7,** 98–107.

DOUGLAS, M. *Purity and danger.* New York: Praeger, 1966.

DURKHEIM, E. *The rules of sociological method.* New York: Free Press, 1950.

EDGERTON, R. B. Pokot intersexuality: An East African example of the resolution of sexual incongruity. *American Anthropologist,* 1964, **66,** 1288–1298.

ERIKSON, K. T. *Wayward puritans.* New York: John Wiley and Sons, 1966.

FARIS, R., AND DUNHAM, W. *Mental disorders in urban areas.* Chicago: University of Chicago Press, 1939.

Faulkner, W. *As I lay dying.* New York: Random House, 1946.

Gibbs, J. P. Issues in defining deviant behavior. In R. A. Scott and J. Douglas (Eds.), *Theoretical perspectives on deviance.* New York: Basic Books, 1972.

Gibbs, J. P., and Martin, W. *Status integration and suicide.* Eugene, Ore.: University of Oregon Press, 1964.

Glass, A. J. Psychotherapy in the combat zone. Symposium on Stress presented at the Army Medical Service Graduate School, Washington, D.C., 1953.

Goffman, E. *Asylums.* Chicago: Aldine, 1961.

Goffman, E. *Stigma.* Englewood Cliffs, N.J.: Prentice-Hall, 1963.

Gouldner, A. Sociologist as partisan. *American Sociologist,* 1968, **5,** 103–116.

Gove, W. Societal reaction as an explanation of mental illness: An evaluation. *American Sociological Review,* 1970, **35,** 873–884.

Haney, C., Banks, C., and Zimbardo, P. G. Interpersonal dynamics in a simulated prison. *International Journal of Crime and Penology,* 1973, **1,** 69–97.

Hooten, E. *The American criminal.* Cambridge, Mass.: Harvard University Press, 1939. (a)

Hooten, E. *Crime and man.* Cambridge, Mass.: Harvard University Press, 1939. (b)

Howard, A. Learning to be Rotuman: Enculturation in the South Pacific. New York: Teachers College Press, 1970.

Hughes, H. M. (Ed.) *The fantastic lodge: Autobiography of a girl drug addict.* New York: Fawcett World Library, 1971.

Kinsey, A. C., Pomeroy, W., and Martin, C. *Sexual behavior in the human male.* Philadelphia: Saunders, 1948.

Kuhn, T. S. *The structure of scientific revolution.* Chicago: University of Chicago Press, 1962.

Leighton, D. C., Harding, J. S., Macklin, D. B., Macmillan, A. M., and Leighton, A. H. *The character of danger.* New York: Basic Books, 1963.

Lemert, E. M. *Social pathology.* New York: McGraw-Hill, 1951.

Lemert, E. M. *Human deviance, social problems, and social control.* Englewood Cliffs, N.J.: Prentice-Hall, 1967.

Lombroso, C. *Crime: Its causes and remedies.* Boston: Little, Brown, 1918.

McCord, W., and McCord, J. *Psychopathy and delinquency.* New York: Grune and Stratton, 1956.

McCord, W., and McCord, J. *The origins of alcoholism.* Palo Alto, Calif.: Stanford University Press, 1960.

Matza, D. *Becoming deviant.* Englewood Cliffs, N.J.: Prentice-Hall, 1969.

Mead, G. H. *Mind, self, and society.* Chicago: University of Chicago Press, 1934.

Merton, R. K. *Social theory and social structure.* (Enlarged ed.) New York: Free Press, 1968.

Pasamanick, B. A survey of mental disorder in an urban population. IV. An approach to total prevalence rates. *Archives of General Psychiatry,* 1961, **5,** 151–155.

PILIAVIN, I., AND BRIAR, S. Police encounters with juveniles. *American Journal of Sociology,* September 1964, **70,** 206–214.

QUINNEY, R. *The problem of crime.* New York: Dodd, Mead, 1970.

REDL, F., AND WINEMAN, D. *The aggressive child.* New York: Free Press, 1957.

ROSZAK, T. *The making of a counter culture.* Garden City, N.Y.: Doubleday, 1969.

ROTHMAN, D. J. *Discovery of the asylum.* Boston: Little, Brown, 1971.

SCHEFF, T. J. *Being mentally ill: A sociological theory.* Chicago: Aldine, 1966.

SCHUR, E. *Crimes without victims.* Englewood Cliffs, N.J.: Prentice-Hall, 1965.

SCHUR, E. *Labeling deviant behavior.* New York: Harper and Row, 1971.

SCOTT, R. A. *The making of blind men.* New York: Russell Sage, 1969.

SCOTT, R. A. The construction of conceptions of stigma by professional experts. In J. D. Douglas (Ed.), *Deviance and respectability.* New York: Basic Books, 1970.

SCOTT, R. A. A framework for the analysis of deviance as a property of social order. In R. A. Scott and J. D. Douglas (Eds.), *Theoretical perspectives on deviance.* New York: Basic Books, 1972.

SCOTT, R. A. Deviance, sanctions, and social integration in small-scale societies. *Social Forces,* March 1976, **54,** 604–620.

SELLIN, T. *Culture conflict and crime.* New York: Social Science Research Council, 1938.

SHELDON, W., HARTLE, E., AND McDERMOTT, E. *Varieties of delinquent youth.* New York: Harper, 1949.

SROLE, L., LANGNER, T. S., MICHAEL, S. T., OPLER, M. K., AND RENNIE, T. A. C. *Mental health in the metropolis.* New York: McGraw-Hill, 1962.

SUTHERLAND, E., AND CRESSEY, D. *Principles of criminology.* Philadelphia: Lippincott, 1960.

SZASZ, T. S. *The myth of mental illness.* New York: Harper and Row, 1961.

U.S. COMMISSION ON MARIHUANA AND DRUG ABUSE. *Marihuana: A signal of misunderstanding.* The Technical Papers of the First Report of the National Commission on Marihuana and Drug Abuse. Vol. 1. Washington, D.C.: Government Printing Office, 1972.

U.S. DEPARTMENT OF HEALTH, EDUCATION, AND WELFARE. Health Services and Mental Health Administration/National Institute of Mental Health. National Institute on Alcohol Abuse and Alcoholism. *First special report to the U.S. Congress on alcohol and health.* Washington, D.C.: Government Printing Office, 1971.

WHEELER, S. Delinquency and crime. In H. S. Becker (Ed.), *Social problems.* New York: John Wiley and Sons, 1966.

WHEELER, S. Deviant behavior. In N. J. Smelser (Ed.), *Sociology.* New York: John Wiley and Sons, 1967.

WOLFE, T. *The electric kool-aid acid test.* New York: Farrar, Straus and Giroux, 1968.

YOUNG, J. Working-class criminology. In I. Taylor, P. Walton, and J. Young (Eds.), *Critical criminology.* New York: Harper and Row, 1974.

7

Attitudes

One hundred years ago, many white Americans were convinced that Indians were primitive savages, though some had never seen an Indian and most had never known one personally. Over the next seventy or so years, many of those convictions persisted. Anyone who doubts that need only to watch a western movie made in the 1930s or 1940s. According to the Hollywood of that time, Indians spoke in grunting monosyllables, were given to torturing and scalping whites, and engaged in unseemly rites on behalf of pagan spirits.

During the last few decades, however, perspectives have changed. We have become more aware of the historical wrongs done to American Indians because of racist beliefs in the superiority and manifest destiny of the white race. And some white people have begun to see the westward movement of the late nineteenth century as the invasion and destruction of an indigenous population. Yet, social stereotypes of the Indian have not disappeared; they have only been transformed. Today some people think that Indians are drunkards or unintelligent, or, from a more liberal perspective, some feel that all Indians are poor and that they have the same problems as poor black and Hispanic Americans. Most social scientists would agree that both hostile stereotypes and "friendly" generalizations are gross oversimplifications.

239

Why do people have erroneous attitudes toward American Indians? Why do others develop similar misconceptions about blacks, Jews, Orientals, or any other racial or ethnic group? Then again, why is it that some people have no apparent racial, ethnic, or sexual biases? How do attitudes about people develop? How can attitudes be measured and studied? How do they relate to behavior? What function or dysfunction do they serve for society and the individual?

The study of attitudes is one of the oldest and most significant areas of social psychological research. Two of the earliest researchers in the field, W. I. Thomas and Florian Znaniecki (1918), went so far as to say that "social psychology is precisely the science of attitudes." While there are not many people who would make that assertion today, there is no doubt of the continuing importance of the subject. William McGuire (1968) best summed up current thinking about the field: "This topic . . . seems of such intrinsic fascination that we expect [it] to attract a high level of research in the future as in the past."

Although people have attitudes about many things—drugs, ecology, political issues, censorship, sex—most of the literature and concern in this field relates to the attitudes people develop toward members of other racial and ethnic groups. What researchers have learned and may one day discover will, perhaps, help the diverse people of the world live together in some kind of harmony.

What Is an Attitude?

An *attitude* is a predisposition toward any person, idea, or object that contains cognitive, affective, and behavioral components. In other words, any one of our dispositions is an attitude if it contains, in some part, aspects of knowing, feeling, and acting. Zimbardo and Ebbesen (1970, p. 7) define each of the three components as follows:

The affective component consists of a person's evaluation of, liking of, or emotional response to, some object or person. The cognitive component has been conceptualized as a person's beliefs about, or factual knowledge of, the object or person. The behavioral component involves the person's overt behavior directed toward the object or person.

Consider an object—for example, a piece of legislation to outlaw school busing. A person will base his position on busing on some apparent or real facts (cognitive component). He may think that busing is the best way to achieve court-ordered integration. Also, he may have a positive feeling about integration (affective component). As a result, he writes, or at least is inclined to write, letters to his congressional representatives telling them to vote against the proposed bill (behavioral component). We would say, therefore, that his attitude toward the piece of legislation is negative. Let us now examine each of the three components of an attitude.

The cognitive component

The *cognitive component* refers to the way the object or person is perceived—it is the mental picture formed in the individual's head, and includes all the person's thoughts, beliefs, and knowledge about the object. In attitudes toward racial or ethnic groups, the cognitive component is frequently referred to as the *stereotype*. In our illustration above, although our subject might not support the piece of legislation on the issue of busing itself, dozens of his cognitions may enter the picture. For example, although the person may believe that the antibusing law is unconstitutional, a bad law, or possibly even a racist measure, he might also believe that busing causes deterioration of neighborhoods or raises taxes. Sometimes the issue might be further complicated by unpleasant associations. A person might favor busing, but on finding that his views coincide with those of people whose positions he generally finds distasteful, he might begin to find busing less desirable.

In addition, the relative importance of cognitions will vary. Perhaps, to con-

tinue our example, the person does not mind the increase in taxes if it will allow his children the opportunity of knowing children of other races. The importance of each cognition will be determined in large part by the affective or feeling component. Mildly negative feelings about higher taxes are overbalanced by stronger positive feelings toward the benefits of racially mixed classrooms. It would seem, then, that the person would act to defeat the antibusing bill and above all, would send his children to the school in question. Yet that is not necessarily true. A whole group of new cognitions may enter the picture. He might decide finally that a private school would insure a better education for his children after all.

Then there is the possibility that the issue will be further clouded by opposing attitudes held at the same time. This might sound impossible, but is actually quite common. One can be both for comprehensive busing *and* against it at the same time. A mother of an eight-year-old might cognitively give full support to the busing of school children to achieve racial integration, but might be reluctant to have her own little girl sit on a bus for an hour each day to get to a school on the other side of town.

In a more concrete example, S. R. Verba and his colleagues (1967) sampled public opinion about the Vietnam war when the war was at its peak. These investigators found that many of the people who were in favor of invading North Vietnam also tended to favor bringing all American troops home. Thus, the same individuals were for escalation and deescalation of the war at the same time.

Affect: The emotional component

From the foregoing discussion, it may seem that attitude study involves unraveling data and explanations potentially as slippery as a plate full of spaghetti. But to the contrary, studies have shown that most people do not go through an elaborate mental argument in forming attitudes. Attitudes are much simpler. After all, a predisposition implies an oversimplification, a generalization. It says that if something was true of a prior situation, it will be true again as long as there are similarities—sometimes only superficial similarities at that. Consider the way most people phrase an attitude. They are not likely to say, "After considering the pros and cons on the issue, I am of the attitude. . . ." More often, an attitude is expressed like this: "Busing is bad," "Men with long hair are immoral," "I like rock 'n' roll," and so on. These are sweeping generalizations—opinions that do not present complex arguments but do reflect strong emotion. It has been shown that when a person is thoroughly convinced by arguments, the affect of support will linger long after the reasons are forgotten.

That feelings tend to be more important than cognitions can be seen constantly in daily life. Two people can have similar information and yet come out as vociferous foes on a particular issue. Spokespersons for the atomic energy industry and conservationists opposed to the use of atomic energy, for example, both use the same facts in their arguments, but base their appeals on emotion. The former hold out the prospect of a nation without power, whereas the latter depict a devastating nuclear accident in the future. Other examples of this kind of appeal are numerous. It is commonly believed—not unjustifiably—that those who have an emotional stake in a social issue are likely to do more work for it than those who are convinced of its correctness but are unmoved by the issue.

Because attitudes are rooted in feelings, they tend to be enduring. We are inclined to hold on to our predispositions in the face of attack. Added information will scarcely make a dent in our attitudes. For example, an employer who believes that black workers are inefficient would probably consider a diligent and careful black person in his employ as an exception rather than change his attitude toward black workers.

Behavioral component

The *behavioral,* or *conative,* component of an attitude refers to the individual's actions toward an object or person. In our illustration of school busing, for example, the behavioral component would be the act of sending letters to the representatives in Congress, urging them to vote against the bill.

The behavioral component is influenced by the cognitive and affective components. A person who hates Jews will most likely discriminate against them whenever possible. He may refuse to shop in a store owned by a Jew, for example, or he may attempt to prevent Jews from moving into his neighborhood.

Facts, values, and opinions

In everyday situations, people tend to confuse attitudes with such related concepts as facts, values, and opinions. In what way do attitudes differ? Let us first consider facts. Although some facts may go into forming attitudes, facts contain no emotional component. If a fact is disproved, a person will readily concede the error. A person who asserts that the highest mountain in America is 14,000 feet high usually has no stake in that assertion and would be willing to change it upon learning of a 20,000-foot peak. However, facts can become distorted by, and associated with, attitudes. Such facts will be considered true even in the face of contrary evidence. A recent poll in West Germany on anti-Semitism, for example, revealed that many Germans thought there were over 200,000 Jews presently in that country. In fact, the number is little more than one-tenth of that.

Just as attitudes should not be confused with facts, so, too, they should not be mistaken for beliefs, values, or opinions. A *belief* attributes a cognition to an object; that is, when we say America is racist, we attribute racism to America. Similarly, the statement that elephants have good memories is a belief which attributes the property of good memories to the object, elephants. A belief is based more on fact or presumed fact and less on emotion than an attitude. However, several beliefs may be associated with one attitude.

A *value* is an underlying principle, usually a moral or ethical imperative. A value statement might be, "Racism is wrong." Values often underlie attitudes. For instance, the value that asserts a wrongness about racism will underlie attitude statements like "Integration is a good idea," "Busing will improve education," or "Black workers should be given equal access to jobs." While we have many attitudes and beliefs, we have only a few values. They are a basic framework on which our cognitions are based.

Finally, an *opinion* is defined by social psychologists as the verbal expression of an attitude, belief, or value. It is not the same as an attitude because in itself it does not necessarily contain an affective component, nor does it imply a tendency to action. One can state the opinion that writing to your congressman is a good idea, and yet only assert what is presumed to be a fact. If a person who did not agree could be shown that writing to a congressman is a good idea, that person might readily change his mind.

Prejudice, racism, sexism, and discrimination

Before examining the questions of how attitudes are measured and formed, we should examine four more terms that will appear frequently in this chapter. Prejudice, racism, and discrimination are often linked together in research as well as in common daily usage. They are, however, distinctly different concepts.

Prejudice is a negative attitude usually directed toward specific groups of people but not necessarily toward racial or ethnic groups. Richard Ashmore (1970, p. 253) more precisely defines prejudice as "a negative attitude toward a socially defined group and toward any person perceived to be a member of that group." Thus, a person may be prejudiced against black people, men with long hair, military officers, athletes, actors, women executives, or any other distinct group. Prejudice develops out of an inability to think of people as individuals. Instead, a person perceives a characteristic of one or more members of a group and generalizes that characteristic to all the members of the group. The attribute may be true to some extent, but usually is basically inaccurate. One common misconception of this nature is the idea that all Jews are wealthy and that they hold economic power in the world far out of proportion to their numbers. General Brown, the Army Chief of Staff, echoed this belief when he stated that Jews controlled the banks in America. However, almost a quarter of a million Jews in New York City alone live below the poverty line.

Racism is not just a prejudiced attitude directed toward racial groups. It goes beyond that. According to the U.S. Commission on Civil Rights, racism is "an attitude, action, or institutional structure which subordinates a person because of his or her color." Racism, then, not only involves an antagonism toward a racial group, but seeks to relegate that group to an inferior status as well. For example, the racist attitude that Indians are primitive becomes a reason for denying an Indian a job. It is possible that racial prejudice may not be racist. A comment such as "All black people like overly loud music" may indicate some prejudice, is undoubtedly false, and yet may not be racist.

Sexism is the same as racism except that the targets, rather than nonwhite people, are women. A company, for example, with no blacks, Hispanics, or women at the management level is open to the charges of both racism and sexism. In fact, racism and sexism are usually found together. Interestingly enough, this common phenomenon has favored black women and may explain the relatively large number of extraordinary black women in public life. The presence of one black woman occupying a conspicuous position automatically absolves a company or institution of both racism and sexism.

Prejudice and racism are primarily attitudes, whereas *discrimination* refers only to behavior. Acts that favor one person over another simply because of a group affiliation are discriminatory. Discrimination may go with prejudice and racism, but not always. A person may have prejudiced attitudes and yet not discriminate. A storekeeper, for example, may be prejudiced against blacks but hire them because his store is in a black neighborhood and black salespeople would be good for business. Conversely, a person might support discrimination, but not be prejudiced. Thus, a person may work for a company that practices discrimination, live in an apartment house that restricts its tenancy to specific groups, or belong to a social group that restricts membership to certain groups, even though the individual herself is not prejudiced.

The Measurement of Attitudes

The above example leads us to the next important question in our study of attitudes: Is there any way to pinpoint and measure an individual's attitudes? As the natural sciences have taught us, a discipline that can quantify and measure the phenomena it studies will progress much faster than one that cannot. Social psychologists have attempted in various ways to measure what people's attitudes are and how they are related to each other and to behavior.

Most of the techniques for measuring attitudes that have been developed since the first studies in the 1920s involve some form of self-reporting. People are asked to respond in a variety of ways to an attitude object. Some techniques reflect only a verbal statement of opinions. Others measure affect, and still others examine behavior. A few studies integrate two or three of these elements. Without any intention of being complete, here are five scales of measurement that have proven to be important in the study of attitudes.

The Thurstone scale

Louis Thurstone (1928) believed that attitudes could be measured by scaling people's opinions. He felt that in theory the best way to measure attitudes was to ask, for example, "Are you for or against black aspirations?" However, he realized that unless a respondent had a completely positive or negative attitude, she would want to add qualifiers. "Yes," she might say, "I'm in favor of black aspirations for equality. It's the only fair thing, but I don't want to be denied admission to law school to make a place for a black student whose record is not as good as mine." Of course, an interviewer might be present to probe more deeply, but the more an attitude is qualified, the more difficult it becomes to rate the answers on a scale. Therefore, Thurstone concluded that the best way to measure an attitude would be to take a group of simple, direct, and wide-ranging statements on an issue, ask subjects for a response to each, and sum up the results.

However, Thurstone's procedures for creating an appropriate list of statements were quite complex. His first step was to select and define as precisely as possible the attitude he wished to measure. He then formulated a large number (fifty or more) of simple, unambiguous statements about the attitude object. Thurstone suggested that there should be extensive editing of the original list to refine the statements. He offered five criteria for the editing process: (1) statements should be brief; (2) they should be stated so that they can be endorsed or rejected; (3) they should be relevant to the issue; (4) they should be unambiguous; (5) they should represent the entire range of possible opinions about the issue.

Thurstone's next step was to distribute the statements to a large number of judges (as many as 300) who would objectively and independently indicate whether they thought a statement represented a positive (favorable) or negative (unfavorable) attitude toward the object. (Each statement was typed on an index card.) After evaluating the statements, each judge then placed the card in one of eleven piles which represented a continuum, or scale. For example, if a judge thought a statement expressed a strong positive position toward the attitude object, he placed it on the first pile. In the second pile were placed the next strongest positive statements, and so on, up to the eleventh pile, on which were placed statements that expressed strong negative positions. In the sixth pile, which was just about in the center of the scale, were placed neutral statements—those that were neither favorable nor unfavorable.

Next, a scale value, showing the degree of favorableness or unfavorableness toward the object, was computed for each statement. This was done by taking an average—a mean score—of all the judgments for each item. For example, suppose that the investigator was trying to determine attitudes toward blacks and one statement read "Black families lower neighborhood property values." Suppose further that the distribution of scores about this statement looked like Figure 7-1:

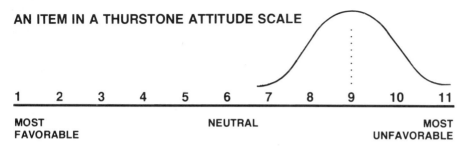

AN ITEM IN A THURSTONE ATTITUDE SCALE

| 1 | 2 | 3 | 4 | 5 | 6 | 7 | 8 | 9 | 10 | 11 |

MOST FAVORABLE   NEUTRAL   MOST UNFAVORABLE

Figure 7–1. A hypothetical scale value for evaluations of the statement, "Black families lower neighborhood property values." Its position on the attitude continuum would be 9. Such a scale value indicates that the majority of the judges felt that this statement expressed an attitude that is highly unfavorable toward blacks.

This scaling process was repeated for all the fifty or so original statements; those which were found to be ambiguous—that is, those which the judges could not agree on—were discarded. The researcher then selected about twenty or twenty-five of the unambiguous statements whose average scale values were distributed as evenly as possible over the eleven-point scale.

Thurstone's scale is probably the easiest scale from the subject's point of view, with clear and simple statements that require only a yes or no answer. Also, given the range of statements, a person should feel that his viewpoint has been adequately considered. As C. Selltiz and her colleagues (1959) point out, the Thurstone scale has been used effectively to measure attitudes toward a wide range of subjects, including war, capital punishment, various ethnic groups, and religious institutions. However, it does have its limitations. Among the most important of these is the question of the influence of the feelings and socioeconomic backgrounds of the judges in their scaling of the however, that willingness to engage in deviant behavior is one thing and ability to do it is quite another. Being willing means only that the subject may try it; she may change her mind when faced with the concrete situation of the deviant action. The important point is that the person has a choice and exercises it.

Let us suppose that the person chooses not to commit the deviant act. In this case, Matza argues, she will have discovered the self-truth that she is not willing after all. The true meaning of the preceding impulse is thereby revealed to the person in the course of her attempt to act on it. This does not mean that the issue is forever settled in her mind, only that she is unwilling at this time. She may reconsider the matter later.

What happens if the person does engage in the deviant behavior? Hurdling the invitational edge required an act of will. The person pondered both herself and the situation, and the product was an act of behavior. But hurdling the invitational edge does not automatically confer a deviant identity upon the individual. It only identifies her as a person who has tried something once. Whether or not she continues depends on a great deal more. For example, how compatible has the person found the deviant action to be with her sense of herself? If it is a matter of taking drugs, does she enjoy it or does she fear it? If she has stolen something, did it give her a thrill or just a hollow feeling, or perhaps make her feel guilty? By engaging in the deviant behavior, the person is now in a position to know these things concretely. When she was only willing to try the deviant act, she contemplated its suitability for herself in a hypothetical way, but now she has the full knowledge of commission and can judge more realistically the degree of compatibility between herself and the activity. She may decide to engage in the deviant activity further, or drop it.

As the person gains more and more experience with the activity, its meaning becomes enriched, thereby deepening the process of determining the *affinity* of the subject and the activity. Matza stresses the importance of learning the technique; that is, learning the actual things that one must do in order to engage in the deviant behavior (1969, p. 120). If you do not learn how to inhale marijuana, you cannot be turned on by it and can never, therefore, determine correctly how well attuned you are to it. Similarly, a person who wants to shoplift must learn the techniques of avoiding detection. Matza points out (1969, p. 121) that the significance of learning the technique is the meaning of affinity. "The *subject* engaged in a *project* is presented with a method by which the two may be related, and their fit actually considered."

The terms of the reconsideration broaden as the process continues. At first she thinks only in terms of how well attuned she is to the deviant activity, but as she decides to do it again and again she begins to reconsider all aspects of herself. She may have enjoyed using drugs a few times, but now she must consider the meaning of being a drug user in the light of everything else she items (Selltiz et al., 1959). Hovland and Sherif (1952), for example, found that in one Thurstone-type questionnaire which measured attitudes toward blacks, there were wide differences between the scale values assigned by pro-black judges who were both black and white and anti-black judges who were white. Moreover, the Thurstone scale is often inconclusive at the individual level, and it has the added drawback of being immensely difficult to construct. Many social psychologists, in fact, believe that it is unnecessarily difficult. As a result, there have been attempts over the years to simplify it.

The Likert scale

Rensis Likert developed a scale, a few years after Thurstone's, which was similar to his predecessor's in some respects. He, too, used a series of statements and measured attitudes on the basis of the average of the responses. However, there are a number of important differences between the Likert and Thurstone scales. In particular, Likert objected to the massive forces required to put a Thurstone scale together. "It does seem legitimate to inquire," he wrote, "whether it actually does its work better than simpler scales which may be employed" (1932). Moreover, unlike Thurstone, Likert did not attempt to use items that are evenly distributed over a continuum of favorableness–unfavorableness. Instead, he sought statements that were either favorable or unfavorable toward the attitude object. In short, his statements represented extreme views on an issue.

After formulating his statements, Likert distributed them to a small number of judges who had been selected randomly from the pool of subjects to be tested. The judges were instructed to indicate the degree to which they agreed or disagreed with each statement by checking one of the following options on a five-point scale: strongly agree, agree, undecided (neutral), disagree, strongly disagree. On a measure of attitudes toward blacks, for example, one item on the questionnaire might look like Figure 7–2:

I would never marry a black.

strongly agree	agree	neutral	disagree	strongly disagree
5	4	3	2	1

Figure 7–2. An item on a Likert-type attitude scale.

Thus, a score of 5 is given to the strong agreement response, whereas the strong disagreement response rates a score of 1. In this way, each statement is given a scale value of from 1 to 5.

Only those statements that produced the widest range of attitudes were used.

Likert sought to eliminate those statements which, though they might bear on the subject, might be too theoretical to reflect attitudes, or might be interpreted in more than one way. A statement like "Integration is historically inevitable" might at first glance seem like an appropriate, simple statement. But some who might agree with it might, nevertheless, still prefer segregation. Likert wanted statements that showed an internal consistency in the scaling of an attitude. He objected to tests that indicated erratic patterns.

The Likert scale is one of the most popular today because it is one of the easiest to construct. In fact, many researchers have simplified the process further. They merely take educated guesses about effective statements and eliminate judges entirely. It is a scale that almost anyone, from student to expert, can construct, provided they keep Likert's principles in mind.

The Bogardus scale

No matter how refined the statements are in either the Likert or Thurstone scale, there is still the likelihood that internal consistency will never be achieved. There will always be people who will answer a question for completely unpredictable, idiosyncratic reasons. One alternative is called a *unidimensional scale.* This device is designed to narrow an issue not simply to a single attitude, but to a single underlying dimension of that attitude. Such a scale was devised by Emory Bogardus in 1925. This technique, known as the *social distance scale*, quantitatively measures the degree of distance a person wishes to maintain in relationship to people of other groups. With the Bogardus scale, the subject is asked to check any or all of seven statements with respect to other ethnic groups, as in Figure 7-3.

According to my first feeling reactions, I would willingly admit black people (as a class, and not the best I have known, nor the worst members) to one or more of the following classifications:

_____	**close kinship by marriage**	1
_____	**membership in my club as personal friends**	2
_____	**neighbors on my street**	3
_____	**employment in my occupation**	4
_____	**citizenship in my country**	5
_____	**only as visitors to my country**	6
_____	**would exclude from my country**	7

Figure 7–3.
An example of
items in a Bogardus-type
social distance scale
to measure attitudes.

SOURCE: Adapted from Bogardus, E. S. Measuring social distances. In K. Thomas (Ed.), *Attitudes and behaviour: Selected readings.* Middlesex, England: Penguin Books, Ltd., 1971. Page 88.

The numbers at the right indicate the degree of social distance represented by each statement: the higher the number, the greater the social distance. Thus, a person willing to allow the closest relationship—kinship—is presumed to be the least prejudiced, while one who would deny admission of a group to his country is considered the most prejudiced.

Although there is undoubtedly some validity in Bogardus's technique, his results reveal that acceptance of a close relationship does not always mean acceptance of a more distant one. Also, there is no guarantee that expressions of social distance reflect how people will behave. Would 97 percent of the people questioned resign from a club if blacks were allowed to join?

The semantic-differential scale

The semantic-differential scale developed by Osgood, Suci, and Tannenbaum (1957) requires respondents to rate attitude objects on a very different basis than do the studies we have looked at thus far. Rather than ask for a variation of the positive/negative rating, the researchers asked subjects to rate objects along a scale of bipolar adjectives. These might include good/bad, active/passive, wise/foolish, etc. The scale is divided into eight parts, so that a 7 might mean that a respondent views blacks as more bad than good, whereas a score of 4 would indicate relative neutrality. An individual's attitude score is obtained by tallying all of his responses. Typically, the higher the score, the more positive is the subject's attitude toward the object, person, or issue in question.

Osgood, Suci, and Tannenbaum argued that this kind of measure is at least as valid as any other and that it would have the added interest of discriminating between those who base their attitudes on extreme emotional factors and those who are more thoughtful. The former, it was predicted, would advocate all-or-nothing positions. They would tend toward the simplest, most extreme evaluations, and their scores would fall on one side of the scale or the other. Sophisticated thinkers, on the other hand, would "show less tendency to polarize . . . and the use of factors other than the evaluative."

Later refinements developed three different categories of attitude dimensions. The category of feeling—i.e., good/bad—was called the *evaluative* dimension; that of strength—strong/weak—was referred to as the dimension of *potency*; and finally, adjectives such as fast/slow comprised terms of *activity*. In Figure 7–4, for example, subjects were asked to circle one number on each line in respect to an object of an attitude.

The semantic-differential scale has definite advantages. It is easy to construct. Almost any previous scale can be a model for any other regardless of the variable being studied, because the adjectives are independent of any variable.

Thus, it can be used to measure attitudes toward all manner of phenomena, from ethnic groups to political parties, to the desirability of having children.

The F-scale

The techniques of measurement discussed so far have, for all their differences, two things in common: First, they seek to measure attitudes on one issue and more often on only one component of that issue. Second, the questions or statements posed to the subjects are directly concerned with the object of the attitude (i.e., if the attitude is that toward race, the questions are about black people). Neither point sounds unreasonable. Why try to devise a test that will measure two or more variables at the same time? And, one might ask, what would be the point of measuring an attitude without ever stating the attitude object? How can a researcher determine how a person feels about an issue by asking about something else?

Nevertheless, T. W. Adorno, Else Frenkel-Brunswik, Donald J. Levinson, and R. Nevitt Sanford (1950) attempted to discover what they considered "anti-democratic" tendencies of individual personalities, as well as to measure anti-Semitism without specifically mentioning Jews or delving into any political or economic questions. These investigators felt that some people tend to minimize their prejudices when they are asked about them. Indeed, there are

Circle one number on each line in respect to your attitude toward Puerto Rican people in continental United States.

Evaluation scale

Good	7	6	5	4	3	2	1	Bad
Pretty	7	6	5	4	3	2	1	Ugly
Wise	7	6	5	4	3	2	1	Foolish

Potency scale

Large	7	6	5	4	3	2	1	Small
Strong	7	6	5	4	3	2	1	Weak
Heavy	7	6	5	4	3	2	1	Light

Activity scale

Fast	7	6	5	4	3	2	1	Slow
Active	7	6	5	4	3	2	1	Passive
Sharp	7	6	5	4	3	2	1	Dull

Figure 7–4. Items in a semantic-differential scale as developed by Osgood, Suci, and Tannenbaum.

SOURCE: Adapted from Osgood, C. E., Suci, G. J., and Tannenbaum, P. H. *The measurement of meaning.* Urbana, Ill.: University of Illinois Press, 1957.

people who might say, without lying consciously, that they would not object to Jews moving in next door. And yet, history has shown that the same people have supported political movements or candidates that advocated discrimination or outright genocide.

Adorno and his team proceeded to develop a test that would explore a range of variables that seemed related to an antidemocratic personality. The selection of the variables was made by a study of the writings of anti-Semitic agitators, by a study of theoretical works on fascism and anti-Semitism, and by assessing previous questionnaires. Out of the selection process, they chose a number of variables to test, such as conventionalism, superstition and stereotypy, power and "toughness," cynicism, and sex (especially an exaggerated concern with sexual "goings-on"). These variables were presented in a Likert-type test in a series of statements to be scored on a range of +3 to −3. In no case were Jews (or any other ethnic group) mentioned, or any political issues.

The results of the test were rated on what was called the F-scale—F standing for fascism. There were several versions of the test. In each case, those subjects who showed an antidemocratic personality—and thus were presumed susceptible to anti-Semitism—also proved to be prejudiced against Jews on more traditional attitude measures. The F-scale studies show that attitudes can be studied as a dimension of a larger concept—personality. A measurement of the concept predicts a score on the attitude, whereas the more traditional scales measure the attitude directly as an unrelated variable.

Limitations of self-reporting scales

As Cook and Selltiz (1964) point out, there are a number of difficulties with most self-reporting attitude-measurement scales. First, the implications of the questions are obvious to the subject. "Thus," say Cook and Selltiz, "a person who wishes to give a certain picture of himself—whether in order to impress the tester favorably, or to preserve his own self-image, or for some other reason—can rather easily do so." After all, no one likes to be thought of as a bigot or a racist, even though he may actually be one.

Recently, several techniques have been introduced to deal with this problem. The simplest and most frequently used is to assure the subject that he will remain completely anonymous, and to emphasize the fact that honest answers are necessary for the advancement of scientific knowledge. The researcher can also attempt to establish rapport with the subjects, informing them that he will not disapprove of their views, no matter how extreme they are.

Another limitation to self-reporting tests is the fact that certain individuals tend either to agree or disagree with most items regardless of content. Others are apt to give extreme (or moderate) answers, no matter what their position on the issue. Finally, despite any efforts on the part of the researchers, there is the possibility that responses do not correspond with the private beliefs or opinions of a subject. In such cases, factors other than those being tested may influence the individual's responses. For example, a subject who is not prejudiced against blacks may oppose laws making discrimination in the sale of housing to blacks illegal because he may feel that a property owner has the right to sell or not to sell his property to whomever he wishes.

Other attitude-measuring techniques

In addition to the above self-reporting techniques, there are a number of other, less frequently used techniques for measuring attitudes (Ashmore, 1970; Cook and Selltiz, 1964). The first of these techniques is the observation of overt behavior, in which actual behavior toward an object or person is observed and measured. As with self-reporting scales, the underlying assumption here is that there is a positive correlation between an act and the attitude which may underlie the act. If a subject is friendly toward Jews or blacks, for example, the researcher assumes that the subject has a favorable attitude toward these groups.

Albert Mehrabian (1967, 1968) decided to study the behavioral aspect of attitudes using some of the ideas from proxemics, or nonverbal communication. *Proxemics*, discussed in chapter 9, is concerned with "the degree of closeness, directness, or intimacy of the nonverbal interaction between two communicants." By measuring the distance, eye contact, and body tension involved when two people interact, Mehrabian believes he can gauge the subjects' attitudes toward one another. Negative attitudes, for example, may be associated with greater distance, less eye contact, and the tendency to lean back and away from another individual when interacting.

Another attitude-scaling technique is the measurement of physiological reactions, such as pupil dilation, heart rate, and the galvanic skin response (GSR). Of these, the GSR has been used most frequently, particularly in the study of prejudice. However, this technique, along with some of the other physiological techniques, is limited, in that it can detect only extreme responses. (See chapter 12 for a detailed description of GSR.)

Finally, two other attitude-measuring techniques available are the projective test and the measurement of performance on objective tasks. In a projective test, an individual is given a picture of a scene or a character which is deliberately ambiguous. The subject is asked to make up a story or complete some sentences about the people in the picture—for example, a group of children, both black and white, or a black girl and a white girl sitting at a table. Measuring the subject's performance on an objective test involves presenting him with specific tasks. The assumption behind such tests is that attitudes influence certain types of performance. For example, a subject may be asked to memorize material. Some of the material may be favorable to the attitude object, some of it may be unfavorable, and some of it may be neutral. Material with which the subject is comfortable—that is, which corresponds to his attitudes or beliefs—is more easily learned than material that he disagrees with. As Ashmore (1970, pp. 254–255) notes, both of these techniques are seldom used. The projective test techniques "are often unreliable, difficult to interpret, and expensive," whereas the objective tasks "are generally somewhat crude and imprecise."

Attitude Formation

How do we arrive at our attitudes? There are so many possible influences, so many ways in which we may be influenced. Although it is important, direct personal experience with the target of the attitude is not the explanation. Horowitz (1947) found that contact with "nice" blacks is not as important as contact with the prevailing attitudes toward them among others in the society. In truth, we have attitudes toward people we have never met and things we have never seen or heard or done. Can we know that a South Pacific island is a wonderful place to visit without having been there? Or can a voter know whether a candidate for office is honest or crazy, or just plain incompetent without prolonged personal contact? Yet, people develop attractions or repulsions to candidates, sometimes for no apparent reason.

The fact is that virtually anything and anyone can shape attitudes. In the case of the attitudes of whites toward American Indians, for example, some possible influences include the movies, old and new; books and reports on Indian life; history as taught in public school; protests by Indian groups which may reinforce existing attitudes, either pro or con; and personal knowledge. The cultural milieu—the shared values and beliefs that establish norms—also molds our attitudes. For example, one study by Pettigrew (1971) found that 75 percent of all Americans who are prejudiced against blacks hold such an attitude chiefly because of the influence of American culture, which, by and large, is racist.

Some people in our lives seem to be especially important in attitude formation. One's immediate family—parents, brothers, and sisters—appears to be foremost. A study by Jennings and Niemi (1968) showed that children of high school age tend to support the same political candidates as their parents. For some people, it lasts well beyond adolescence. There are many who will boast of being a sixth-generation Republican. Children also tend to form prejudices against blacks, Jews, and other ethnic groups under the influence of their parents. Thus, Epstein and Komorita (1966) found that both white and black elementary school children held the same prejudiced attitudes toward minority or ethnic groups as their parents.

As important as parents are in shaping the attitudes of their children, however, their influence should not be overemphasized. It seems that as a child grows older, the impact of parental influence begins to diminish. From late adolescence on, attitudes begin to change. Hess and Torney (1967), for example, found that whereas 80 percent of elementary school children shared their fathers' attitudes toward political parties, only about 55 percent of college students did. During the adolescent and postadolescent years, then, new groups of influences enter one's life. Three of the most important of these are the mass media, peers, and the milieu of such institutions as schools, churches, and work organizations. Since the mass media are also important factors in attitude change, their influence will be discussed in chapter 8.

Peers

In late adolescence, peers become the primary reference group, and the major influence on a person's attitudes. Studies of college students have shown that

Using projective techniques, subjects are asked to make up a story concerning these two girls.

friends/peers affect a wide range of attitudes, such as goals, political ideas, and racial and ethnic prejudices. A study by Margolis (1971), for example, showed that black university students who dated or formed close friendships with whites were most concerned with the opinions of their black peers about such relationships.

The classic study on peer influence was conducted from 1935 to 1939 by T. M. Newcomb (1943) with students at Bennington College. At that time, Bennington was the most expensive college in the United States. The students were almost entirely white and came from affluent, conservative families. On the other hand, the school was noted for its intellectual freedom and liberal atmosphere. Newcomb sought to discover how the young women were affected by this clash of conservative upbringing and liberal campus atmosphere. He studied the attitudes in all college classes over a period of four years and he found that most students became progressively more liberal. To give one example, more than 60 percent of the students' parents favored Alf Landon, the Republican candidate for president in the 1936 elections. Among the freshman class at Bennington that year, 62 percent endorsed their parents' choice. Among the sophomores, that figure had declined to 43 percent. The juniors and seniors, however, were overwhelmingly opposed to the Republican candidate. Only 15 percent endorsed him. Conversely, a mere 29 percent of the freshmen supported the Democrat Roosevelt, compared to 54 percent of the upper classes. Thirty percent of the juniors and seniors favored socialist or communist candidates—more than three times the percentage among the freshmen.

Most telling of the significance of peer influence was the fact that those women who became more liberal were the students most active in the college's social life. On the other hand, those who remained conservative tended to be isolated and aloof. Furthermore, the conservatives maintained strong family ties. Said one, "As soon as I felt really secure here, I decided not to let the college atmosphere affect me too much. Every time I've tried to rebel against my family I've found how terribly wrong I am, and I've very naturally kept to my parents' attitudes" (Newcomb, 1943, p. 124).

During the surge of college radicalism in the 1960s, many adults expressed the belief that student radical politics was a passing stage. When the "kids" grew older and had more responsibilities, they would "grow up" and adopt political views more in line with their own. But the Newcomb study seems to suggest otherwise. To determine how lasting the political liberalism of the Bennington students was, Newcomb (1967) did a follow-up study twenty-five years later. He found that political liberalism endured. For example, in the 1960 presidential election, 60 percent of the Bennington graduates preferred Kennedy. That figure was double the percentage of women from similar economic and social backgrounds nationwide. Likewise, conservatives at Bennington remained conservative and tended to vote for Nixon. Why should this be so? Newcomb pointed out that once the women had graduated, they sought situations that were consistent with the attitudes they had developed in college. Jobs, husbands, and social relationships were chosen at least in part according to college-formed attitudes.

The effect of peers on behavior is evident in another study by DeFleur and Westie (1958). In this experiment, subjects were asked to indicate if they were willing to pose for friendly pictures with people of a different race. They were also given the option of permitting the photos to be used in various situations, from laboratory work to a nationwide publicity campaign. After the students had made their decisions, the researchers asked whether any reference group influenced their choices—that is, whether they were acting with the approval or censure of any group in mind. Seventy-one percent said yes, they were concerned about their image with respect to one or more reference groups. Although sixty different groups were named, nearly all who named a group said that peers were a factor. On the other hand, for only a third was their family an important consideration. Thus, for a majority of the students, their decision was peer-directed.

Schools and other institutions

There is no doubt of the importance of peers in the formation of attitudes. But often, as in the case of the university, the institutional environment of the group is also significant. This is especially true of schools and universities. As Edgar Z. Friedenberg pointed out in his classic study *Coming of Age in America* (1963), schools try to promote social values and attitudes. It was his contention that that effort seemed to be more important in many schools than teaching students how to use their minds. One of his results suggested that all but a handful of students had views that coincided with the attitudes of teachers and administrators. Those attitudes were not necessarily voiced by people in positions of authority, but nearly all of them articulated the attitudes by example or by implication.

To understand institutional influences, let us consider the university. Besides peers, students come into contact with teachers and administrators who are often creative and intelligent, and usually respected for their knowledge and authority in certain fields. What they have to say and what they do will be regarded with more than passing interest. Newcomb acknowledged the part the Bennington faculty played in establishing the liberal ambiance at the school. In addition, a student at a university studies a wide range of material. For example, black and other minority studies programs can give whites a better understanding of minorities. This may account for the small degree of racial prejudice found on college campuses. It is not surprising to find that studies (for example, Caffrey, Anderson, and Garrison, 1969) have shown that even among southern schools, juniors and seniors are significantly less prejudiced than freshmen. Another study by Selznick and Steinberg (1969) found that the more educated an individual, the less likely he was to be anti-Semitic. These investigators have hypothesized that the reason behind this phenomenon may be the impact of college education on the individual's thinking processes.

However, the university does more than merely provide information. It also, and more importantly, teaches students to think for themselves. A student's prejudices are unlikely to last long when he or she begins to challenge prior assumptions and any tendency to oversimplification. In that kind of environment, easy generalizations are revised; simplistic ideas give way to more complex thought.

In addition to schools, almost any institution a person is connected with may be influential in forming attitudes. Peer pressure, the realities of the business and social world, and other factors, almost make an institutional perspective inevitable. Many of those involved in the Watergate scandal, to

The school bus —time-honored, unchanged in appearance for two generations, as familiar a sight as the schoolhouse itself— has become the target of racial controversy.

give one example, reported that from the perspective of the Nixon White House, they had come to see the administration/presidency/country as beset by enemies that included virtually every critic. Some of those who reported this experience were not entirely certain how that attitude could have become so thoroughly ingrained that they, law-and-order advocates, could repeatedly break the law without a question or a qualm. Yet there is every likelihood that had they not accepted those attitudes, they would have been isolated and perhaps dismissed from their jobs.

Other than institutions of employment, organized religions are probably the institutions with the greatest number of members. Since the churches preach certain moral values, is it reasonable to assume that church members are free of ethnic and racial prejudices? Studies have indicated that the significant variable is not whether a person goes to church, but why he goes. Those people who go to church for social rather than religious reasons, and who attend church only a few times a month, tend to be more prejudiced than those who never go at all. On the other hand, people who truly may be said to be religious—those who attend church at least eleven times a month—are found to be least prejudiced (Struening, 1963). The influence of a church, says Struening, is related to the function it plays. If it is a basic part of a person's life, he or she will adopt its principles; if it is a status symbol, its precepts are not important. This can probably be applied to many other institutions. People who are in a group only for what they can get out of it are likely to develop different attitudes than those who join with the hope of learning, doing, or otherwise contributing to what they consider an important enterprise.

Attitudes and Behavior

Although all people have formed attitudes, few find an opportunity to act in any methodical fashion in accordance with their attitudes. The police officer who hates blacks in general may find himself offering advice to a young black boy at the station house who is in trouble with the law. A college woman from an anti-Semitic family who never knew any Jews may find herself in love with a Jewish classmate. What does the research tell us about the extent to which people behave in accordance with their attitudes?

The LaPiere study

DeFleur and Westie (1958) named the readiness to translate attitudes into overt action *salience*. At first consideration, one might expect the level of salience to be high. We expect someone who is anti-black to move out of a neighborhood if there is an influx of black people (assuming he can afford to move), to leave an organization that permits black membership, or to vote for a racist candidate. However, none of this is necessarily true. People who verbally attack black people in private conversations might not discriminate against them. On the other hand, some who decry racism may be the first to move out of the neighborhood when a black family moves in next door.

To test these propositions, Richard LaPiere, in a famous 1934 study, traveled all over the United States with a Chinese student and his wife. They traveled over 10,000 miles together, staying in 66 hotels or other sleeping accommodations, and were served in 184 restaurants. During that time, there was only one refusal of service, and that was at a second-class California auto camp (a motel), where the proprietor flatly stated, "I don't take Japs." Yet in much better establishments, LaPiere and the couple were treated well, if not graciously. The Chinese couple also visited a few hotels and restaurants alone. In no case were they refused service, and on the whole, were treated as well as when they were in LaPiere's Company.

Six months later, LaPiere sent a questionnaire to all the places that he and the couple had visited. The essential question was, "Will you accept members of the Chinese race as guests in your establishment?" Of the 81 restaurants that replied, 75 said they would *not* accept Chinese customers, while the remaining 6 said that it depended on circumstances. Out of 47 hotels, 43 said no, 3 mentioned circumstances, and a single one said yes. It should be noted that in the 1930s such discrimination would not have been illegal and was, in fact, fairly common. In spite of that, the couple suffered little of it. The results seemed unmistakable: there was almost no correlation between behavior and attitudes.

LaPiere, for one, was convinced of it. He concluded his article by saying that he saw no reason why researchers should spend so much time on pencil-and-paper attitude studies. "It would seem far more worthwhile," he stated, "to make a shrewd guess regarding that which is essential than to accurately measure that which is likely to prove quite irrelevant."

However, there was immediate criticism. A few suggested that some of the establishments may not have known that the couple were Chinese. The couple spoke unaccented English which LaPiere himself said reduced tense situations. Other critics of the study pointed to the fact that the couple were usually in the company of a white man. In addition, they tended to look well-groomed, respectable, westernized, and especially genial. (LaPiere wrote, "My Chinese friends were skillful smilers, which may account, in part, for the fact that we received but one rebuff in all our experience.") At the time, Orientals were subjects of crude stereotypes that may have led some proprietors to believe that Orientals were typically barefooted, straw-hatted peasants. The sight of middle-class people may well have been disorienting. Prejudice, after all, is oversimplification, based on generalized information. When the suppositions are undercut by obvious facts, the nature of the object may be denied. Finally, it was pointed out that LaPiere dealt with clerks and not top management. Those at the bottom may not have been told to refuse service to Orientals—especially in remote areas where Orientals seldom, if ever, appeared.

The criticism of LaPiere's study can be summarized simply: the results were due to special circumstances. Yet the same criticism might be applied to all attitude research. A person may respond to a question about blacks in different ways depending on who is asking the question. How one feels on a given day might alter the response; if your car was demolished just before you took an attitude test, you might be more hostile and aggressive than on another day. Another point in LaPiere's favor is that several other studies have supported his conclusion that there are great inconsistencies between attitudes and behavior. In an important article which summarizes studies of the relationship between attitudes and behavior, Wicker (1969, p. 161) wrote: "These studies suggest that it is considerably more likely that attitudes will be unrelated, or only slightly related, to overt behavior than that attitudes will be closely related to actions."

Attitudes and multiple acts.   With this in mind, Fishbein and Ajzen (1974) decided to test a different type of hypothesis. The LaPiere study and most other attitude/behavior research tested one act in relation to an attitude. But what about multiple acts? Was inconsistency still the rule? Or might people be inconsistent on occasion while generally acting in accord with their attitudes? The two researchers chose to do a series of tests relating religious attitudes with behavior. First, sixty-two undergraduate students (male and female) were asked to fill out self-reports of religious behavior. Questions included, "Do you pray before or after meals," "Do you donate money to religious institutions," and so on. Next, the subjects were asked about behavioral intentions: would they have a religious marriage, and so on. Finally, the students filled out five different attitude tests based on semantic-differential, Likert, Guttman, Thurstone, and Guilford scales. The results in all cases were what Fishbein and Ajzen had anticipated. "All attitude scales correlated highly with multiple-act criteria, while the prediction for single-act criteria tended to be low and 'nonsignificant.'" Thus, there is a high degree of salience overall, but not in respect to any particular behavior. In an earlier study (1967, p. 485), Fishbein found the same result:

We have frequently measured a subject's attitude toward Negroes, and then we have attempted to predict whether the subject would ride with, work with, or cooperate with Negroes. But it is unlikely that the subject's beliefs about the particular Negroes he comes in contact with are similar to his beliefs about Negroes in general.

Factors influencing inconsistency. What are some of the factors that might influence the inconsistency between attitudes and behavior? Insko and Schopler (1967) suggest that the attitude being measured may not be as strong as some of the individual's other attitudes. For example, a person may refuse to contribute to a civil rights organization not because he does not believe in equality for blacks, but because he has other, more pressing, obligations. In other words, his attitudes toward paying rent and feeding his family may predominate over those toward helping blacks achieve equality.

In another study, Carr and Roberts (1965) show that certain aspects of the situation are important. This phenomenon was hinted at in our discussion of the criticism of LaPiere's study. Carr and Roberts found that some black college students did not join in a black march for racial equality because they were pressured against doing so by their parents. Similarly, other black students reported that the only reason for their participation in the march was that fellow students had pressured them into taking part. Presumably, in both cases, the black students held favorable attitudes toward the demonstration. But for different situational reasons, their attitudes and behavior were not consistent.

Finally, studies have shown that the expected consequences of one's actions can influence the attitude–behavior relationship. Kutner, Wilkins, and Yarrow (1952), for instance, believe that many a prejudiced hotelkeeper accommodates blacks and other ethnic groups because he fears being prosecuted by the authorities for discrimination.

Does behavior influence attitudes? An interesting theory involving the inconsistency between behavior and attitudes has been proposed by Dwayne Bem (1968, 1970, 1972). Bem (see chapter 10 for a detailed discussion of Bem's research) holds that it is our behavior that influences our attitudes, rather than the other way around. Thus, according to Bem's theory (1970, p. 2):

Individuals come to "know" their own attitudes, emotions, and other internal states partially by inferring them from observations of their own overt behavior and/or the circumstances in which this behavior occurs. Thus, to the extent that internal cues are weak, ambiguous, or uninterpretable, the individual is functionally in the same position as an outside observer.

In other words, one cannot directly perceive his internal states; rather, he can only infer them by observing his own behavior. For example, when an individual who is asked, "Do you like brown bread?" replies, "I guess I do, I'm always eating it," it is obvious that the person's action is the source of his attitude.

Indeed, his reply is functionally equivalent to the reply his wife might give for him: "I guess he does, he is always eating it." Only to the extent that "brown

FOUR STYLES OF RELATING TO GOVERNMENT

There are many theories about how democracy should function, but few focus on the role that the people play in political life, or on their attitudes toward government. Traditional democratic theories envisage "the people" on the one hand, and "public officials" on the other: the behavior of the public officials is to be guided by the wishes of the people. But Lester Milbrath (1977) believes that such theories are too simple: they fail to account for the realities of the complex relationships between people and their rulers. For example, he has made four classifications of political activist, each with a different complex of attitudes toward government. Each of these types contributes differently to the political system, and each has different expectations of the system.

Milbrath's first type of activist is the party and campaign activist. The investigator found that these individuals are the gladiators of political contests. They participate in a political party between elections as well as at election time, they take an active part in a political campaign, they give money to help a party or candidate, they work to get people registered to vote, they try to convince people to vote for their party their way, and they join groups working to improve community life. Only a relatively small proportion of people take a party and campaign activist attitude toward the political system; such activists constitute about 15 percent of the population of the United States.

Activists of the second type are the protesters, those who have dissenting attitudes toward government. Characteristics of such individuals include participation in street demonstrations, public protest against government policies they feel are morally wrong, and even refusal to obey laws they consider unjust. With the exception of the last item, the proportion of whites joining in such events ranges from 1 to 5 percent; the proportion of blacks ranges from 5 to 19 percent. It is clear that the great majority of both blacks and whites feel little responsibility to engage in protest activities. Even more striking is the sizable proportion of those who believe it is wrong.

Third are the communicators. These individuals keep themselves informed about politics, send messages of support as well as messages of protest to government policy makers, engage in political discussion, and write letters to the editors of newspapers. The communicator mode seems to require a high level of education, of information about politics, and of interest in politics. Communicators tend to be more critical of government than party activists or patriots but generally do not use protesting activities to express their critical views.

Milbrath's last type may be called the community activist. Characteristics of these individuals include forming groups to deal with local social problems, working with existing groups to solve local problems, and contacting public officials about social problems. In many ways, community activists are similar to party and campaign activists: both cluster into the general activist pattern and both have high levels of psychological involvement in community matters. The main difference is that community activists are much less concerned with party and campaign politics than are party activists. Approximately 20 percent of Americans may be considered to be community activists (Milbrath, 1977).

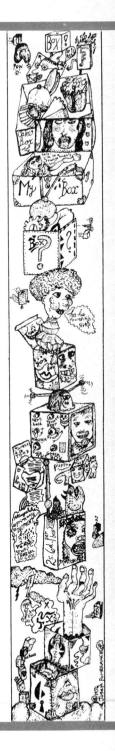

bread" elicits strongly conditioned internal responses, might he have additional evidence, not currently available to his wife, on which to base his self-descriptive statement (Bem, 1968, p. 200).

According to Bem's theory, an individual might work with a Hispanic person. As fellow workers they might eat lunch together, tell jokes, talk about their families. When asked, the individual might say, "Yes, I guess I do like Mexicans. After all, I eat lunch with Maria every day."

Theories of Attitude Formation

How are attitudes formed? This is a formidable question, one that is not answered easily. Actually, there are no answers, only a number of approaches, none of which excludes any other. It is quite likely, in fact, that all the theories we will discuss are true to some degree. Approaches to the issue reflect each scholar's theoretical orientation. The following perspectives are representative of the current thinking among social psychologists and are the basis of considerable research.

Four approaches will be covered: learning theory, historical and economic approaches, functionalism, and cognitive theories. The first approach is based on theories of conditioning. Historical and economic approaches tend to be more political than scientific, but are useful in that they see the individual as a part of society rather than isolated from it. Functionalism relates attitudes to individual needs and is often associated with theories of psychoanalysis and other "depth" psychologies. Finally, cognitive theories suggest that people seek overall cognitive systems in which attitudes are used to keep behavior and cognitions in balance.

Learning theory

In some sense, all major theories of attitude formation are "learning" theories. Several scholars, such as McGuire (1968), have suggested that physiological and genetic factors may be involved, but these ideas are either too limited in scope or too difficult, if not impossible, to research. However, in this context we refer to only those approaches that emphasize conditioning, stimulus/response, reinforcement, and other elements of what is commonly called behaviorism, as learning theory. The learning theory approach is straightforward and concrete, and it has been supported by a considerable amount of research.

Although there are variations, learning theory proponents believe, essentially, that attitudes are acquired much in the same way that facts, concepts, ideologies, ways of thinking, and habits are acquired. We learn facts, but we also learn emotions associated with them. It is the pairing of facts with emotions that results in the development of attitudes. A cognition is associated with an emotional evaluation of prior cognitions.

Foremost among the supporters of learning theory as applied to attitudes are Byrne and Clore (1970) and Staats and Staats (1958). According to these investigators, emotional responses can be elicited by numerous environmental stimuli. A new stimulus is able to elicit the same emotional responses as the old stimulus if the new stimulus becomes associated with the old one. Thus, if an individual experiences unpleasant feelings when he is exposed simultaneously to a loud noise and an electric shock, then words that are repeatedly associated with the noise and the shock will also elicit an unpleasant emotional response. Staats, Staats, and Crawford (1962), for example, found that individuals who were subjected to a loud noise or an electric shock every time they heard the word "large" developed a negative attitude toward the word. Along the same lines, Zanna, Kiesler, and Pilkonis (1970) conducted another experiment using the words "light" and "dark," and obtained similar results.

Several factors may play a part in the establishment of such associations. One may be reinforcement. A predisposition that is encouraged by rewards, praise, or social acceptance will be likely to be enduring. The emotional gratifications of the rewards become associated with the object. On the other hand, negative reinforcements—punishments, criticism, and so on—will lead to a negative attitude toward the object.

Imitation also may play a part. Just as people imitate the behavior of others, they might imitate attitudes as well. Anyone might serve as a model: teachers, parents, friends, celebrities. Children, most obviously, copy parents' apparent attitudes—that is, their behavior with respect to an object. That often proves more powerful than anything that parents might say.

Of course, not all attitudes are formed as a direct result of personal experience, of watching the behavior of models, or of encouragement from others. An attitude may develop indirectly from an emotional association with another attitude. Individuals form attitudes based on association between an object and another attitude. For example, white people who believe that black neighborhoods always become slums may become anti-black without any personal contact with either blacks or slums. The logic is as follows: these people have strong positive associations with clean, well-cared-for homes; since blacks have become paired with dirty, run-down slums which evoke a strong negative response, blacks as a group begin to evoke a negative response as well.

One significant experiment showed how elements of learning theory might be used to help change attitudes toward minority groups. The study by Litcher and Johnson (1968) involved second-grade schoolchildren in a nearly all-white midwestern city. The children had had virtually no personal contacts with blacks. Blacks were not a significant economic or social factor in the community and therefore could not be presumed to be a personal threat to anyone. In spite of that, preliminary tests showed that the children's attitudes toward blacks were largely negative.

The researchers gave an experimental group of second-graders a reading text that was multiethnic, while a control group used a text that portrayed only white people. In all other respects the books were similar. Characters in both books were like the children themselves—middle class and white-skinned. Four teachers in two schools taught both experimental and control classes, trying as much as possible to conduct all the classes in the same way. At the end of the experiment, Litcher and Johnson retested the children's attitudes toward blacks. The retest showed that the experimental group had significantly more favorable attitudes toward blacks than those in the control group. The importance of the results is quite clear. There are indirect ways of reducing prejudice, in this case, by including blacks in the category of familiar middle-class people, not as either foreign or threatening. The experiment clearly changed the associations the children had made with reference to black people.

Historical and economic approaches

In defining racism, we noted that it includes the social and economic subordination of people on the basis of color. Social and economic subordination cannot be entirely understood without reference to the social and economic structures that maintain it. Since some individuals and institutions find racial and ethnic prejudices beneficial, they have, intentionally or not, encouraged and passed along these prejudices until racism has become an institution in itself. Secord and Backman (1964, p. 421), for example, state that political leaders frequently support the maintenance of prejudice, thus helping to institutionalize it. Political leaders, say these investigators, "are likely to rise to power to the extent that they represent the norms characteristic of the voting populace. Persons holding attitudes at variance with the norms are not likely to be successful in elections. Thus, as these leaders acquire power, they exert further influence in support of the status quo. This process has probably been extremely important in the South in the past in maintaining prejudice toward the Negro." Racial problems, under the guise of law and order or school busing, continue to be an important political issue. Each official elected on a racist political platform arouses and reinforces racist attitudes.

Karl Marx was one of the first to articulate a historical view of prejudice. To him, prejudice is a way in which the ruling class exploits the laboring masses: prejudices are perpetuated by creating enemies to divert the masses from their real concerns. This also explains why the people who are exploited themselves become the fiercest exponents of prejudice. Trotsky, presenting the Marxist view of the Arab–Jewish conflict in the late 1930s, suggested that entrenched interests—religious hierarchies, capitalists, and so on—were encouraging religious and ethnic antagonisms so that the working classes would be deflected from their real concerns—that is, their exploitation by the ruling classes—by directing their discontent onto their fellow workers from a different religious, racial, or ethnic background.

In the case of the Arabs and the Jews, Trotsky felt that both sides were to blame. But a more frequent problem in history has been the instances of prejudice against relatively powerless minorities. Jews in particular have been used as a focus of discontent—a strategy called *scapegoatism*. Knowing that the Jewish people were helpless to resist, and playing on the religious beliefs and superstitions of the peasantry, leaders such as the Russian Czars would launch periodic attacks on the Jews. Sometimes the purported reason for the assaults would be religious. But economic motives were also apparent. Jewish property was often seized both in Christian and Moslem countries.

While the ruling class wound up with most of that property, ways were found making Jews economic pariahs to the poor who would help by enlisting mass support for organized ethnic persecution. The Polish noblemen, for ex-

The Jew, always a stranger in another's country, has been used as a scapegoat throughout Western history to divert the attention of the indigenous population from its real interests.

ample, used to have Jewish tax collectors, so that the peasants would associate the Jews with the hated taxes. Jews also were denied the right to own land and thus often turned to the business of moneylending, a profession not only calculated to produce enemies but actually considered sinful by the Catholic church.

Colonialism represents another example of the ways in which prejudice has been used. While the industrial powers were motivated almost entirely by self-interest in their exploitation of colonial empires, they justified colonialism by saying that they were bringing civilization and religion to the heathen. But such a claim in itself fosters contempt and prejudice. According to the colonizers, Asians, Africans, and other nonwhites were backward, half-human, and thus expendable. The American Indian "got in the way of progress." To portray them as savages and to foster prejudice was almost mandatory for those who wished to exploit Indian lands and resources.

Black people are at times thought of as colonial people even within their own country. Kenneth Clark (1965), for example, has demonstrated that Harlem—the predominantly black community in New York City—has many of the characteristics of a colony. As colonials, subordinate and treated as inferiors, blacks can be paid less and forced to accept menial positions. Substandard housing is justified by people who say, "They'll only wreck proper housing, so why bother?" Although history and economic circumstances may not tell the whole story of how attitudes develop, nevertheless attitudes cannot be understood without reference to such economic and social forces.

Functionalism

In a sense, we choose our attitudes. Why we choose one over another is a question that has been examined from several perspectives. The functionalist approach says that we choose attitudes that meet particular psychological needs. In other words, our attitudes serve psychological functions, and how we choose will depend on our individual concerns. Psychological factors applicable to one attitude may not necessarily be factors in another case. Further, two people may arrive at the same attitude for entirely different reasons. Daniel Katz (1960) has identified four attitude functions: the instrumental, adjustive, or utilitarian function; the ego-defensive function; the value-expressive function; and the knowledge function.

The instrumental, adjustive, or utilitarian function. This function relates to the learning theory models. A person tries to develop attitudes that provide the most benefit. Included in this category is economic self-interest. Prejudice against blacks, women, or any minority group may well be beneficial to those who practice it.

The ego-defensive function. The ego-defensive function is one that is most closely allied with depth psychology. Any theory that accepts unconscious thoughts and impulses regards many of our attitudes—especially negative ones—as ego-defensive. Individuals protect themselves and their self-images through their attitudes, which serve to reduce anxiety and deflect emotional conflicts. Consider, for example, the case of a man who fears that he is a homosexual. This person could develop an antihomosexual attitude, rationalizing that such an attitude will crush his impulse to engage in homosexual acts.

How we feel about ourselves has important consequences. A negative self-image can lead to hostility toward almost anyone else. People who feel inferior will bolster their egos by taking a superior attitude with respect to others. Minority groups, especially if they are oppressed, are good targets because they cannot fight back, thus proving their inferiority. Katz points out that in a case in which no handy object of prejudice exists, a disturbed person might try to create one.

It should be added that the ego-defensive function need not produce negative results. Pacifism may emerge from a fear of aggression or physical injury; ideas about human brotherhood may develop from fears of inadequacy in competition, and so on. Almost any predisposition, in fact, might spring from a defensive reaction.

The value-expressive function. On the other hand, it is quite possible that attitudes may stem from self-esteem and a positive self-image. An attitude might be the expression of a central value system, a way of saying, "This is what I am. This is what I stand for." A person who considers himself fair-minded and liberal may be supportive of black political and social aspirations. It may not matter what he can get out of it. The personal satisfaction of doing right may be reward enough. This is not to say that many people are able to maintain and assert beliefs and attitudes without any kind of support whatsoever (though some have done so). But the initial motivation may be simply a matter of deeply felt principle.

The knowledge function. Often attitudes are of no practical use at all. The object involved is insignificant or nonthreatening; yet an individual will develop an attitude toward it. According to Katz, everyone wishes to understand and order his universe. Many bits of knowledge seen on television, read in newspapers, or perceived in passing will be assimilated into a whole. The world is more comprehensible that way, and people are provided with a guide for dealing with new experiences. Overall, the functional approach has been of less interest to social psychologists than to psychohistorians who wish to explain events after the fact. Part of the difficulty is that tests designed to read the unconscious mind are harder to construct and interpret than opinion and behavior measures. However, as we have seen, a test like the F-scale is one example in which personality traits can be explored with results that correlate highly with more traditional measures of attitudes.

Cognitive theories

The theories thus far presented, however significant, tend not to deal with the fact that attitudes are subjected constantly to new and often contradictory material. Some cognitions will support an attitude, whereas others will challenge it. What happens to the attitude then? Although we may cling to an attitude more tenaciously than we do to fact, new information must nevertheless be processed. Challenging new information is not necessarily rejected automatically. How do we handle new information?

In considering these questions further, it becomes impossible to think of one attitude in isolation. What is the significance of that new information? What is our attitude toward the source? How strong was our original attitude? Consider for a moment a person who opposes racial integration. If that person learns suddenly that a valued friend supports integration, he or she must deal with that fact. Perhaps the person begins to question his own beliefs on integration, or perhaps the friend becomes less valued. Or, the person's self-image may suffer. Much interest in recent years has focused on this question, the question of how attitudes fit into an overall cognitive structure. Basically, the cognitive theories are all concerned with the question of consistency, and all have one point in common: given inconsistency, people have a tendency to change toward consistency. Although people need not be consistent in everything they say or do, contradictions produce conflict, tension, and anxiety until there is a resolution.

McGuire (1966) offers a number of ways in which attitudes may be inconsistent. Some of these are: (1) Two attitudes may be logically inconsistent—i.e., a person might be disposed to X and not X at the same time although the contradiction is apparent only when the issue has to be faced. (2) Social roles may produce inconsistency. (3) Situations change, rendering some attitudes obsolete or useless. (4) Pressure may force a person to adopt an attitude that is inconsistent with another. There are other possible reasons for inconsistency, of course, but these are the most evident and recognizable. The research question here is not the reason for inconsistency, but the way people deal with it.

Balance theory.   The balance theory of Fritz Heider (1958), one of the first cognitive consistency theories, posed a triangular relationship between a person and two attitude objects as an illustration. Heider, however, was more interested in affective relations rather than inconsistencies in logic, and therefore one of the attitude objects was always another person.

Heider's theory attempts to tease out the nature of the relationships among three entities: P (the person who perceives the relationship); O (another person); and X (some object). P can either like (+) or dislike (−) the other two entities. At any time, the relationship between any of the members in the triangle could be balanced (i.e., consistent) or unbalanced (inconsistent). In Heider's words, "In the case of three entities, a balanced state exists if all three relations are positive in all respects or if two are negative and one positive." Let us see how this theory works in a concrete example.

A person, P, has an attitude toward person O, a friend, and another attitude toward object X, black aspirations. P likes his friend O (+) and also has a favorable attitude toward the aspirations of black people (+). If P discovers that O has similar attitudes toward blacks, then the situation is balanced. The diagram shows that there is no inconsistency of feelings:

However, what happens if P finds out that his friend has attitudes toward blacks that are mainly negative? The situation is unbalanced:

Also unbalanced would be the situation in which P dislikes O and supports blacks, only to find that O supports blacks:

In either of these situations, Heider maintains, some kind of resolution is necessary. In the first instance, either P would like O less or he would be less supportive of black aspirations. In the second, either P would like O more or he would have a less favorable attitude toward blacks. How the problem would be resolved is less important to Heider than his contention that it has to be resolved in order to bring the two attitudes into balance. Thus, basic to Heider's theory is the proposition that an unbalanced relationship generates strain or tension; this strain causes the member or members experiencing it to act to restore the balance.

Heider's theory is useful in that it is easy to follow conceptually, that it diagrams attitude changes in a simple, direct way, and that it focuses on interpersonal relations. In addition, it demonstrates that inconsistencies may be resolved in different ways. However, the theory also has a number of limitations. For one thing, it cannot indicate how a person will act to resolve an imbalance. Furthermore, as Zajonc (1960) points out, it is possible that some unbalanced situations may remain stable and generate no pressures toward balance. Suppose, says Zajonc, a person likes neither the British nor their national game, cricket. If one of these attitudes were different (if the person liked the British, say, but hated cricket), then, according to balance theory, this person would be under pressure to change one these attitudes to bring about balance. However, there are doubtless many individuals who hold inconsistent attitudes toward the British and cricket. Zajonc concludes, "Attitudes depend at least to some extent on the relationship of the attitude object to the individual's needs and fears, and . . . these may be stronger than forces toward balance. There are in this world things to be avoided and feared. A child bitten by a dog will not develop favorable attitudes toward dogs. And no matter how much he likes Popeye you can't make him like spinach, although according to balance theory he should" (p. 285).

Congruity theory. An approach related to Heider's balance theory is the congruity theory advanced by Osgood and Tannenbaum (1955). According to these investigators, the principle of congruity governs all human thinking. This principle states that changes in evaluation or attitude always occur in the direction of increased congruity with the existing frame of reference. In other words, our attitudes change so that inconsistency is reduced or eliminated and congruity is achieved.

Congruity theory is basically concerned with the ways one individual's evaluation of an object affects another person's attitudes. Thus, if a student's English professor praises a certain novel, what effect does this criticism have on the student's attitude toward both the teacher and the novel? Individuals toward whom we have positive attitudes, say Osgood and Tannenbaum, should have positive attitudes toward objects we approve of. "In the simplest of states in which human thinking operates," write the investigators, "sources we like should always sponsor ideas we like and denounce ideas we are against, and vice versa" (p. 44).

ATTITUDES TOWARD SEX:
ONE MAN'S PERVERSION IS ANOTHER MAN'S PRACTICE

Nearly everyone knows that different people in a society have different attitudes toward certain kinds of behavior. A black teenager living in an urban ghetto, for example, has different feelings about the police and other law-enforcement officials than does a white youth from a middle-class suburb. The same holds true for attitudes toward dress, religion, education, and many other human activities. It should come as no surprise, then, that attitudes toward sex also vary. This was documented empirically in 1948 by Kinsey, Pomeroy, and Martin in the first volume of their now-famous study, *Sexual Behavior in the Human Male.*

To collect their data, the researchers interviewed over 12,000 men whom they classified according to such variables as marital status, age, education, and occupation. The authors were curious to learn whether sexual attitudes are generally the same for men—regardless of their background characteristics—who live in the same culture and historical period. Their research findings revealed that the way men think of sex and what they consider normal varies considerably within the same society.

Take, for instance, the question of positions in intercourse. Kinsey writes, "Most persons will be surprised to learn that positions in intercourse are as much a product of human cultures as languages and clothing, and that the common English–American position is rare in some other cultures." According to Kinsey, coitus with the female supine on her back and the man lying on top—the "missionary position"—is a relatively recent phenomenon dating from the onset of Christianity. His data show that American men in different social classes favor some positions over others, and that the frequency with which all the positions are used changes for each class.

But nowhere is this difference in attitude more startling than in the disagreement surrounding the female breast. "The upper-level male considers it natural that the female breast should interest him, and that he should want to manipulate it, both by hand and by mouth," says Kinsey. "The biologic origin of this interest is, however, open to question, because many lower-level males do not find the female breast similarly interesting and have little inclination to manipulate it, either by hand or by mouth. Many lower-level males rate such mouth–breast contacts as perversions, and some of them dismiss the idea with considerable disgust, as something that only a baby does when nursing from the mother's breast."

Biblically, masturbation was considered sinful, and an element of wrong-doing associated with masturbation lingered as late as 1948. Kinsey writes, "At lower levels, and particularly among the older generations of the lowest levels, masturbation may be looked down upon as abnormal, a perversion, and an infantile substitute for sociosexual contacts . . . The upper level more or less allows masturbation as not exactly desirable nor exactly commendable, but not as immoral as a sociosexual contact."

The attitudes Kinsey discovered to be true of men in 1948 may no longer hold in detail. The importance of Kinsey's research is that it demonstrated that sexual attitudes can be measured, and that it made possible all the research on sexuality and sexual dysfunction that has followed.

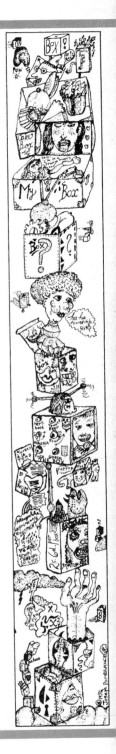

To illustrate, let us elaborate on the above example. Suppose that Joel is an English literature major in college and deeply respects a certain professor who specializes in the modern American novel. Suppose further that Joel thinks highly of Ernest Hemingway's novel *The Old Man and the Sea*. Now, if Joel's professor praises the novel, there will be congruity in Joel's attitude toward both. In short, a positive source has made a positive evaluation of a positive object, producing congruity. Similarly, Joel's attitude will be congruous if a negative source embraces a negative object (a teacher Joel does not regard too highly, for example, may rave about a novel that Joel does not like); if a positive source criticizes a negative object (if a teacher whom Joel respects condemns a trashy novel); or if a negative source denounces a positive object (the poorly respected teacher condemns *The Old Man and the Sea*).

Osgood and Tannenbaum have quantified attitudes by devising a seven-point scale: $+3, +2, +1, 0, -1, -2, -3$, as discussed in the measurement of attitudes earlier in the chapter. The way the scale works is best explained by examining how an incongruous situation affects a person's attitudes. Consider, for example, a liberal Democrat who assigns a value of -2 to his attitude toward the policies of a conservative Republican president. Suppose the same Democrat ranks his attitudes toward ecological issues at $+3$. Now, what will happen to this Democrat's attitudes when the president endorses an ecology bill that would prevent offshore drilling for oil? According to congruity theory, the Democrat will change his evaluation both of the president and the ecology bill. In effect, he will attempt to produce a state of cognitive congruency by mentally moving the two entities closer together in his value system.

Thus, congruity theory predicts that the president's position will rise slightly in the Democrat's eyes, whereas the ecology bill will fall a little. The Democrat, for example, might reevaluate the president, raising his attitude value toward the chief executive to the neutral point of zero, whereas his attitude value toward the ecology bill might drop one increment, to $+2$. Thus, by shifting one's attitudes, one moves toward congruity and feels less ill at ease with an incongruous situation. How do Osgood and Tannenbaum determine which will change most? The object that is most polarized in the subject's mind—that is, the object or person that is regarded most positively or negatively by the individual—will change least, because such an object has a stronger place in the person's value system. Thus, as we saw, the Democrat's attitude toward the conservative Republican president changed more than his attitude toward the energy bill.

Besides being able to measure and predict both the magnitude and direction of an attitude change more accurately, congruity theory also includes another element which enables the individual to correct for any incredulity that may exist in an incongruous situation. If a source makes an overly extreme assertion about an object that is simply too farfetched to be believed, the individual can recognize this and will not change his attitudes toward either the source or the object being judged. Thus, if an individual was told that the American Legion convention had agreed to grant total amnesty to all those who evaded the draft or deserted from military service during the Vietnam war, he would find this statement incredible and probably would not change his attitude toward either the American Legion or the war resisters.

As Zajonc (1960) points out, the congruity theory has a certain advantage over other cognitive consistency theories, particularly Heider's balance theory. Since the principles of congruity are formulated in quantitative terms, investigators can measure both the extent and direction of attitude change. And the predictions of attitude change based on quantitative techniques have found some support in studies by Osgood and Tannenbaum and others. As Zajonc states, "While balance theory allows merely a dichotomy of attitudes, either positive or negative, the principle of congruity allows refined measurements using Osgood's method of semantic differential" (p. 270).

Finally, Jones and Gerard (1967, p. 127) offer this caveat about cognitive consistency theories:

It would be a mistake to exaggerate the prevalence of internal consistency in cognitive organization. Man is not completely rational, nor does he always succeed in bringing his beliefs and values into line with his attitudes. Each of us finds ways to live with inconsistency. These usually involve some form of self-deception, or of segregating inconsistent cognitions. But the more basic point is that there are pressures toward balance—strains toward consistency—that animate our information-seeking activities, our reactions to other persons, and many other features of social life.

Summary

An attitude may be defined as a predisposition toward any person, idea, or object that contains cognitive, affective, and behavioral components. The cognitive component consists of the individual's beliefs or knowledge about the attitude object. The affective component refers to the person's emotional responses toward the object, and the behavioral component involves the person's overt behavior toward the object or person.

In daily life, attitudes are often confused with such related concepts as beliefs, values, and opinions. A belief differs from an attitude in that it is based more on fact and less on emotion than an attitude. A value is an underlying ethical imperative, and an opinion is the verbal expression of an attitude, belief, or value.

The study of attitudes made great progress when social psychologists devised ways to measure them. Five measurement scales have been proven to be important in the analysis of attitudes. The first of these, the Thurstone scale, asks subjects to respond to a group of simple questions about an attitude object, then sums up the results. The Likert scale is similar but less complex, and the Bogardus social distance scale quantitatively measures the degree of distance a person wishes to maintain in relationship to members of other groups. The fourth attitude-measuring technique, the semantic-differential scale, differs from the others in that subjects are asked to rate objects along a continuum of bipolar adjectives. Finally, the F (Fascism) scale attempts to tap the subjects' attitudes indirectly by measuring a range of variables that are related to an antidemocratic personality.

The forces which shape our attitudes are many and varied, but two of the most important are our peers and institutions such as schools. Peers, which become important to the individual in late adolescence, affect a wide range of attitudes, such as goals, political ideas, and racial and ethnic prejudices. Studies have shown that schools, institutions of employment, and organized religions are also highly influential in molding attitudes.

Most people have formed attitudes, but few find an opportunity to act in accordance with their attitudes. One classic study by Richard LaPiere, for example, found that although hotel owners had indicated in writing they would not rent a room to Orientals, they did not refuse to accommodate a Chinese couple.

A number of theories have been proposed to explain how attitudes are formed. Learning theory holds that our attitudes are shaped by conditioning. Historical and economic approaches, such as Marxism, hold that attitudes are shaped by social forces. The functionalist viewpoint relates attitude formation to individual needs and is often associated with psychoanalysis and other depth psychologies. Finally, cognitive approaches, such as Heider's balance theory and Osgood and Tannenbaum's congruity theory, suggest that we seek overall cognitive systems in which attitudes are used to keep behavior and cognitions in balance.

Bibliography

ADORNO, T. W., FRENKEL-BRUNSWIK, E., LEVINSON, D. J., AND SANFORD, R. N. *The authoritarian personality.* New York: Harper, 1950.

ASHMORE, R. D. Prejudice: Causes and cures. In B. E. Collins (Ed.), *Social psychology.* Reading, Mass.: Addison-Wesley, 1970.

BEM, D. J. Attitudes as self-descriptions: Another look at the attitude–behavior link. In A. G. Greenwald, T. C. Brock, and T. M. Ostrom (Eds.), *Psychological foundations of attitudes*. New York: Academic Press, 1968.

BEM, D. *Beliefs, attitudes and human affairs*. Belmont, Calif.: Brooks/Cole, 1970.

BEM, D. J. Self-perception theory. In L. Berkowitz (Ed.), *Advances in experimental social psychology*. Vol. 6. New York: Academic Press, 1972.

BOGARDUS, E. S. Measuring social distances. In K. Thomas (Ed.), *Attitudes and behaviour: Selected readings*. Middlesex, England: Penguin Books, 1971.

BYRNE, D., AND CLORE, G. L. A reinforcement model of evaluative responses. *Personality: An International Journal*, 1970, **1**, 103–128.

CAFFREY, B., ANDERSON, S., AND GARRISON, J. Changes in racial attitudes of white southerners after exposure to the atmosphere of a southern university. *Psychological Reports*, 1969, **25**, 555–558.

CARR, L., AND ROBERTS, S. O. Correlates of civil-rights participation. *Journal of Social Psychology*, 1965, **67**, 259–267.

CLARK, K. *Dark ghetto*. New York: Harper and Row, 1965.

COOK, S. W., AND SELLTIZ, C. A multiple-indicator approach to attitude measurement. *Psychological Bulletin*, 1964, **2**, 36–55.

DEFLEUR, M. L., AND WESTIE, F. R. Verbal attitudes and overt acts: An experiment on the salience of attitudes. *American Sociological Review*, December 1958, **23**(6), 667–673.

EPSTEIN, R., AND KOMORITA, S. Childhood prejudice as a function of parental ethnocentrism, punitiveness, and outgroup characteristics. *Journal of Personality and Social Psychology*, 1966, **3**, 259–264.

FISHBEIN, M. Attitude and the prediction of behavior. In M. Fishbein (Ed.), *Readings in attitude theory and measurement*. New York: John Wiley, 1967.

FISHBEIN, M., AND AJZEN, I. Attitudes towards objects as predictors of single and multiple behavior criteria. *Psychological Review*, 1974, **81**, 59–74.

FRIEDENBERG, E. Z. *Coming of age in America: Growth and acquiescence*. New York: Random House, 1963.

HEIDER, F. *The psychology of interpersonal relations*. New York: John Wiley, 1958.

HESS, R., AND TORNEY, J. *The development of political attitudes in children*. Chicago: Aldine, 1967.

HIMMELWEIT, H. T., OPPENHEIM, A. N., AND VINCE, P. *Television and the child*. London: Oxford University Press, 1960.

HOROWITZ, E. L. Development of attitude toward Negroes. In T. M. Newcomb and E. L. Hartley (Eds.), *Readings in social psychology*. New York: Holt, Rinehart and Winston, 1947.

HOVLAND, C. I., AND SHERIF, M. Judgmental phenomena and scales of attitude measurement: Item displacement in Thurstone scales. *Journal of Abnormal and Social Psychology*, 1952, **47**, 822–832.

INSKO, C. A., AND SCHOPLER, J. Triadic consistency: A statement of affective–cognitive–conative consistency. *Psychological Review*, 1967, **74**, 361–376.

JENNINGS, M., AND NIEMI, R. The transmission of political values from parent to child. *American Political Science Review*, 1968, **62**, 169–184.

JONES, E. E., AND GERARD, H. B. *Foundations of social psychology.* New York: John Wiley, 1967.

KATZ, D. The functional approach to the study of attitudes. *Public Opinion Quarterly*, 1960, **24**, 163–204.

KINSEY, A. C., POMEROY, W. B., AND MARTIN, C. E. *Sexual behavior in the human male.* Philadelphia: W. B. Saunders, 1948.

KUTNER, B., WILKINS, C., AND YARROW, P. R. Verbal attitudes and overt behavior involving racial prejudice. *Journal of Abnormal and Social Psychology*, 1952, **47**, 649–652.

LAPIERE, R. T. Attitudes vs. actions. *Social Forces*, 1934, **13**, 230–237.

LIKERT, R. A technique for the measurement of attitudes. *Archives of Psychology*, 1932, **140.**

LITCHER, J., AND JOHNSON, D. W. Changes in attitudes toward Negroes of white elementary school students after use of multi-ethnic readers. *Journal of Educational Psychology*, 1969, **60**, 148–152.

McGUIRE, W. J. Attitudes and opinions. *Annual Review of Psychology*, 1966, **17**, 475–514.

McGUIRE, W. J. The nature of attitudes and attitude change. In G. Lindzey and E. Aronson (Eds.), *The handbook of social psychology.* (2nd ed.) Vol. 3. Reading, Mass.: Addison-Wesley, 1968.

MARGOLIS, C. The black student in political strife. *Proceedings of the Seventy-ninth Annual Convention of the American Psychological Association*, 1971, **6**, 395–396.

MEHRABIAN, A. Orientation behaviors and nonverbal attitude communication. *Journal of Communication*, 1967, **17**, 324–332.

MEHRABIAN, A. Inference of attitude from the posture, orientation, and distance of a communicator. *Journal of Consulting and Clinical Psychology*, 1968, **32**, 296–308.

MILBRATH, L. W. AND GOEL, M. L. *Political participation.* (Rev. ed.) Chicago: Rand McNally, 1977.

NEWCOMB, T. M. *Personality and social change.* New York: Dryden, 1943.

NEWCOMB, T. M., KOENIG, T. K., FLACKS, R., AND WARWICK, D. *Persistence and change: Bennington College and its students after 25 years.* New York: John Wiley, 1967.

OSGOOD, C. E., SUCI, G. J., AND TANNENBAUM, P. H. *The measurement of meaning.* Urbana, Ill.: University of Illinois Press, 1957.

OSGOOD, C. E., AND TANNENBAUM, P. H. The principle of congruity in the prediction of attitude change. *Psychological Review*, 1955, **62**(1), 42–55.

PETTIGREW, T. Race relations. In R. Merton and R. Nisbet (Eds.), *Contemporary social problems.* New York: Harcourt Brace Jovanovich, 1971.

SECORD, P. F., AND BACKMAN, C. *Social psychology.* New York: McGraw-Hill, 1964.

SELLTIZ, C., JAHODA, M., DEUTSCH, M., AND COOK, S. W. *Research methods in social relations.* New York: Holt, Rinehart and Winston, 1959.

SELZNICK, G., AND STEINBERG, S. *The tenacity of prejudice: Anti-Semitism in contemporary America.* New York: Harper Torchbooks, 1969.

STAATS, A. W., AND STAATS, C. K. Attitudes established by classical conditioning. *Journal of Abnormal and Social Psychology,* 1958, **57,** 37–40.

STAATS, A. W., STAATS, C. K., AND CRAWFORD, H. First-order conditioning of meaning and the parallel conditioning of a GSR. *Journal of General Psychology,* 1962, **67,** 159–167.

STRUENING, E. Anti-democratic attitudes in a midwestern university. In H. Remmers (Ed.), *Anti-democratic attitudes in American schools.* Evanston, Ill.: Northwestern University Press, 1963.

THOMAS, W. I., AND ZNANIECKI, F. *The Polish peasant in Europe and America.* Vol. 2. Boston: Badger, 1918.

THURSTONE, L. L. Attitudes can be measured. *American Journal of Sociology,* 1928, **33,** 529–554.

VERBA, S. R., BRODY, A., PARKER, E. B., NIE, N. H., POLSBY, N. W., EKMAN, P., AND BLACK, G. S. Public opinion and the war in Vietnam. *American Political Science Review,* 1967, **61,** 317–333.

WICKER, A. W. Attitudes vs. actions: The relationship of verbal and overt behavioral responses to attitude objects. *Journal of Social Issues,* 1969, **25,** 41–78.

ZAJONC, R. B. Balance, congruity and dissonance. *Public Opinion Quarterly,* 1960, **24**(2), 280–286.

ZANNA, M. P., KIESLER, C. A., AND PILKONIS, P. A. Positive and negative attitudinal affect established by classical conditioning. *Journal of Personality and Social Psychology,* 1970, **14,** 321–328.

ZIMBARDO, P., AND EBBESEN, E. B. *Influencing attitudes and changing behavior.* Reading, Mass.: Addison-Wesley, 1970.

8

Attitude Change

When author Norman Mailer, during the 1976 presidential campaign, sought to uncover President Carter's roots, he paid a visit to the then candidate's home in Plains, Georgia. He had anticipated "a dry and dusty town with barren vistas, ramshackle warehouses and timeless, fly-buzzing, sunbaked afternoons." He found, instead, a town that "felt peaceful and prosperous. It had the sweet, deep green of an old-fashioned town [and] . . . a promise that the mysterious gentility of American life was present" (Mailer, 1976).

Mailer's journey to Plains illustrates an elementary case of attitude change. In chapter 7 an attitude was defined as a predisposition toward any person, idea, or object that contains cognitive, affective, and behavioral components. Mailer, a Northern intellectual with well-known antiestablishment political views, had a negative stereotype of Southern small towns. However, when he encountered evidence to the contrary, he changed his attitude. Unfortunately, attitude change is rarely this simple. Most attitudes are concerned with things that are difficult or impossible to verify objectively, since they are highly subjective. Attitudes concerning the motives of politicians, the causes of inflation, or predictions of the future are not directly testable (Hovland, Lumsdaine, and Sheffield, 1949). Consider the following two questions:

1. Are you more prejudiced or less prejudiced against various minority groups now than when you were younger? If there were shifts in your attitude, what caused them?

281

2. How did you arrive at your current attitude toward spectator sports? Do you like some and become bored by others? Has your attitude changed over the years, and why?

Can you explain your own shifts in attitude on these two subjects? Do you know what was the cause of your shifts, or, an equally interesting and difficult question, how you have maintained a consistency in your attitudes toward one or both of these subjects?

Unlike many other aspects of social psychology, knowledge and information concerning attitude change are of crucial interest to politicians, the advertising industry and their clients, and virtually to anyone who has a message or a product that he wants to proselytize. A study of attitude change seeks to understand the relationship between the sender, the message, and the recipient.

Persuasion: An Art of Many Variables

Every day all of us are the targets of messages that try to manipulate our thoughts and behavior. Carl Hovland and his colleagues at Yale undertook a systematic program of research concerning the art of persuasion, organized around the famous question, "Who says what to whom and with what effect?" (Smith, Laswell, and Casey, 1946). Their research, and that of their followers, have concentrated on the effects of various kinds of communication upon opinion and attitude change. They conceptualized the structure of communication as consisting of three parts: the source of the communication, the nature of the communication, and the target of the communication, or the audience. The attempt to persuade someone to change his opinion or attitude centers around the variables associated with these three elements.

The Source

A frequently used method of persuasion in advertising involves the endorsement of a product by a famous, successful person—a person with *prestige.* Advertising promotions have featured Joe DiMaggio, gray-haired, handsome, and distinguished, pointing out the advantages of a bank. In this case, the bank gains the endorsement of a famous athlete who also looks like a man who would give good advice about how to handle money and banking business. Bill Cosby, the black comedian, has lent his magic as well as his racial endorsement to a major car manufacturer, and Robert Morley has, with British wit and charm, been selling British Airways to the American public. Such ads are based on the assumption that the source of the communication plays an important role in attitude change.

Prestige of the communicator. Investigators have found that the prestige of the person communicating an attitude greatly affects the degree to which the target subject changes his attitude. Generally, the greater the prestige of the source, the more the target will change his attitude. For example, in a study by Aronson, Turner, and Carlsmith (1963), subjects were asked for their opinions of several samples of poetry written by different modern poets. After the subjects had negatively evaluated one of the samples, they were then told that someone else had found the same sample quite good. Some of the students were told that this positive evaluation came from T. S. Eliot, the noted Anglo-American poet. Other subjects were told that the judgment was made by a Ms. Agnes Stearns, a student at a southern state teachers' college.

Next, all of the students were instructed to reevaluate the original poetry sample. Not unexpectedly, some of the subjects changed their attitudes toward the poetry. But more of the subjects who had read T. S. Eliot's opinion reversed their initial judgments than did those who had read Agnes Stearns's evaluation. Thus, the opinion of the high-prestige source induced more change in attitude than did that of the low-prestige individual.

Another aspect of the prestige variable is the *trustworthiness* of the communicator. Hovland and Weiss (1951) exposed subjects to identical communications concerned with four topics that were controversial at the time: whether antihistamines should be sold without a doctor's prescription; whether it would be feasible for the United States to construct an atomic submarine; whether the steel industry was responsible for the current steel shortage; and whether home television would lead to the decline of movie theaters. For example, the communication concerning the effect of television on movie houses was attributed either to *Fortune* magazine or to a certain syndicated movie-gossip columnist. Audience opinion was measured both be-

Net Change of Opinion from Immediately after Communication to Four Weeks Later According to Credibility of Source

		High Credibility	Low Credibility
	Antihistamines	− 6.5%	6.7%
Topic of communication	Atomic submarines	−16.	13.
	Steel shortage	−11.4	15.4
	Future of movies	− 9.7	− 6.7

Figure 8–1. After a four-week period both high- and low-credibility source effects are reduced—a demonstration of the "sleeper" effect.

SOURCE: Adapted from Hovland, C. I., and Weiss, W. The influence of source credibility on communication effectiveness. *Public Opinion Quarterly*, 1951, **15**, 645.

fore and after reading the communication. Results showed that the communication allegedly produced by *Fortune* was more influential than that ostensibly made by the gossip columnist. Similar results were obtained with the antihistamine issue.

Ulterior motives.   If attractive prestige figures promote a product, does that mean that everyone will run out and buy it? One reason this does not happen is the perceived *ulterior motive* of the source. If a person is perceived as arguing in his own interest, the persuasiveness of the message becomes less forceful. When Muhammad Ali takes to the airwaves to promote a men's cologne, the audience may suspect that the money which Ali is receiving for the commercial may have influenced him more than his admiration for the product. The *intentions* of a communicator contribute to his or her effectiveness.

This variable was cleverly manipulated in an experiment by Walster, Aronson, and Abrahams (1966) which showed that someone usually labeled socially unacceptable (a convicted felon) could be as influential as a respected public official. In the experiment, half of the audience received a newspaper clipping arguing a strong "law-and-order" position: felons are reciving too lenient treatment and therefore the power of the police and the courts should be increased. The other half of the audience received a newspaper clipping in which the argument was the reverse: the police and courts had too much power and, therefore, the rights of defendants should be protected. In addition, the source of the communication was varied. Half of the audience was led to believe that their clipping was written by G. William Stephens, a tough prosecuting attorney, and the other half was led to think that Joe "The Shoulder" Napolitano, convicted heroin dealer, was the author.

The four conditions of the experiment are shown in Figure 8–2. The experimenters hypothesized that attitude change should occur only in conditions II and III, where the source of the communication has nothing to gain personally by advocating his position. As predicted, the results of the experiment showed that the greatest opinion change occurred in the conditions in which the prosecutor argued for less court power and the convicted criminal argued for more. The source was most effective when his argument ran counter to his own interests.

The sleeper effect.   Another problem of advertisers, propagandists, and others using persuasive appeals is the lapse of time following a communication. There is evidence that a given source has its greatest impact immediately after a presentation, and that this dissipates as time goes by.

Kelman and Hovland (1953) discovered this phenomenon in an experiment with high school students who were exposed to a statement advocating that juvenile delinquents be treated less harshly by the judicial system. The person reading the statement adopted one of two guises: either he appeared to be knowledgeable, fair, and responsible about the issue (positive source), or he seemed uninformed, biased, and irresponsible. After listening to the presentation, the subjects were instructed to give their opinions on the question.

Three weeks later, the students were again queried concerning their attitudes toward the treatment of juvenile delinquents. This time, however, half of the students in each condition (either positive or negative source) were reminded of the communicator, whereas no mention was made of the source to the remaining students. Those students who were not reminded of the source differed very little. This demonstrated that the effect of the positive source, which had been much more powerful immediately following the communication, disappeared over the three-week period. Kelman and Hovland attribute this to the fact that people forget the source of a communication more quickly than they forget the content. However, when reminded of the source, the differences produced by the positive and negative sources remained approximately the same as they had been three weeks earlier.

Kelman and Hovland found most significant the change to agreement with the communication of those subjects exposed to the negative source who were not reminded of its origin. They labeled this the *sleeper effect.* That is, the association of the negative qualities attributed to the source weakens over time; the memory of the message itself will be as strong as it would have been if the source originally had been positive. Thus, even when a discredited source makes a pronouncement, the message cannot be dismissed as nonsense. People will remember it and forget the mendacity of the source.

**Prediction of Attitude Change
from Perceived Motives of Source**

SOURCE

MESSAGE	Prosecuting attorney	Convicted felon
Harsher toward criminals	I	II
More liberal	III	IV

Figure 8--2. Attitude change should occur in conditions II and III. A source has greater credibility when his message runs counter to his interests.

Communication interference.   These experiments concerning the source of the communication demonstrate, on the one hand, that prestige, trustworthiness, and attractiveness increase a communicator's effectiveness. On the other hand, perceived intentions, particularly the harboring of ulterior motives, and time (the sleeper effect) may work to decrease the effectiveness of the source. In some cases these factors might even cancel the effect of the source. Why, then, do advertisers seek attractive celebrities to endorse their products publicly? The answer lies in the phenomenon called *communication interference* (Freedman, Carlsmith, and Sears, 1970). This refers to factors which stop or inhibit the transmission of a message, particularly audience resistance. If a message cannot even reach its target, then obviously no persuasion or attitude change is possible. Thus, the value of having a well-known, attractive, and prestigious source may lie not so much in the person as a source, but in persuading the audience to give their attention to the message—overcoming interference effects.

The nature of the communication

The nature and presentation of a communication play an important role in determining its effectiveness. Suppose that you were given an opportunity to convince an audience to take a particular view of an issue. Let us say, for argument's sake, that you believe strongly that dogs should be banned from urban centers for sanitary reasons. Consider these three important questions:

1. Is it preferable to present both sides of the issue or only the one which you are advocating?

2. If you decide that both sides are to be presented, is it better to present your position first or last? This is analogous to a debate or courtroom situation in which the order of presentation may have an important effect.

3. Finally, what type of audience should you select to present your opinions to? Should you speak before the American Kennel Club or seek a more receptive audience? The discrepancy between the audience's initial opinion and that advocated by the communicator must be taken into account.

One-sided versus two-sided arguments.   Now that we have settled on an issue (banning dogs from cities), the decision must be made as to whether an audience will be more receptive if both sides of the question are presented. On the one hand, if a communicator presents both sides of an argument, the audience might say "What a fair-minded person!" and be more receptive to his position. On the other hand, even a mention of the opposing view might leave the audience confused, especially if the argument is presented well. There is no simple answer here. Research has shown that the characteristics of the audience are an important factor. If an audience is intelligent and well informed, it is usually knowledgeable about some of the counterarguments and may resent a one-sided communication as an affront to its intelligence (Aronson, 1976). However, if the audience is not knowledgeable or the issue is a relatively new one, then a single presentation is advisable.

Another factor is the initial opinion of the audience. If the audience is already predisposed toward the communicator's point of view (for example, the Dog-Haters' League), then a one-sided communication will have a greater impact. If, however, the audience is leaning in the opposite direction, then a two-sided communication is more effective (Hovland, Lumsdaine, and Sheffield, 1949). Outside of the laboratory, however, few communicators ever provide a balanced presentation.

The order of presentation. An interesting phenomenon often occurs in the field of memory research. If a person is given a list of words to memorize, analogous to a shopping list, the position of the words on the list is an important factor in determining which words will be remembered—the *serial-position effect.* Usually the first and last items on a list are remembered best. This is called the *primacy effect* and the *recency effect*, respectively. When two opposing arguments are to be presented, should the communicator create a primacy or recency effect? Not only does the source want to be persuasive but she wants the audience to remember her message as well.

Miller and Campbell (1959) investigated this problem and found that the lengths of time between the presentation of the two views, and between the second communication and the measurement of the attitude, are the important factors. The experimenters presented to their subjects (the audience) a condensed version of a transcript from an actual jury trial, with the arguments for the plaintiff and for the defendant placed in two separate blocks. A primacy effect occurred when the second communication was presented right after the first, followed by a delay in the measurement of the audience's attitudes. This is analogous to a jury trial in which summations of both sides are given, followed by a delay while the jury deliberates the verdict. If the results of the experiment can indeed be generalized to a courtroom setting, then it is the attorney presenting the first summation who has the advantage. However, if there is a delay between the first and second communications and the attitudes of the audience are measured immediately after the second communication, then the last communication is more influential (recency effect).

The audience

The audience is the target of the communication: the object of the persuasion effort. Research shows that the characteristics of the audience are important to the outcome of attitude change.

Self-esteem. Some people are more easily persuaded than others. Hovland and Janis (1959) found that one factor which affects the persuasibility of an individual is level of self-esteem. A person who feels inadequate is more easily influenced than an individual who thinks highly of himself. Cohen (1959), after determining the levels of self-esteem of individual subjects, found that those with high self-esteem try to influence other people more than individuals who are low in self-esteem. Moreover, it is much easier to pressure a person with low self-esteem to change his attitude about an issue. In a related finding, Sears (1967) determined that individuals whose views were criticized became more persuasible because they were made to feel more anxious.

People with low self-esteem place a low value on their opinions. This makes them less reluctant to give them up when confronted with differing opinions. Festinger's (1954) *theory of social comparison* suggests that a person who is sure of his opinions would be less inclined to look toward others for confirmation. However, the person with low self-esteem will more readily seek out the opinions of others and be more willing to readjust his own accordingly.

Fear arousal. A controversial area of attitude change, and one which has spurred much research, is the effect of a fear-arousing communication on an audience. Are people more likely to change their attitudes if they are frightened by a message? Or, do frightening messages boomerang because people "tune out" as a way of defending themselves against them? To put the question another way, do people respond realistically to fear-arousing messages by changing their attitudes in ways advocated by the communication, or do they employ what Freud called *defense mechanisms* (denial, repression, etc.) to alleviate their fright? For example, what would be the best tactic for the American Cancer Society to persuade people to stop smoking?

*A woman speaker,
because of societal prejudice
against women,
may have difficulty
in establishing credibility
and persuading an audience.*

Janis and Feshbach (1953) started the debate concerning fear arousal in a study using the prevention of tooth decay as a message. They showed a film to high school students that stressed the importance of brushing the teeth after eating. There were three different versions of the film, each one coinciding with a different experimental condition. In the high-fear condition the students were shown horrible pictures of rotting, discolored teeth and diseased gums. The mild-fear group was exposed to less shocking pictures, and the no-fear subjects did not see any pictures of decayed teeth. When questioned a week later, the students in the no-fear group had taken more positive action toward the prevention of tooth decay than students in the other two conditions. This led Janis and Feshbach to conclude that the arousal of fear has a *boomerang effect,* and that maximum attitude change is produced by persuasive messages which are not fear-arousing.

Subsequent studies, however, produced conflicting results. For example, Dabbs and Leventhal (1966) conducted an experiment similar to the Janis and Feshbach study advocating tetanus shots for college students. A high-fear condition was established by a dramatic presentation involving an explicit description of the symptoms and the course of the disease. A moderate-fear group received some information about the disease, with no particular emphasis placed on the symptoms. The no-fear subjects were told only about the advisability of getting the shots. After the presentation, the subjects were asked about their intentions of getting shots and, in addition, the university health service kept a record of the number of students who received inoculations during the following month. The results are the reverse of what Janis and Feshbach found. In this experiment, high fear-arousal motivated not only attitude change but, more important, behavior change as well. Other experiments (for example, Leventhal and Singer, 1966; Leventhal, Singer, and Jones, 1965) have also supported this relationship.

Whenever conflicting results are generated between two similar experiments, social scientists are motivated to resolve them. They first look for methodological flaws in the experiments and then, barring these, they look for a variable which explains both sets of results. We saw how this was done with the discrepancy experiments, using the level of prestige to resolve the disparate findings. Leventhal (1970) has supplied an explanation for the conflicting results in fear arousal. In order to understand it, let us take a further look at the Dabbs and Leventhal experiment. There was an additional variable, not discussed above, which we shall call *directiveness.* Some of the students in all three groups were explicitly informed that the health service offered the tetanus inoculation and were given a map locating the service. Of these, 28 percent actually went for the shot, whereas of the group which received no specific instructions, only 3 percent received the inoculation.

The crucial variable seems to be providing explicit instructions on how to reduce the aroused fear. This is illustrated by Leventhal's (1970) cigarette experiment, in which he found that a high-fear communication produced a much greater intent to stop smoking than a low-fear message. Unless the high-fear message was accompanied by specific instructions, such as "Buy a magazine instead of a pack of cigarettes," the amount of cigarette smoking was not significantly reduced. However, specific instructions without a fear-arousing communication are ineffective. The best results are produced by the combination of fear arousal and directiveness, with subjects in this condition smoking significantly less four months after the experiment.

The inoculation effect.   In the last section it was suggested that people might employ defense mechanisms to reject threatening messages. William McGuire and his associates have been concerned with a different aspect of resisting persuasive messages. They asked if it were not possible to create a defense against persuasion. "Defense" in this case does not involve unconscious mechanisms, but is based on a medical analogy. McGuire likens the target in the attitude-change situation to a person being attacked by a virus. If a person has no natural defenses or antibodies against the attack, then the virus can do great damage. In medicine there are two ways to increase resistance to a disease: the body can be strengthened generally by prescribing vitamin supplements, good food, exercise, and such; or the body can be provided with the opportunity to produce antibodies. This is done by inoculating with a small amount of the virus—not enough to endanger health, but enough to stimulate the production of antibodies. When an individual then encounters a full-blown attack by the virus, his body will have the antibodies as a defense against the disease (McGuire and Papageorgis, 1961).

McGuire reasoned that the same can be done for a persuasive attack. McGuire and Papageorgis (1961) first identified a number of cultural truisms—opinions so extensively held in our culture that they are rarely questioned. The following were selected for use in their study:

1. Everyone should get a chest X-ray each year in order to detect any possible tuberculosis symptoms at an early stage of the disease.
2. Penicillin has been, almost without exception, of great benefit to mankind.
3. Most forms of mental illness are not contagious.
4. Every person should brush his teeth after each meal.

The experimenters reasoned that these cultural truisms were analogous to defenseless bodies facing an attack of a virus to which there was no natural immunity in the population.

McGuire and Papageorgis asked their subjects to rate the extent of their agreement or disagreement with the four statements. They then divided the subjects into three groups. A *support* group received support for their initial opinions, which, in the medical model, would be analogous to giving the person vitamin supplements. In the *inoculation* condition, the group was subjected to a mild attack on their opinions (an inoculation) which could be easily refuted. A control group received neither support nor the inoculation. The positions of all subjects were then strongly attacked. The results show that the subjects in the inoculation condition evidenced the least amount of attitude change, whereas those in the support and control groups showed a significantly greater amount of change in their positions.

The reasons why subjecting a person to a mild attack on his opinions makes him more resistant to a later forceful attack are still not well understood. Undoubtedly, it gives the individual motivation and practice in refuting a later attack. In line with this thinking, Freedman and Sears (1965) conducted a study in which teenagers heard a talk entitled "Why Teenagers Should Not Be Allowed to Drive." In one condition the subjects were told ten minutes in advance that they were going to hear the talk and were informed of the title. A control group was given no advance warning. The experimenters found that the group that had been given advance notice was less influenced by the presentation than the control group. The important element operating in these studies seems to be time; a person needs enough time to organize a refutation. This can be done either by subjecting his views to a mild attack or by forewarning him. In both cases the subject has time to prepare a defense.

This section has concentrated on the structure of communication. The studies by Hovland, his co-workers, and those that followed his approach have a distinctly empirical flavor. This empirical approach has led to a great deal of knowledge and research concerning the variables which influence attitude change. That is, they have looked at the communication process as a group of isolated, independent variables, without any overall theory of communication to aid in predicting which variables are important.

Theories of Attitude Change

A theory of attitude change must explain why attitude change occurs, the process of change, and in what situations it can be expected. Attitude change has been included in most theoretical perspectives, including learning theory, cognitive psychology, and even psychoanalysis. An early theory of attitude change, stemming from the behaviorist perspective, is reinforcement theory (Hovland, Janis, and Kelley, 1953).

Reinforcement theory

According to Hovland, Janis, and Kelley (1953), attitudes and opinions are responses, learned like any other response. In particular, attitudes "are oriented toward approaching or avoiding a given object, person, group, or symbol" (p. 4). Under certain conditions, exposure to a persuasive communication may induce a person to change his opinion or attitude. This change is the same as the acquisition of any new habit: there must be some incentive or reinforcement, usually in the form of a reward or of the avoidance of an unpleasant situation. For example, a child growing up in Chicago may "learn" to like the Chicago Bears football team because all his friends do. Social acceptance acts as a powerful reinforcer or incentive to the learning of an attitude. If the boy then moves to Los Angeles, he may find that his opinion of the Bears is no longer rewarded, and may switch his allegiance to the Rams, because he finds that rooting for the home team leads to greater acceptance. In this case, change occurs because learning a new response brings greater reinforcement than the old one.

When an individual is exposed to a persuasive communication which advocates an attitude different from her own, two things occur, according to Hovland and his colleagues. She responds with her own attitude and with the position suggested by the communication. The acceptance of a new opinion is contingent upon the incentives suggested by the communication. These incentives take the form of rewards and punishments which follow upon the acceptance of the new opinion. If the reinforcement is greater than that for opinions already held, then change occurs.

Most research in this area has concentrated on using social approval as a reinforcer. For example, Ekman (1958) studied the use of both verbal and nonverbal signs of approval to condition a negative attitude toward capital punishment. A sixty-three-item questionnaire related to the use of capital punishment was administered individually to each subject, with no reinforcement given for the first twenty-one items. The remaining items were reinforced. The verbal reinforcer was the response "good" and the nonverbal incentive was a head nod, smile, and a slight movement forward. The results showed that the number of anti-capital-punishment responses increased as a result of both types of social approval. Other experiments have replicated these results, employing similar types of reinforcement (Calvin, 1962; Krasner, Knowles, and Ullmann, 1965).

Although Hovland, Janis, and Kelley's theory stimulated a good deal of research, it is no longer as important as it was. Three factors have contributed to its decline. First, behaviorism, on which learning theory is based, has, to a great extent, been supplemented with newer theoretical approaches. Secondly, there is some doubt that inducing a person to express an opinion by means of social approval or other types of reinforcement is tantamount to a change in attitude (Insko, 1967). It may reflect only compliance (Kelman, 1961), the most superficial level of social influence. *Compliance,* according to Kelman, refers to the statement of an opinion only for the purpose of obtaining a reward or avoiding a punishment. This is the level of social influence that experiments

WAS PATTY HEARST BRAINWASHED?

When Patricia Hearst, member of the prominent publishing family, was put on trial for bank robbery, her lawyer, F. Lee Bailey, used the argument that she had been brainwashed as his principal defense tactic. He argued that since she had been brainwashed, she was not herself and therefore was not responsible for her actions. Bailey sought to make the analogy between a judgment of legal insanity and brainwashing. A plea of insanity would condemn the defendent to years in a mental institution, whereas brainwashing could be quickly remedied and the victim brought back to herself. In the trial he had to prove that his client had, indeed, been brainwashed and that brainwashing was a legitimate defense, as is, for example, insanity or acting in self-defense.

Patty Hearst had been kidnapped as a political gesture by an extreme left-wing organization, the Symbionese Liberation Army. Several months after her capture, tapes were released to the media in which Hearst could be heard denouncing capitalist society, and her parents as members of the ruling class as well. At the same time, she announced her decision to join the SLA and to adopt the name "Tania." At no time prior to her kidnapping had Hearst ever been heard to voice such sentiments. Did the SLA brainwash her? If not, how could her parents, her lawyer, and the jury make sense of her dramatic change in attitude?

In an article in a popular magazine, Bailey (1976) describes his impressions on first being introduced to Hearst. He writes that he was amazed to find a woman acting so much like a robot. She seemed physically and emotionally numb, and he uses the word "anesthetized" to describe her responses. He found her emotionally fragile, as if in a state of shock, and noted that she seemed to be functioning with less than normal alertness.

Bailey believed Patty Hearst was brainwashed. At her trial, under the questioning by Bailey. Hearst revealed that she had been subjected to constant pressure from SLA members. According to her testimony, she was kept gagged, bound, and blindfolded for a number of weeks in a tiny closet. She was unable to eat for many days. She was questioned unceasingly by Cinque, the group's leader, and threatened with sexual abuse and death. In consequence, she became convinced that she might at any time be killed at the whim of her captors. The SLA even convinced her that she was a sacrificial victim, abandoned by her parents and government—doomed to death unless she joined the SLA.

When Hearst was being held in jail prior to her trial, Bailey noted that she was unable to remember events from her captivity. Although he thought she was demonstrating odd behavior, one of the psychiatrists described her as "a returned prisoner of war—one who has endured an experience that cannot be revealed for fear the unbearable emotions of that ordeal will return and tear the fragile survivor apart." She was unable to remember incidents connected with the past, even the time before she was kidnapped, and she was unable to gauge time. About the holdup of a sporting goods store, she said, "I can't believe I didn't just let them get caught and turn myself in."

Unfortunately for Hearst, the jury was not convinced by Bailey's defense. They accepted neither the brainwashing testimony nor the legitimacy of brainwashing as a defense.

such as Ekman's (1958) reflect. However, for a statement to reflect a person's true attitude, it must come from a deeper, internalized level.

Perhaps the most important reason for the decline in influence of the reinforcement approach was the formulation of the *theory of cognitive dissonance.* As we will see in the next section, cognitive dissonance is often at variance with reinforcement theory. It makes predictions which seem contrary to common sense: sometimes, according to dissonance theory, the least amount of reinforcement produces the greatest attitude change.

Cognitive dissonance

The theory of cognitive dissonance, introduced by Leon Festinger in 1957, has been influential in social psychology because it makes such surprising predictions. An important element in the theory is *cognition*—that is, knowledge of any kind. Cognitions include facts, behavior, beliefs, opinions, or anything else of which a person is aware. Everyone has countless cognitions, and the basic notion of Festinger's theory is that we strive for *cognitive consistency.* That is, we seek to make our cognitions consistent, or in agreement, each with the other. This is not always possible, however. For example, consider the student who has a high opinion of his intellectual abilities. This same student then fails an exam. The first cognition, the belief that he is smart, is inconsistent with another—the fact that he failed the test. When two cognitions are inconsistent, as in this case, they are said to be *dissonant,* and the person is in a state of *cognitive dissonance.*

Two cognitions are dissonant if the opposite of one follows from the other. As another example, consider a doctor who smokes: the fact that he smokes is not consistent with his knowledge that smoking cigarettes is highly correlated with lung cancer. The first cognition, smoking, is in a dissonant relationship with the second, that smoking causes a dread disease.

Magnitude of dissonance. The degree of dissonance depends on two factors: first, the importance of the cognition to the individual, and second, the proportion of relevant cognitions to total cognitions concerning a particular issue which are dissonant. Let us start with the first factor: if the cognitions involved are of little consequence to the person, little dissonance is produced, even though the cognitions may be in a dissonant relationship. For example, when a small item is bought in a store where one knows the merchandise is overpriced, dissonance may be created but its magnitude will be low. On the other hand, failing an examination might produce a high level of dissonance because of its importance to the student. The subjective nature of the determination of "importance" leaves the theory open to criticism because the relevance of particular cognitions varies from person to person (Insko, 1967).

Secondly, the magnitude of dissonance increases as the number of cognitions that are in a dissonant relationship increase. Thus, the more smokers our doctor friend observes who succumb to lung cancer, the greater the dissonance created by his continuing to smoke. Similarly, the bright student who fails an exam has a greater degree of dissonance when he learns that other students whom he does not consider particularly intelligent passed the exam.

Dissonance reduction. Festinger postulates that as the level of dissonance between cognitions increases, a person feels more and more pressure to reduce it. The basic assumption of the theory is that people are motivated to behave and think consistently. In this sense, dissonance can be seen as having properties like those of other negative drives, such as fear, in that the person is motivated to reduce or eliminate the pressure.

Cognitions are not static and their rigidity varies according to their importance. These facts set a limit to the magnitude of dissonance. As Festinger puts it: *"The maximum dissonance that can possibly exist between any two elements is equal to the total resistance to change of the less resistant element"* (1957, p. 28). As the least resistant cognition changes, dissonance is reduced by means of a process of self-justification (Aronson, 1976). There are three ways in which this process can take place: by reducing the importance of the dissonant cognitions, by adding consonant cognitions, or by changing one of the cognitions so that they are no longer inconsistent. For example, the person who does not like his job but continues to work is in a state of cognitive dissonance. He may seek to justify staying at that job by lessening the importance of the negative aspects of his work. Or the person may enhance the cognitions consonant with staying on the job, such as "the pay is good," or "the benefits are substantial." The third method, that of changing one of the cognitions, can result in two different outcomes. He may change his attitude toward the job and come to view it favorably, or he may quit. However, making the decision to quit, as we shall see in the next section, may create a new dissonant situation as the person seeks to justify the decision.

Postdecisional dissonance. When an important decision must be made, such as choosing a car, a career, or a college, conflict is engendered by the consideration of the possible alternatives. After the decision has been made, the conflict is resolved but dissonance is produced. All of the positive aspects of the unchosen alternatives, along with the negative aspects of the chosen alternative, are in dissonance with the decision. For example, suppose one is forced to choose between two jobs, one of which is high-paying but stressful and insecure, while the other pays less but is comfortable and relatively secure. Whichever job is chosen, dissonance will be produced. If the person chooses the secure job, then the relatively low pay will be dissonant with the decision. On the other hand, the stress and fear of being fired will be dissonant with the choice of the high-paying job.

This type of dissonance can be reduced by reevaluating the alternatives. After the choice is made, the person will seek justification for making that choice. Thus, a person in this situation will tend to increase the attractiveness and value of the chosen alternative as well as decrease the attractiveness of the unchosen alternative. This reevaluation process to reduce dissonance is illustrated in an experiment by Brehm (1956). College women were asked to rate the desirability of such products as a toaster, portable radio, automatic coffee maker, and so on. There were eight items in all, and to compensate the women for their time, they were told that they would be able to pick one of the items to take with them. They were then informed that because of short supply, they would have to choose between one of two items. Dissonance theory predicts that higher levels of dissonance are produced if a person has to make a choice between two similar items rather than between two disparate items. Therefore, in the high-dissonance condition, the subjects were given a choice between two similarly rated items, whereas the choice in the low-dissonance condition was between two items far apart in the desirability ratings. After making their choice, the subjects were asked to rate all of the items again. The final ratings revealed that there was a strong tendency to increase the evaluation of the chosen object, whereas the rejected alternative decreased in attractiveness. This was true for both high and low dissonance, with a greater change in the high-dissonance condition. Thus, in either case, the effort to reduce dissonance involved tipping the scales decisively in favor of the actual decision.

An interesting aspect of postdecisional dissonance is that reevaluation occurs only when the outcome of the decision is certain. If it appears that there is a chance that a rejected alternative might still be obtainable, no dissonance is produced, and therefore no reevaluation is necessary. Jecker (1964), in an experiment similar to Brehm's, asked students to choose between two popular records; they were assured they would be permitted to keep the one they selected. One group of subjects were then told that there was a good chance that they would also receive the unchosen record; the second group was told that there was a slight chance this would happen; a third group was told that there was no chance at all. Only in this last group, when there was no chance of receiving the rejected alternative, did a significant change in attitude toward the selected record occur.

Disconfirmed expectancies. When something is expected and the anticipated event does not occur, it is not only disappointing but dissonance-producing as well. If one pays $5,000 for a new car and it turns out to be a "lemon," dissonance is produced between the expectation of performance and the failure of that expectation to materialize. One way of resolving this situation is to try to justify the purchase on the grounds that it was a good idea even though it did not work out. This was the reaction of a group of people who prophesied that the world was coming to an end.

Festinger, Riecken, and Schachter (1956) did a study in which they observed a small group of people who believed that the world was going to end. (See chapter 1 for the methodology of this research.) In addition, the leader of the group made a prophecy as to the specific date on which this event was to take place. The group avoided publicity and quietly went about preparing for "doomsday." Festinger and his colleagues saw this as an excellent example of a dissonance-producing situation because of the discrepancy between the group's commitment to their beliefs, on the one hand, and the fact that there was very little likelihood that the prediction would come true, on the other. As Festinger wrote (Festinger, in Evans, 1976): "If you really believe the second coming is going to occur and the world as it exists today is going to vanish, you don't go about your life in a normal manner. Material possessions don't mean anything, jobs don't mean anything. You just prepare for the second coming."

When the predicted doomsday came and went, members of the group did, indeed, experience a high level of dissonance, as evidenced by their subsequent behavior. Assuming their experience of a high level of dissonance, what did they do to reduce it? They chose, in the first place, to cling to their doomsday belief. Therefore, in some way they had to justify quitting their jobs and abandoning their material possessions. To bring their cognitions into some kind of harmony, they chose to create a new cognition to rectify the failure of the old one: their leader proceeded to set a new date for doomsday. Furthermore, this time the members did not keep their ideas to themselves but went out into the community to try to gain support for the correctness of their views. It seems that if a disconfirmed expectation is important enough to an individual, it may be easier for him to maintain his belief by trying to convince others that it is basically sound rather than to admit that it was wrong in the first place.

Of course, belief in the face of continued disconfirmation cannot be sustained indefinitely. One group, a UFO cult (Balch and Taylor, 1976), expected for months to be momentarily "beamed up" to a spaceship. Although the group proselytized for a while, like the group in the Festinger study, gradually, the members all left, one by one. They did not regret what they had done (this group also gave up their worldly possessions), but reduced their dissonance by emphasizing what they had learned from the experience.

Attitude-discrepant behavior. When an individual performs an action which is inconsistent with a belief or an attitude she holds, a third type of dissonant situation is created. For example, if one believes that a particular acquaintance cheats at cards, it is discrepant to play poker with that person. Similarly, if one's attitude toward communism is quite negative, a visit to the Soviet Union might prove to be dissonance-provoking. Most of the time our behavior is consistent with our attitudes; yet there are bound to be situations in which we engage in attitude-discrepant behavior. A person may detest social psychology, yet study it diligently. Or one may think that his $20,000-a-year job is a waste of time but go to work every day. In these situations we have sufficient justification for our behavior. The social psychology student may work to get a good grade; the job holder, for the money. Cognitive dissonance theory has concentrated on situations in which there is insufficient justification for an action, however, because it is just these situations that produce attitude change.

The classic experiment demonstrating the application of cognitive dissonance to attitude change was conducted by Festinger and Carlsmith (1959). In this experiment, each subject was required to perform a tedious set of tasks. The experimenters then induced the subject to tell another person that the tasks were interesting and enjoyable. Some of the subjects were offered $20 to do this, while others were offered only $1. A control group also performed the boring tasks, but these subjects were not asked to lie. The experimental subjects then were asked how much they had enjoyed the tasks and how willing they were to participate in a similar experiment. Those subjects who received $1 for lying actually rated the experiment more enjoyable than the subjects who received $20. Why?

Clearly the situation is dissonance-producing. Doing something very boring and then stating that it is enjoyable is attitude-discrepant. The $20 subjects can reduce their dissonance by adding the cognition that they were paid a good sum of money for a little lie; this group had sufficient justification for their actions. One dollar, however, is not a sufficient sum to warrant telling a lie. This group reduced their dissonance in the only remaining way: they changed their attitudes toward the tasks.

This study and others like it (Mills, 1958) created a good deal of criticism when they first appeared, because they produced outcomes that ran counter to learning theory. Learning theory would predict that reinforcement following a response usually increases that response: the greater the magnitude of the reinforcement, the greater the likelihhood of the response. That would mean that the $20 subjects, in Festinger and Carlsmith's experiment, should enjoy the tasks more. However, perhaps we should ask again what is being reinforced: the performance of the tasks, or convincing someone of an untruth? If the $20 subject were asked "How much do you enjoy lying?," the results might be different. That is not to say that cognitive dissonance is not valid; it does mean that its findings do not necessarily contradict learning theory.

Attitude change as a result of cognitive dissonance does not occur only in situations of insufficient reward. In one experiment (Zimbardo, Weisenberg, Firestone, and Levy, 1965), subjects were actually induced to eat grasshoppers! In one condition, the experimenter was very warm and friendly, whereas in the other condition, the experimenter was cold and austere. After they ingested the insects, the subjects were asked how much they liked them. The subjects who had the "cold" experimenter rated the grasshoppers higher than the subjects who had the "warm" experimenter. The latter group had sufficient justification for eating grasshoppers—they were doing it because the experimenter was "so nice." The group with the "cold" experimenter, however, lacking this justification, changed their attitudes toward eating grasshoppers. Thus, according to dissonance theory, the important element in producing attitude change is that there be insufficient justification for performing discrepant behavior. If a person is coerced or threatened into performing a contradictory act, no dissonance is created (Aronson and Carlsmith, 1963; Freedman, 1965) because the person is merely complying under pressure. However, only when the individual perceives that he or she has a choice in the situation (David and Jones, 1960) is the person compelled to justify his actions by changing his attitudes in order to gain cognitive consistency.

Attitudes and the Mass Media

A great quantity of information is transmitted every day by the mass media, including television, radio, movies, newspapers, books, and magazines. All are concerned with communicating on a mass basis. Brown (1963) defines *mass communication* as that "which is directed towards a relatively large, heterogeneous, and anonymous audience" (p. 142). This audience is the essential characteristic of mass communication. The research question, then, becomes a study of the effects of messages reaching millions of people almost simultaneously. How are the effects of mass communication different from the effects of personal communication?

Before the printing press was invented by Gutenberg in the fifteenth century, information traveled mostly by word of mouth. It might have taken weeks, months, or even years for information to reach those concerned with it. One is reminded of the Battle of New Orleans fought during the War of 1812. The war was actually over, but the combatants in far-away Louisiana had no way of knowing this and a savage battle ensued. Today, with television, we become aware of events instantly. A whole nation watched as Jack Ruby shot Lee Harvey Oswald, followed a few days later by the funeral of an assassinated president, wiith close-ups of the grieving family. In 1969 people crowded around their television sets to watch strangely clad men bounce buoyantly around the moon. Nor is the TV camera a passive observer of events. Situations are created for it, as the presidential debates of 1960 and 1976 attest.

How have these technological feats affected us? In order to answer this question, it is necessary to deal with two aspects of mass communication: its *content,* and the media as a *process.* Since television is the most powerful of the mass media, most of this section will be based on the effects of television, but what is presented is true to some extent of all the media.

The content of mass media

Brown (1963) states that mass communication has four functions:
1. the surveillance of the environment, or supplying the *news;*
2. commentaries on the news which take the form of *propaganda,* or *editorializing;*
3. the transmission of the social heritage, or *education;* and
4. entertainment.

Since our main concern is with attitude change, it is necessary to look at the role of propaganda in relation to the other three functions.

News is a relatively recent innovation. Before the advent of newspapers, there was really no such thing as news *per se;* the closest thing to it was local gossip. It was not thought necessary by the local and national authorities to share general information with the public, unless it was to manipulate it for some purpose, such as building support for fighting a war. One might say that the mass media in the form of newspapers invented news.

Propaganda, however, is different from news in that it is a deliberate attempt at indoctrination. Propaganda is most obvious in totalitarian societies where the government controls the mass media. In these countries the mass media are looked upon as natural extensions of the government and as tools to promote its policies. In the United States and other Western countries, however, propaganda usually poses as one of the three other functions of mass media: news, education, or entertainment. In retrospect, we can view the "yellow journalism" of the 1890s as a deliberate attempt to manipulate opinion, although at the time it was perceived as news (DeFleur and Ball-Rokeach, 1975). More recently, during the Vietnam war, the nightly television newscasters reported the daily body count in which the enemy dead were usually reported as ten to the American one—often a gross distortion. News about events in a war, however, is controlled by the armed forces by means of censorship and control of access to information. Thus, war news must be considered government propaganda even when it is presented by private enterprise as part of a regular news program.

Propaganda also poses as entertainment. One weapon of the propagandist is to suggest that his message is consonant with the existing beliefs and attitudes of his audience (Brown, 1963). An excellent way to manipulate this situation is to induce the audience to identify with the hero. For example, the Hollywood motion pictures made during World War II portrayed John Wayne or William Bendix as personifying the highest ideals of American democracy. These films served their purpose well, but were particularly effective because they were never clearly labeled as propaganda; they were sold as entertainment.

Perhaps the clearest examples of the influence of television, since it is purposeful, are the commercials by which buying habits are manipulated. Although products that have been advertised on television and radio have sometimes failed, in most cases television is successful in raising product awareness. One restaurant chain, for example, reported that in an area where they had outlets, television advertising boosted awareness among customers by 35 percent. In addition to awareness, of course, there are the actual sales of products. Some commodities, especially over-the-counter drugs, continue to sell well despite the fact that consumer studies have shown that unadvertised but comparable products are available for much less money (Bem, 1970).

Another influence of the mass media is concerned not with what is shown but what is omitted. This selectivity is especially powerful on television, where there is so much money involved that many issues and topics get shuffled aside. More important, controversial issues may be rejected for fear of offending segments of the audience. This fact has led Edith Efron to call television "the timid giant" (McLuhan, 1964).

Even the extent of exposure can make a difference. Efron (1971) developed a concept she calls the *parallel principle,* by which she means that the decision of a network to select or omit opinions on the news reflects an editorial bias. She studied the 1968 presidential election, suspecting that all three networks were editorially biased against Richard Nixon. Then she collected her data by counting the number of words spoken for or against the major candidates on the evening news of the three major networks, beginning seven weeks prior to the election. Figure 8-3 shows the results of this study. Soon after Nixon was elected, members of his administration charged that the media were anti-Nixon. Efron's study supports this contention.

The presidential debates of 1960 and 1976 also reflect the exclusionary power of television. No representatives of any political party other than those of the Democratic and Republican parties were present. This places television in the position of appearing officially neutral, while effectively banning opinion coming from the right or left of the political spectrum. Prior to television, the two-party system was a tradition. The selectivity of television has further institutionalized that tradition.

On the other hand, national television may give coverage to issues omitted at the local level. For example, before the advent of television, Southern blacks could get news only from local radio stations and newspapers, which censored much of the racial news, particularly that dealing with the civil rights movement (Bagdikian, 1971). In the 1950s, however, blacks got uncensored reports of events in the civil rights movement from national television reports. Thus, television provided Southern blacks with in-depth reports on racial news. According to Bagdikian, this access to uncensored news may have raised the consciousness of blacks, and so played a key role in the social changes brought about by the civil rights movement of the 1960s.

The logical question that emerges is, can the media induce members of the public to change their minds about political candidates? Two studies have produced evidence indicating that the media have little influence on the process of voter decision-making. In a classic study by Lazarsfeld, Berelson, and Gaudet (1948), for instance, it was found that the media during the 1940 election—consisting chiefly of radio and the press—had little effect on swaying individuals to vote one way or the other. This study did, however, uncover one important fact about the impact of the media on the opinions of the electorate: people tended to turn to *opinion leaders* for interpretations of the information transmitted by radio, newspapers, and magazines. This phenomenon is referred to by Katz (1957) as the "two-step" process of communication. The opinion leaders were influenced by what they read and heard in the media, and their opinions, in turn, influenced the individuals who looked to them for clarification. Thus, we can say that most people appear to be influenced by the media, either directly or indirectly.

A later study by Wilbur Schramm (1967) supported the findings of Lazarsfeld and his colleagues. Schramm found that the media (including radio, television, and the press) have little effect on behavior if the message is not mediated by the personal contact of some opinion leader or authority figure. In connection with such mediating factors, a study by Joseph Klapper (1957) suggests that the media do not change attitudes or beliefs; rather, they reinforce existing ones. Individuals tend to select those messages from the media that support their own attitudes and beliefs. Thus, speeches by political candidates are aimed at reinforcing the views of their constituents rather than at attempting to convert individuals who support the opposition.

**A Comparison of the Number of Words
Spoken on the Three Major TV Networks
for and against the 1968 Presidential Candidates**

Figure 8–3. A count of the words spoken for and against the candidates shows that although Nixon was the target of much more unfavorable notice, he received more attention.

	For	Against
Nixon	1,620	17,000
Humphrey	7,458	8,307

SOURCE: Adapted from Efron, E. *The news twisters*. New York: Manor Books, 1971. Pp. 32–35.

The process of television

So far we have concentrated primarily on the product of mass media, the content. However, Marshall McLuhan has been concerned with the effects generated by the technological qualities of the media themselves (1964). McLuhan's main contention is that every technological innovation is an extension of man. The printing press was an extension of the hand, just as the telescope is an extension of the eye. This idea can be expressed vividly by considering the Viking landings on Mars. Each Viking contains an "arm," a mechanical scoop to analyze soil samples. This arm thus is an extension of man's natural arm over millions of miles. McLuhan views the electronic media, such as television and the computer, as an extension of man's nervous system. Each technological feat, and therefore each extension, changes our environment. This is why McLuhan feels that the structure of a given medium is much more important than its content—because of its environmental impact. McLuhan summarizes this idea in his famous statement, "The medium is the message."

Each medium has certain properties which influence human behavior. Television, for example, because of its low picture definition, is a "cool" medium, since it requires the viewer to participate in filling in the picture. Conversely, radio is a "hot" medium because the listener is not required to be so involved in completing the transmission. Hot media are better vehicles for transmitting action and emotion. Therefore, motion pictures are considered a hot medium. A cool medium such as television tends to exaggerate such subtleties as a raised eyebrow or a particular intonation. Another characteristic of television, according to McLuhan, is that it is tactile, because of the necessary involvement of the viewer (McLuhan, 1964).

McLuhan's theory, although it has received widespread recognition, has not been adopted by many researchers. Most social psychologists have rejected McLuhan's technological determinism as being too extreme. They feel that both media content and structure are important. Furthermore, many social scientists are wary of any explanation that points to a single factor as the cause of a particular social phenomenon (DeFleur and Ball-Rokeach, 1975).

Dependency. The concept of the effect of communication presented by De-Fleur and Ball-Rokeach (1975) is concerned with the fact that in an urban, industrialized society, man is becoming more and more dependent on mass-media information sources. This *dependency* takes the form of satisfying certain needs, such as the need to understand one's social world and the need for *fantasy-escape,* brought on by the stress of the urban environment. With increased dependency, there is a greater probability that the information supplied by the media will alter various attitudes and beliefs. Urban environments tend to be alienating so that the traditional lines of personal communication break down. Therefore, the person in this setting becomes more dependent on the mass media for *interpretation of reality*, rather than relying on the comparisons supplied by other people. Thus, the mass media play an ever-increasing role in attitude formation and change. The public relies on the media for the formation of attitudes toward changing conceptions of communism, energy crises, sex, and political corruption, to name just a few of the important issues of the last decade. Dependency is another concept, like those of McLuhan, that is concerned with the media as process. Rather than attending to the messages of the media or the lack thereof, dependency on the media itself is seen as the source of attitude change.

Brainwashing

In our society the term *brainwashing* is frequently applied to anyone who has a strong commitment to a belief which we cannot understand. It is as if we felt that the person's ideas are so alien that they must have been forced on him. The concept of brainwashing also has been used to explain a rapid change in attitudes and beliefs, for example, to account for a religious or political conversion. Distrust of such institutions as the military or public education may bring forth charges of brainwashing. The term itself was coined by an American journalist, Edward Hunter (1951), as a translation of the Chinese *hsi nao*, which means, literally, "wash brain." Hunter heard the term used by Chinese informants following the Chinese revolution.

In this country, brainwashing gained currency during the Korean war, when both the Koreans and the Chinese used brainwashing or thought-reform techniques in an attempt to coerce American prisoners of war to renounce their attitudes, beliefs, and values and adopt those of their captors. Following the repatriation of the prisoners, a rash of articles appeared which added to the confusion concerning these techniques. Some prisoners reported that the brainwashing techniques were so terrifying that no one could possibly withstand them, whereas other articles denounced the American soldiers who had succumbed (Schein, 1956).

Recently the concept of brainwashing has reemerged in the mass media. For example, the defense in the Patty Hearst case rested on an attempt to show that she had been brainwashed by her kidnappers. Another instance is the outrage of many parents in recent years over the techniques allegedly used by certain religious groups, such as the Jesus People and the Unification Church, in converting their children. A typical comment from one parent was that a religious cult was using "mind control" to hold her daughter, implying that her conversion was not of her own volition (*New York Times*, October 15,

1976). Given the fear and confusion surrounding this subject, it might be useful to try to understand it better. Let us begin by examining the ordeal of one man who was subjected to Chinese thought reform.

The case of Dr. Vincent.   The experiences of Dr. Charles Vincent were reported by Robert J. Lifton (1961), who interviewed former prisoners of the Chinese Communists in Hong Kong in 1954. Dr. Vincent was a Frenchman who had remained in China after the revolution to carry on his medical practice, until he was arrested and sent to a "reeducation center." He was placed in an eight-by-twelve-foot bare cell, in which there were other prisoners who immediately began heaping invectives on him, such as "spy," "criminal," and "imperialist." Dr. Vincent was very confused because not only did he not know why he had been arrested, but he could not understand why his fellow prisoners were abusing him.

Then his cellmates began to demand that he confess his "crimes" to the government. During interrogation Dr. Vincent was urged to confess, and when he told them he was not guilty of any crimes, they put him in chains and handcuffed his hands behind his back. He remained handcuffed for several days, not being allowed to sleep or bathe. When Vincent protested that he was innocent, his cellmates told him that his guilt was self-evident by the fact that he was in prison. "The government does not arrest innocent men," one of the inmates explained to him. After a few days of this treatment, Dr. Vincent decided that the only way to improve his situation would be to fabricate a confession. He did so, with the guidance of his captors. The chains were removed and he gradually received more lenient treatment. Vincent confessed to being a spy and implicated and denounced friends and associates supposedly involved in the fictitious spy ring.

Later in his prison stay, Vincent took part in "reeducating" other prisoners, a process called the "struggle." When Lifton interviewed Dr. Vincent for the first time, Vincent explained that thought reform or brainwashing could be viewed in two ways:

From the imperialist side we are not criminals; from the people's side we are criminals. If we look at this from the imperialists' side, reeducation is a kind of compulsion. But if we look at it from the people's side, it is to die and be born again" (Lifton, 1961, p. 44).

Elements of brainwashing

Certain elements in the case of Dr. Vincent can be generalized to all brainwashing procedures. These elements or psychological steps are designed to bring about "the penetration by the psychological forces of the environment into the inner emotions of the individual person . . ." (Lifton, 1961, p. 66). That is, the usual barriers between the person and the environment are first broken down and then the continued psychological survival of the person becomes contingent upon accepting attitudes and beliefs from the outside. This environmental "press" is the central factor in brainwashing. Ego and everything else that determines identity give way to the pressure from the outside. Then the individual comes to reject his former identity and construct another in accordance with the precepts of his captors. This is not mere compliance in the sense in which Kelman (1961) uses the term, but a rebuilding of the person's psyche. As Dr. Vincent put it, it is "to die and be born again." The essential elements of this process are:

1. *A rigid environment.* A rigid, controlled environment enables the brainwasher to exert maximum environmental pressure on the individual, and at the same time to remove the person from familiar surroundings, including family and friends, which support old ways of thinking and acting. A prison or hospital, with its physical barriers, is ideal for this, of course, but the same thing can be accomplished in a religious commune or in a military training camp.

2. *A loss of identity.* From the beginning, Dr. Vincent was told that he was not a doctor, but a "criminal" and a "spy." These assertions, coupled with physical torture and the humiliating "struggles" with his fellow prisoners, brought about a loss of Vincent's sense of self, a sense of who he was as a person. Building a sense of identity, as Erikson (1963) has detailed, is a lifelong process, a process which can be terminated rapidly under extreme environmental pressure.

3. *Extreme emotional arousal.* Many researchers feel that this is the *sine qua non* of brainwashing. Sargant (1959), taking a Pavlovian approach to brainwashing, states that brainwashing takes place only when the brain is overstimulated. Intense emotional excitement causes the brain to go into an

KOREAN PRISONERS OF WAR: TRAITORS OR VICTIMS?

What is brainwashing? How does it work? Why is it so effective? At the end of the Korean War in 1953, an American psychiatrist, Edgar Schein (1956), began to answer these questions by examining returned prisoners of war who had been brainwashed by the Chinese. At the time, the concept was little understood, and there were conflicting ideas about the methods and techniques of brainwashing. A composite of the interviews showed that the Chinese were able to undermine the belief structures of the prisoners by maintaining ceaseless psychological pressure. Two basic tactics made the program successful: the Chinese effectively prevented the men from forming close personal ties, and they used a system of rewards and punishments to reinforce "correct" behavior.

When the prisoners were first captured, the Chinese created an atmosphere of friendliness and leniency which would later be useful in making some men receptive to their ideas. In the next few weeks, however, the men were inadequately clothed and fed, and threatened with severe punishments and the possibility of death. But they were also told that if they were "cooperative," nothing would happen to them. In this atmosphere of fear, individual prisoners began to look out for themselves, and the team spirit dissolved.

Once interned in the permanent camps, the prisoners were segregated according to race, nationality, and rank. The psychiatrists discovered that the Chinese organized camp life around a whole set of social conditions which would be useful in bringing the Americans around to their way of thinking. First, all sources of information were cut off, and the prisoners became dependent on their captors to find out what was going on in the outside world. Then the Chinese eavesdropped on the prisoners, creating a general air of mistrust which made the men suspicious of each other and wary of congregating in groups. Finally, the Chinese made efforts to recruit volunteers to serve as their lackeys. These men were hand-picked by their captors, but the prisoners were forced to "elect" them.

The actual indoctrination was equally pervasive. Prisoners were required to attend daily lectures and watch propaganda movies. The most powerful tool was the testimonials of prisoners supporting the Communists. Schein found that if even one man became convinced, it was no longer possible for some of the others to resist indoctrination.

The Chinese also required the men to hold group discussions about the indoctrination material. The prisoners were questioned constantly about their nonmilitary lives and badgered when their answers did not collaborate with past accounts. In time, some men believed that the Chinese could find out anything about anybody. Also, the Chinese made the prisoners "confess" to relatively minor infractions of camp rules. These verbal or written confessions were a regular feature of camp life.

Finally, the Chinese used a system of rewards and punishments. Prisoners were enticed to collaborate with the promise of release, communication with the outside world, and the luxury of personal items or food. They were also warned repeatedly that horrible punishments awaited those who refused to participate.

Brainwashing, then, is an accumulation of tactics. The Chinese were successful because they maintained an environment of unrelenting psychological stress. They promised relief but dangled the possibility of unknown terrors before the prisoners.

inhibitory state as a protective device. It is in this inhibitory state, according to Sargant, that brainwashing and religious conversion can occur.

4. *Guilt.* One of the most pervasive aspects of Dr. Vincent's experience was the constant assertions that he was guilty of a crime. This guilt was supported by a circular reasoning that followed this sequence: accusation, Vincent's refutation, and then support for the accusation by invoking the environment. Statements such as "You must be guilty because you are in prison," and "The government does not arrest an innocent man" are examples of this process. This tautological reasoning, together with the breakdown of identity, left Vincent feeling that he was a guilty person, a criminal.

5. *Confession.* The pervasive feelings of guilt create a compulsion to confess even though the confession may have to be fictionalized. This is often the case in religious conversion, in which the sinner is urged to confess his sins. That confession in brainwashing leads to attitude change is consonant with cognitive dissonance theory and self-perception theory: the confession is attitude-discrepant behavior and thus leads to attitude change, if there is no external force motivating that behavior. To the outside observer, brainwashing is nothing but external force, but to the prisoner or potential religious convert, the intense guilt feelings that have been created in him lead to the confession. The confession, being a lie to begin with, becomes true to the confessor to account for the feelings of wrongdoing or sin.

6. *Negative and positive reinforcement. Negative reinforcement* is the alleviation of a painful or unpleasant state. We saw this in Dr. Vincent's case when the chains and handcuffs were removed following the initiation of his confession. This encouraged him to confess in order to avoid further torture. Later during his stay in prison, the companionship of his fellow prisoners, *positive reinforcement,* helped support his new attitudes.

Religious conversion

Some types of religious conversion are accomplished by techniques similar to brainwashing. One researcher had an experience with a group of "Jesus Freaks" that illustrates the use of these techniques. This group travels the Staten Island Ferry in New York looking for converts. They usually seek a young person sitting alone and begin by accosting him with questions such as "How do you feel about Jesus," "Is Jesus in your heart," and "Do you read the Bible." Any protestation is met by turning to a page in the Bible which refutes the protest. This encounter goes on until the half-hour ferry ride is over. There are two similarities here to the case of Dr. Vincent. First there is the "struggle," in which the "Jesus Freaks" confront the person in a rather hostile way. The second is the tautological reasoning involved in presenting Biblical quotations. "Of course it is true; it is in the Bible" is very similar to "Of course you are guilty; you are in jail." In both cases the environment is pressed on the individual.

If the potential convert accepts an invitation to the group's communal house, the pressure becomes more intense. Challenges to his identity occur within minutes of his arrival with suggestions that what he does, and what his conception of himself is, are unimportant compared to the glory of pursuing God, Jesus, and the Bible, and making converts.

The communal house is, in its way, as controlled an environment for the convert as a prison. All conversation is focused on him and on persuading him to accept the group's attitudes and ideas. The guilt process is initiated by talk of sin and more sin. The Bible is again referred to with the quote "All men are sinners," followed by the syllogism "All men are sinners, and since you are a man, then you are a sinner." Similar experiences have been reported by other researchers (e.g. Harder et al., 1972; Rice, 1976), all of whom stress the intense group pressure placed on the individual.

To compare a conversion to brainwashing is not to condemn either tactic, but only to point out that they contain certain similarities. In fact, attitude change can be viewed as a continuum ranging at one end from simple persuasion techniques which induce compliance, to conversion and brainwashing at the other end. Points along the continuum include the inoculation effect, cognitive dissonance, and fear arousal. Each process, from persuasion to brainwashing, involves a subsequent increase in pressure from the environmental scenario arranged by the persuader until, finally, the self is no longer able to maintain its integrity, is destroyed, and is recreated in the image of the persuader.

Summary

The study of attitude change seeks to understand the relationship between a communication and its recipient. The attempt to persuade someone to change his attitudes centers around three parts of the communication: its source, its nature, and its target. The prestige of the person communicating an attitude greatly affects the degree to which the target subject changes his attitude. Similarly, sources which are either attractive or trustworthy wield greater influence than those which are not. It has also been found that the intentions of the communicator contribute to his or her effectiveness: the source is most effective when no ulterior motive is perceived.

The nature and presentation of a communication play an important role in determining its effectiveness. Among the elements that affect the way the communication is received are whether one or both sides of the argument are presented, the order in which the arguments are presented, and the degree of discrepancy that exists between the attitudes of the source and those of the audience.

The characteristics of the audience also affect the outcome of the attitude change after the message has been delivered. A person with low self-esteem, for example, is more easily influenced than one who thinks highly of himself. Although there is some debate on the subject, there is also evidence that a fear-arousing message can motivate attitude change. Moreover, a person can be "inoculated" against accepting a communication aimed at changing his attitudes by subjecting him to a mild attack of his opinions.

A number of theories have been advanced to explain attitude change. According to reinforcement theory, for example, attitudes are responses learned as are any other responses. An attitude that is positively reinforced is adopted; one that is negatively reinforced is rejected. Opposed to reinforcement theory is the cognitive dissonance approach. This theory posits that we strive for cognitive consistency. As the level of dissonance between cognitions increases, the person feels greater pressure to reduce it. Postdecisional dissonance, disconfirmed expectancies, and attitude-discrepant behavior are other important elements of cognitive dissonance theory.

Currently, the perspective in social psychology that is receiving a good deal of attention is attribution theory. This approach suggests that we infer the motives of others by attributing their actions to either environmental pressures or internal causes.

The mass media, particularly television, are responsible for attitude change as well as attitude formation. Two aspects of mass communication are essential for our understanding of its effects on attitudes: the content of the media and the media as a process. Mass communication has four kinds of content: news, propaganda, education, and entertainment. In the United States, propaganda is communication in the guise of the other three. Studies have shown that the media influence political attitudes, either directly or indirectly, through opinion leaders.

Marshall McLuhan has divided media into two categories: hot and cool. A cool medium, such as television, requires the viewer to participate in completing the picture transmitted to him. Radio, by contrast, is a hot medium because the listener is not so involved.

Another explanation for rapid change in attitudes is brainwashing. All brainwashing procedures contain six elements: a rigid environment, a loss of identity, extreme emotional arousal, guilt, confession, and reinforcement. Some types of religious conversion are accomplished by techniques similar to those used in brainwashing.

Bibliography

ARONSON, E. *The social animal.* (2nd ed.) San Francisco: W. H. Freeman, 1976.

ARONSON, E., AND CARLSMITH, J. M. The effect of severity of threat on the devaluation of forbidden behavior. *Journal of Abnormal and Social Psychology,* 1963, **66,** 584–588.

ARONSON, E., TURNER, J., AND CARLSMITH, J. M. Communication credibility and communication discrepancy as determinants of opinion change. *Journal of Abnormal and Social Psychology,* 1963, 6 7, 31–36.

BAGDIKIAN, B. H. *The information machines.* New York: Harper and Row, 1971.

BAILEY, F. L. Patty Hearst: The untold story. *Ladies' Home Journal,* September 1976, **93,** 36.

BALCH, R. W., AND TAYLOR, D. Salvation in a UFO. *Psychology Today,* October 1976, p. 58.

BREHM, J. Post-decision changes in the desirability of alternatives. *Journal of Abnormal and Social Psychology,* 1956, **52,** 384–389.

BROWN, J. A. C. *Techniques of persuasion: From propaganda to brainwashing.* Baltimore: Penguin Books, 1963.

CALVIN, A. Social reinforcement. *Journal of Social Psychology,* 1962, **56,** 15–19.

COHEN, A. R. Some implications of self-esteem from social influence. In C. Hovland and I. L. Janis (Eds.), *Personality and persuasibility.* New Haven, Conn.: Yale University Press, 1959.

DABBS, J. M., JR., AND LEVENTHAL, H. Effects of varying the recommendations in a fear-arousing communication. *Journal of Personality and Social Psychology,* 1966, **4,** 525–531.

DAVIS, K. E., AND JONES, E. E. Changes in interpersonal perception as a means of reducing cognitive dissonance. *Journal of Abnormal and Social Psychology,* 1960, 6 1, 402–410.

DeFLEUR, M. L., AND BALL-ROKEACH, S. *Theories of mass communication.* (3rd ed.) New York: David McKay, 1975.

EFRON, E. *The news twisters.* New York: Manor Books, 1971.

EKMAN, P: A. A comparison of verbal and nonverbal behavior as reinforcing stimuli of opinion responses. Unpublished doctoral dissertation, Adelphi College, 1958.

ERIKSON, E. H. *Childhood and society.* (2nd ed.) New York: W. W. Norton, 1963.

EVANS, R. I. (Ed.) *The making of psychology.* New York: Alfred A. Knopf, 1976.

FESTINGER, L. *A theory of cognitive dissonance.* Stanford, Calif.: Stanford University Press, 1957.

FESTINGER, L., AND CARLSMITH, J. M. Cognitive consequences of forced compliance. *Journal of Abnormal and Social Psychology,* 1959, **58,** 203–210.

FESTINGER, L., RIECKEN, H., AND SCHACHTER, S. *When prophecy fails.* Minneapolis: University of Minnesota Press, 1956.

FREEDMAN, J. L. Long-term behavioral effects of cognitive dissonance. *Journal of Experimental Social Psychology*, 1965, **1**, 145–155.

FREEDMAN, J. L., CARLSMITH, J. M., AND SEARS, D. *Social psychology*. Englewood Cliffs, N.J.: Prentice-Hall, 1970.

FREEDMAN, J. L., AND SEARS, D. O. Warning, distraction, and resistance to influence. *Journal of Personality and Social Psychology*, 1965, **1**, 262–265.

HARDER, M. W., RICHARDSON, J. T., AND SIMMONDS, R. D. Jesus people. *Psychology Today*, December 1972, p. 45.

HOVLAND, C., AND JANIS, I. L. (Eds.) *Personality and persuasibility*. New Haven, Conn.: Yale University Press, 1959.

HOVLAND, C., JANIS, I. L., AND KELLEY, H. *Communication and persuasion*. New Haven, Conn.: Yale University Press, 1953.

HOVLAND, C. I., LUMSDAINE, A. A., AND SHEFFIELD, F. D. *Studies in social psychology in World War II. Vol. 3. Experiments on mass communication*. Princeton, N.J.: Princeton University Press, 1949.

HOVLAND, C., AND WEISS, W. The influence of source credibility on communication effectiveness. *Public Opinion Quarterly*, 1951, **15**, 635–650.

HUNTER, E. *Brain-washing in Red China*. New York: Vanguard Press, 1951.

INSKO, C. A. *Theories of attitude change*. Englewood Cliffs, N.J.: Prentice-Hall, 1967.

JANIS, I. L., AND FESHBACH, S. Effects of fear-arousing communications. *Journal of Abnormal and Social Psychology*, 1953, **48**, 78–92.

JECKER, J. The cognitive effects of conflict and dissonance. In L. Festinger (Ed.), *Conflict, decision and dissonance*. Stanford, Calif.: Stanford University Press, 1964.

KELMAN, H. C. Processes of opinion change. *Public Opinion Quarterly*, 1961, **25**, 57–78.

KELMAN, H. C., AND HOVLAND, C. Reinstatement of the communicator in delayed measurement of opinion change. *Journal of Abnormal and Social Psychology*, 1953, **48**, 327–355.

KRASNER, L., KNOWLES, J., AND ULLMANN, L. Effects of verbal conditioning of attitudes on subsequent motor performance. *Journal of Personality and Social Psychology*, 1965, **1**, 407–412.

LAZARSFELD, P., BERELSON, B., AND GAUDET, H. *The people's choice*. New York: Columbia University Press, 1948.

LEVENTHAL, H. Findings and theory in the study of fear communications. In L. Berkowitz (Ed.), *Advances in experimental social psychology*. Vol. 5. New York: Academic Press, 1970.

LEVENTHAL, H., AND SINGER, R. P. Affect arousal and positioning of recommendations in persuasive communication. *Journal of Personality and Social Psychology*, 1966, **4**, 137–146.

LEVENTHAL, H., SINGER, R. P., AND JONES, S. Effects of fear and specificity of recommendation upon attitudes and behavior. *Journal of Personality and Social Psychology*, 1965, **2**, 20–29.

LIFTON, R. J. *Thought reform and the psychology of totalism*. New York: W. W. Norton, 1961.

MCGUIRE, W. J., AND PAPAGEORGIS, D. The relative efficacy of various types of prior belief-defense in producing immunity against persuasion. *Journal of Abnormal and Social Psychology,* 1961, **62,** 327–337.

McLuhan, M. *Understanding media.* New York: McGraw-Hill, 1964.

Mailer, N. The search for Carter. *New York Times Magazine,* September 26, 1976, p. 19.

Miller, N., and Campbell, D. Recency and primacy in persuasion as a function of the timing of speeches and measurements. *Journal of Abnormal and Social Psychology,* 1959, **59,** 1–9.

Mills, J. Changes in moral attitudes following temptation. *Journal of Personality,* 1958, **26,** 517–531.

Rice, B. Messiah from Korea: Honor thy Father Moon. *Psychology Today,* January 1976, pp. 36–47.

Sargant, W. *Battle for the mind: A physiology of conversion and brainwashing.* New York: Harper and Row, 1959.

Schein, E. H. The Chinese indoctrination program for prisoners of war: A study of attempted "brainwashing." *Psychiatry,* 1956, **19,** 149–172.

Sears, D. O. Opinion formation and information preferences in an adversary situation. *Journal of Experimental Social Psychology,* 1967, **2,** 130–142.

Walster, E., Aronson, E., and Abrahams, D. On increasing the persuasiveness of a low-prestige communicator. *Journal of Experimental Social Psychology,* 1966, **2,** 325–342.

Zimbardo, P., Weisenberg, M., Firestone, I., and Levy, B. Communication effectiveness in producing public conformity and private attitude change. *Journal of Personality,* 1965, **33,** 233–255.

9

Language and Communication

This communication—the book you are now reading—is a purely verbal one, or as close to it as you are ever likely to get. No doubt the design of the typeface, the layout of the page, the feel of the paper may convey ideas to you that cannot be found in the words alone, but the communication would be even farther from the written word if you listened to the text read aloud on a record. For then the reader's tone of voice, reading speed, loudness, and other vocal characteristics would soon give you the impression that she found this material profoundly intriguing—or that she considered it rubbish, or that she didn't understand it and couldn't care less because she was recording for pay. The mixture of verbal and nonverbal communication would be still more inextricable if the reader were in a lecture room, not on a record; and even more if she were speaking extemporaneously, giving full play to facial expression and gesture.

It seems, then, that if a communication is verbal, it is mixed with nonverbal elements. But is there any purely nonverbal communication, among human beings at least? A smile, perhaps? An upraised middle finger? A slow, hip-swinging gait? One investigator, F. E. X. Dance, exploring the difference between vocal and nonverbal communication, points out that:

a scream . . . may be vocal and nonverbal on the reflex discharge level. [But] when interpreted by a passerby [it] may have meaning . . . beyond the meaning to the screamer. Thus, the passerby's meaning . . . is interpreted by him *in terms of*

315

words and becomes both vocal *and* verbal. A traffic signal derives its meaning from the observer's past experiences in learning law and order through words. The traffic signal, then, is nonvocal and verbal (1967, p. 290. Italics added).

Well, of course, you may say, a red traffic semaphore means "stop," and "stop" is a word, but what is the verbal meaning of Bach's *Brandenburg Concerto No. 4?* What is the verbal meaning of an abstract painting or a modern ballet?

No empirical research in psychology will answer these questions, but it is thanks to psychology that much of human communication is now known to involve both verbal and nonverbal factors—so much so, in fact, that we are forced to wonder whether this is true of all human communication. The terms "verbal" and "nonverbal," moreover, cover a great variety of things, for one of the main accomplishments of the scientific study of communication has been to discover several factors that influence communication far more than had previously been supposed.

An obvious requirement in verbal communication is that the listener be able to recognize the words. But researchers have shown that this can be quite difficult, even when the words are spoken clearly and the listener is paying close attention. For example, in one study, individual words and short phrases were cut out of an ordinary conversation that had been recorded on tape. Professional cutting and splicing techniques were used to minimize sound distortion. When the separate words and phrases were spliced into a blank tape and played to subjects who had not heard the original conversation, they recognized only 50 percent of the single words heard in isolation, but 80 percent of the phrases consisting of two, three, or four words (Pollack and Pickett, 1964). The researchers conclude that you cannot even hear words correctly unless you already have some idea of their general context.

In addition to winks and words, then, communication seems to involve thought. It certainly has been argued, as we will see later in this chapter, that language limits thought. It has also been argued that people could never learn a language, or at least not the grammar, unless they had some innate capacity for it. Does this mean we must posit some kind of language gene? Language does seem to be learned in stages, and these stages are said to correspond to certain stages of cognitive development recognized by many psychologists. If correct, this correspondence would establish a general link between heredity and language, though nothing as specific as a language gene. The individual, however, does not communicate solely with himself. And so we must add another factor to the list: society.

Before we begin, however, we should remind ourselves that although communication has many aspects, there are also many things in this world that have nothing to do with communication at all. Suppose you see a woman scratching her leg. What does she mean by it? But take an easier example: a dog walks wearily out of the sun and lies down in the shade to pant, his tongue lolling and dripping. Is this his way of telling you he's hot? Do the crocuses come up to let people know it's spring? Not every gesture or word is necessarily a communication to be interpreted. Even in today's communications-conscious world, it is possible for a woman to scratch her leg because it itches.

Nonverbal Communication

The first dictionary (Chinese, with 40,000 characters) was compiled before 1000 B.C. However, nonverbal communication has been studied systematically only in recent decades, even though our anthropoid ancestors must have communicated nonverbally long before they used language. Of course, words and grammar lend themselves to the study of communication more readily than do grins and growls, and most nonverbal communication accompanies speech rather than replacing it.

Exactly what are the varieties of nonverbal communication? "The human face alone," Birdwhistell (1970) says, "is capable of making some 250,000 different expressions." Estimates of how many different nonverbal signs people all over the world use, and to what categories these signs can conveniently be assigned, differ from expert to expert. However, all nonverbal communication can be divided into three categories: moving and silent, still and silent, and vocal. Head noddings, hand gestures, and foot swingings are silent motions. So are smiles and frowns. This is probably the most important category of nonverbal communications, and it is called *kinesic* behavior. Stroking, holding, hitting, and other touching behavior may also be included in kinesics.

Even when still and silent, the human body may "speak" in several ways. Posture in standing, sitting, crouching, or reclining is one way. Another is in the distance people put between them, or more generally in the use and perception of personal and social space—a communications medium called *proxemics.* Another way is in breath and body odors, physique, and general attractiveness. People also communicate by means of signs that are not part of their bodies: masks, false eyelashes, lipstick, eyeglasses, clothes. What is a person telling you if she smokes with an amber and gold cigarette holder? If she decorates her apartment with Louis Quinze furniture? If dirty dishes have been left in the sink for three days?

A third category, known as *paralanguage,* consists of signs that are vocal and yet nonverbal. Many of them, however, are part of a verbal utterance. In writing, we try to indicate them with punctuation: "Virginia is a nice girl." "Virginia is a nice girl?" "Virginia is a nice girl!" Or with italics: "Well, you'll *never* guess what she told *Madge.*" Other vocalizations have nothing to do with words. There may be no message in a sneeze, a cough, or a hiccup, but there usually is in a laugh, a sigh, a moan.

Learned or instinctive?

Perhaps one of the reasons people have become so interested recently in non-verbal communication is that they believe it to reveal the truth, especially the truth concerning feelings. Thus, it is felt that if you can understand the non-verbal indicators in a person's behavior you will know what he is really feeling. The polygraph lie-detecting procedure, in fact, is based on just that assumption. "Did you take the money out of the till?" the polygraph technician asks. "No," the suspect replies, and the indicators for his blood pressure, breathing, and skin perspiration jump. But can the sweat in the palm of your hand be called communication and can you be taught to control it?

Birdwhistell, in keeping with his determination to investigate human kinesics as a nonverbal language, might exclude such reactions as sweaty palms from his field of interest because, except in the rare case of being measured with special equipment, they do not "systematically influence the behavior of other members of any particular group" (1970). Just as speech does not communicate unless it is audible, body activity does not communicate unless it is visible. Furthermore, Birdwhistell has been carrying out his investigations on the hypothesis that the systematic gestures practiced by the members of a community are a function of the social system to which they belong—that is, the *meanings* of gestures, just like the meanings of words, are culture-bound. Although cross-cultural studies of facial expressions and other kinesic signs are still being conducted, Birdwhistell believes that no gestures will be found that have the same meaning in all societies; gestures and their significance must be learned.

Some evidence, however, seems to point in the opposite direction. Paul Ekman, Richard Sorenson, and Wallace Friesen (1969) have found "evidence of pan-cultural elements in facial displays of affect." Their studies show that observers in New Guinea, Borneo, the United States, Brazil, and Japan "recognize some of the same emotions when they are shown a standard set of facial photographs. This finding contradicts the theory that facial displays of emotion are socially learned and therefore culturally variable" (Ekman et al., 1969).

The researchers based their study on Tomkins's theory of personality, which postulated genetically derived programs which were linked to universal facial displays, such as interest, joy, surprise, fear, anger, distress, disgust–contempt, and shame. Ekman and his colleagues felt that it is possible to distinguish facial displays which are pan-cultural from those that are culturally variable. To reveal the pan-cultural elements in facial displays which express the emotions listed above, these investigators obtained samples (photographs) that expressed cultural universals.

Subjects who were from such diverse societies as the United States, Brazil, Japan, New Guinea, and Borneo were asked to select a word from a list of six emotions for each picture.

Although Figure 9–1 indicates that the preliterate groups from New Guinea and Borneo gave the predicted response far less often than did the literate groups, there is, nevertheless, justification for saying that facial displays communicate specific emotions cross-culturally, and that, therefore, there is reason to suspect that such displays have a genetic derivation. However, as the discussion on socialization in chapter 2 indicated, learning and heredity are closely intertwined. The child must gain proficiency in reading the facial expressions of those around her even as she learns to understand words.

Kinesics

The Samoans use an eyebrow flash to express "yes," while a Greek expresses "no" by jerking his head back (Eibl-Eibesfeldt, 1972). And even within one culture, the meaning of a gesture can be affected by the communicators' ranks, ages, and sexes; by the time and place of the encounter; and by the communicators' purposes. However, kinesics, the study of gestures, is usually approached not by an investigation of meanings but by precise description. Picture two soldiers standing on the side of the road thumbing a ride. Here is how Birdwhistell describes their motions as a car goes by:

The two soldiers stood in parallel, arms akimbo with an intrafemoral index of 45 degrees. In unison, each raised his right upper arm to about an 80-degree angle, moved the arm in an anterior–posterior sweep with a double pivot at shoulder and

Rates of Recognition of Six Affects among Samples from the United States, Brazil, Japan, New Guinea, and Borneo
(in percents)

Affect Category	United States	Brazil	Japan	New Guinea Pidgin responses	New Guinea Fore responses	Borneo
Happy	97	97	87	99	82	92
Fear	88	77	71	46	54	40
Disgust-contempt	82	86	82	29	44	
Anger	69	82	63	56	50	64
Surprise	91	82	87	38		36
Sadness	73	82	74	55		52

Figure 9–1. The table shows the percentage of responses in each cultural grouping identifying photographs that the researchers hypothesized show universally recognizable emotions.

SOURCE: Adapted from Ekman, P., Sorenson, E. R., and Friesen, W. Pan-cultural elements in facial displays of emotion. *Science*, April 4, 1969, **164**, 87.

elbow; the four fingers of the right hand were curled and the thumb was pos-
teriorly hooked; the right palm faced the body. Their left arms were held closer to
the body with an elbow bend of about 90 degrees. The left four fingers were curled
and the thumb was partially hidden as it crooked into their respective belts (1970,
p. 176).

Birdwhistell, who invented the word *kinesics* and is the most important
investigator in the field, has also devised a set of symbols called *kinegraphs*
that can be used to record facial expressions and body motions. This system of
notation elaborates variants of eight base symbols for eight sections of the
body: total head; face; trunk; shoulder, arm, and wrist; hand and finger; hip,
leg, and ankle; foot activity and walking; and neck movements. Unlike business letters and music, however, which can be taken by dictation, kinesic
sequences are usually too rapid to be recorded in the field with pencil and
paper. Instead, they are taken on film, so that later the movie can be studied as
many times as necessary, perhaps in slow motion, to discern and note down
every gesture in the sequence.

Not every gesture that can be recorded in this system has meaning by itself.
Most of them are components of meaningful expressions, like the individual
letters or sounds in words. Birdwhistell calls them *kines* and believes that they
combine to form *kinemorphemes*—kinesic words. The kinemorphemes, he
believes, further combine syntactically "into extended linked behavioral organizations, the *complex kinemorphic constructions*, which have many of the
properties of the spoken syntactic sentence" (1965).

Birdwhistell carries the analogy between kinesics and language too far for
some investigators. It has been objected, for example, that whereas the putting
together of sounds or letters to form words is governed by rules, the assembling
of movements does not seem to be based on rules that are internal to the
movements themselves. On the contrary, the boundaries of groupings of
movements seem to be governed by unit formation in the speech that is going
on at the same time (Dittmann, 1971).

But efforts to establish a kinegraphic alphabet and perhaps to compile a
kinesic dictionary began only a few decades ago. We are still a long way from
knowing exactly what kinesics are and how they are structured. While this
work has been going on, however, other investigators have been trying to
classify the sorts of things that kinesics do.

Functions of kinesics. Ekman and Friesen believe there is one class of
kinesics that stands for an idea that can just as well be expressed in words
(1969). Often gestures rather than words are used because the receiver of the
message cannot hear the sender. A motorist, for example, can see the hitchhiker's swinging thumb, but he cannot hear the spoken request, "Can you give
me a ride?" The thumb, moreover, does not tell the motorist anything about

the hitchhiker's emotions. It tells him in what direction the hitchhiker is going, but this information is redundant because the hitchhiker stands on one side of the road and solicits only the cars going in that direction. That the thumb carries little or no meaning beyond "Can you give me a ride" is demonstrated by the practice of some hitchhikers who hold up a piece of cardboard with their destination written on it.

Gestures of this type also may be used for ironic effect. One may wish to be insolent toward a person within hearing, for example, and to have it perceived by a third party but not by the person himself. While the person is not looking, one flashes the upraised middle finger to convey a mild obscenity. For added emphasis, the sender hits his upper arm with his other hand. The motions used by ground personnel to guide a taxiing airplane into its berth, the sign language of the deaf, and the gestures used by underwater swimmers all belong to this class of kinesics, which Ekman and Friesen call *emblems*. We use them about as consciously as we do words.

Another class of kinesics, the *illustrators*, accompany speech. A hand chops down to emphasize a word; the eyes squint as the person says "We came out into the bright sunlight"; the arms fold and the shoulders rise to illustrate "By then I was freezing"; the tongue licks the lips for "It was the best pasta I've ever tasted." Some illustrators are vague, such as the motions that trace a line of thought; others are quite specific, as in pointing at the object under discussion. But none of them is used in the absence of speech. Some cultural groups possess a rich vocabulary of illustrators, whereas others tend to rely to a greater extent on the spoken word. We use illustrators intentionally, though not quite as deliberately as we use emblems.

Our conscious control is much more ambiguous over a third class of kinesics, the *affect displays*. They can be intentional; indeed, they can be "put on" to communicate emotions we do not feel. For example, a young bride shows surprise upon unwrapping a present, even though she knew what it was all along, or a person smiles approval at tasting a friend's homemade bread even though it's as dense as a rock. Usually, however, our affect displays are a spontaneous reflection of what we are really feeling. We may consciously intensify or prolong them if we want others to see them, but the first impulse seems to be involuntary.

Psychotherapists have been particularly interested in affect displays because they sometimes contradict what a patient is saying or otherwise reveal feelings the patient would like to hide. A typical example is the patient who speaks approvingly of a friend and, as far as the therapist can tell, holds a pleasant expression on her face; but when the movie of the session is played back in slow motion (four frames per second instead of the normal twenty-four), a wave of anger is seen to pass over her features. Haggard and Isaacs (1966) found through their study of facial expressions on film that no expression briefer than two-fifths of a second is likely to be identified; expressions that last no longer than one-fifth of a second escape notice altogether; and expressions of an intermediate duration are perceived only as changes. In Haggard and Isaacs's terminology, expressions too brief to be perceived or identified are known as *micromomentary*.

But if an expression is too brief to be perceived, is it a communication at all? When you were alone, have you ever smiled at coming across something you thought you had lost? Have you ever scowled when you stubbed your toe? Eibl-Eibesfeldt (1970) says the anger syndrome can be observed even in people born deaf and blind. The line between voluntary and involuntary action is hard to draw when it comes to affect displays. The involuntary revealing of emotion, therefore, can scarcely be called communication, since there is no communicative intent. Perhaps it is best classified as perception, since the burden is on the observer to make the interpretation.

Affect displays can, of course, augment or contradict what the person is saying verbally, and can equally well occur without verbal accompaniment. A fourth class of kinesics, the *regulators*, have no use aside from verbal communication. Mainly head nods and eye movements, they tell a listener when to be quiet and listen or when to come in with feedback. When produced by the listener, regulators tell the speaker to elaborate or repeat, to go on, to speed up or get more interesting, and to let the listener speak. The use of regulators seems to differ from one social class to another and from culture to culture, yet people are not clearly aware of using them. Most people, for example, nod their head, perhaps making an "m-hm" sound at the same time, almost without knowing it.

Can you see the fear on this woman's face or does it help to know that the picture was taken less than half an hour after a bomb had gone off in her neighborhood in Belfast?

Windows of the soul.   Eye movements can be used as illustrators, and in our culture they are among the most important regulators. When two people are carrying on a conversation, for example, the speaker looks at the listener as he comes to the end of his speech. This is a signal for the listener to begin speaking. The second speaker looks away as he starts his speech, while the first speaker continues to look at him (Kendon, 1967). Traditionally, the eyes have been considered the clearest expression of emotion. Lovers drink deep of each other's eyes—and so do haters. The long, hard stare has definitely been associated with aggressiveness (Moore and Gilliland, 1921). The proposition that the more you like a person, the more you make eye contact with her, has been only partially confirmed by studies conducted by Mehrabian (1969). Subjects made less eye contact with people they disliked than with those toward whom they were neutral, but they made as much if not more eye contact with the latter than with people they liked very much.

Ekman does not believe that the eyes are the best indicators for all six of the expressions he calls basic. Only sadness and fear are recognized primarily through observation of the eye area; happiness and surprise seem to be revealed in the eye area and the lower face; disgust is shown in the lower face alone, and anger in the lower face plus the brows and forehead (Ekman, Friesen, and Tomkins, 1971).

Do a liar's eyes give him away? Ekman and Friesen made a film of a patient they knew was engaging in deception: actually anxious, confused, and troubled by delusions, the person tried to appear healthy and content. The experimenters showed the film to three groups of observers. One group saw only the patient's head and face; another saw only the patient's body from the neck down; and the third group saw the patient whole. Observers who saw only the face and head described the patient as cheerful, pleasant, sensitive, kind, cooperative, warm, talkative—and honest. Those who saw only the body perceived the patient as confused, worried, tense, cautious, and defensive. The observers who saw both face and body characterized the person as alert, active, and changeable (Ekman and Friesen, 1969).

Proxemics and other motionless communication

Edward T. Hall has analyzed proxemics and devised a notation for it in the same way as Birdwhistell has analyzed and notated kinesics. And just as Birdwhistell records the positions and motions observed in eight sections of the human body, Hall records the variables observed in eight factors that he believes structure the space between people during interaction (1963). The first factor in Hall's analysis identifies the interactant's *posture and sex* in only six combinations: male prone, male sitting or squatting, male standing, and the same three postures for a female. These combinations can be coded by number

(1–6), by abbreviation (m/pr, m/si, etc.), or by pictograph, whichever the investigator finds most convenient.

Posture has, of course, been analyzed in much greater detail. Gordon Hewes says the human body can assume about 1,000 steady postures, though far fewer are customary in any one culture. Cross-cultural differences in postural repertoires are sometimes due to environmental factors: People who live where the ground is usually wet or cold, for example, do not often sit on it. In other cases, the selection of customary postures seems to be purely cultural. The Japanese would not lack for chairs if they wanted to sit like Americans, but they often prefer sitting on the floor. In the theater they sometimes squat on their heels in their seats, Hewes reports, because it is more comfortable for them (1957).

Hall's second factor distinguishes nine *positions* in which two interactants can face each other or face apart. In the position coded zero, the two interactants are facing each other directly, their shoulders parallel. In the next position on the compass, coded 1, they face each other with their shoulders at a 45-degree angle. The positions move on around the compass in 45-degree increments: By position 4, the two interactants are facing the same direction, shoulder to shoulder; position 8, with the interactants back to back, is the obverse of position 1.

The distance between interactants and their potential for touching each other constitute what Hall calls the *kinesthetic dimension.* For his notational system he distinguishes eleven significantly different distances, from touching with the head or trunk to being unable to touch without a stick or some other extension. Another, simpler analysis of this dimension divides it into four zones: intimate, personal, social, and public. The distance between middle-class Americans is intimate when it is one and one-half feet or less; that is, they are generally uncomfortable interacting any closer than this unless the interaction is between intimates. For informal contact between friends, Americans prefer a distance of one and one-half to four feet—the personal zone. Acquaintances communicate most comfortably in the social zone, or at a distance of 4 to 12 feet; and beyond 12 feet interactors are in the social zone. Communication at public distance becomes formalized as public speaking.

How well the interactants know each other is only one of the factors that influence the preferred distance between them. Another is relative rank: A general keeps more distance between himself and a private than between himself and another general. And of course, the whole system of zones and distances depends on one's culture. Many North Americans, for example, prefer to carry on their personal and social interactions at a greater distance than do Latin Americans, a preference that the Latin Americans often interpret as a sign of coldness.

Hall rates the factor of touching on a scale of 0 to 6, from caressing and holding to no contact at all. Although Hall differentiates touching behavior from distance, the two are often related. For example, Arabs often stand very close to each other (by North American standards) while talking; they also transmit casual messages to friends and even to strangers by touch. Hall speculates that this behavioral difference reflects different concepts of the self. People in North America think of themselves as including their skin, and perhaps their clothes and a few inches of space on all sides as well, whereas the Arab's self is deep within him. Strictly speaking, his skin is no part of himself, and so no offense can be given by impersonal touching (1966).

Arabs also tend to look each other straight in the eye while talking, whereas Navahos keep each other in view only peripherally. This factor is called *visual* code. *Thermal* code—the heat we feel an interactant's body giving off—and *olfactory* code, from perfume to flatus, also can be measured separately, though Hall admits we know little about their part in structuring an interaction. The final factor in his analysis is *loudness of voice.*

Paralanguage

The quality of the speaking voice is still another of the many signs that are vocal and yet not verbal. Besides relative loudness or softness, the speaking voice is characterized by average pitch, pitch variability, articulation, resonance, tempo, breathiness, nasality, throatiness, orotundity, flatness, and other qualities identified by various investigators (Trager, 1958; Addington, 1968). In many cases we use one or a combination of these qualities to clarify the meaning of our speech. The most striking example is sarcasm, when we show by vocal cues (often accompanied by eloquent facial expressions as well

The distance between a public speaker and his audience would be classified by Edward Hall as the social zone. These four generals seem to have a common conception of how to sit when on public display.

as gestures) that we mean the very opposite of what our words would seem to say. The bitter effect of sarcasm usually conveys contempt that words by themselves could not adequately express.

As indispensable transmitters of the message we want to communicate, vocal cues are chosen, timed, and produced quite deliberately. But it is with considerable difficulty and limited success that we fake the vocal cues that enable listeners to guess our age, sex, and social status (Harms, 1961; Ellis, 1967). One investigator also found that listeners could tell black and white Americans apart by their voices (Nerbonne, 1967), but this was disconfirmed by an informal study which used speakers who had all grown up in the same neighborhood in Milwaukee (Knapp, 1972).

Some people, but not all, are quite skillful at communicating emotion with their voices (Davitz and Davitz, 1959); and the same people are usually the ones best able to recognize emotion expressed in others' voices. Davitz found that these sensitive listeners and expressive speakers are usually good at expressing emotion facially as well (Davitz, 1964). But how do they do it? Which vocal qualities convey which emotions?

Since the vocal code for emotional expression is not the same for one socioeconomic level as it is for another, it can be assumed that this ability is culturally determined, and therefore learned. Investigators are trying to break the code used by middle-class Americans. Information summarized by Davitz, for example, gives the vocal characteristics of anger as loudness, high pitch, blaring timbre, rapid speech, irregular up-and-down inflection, irregular rhythm, and clipped enunciation; the characteristics of affection are softness, low pitch, resonant timbre, slow speech, steady and slightly upward inflection, regular rhythm, and slurred enunciation (1964). Is there a culture in which "I love you," in order to sound sincere, must be yelled at the top of one's lungs? The scientific study of nonverbal communication, still in its infancy, has many such questions to investigate.

Language

We have long been in the habit of thinking of Language with a capital L, for it is this ability that makes us feel qualitatively superior to the rest of creation. This glittering crown, Language, seems to have almost magical properties. We think it sets us as far above the apes as they are above clams: it seemed a quantum jump in evolution. Those scientists who have communicated in English with the chimpanzees Washoe and Sara, as well as those who have worked with whales and dolphins, might well dispute this claim to superiority because of language and the cultural accumulation it makes possible. The fact that we may not be the sole inhabitants of the planet who communicate by

UNIFORMS: THE UNSPOKEN LANGUAGE

"The redcoats are coming!" was a common cry in revolutionary times to warn American colonists of the coming of the hated red-uniformed British troops. From the time of the eagle-crested Roman legions, to the invasions of the Mongols and the Huns, right down to the man in the gray flannel suit, the uniform has been a way for people to distinguish friend from foe, their betters from their inferiors on the social ladder. The uniform is a reliable form of communication.

In more rigidly divided societies, as in feudal times, uniforms, or the modes of dress appropriate to each class or trade, have helped people to recognize one another. Shoemakers and bankers wore one type of clothing; warriors and princes, another.

According to sociologists Nathan Joseph and Nicholas Alex (1972), "The uniform makes the wearer's status much more visible than other types of dress." Sometimes the anonymity of the uniform will even help hide discrepancies in status that would otherwise be apparent. "Ironically, the explicit symbolism of the uniform facilitates its counterfeiting. It was much easier for the cobbler from Koepnick to assume the status of captain in the Kaiser's army than for Liza Doolittle to simulate membership in the English upper class. The cobbler's claim in status was legitimized by his appearance in easily identifiable and guaranteed symbols, while for Liza status had to be legitimized by appropriate behavior as well as appearance."

In sharp contrast, dressing up in costumes is a way of confusing and even destroying status. Much of the fun of the Mardi Gras or carnival season is the ability to pass as a queen when one is a kitchen girl or a tramp when one is a member of the upper class.

Uniforms also are a way of reinforcing the idea that the wearers of the uniform will act in a certain way. It is assumed, for example, that men who wear company uniforms at gas stations will know how to service cars. The uniform is a leveler of personal differences: individuals in uniform become part of the larger group—the navy or the fire department—and submerge their own beliefs into the larger one of the nation, team, or company. If the uniformed person is a policeman, we expect him to uphold certain beliefs and reinforce others, even if he does not believe or practice them in his private life. In fact, some policemen like to wear civilian dress to and from work to avoid being on call at all times.

Sometimes, when a uniform is connected with a country or a national policy that is unpopular, the uniform itself may become a protest. When the war in Vietnam began to arouse public outcry, military styles of dress became fashionable. Military uniforms, turned into stylish fashions, became a way of mocking the draft and military service. As more and more people began to wear surplus army clothes, workboots, and fatigues, they formed an "army" of dissenters, recognizable to society at large and to each other by a particular code of dress. In this way, it could be said that there was a "uniform" of protest.

Uniforms, like other forms of dress, are a language—a form of nonverbal communication indicating social status, political opinions, lifestyle, occupation, and ideologies. The uniform implies that its wearer will act in a certain way, belong to a certain class, or perform special functions.

means of a spoken language does not diminish in any way the miracle of language as a means of communication, nor the astonishing feat displayed by children who are able to learn their native tongues with such relative ease.

Learning to talk

Despite the great differences in the way various languages sound, the different items and ideas that are tagged with words, the different ways in which words are combined grammatically, and even despite the different ways children are brought up in various societies, the early stages of learning to talk seem to be about the same all over the world (Ervin-Tripp, 1973). Babies cry and scream with their first breath, start to coo in the second month of life, and laugh in the third. They show signs of imitating the intonations of adult speech, or at least the intonation that sounds like a request, by the seventh month (Tonkava-Yampol'skaya, 1973). But these vocalizations are usually defined as nonverbal. One investigator, however, argues that babbling is the child's first real attempt at verbal expression, for it begins when the child can understand a few of the words he hears around him and is dropped as soon as he can talk with some fluency (Engel, 1973).

In his early babbling, a child produces most or all of the many sounds in the human vocal repertoire, but since his native language uses only a select few, he hears only these sounds in the speech of others and gains people's attention more often by producing them. The result, of course, is that the "foreign" sounds gradually disappear from his babbling. Most children can deliberately pronounce a few syllables of their native language by the time they are one year old. In many, if not all languages, these first syllables are duplicated, as in "choo-choo," "ma-ma," "baby" (often pronounced "bay-bay").

With each successive month, the child adds a few words to his speaking vocabulary and many more to his comprehension, but it is not until the age of about eighteen months that he puts two words together to convey a new meaning. According to M. Braine (1963), the child's first combinations add an *X word* to a *pivot*. The investigator's son, for example, first said "See hat," then "See sock," "See horsie," and "See boy." When the child has added many of the other words he can pronounce (X words) to the pivot, he knows how that pivot works and starts with another one, perhaps "more" or "all gone" or "my." At this stage, X words are sometimes used alone; pivots only in combination, and always in the same position, initial or final. Most X words are nouns; pivots usually are not. In the second stage, the child loses interest in pivots and begins to put two nouns together, as in "Mommy store" (Braine, 1963).

From the context and the child's vocal cues and gestures, it usually will be clear that this two-word sentence means "Mommy has gone to the store," and the response will be to the full sentence intended: "That's right," or "No, she's only down doing the laundry." Few adults will think it important to correct the child's grammar: "Mommy *has gone* to the store. Can you say 'has gone'?" Indeed, at this stage the child would probably pay no attention to such a correction. He ignores such words as "has," "gone," and "to" in the speech of others and has no use for them himself, since nonverbal cues replace grammar to clear up the ambiguities of one- and two-word sentences. Given the appropriate context, tone of voice, and gestures, he will respond the same way to "Give Daddy your shirt," "Give your shirt to Daddy," and "Give Daddy to your shirt," apparently noticing little difference between them (Wetstone and Friedlander, 1973).

Words such as the auxiliary verb "has" and the preposition "to" are obviously more difficult to understand than such nouns as "shirt" and "store" and such verbs as "give" and "look." Terms of comparison and relation give rise to some odd confusions. Many children, for example, seem to understand "more," "big," and "long" before they do "less," "little," and "short." When a three-year-old says two things are different, he may mean they are the same (Donaldson and Balfour, 1968).

Auxiliary verbs, prepositions and conjunctions, word order, such word endings as "-ed" and "-ing," and transformations such as "go, gone, went" are the materials of grammar. Their function, as we have just seen, is to make language as clear and unambiguous as possible with a minimum of help from nonverbal cues. But what an abstract, complicated task this is! Just take the word "but," for example. The *American Heritage Dictionary* devotes a six-inch column to a description of the subtleties of the three-letter word "but." Such niceties of language cannot be taught to a three-year-old.

And yet, children do learn it, mostly by the age of five or six. Handicapped, institutionalized, abused—almost all children learn it in spite of every obstacle. Fortunately, the only obstacle for many is the difficulty of grammar itself. They have an abundance of models to imitate. Direct conversation with people serves to correct their grammatical usage and help them to expand their sentences. In *Verbal Behavior* (1957), for example, Skinner argued that language is not radically different from any other kind of behavior, and is acquired by the same sorts of conditioning that give rise to all our habits and knowledge. That is, we become more and more likely to perform certain actions, such as uttering certain sounds, in certain circumstances because they usually lead to predictable consequences. And indeed, this explanation does seem adequate to show how we learn the meanings of commonly used nouns and verbs. It is a matter of associating a sound with an action or thing. Some psycholinguists believe, however, that grammar is too difficult and too subtle to be learned just by imitation. What, for example, is the thing associated with the word "but"?

The child learns words by imitation. He does not make them up but hears them spoken again and again, learns what they refer to, and tries to pronounce them as he hears them. On the other hand, most adult sentences are original—made up for the occasion. The child may hear them once and never again. Nevertheless, a child soon speaks sentences that he has never heard before. Evidently he does not learn specific *sentences*, but *rules* that dictate the combination of words to form sentences. However, no one teaches him these rules as such.

Normally children make this leap from single words to well-formed adult sentences between the ages of eighteen months and five years, a period of three and one-half years. All the more amazing, then, that Isabelle, a socially isolated child found in Ohio in 1937, accomplished the same thing in a much shorter time. As Roger Brown tells the story, Isabelle was six and one-half years old when she was found.

She was the illegitimate child of a deaf mute, and mother and child had lived most of the time in a darkened room away from the rest of the family. Isabelle behaved in many ways like a wild animal. She was fearful and hostile. She had no speech and made only a croaking noise. At first she seemed deaf, so unused were her senses.

Isabelle was taken away and given excellent care by doctors and clinical psychologists. Although her first score on the Stanford-Binet was nineteen months, practically at the zero point of the scale, a program of speech training was, nevertheless, undertaken. A week of intensive work was required to elicit even a first vocalization. Yet a little more than two months later she was beginning to put sentences together. Nine months after that, she could identify words and sentences on the printed page and write very well. Isabelle passed through the usual stages of linguistic development at a greatly accelerated rate. She covered in two years the learning that ordinarily occupies six years. By the age of eight and one-half Isabelle had a normal IQ and was not easily distinguished from ordinary children her age. In this case speech behaved like many other human and animal performances; the delayed subject progressed at an accelerated rate, presumably because of her maturity (Summarized by Brown, 1958, pp. 191–192, from Davis, 1947).

The story of Isabelle is an extreme example of the maturation processes that seem to take place in learning to speak a language. Indeed, a Piagetian would find it very interesting to note that when Isabelle began her education, she was just at the age when most children emerge from what Piaget calls the preoperational period and enter the period he identifies as that of concrete operations (see chapter 2). If the maturation of her cognitive capacities had not been retarded by her social isolation, she would have been just about ready to overcome the egocentricity, the inability to reverse sequences in thought, and the other limitations that characterize preoperational intelligence. Two capabilities that appear for the first time in the period of concrete operations, taking the other person's viewpoint and classifying objects by category, would obviously be very useful in learning to speak. The "operations" in Piaget's term "concrete operations" are mental processes in which objects can be conceptualized in more than one way, as, for example, when a child thinks of the category "cows" and the category "horses" at the same time, and understands that they both belong to the category "livestock." This newfound ability to classify things and understand the relationships between classes is only a step away from the grasp of the form of entities—the realization that not only is there a class of concrete red objects but also the formal quality of redness. In the period of concrete operations when the child becomes able to take the viewpoint of another it becomes possible for the child to listen to her own words and thus to say what she imagines the other will understand.

Retracing the steps of language acquisition that we have just described, other correspondences with Piaget's stages of cognitive development can be found. For example, when the child intentionally produces her first recognizable syllables, she is usually in the fourth stage of Piaget's sensorimotor period, the stage when Piaget says the child's own intention becomes the primary motivating factor for starting an activity. And when the child forms her first two-word sentences she has usually reached the stage in which Piaget says she has just become capable of imagining things even though they are not physically present to her.

More direct evidence that language learning follows a maturational sequence is provided by a study in which Roger Brown and his assistants tape-recorded much of the ordinary speech of three children for almost two years. The investigators scanned the children's speech for the appearance of fourteen elements of grammar, as well as verb endings such as "-ed," "-en," "-ing," and the inversion of word order to form an interrogative sentence. During the study, all three children increased the length of their sentences from an average of one or two words to an average of four or five. All three mastered the use of most of the fourteen grammatical elements Brown was investigating, though they received no coaching. What was most remarkable, however, was that they all mastered these elements in the same sequence (Brown, 1973).

Is there, then, some sort of innate capacity for learning grammar? Noam Chomsky believes there is:

As a precondition for language learning, [a child] must possess, first, a linguistic theory that specifies the form of the grammar of a possible human language, and, second, a strategy for selecting a grammar of the appropriate form that is compatible with the primary linguistic data [that is, examples of linguistic performance that are taken to be well-formed sentences, examples designated as nonsentences, and other information]. As a long-range task for general linguistics, we might set the problem of developing an account of this innate linguistic theory that provides the basis for language learning (Chomsky, 1967, p. 102).

Thus, according to Chomsky, a person is born with a potential capacity to use language. The ability to communicate by means of language is not learned in the same way as one learns to tie one's shoe or drive a car. Biological inheritance and maturation provide every normal person with an innate theory "that specifies the form of the grammar of a possible human language"—his native language being one of the many possible. The task of linguistics, then, is to give an account of this innate theory and the task for psycholinguistics becomes that of describing how the child selects "a grammar of the appropriate form that is compatible" with the particular language he is learning.

George A. Miller, speaking for some (but by no means all) psycholinguists, agrees that if investigators wish to deal realistically with the problem of language, they will have to talk "about innate and universal human capacities instead of special methods of teaching vocal responses" (1965). But to Miller, the psychological study of language involves more than learning theory plus a large biological component. The investigator must also ask how the language learner tests hypotheses about particular rules of grammar.

That learning a language is not just a matter of forming the appropriate habits seems evident from the kinds of mistakes that children make. When beginning to use the past tense, for example, a child may say "Leon runned around the corner," though she has never heard "runned" before; it is simply a misapplication of an otherwise valid rule that the past tense is formed in English by adding "-ed" to the verb. The main question for psycholinguistics, then, seems to be: Where and how did she get that rule in the first place?

Language and thought

French encyclopedist Denis Diderot believed that our thoughts have a natural order, and that of all the ancient and modern languages, the one in which the order of words corresponds most closely to the natural order of thoughts is, by some amazing coincidence, none other than French: "French is made to instruct, to clarify and convince; Greek, Latin, Italian, English, to persuade, to move and deceive: speak Greek, Latin, Italian to the people; but speak French to the sage."

Modern investigators find nothing at all surprising about this correspondence between languages and "natural" processes, though they believe that Diderot put the cart before the horse. Diderot's thoughts tended to follow the order of words in French because his use of the language had trained his mind to think in that order. A different order of thoughts would seem natural to native speakers of Eskimo or Arabic, and that order would resemble the order of words in their language.

Actually, it is not the order of thoughts that interests investigators today so much as it is the content. Since thoughts themselves are hard to study except through language, anyone wishing to explore the relationship between language and the mind must start with some mental function that can be mea-

ANATOMY OF A RUMOR

A rumor, according to Tamotsu Shibutani (1966), is improvised news. "Human society," he says, "is a communicative process in which coordinated activities can go on so long as men support one another's perspectives." With the world in a constant state of flux, knowledge must keep pace with changes. In ambiguous situations where there is no certainty of knowing, rumors are born. "Men alter their orientations together." A reasonable account is pieced together from fragments. The rumor of the miracle of Sabena Grande was an example given by Shibutani of a rumor created by intense emotion.

On May 25, 1953, more than 100,000 people gathered on ten acres of land in predominantly Catholic Sabena Grande, Puerto Rico. The crowd was awaiting a miracle—the appearance of the Virgin Mary. The crowd had learned of the miracle from seven local schoolchildren who claimed that they had seen the Virgin appear daily at noontime at a well, and that the Virgin had vowed to reappear this very day at 11:00 A.M.

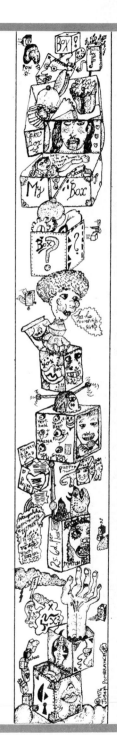

The mayor of a nearby town soon erected an altar at the well. The children's parents encouraged them to continue visiting the site, where they led groups of pilgrims in prayer. Some of the worshippers formed processions. As news of the event spread, the numbers of the faithful hoping for a glimpse of the Virgin swelled. In a short time, people were pouring in from all over Puerto Rico, Haiti, Cuba, and as far away as New York. As the throng increased, so did the news coverage. A local radio station, for example, began daily broadcasts from the site, and newspaper reporters swarmed into the area.

The crowd surged around the well, which was surrounded on three sides by steep hills. No one knew what to expect, but soon some people said they saw the Virgin hovering in the clouds. People who had been ill insisted that they had been cured. Then reports that the Virgin had been sighted spread through the crowd. Shortly after 11 o'clock, some people claimed that the Virgin, dressed in black, was walking down the west hill toward the well. Upon further investigation, however, this figure turned out to be an old woman wearing black. Some eager individuals reported seeing the Virgin walking up the east hill—this time wearing a white robe. But closer scrutiny revealed an old man in a white shirt. The crowd started to dwindle at noon. By 5:00 P.M. a mass exodus of the area began.

The Virgin was never known to have appeared, but in the years that followed, people continued to visit Sabena Grande—as many as 3,000 on a weekend. The pilgrims washed themselves in the well water and bottled it to take home. They collected pebbles and stones as religious objects and donated money for the upkeep of the shrine.

To this day, the miracle has not received the stamp of approval of the Catholic church. But the idea that something unusual had occurred at the well was firmly planted in the minds of the participants. Some people were certain that they had not seen the Virgin but still believed the children. Some who had been doubtful at first came away believing, although they had witnessed nothing out of the ordinary. Others maintained that they had been cured of illness. Still others who had scoffed at the outset were reassured that it was all a hoax.

sured wordlessly. Roger Brown and Eric Lenneberg (1954) chose the function of *color discrimination*. They noted that in the Iakuti language one word covers both the hues that in English are called green and blue. Is it possible, they wondered, that Iakuti speakers do not distinguish between green and blue as readily as English speakers do? But since Brown and Lenneberg were not able personally to question Iakuti speakers about their color perceptions, they designed their experiment to answer a slightly different question: Does having a short, commonly used word for a color make it easier to recognize?

First the experimenters asked native English-speaking subjects to name several colors that they saw flashed on cards. This showed the experimenters which colors are codable (have an unambiguous, quickly given name in English) and which are not. The subjects answered most rapidly and agreed most often on such colors as red, orange, yellow, and green, with such colors as powder blue, for example, receiving lower codability scores. Next, the experimenters showed each subject four colors on a single card, removed them, and then asked the subject to point to the same four colors on a large chart displaying 120 of them. As expected, the more codable the color, the easier it was to recognize, especially when the interval between the showing of the original colors and the identification was not more than a few seconds (Brown and Lenneberg, 1954).

The same experiment was later conducted using Zuni subjects, whose language has a single word for both orange and yellow. Monolingual Zunis in their recognition task often confused orange and yellow, an error that English speakers never make. Zunis who spoke both English and their native tongue confused the two colors half as often as their monolingual compatriots (Lenneberg and Roberts, 1953).

The rainbow is a continuous band that can be divided into segments in any way desired, and to each segment any name can be attached. A similar arbitrariness in dissection and naming is possible with many other aspects of the world. In English, for example, a distinction is made between lakes and seas, whereas in German they are all *Seen*. But these interlinguistic differences in what words cover, the *lexical* differences, account for only part of the gap between languages; the rest is a matter of grammar. The psycholinguist must also ask, therefore, whether grammatical differences affect cognition.

Brown (1957) sought to answer this question by showing young children a picture that comprised three unfamiliar elements, an action, an object, and a substance. One of the pictures he used, for example, showed a pair of hands kneading some confetti-like material above a round container. The children had never seen kneading before and had no name for it, nor had they ever seen or heard of confetti, or that particular kind of container. When the experimenter showed the child the picture, he uttered a name: "niss," "sib," or "latt." Then he gave the child three new pictures, one of the action alone (the hands kneading, for example), one of the object alone (the container), and one of the substance alone (the confetti), saying "Now show me another picture of. . . ."

How was the child to know which of the three elements the experimenter meant? When he uttered the name the first time, he characterized it grammatically, using it as a verb, as a particular noun, or as a mass noun: "Do you know what it means to sib? In this picture you can see some sibbing," or "Do you know what a sib is? In this picture you can see a sib," or "Have you ever seen any sib? In this picture you can see some sib." The results of the experiment were very clear. When the new word was introduced as a verb, ten out of sixteen children chose the picture of an action. When the word was a particular noun, eleven of the sixteen chose the object; and when the word was a mass noun, twelve picked the substance. "There is a sense, then," Brown concludes, "in which this grammatical feature of a language affects the cognition of those who speak the language. Differences between languages in their parts of speech may be diagnostic of differences in the cognitive psychologies of those who use the languages" (Brown, 1957, p. 5).

Linguistic relativity. One cannot generalize very widely from empirical studies such as these, and Brown is careful to state his conclusion in modest terms. These studies were suggested, however, by the hypothesis of *linguistic relativity,* which ascribes to language the power to determine the individual's entire *Weltanschuung.* Benjamin Lee Whorf, perhaps the most forceful exponent of this theory, boldly asserts that language "is not merely a reproducing instrument for voicing ideas but rather is itself the shaper of ideas, the program and guide for the individual's mental activity, for his analysis of impressions, for his synthesis of his mental stock in trade." In Whorf's view, language takes on a coercive, almost inescapable power over the thinker. "We cut nature up, organize it into concepts, and ascribe significances as we do," he wrote, "largely because we are parties to an agreement to organize it in this way." Admittedly, this agreement is "an implicit and unstated one, BUT ITS TERMS ARE ABSOLUTELY OBLIGATORY . . ." (Whorf, 1940, in Carroll, 1956, pp. 212–214).

It was largely through a study of native American languages that Whorf arrived at this theory. In Hopi, he found, space is not conceived as homogeneous and instantaneous, the way Newton (and most other speakers of Indo-European languages) assumed it to be. Nor does Hopi have any general notion of time as a flowing continuum in which everything in the universe goes along at a constant rate. These two conceptions, of a static three-dimensional infinite space and a kinetic one-dimensional uniformly flowing time, are what Whorf calls cosmic forms—the metaphysics underlying our own language, thinking, and culture. Although these two cosmic forms are foreign to the Hopi way of thinking, the Hopi do impose upon the universe two grand cosmic forms of their own and these, Whorf claims, have been shaped by their language.

However, most students of linguistics today do not accept the Whorfian hypothesis that languages constrain and determine modes of thought. Joshua Fishman (1971) points out that "languages primarily reflect rather than create socio-cultural regularities in values and orientation, and that languages throughout the world share a far larger number of structural universals than has heretofore been recognized." In addition, after many years of intensive research, no one has yet been able to demonstrate a "cognitive difference between two populations on the basis of the grammatical or other structural differences in their languages alone" (Fishman, 1971). Furthermore, languages change, expand, and contract as the socio-cultural realities of their users change. Thus a language is a reflection of the thought of its users rather than a constraint on the ability to think.

The Sociology of Language

"A bas l'anglais!" cry the French Canadians, demanding that only French be used in their public schools. Meanwhile, back in France, the Bretons rebel against learning French. Flemings in Belgium protest vociferously against anything less than full equality for Dutch in the Brussels area. Welsh nationalists daub out English signs along the roadways in Wales and many Irish revivalists seek even stronger governmental support for the restoration of Irish than that made available during half a century of Irish independence. Jews throughout the world protest the Soviet government's refusal to publish Yiddish writers and the forced closing of Yiddish schools and theaters, and some Puerto Rican nationalists strive for less, or no, English in Puerto Rican official life.

All these examples feed into the broad data pool of the modern sociology of language (Fishman, Ferguson, and Das Gupta, 1968). The choice of which language is to be spoken can become a political issue at the national level. At the personal level it is a choice made by every bilingual speaker with little conscious thought. The same is true of people who know only one language, for they have a choice of varieties of that language. When you talk with your professor's wife at a departmental party, for example, you do not use the same variety of English as you do with your fellow campers while rustling up some grub in the wilderness.

How do we know which of the different language varieties to use in a given situation? What factors determine our choices? The study of these questions is included in that branch of learning known as the *descriptive sociology of language.* The descriptive sociology of language aims first to identify various speech and writing communities—communities that share a particular way of using a particular language, or, in the case of communities many of whose members are bilingual, the manner in which two or more languages are used. The next task is to describe the generally accepted social organization of the language or languages within a speech and writing community—who speaks what language variety or what language to whom, when, and to what end.

Descriptive sociology of language

One of the basic insights of the descriptive sociology of language is that members of social networks and communities do not always display either the same language usage or the same behavior toward language (Labov, 1971). For example, in Belgium both French and Dutch are spoken. Government officials in Brussels who are of Flemish origin (their first language is Dutch) do not always speak Dutch to one another. Not only are there occasions when they speak French to each other instead of Dutch, but there are some occasions when they speak standard Dutch and others when they use a regional variety of Dutch with each other. Indeed, some of them also use different varieties of French with each other as well, one variety being particularly loaded with government officialese, another corresponding to the nontechnical conversational French of the highly educated circles in Belgium, and still another being not only a more colloquial French but the colloquial French of those who are Flemings. The descriptive sociology of language is the study of the systematic nature of the alternations between one variety and another among individuals who share a repertoire of varieties (Fishman, 1970; Fishman, Cooper, Ma et al., 1971). However, multilingual speech networks or communities, such as those of most Puerto Ricans in the continental United States and many in Puerto Rico as well, are not the only groups that utilize a repertoire of language varieties. In monolingual speech communities the linguistic repertoire may consist of social class and regional varieties, or even of social class, regional, and occupational or situational varieties of the same language. A young man who sometimes says "I sure hope yuz guys'll shut the lights before leavin'" also is quite likely to say, or at least to write, "Kindly extinguish all illumination prior to vacating the premises." It's all a question of when to say the one and when to say the other, when interacting with individuals who could understand both equally well, but who would consider use of the one when the other is called for a serious *faux pas.*

Situational shifting. Members of social networks who share a linguistic repertoire know when to shift from one variety to another (Ervin, 1964). Which language usage or behavior a person will choose depends on the situation. A shift in situation, for example, may require a shift in language variety. A shift in language variety may signal a shift in the relationship between members of a social network, or a shift in topic and purpose of their interaction, or a shift in the privacy or locale of their interaction (Blom and Gumperz, 1972).

How does a speaker define a situation? Investigators have found that it is defined by the relationship between the interlocutors, the topic under discussion, and the setting. The boundaries that differentiate between classes of situations must be empirically determined by the investigator, and constitute one of the major tasks of descriptive sociology of language. Sociolinguists use the methods of participant observation, surveys, experimental procedures, and depth interviews in their effort to differentiate the situations that require one language variety from those which require another variety (Fishman, 1971).

Domains. All the situations that require one language variety constitute what sociolinguists call a *domain.* In a study of bilingual Puerto Ricans in and around New York, for example, Lawrence Greenfield identified five domains that accounted for all the situations he had observed in more than a year of study (1972). The five domains were family, friendship, religion, employment, and education. Greenfield's subjects were likely to use Spanish in the domain of friendship and likelier still to use it in the family. They were fairly likely to use English in the domain of religion, more likely to use it in employment, and most likely in education.

As Figure 9–2 shows, a typical situation can be constructed for each domain. If all three elements of any situation are typical for one domain, they are congruous; that is, a person in that situation has little difficulty deciding what language variety to use. But which language, for example, would two Puerto Rican friends playing on a New York beach use to address a bilingual teacher they know who happens along? The answer, Greenfield hypothesized, is that the participants would try to minimize the incongruity. Thus, the two friends

USE OF SPANISH AND ENGLISH IN FIVE DOMAINS

DOMAIN	SITUATION			LANGUAGE	VALUE
	Interlocutor	Place	Topic		
Family	parent	home	how to be a good son or daughter	Spanish most likely	intimacy
Friendship	friend	beach	how to play a certain game	Spanish likely	intimacy
Religion	priest	church	how to be a good Christian	English likely	status
Employment	employer	workplace	how to do one's job better	English more likely	status
Education	teacher	school	how to solve an algebra problem	English most likely	status

Figure 9–2. A bilingual Puerto Rican living in New York City will use the language appropriate to the situation.

SOURCE: Adapted by J. Fishman from data from L. Greenfield Spanish and English usage self-ratings in various situational contexts. In J. A. Fishman (Ed.), *Advances in the sociology of language.* II. The Hague: Mouton, 1972.

on the beach would talk with the teacher about some topic appropriate either to school or to some concern of the two students. This choice of a topic would make the situation congruous enough to determine the appropriate choice of a language. In order to test this assumption, Greenfield (1972) presented his subjects with two incongruent components—a person from one domain and a place from another domain—and asked them to select a third component in order to complete the situation, and then to indicate whether they would be more likely to use Spanish or English in the situation. Greenfield found that the third component was almost always selected from one of the two incongruent domains. Furthermore, in their attempts to render a seemingly incongruous situation somewhat more congruent, his subjects' language preferences left the relationship between domains and language choice substantially unaltered. Thus, all domains became somewhat less different from each other than they had been in the fully incongruent situations. Language choice is much more clear-cut and polarized in usual situations than in unusual situations which must be resolved by individual interpretation.

Metaphorical switching. Sometimes, too, a person shifts the language variety she is using even though the situation has not changed at all. The switch is usually momentary, and the person's interlocutors do not follow her in using the inappropriate language variety themselves. Such a shift is a case of *metaphorical switching*, done for humor or emphasis. If the person knows all her interlocutors well, metaphorical switching may have exactly the effect she intended; otherwise the possibility of giving offense is great, for most people are members of more than one speech community, each with somewhat different sociolinguistic norms. For example, a switch to Cockney among the upper-class English may well elicit a brief raising of eyebrows or a pause in the conversation, until it is clear from the speaker's demeanor that only a humorous interlude was intended. Metaphorical switching can be risky and is a luxury that can be afforded only by those who share not only the same set of situational norms but also the same view as to their violability (Blom and Gumperz, 1972; Kimple, Cooper, and Fishman, 1969).

The dynamic sociology of language

The dynamic sociology of language studies seeks to explain the changes in the choice and use of language by a speech community over time. For example, when the members of differing speech communities are brought into greater interaction with each other, the linguistic repertoire of each may undergo change. Thus, most immigrants to the United States experience sufficient interaction with English-speaking Americans, particularly in the work domain and in the education domain, to learn English. This also has long been true for

French-Canadians in large industrial centers such as Montreal. Yet, how differently these two processes of linguistic repertoire change have worked out. In the United States the immigrants largely lose their mother tongues within one, two, or at most three generations. In Montreal each new French-Canadian generation starts off monolingual in French and then acquires English later in life without, however, handing on this second language to the next generation as its initial language. The case of the American immigrants is an example of unstable bilingualism; of the French-Canadians, stable bilingualism. How can we best describe and account for this difference in outcome between two populations, each of which was forced to acquire English for the purpose of upward mobility.

Unstable bilingualism. American immigrants needed English both as a *lingua franca*—a common tongue—because they came from so many different speech communities, and as a passport to social and economic advancement. Because of the severe dislocation from their "old-country" rural or small-town ways of life to the new American urban context, it became impossible for them to sustain their home and family patterns—the domain separation on which the survival of their native tongue depended. Furthermore, those immigrants whose English was better, progressed more rapidly on the American scene and became models within the immigrant community. Thus, the home and immigrant life itself became domains of English, particularly under the additional imperatives of the American school and the Americanizing and amalgamating efforts of American churches. As a result, children of immigrants soon became bilingual even within the family and immigrant contexts. Thus, the immigrant speech networks have survived only in those few cases where immigrants of a single background clearly predominated, as in the case of German- and Scandinavian-language islands in the midwest, or where the social mobility of the immigrants was sharply restricted, as in the case of Spanish speakers in the southwest. Almost everywhere else, economic advancement and the dislocation of traditional home and community practices went hand in hand. There was ultimately no domain in which the non-English ethnic language alone was absolutely required, and as a result, there was no domain in which it was retained (Haugen, 1953; Fishman, 1966).

Stable bilingualism. In Montreal the situation was, and still is, much different. French speakers were initially exposed to English instruction and to English jobs only slowly over a long period of time. Elementary schools long remained entirely French, as did their churches, and even secondary schools were French and under church auspices. The result was that the children remained monolingual and French-speaking as long as they were restricted to home, neighborhood, and church. They became increasingly bilingual as they passed through more advanced levels of the school and work domains, but then reverted increasingly to French monolingualism if school and work careers were kept at lower levels. As a result, the domains of English and the domains of French were kept quite separate (Lieberson, 1965, 1970).

However, something new has recently been added to the Montreal picture. French-Canadian education has expanded to the point where it produces more well-qualified individuals than can be assimilated into the various English-managed enterprises. As a result, French-speaking elites increasingly have claimed and formed their own enterprises in these domains. For them English has become increasingly superfluous in view of the lack of domain separation and situational need. In addition, speaking English has become symbolic of the subordinate position of these French elites and is opposed on political grounds (Lieberson, 1970; Hughes, 1972).

These two sociolinguistic patterns, those of the American immigrant and the French-Canadian nationalist, are not unique. They have been repeated many times in the past century. For example, the Hispanicization of indigenous Indian populations moving to urban centers throughout Latin America has followed the same path as that of the anglicization of immigrants to the United States.

Bilingualism and diglossia

Sociolinguists speak of individuals as *bilingual,* and a society or nation is referred to as *diglossic.* A society is diglossic when its members use two or more languages for intrasocietal purposes. In such societies there is one set of behaviors, attitudes, and values that attain realization through one language, and a different set of behaviors, attitudes, and values that attain realization through another language. Both sets are fully accepted as culturally legitimate and complementary; they seldom come into conflict because they are functionally separated. As Ferguson observed (1959), one of the languages in a diglossic society can usually be designated the high language and the other the low. The term "diglossic" has also been extended to apply not only to societies in which two or more officially recognized languages are used, but also to those communities featuring separate dialects, registers, or functionally differentiated varieties of any kind (Gumperz, 1961, 1966).

Both diglossia and bilingualism. A speech community may be marked by *both diglossia and bilingualism.* In Paraguay (Rubin, 1962, 1968), almost the entire population utilizes Spanish (high) and Guarani (low). The indigenous rural population has added Spanish to its linguistic repertoire in connection with matters of education, religion, government, and high culture, and has emphasized social distance or status differences. Since the majority of city dwellers are relatively recent country folk, they maintain Guarani for matters of intimacy and primary group solidarity. However, it should be noted that Guarani is not an official language: that is, it is not recognized and utilized for purposes of government, formal education, and the courts. The high (Spanish) variety alone is officially recognized without, however, threatening the acceptance or stability of the low (Guarani) variety within the speech community.

Below the level of nationwide functioning, there are many examples of the presence of stable diglossia and widespread bilingualism. Before World War I, traditional Eastern European Jewish males utilized both Hebrew (high) and Yiddish (low) with each other, depending on the situation, and, in more recent days, their orthodox descendants have continued this pattern, adding a Western language, notably English (Fishman, 1965b; Weinreich, 1962). A similar example is that of upper- and middle-class males throughout the Arabic world in conjunction with the use of the classical Koranic and the vernacular, Egyptian, Syrian, Lebanese, Iraqi, etc. Arabic and, not infrequently, also a Western language—French or English—may be spoken or written for purposes of business or technological communication (Blanc, 1964; Ferguson, 1959; Nader, 1962).

In all of these examples there is a fairly large and complex speech community whose members have available both a range of compartmentalized roles and ready access to these roles. If the members of these speech communities were restricted to fewer roles, then their linguistic repertoires would also be more restricted, making separate languages or varieties unnecessary. In addition, were the roles not compartmentalized, that is, not associated with sepa-

BILINGUALISM AND DIGLOSSIA

Diglossia: in which two languages are utilized in the society

		PRESENT	NOT PRESENT
Bilingualism: in which an individual utilizes two languages	**PRESENT**	diglossia and bilingualism	bilingualism without diglossia
	NOT PRESENT	diglossia without bilingualism	neither diglossia nor bilingualism

Figure 9–3. Diglossia and bilingualism do not necessarily occur together. Either may be present or absent in a particular nation.

rate though complementary domains, one language or variety would displace the other. Finally, were widespread access not available to the variety of compartmentalized roles, then the bilingual population would be a small, privileged caste or class, as it has been in traditional India and Russia, rather than a broadly based population segment.

Diglossia without bilingualism.   In the case of diglossia without bilingualism, two or more speech communities are united religiously, politically, or economically into a single functioning unit despite important sociocultural cleavages in which two or more languages are spoken. However, one or both of the speech communities are marked by relatively impermeable group boundaries. Outsiders who are not born into the speech community are severely restricted in their access to roles and language. Linguistic repertoires in one or both groups thus are limited because of role specialization.

European elites, for example, often stood in this relationship with their countrymen. These elites utilized French or some other fashionable high tongue, and the masses utilized another, not necessarily linguistically related, language. Since the majority of the elites and the majority of the masses never interacted, they did not form a single speech community and their necessary communications were by means of translators or interpreters. Nevertheless, the two groups were joined politically and economically into a unity, with an upper and a lower class, each with a language appropriate to its own restricted concerns. A modern example of diglossia without bilingualism can be found in India (the Brahmins and the Untouchables).

In general, this pattern is characteristic of nations that are economically underdeveloped and combine groups that are locked into the extremes of the social spectrum—very rich and very poor. Obviously, such polities are bound to experience language problems when their social patterns begin to alter in the direction of industrialization, widespread literacy, education, and modernization. Political and economic development of the lower classes is likely to lead to secessionism or to demands for equality for the submerged languages. The language problems of Wales, Canada, and Belgium stem from origins such as these.

Bilingualism without diglossia.   We turn next to those situations in which there is *bilingualism without diglossia,* the situation in which many people speak two languages without well-established or separate functions for either. Under what circumstances do these bilinguals function without the benefit of a well-understood and widely accepted social consensus as to which language is to be used, between which interlocutors, for communication concerning what topics, or toward what ends? Briefly put, these are circumstances of rapid social change, of great social unrest, and of widespread abandonment of prior norms before the consolidation of new ones.

The needs as well as the consequences of rapid and massive industrialization frequently have caused members of a working-class speech community, particularly dislocated immigrants and their children, to abandon their traditional sociocultural patterns and language. They learn, or are taught, the language of their employers much sooner than they are absorbed into the cultural patterns and privileges of the people who speak that language. Some react to this imbalance by stressing the newly gained language of education and industry, whereas others react by seeking to replace the latter with an elaborated version of their largely preindustrial and preurban tongue. Thus, the mother tongue of these people and the new language are used in a seemingly random fashion (Nahirny and Fishman, 1965; Fishman, 1965d). The language of work and of the school comes to be used at home.

If an awareness of the two varieties as separate languages is also absent, a pidginization and creolization process will be set into motion. Instead of using two or more languages carefully separated by domain and interlocutor, people in this situation may use several intervening varieties. Such fused varieties may, within time, become the mother tongue and only tongue of a new generation. Thus, bilingualism without diglossia tends to be societally transitional, both in terms of the linguistic repertoires of speech communities and in terms of the speech varieties involved.

Many studies of bilingualism and intelligence, or of bilingualism and school achievement, have been conducted within the context of bilingualism without diglossia, often without sufficient understanding on the part of investigators that this was but one of several possible contexts for the study of bilingualism. As a result, there have been false generalizations of the disadvantages of bilingualism. Poor scores have been related to bilingualism rather than to the presence of disadvantageous social patterns (Fishman, 1965a; Fishman et al., 1966).

Neither diglossia nor bilingualism. This situation, if it exists, would be found only in very small, isolated, and undifferentiated speech communities (Gumperz, 1962; Fishman, 1965c). Given little role differentiation or specialization and frequent face-to-face interaction between all members of the speech community, no fully developed varieties may establish themselves, particularly if no regular contacts with other speech communities are maintained. Nevertheless, such groups—be they bands or clans—are easier to hypothesize than to find. All communities seem to have certain ceremonies or pursuits for which access is limited, if only on an age basis. Thus, all linguistic repertoires contain certain terms that are unknown to certain members of the speech community, certain terms that are used differently by one subset of speakers than by another. In addition, such factors as exogamy, conquest, expansion of population, economic growth, and contact with others all lead to internal diversification and, consequently, to repertoire diversification. Such diversification is the beginning of bilingualism. Its societal normification is the hallmark of diglossia. Therefore, quadrant four tends to be self-liquidating.

In quite a surprising way, the sociology of language draws on the politics and economics of emerging nations, the psychology of bilingualism, the social psychology of social interaction and perception of the other, and the sociology of social function, status, and role. All these factors must be taken into consideration when a description or an explanation of an individual's or a people's language choices is made. Indeed, in Great Britain even today, social mobility is possible only for people who can speak upper-class English, as George Bernard Shaw was only too eager to show in *Pygmalion*. Thus, language has become another area in which choices made automatically, without conscious thought, have been seen as problematic by social scientists who come to far-reaching and unexpected explanations and conclusions.

Summary

Communication involves words, gestures, ideas, and society. Nonverbal communication can be divided into three categories: moving and silent, still and silent, and vocal. Moving silent communication, or kinesic behavior, is the most important form of nonverbal communication. Another important form is proxemics, the use and perception of personal and social space.

There is some question whether nonverbal communication is inherited or acquired through learning. Since there is justification for saying that facial gestures communicate certain emotions cross-culturally, there is reason to suspect that such gestures are genetically determined. However, learning and heredity are so intertwined that this point is difficult to prove.

Despite the great differences in the way various languages sound, the early stages of learning to talk seem to be about the same the world over. The child starts out by babbling, and by the eighteenth month begins putting two words together to convey new meanings. Normally, children make the leap from single words to well-formed sentences between the ages of eighteen months and five years. Some investigators, notably the linguist Noam Chomsky, believe that the child has an innate capacity for learning the rules of grammar.

Much new information concerning the relationship between language and society has been provided by researchers who study the sociology of language. A basic insight of the descriptive sociology of language is that members of communities do not always display either the same language usage or the same behavior toward language; these things depend on the situation in which a speaker finds himself. All situations that require one language variety constitute a domain.

The dynamic sociology of language studies seeks to explain the changes in the choice and use of language by a speech community over time. When members of differing speech communities interact, the linguistic repertoire of each may change. This can lead to either stable bilingualism or unstable bilingualism.

A concept related to bilingualism is diglossia. A society is diglossic when its members use two or more languages for intrasocietal purposes. Diglossia and bilingualism do not necessarily occur together. Either may be present or absent in a particular nation. Only very small, isolated, and undifferentiated speech communities are neither diglossic nor bilingual.

Bibliography

ADDINGTON, D. W. The relationship of selected vocal characteristics to personality perception. *Speech Monographs*, 1968, **35**, 492–503.

BERGER, P., AND LUCKMANN, T. *The social construction of reality*. Garden City, N.Y.: Doubleday, 1966.

BIRDWHISTELL, R. L. Communication without words. In P. Alexandre (Ed.), *L'Aventure humaine*. Paris: Société d'Etudes Litteraires et Artistiques, 1965.

BIRDWHISTELL, R. L. *Kinesics and context: Essays on body motion communication*. Philadelphia: University of Pennsylvania Press, 1970.

BLANC, H. *Communal dialects of Baghdad*. Cambridge, Mass.: Harvard University Press, 1964.

BLOM, J.-P., AND GUMPERZ, J. J. Some social determinants of verbal behavior. In J. J. Gumperz and D. Hymes (Eds.), *Directions in sociolinguistics*. New York: Holt, Rinehart and Winston, 1972.

BRAINE, M. D. S. The ontogeny of English phrase structure: The first phase. *Language*, 1963, **39**, 1–13.

BROWN, R. W. Linguistic determinism and the part of speech. *Journal of Abnormal and Social Psychology*, July 1957, **55**, 1–5.

BROWN, R. W. *Words and things*. New York: Free Press, 1958.

BROWN, R. W. *First language: The early stages*. Cambridge, Mass.: Harvard University Press, 1973.

BROWN, R. W., AND LENNEBERG, E. H. A study in language and cognition. *Journal of Abnormal and Social Psychology*, 1954, **49**, 454–462.

CHOMSKY, N. Methodological preliminaries. In L. A. Jakobovits and M. S. Miron (Eds.), *Readings in the psychology of language*. Englewood Cliffs, N.J.: Prentice-Hall, 1967.

DANCE, F. E. X. Toward a theory of human communication. In F. E. X. Dance (Ed.), *Human communication theory*. New York: Holt, Rinehart and Winston, 1967.

DAVITZ, J. R. *The communication of emotional meaning*. New York: McGraw-Hill, 1964.

DAVITZ, J. R., AND DAVITZ, L. The communication of feelings by content-free speech. *Journal of Communication*, 1959, **9**, 6–13.

DITTMANN, A. T. Review of kinesics in context. *Psychiatry*, 1971, **34**, 334–342.

DONALDSON, M., AND BALFOUR, G. Less is more: A study of language comprehension in children. *British Journal of Psychology*, 1968, **59**, 461–472.

EIBL-EIBESFELDT, I. The expressive behavior of the deaf and blind born. In M. von Cranach and I. Vine (Eds.), *Non-verbal behaviour and expressive movements*. London: Academic Press, 1970.

EIBL-EIBESFELDT, I. Similarities and differences between cultures in expressive movements. In R. E. Hinde (Ed.), *Non-verbal communication*. Cambridge: University Press, 1972.

EISENBERG, A. M., AND SMITH, R. R., JR. *Nonverbal communication*. Indianapolis: Bobbs-Merrill, 1971.

EKMAN, P., AND FRIESEN, W. Nonverbal leakage and clues to deception. *Psychiatry*, 1969, **32**, 88–106.

EKMAN, P., FRIESEN, W., AND TOMKINS, S. S. Facial affect scoring technique: A first validity study. *Semiotica*, 1971, **3**, 37–58.

EKMAN, P., SORENSON, E. R., AND FRIESEN, W. Pan-cultural elements in facial displays of emotion. *Science*, April 4, 1969, **164**, 86–88.

ELLIS, D. S. Speech and social status in America. *Social Forces*, 1967, **45**, 431–451.

ENGEL, W. The development from sound to phoneme in child language. In C. A. Ferguson and D. I. Slobin (Eds.), *Studies of child language development*. New York: Holt, Rinehart and Winston, 1973.

ERVIN, S. M. An analysis of the interaction of language, topic, and listener. *American Anthropologist*, 1964, **66** (Part 2), 86–102.

ERVIN-TRIPP, S. M. Imitation and structural change in children's language. In C. A. Ferguson and D. I. Slobin (Eds.), *Studies of child language development*. New York: Scribner's, 1973.

FERGUSON, C. A. Diglossia. *Word*, 1959, **15**, 325–340.

FISHMAN, J. A. *Yiddish in America*. Bloomington: Indiana University Research Center in Anthropology, Folklore, and Linguistics, 1965. (a)

FISHMAN, J. A. *Sociolinguistics: A brief introduction*. Rowley, Mass.: Newbury House, 1970.

FISHMAN, J. A. The sociology of language: An interdisciplinary social science approach to language in society. In J. A. Fishman (Ed.), *Advances in the sociology of language*. I. The Hague: Mouton, 1971.

FISHMAN, J. A., et al. *Language loyalty in the United States*. The Hague: Mouton, 1966.

FISHMAN, J. A., COOPER,, R. L., MA., R., et al. *Bilingualism in the barrio*. Language Sciences Monograph Series. Bloomington: Indiana University, 1971.

FISHMAN, J. A. Varieties of ethnicity and language consciousness. *Georgetown University Monograph Series on Languages and Linguistics*, 1965, **18**, 69–79. (b)

FISHMAN, J. A. Who speaks what language to whom and when? *Linguistique*, 1965, **2**, 67–88. (c)

FISHMAN, J. A. Language maintenance and language shift: The American immigrant case within a general theoretical perspective. *Sociologus*, 1965, **16**, 19–38. (d)

FISHMAN, J. A. Bilingual sequences at the societal level. *On Teaching English to*

Speakers of Other Languages, 1966, **2**, 139–144.

FISHMAN, J. A., FERGUSON, C. A., AND DAS GUTPA, J. (Eds.), *Language problems of developing nations*. New York: John Wiley and Sons, 1968.

GREENFIELD, L. Spanish and English usage self-ratings in various situational contexts. In J. A. Fishman (Ed.), *Advances in the sociology of language*. II. The Hague: Mouton, 1972.

GUMPERZ, J. J. Speech variations and the study of Indian civilization. *American Anthropologist*, 1961, **63**, 976–988.

GUMPERZ, J. J. Types of linguistic communities. *Anthropological Linguistics*, 1962, **4**(1), 28–40.

GUMPERZ, J. J. On the ethnology of linguistic change. In W. Bright (Ed.), *Sociolinguistics*. The Hague: Mouton, 1966.

HAGGARD, E. A., AND ISAACS, K. S. Micromomentary facial expressions as indicators of ego mechanisms in psychotherapy. In L. A. Gottschalk and A. H. Auerbach (Eds.), *Methods of research in psychotherapy*. New York: Appleton-Century-Crofts, 1966.

HALL, E. T. *The silent language*. Garden City, N.Y.: Doubleday, 1959.

HALL, E. T. A system for the notation of proxemic behavior. *American Anthropologist*, 1963, **65**, 1003–1026.

HALL, E. T. *The hidden dimension*. Garden City, N.Y.: Doubleday, 1966.

HARMS, L. S. Listener judgments of status cues in speech. *Quarterly Journal of Speech*, 1961, **47**, 164–168.

HAUGEN, E. *The Norwegian language in America*. Philadelphia: University of Pennsylvania Press, 1953.

HERTZLER, J. O. *Laughter: A socio-scientific analysis*. New York: Exposition Press, 1970.

HEWES, G. The anthropology of posture. *Scientific American*, 1957, **196**(2).

HUGHES, E. The linguistic division of labor in Montreal. In J. A. Fishman (Ed.), *Advances in the sociology of language*. II. The Hague: Mouton, 1972.

JOSEPH, N., AND ALEX, N. The uniform: A sociological perspective. *American Journal of Sociology*, 1972, **77**(4), 719–730.

KENDON, A. Some functions of gaze direction in social interaction. *Acta Psychologica*, 1967, **26**, 22–63.

KIMPLE, J., JR., COOPER, R. L., AND FISHMAN, J. A. Language switching in the interpretation of conversations. *Lingus*, 1969, **23**, 127–134.

KNAPP, M. L. *Nonverbal communication in human interaction*. New York: Holt, Rinehart and Winston, 1972.

LABOV, W. Language in society. In J. A. Fishman (Ed.), *Advances in the sociology of language*. I. The Hague: Mouton, 1971.

LENNEBERG, E. H., AND ROBERTS, J. M. The denotata of color terms. Paper presented at the meeting of the Linguistic Society of America, Bloomington, Indiana, August, 1953.

LIEBERSON, S. Bilingualism in Montreal: A demographic analysis. *American Journal of Sociology*, 1965, **71**, 10–25.

LIEBERSON, S. *Language and ethnic relations in Canada*. New York: John Wiley and Sons, 1970.

MEHRABIAN, A. Significance of posture and position in the communication of attitude and status relationships. *Psychological Bulletin*, 1969, **71**, 359–372.

MILLER, G. A. Some preliminaries to psycholinguistics. *American Psychologist*, 1965, **20**, 15–20.

MOORE, H. T., AND GILLILAND, A. R. The measure of aggressiveness. *Journal of Applied Psychology*, 1921, **5**, 97–118.

NADER, L. A note on attitudes and the use of language. *Anthropological Linguistics*, 1962, **4**(6), 24–29.

NAHIRNY, V. C., AND FISHMAN, J. A. American immigrant groups: Ethnic identification and the problem of generations. *Sociological Review*, 1965, **13**, 311–326.

NERBONNE, G. P. The identification of speaker characteristics on the basis of aural cues. Doctoral dissertation, Michigan State University, 1967.

POLLACK, I., AND PICKETT, J. M. The intelligibility of excerpts from conversation. *Language and Speech*, 1964, **6**, 165–171.

RUBIN, J. Bilingualism in Paraguay. *Anthropological Linguistics*, 1962, **4**(1), 52–58.

RUBIN, J. Language and education in Paraguay. In J. A. Fishman, C. A. Ferguson, and J. Das Gupta (Eds.), *Language problems in developing nations*. New York: John Wiley and Sons, 1968.

SAPIR, E. (Selected writings) In D. G. Mandelbaum (Ed.), *Selected writings of Edward Sapir*. Berkeley: University of California Press, 1951.

SAPIR, E. *Culture, language, and personality*. Berkeley: University of California Press, 1956.

SEBCOK, T. A. Animal communication. *International Social Science Journal*, 1967, **19**(1), 88–95.

SHIBUTANI, T. *Improvised news: A sociological study of rumor*. Indianapolis: Bobbs-Merrill, 1966.

SKINNER, B. F. *Verbal behavior*. New York: Appleton-Century-Crofts, 1957.

TONKAVA-YAMPOL'SKAYA, R. V. Development of speech intonation in infants during the first two years of life. In C. A. Ferguson and D. I. Slobin (Eds.), *Studies of child language development*. New York: Holt, Rinehart and Winston, 1973.

TRAGER, G. L. Paralanguage: A first approximation. *Studies in Linguistics*, 1958, **13**, 1–12.

WEINREICH, U. Multilingual dialectology and the new Yiddish atlas. *Anthropological Linguistics*, 1962, **4**(1), 6–22.

WETSTONE, H., AND FRIEDLANDER, B. The effect of word order on young children's responses to simple questions and commands. *Child Development*, 1973, **44**, 734–740.

WHORF, B. L. (Selected writings) In J. B. Carroll (Ed.), *Language, thought, and reality: Selected writings of Benjamin Lee Whorf*. Cambridge, Mass.: MIT Press, 1956.

10

Perception

Jessica walks into Room 310 in the psychology building the first day of her class. The instructor's back is to the class. It's a woman. She is writing the title of the text on the board. She turns around and faces the class. She's pretty. She's young. What will she be like as a teacher? She looks serious. Will her lectures be tedious? Will we all get a chance to talk? Will her exams be hard? Will she really read my papers? One of the students asks a question. It seems an obvious point. The girl next to her seems to mirror her thoughts, muttering "stupid" under her breath. Jessica feels an attraction to her. Then Jessica begins to wonder about her decision to major in psychology. Is she really interested in the field or was she flattered because of her A from Professor Wright in the intro course? In a short minute or two, perceptions of other people, thoughts about oneself, judgments to be made about others, about oneself—all crowd the brain.

In addition to social stimuli, there are countless sensory stimulations from the physical environment. Scores of sounds are contained in a single spoken sentence. The squeeze of a hand brings hundreds of different charges to the brain. And there is an entire array of stimuli, different in quality, which emerge from the internal world of oneself. In the movement of a single muscle, the brain receives innumerable messages. The stomach, bladder, lungs, genitals, and heart supply additional information as to their condition. And to add

351

to the confusion there is the incessant intrusion of the past, ushered in by the process of memory. The entire flux swirls into our experience, and the tumult is renewed with each passing moment. The world becomes, in the words of William James, "a booming, buzzing confusion."

Perhaps this description does not agree with your own perception of others and yourself. You might say that the world appears orderly and stable; your bodily activities appear clear and distinct. Seldom do you feel overwhelmed and confused by the pandemonium of experience. This reaction is perfectly justified. However, it is just this discrepancy between what we objectively know to be a virtual chaos of inputs to our senses, and the adult perception of an organized world, that furnishes the cutting edge to our discussion. Like Jessica, we are continuously receiving information, almost unconsciously registering the familiar in the environment, refusing to notice much of the strange, and questioning and sorting as much of the unfamiliar as we can deal with. This organizing of the environment, both social and physical, into components that can be categorized and made to fit into the knowledge of reality that we already have is accomplished by means of *concepts*. For it is primarily the capacity of the human being to form concepts that stands between him and chaos. And it is this same ability that guides and directs the individual's social conduct.

Concepts

Conceptualization is the process of treating different stimuli as equivalent. When noticeably different stimuli, or the same stimulus encountered on successive occasions, are placed in a single class or category, given the same label, or identified as being equivalent, conceptualization has occurred. No two individuals smile in the same way; yet we have the ability to abstract a few similarities of these muscular contortions (e.g., an upturned mouth) and form a concept. The concept of "color" is formed by abstracting the quality of chromaticity, whether it be green, yellow, or blue.

Nor is this process of conceptualization an isolated event. The very act of perceiving an object or another person is guided by our concepts. A round ceramic object may be perceived as a candy dish, a cereal bowl, or an ashtray, depending on our concept of what these objects should look like. As Bruner (1957a) puts it, "All perceptual experience is necessarily the end product of a categorization process." An individual is stimulated by a certain object and she responds by referring the object to a certain concept or category.

Social concepts play a particularly important role in how we perceive our social world, a world where the ability to label the behavior of others and the self is critical to our social endeavors. Our behavior toward others is partly determined by our conceptions of them. In addition, our actions are strongly influenced by our conceptions of self. To see oneself as "inferior," for example, is to imply an entire series of activities in which one would not engage if he viewed himself as "superior." The conception of oneself as "intelligent" or "religious" will lead one down paths not followed by those who consider themselves "average" in intelligence or "atheistic." As Henry David Thoreau once wrote, "What a man thinks of himself . . . indicates his fate."

Thus, the main concern of this chapter is with the process of conceptualization in interpersonal relations. Our major supposition is that understanding social behavior requires our taking into account these conceptual processes. However, we must first take a look at the functions of concepts in order to appreciate the relatedness of concepts to the social world.

Social Perception: Applying Concepts to People

Faced with the flux in another's behavior, confronted with the complexity of oneself, how do we choose from the storehouse of concepts available to us? What determines which concept we will apply on any given occasion? In most cases, we have only clues. We must take what little information is available, make wide-ranging decisions, and behave accordingly. We must commit ourselves to behavior with less than full confidence. People cannot be tested for the purpose of verifying our perceptions of them. Males, for example, typically invite females out with little knowledge of their particular charms or wiles, and females accept such invitations with little knowledge of the males' intent. We vote for political candidates with minimal knowledge of their actual abilities and attitudes. And we judge our own motives and capabilities with little consistent information about ourselves.

In each of these cases we use information that is ambiguous, inconsistent, or insufficient to form judgments that carry us beyond the present circumstance. A girl may be judged "good fun" simply because she has an attractive appearance; a male may be judged as honorable simply because his academic grades are good. Political candidates are only too aware that their administrative capabilities may be judged by their belief in God or by the accomplishments of their female relatives. A man may decide that he is cut out to be a doctor on the basis of his undergraduate grades in chemistry. In each of these cases we are going beyond the information given (Bruner, 1957b). Nevertheless, we all form concepts, make judgments, and act, despite the ambiguity and insufficiency of information.

Association of concepts

Psychologists in the Freudian tradition have long been interested in ways of tapping the unconscious. One popular method of exploring unconscious thought is to give the patient a series of words and have him respond to each with the first word that comes to mind. If the word "knife" is presented, the patient might say "fork" or "cut," or to the stimulus "mother," he might quickly respond with "father." Uncommon associations, such as responding to "knife" with the word "father" or long pauses before responding, signal the psychologist to probe more deeply. The reasoning behind this procedure is that for most people within a cultural tradition, certain associations are common; uncommon associations and long pauses indicate to a Freudian analyst that unconscious forces are interfering with the normal associations.

For our purposes, however, the procedure demonstrates that concepts are not learned in a vacuum, independent of each other. Rather, there are strong learned associations among them, such that when one is present, others are called to mind. If asked to do so, most of us would have little difficulty in rapidly responding to the word "knife" with a long string of associations, and many of these associations would be very typical within our culture.

This association of concepts can occur through such diverse processes as frequency, proximity, or similarity, or through reinforcement. Two concepts such as "popcorn" and "movies" can become linked because they frequently co-occur. "Mailbox" and "street corner" may become associated because they are often located near each other. The first association to "pen" is usually "pencil" because, as writing implements, they are similar items. Reinforcement also serves to associate concepts. A reinforcer, in learning theory, is anything that increases a response. In this sense, organisms are reinforcement-seeking and will associate concepts which have led to reinforcement in the past. Children quickly learn to associate "supermarket" with "cookies" because cookies are sweet and act as reinforcers. Sex serves to link concepts together. A particular perfume may evoke the memory of a certain woman, or a restaurant may be associated with a certain lover.

But not all concept linkages directly reflect the world of physical properties. Another important source is the language, as it is spoken and written. And if we hear the sentence fragment, "The boy hit . . . ," we expect the next concept to refer to an object. The fact that nouns typically follow transitive verbs in our language has taught us to expect this.

The important thing, however, is that no matter how concepts become associated, one concept is able to elicit or evoke another concept. When a concept is regularly evoked by another concept, it is said to be *salient*. "Cat" is a salient concept in respect to "dog"; "Jingle Bells" is salient in respect to "Christmas." Each time concepts are associated, the *association strength* between the concepts is incremented. Therefore, a concept with a high association strength will become salient with reference to the concept which stimulates it. This is why certain complex social phenomena have to be learned. People learn to associate the concept through repeated usage.

The degree of saliency determines *expectancy*—a person's anticipation of what is to occur. If one concept is regularly associated with another concept, one comes to expect the second concept. For example, "mugging" may be a salient concept, for many, to "New York," and visitors to that city may be wary because these concepts have been linked many times in the past. The smell of cooking generates the expectancy of dinner. Through the association of concepts we can anticipate events and act accordingly.

Warmth and beyond: An application

We can now turn to one of the classic studies of social perception and see how our analysis of concept association applies. In 1946, Solomon Asch published an engaging set of research findings. The methodology was simple. Undergraduates at Swarthmore College were given a list of traits that could be used to describe a person. As you read these same traits, you might try to conjure up a mental picture of the type of person (other than yourself) to whom they refer: "intelligent, skillful, industrious, warm, determined, practical, cautious." Asch asked his students to write a brief description of the person to whom these traits applied, and to indicate on a separate checklist which of a series of other adjectives would best describe such a person. A second group of students participated in the very same procedure, with one modification. The word "cold" was substituted for "warm" in the original list. The major focus of the study was on the effects of this single substitution on the subsequent descriptions and ratings which the students made.

Three important findings emerged. First, students had little difficulty in expanding these few traits into meaty personality sketches of the fictitious person. For example, when "warm" was included in the list, one student wrote of a scientist who performed numerous experiments and who persevered in the face of numerous setbacks. "He was driven," wrote the student, "by the desire to accomplish something that would be of benefit." This finding nicely documents our earlier discussion of how persons use minimal amounts of information to draw wide-ranging conclusions about others.

The second major finding was that the substitution of "cold" for "warm" made a profound difference in both the quality of the resulting sketches and the adjectives chosen as descriptive. In contrast to the humanist–scientist image stimulated by the list containing "warm," the insertion of "cold" produced sketches of a person who was calculating, unsympathetic, and snobbish.

Whereas 91 percent of the students saw the warm individual as "generous," only 8 percent saw the cold-stimulus person as having this characteristic. Similarly, when "warm" was used, the individual was seen as much more "popular, happy, and humorous." In an interesting extension of the Asch study, Veness and Brierley (1963) used voice intonations to create the impression of warm and cold, and essentially repeated Asch's early findings.

The third major finding was that the traits "warm" and "cold" were *central*. That is, when they were substituted for each other, vast differences appeared in subjects' impressions. However, when the traits "polite" and "blunt" were used in the slots previously occupied by "warm" and "cold," the differences in subsequent ratings were far less pronounced. These results were puzzling. Why should some traits have such a strong impact on impressions and others make such little difference? One answer to this question was provided by Wishner (1960). Wishner used all the adjectives that had appeared in the original study. Rather than rating a fictitious person, he had students in ten different sections of a psychology course rate their instructors on all traits. In this way he was able to determine the correlation of each trait with all others. Thus he found that an instructor rated as "warm" was also very likely to be rated as "sociable," but that "warm" teachers were not rated as "persistent." The correlations of traits thus indicated the degree of association between each of the traits.

A trait term was found to be central when it had a high degree of association with the other adjectives used for rating. Thus, it was held that "warm" and "cold" were central in the original study because they were strongly associated with other terms on the checklist (e.g. "popular" and "happy"). According to this line of reasoning, "polite" and "blunt" would have less effect on impressions because they were not strongly associated with the particular adjectives on the checklist. However, research by Archer (1960) and Tenbrunsel et al. (1968) strongly suggests that some concepts have a greater number of associations than others. In reaction to some concepts, for example, people can rapidly reel off a series of associations. For others, they may struggle in providing more than a few. The capacity of a concept to elicit associations may also be called its *association value.* The association value or centrality of terms such as "intelligent" or "friendly" is high in our culture. Trait terms such as "well-intentioned" or "civil" may be less well connected to other concepts.

Let us ask how centrality might affect our day-to-day perceptions of others. If an individual falls easily into the categories of "intelligent" and "friendly," an entire set of dispositions is triggered. Our behavior toward him is more channeled, and the way he is treated by others is more homogeneous. The person who cannot be described by a central trait—for example, the man whose most marked characteristic is that he is civil and well-intentioned—

may expect much more caution on the part of others in the way they will judge him, and much more variation in their behavior.

A study by Kelley (1950) demonstrates this last point and expands importantly on Asch's original work. Kelley announced to the sections of his psychology course that they would be visited by a guest lecturer who would lead their

Choice of Traits Found to be Congruous with Warm/Cold and Polite/Blunt (in percents)

TRAITS	EXPERIMENT A		EXPERIMENT B	
	"WARM" N=90	"COLD" N=76	"POLITE" N=20	"BLUNT" N=26
1. generous	91	8	36	58
2. wise	65	25	30	50
3. happy	90	34	75	65
4. good-natured	94	17	87	56
5. humorous	77	13	71	48
6. sociable	91	38	83	68
7. popular	84	28	94	56
8. reliable	94	99	95	100
9. important	88	99	94	96
10. humane	86	31	59	77
11. good-looking	77	69	93	79
12. persistent	100	97	100	100
13. serious	100	99	100	100
14. restrained	77	89	82	77
15. altruistic	69	18	29	46
16. imaginative	51	19	33	31
17. strong	98	95	100	100
18. honest	98	94	87	100

Figure 10–1. Subjects describing an imaginary individual with a trait list that includes the word "warm" perceive the same individual quite differently when "cold" is substituted for "warm" on the list. Ninety-one percent of the subjects rated an individual described as warm also to be generous, whereas only 8 percent saw the person described as cold to have this characteristic. The substitution of "polite" and "blunt" for "warm" and "cold" on the trait list has a less pronounced effect on the subjects' rating.

SOURCE: Adapted from Asch, S. E. Forming impressions of personality. *Journal of Abnormal and Social Psychology*, 1946, **41**, 263.

discussion for the day. Before the visitor arrived, notes were distributed to the students in the class providing them with biographical information about the visitor. For half the students in the class, the guest was described with Asch's first list of traits, including "warm"; the other half received the same list with "cold" substituted. The guest then arrived and led the class in a twenty-minute discussion. After he departed, students rated him using the same adjectives used in the original Asch study. In spite of the fact that the students had had twenty minutes in which to confront him at close range—to watch and listen to him—their ratings of him were found to be highly biased by the single insertion of "warm" or "cold" into the preliminary descriptions. Students who were told of his warmth indeed came to see him as warm and in ways associated with warmth; the single mention of his coldness biased their perception of him in the opposite direction.

Another way of looking at the centrality of some traits as opposed to others is provided by the *semantic differential*. (See chapter 7 for measurement of the semantic differential.) Osgood, Suci, and Tannenbaum (1957) found that the connotative meaning of most words can be expressed in terms of three basic dimensions: an *evaluative* dimension (good–bad), a *potency* dimension (strong–weak), and an *activity* dimension (active–passive). The meanings that words connote are emotional, usually expressing a preference or an evaluation. Words such as "warm" and "cold" carry a great deal of connotative meaning, especially on the evaluative dimension, which was found to outweigh the potency and activity dimensions.

These dimensions are derived by taking target words and asking people where they fit on a continuum created by bipolar adjectives, such as angular–round, clean–dirty, good–bad, stale–fresh, and so forth. The three basic dimensions create a *semantic space* in which target words can be located and compared with other target words. For example, "rosebud" was found to connote good, impotent, and passive associations on the three dimensions, whereas "quicksand" had associations of bad, strong, and passive (Osgood, 1952).

In terms of our conceptual model, it was previously stated that centrality is related to a high degree of association to other words. One of the traditional definitions of "meaning" has been the number of associations that a word elicits (Noble, 1952). For example, "iguana" will probably be less meaningful to the reader than "dog" or "cat" because in most cases, people have fewer associations to "iguana." Therefore, "warm" and "cold," which have a high degree of connotative meaning, would be central because of the number of associations that they evoke.

This relates to our discussion of saliency. If "warm" or "cold" evokes many associations, then it would follow that many words would, in turn, elicit the central trait. In this sense, a cluster of concepts could "converge" on a central trait, with each element in the cluster contributing its own association strength to make that trait salient. For example, "tall" and "dark," taken separately, may not evoke "handsome" because there may be low association strength between each and the concept "handsome." However, taken together, their combined association strength might serve to make "handsome" salient. In this way, certain traits may become central because of the combined association strengths of many related traits.

The associational process we have outlined thus far has both adaptive and injurious consequences. When we are forced to make judgments about a person with incomplete information at our disposal, the associational process may be very useful. Because associations are at least partially based on real-world observation, they provide us with best guesses about the character and probable behavior of others. On the other hand, our first impression may present strong biases which may be hard to correct. Consider meeting a person for the first time who has just broken up with his girlfriend. We might easily judge this person to be hostile as well as depressing to be with, and avoid future encounters that might serve as a corrective to our mistaken impression.

Settings

As we have seen, people utilize limited information to form far-reaching judgments about others. Such judgments are often influenced by an association with the *setting* in which we encounter the person rather than the person himself. Thus, if we see a man in a business suit enter a bank in the middle of the morning, we expect that he will carry out a normal transaction within. Our concept world, based on previous observations, gears us to expect this, and we might well describe the man as "honest" and "industrious" if asked about his probable character. This, of course, is one reason that daylight bank robberies are successful. People's expectations are so geared that they fail to notice the transaction, which includes a weapon and money being deposited quickly into a paper bag. Our assessments of what people are like and what they will do is thus based on concepts associated with particular environmental contexts.

Goffman (1963) has pointed out that people are under great pressure to perform certain behaviors in specified places. If at a party, one must perform as a guest, smiling a certain percent of the time, placing limits on one's vocabulary in specified ways, and standing in certain postures. If confined to a mental institution, there are other prescriptions concerning how one is to behave, and if a patient does not perform them properly he may be punished. Because behavior is specific to situations, and because both the behavior and the situations are conceptualized, concept associations are formed. Thereafter, environmental contexts will be used to judge people according to the settings in which they are found. Indeed, people often seek certain environments so that the color or tone of the situational context will lead them to be more favorably judged by others. Goffman (1959) sees these settings as "stages" for a "performance," stages which often lead to subtle social changes: "[An] example can be found in the recent development of the medical profession where we find that it is increasingly important for a doctor to have access to the elaborate scientific stage provided by large hospitals" (Goffman, 1959).

Some of the clearest demonstrations of the effects of settings can be found in the literature of the judgments of emotions. The problem of how well people are able to recognize various emotions in others has a long-standing history stemming originally from Darwin's writings in 1872. Much of this research has used pictorial representations of people in various poses or with various facial expressions. The subject's task is to identify the emotion portrayed. Since the 1920s, research has consistently shown (Landis, 1929; Frijda, 1958) that the background in which the stimulus person is pictured is of extreme importance in determining the judgments that are applied. So strong are these effects, and so much do they increase judgmental accuracy, that some (e.g. Coleman, 1949) have felt that there is really very little consistent information conveyed in the face and body alone. The setting may furnish the strongest cues for ascribing emotions to others. For example, consider a person laughing: only situational cues can reveal whether this action is expressive of happiness or embarrassment.

Situational cues are hardly infallible aids in making judgments of others. One source of error in such cases is the differing level of involvement of the perceiver and the perceived. For example, we might judge the manager of a baseball team as "very happy" when he squeaks through the first seven games of the season without a loss. However, the manager himself may be in the throes of agony, as he considers how difficult it has been for his team to win against the poorest teams in the league. An intriguing experimental example of misjudgment is provided by Deutsch (1960). Subjects worked on a task together. One group of subjects in this experiment received strong criticisms of their work from another person in their task-group. These subjects then rated their critic on a variety of evaluative dimensions. A second group of subjects was apprised of what had happened—that one of the group members had been criticized by another. Their task, however, was to *predict* the ratings of the critic made by the targets of his criticism. In essence, this second group was to judge the emotional reactions of the first group on the basis of what they knew about the situation. The results indicated that the bystanders vastly overrated

DARWIN: THE EXPRESSION OF EMOTION

Do our facial expressions serve as barometers of our inner thoughts and feelings? This question is currently receiving some attention from social psychologists, many of whom were inspired by the ground-breaking work of Charles Darwin. In 1872 Darwin startled his contemporaries by claiming that his study of facial expressions supplied additional evidence supporting the relationship of various species and the overall evolutionary process. He published his findings as *The Expression of the Emotions in Man and Animals,* and forced Victorian society to rethink its ideas about the exclusivity of man in the natural world.

"With mankind some expressions, such as the bristling of the hair under the influence of extreme terror, or the uncovering of the teeth under that of furious rage, can hardly be understood, except on the belief that man once existed in a much lower and animal-like condition. The community of certain expressions in distinct and allied species, as in the movements of the same facial muscles during laughter by man and various monkeys, is rendered somewhat more intelligible, if we believe in their descent from a common progenitor" (p. 12).

Darwin was ingenious in finding data to support his contentions. For example, he used photographs of the facial expressions of an old man. Darwin writes, "It fortunately occurred to me to show several of the best [photographic] plates without explanation, to twenty educated persons of various ages and both sexes, asking them by what emotion or feeling the old man was supposed to be agitated. . . . Several of the expressions were instantly recognized by almost everyone. . . . On the other hand, the most widely different judgments were pronounced in regard to some of them. This exhibition was of use in another way, by convincing me how easily we may be misguided by our imagination" (p. 14).

Darwin observed infants. He was interested in the forcefulness with which they express their feelings; whereas he observed that later in life people have learned to mask their emotions to a great extent. In the same vein, he solicited observations of the insane from the director of an "immense asylum"; the insane "ought to be studied, as they are liable to the strongest passions and give uncontrollable vent to them" (p. 13). It occurred to Darwin to study the works of art of great painters and sculptors, because they are such close and careful observers of life. However, he found beauty to be the main object in a work of art, and emotions contort the face; artists seem to prefer to use composition and details to convey meaning and emotion.

Another source of evidence sought by Darwin was the expressions and gestures of "all the races of mankind, especially those who have associated but little with Europeans. Whenever the same movements of the features or body express the same emotions in several distinct races of man, we may infer with much probability that such expressions are true ones—that is, are innate or instinctive" (p. 15). He circulated a questionnaire among missionaries and other world travelers, received many replies, and was confirmed in his hypothesis that "the same state of mind is expressed throughout the world with remarkable uniformity" (p. 17).

Thus did Darwin seek to understand the "cause or origin of the several expressions" and to apply his conclusion "with satisfactory results both to man and the lower animals" (p. 19).

the emotional impact of the criticism. They attributed to the criticized team members much more hostility than they actually felt. Deutsch concluded that people seem to operate on the basis of a *pathetic fallacy*. They seem to overestimate the pain or misery of the afflicted.

Similarities

Psychologists have long sought to measure accuracy in social perception. One popular method for assessing this talent has been to compare the personality ratings people make of relative strangers with the strangers' own self-ratings (Dymond, 1949; Estes, 1938). It was reasoned that those who came closest to the self-ratings of the strangers were most skilled at social judgments. Later, however, an important flaw was discovered in this method. If subjects were asked to rate themselves along the same dimensions the relative

When other clues are ambiguous, the setting may serve to define social class.

stranger was to use, an interesting thing happened. A high correlation emerged between the self-ratings and the predictions made about the stranger. People seemed to assume the stranger was much like themselves. The discovery of this set toward *assumed similarity* (Gage and Cronbach, 1955) threw the entire line of earlier research into question. After all, if people simply assume that others answer as they do, then they would automatically get a high score if the stranger happened to be similar to them in personality and a low score if he did not. What were thought to be accurate scores were highly biased by the degree of chance-determined similarity between the judge and the target.

Although the discovery of assumed similarity biases and other methodological flaws frustrated the search for accurate social judges, the issue of assumed similarity gained its own importance. Why should people assume that others are like themselves? The model of concept association suggests that people are aware of the association between their own background characteristics and their lifestyle. This awareness can become critical, for example, when people visit another culture and see how much their values, clothes, and manners depend on their being raised in a different tradition. Thus, background characteristics and behavior are closely linked associations.

In predicting another's behavior, one usually has some indication of background characteristics, even if limited to sex, style of dress, age, or skin color. If these characteristics at all approximate one's own, what is the best guess that can be made about the other's behavior? In the absence of further information, the most optimal strategy would be to predict that he would respond as one would oneself. Thus, the extent to which a person uses himself to predict the behavior of another should depend on the degree of similarity he sees between their social characteristics. A male would be more likely to use himself as a baseline to judge other males rather than females, people his age as opposed to those younger or older, and so on. From their review of the literature, Gage and Cronbach (1955) conclude that there is good empirical support for such reasoning.

It should also hold that if an individual is provided with information about another's behavior, and there is similarity between this behavior and her own, she would tend to predict that the other has social characteristics similar to her own. Thus, if we find ourselves at the same concerts, movies, or plays as another, and see that she dresses much as we do, we may well assume that she is similar to us in education, social class, age, and so on. In making judgments about another's background, then, people will make equal use of the associations holding between their own behavior and their social characteristics.

There are dangers, however, in this process. If a person is considered dissimilar in background (race, religion, and so on), we may neglect the fact that he may have needs and aspirations that are similar to our own. One reason why equal-status contacts between blacks and whites are effective in reducing prejudice (Deutsch and Collins, 1951) may be that an opportunity is afforded to members of both races to realize that a dissimilar racial background may mask not only similarities of other social characteristics but many behavioral similarities. On the other hand, assuming similarity with people of like backgrounds also has its pitfalls. To the extent that we maintain stable perceptions of self, we may be insensitive to changes that occur in another. To assume that a good friend will always prefer what we choose is to deny his possibilities for independent growth. Or, if perception of others is based on perception of self, then marked fluctuations may have nothing at all to do with their behavior, but may depend solely on fluctuations in self-perception. The hungry husband may be led to believe that the remainder of the family must be hungry as well, and demand dinner at what for them is an unreasonably early hour.

Using self to judge others. While people use themselves as reference points for judging others as similar to the self, they also tend to perceive others in relationship to their judgments of self. Let us begin by examining some data supplied by Peabody (1967). In this study, subjects received a list of adjectives descriptive of people. The list included such traits as dominating, rebellious, and friendly. The subject was to assume that each of these traits described the reactions of one person (P) to the characteristics of some other person (O). He was then to choose from a list of fourteen characteristics those which most reasonably could have produced P's reaction in each case. In other words, what must O have been like to produce P's reactions of domination, rebelliousness, and so on. The results showed remarkable agreement among the fifty subjects. A full 92 percent agreed that O's being "submissive" was the most likely cause of "dominating" behavior in P; 90 percent felt that "aggressive" behavior by O was the most likely cause of "tenseness" in P; "sexually arousing" behavior on the part of O was seen as the most likely cause of P's "sexual arousal" by 94 percent; and there was total agreement among subjects that O's "friendly" behavior was the most likely cause of P's "friendliness." These data demonstrate that people have highly developed ideas about cause and effect in social life. They make a connection between certain forms of behavior on the part of one person with certain reactions in another. As a result, they carry with them series of associated concepts about what leads to what in social interaction.

Thus, if we can identify how we have behaved toward another, this knowledge is likely to influence our perception of his reaction. The concepts that will be most salient are those most closely associated with the interpretation we have made of our own behavior. Peabody's research suggests that if we see our own actions as "dominating," we would be prepared to interpret the other's reaction as "submissive." These two concepts are associated, so that when we observe "dominance," the concept of "submissiveness" is highly salient to our interpretation of what follows. In the same way, if we feel that we are being "aggressive," we might be prepared to see the other as "tense"; if we feel we have been "friendly," we may interpret the other's reactions as "friendly"; and if we feel "sexually aroused" we classify the other's reaction to us as "arousal." These perceptions may, of course, be quite incorrect. With lack of social feedback, the process may create an autistic, if not a paranoid, perception of the social world. For a girl to wear what she feels is a "pretty dress" may cause her to feel "admired" by others, thus boosting her esteem throughout an entire day although no one has really noticed her at all. A speaker who feels that the points he is making are "excellent" may automatically assume that his audience is "appreciative," and feel self-assured and at ease as a result. And one who has committed a "crime" may well feel that others are "suspicious," and react furtively as a result. Perceptions of our own behavior bias our perception of others' reactions.

This same process suggests that not only do we judge others' reactions in terms of our behavior toward them, but that we judge others' behavior toward us in terms of our reactions. Sometimes a person is more conversant with his own reactions than he is with what the other has done to produce them. For example, we sometimes hear such comments as, "I don't know why I don't like him, but I just don't," or "I don't know what it is he does, but every time I leave his classroom I feel angry inside." The person has a concept for his reaction, but not one for the behavior that produced his reaction. At this point the process of association comes to bear. In searching for a cause to explain his reaction, the person may use the most salient concepts available to him. Namely, he will use those which have the highest degree of association with the concept he uses to understand his own behavior. If his reaction is one of dislike, he may look for behavior in the other which can be classified as "unfriendly"; if he feels angry after talking with the other, the anger will be justified when he has pinpointed aspects of the other's behavior that appear "aggressive."

The ambiguity of behavior

The tendency to judge others in terms of self is potentially a misleading one, since it is possible to find at least some support for almost any label one wishes to apply to the other—regardless of his behavior. In almost any segment of behavior, it is possible to find some justification for perceiving an act to be "friendly," "unfriendly," "aggressive," "passive," and so on. This point can be illustrated with the following dialogue:

MARVIN: Mother, I would like to introduce you to Mary Ann Adams. Mary Ann, this is my mother.

MARY ANN: How do you do, Mrs. Snow.

MOTHER: So nice to meet you, dear. Marvin has spoken so often of you.

MARY ANN: And he of you, too, Mrs. Snow.

MOTHER: Marvin mentioned he met you when you were waitressing at the college, isn't that so?

MARY ANN: Well, not exactly, I was working at the cafe, but I was also in school.

MOTHER: Come, make yourself comfortable, Mary Ann. You must excuse the clutter, but Marvin has been so busy lately—well, you must know—that I just can't keep things up myself anymore. I really need someone around more, now that dear Edwin has passed away.

MARY ANN: Yes, it's fine . . I mean . . I was sorry to hear about his death. My condolences, but the *house* looks just fine.

MOTHER: Thank you, Mary Ann. Now let's have a nice chat while Marvin fetches the tea. I can see we will get along just fine. After all we *do* have a common interest!

What can be said of Marvin's mother in this little scene? Is she friendly or unfriendly, dominating or submissive? Certainly her greeting to Mary Ann is most cordial and indicates that she is also aware of Marvin's high regard for the girl. And she expresses interest in Mary Ann by asking about her first meeting with her son. She also invites her to make herself comfortable, and to have a "nice chat" when she might otherwise have excused herself to fetch tea. And she expresses directly her confidence that they will get along. One might thus conclude that she was very "friendly." On the other hand, her initial question concerning Mary Ann's waitressing could be perceived as unflattering, if not barbed. Her reference to Marvin's being so busy lately, and the fact that she needs "someone around more" could easily be construed as a criticism of Mary Ann's pirating her son. Her last sentence also smacks of competitiveness. Observing this, one might feel that she was very "unfriendly." In the same way, her pointed question about the waitressing, her channeling Mary Ann into sitting down and then chatting at a time convenient for herself, and her sending Marvin for the tea, could all be labeled as "dominating." Yet, her request to be excused for the clutter, her statement of dependency and inadequacy in the face of her husband's death, and even her request for Marvin to fetch the tea (being unable herself?) could all be perceived as "submissive."

The point is that much of our social categorizing rests on just such ambiguity. Interactions between people generate questions which often must be hastily answered with a label so that the interaction may continue. Can you imagine what would happen if Mary Ann continually interrupted Marvin's mother to ask if her statements indicated friendliness or submissiveness? Usually we must make assumptions about another's behavior which are generated by those concepts we would apply to ourselves in an identical situation.

Emotion and Perception

Perceptions, as we have seen, are the concepts we have about ourselves and others. How do our emotions affect the way we judge others? Do our emotions bias our perceptions? For example, an individual in love may find his beloved to be beautiful, intelligent, and diligent when all his friends, who remain emotionally uninvolved, would agree that she is quite stupid and lazy. Research shows that concepts often carry strong emotional associations. In their work on the semantic differential, for example, Osgood and his associates (1957) tapped the affective or emotional associations of various concepts. This research demonstrates the extreme ease with which people of all cultures assign an emotional value (along a positive–negative dimension) to concepts. People react with strong positive ratings when certain words are presented, and with very negative ratings to others.

In addition, Osgood's measures of affective associations have been very useful in studying the emotional content of social issues. For example, in 1970, Kenneth and Mary Gergen used a single positive–negative rating scale to examine the affective meaning that various national symbols held for demonstrators against the Vietnam war. The results proved very interesting at the time, as the demonstrators had been criticized nationally for their communist, revolutionary, and anarchist viewpoints. For this sample of over 5,000 students, three of the concepts with the most positive affective meaning were "The Constitution," "The Bill of Rights," and "Thomas Jefferson." Most rejected by the activists was the concept of "The President." It appears that the demonstrators were deeply dedicated to what most people would consider to be the fundamentals of American democracy and rejected what they felt to be deviations from these traditions. This research supports the assumption that many concepts carry with them some degree of affect, varying from positive to negative. However, we have not yet dealt with the central questions: How does emotion influence the way we judge others? Do our emotions bias our perception? Let us examine two cases that are relevant to the biasing effect of emotion: racial prejudice and the halo effect.

Skin color and racism

There is substantial evidence to indicate that almost universally, the emotional impact of the color black is negative. Research with the semantic differential, for example, shows that students in the United States, Europe, and Asia all negatively evaluate the concept "black," while the concept of "white" is reacted to much more positively (Williams, Morland, and Underwood, 1970). How can we understand such reactions?

With a little speculation about childhood experience, one answer becomes clear. The initial learning of the concept "black" is accompanied by negative emotional reactions. Two types of experience can be singled out as potentially producing this reaction: the child's reaction to night versus day, and his cleanliness training. Night is often a period in which the child is isolated, without comfort or bodily gratification. Moreover, night is a screen on which the child can project his worst fears. Any sort of demon can exist "out there in the black." With the coming of light, family and environment are again in view; sustenance and security are again present. Dollard and Miller (1950) have best

RATINGS OF 10 COLORS BY STUDENTS FROM DIFFERENT COUNTRIES

Group	White	Black	Brown	Yellow	Red	Blue	Green	Purple	Orange	Gray
American (Cauc.)	1.82	5.03	4.37	2.75	3.17	2.02	2.34	3.18	3.52	4.56
American (Negroes)	2.05	4.11	3.82	2.52	3.08	2.28	2.78	4.00	3.05	4.23
Germans	1.96	3.69	4.85	3.60	2.63	2.13	2.95	2.68	3.12	4.67
Danes	2.20	4.07	4.31	3.20	2.87	2.27	2.70	4.33	3.54	4.33
Chinese	1.59	4.81	4.29	2.48	2.97	2.20	2.80	3.25	3.03	4.71
Indians	1.89	5.00	3.60	3.20	3.45	3.07	2.95	3.86	2.63	3.87

Figure 10–2. Is black really beautiful? No, say university students from five different countries. Some 570 students took a semantic-differential test that contained twelve adjective rating scales. In the table above, low numbers represent positive ratings. The students gave the color white the highest rating. Black and gray, by contrast, received the lowest scores.

SOURCE: Adapted from Williams, J. E., Morland, J. K., and Underwood, W. L. Connotations of color names in the United States, Europe, and Asia. *Journal of Social Psychology*, October 1970, **82**(1), 7.

outlined the profound significance of childhood cleanliness training. These authors argue that, particularly in Western culture, children are taught to abhor the presence of dirt and other dark substances, whether on his body or in his surroundings. Whiteness is sanctified in the cultural myth that "cleanliness is next to Godliness."

Once the basic association between concept and emotion has been formed, objects and, most importantly, people that fall into the concept range may elicit the emotion. Black skin itself, then, may dispose one negatively—regardless of the skin color of the observer. Laboratory research by Williams and Edwards (1969) provides support for this line of thinking. White kindergarten children were presented with a series of picture pairs. One picture in each pair was white and the other black. A white dog and a black dog appeared together, a white horse and a black horse, and so on. For each pair, the child was asked to make guesses about the attributes of the various animals and objects. Thus, in the case of the dogs, the experimenter asked such questions as "which is the clean doggy," "which is the bad doggy," and "which is the naughty doggy." Whenever the child answered that the black animal or object possessed the positive attributes or assigned negative attributes to the white choice, he was rewarded with candy; punishment for associating positive responses with white choices was achieved by taking pennies away from a stack that had been given to the child at the outset. Control-group children participated in the same task but with no reinforcement for their choices.

It was first found that the reinforcement procedure was effective in weakening the children's general tendency to assign negative attributes to black objects. The children learned through this procedure that "black is beautiful." After the learning task, the children were asked about the attributes of pictures of various pairs of human figures. In each case one of the pictures was of a white person and the other of a black. On one trial the child was told, "Here are two girls. Everyone says that one of them is very pretty. Which is the pretty girl?" The researchers wanted to know whether the learning of a negative reaction to white and a positive reaction to black would carry over to this test of racial attitudes. The results showed that the reinforced subjects assigned more positive attributes and fewer negative attributes to the black figures than did the control subjects. Seventy percent of the children in the control condition displayed a significant degree of anti-Negro prejudice on this task, compared to only 48 percent in the reinforced group. It does seem, then, that our emotional associations to color are carried over to our perception of others. If the emotional associations to black are formed at an early age, as suggested, it may be that this association has to be unlearned if successful race relations are to be established.

The halo effect

A second application of our earlier segment relating to concepts and emotion stems from a curious tendency noticed by psychologists early in the century. It appeared that when people were engaged in rating or assigning traits to others, strong biases emerged. Traits that seemed to be independent of each other in real life were highly correlated in people's ratings of each other. There is little reason to believe, for instance, that people who are physically attractive are more intelligent, or that a person who is insincere is also less considerate. And

**Stereotypes of Lower-class Whites
and Lower-class Negroes by
92 White and 180 Negro Subjects**

Reactions of White Subjects

LOWER-CLASS WHITES		LOWER-CLASS NEGROES	
Trait	Per Cent	Trait	Per Cent
Happy-go-lucky	20	Superstitious	66
Materialistic	20	Lazy	39
Ignorant	19	Physically dirty	34
Lazy	19	Unreliable	34
Loud	19	Musical	30
Rude	19	Loud	26
Unreliable	17	Ignorant	26
Pleasure-loving	16	Happy-go-lucky	24
Physically dirty	15	Ostentatious	19
Practical	14	Pleasure-loving	17

Reactions of Negro Subjects

Physically dirty	36	Loud	55
Ignorant	34	Superstitious	44
Rude	33	Very religious	35
Lazy	19	Lazy	28
Loud	18	Ignorant	26
Deceitful	18	Physically dirty	21
Sly	14	Sensitive	19
Stubborn	14	Happy-go-lucky	17
Superstitious	14	Talkative	15
Tradition-loving	14	Pugnacious	14
		Rude	14

Figure 10–3. Perceptions of others are often biased by the stereotypes we have of the group to which they belong. This table, compiled in 1956 from data gathered in the early fifties, reflects the kinds of stereotype that the civil rights movement of the 1960s sought to destroy.

SOURCE: Bayton, J. A., McAlister, L. B., and Hamer, J. Race–class stereotypes. *Journal of Negro Education*, Winter 1956, 75–78, Table 2.

yet, in examining the ratings people make of others, a high correlation is typically found among such traits. In particular, the correlation is based on the evaluative connotations of a single trait. If one positive or socially desirable trait is assigned, there is a high probability that many others also will be. This perceptual bias has been appropriately termed the *halo effect*, and its implications are critical. It jars us as most unfair, for example, that people are successful in the business world, in the arts, in academia, or in politics, not because they have outstanding skill, but because of their attractive appearance, good "social background," their smile, or charming manner. The halo effect may play a strong part here: those who are seen as friendly and sociable are also more likely to be viewed as skillful, intelligent, and creative, and to be rewarded accordingly. As Dion, Berscheid, and Walster (1972) have shown, both male and female college students assign more desirable personality traits, such as kindness, poise, and sociability, to physically attractive persons (of both sexes) than to unattractive ones. They also tend to project better futures, such as getting good jobs or marrying well, for those who are more attractive.

Another arena in which the halo effect may have pernicious consequences is in the classroom. A teacher's opinions of a student's intelligence may well be influenced by the student's personal appearance, his manners, his family background, and other irrelevancies. And as Rosenthal and Jacobson (1968) have shown, such biases not only affect the teacher's behavior toward the student, but may ultimately affect the student's academic performance. When a student is thought to be mediocre, he will generally perform in a mediocre fashion; when respected and liked, his desire to perform well is increased. Thus, a person whose perceptions are biased by the halo effect can create a self-fulfilling prophecy; that is, he can cause the target person to assume the traits attributed to her.

Self-Perception

That we should use judgments about ourselves as clues to interpret another's behavior may mislead us, but in an ambiguous world it may constitute the best guess. However, the reverse is also true. We are ambiguous creatures even to ourselves, and often find it difficult to interpret our own behavior. In such cases we may also rely on what we know of others—their behavior toward us and the evidence of their feelings about us. To appreciate this point fully, it is first necessary to realize that one's perception of self is highly malleable and subject to great fluctuation from one situation to another. Certainly, of course, there are some concepts of self that are so well learned that little fluctuation occurs. One's concepts of self as male or female, black or white, Catholic or Protestant, married or single, are so frequently verified that we seldom change our identifying labels in these areas. And yet, there are innumerable concepts of self that may be easily modified. One's concept of self as "strong," "graceful," "capable," "intelligent," "attractive," or "energetic" may be highly dependent on time and circumstance.

Horoscopes make very good use of the human faculty for reconceptualizing self. Typically, one's horoscope contains a set of traits that are to be applied to self. Sagittarians, as an example, are supposed to be "cheerful" and "impulsive." Because self-experience is multiplex, it is quite easy to find at least some support for any given concept within the welter of available data. All of us think of ourselves at one time or another as "cheerful" or "impulsive." Thus, the ambiguity of the labels, and the multiple interpretations available for any given behavior, make it possible for almost anyone to find her horoscope miraculously descriptive.

Modifying self-concepts

Social psychologists have found that they can quite readily modify self-perceptions and have conducted experiments along these lines in order to show the extent to which a person's self-perception is affected by others. In a study by Gergen (1965), for example, coeds were placed in an interview situation in which they were asked questions about themselves. During this period, the interviewer showed subtle agreement (smiles, nods) whenever the student made a positive evaluation of herself. When she criticized herself, the interviewer subtly disagreed by remaining silent or shaking her head. As a result of this reinforcement, subjects began to evaluate themselves more and more positively as the interview progressed. After the interviewer departed, the subjects were asked to rate themselves as honestly as possible on a self-esteem measure. Scores on this measure were compared with scores obtained on the same measure some weeks earlier. A marked increase in self-esteem was found to result from the reinforcement procedure. This increase in self-esteem also differed significantly from the slight increase found in a nonreinforced control group. One girl remarked later that she had, for some unknown reason, felt happy for the remainder of the day. In a second study (Gergen and Gibbs, 1966), simply having people think of how they might impress others with themselves was sufficient to increase their subsequent evaluations of self.

Along these same lines, there is a supposedly true tale about a group of students who chose the most unpopular and unattractive girl in their class, and decided to respond to her as if she were a campus beauty queen. As the semester drew on, a remarkable change began to occur. The girl began to wear more attractive clothing, her grooming improved, and her disposition became more and more pleasant. By the end of the semester the males were no longer plotting collective intrigues; they were too busy competing with each other for dates with the girl. It seems quite likely that the girl, when exposed to a homogeneous set of reactions to herself, began to redefine herself. Believing herself to be attractive, she behaved accordingly.

There are a wide number of factors that affect one's concept of self (see Gergen, 1971). Yet, because another views us in a certain way, it does not mean that we will automatically change our self-concept. Under what conditions does one seek information about oneself? One such circumstance that has been studied experimentally is the ambiguous situation.

Clarifying self-concepts

The impetus for investigating information-seeking in uncertain or ambiguous situations originated in Leon Festinger's theory of social comparison. Festinger (1954) states that people seek to verify their opinions. Opinions, in this sense, can be concepts about the environment, a situation, or the self. Furthermore, when objective, nonsocial information is not available for evaluating opinions, people turn to others. The seeking of clarification of ambiguous opinions, however, may lead to a change of opinion in the direction of those held by

Will this woman's concept of herself as a singer and artist be validated by the audience?

others who are available for comparison. This can occur because, according to Festinger, we seek to compare ourselves with others whom we judge to be similar.

Emotional experience often seems quite clear. We think we know when we are "angry" as well as "happy" or "sad." There is normally no confusion about what emotion is present. There are studies, however, that strongly indicate that any state of emotional arousal can be equated with an arousal of the sympathetic nervous system. Thus, a similar physiological state may be aroused with every emotion. One of the most influential experiments in this area was conducted by Schachter and Singer (1962). The researchers injected certain subjects with epinephrine, a drug which causes physiological arousal. They hypothesized that those subjects would be under a certain pressure to label their aroused state, and, lacking objective information, would look to situational factors for an explanation. Indeed, this was the case as the subjects in the experimental groups labeled their feelings and directed their behavior according to the events surrounding them. Subjects who received a placebo instead of epinephrine, or who had been given objective information about the effects of the drug, did not engage in this process. (This experiment is discussed in chapter 12.)

From this evidence, we must conclude that the concepts we have for emotions are primarily learned, and we must be taught when and under what circumstances to apply these concepts to ourselves. On a physiological level we may experience little more than a general level of arousal; whether we label this state "resentment," "hatred," or "jealousy" may be entirely dependent on how we have learned to label this arousal under given circumstances. When a person interferes with our activities, we may say we feel "resentful"; when he insults us we may feel "hatred"; and when he possesses that which we desire we may feel "envy." Physically we will experience the emotions in the same way. Only the conceptual label has changed.

The Effects of Motivation on Perception

Motives furnish additional wellsprings of behavior. Desires to obtain money, power, and social acceptance often lie at the center of a person's social existence. Motives are also a major source of bias in the way an individual interprets his environment; motivation influences the concepts we use in dealing with the world of physical reality. Although an array of phenomena has been studied, research findings can be summarized in one sweeping principle: for the most part, perception is self-enhancing. We tend to interpret the world in such a way as to maximize self-gratification. We tend to make the world appear more favorable to us than perhaps it actually is, and by the same token, we avoid perceiving those aspects of life that are painful or unpleasurable.

Approach motivation

Research concerned with the self-enhancement of perception usually falls into one of two categories: *approach* motives and *avoidance* motives. In the first case, the person is motivated to perceive some desired end, such as food or social acceptance, and in the second he wishes to deny or avoid a distasteful or painful situation.

One way to examine the relationship between approach motivation and perception is to deny a person a basic need such as food, and then to observe the effects of such deprivation on his perception. In a number of the early studies, subjects were deprived of food for varying lengths of time, and then asked to identify vague or amorphous figures or to recognize words (some of them food-related) flashed at them for a brief instant (cf. McClelland and Atkinson, 1948; Wispé and Drambarcan, 1953). The results of such procedures were fairly consistent. Food-deprived subjects were more likely to label the

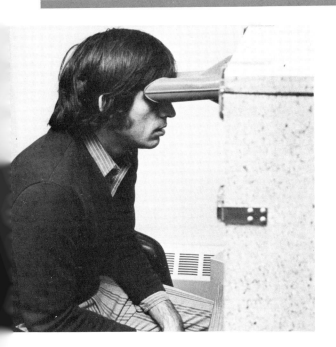 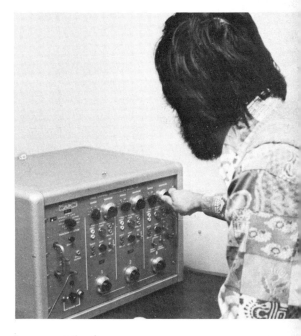

The tachistoscope is a device for projecting transient images. The hungry subject will identify such amorphous figures as food related objects.

ambiguous figures as food or food-related, and to recognize food-related words more rapidly. Such perceptual biases might well be anticipated. Goal concepts are highly salient; that is, food is the most salient stimulus in the environment for an extremely hungry person; expectations are centered on gratification; and therefore, it should not be surprising that as a part of the search of the environment, subjects would be biased in favor of identifying words and pictures of food more readily.

But let us move from the perception of food to the perception of people. What influence does approach motivation have on the way in which we perceive others? A classic study by Pepitone (1949) provides us with one good answer. Pepitone offered high school students the opportunity to win a free ticket to a basketball game. Motivation was varied by informing one group (high motivation condition) that the tickets were to an important college game, and a second group (low motivation condition); that the tickets were for an unimportant high school game. In order to obtain the tickets, each student had to be approved by a visiting panel of coaches that would ask his opinions about various aspects of the sport. In one section of the experiment, the subjects faced a panel of three members, each of whom was instructed to behave in a particular way. One panel member was privately instructed to respond in a very friendly manner to all that the subject said (Mr. Friendly), a second was to be more neutral in his reaction to the subject (Mr. Neutral), and the third was to respond to the subject in a generally uncharitable and critical fashion (Mr. Negative). After the interview, the subject was asked to rate the panel members as to how approving, as well as how powerful, he perceived each to be in determining whether he would be granted the ticket.

The ratings of the panel members by the subjects showed unmistakable distortions to favor self-gratification. Although Mr. Friendly maintained the same role throughout, subjects in the high motivation condition rated him as significantly more approving and significantly more powerful than subjects in the low motivation condition. In addition, it was found that regardless of motivation, Mr. Friendly was seen as more powerful than either Mr. Neutral or Mr. Negative. This experiment was designed to show two aspects of approach behavior in relation to distortion in the perception of other people. The experimenter, Mr. Friendly, not only gained greater approval because he was perceived as friendly, but for those who were in most need, he appeared to be more able to offer satisfaction.

Avoidance motivation and perceptual defense

When we turn to avoidance motivation, the immediate question is whether we will find the reverse of what we found in approach motivation. If we are more likely to perceive that which gives us pleasure, are we less likely to perceive the painful? Thinking about this issue originated with Freud and his theory that psychic forces prevent painful or disruptive thoughts from entering consciousness. In the 1940s, Freudian thinking evolved the intriguing hypothesis of *perceptual defense,* a hypothesis that has stimulated research to the present. According to the perceptual defense hypothesis, if you feared a particular person or hated a particular food, you would be less likely to notice the person in a crowd or see the food on a menu. It was initially felt that unconscious forces were at play in producing perceptual defense. The person was said to "subceive"—that is, unconsciously to monitor his environment for threatening or painful material and to impede the entry of such material into consciousness. However, there is little reason to think in such mysterious terms as "unconscious monitoring." Rather, it seems quite likely that concepts related to pain will be less salient to the person, thus, less likely to be used in categorizing stimuli. Further, the concepts we use in searching the environment are more likely to be relevant to pain avoidance than to its onset.

Early studies in the area often used materials known to be emotionally threatening and compared the rapidity with which they were recognized with emotionally neutral materials. Thus, for example, McGinnies (1949) had subjects view words through a tachistoscope, which allowed him control over the amount of time each word was exposed. Obscene or taboo words were interspersed randomly with words that were more neutral in impact. First the words were exposed for very brief intervals (less than one-tenth of a second), and gradually the exposure time was increased. It was predicted, and found, that it took more time for subjects to recognize the taboo than the neutral words. Although the findings seemed to demonstrate perceptual defense, the methodology was criticized. First, it was argued that subjects were more hesitant to admit they saw obscene words in a psychological experiment. Second, since taboo words occurred infrequently in the middle-class milieu of that time, it was suggested that they would be less familiar to the subjects.

Later studies overcame these difficulties. Nonsense syllables were used which enabled the experimenter to rule out embarrassment and previous familiarity as explanations. Then, in order to create avoidance motivation, certain syllables were associated with electric shock. The question was, with an equal number of exposures, would those words previously associated with shock be less rapidly seen? A number of investigations answered the question in the affirmative (cf. Rosen, 1954; Eriksen and Browne, 1956; Dulaney, 1957).

It is also important to notice in these latter studies that self-gratification is obtained in the absence of the pain-associated stimulus. That is, greater pleasure is achieved when the subject does not think of nonsense words associated with shock, does not expect them, and does not search for them. However, if people always underwent perceptual failure when pain was near at hand, there would be grave repercussions indeed. One would be less apt to see an oncoming vehicle when crossing the street or less sensitive to taking the wrong bottle from the medicine chest. In fact, we are usually more sensitive in such cases, and the primary reason is that self-gratification is greater when we notice than when we do not. It thus follows that perceptual defense should not occur when self-gratification can be achieved by noticing a pain-associated stimulus. This is precisely what has been found in a number of experiments (Reece, 1954; Rosen, 1954; Dulaney, 1957). When electric shock is associated with a group of nonsense syllables and the shock can be avoided by recognizing these syllables, recognition time is markedly decreased. Rather than perceptual defense, perceptual enhancement takes place.

Attribution and the Concept of Will

The concept of free will has long been debated, especially by behavioral scientists. Do people have sufficient control over all the aspects of their lives to be held responsible for their actions? Are they the causes of their own behavior?

When we begin thinking about social perception, however, the matter becomes more complicated. People (including behavioral scientists) do use the concept of will in their daily lives to interpret themselves and others. We say, "I decided on my own to do it," "I am determined to do it," "I did it of my own free will," "I am going voluntarily," "John chose not to act," "Mary is certainly self-determined," "He has strong willpower," "I don't intend to pay," and so on. Each of these sentences reveals our supposition that people are capable of willing or causing their own actions. And in dealing with others, it becomes an important consideration to determine whether or not their actions are intended. If we feel that a person intended the harm he has done us, our response is quite different than if we feel it was an accident or unavoidable. The supposition of will is spelled out even more clearly in our legal codes, which make clear distinctions between acts that are under the person's control and those that are not. A person is held responsible for the former and receives stiffer penalties accordingly. The difference between murder and manslaughter is not in the act itself but in the intention of the accused.

A classic experiment by Thibaut and Riecken (1955) illustrates the problem. The experimenters had their subjects make a reasonable request of either a high-status or low-status confederate, and in both cases he complied with the request. Questioning of the subjects afterward revealed that they viewed the compliance of the high-status confederate as being caused by his own "free will": that he was the originator of his actions. The cause of the compliance of the low-status confederate was perceived as due to external factors, forces outside the low-status confederate which caused his behavior. The subjects were making a distinction about the *locus* of causality, whether it was *internal* or *external* to the individual. The problem, then, in social perception is not in determining whether behavior is actually a product of free will, but how the causes of another's behavior are perceived—whether internal (of his own free will) or external (caused by some factor or factors in the environment)—and what the consequences are that follow from that perception.

When are we most likely to interpret behavior as internally caused? What factors give rise to this particular interpretation of behavior? As we have pointed out, social perception involves ascribing characteristics to events— that is, labeling or fitting concepts to them. From this viewpoint, the problem is to identify the conditions under which the person labels an observable action as willful or not. This labeling is known as the *attribution process*, a process, according to Jones and Goethals, that occurs "when an observer causally interprets a given set of information" (1971). The information may include behavior, the consequences of behavior, or the circumstances under which the behavior occurs. Of particular interest, of course, is the way in which attributions may be biased. Let us turn to some of the factors involved in attributing causes, and the ways in which such attributions are biased.

Internal or external attribution

There is strong experimental support for the notion that an action seen as pushed or forced by external circumstances is not seen as willed. De Charms (1968) reports studies in which children as well as high school students built mechanical models. In one condition the students were given no directives for completing the model; they had to figure out how to do it themselves. In a second condition, students were given complete instructions that outlined each and every step. After completing the models, the subjects in the first condition rated themselves as feeling significantly more free. Compared to the other group, they felt that their behavior was less guided by forces beyond their control. Interestingly enough, they also enjoyed their work to a greater extent when left to rely on their own ability.

In turning to the perception of others, we find similar results. Steiner and Field (1960) had subjects participate in three-man discussion groups. The discussions dealt with the issue of racial integration. In some discussion groups the experimenter publicly assigned one of the group members (actually an experimental confederate) the task of presenting the prosegregation side of the argument. For other groups, the confederate took the same prosegregationist position, but in this case it was not apparent that he was instructed to do so. Ratings of the confederate made after the discussion showed that where the prosegregationist position was adopted out of duress, subjects were much less trusting of his opinions. His opinions did not appear to be self-determined or voluntary, and thus, did not seem to be really his own.

Goal attractiveness operates in the same fashion as forces that push the person toward certain goals. That is, we see an action as less willful if done for great reward. It is quite fitting to respond to a boss who is questioning one about why he or she is taking a position in another firm with "The offer is just so attractive that I am forced to take it." The reply suggests that the act is unwilled and thus not subject to punishment. The individual could not reasonably take any other course.

Research findings support this line of argument. In one study (Gergen and Swap, 1977), subjects were given several situation-sketches to read. As an example, they were to imagine themselves in a juvenile gang, and as a result of group pressure, forced into committing a certain crime. Subjects were then asked to rate the extent to which they would feel their behavior to be a true expression of will and to rate the amount of responsibility they would feel for their actions. Consistent with our discussion thus far, there was a high degree of correlation between rated willfulness and responsibility. When people ascribe will to themselves, they also feel responsible for their actions. Furthermore, ratings showed that increasing the attractiveness of a goal significantly decreased the subjects' feelings of will and responsibility. In the case of the juvenile gang situation, for example, subjects rated their feelings of will when the value of the object stolen was low, and then again under conditions in which the object was of great value. Significantly more involvement of will was indicated with the low-valued objects.

All these data lend support to the first of our propositions: the less environmental compulsion in evidence (either pushing or pulling the person toward certain behavior), the more we attribute willfulness or intention to the actor. We see the actor himself as the cause of his own behavior and we hold him responsible as well as give him credit. When we perceive external pressures, we attribute cause for the behavior to these forces, and forgive, excuse, or withhold credit.

The mind and the body

The mind/body dichotomy has ancient roots in Western culture. Aristotle, for one, wrote an extensive account of the thinking, choosing, and evaluating carried out by the "rational soul." The rational soul was contrasted to the more vegetative and animalistic characteristics, the bodily aspects, of man. In later Christian writing, the notion of the rational soul is modified and becomes the "holy spirit" as opposed to the "flesh." As Paul wrote in his letter to the Galationa, ". . . the desires of the flesh are against the spirit, and the desires of

THE TALE OF RASHOMON

What we think has been the course of events that we have experienced is subject to a constantly shifting balance of reality. Our own view of the actions of others may or may not coincide with their sense of reality. Emotions, biases, desires, and other motives distort the perceptions of participants in seemingly straightforward, unalterable events.

The telling of a tale several times over through the perspectives of the different participants has proved an effective literary device. The famous Japanese tale of Rashomon is told in this fashion. In the story, a man and his young wife are enticed into a grove by a bandit who rapes the wife. Then, the various people who were involved in the crime, or who knew the couple, recount the incident as they perceived it. In all, there are seven testimonies—the bandit, the wife, a spirit speaking for the slain husband, a woodcutter who found the body of the husband, a traveling priest, a policeman, and the mother of the wife.

In the story as told by the bandit, he admits he killed the husband, but claims he was enticed into doing so by the wife. Once in the grove, he overcame the husband, gagged him with leaves, and trussed him up with rope. Then he admits that he raped the man's wife. He claims that then the woman begged him to fight her husband. She intended to marry the survivor, for she could not bear to live with the knowledge that two men knew of her degradation. The bandit fought the husband and managed to kill him. He claims he was motivated only by the imploring glances of the woman, which kindled an insane passion in him. When he turned to claim the woman, he found that she had run away. The bandit then fled the scene of the crime.

According to the wife, the bandit's story is false. After the bandit raped her, she said, he turned to her husband and laughed mockingly. She ran to her bound and gagged husband and was thunderstruck by the look in his eyes, which she described as "a cold light, a look of loathing." She fainted. When she came to, the bandit was gone, but now she was certain, by the look in her husband's eyes, that he despised her. "Kill me," she claims, is what her husband's eyes told her. She resolved to kill him and then herself. Unfortunately, after she had killed her husband with her own small sword, she was unable to kill herself.

The spirit of the dead man bitterly claims that his wife misunderstood. The spirit claims that the robber tried to convince the woman to become his wife. While the robber talked, she looked into her husband's eyes and he tried to convey his trust to her. When the wife agreed to go with the bandit, the husband's spirit claims she suddenly said, "Kill him. I cannot marry you as long as he lives." The bandit then asked the husband whether he wanted his wife to be killed for her disloyalty. The husband hesitated, and his wife ran into the woods. Then the brigand untied the man and escaped into the woods. The husband found his wife's small sword lying on the ground and stabbed himself.

Which version is true? No one will ever know. The husband and wife each acted according to impulses and impressions that they believed they were reading in each other's eyes. Like life, the story is ambiguous: there are opportunities for alternative interpretations of the same event and each witness is activated by his or her own personal desires and motivations.

the spirit are against the flesh." Descartes' influential writings of the seventeenth century spoke of mind (soul) as pure thought, that which uniquely pertains to "our nature," as contrasted with the bodily functions. Cartesian dualism still has a strong influence on current thinking. Mind, the rational function, is seen as being able to anticipate, to plan, and to engage in logic, intent, and will. Emotion is viewed as opposed to these activities, as a threat to subvert the sound logic of the mind. Because of this antithesis, and their arousal component, emotions have been relegated to the bodily arena.

It seems that the more rational an action appears to be, the more willfulness, cause, and intention we ascribe to it. Behavior stemming primarily from bodily needs or from the emotions is perceived as less willed—therefore less responsible. Our legal codes also reflect this usage. Thus, we hold an individual as being less responsible if a crime appears to be the result of spontaneous rage rather than rational planning. In Italy, the killing of a spouse in the arms of a lover is deemed a "crime of passion," and sometimes excused without sentence. We are hardly surprised in our culture to hear a person say, "I couldn't help it, I was just overwhelmed with emotion," or "I didn't mean to, I was just so hungry." It seems peculiar in Western culture that the body is treated as such a second-class citizen—an inferior baggage which wrests control from the "true self."

In keeping with this line of reasoning, a study by Jones, Hester, Farina, and Davis (1959) is of great interest. Common observation, as well as our legal codes, indicates that people tend to think of the mentally unbalanced as not acting willfully, but as being driven by irrational or emotional impulses. As a result, when we are treated badly by someone who is disturbed, we are less affected than if we perceive that person to be normal. We feel that he does not really intend his actions, and would act differently toward us if he were in full possession of his rational capacities. The experiment of Jones and his colleagues supports this line of reasoning. Female college students were placed in a situation in which they received criticism from another student. One group of subjects was led to believe that the person who criticized them was maladjusted; another group felt that their critic was quite normal. The actual criticism was the same for both groups. Members of a third group were bystanders who observed the critics and their targets. These ratings of the experimenter-critic by the experimental and control groups were compared with ratings made by subject-bystanders. The results showed that when criticized subjects rated the maladjusted critic, they were less negative than the bystanders. In effect, they seemed to forgive the maladjusted girl because she couldn't help it. On the other hand, in rating the well-adjusted critic, the results were reversed. The criticized subjects were much harsher in their judgments than the bystanders. They were seemingly stunned as a result of the intentional assault of the other.

We have discussed the emotional and the irrational as sources for the attribution of the causes of behavior. A third factor in attributing the causes of others' behavior is effort. It is proposed that the greater the effort accompanying a given action, the greater willfulness is attributed to the person. This connection between will and effort was noted as early as 1920 when Wheeler argued from his data that the concept of volition should be entirely equated with feelings of physical strain. But common usage also reveals the connection. When we see a person doggedly persist at a task, we speak of his being "strong-willed" or "determined." With actions of little effort—the brushing of a fly from one's hand, the snuffing of a cigarette—we are likely to attribute little intention or decision.

While there is little direct evidence of effort related to perceiving others, there are supporting data concerning self-perception. In the Gergen and Swap study, subjects were asked about their feelings of will and responsibility under conditions in which effort was either high or low. In one case the robbery required great physical stress; in another it was done casually. In one instance a race at a track-meet was said to be difficult to win; in a second, it was simple. In one situation an examination was difficult to pass, and in a second, easy. In each of these cases, subjects rated their actions as being a greater expression of will under the high-effort conditions.

Attribution: Self versus others

Earlier we said that there is no special reason to believe that the factors influencing attributions of willfulness or intentionality to self are different from those determining our perception of will in the behavior of others. However, Jones and Nisbett (1971) have argued that there are important differences between the attribution of cause in self and the attribution of cause in the perception of others. Although the same factors may operate in both cases, the differences are such that people will generally attribute more willful activity to others than to themselves over a broad range of situations, and to see themselves as acting under situational constraints. Why should this be so?

Jones and Nisbett offer several explanations. First, they reason that the actor typically has more information about the history behind his own actions than he has in the case of others. When an individual selects her college major, for example, she will be aware that her father desires her to become a lawyer, and thus she would probably see a pre-law decision on her part as partly controlled by knowledge of her father's wishes and less by her own will; she would be less likely to know of similar situations faced by her classmates and would thus see their decision to enter pre-law as more under their own control. Furthermore, most individuals will attend the forces impinging on them from the environment as they make decisions and engage in activity. Explanations of behavior are likely to be in terms of those impinging forces. Such explanations would place less emphasis on internal willfulness. However, in observing others, our focal point is typically their actions, and not the environment that shapes their decisions. Thus, in accounting for the behavior of others, we will attribute less to the environment and more to their intentions.

How do these suppositions bear up empirically? Nisbett, along with his colleagues, Caputo, Legant, and Marecek (1973), studied the matter by asking male college students to write brief descriptions, first of their reasons for selecting their major field of concentration, and then of their reasons for finding attractive the woman of greatest interest to them at the moment. After writing descriptions of their own reasons for these two investments, they were asked to answer the same questions as their best friend would. All answers to the questions were then coded, and special attention was given to whether each response explained the behavior in terms of *environmental factors* or in terms of *personal causality*. An environmental response to the question of selecting a major might be in terms of "the great possibilities for advancement" or "the high wages offered"; an environmental choice of girlfriend might be "She is constantly warm and encouraging to me." In contrast, an explanation in terms of personal causality might emphasize a deep interest in, or love for, the field of study, or the freedom of self-expression and capacity for openness felt in the company of the woman. A tally of the frequency with which the two categories were used in explaining both their own and their best friends' behavior fully supported the Jones and Nisbett thesis. In both cases, students were more likely to describe their own choices in terms of the environment and their friends' choices in terms of internal causation. Apparently we see our friends acting more as they please, and ourselves more bound by circumstance.

While the Jones and Nisbett arguments make a good deal of sense, we must be careful not to overgeneralize. Their arguments are more relevant at some times than others, and it is dangerous to speak in terms of "generally." One major reason that we may not always see our own behavior as less willful than the behavior of others stems from our earlier arguments of emotional biases in social perception. We are quite capable of altering the labels we attach to our behavior and to others according to our needs and desires. Since matters of willful intent are not only ambiguous but tied to responsibility, there is opportunity for bias. That is, if our actions turn out to be meritorious, we will be likely to attribute the actions to personal causation; however, if our actions end in failure, we will be more likely to prefer to escape the responsibility. Such results have emerged from empirical studies.

Research on attribution has far-reaching implications. For example, the way in which punishment is meted out in society is linked to intention. The assumption is made that people are the causes of their own behavior. A criminal who intentionally carries out a crime receives a heavier sentence than one who can show extenuating circumstances. A child is more forcefully punished when he is perceived to misbehave willfully than if the same misbehavior stems from exhaustion or it is perceived that his sister put him up to it. Government officials are criticized more vehemently for misconduct based on voluntary decisions than on misconduct forced by circumstance. And yet, as the present research indicates, the perception of oneself as the cause of our own behavior is viewed in a different light than the perception of the cause of others' behavior. This would make willful and intentional behavior far more arbitrary than is commonly supposed, since the extent of the intentionality lies in the mind of the beholder. Furthermore, those who are perceived as being most like us are viewed as less willful and more caught up by circumstance than those who are different. Thus, middle-class criminals, such as politicians and corporation executives, who commit white-collar crimes are likely to receive light sentences. Criminals who are poor and from different racial backgrounds are likely to receive harsher sentences, since the circumstances surrounding such people and their actions are less familiar to the middle-class members of the judiciary system.

Summary

Concepts organize the environment into compartments that can be categorized and shaped to fit the knowledge we already have. Social concepts are important in that our behavior toward others is determined largely by our concepts of them.

Applying concepts to people is difficult because in most cases, we must act only on the clues. One way to increase the information value of a given situation is to associate many concepts with one another. Concept association is facilitated through such factors as frequency, proximity, similarity, and reinforcement. When one concept is regularly evoked by another, it is said to be salient. A concept's degree of saliency determines expectancy—an individual's anticipation of how another will behave. Those ideas which have very high degrees of saliency are known as central concepts because they trigger entire sets of concepts.

Our assessment of what people are and how they will behave is based on concepts associated with particular settings. An individual can predict how another person will behave by gauging the degree of similarity that exists between them. Moreover, we judge another person's behavior toward us in terms of our own reactions.

Studies have shown that emotions bias our perceptions. There is evidence, for example, that indicates that the color black has a negative emotional impact, whereas the color white has a positive emotional impact. Researchers also have found that traits which are apparently independent of one another in real life are highly correlated in our ratings of other people. This phenomenon is referred to as the halo effect.

We often interpret our own behavior in light of the behavior of others toward us. Thus, we seek to verify our concepts about the self by turning to others. By affiliating with others who are in a similar situation, we can reduce uncertainty about our conception of ourselves. Not only are we dependent on the environment for clues to our own self-perceptions and emotions, but we even use our own behavior as an indicator for what we feel.

Motives influence the concepts we use in dealing with the outside world. We tend to make the world appear more favorable to us than it actually is, and we tend to avoid perceiving those aspects of life that are painful or unpleasant.

People use the concept of free will to interpret the behavior of themselves and others. The causes of another's behavior are perceived as either internal (that is, of their own free will) or external (that is, the result of some environmental factor). An individual labels an act as willful or not through the process of attribution. In many cases, an act that is perceived as forced by external circumstances is not seen as deliberately willed. By the same token, the more rational an act appears to be, the more willfulness or intention we attribute to it. People generally attribute more willful activity to others than to themselves; they see themselves as acting under situational constraints. Moreover, those who are perceived as being most like us are viewed as less willful and more caught up in circumstance than those who are different.

Bibliography

ARCHER, E. J. Re-evaluation of the meaningfulness of all possible CVC trigrams. *Psychological Monographs*, 1960, **74** (10, Whole No. 497).

ASCH, S. E. Forming impressions of personality. *Journal of Abnormal and Social Psychology*, 1946, **41**, 258–290.

BAYTON, J. A., McALISTER, L. B., AND HAMER, J. Race–class stereotypes. *Journal of Negro Education*, Winter 1956, 75–78.

BRUNER, J. S. On perceptual readiness. *Psychological Review*, 1957, **64**, 123–152. (a)

BRUNER, J. S. Going beyond the information given. In *Contemporary approaches to cognition*. Symposium presented at the University of Colorado. Cambridge, Mass.: Harvard University Press, 1957. (b)

COLEMAN, J. C. Facial expressions of emotions. *Psychological Monographs*, 1949, **63** (1, Whole No. 296).

DARWIN, C. *The expression of the emotions in man and animals.* Chicago: University of Chicago Press, 1965.

DE CHARMS, R. *Personal causation, the internal affective determinants of behavior.* New York: Academic Press, 1968.

DEUTSCH, M. The pathetic fallacy: An observer error in social perception. *Journal of Personality*, 1960, **28**, 317–332.

DEUTSCH, M., AND COLLINS, M. E. *Interracial housing.* Minneapolis: University of Minnesota Press, 1951.

DION, K., BERSCHEID, E., AND WALSTER, E. What is beautiful is good. *Journal of Personality and Social Psychology*, 1972, **24**, 285–290.

DOLLARD, J., AND MILLER, N. *Personality and psychotherapy.* New York: McGraw-Hill, 1950.

DULANEY, D. E., JR. Avoidance learning of perceptual defense and vigilance. *Journal of Abnormal and Social Psychology*, 1957, **55**, 333–338.

DYMOND, R. F. A scale for the measurement of empathic ability. *Journal of Consulting Psychology*, 1949, **13**, 127–133.

ERIKSEN, C. W., AND BROWNE, C. T. An experimental and theoretical analysis of perceptual defense. *Journal of Abnormal and Social Psychology*, 1956, **52**, 224–230.

ESTES, S. G. Judging personality from expressive behavior. *Journal of Abnormal and Social Psychology*, 1938, **33**, 217–236.

FESTINGER, L. A theory of social comparison processes. *Human Relations*, 1954, **7**, 117–140.

FRIJDA, N. H. Facial expression and situational cues. *Journal of Abnormal and Social Psychology*, 1958, **57**, 149–155.

GAGE, N. L., AND CRONBACH, L. J. Conceptual and methodological problems in interpersonal perception. *Psychological Review*, 1955, **62**, 411–422.

GERGEN, K. J. Interaction goals and personalistic feedback as factors affecting the presentation of self. *Journal of Personality and Social Psychology,* 1965, **1**, 413–424.

GERGEN, K. J. *The concept of self.* New York: Holt, Rinehart and Winston, 1971.

GERGEN, K. J., AND GIBBS, M. S. Role playing and modifying the self-concept. Paper presented at meeting of the Eastern Psychological Association, 1966.

GERGEN, K. J., AND SWAP, W. As described in Gergen, K. The social construction of self-knowledge. In T. Mischel (Ed.), *The self in psychology.* Oxford, England: Blackwell-Oxford, 1977.

GOFFMAN, E. *The presentation of self in everyday life.* Garden City, N.Y.: Doubleday, 1959.

GOFFMAN, E. *Stigma.* Englewood Cliffs, N.J.: Prentice-Hall, 1963.

JONES, E. E., AND GOETHALS, G. R. Order effects in impression formation: Attribution context and the nature of the entity. In E. E. Jones et al. (Eds.), *Attribution: Perceiving the causes of behavior.* Morristown, N.J.: General Learning Press, 1971.

JONES, E. E., AND NISBETT, R. E. *The actor and the observer: Divergent perceptions of the causes of behavior.* Morristown, N.J.: General Learning Press, 1971.

JONES, E. E., HESTER, S. L., FARINA, A., AND DAVIS, K. E. Reactions to unfavorable personal evaluations as a function of the evaluator's perceived adjustment. *Journal of Abnormal and Social Psychology,* 1959, **59**, 363–370.

KELLEY, H. H. The warm–cold variable in first impressions of persons. *Journal of Personality,* 1950, **18**, 431–439.

LANDIS, C. The interpretation of facial expression in emotion. *Journal of General Psychology,* 1929, **2**, 59–72.

McCLELLAND, D. C., AND ATKINSON, J. W. The projective expression of needs. 1. The effects of different intensities of the hunger drive on perception. *Journal of Psychology,* 1948, **25**, 205–222.

McGINNIES, E. Emotionality and perceptual defense. *Psychological Review,* 1949, **56**, 244–251.

NISBETT, R., CAPUTO, G. C., LEGANT, P., AND MARECEK, J. Behavior as viewed by the actor and as viewed by the observer. *Journal of Personality and Social Psychology,* 1973, **27**, 154–164.

NOBLE, C. E. An analysis of meaning. *Psychological Review,* 1952, **59**, 421–430.

OSGOOD, C. E. The nature and measurement of meaning. *Psychological Bulletin,* 1952, **49**, 197–237.

OSGOOD, C. E., SUCI, G. J., AND TANNENBAUM, P. H. *The measurement of meaning.* Urbana, Ill.: University of Illinois Press, 1957.

PEABODY, D. Trait inferences: Evaluative and descriptive aspects. *Journal of Personality and Social Psychology Monograph,* 1967, **7**(14, Whole No. 644), Part 2.

PEPITONE, A. Motivational effects in social perception. *Human Relations,* 1949, **3**, 57–76.

REECE, M. M. The effect of shock on recognition thresholds. *Journal of Abnormal and Social Psychology,* 1954, **49,** 165–172.

ROSEN, A. C. Change in perceptual threshold as a protective function of the organism. *Journal of Personality,* 1954, **23,** 182–195.

ROSENTHAL, R., AND JACOBSON, L. *Pygmalion in the classroom: Teacher expectation and pupil's intellectual ability.* New York: Holt, Rinehart and Winston, 1968.

SCHACHTER, S., AND SINGER, J. E. Cognitive, social, and physiological determinants of emotional state. *Psychological Review,* 1962, **39,** 379–399.

STEINER, I. D., AND FIELD, W. L. Role assignment and interpersonal influence. *Journal of Abnormal and Social Psychology,* 1960, **61,** 239–245.

TENBRUNSEL, T. W., NISHBALL, E. R., AND RYCHLAK, J. F. The idiographic relationship between association value and reinforcement value, and the nature of meaning. *Journal of Personality,* 1968, **36,** 126–137.

THIBAUT, J. W., AND RIECKEN, H. W. Some determinants and consequences of the perception of social causality. *Journal of Personality,* 1955, **24,** 113–133.

VENESS, T., AND BRIERLEY, D. W. Forming impressions of personality: Two experiments. *British Journal of Social and Clinical Psychology,* 1963, **2,** 11–19.

WHEELER, R. H. Theories of will and kinaesthetic sensations. *Psychological Review,* 1920, **27,** 351–360.

WILLIAMS, J. E., AND EDWARDS, C. D. An exploratory study of the modification of color concepts and racial attitudes in pre-school children. *Child Development,* 1969, **40**(3), 737–750.

WILLIAMS, J. E., MORLAND, J. K., AND UNDERWOOD, W. L. Connotations of color names in the United States, Europe and Asia. *Journal of Social Psychology,* 1970, **82,** 3–14.

WISHNER, J. Reanalysis of "impressions of personality." *Psychological Review,* 1960, **67,** 96–112.

WISPE, L. G., AND DRAMBARCAN, N. C. Physiological need, word frequency and visual duration thresholds. *Journal of Experimental Psychology,* 1953, **46,** 25–31.

11

Motives

Our lives are filled with other people. We fear them. We love them. We hate them. We tolerate, ignore, admire, respect, and disapprove of them. The bouncing of emotions and judgments off one person back to the first, and back and forth again, has been amply discussed. In addition to our feelings and perceptions, we have motives in our relationships with others. We not only need other people; we use them. We manipulate, hurt, and maneuver them. It is in this respect that we have said that a basic dimension of social psychology is movement toward and away from other people. People do not just react; they act. They seek out others to give to them, to denigrate them, or to exploit them.

This chapter will be concerned with actual presences and absences, motives toward and away from other people. In an analysis of a large number of studies, for example, U. Foa (1961) finds two independent dimensions of interpersonal behavior: dominance–dependency, and low affiliation–high affiliation. Similarly, Schutz, in the formulation of his theory of social motivation (1958), talks of three basic dimensions: inclusion, or the desire to interact and associate with other people; control, or the desire to establish a satisfactory relationship with other people with respect to control and power; and affection, or the desire to establish a satisfactory relationship with others with respect to love and intimacy. These authors are concerned with motives, the impulse in people that directs them to act, especially in regard to moving toward or away

391

from other people. There are a number of different ways of approaching the subject of motives, but often, different categories and labels employed by individual writers and thinkers refer to the same content. Here, we will talk about aggression, affiliation, attraction, altruism, and power.

Aggression

A violent crime occurs in the United States every forty-eight seconds. Between the years 1945 and 1969 there were fifty-five wars of significant magnitude throughout the world. In the *Leviathan,* the seventeenth-century English philosopher Thomas Hobbes presented the idea that "Homo homini lupus"—man is (like) a wolf to (his fellow) man. Centuries later, other Englishmen, the Beatles, sing that "happiness is a warm gun." We live in a world of violence and aggression. Most historical and anthropological data indicate that aggression directed against other human beings is not unique to our own time and place. There have been exceptions to this rule, but these are few in number, and an entirely peaceful existence tends to be found in cultures not only small in scale but isolated. Aggression, in fact, seems to be so much a part of existence that the language and metaphor of combat are encountered in a wide variety of settings and activities, including the enterprise of social science itself. We talk of the war on poverty, the war between the sexes, the fight against illness and disease, psychological defenses, and character armor.

Americans have ambivalent attitudes toward aggression. On the one hand, we have created a demand for movies, books, and television shows which graphically depict aggression and violence. There is the American Declaration of Independence which asserts the right to use violence when other remedies are not available. And there is the presence of an estimated one and one-half million guns in private homes in the United States. On the other hand, there are religious admonitions against the use of aggression and violence. Peace movements such as those which arose during the war in Vietnam received strong support. There is increasing public concern over aggression and violence in the media, and a strong sentiment for gun control. An interest on the part of social scientists in aggression has been given added impetus by the development of nuclear weapons. These weapons, which make the destruction of all life on the planet a distinct possibility, are a new historical development, probably unique in the history of humanity. Although it is no doubt true that throughout history large groups of people entertained the notion of the end of all life on the planet through a natural or supernatural holocaust, never before have so many people become aware of not only the very real possibility but the exact process by which men may destroy the world.

Nuclear warfare, and other less dramatic, smaller-scale events such as violent crime, have caused many to believe that social scientists must become involved in applied problems. A social science which does not direct itself to human problems is a luxury we can no longer afford. Whereas in the past, much of the study of aggression has been of a relatively abstract nature, recently there has been increasing concern with many applied problems such as suicide, crimes of violence, and urban race riots.

Aggression defined

The *Shorter Oxford English Dictionary* (1956) defines aggression as: "1. an unprovoked attack; the first attack in a quarrel; an assault; 2. the practice of making such attacks." Dollard, Doob, Miller, Mowrer, and Sears, in a classic work on aggression (1939), state that aggression is "a response having for its goal the injury of a living organism." In a more behavioristic vein, Buss (1961) writes that aggression is "a response that delivers noxious stimuli to another organism." Since issues of legality and morality are frequently involved in an examination of aggressive behavior, increasingly it becomes relevant to ask whether a particular definition or explanation of aggression serves the vested interests of a specific segment of society. For example, did some inner-city blacks riot in the sixties because they were unsocialized riffraff? Or did they create a civil disorder to bring attention to the idea that their legitimate aspirations were blocked? Asking one, rather than the other, of these questions leads to very different conclusions about the nature of aggression, blacks, and society. In another similar example, attempts were made to explain campus disturbances in the sixties solely in such psychoanalytic terms as the unresolved oedipal complex. Such explanations are open to the criticism of being not only naive reductionism, insensitive to the social context of behavior, but also an excellent example of blaming the victim (Ryan, 1971), as well as being oriented toward the preservation of the status quo. As Keniston (1970) has stated:

The usefulness of the Oedipus complex in explaining political and historical phenomena is open to challenge. In attempting to understand student revolt, we are, of course, not attempting to understand a universal phenomenon. Rather, we are seeking to explain why at a particular time in modern history (but not at other times), a particular group of young men and women (but not most of their contemporaries), have become intensely concerned with social and political injustices of their world, have devised a new series of tactics, strategies and interpretations of reality, and have set themselves against established institutions and values. . . . If the Oedipus complex is a universal developmental phenomenon, oedipal feelings alone are of little use in accounting for specific groups acting in specific ways at specific historical moments. . . .
This body of work [psychological reductionism of youth activism], while far

from consistent, is beginning to provide intellectual respectability and ideological underpinning for the rejection and even repression of student protest (Keniston, 1970, pp. 6–7).

Any assessment of aggression must also take into account the social context within which the behavior occurs. Thus, Buss (1961) observes that if violent attacks occur within the confines of a socially accepted role, they are not considered aggressive—for example, a parent would scarcely be condemned for punishing a child with a spanking for crossing a dangerous street. Therefore, in systematic considerations of aggression, it is important to keep in mind that implicit in most definitions of aggression is the notion of *motive:* the purpose, goal, or intention of an act. Behaviors are not usually called aggressive if the harm or injury that results is accidental. Most definitions of aggression, particularly those that deal with human behavior in social contexts, include the notion of the aggressor *intending* to aggress.

The aggression of man against man has long been a puzzling phenomenon for students of human behavior. Explanations for aggression have been incorporated into three quite different theoretical perspectives: the psychoanalytic tradition, including the frustration–aggression hypothesis; the ethological tradition; and social learning theory.

Psychoanalytic tradition

Sigmund Freud has had an impact on all areas of social science and can well be considered one of the primary shapers of modern sensibility. In his early work, Freud maintained a fairly consistent hedonism, a belief that the basic motivation for behavior is pleasure. Since he proposed that the impetus for behavior is derived from psychic energy which is biologically based, Freud is generally considered an instinct theorist. The component of the psyche which he postulated to be the seat of the instincts he labeled the *id,* and he viewed aggression as a variant or displacement of id energy or libido.

Freud found it difficult, however, to include the occurrence of the First World War in his theory of human behavior. If the basic drive in human behavior is pleasure, then how can the killing, pain, and mayhem of a major war be explained?

In *Beyond the Pleasure Principle,* published in 1920, Freud moved away from a simple hedonism. He postulated the existence of a death wish, or *thanatos.* All people, he said, have a desire to return to the inorganic state, to die; thus, life consists of a dialogue between the death wish and the more positive life forces labeled *eros.*

According to this, an instinct would be a tendency innate in living organic matter impelling it toward the reinstatement of an earlier condition, one which it had to abandon under the influence of organic elasticity, or, to put it another way, the manifestation of inertia in organic life (Freud, 1920).

Later, Freud sees aggression as a derivative of *thanatos*. Aggression is self-destruction turned outward against substitute objects.

> A person fights with other people and is destructive because his death wish is blocked by the forces of life instincts and by other obstacles in his personality which counteract the death instincts (Hall and Lindzey, 1957, p. 40).

The concept of *thanatos* has not been widely accepted, even among psychoanalysts, and with some exceptions, it is not generally encountered within the literature. Strachey (1957) explained war in terms of the death wish, and Norman O. Brown (1959, 1968) has used the concept extensively in his writings about the nature of reality and society, but most other social scientists have found the idea too mystical and untestable for their liking. Neo-Freudians (Hartmann, Kris, and Lowenstein, 1949) tended to conceptualize aggressive impulses as part of the ego, or the reality-oriented psychic structure, and as a consequence, they portray aggression in less destructive terms.

However, there are a number of other psychoanalytically derived concepts and orientations which have had an impact upon investigations of aggression. (One of these, the oedipal complex, has already been discussed.) Central to all psychoanalytic theory is the orientation that things that happen early in the life of an individual influence his later life. Also central to psychoanalytic theory is the idea of a fixed amount of biologically derived energy which must somehow be discharged. If this energy is not discharged in one way, then it will somehow be discharged in another. These elements of Freudian theory have been incorporated into an explanation of anti-Semitism.

In 1950, four authors, Adorno, Frenkel-Brunswik, Levinson, and Sanford, published *The Authoritarian Personality*, a massive study on racism and prejudice. (See chapter 7 for a full description of the F-scale and the authoritarian personality.) The authors were interested in investigating the psychodynamics of anti-Semitism and finding a relationship between certain personality variables and negative attitudes toward Jews: do people who strongly dislike Jews differ consistently in any other ways from people who do not? Earlier, Jean-Paul Sartre (1946) had answered this question in the affirmative, but his assertion was not based on empirical data. Would the facts, systematically gathered by social scientists, bear him out?

After gathering extensive data, the four authors concluded that there is a cluster of personality traits which distinguishes anti-Semitic subjects from non-anti-Semitic subjects. They also found that these traits are psychodynamically related. Anti-Semitic subjects are generally prejudiced against other minority groups; they tend to be ethnocentric, self-glorifying, and to idealize their parents. They also suffer from status anxiety and tend to use the defense mechanism of projection. This cluster of traits has come to be known as the *authoritarian personality*. People who are authoritarian were typically raised in homes where there was strict discipline, status anxiety, and no toleration of aggression toward authority. Adorno and his colleagues used Freudian theory to explain the authoritarian syndrome. Aggressive impulses which are not allowed expression during childhood and adolescence, they contended, are displaced onto minority-group members later in life. These negative and aggressive impulses have to be manifested sooner or later, and minority groups are convenient targets.

The Authoritarian Personality generated additional work, both critical and supportive (Christie and Cook, 1958; Hyman and Sheatsley, 1954). In a summary statement fifteen years after the original data were published, Roger Brown (1956) stated that "there is a substantial residual probability that the chief conclusion of the questionnaire work is correct: attitudes of anti-Semitism, ethnocentrism, and authoritarianism do generally go together" (p. 523).

Another explanatory concept derived from Freudian theory is that of *catharsis*, which relates to the psychoanalytic idea of a fixed amount of energy that must somehow be discharged. First articulated by Aristotle in his *Poetics* as a purging or release of fears and anxieties by means of the Greek tragic drama, the concept has reappeared most recently in the debate over the relationship between the mass media and aggression. Does exposure to aggression on television lower the amount of aggressive behavior in viewers through the process of catharsis? In other words, does a person who watches another kill or brutalize his victim, after a mounting series of acts by the victim calling for retaliation, find release for his own feelings of aggression? For example, does a man who is furious at his boss because of many injustices feel his desire to injure his boss well up and then abate as he watches a television hero beat up or shoot a drug pusher or cattle rustler in a television drama? Or does watching violence and brutality daily on television increase aggression, as many parents fear? This latter hypothesis would be supported by the common-sense reasoning that a daily fare of dramatized violence hardens the watcher to brutality and may add specific items to his repertory of aggressive acts, as well as by such psychological explanations as modeling and imitating. There appears, in fact, to be evidence (Bandura and Walters, 1963), which will be presented later in this chapter under the heading *social learning theory*, that the latter situation does exist, but there is also some evidence for the existence of catharsis.

Feshbach and Singer (1970), for example, asked seven groups of boys, totaling 665 in number, to watch a minimum of six hours of television per week between 5 P.M. and 9 P.M. daily. The sample of boys was drawn from three private boarding schools and four state residential schools. Some of the boys could choose only from a list of aggressive television shows and others could choose only from a list of nonaggressive shows. The boys were from ten to seventeen years old, and from a wide range of socioeconomic levels. The boys

WHY WOMEN FEAR SUCCESS

Why does one person achieve more than another in life? The answer to this question is difficult because so many variables are involved. However, investigators studying the problem have isolated some of the factors which produce the need to achieve. One of the most obvious of these is sex: women consistently score differently from men on achievement-motivated tests. In 1969, social psychologist Matina Horner set out to discover why this should be so. In her study, she found that most women, especially those with the skills to be successful, actually fear success.

In our culture, says Horner, female intellectual achievement has traditionally been associated with loss of femininity. Too many women have been brought up with the picture of the smart but lonely career woman. As a result, most women faced with a choice prefer to be less successful but more acceptable socially. Horner defined this negative attitude toward success as "the motive to avoid success." She believes that this motive, like the desire to excel, "is a stable disposition within the person, acquired early in life along with other sex-role standards."

To test her hypothesis, she asked both men and women college students to complete the version of this sentence appropriate to their sex: "After first-term finals, Phil or Anne finds himself or herself at the top of his/her medical-school class." Most of the boys predicted rosy futures for Phil, but this is how one woman described Anne's future: "Anne starts proclaiming her surprise and joy. Her fellow classmates are so disgusted with her behavior that they jump on her in a body and beat her. She is maimed for life."

Most of the women's stories projected fears of social rejection as a result of success. Others projected confusion about the definition of womanliness. A smaller group of women ignored the possibility that a woman could place at the top of her class. They explained Anne's success as luck, or suggested she become a nurse.

Next, Horner wanted to know whether competition against men raised the anxiety level of the women. The students were divided into three groups: in one group, students worked on a set of tests in competition with a person of the same sex; in another group, they competed against a person of the opposite sex; and in the last group they worked alone without competition.

Horner found that a large number of men did better when they competed with others. When she studied the results of the group working alone, she found that women who felt ambivalent and anxious about performing in groups did better by themselves. Seventy-seven percent of the women who were afraid of success performed better working alone.

Finally, Horner asked the students to rate on a scale from 1 to 100 "How important was it for you to do well in this situation?" As expected, the high-fear-of-success women said it was more important for them to do well when they worked alone than in either kind of competition. Ironically, it was found that women most anxious about success would be the most successful if freed of their anxiety. Horner concludes that our society punishes women who want to achieve by making them feel like misfits (Horner, 1969).

could watch more than six hours of television per week as long as what they watched was on the designated list. The study extended over a six-week period. The subjects completed questionnaires measuring a wide range of aggressive themes and values both before and after the six-week period. They were also given projective tests and were rated by their peers and by their supervisors.

Results indicated that the boys who watched aggressive shows on television expressed less aggression than those who watched the nonaggressive television. "The frequency of both verbal aggression and physical aggression, whether directed toward peers or authority figures, was reliably higher in the control group exposed to the nonaggressive programs, as compared to the experimental group who had been placed on the aggressive list" (1970, p. 4). These differences were statistically significant in the state residential schools but not in the private schools. Despite the evidence that modeling and imitating occur to a greater extent in media-exposure situations than does catharsis, the fact that Feshbach and his co-workers can demonstrate a cathartic effect must be accounted for.

Frustration–aggression hypothesis. In 1939, a group of psychologists at Yale University (Dollard, Doob, Miller, Mowrer, and Sears) published a classic monograph on aggression called *Frustration and Aggression.* They based many of their ideas on those of Freud but attempted to formulate these concepts in ways that were testable. The main thesis of the monograph was that "aggression is always a consequence of frustration" and "the occurrence of aggressive behavior always presupposes the existence of frustration, and, contrariwise, the existence of frustration always leads to some form of aggression." Although the initial formulation and subsequent revisions were constantly plagued by criticisms of circularity and vagueness, the basic hypothesis influenced research in aggression for more than twenty years.

Two years after the initial publication of the hypothesis, one of the original authors (Miller, 1941) liberalized the hypothesis to say that "frustration produces instigations to a number of different types of responses, one of which is an instigation to some form of aggression" (p. 338). That is, frustration could have consequences other than aggression, and aggression would not inevitably occur as a response to frustration. Miller also made the point that no assumptions were being made as to whether this relationship was learned or innate. In other words, the relationship of aggression and frustration was not necessarily instinctual.

Considerable empirical evidence has accumulated to support the hypothesis of a relationship between frustration and aggression. Barker, Dembo, and Lewin (1941) exposed two groups of children to attractive and likable toys, but allowed only one group to play with the toys. The other group was frustrated by being allowed only to look at them through a window. Observers recorded that the subsequent play behavior of the frustrated group was much more destructive than that of the nonfrustrated group. Hovland and Sears (1940) found a correlation between the lynchings of blacks in the South and economic prosperity from the years 1882 to 1930. When the price of cotton was high, there tended to be fewer lynchings, and when the price of cotton was low, there tended to be more lynchings. Miller and Bugelski (1948) frustrated a group of men working at camp by forcing them to do a rather boring task when they were expecting a big night out on the town. Measures of their attitudes toward Mexicans and Japanese before and after they experienced frustration indicated that the subjects were more negative toward these ethnic groups after the frustrating experience.

The major difficulty with the frustration–aggression hypothesis is, as Berkowitz (1969b) stated, its oversimplification and sweeping generalizations. Doesn't frustration also lead to other behaviors such as displacement or regression? Observers in the Dembo, Barker, and Lewin (1941) study noted that the children in the frustrated group regressed as well as aggressed. Another criticism was noted by Buss (1961) when he stated that threats and attack can frequently elicit stronger aggressive behavior than can frustration. A persistent difficulty with the frustration–aggression hypothesis since its first formulation

Comparison of the Ratings of the Similar Attitude and the Dissimilar Attitude Groups on Interpersonal Attraction and Evaluation

	Similar Attitude	Dissimilar Attitude
Personal Feelings	6.53	1.76
Desirability as Work Partner	6.47	2.65
Intelligence	5.65	3.06
Knowledge of Current Events	4.65	2.65
Morality	5.76	3.47
Adjustment	6.00	2.71

Figure 11–1. Byrne found that a subject has more positive feelings toward a "stranger" when informed that the person has completed an attitude questionnaire in exactly the same way as the subject has. Conversely, subjects dislike "strangers" who hold opposite attitudes.

SOURCE: Adapted from Byrne, D., Ervin, C. R., and Lambreth, J. Continuity between the experimental study of attraction and real-life computer dating. *Journal of Personality and Social Psychology,* 1970, **16,** 157–165.

has been the circularity of the formulation. Unless both frustration and aggression can be precisely defined in terms completely independent of each other, it becomes difficult to avoid arguing that there must have been some frustration because aggression is being observed, and contrariwise, there must have been some aggression, even if it is not observable, because the organism has been frustrated. It is ironic that this criticism can be made, since one of the goals of the authors of the frustration–aggression hypothesis was to make Freud more operational and testable.

In a revision of the frustration–aggression hypothesis, Berkowitz (1969a, 1969b) modified the original formulation in several basic ways. First, he states that frustration creates "only a *readiness* for aggressive acts. Previously acquired aggressive habits can also establish this readiness" (1969b, p. 308). Next, he states that environmentul cuing stimuli play an important role in actually eliciting the aggression. They are not essential for the occurrence of aggression, but increase the probability of its occurrence.

Berkowitz has gathered much experimental data in testing his reformulations. In one series of studies, male subjects were either angered or treated in a neutral fashion by an accomplice of the experimenter. For some of the subjects the accomplice was introduced as a speech major and for others the accomplice was introduced as a physical education major with an interest in boxing. Subjects were then shown one of two seven-minute film clips. One film was a rather bland treatment of English canal boats and the other was a vicious prizefight scene from the film *Champion.* After viewing one of these films, the subject was given an opportunity to shock the accomplice. As predicted, Berkowitz found that the stimulus cues, boxer versus speech major and bland film versus vicious film, interacted with the situational anger or frustration. The strongest shocks were given by those subjects who had been angered by the accomplice, had watched the vicious prizefight film, and had had the accomplice introduced as a physical education major interested in boxing. Thus, the experimenter introduces frustration, followed by an environmental cuing situation (movie of a prizefight), and finally offers the subject a chance to perform an aggressive act against the very person who frustrated him in the first place.

Berkowitz has established a case for his position, but his modifications of the frustration–aggression hypothesis make it significantly different from the one presented by the Yale authors in 1939.

Ethological tradition

Ethology, the study of the behavior of animals in their natural habitats, can be contrasted with experimental psychology with animal subjects, in which most of the research is in the form of experiments in laboratory settings. In 1963,

Konrad Lorenz, one of the major figures in ethology, published a book entitled *Das sogenannte Böse* (The So-called Evil). This appeared in English in 1966 under the title *On Aggression*. Lorenz argues that aggressive behavior is instinctive and that the instinct of aggression serves a major evolutionary purpose: survival by means of the protection by the adults both of the young and of the territory in which they find food and shelter. Lorenz is similar to psychoanalytic thinkers in that he uses the concept of instinct to explain aggression, but he stresses the positive, adaptive function of aggression rather than the destructive elements which were Freud's preoccupation. Lorenz believes that aggression is an inevitable component of life, and as such, must find periodic outlets. This would explain the outbreak of a major war in almost every generation. For modern man, Lorenz says, there are insufficient outlets short of war. He recommends competitive sports as a nondestructive alternative to war, as well as other demanding physical activities—for example, mountain-climbing, back-packing, and sailing.

Reason, and not emotion, according to Lorenz, is the great enemy of human survival. Here again, he differs from Freud, who expressed the hope that human reason would temper the force of the destructive *thanatos*. For Lorenz, it is the emotions which enable humanity to express its deepest, most true behaviors. Reason is a relatively recent evolutionary development and as such, is a villain in the human drama.

According to Konrad Lorenz's theories on aggression, aggression is natural and innate in people. Schooling in karate would be an excellent way to release aggressive energy.

On Aggression has had a great deal of impact, as have several other similar books, such as Ardrey's *The Territorial Imperative* and Morris's *The Naked Ape*, which also discuss instinct and the essential animal nature of humanity. However, instinct theories have come under widespread attack in scientific circles. Lorenz has been accused of using vague language and of a lack of systematic theory (Johnson, 1972). He has been criticized because hc offers mostly anecdotal evidence for his hypotheses, he has ignored the bulk of scientific literature, and he has extrapolated his findings from other species to man without sufficient justification (Montague, 1968). Critics have also pointed out that it is probably a mistake to consider aggression as analogous to such other biological needs as hunger and sex. Johnson (1972) and others have demonstrated experimentally that deprivation of aggression does not necessarily lead to more aggression, as is the case with a drive such as hunger.

In commenting on the theories of both Freud and Lorenz, Kaufmann (1970) has this to say:

> The chief objection to "instinct" theories is not that they deny possible innate, genetically determined tendencies, but, rather, that they constitute, at least theoretically, a terminal position that reverentially accepts the state of the world and offers no systematic prescription for discovering causal relationships (p. 19).

Social learning theory

There have been a considerable number of psychologists who have emphasized learning processes in their accounts of aggression. (See chapter 2 for a full discussion of learning theory.) J. P. Scott (1958, p. 98), for example, after a review of the literature on aggression, concludes that "all research findings point to the fact that there is no physiological evidence of any internal need or spontaneous driving force for fighting; that all stimulation for aggression comes eventually from forces present in the external environment." In other words, an act of aggression, Scott asserts, is learned behavior. The argument is an important one in its implications. If aggressive behavior is learnsd, then it is possible to alter those aspects of the social environment from which the learning of aggression takes place. On the other hand, if all human beings are innately aggressive, then there is no way ultimately of preventing aggression from becoming manifest.

Adherents of social learning theory believe that, in addition to other factors which are generally considered to be operating in a learning situation, the factor of *imitation*, or *modeling*, is important. People can learn behavior patterns by observing the behavior of others. In one series of experiments (Bandura, Ross, and Ross, 1961, 1963), nursery school children were independently rated for their interpersonal aggressiveness and then brought into a room filled with toys, including a large inflated doll usually referred to as a "Bobo doll." One group of children watched adult models punch and kick the doll. Another group observed the same behavior on a television monitor. A third group watched an aggressive model who was dressed like a cat. A number of control groups were used, including one in which the model played in a nonaggressive fashion with the doll. The children were then mildly frustrated and allowed to play with the toys. Their behavior was observed. The authors found that exposure to aggressive models significantly increased aggressive behavior. Furthermore, watching the models on television had as strong an effect as watching them in person. When the model was dressed like a cat, however, it had less influence on the children.

Other studies (Bandura, 1965; Walters and Willows, 1968) have shown that if a child watches a film in which an adult is rewarded for behaving in a novel, aggressive manner, then the child will imitate the adult, and that this imitation occurs more often when the adult is rewarded than when the adult is punished. Bandura and his colleagues believe that there are several processes occurring in these situations. One is modeling, in which the observer may

Child with Bobo doll.

acquire new responses not previously available (Bandura and Walters, 1963, p. 60). There also may be a facilitation of responses already present in the person's repertoire, and a lessening of inhibitions toward the performance of aggressive behaviors.

Aggression as a social problem

The study of aggression has, perhaps more than any other specialty in social psychology, a direct application. Moreover, as we have seen, the tradition within which the researcher works has implications which reach beyond the university walls. Aggression is a social problem, whether aggressive acts are performed by an angry individual, an unruly mob, a politically organized movement for social justice, or a nation at war. When people perform aggressive acts, other people get hurt. The studies that follow are directly oriented toward specific social issues and are concerned with a particular direction for social change.

Civil disorders in the urban ghettos. The sixties in the United States were characterized by many large-scale outbreaks of violence in black urban ghettos. What events precipitated the civil disorders? Who participated? Why did they throw rocks and bottles, set fires which burned blocks of homes, and loot stores? Were the disorders senseless outbursts engaged in primarily by the alienated segments of the population? Or was it the case that ghetto residents used civil disorders as a form of protest against racism? The Kerner Commission (National Advisory Commission on Civil Disorders, 1968) stated:

What most white Americans never fully understood—but what the Negro can never forget—is that white society is deeply implicated in the ghetto. White institutions created it, white institutions maintain it, and white society condones it (p. 2).

Empirical investigations of the civil disorders, the police, and the black participants themselves, did much to uncover the underlying dynamics of the mob actions and to dispel certain misconceptions about what took place.

In discussing the onset of the civil disorders, the Kerner Commission (1968) noted that, because the specific types of precipitating events were so diverse, it was best to think of a particular precipitating event as a trigger that released energy that already existed, rather than as a direct cause of the events that followed. However, in an analysis by Downes (1968), the most frequent category of precipitating events in the ghetto disorders from 1964 to 1968 was some form of altercation between ghetto residents and the police. Marx (1970) also asserts that a basic problem in ghetto areas was the deterioration of police–community relations, such that most ghetto residents attributed little legitimacy to the police. After citing many instances of inappropriate control strategies employed by the police, such as mass firing in response to what was thought to be sniping, and the failure of police to negotiate with rioters, Marx makes the insightful point that in a civil disorder, the police are as subject to psychological phenomena which may result in extreme behavior as are the rioters. These phenomena include emotional contagion, spread of rumor and panic, and lessening of inhibitions. (See chapter 5 for a discussion of mobs and crowds.)

Who riots? Is it true, as the "riffraff" theory asserts, that the lowest segment of the population participates most actively? In an article reviewing the research, Caplan (1970) states that the rioters were, in fact, quite different from the stereotype. Rioters did not differ from nonrioters in terms of absolute income; rioters were not the hard-core unemployed; rioters were more socially and politically integrated into the community than nonrioters; rioters were better educated; and rioters were not recent immigrants to the city. Rioters tended to be politically better informed and active and to have stronger feelings of racial pride.

To explain the aggression of the rioters, Caplan offered a "blocked-opportunity" theory based upon a lack of congruence between aspirations of the "new ghetto man" and the objective conditions of life in the ghetto. Sears and McConahay (1970) talked of increased militancy in the socialization process and an increase in relative deprivation. These authors believe that young black people raised in the North are more aggressive toward, and independent of, whites. They also have increasing aspirations concerning their lives, but these aspirations are coupled with a belief that the social system will prevent the realization of their rising expectations. The general picture which emerged (Allen, 1970) from a large number of investigations was that of proud, representative members of a community, striking back in purposeful, although spontaneous, fashion against individuals and institutions which they perceived as both frustrating them and aggressing toward them.

Why does the image of riffraff participating in mindless violence still persist? Perhaps the best answer comes from Ryan (1971) when he speaks of ideologies which "blame the victim" and thereby relieve the majority of both blame and the responsibility to institute social change. The Kerner Commission, whose members were government figures not known for their social radicalism, placed the blame for the civil disorders squarely on the white community. They made many recommendations for improving the living conditions, education, and employment opportunities for black Americans that for the most part have not been implemented.

Aggression and the environment. Psychologists recently have demonstrated an increasing interest in the relationship between the spatial dimensions of the physical environment and behavior (Friedman and Juhasz, 1974). Much of this work is relevant to the social psychology of aggression. For example, Robert Sommer (1974) has developed the concept of "hard" architecture, which, he feels, bears a direct relationship to aggression and as such, can be considered a social problem. In summarizing the properties of hard architecture, he lists the following characteristics (pp. 25–26):

1. Lack of permeability. A minimum of contact between inside and out. The building has no connection with the surrounding neighborhood.
2. Expensive to construct, alter, or raze. Few possibilities for change and expansion without a gross misfit between building and activities.
3. Clear differentiation of status levels. Every activity and person has a specified location. Minimum contact across status levels or departments.
4. Passive adjustment and psychological withdrawal are encouraged. Little possibility for experimentation or change.
5. Rather than relying mainly on the occupants themselves to provide security with outside assistance when needed, security is assigned to a specialized agency. Eventual replacement of security through people by security through machines.
6. Materials and furnishings selected for ease of purchasing and maintenance, producing uniformity in design and layout.

Sommer believes that hard architecture is the product of a security-state mentality in which people are seen as potential enemies, and there is the conviction that the way to reduce this threat is to create a physical environment which people cannot manipulate. It is Sommer's belief that this strategy further dehumanizes the environment and aggravates the problem rather than solving it. He proposes a strategy of "soft" architecture where the need for people to have impact on their surroundings is recognized and taken into account. This is done both through design features and policy features. Similarly, Friedman and Thompson (1976) have proposed the creative use of color as a vehicle for humanizing the environment and as a way to reduce alienation from the physical environment by providing information about it.

The graffiti situation in the New York City subway system is a good example of a hard architectural approach. Graffiti artists have covered most of the subway cars in the city with large, colorful murals, the content of which consists, for the most part, of the artist's first name and street number. The official reaction of the municipal authorities has been to condemn the graffiti as illegal aggression and to enact laws against it. Large amounts of paint remover have also been purchased. The graffiti artists have proven more than equal to the challenge and even after a huge outlay of money, the graffiti shows no sign of abating. Sommer and others, including the artist Claes Oldenberg, believe that the graffiti should be viewed as attempts to humanize a hard, ugly environment, and the graffiti activity should be encouraged, with perhaps some regulation, instead of being defined as asocial, aggressive behavior.

Oscar Newman (1972) has articulated a number of ideas on building environments and spaces in which people would be safe from the aggression of others. Observing a public housing development in the Bronx where the tenants were extremely fearful of being victimized by criminals, Newman developed a number of design concepts which have proven helpful. He reasoned that increased tenant surveillance of the grounds, greater definition of the functions of the grounds, and an increased sense of possession by the residents were required. A variety of design changes were introduced:

> To highlight the public quality of the major pedestrian walk, the design called for (1) widening of the path, using colored and decoratively scored paving; (2) differentiating small private areas (front lawns) outside each dwelling from the public path with low, symbolic walls; and (3) the addition of public seating in the center of the public path, located at a distance from private dwellings sufficient to eliminate conflicts over use, but close enough to be under constant surveillance by residents.

While many similar ideas have been offered in the past, the increasing contemporary emphasis on physical environment offers the important message to students of aggression that any attempts either to understand or control aggression must take features of the physical environment into account.

Affiliation, Attraction, and Altruism

"It is not good that man should be alone." (Genesis 2:18)
"Who can enjoy alone?" (Milton, *Paradise Lost*)
"One is the loneliest number you'll ever know." (The Beatles)

People come together for reasons other than the desire to harm each other. This coming together of people can be considered one of the basic assumptions of social psychology, and it has been extensively investigated in guises other than aggression. Social psychologists have investigated three such ways of coming together: affiliation, attraction, and altruism. What are the factors which influence affiliation? Anxiety, birth order, fear reduction, and social comparison have all been demonstrated to have a strong impact on affiliative behavior.

Affiliation

Early social psychologists believed that people joined others because of an instinct of gregariousness. Just as animals lived in groups, so, it was postulated, do people. The concept of instinct has not been very popular in American psychology, and over the years other psychologists have pointed out the obvious: most, if not all, of our needs are, at least initially, met by, or satisfied within the presence of, other people. Thus we have ample opportunity to learn to desire the presence of other people. Is the need for other people innate or learned? Both innate and learned are rather general answers, the utility of which is limited unless specific causes and processes of affiliative behavior are identified.

Anxiety, affiliation, and birth order.   The existence of solitary confinement, considered among the most harsh of punishments, illustrates the fact that people do not like to be alone. Even when basic biological needs are being met, most people prefer the presence of others. After observing people in isolation, Schachter (1959) reported that "one of the consequences of isolation appears to be a psychological state which in its extreme form resembles a full-blown anxiety attack" (p. 12). Can the opposite be said to be true? If isolation leads to anxiety, does anxiety result in people wanting to affiliate with others? In an attempt to answer these questions and to explore more fully the relationship between anxiety and affiliation, Schachter and his colleagues performed a series of experiments which have become classics in the study of affiliation.

In the initial study, the subjects, women in the introductory course at the University of Minnesota, were led to believe that they were going to receive a series of electric shocks. Schachter's research design called for both an experimental and a control group. Subjects in the high-anxiety condition were told that the shocks would hurt and be painful, but that there would be no permanent damage. The control subjects in the low-anxiety condition were told that the shocks would barely be felt, and if they were felt at all, they would most likely resemble a tingle or a tickle. The subjects then were told that there would be a ten-minute delay for the setting up of experimental apparatus. The subjects were asked whether they would prefer to wait alone or in the presence of others. The experiment ended when each subject indicated her choice.

As expected, the manipulation of the independent variable, anxiety, did have a strong impact on the choice to wait alone or to wait with others. Of the thirty-two high-anxiety subjects, twenty wanted to wait with others. Only ten of the thirty low-anxiety subjects chose to wait with others.

In a second experiment, all the subjects were told that they would receive shocks, but half the subjects were given the choice of waiting alone or of waiting with others who would also be taking part in the same electric shock experiments. The other half, the control group, were given the choice of either waiting alone or waiting with people who were not participating in the experiments, but merely waiting to see their faculty advisers. Of the ten subjects who could wait with others participating in the experiment, six chose to do so, whereas of the ten given the option of waiting with someone who was waiting to see a faculty adviser, all chose to wait alone. As Schachter said, the adage "misery loves company" should be changed to "misery loves miserable company."

Schachter suggested five hypotheses to explain why anxious subjects wanted to affiliate with other anxious subjects: **1.** the desire either to convince the other person not to participate or to escape themselves, **2.** a desire to obtain cognitive clarity about what the experiment was all about, **3.** direct anxiety reduction, **4.** indirect anxiety reduction, or **5.** self-evaluation. In another experiment it was found that anxious subjects preferred to wait with other people even if they were not allowed to talk to them. This result would seem to support hypotheses three, four, and five.

Upon further analysis of his data, Schachter noted that the affiliative tendency of anxious subjects was significantly higher among subjects who were either firstborn or only children. There is considerable evidence that firstborn have higher achievement needs (Sampson, 1962), are more conforming (Becker and Carrol, 1962), and are raised in a less consistent manner because their parents are novices (Sears, Maccoby, and Levin, 1957). Inconsistent treatment may lead to a more confused self-concept in the firstborn, causing them to seek others for self-evaluation. Schachter (1959) concluded that firstborn college students are more affiliative because of childhood experiences. Similarly, Sampson (1965) stated that the firstborn were more dependent on the mother as infants and this led to a stronger affiliative tendency as an adult.

Are there any other concepts which shed additional light on the affiliative tendency? The two that are most frequently encountered are fear reduction and self-evaluation through social comparison.

Fear reduction. A case could be made that whereas fear, defined as a response to a specific stimulus, leads, as Schachter has shown, to greater affiliation, anxiety should lead to less affiliation. According to psychoanalytic theory, anxiety is aroused by unconscious desires, frequently in the areas of sexuality or aggression—desires that those who have them consider unacceptable. In the situation of fear, which is by definition realistic, others can reassure. But in the situation of anxiety, which is by definition unrealistic, the presence of others may make things worse. The others who are present frequently are not themselves anxious, and often the anxiety-inducing concerns either are subconscious or are not subjects about which one would feel free to talk. The potential for embarrassment in an anxiety-producing situation would be a strong motivation for concealing feelings.

Sarnoff and Zimbardo (1961) performed a study similar to Schachter's, but introduced a variation so that they could manipulate fear and anxiety independently. One group of subjects was treated in a manner similar to Schachter's subjects, with the fear-arousing stimulus being the expectation of electric shock. The manipulation concerned anxiety level. The control subjects, among whom low anxiety was being aroused, were told that they would have to blow whistles, balloons, etc. High-anxiety subjects were told that they would have to suck on nipples, breast shields, and so on. The experimenters believed that the control group would not be made anxious blowing whistles or filling balloons because, although the required behavior was somewhat atypical, it was well within the range of permissible behavior for an adult man. The behavior required of the high-anxiety group was entirely inappropriate and was intended to evoke extreme embarrassment and a host of anxieties. All subjects were then asked to make the same affiliative choice—to wait alone or with someone else.

The results demonstrate that an increase in fear increases affiliation, whereas an increase in anxiety lessens affiliative tendencies. Affiliation is sought by those in whom fear has been aroused, for the purpose of reducing the fear. When anxiety is aroused, other people are avoided.

Attraction

What are the factors which cause people to do more than merely affiliate with each other, and actually to like each other? Three widely investigated causes of attraction have been proximity, similarity, and physical beauty.

Proximity. In general, people who live close to each other are more likely to be attracted to each other than people who do not. This has been shown to be true for groups as diverse as Jibaro Indians, female university students, army recruits, and married MIT students. Kipnis (1972b) has shown that attraction is greater among workers who work close to each other rather than far apart, and Bossard (1932) has presented data showing that marriages are more likely to be contracted by people who live near one another rather than at a distance. In addition, Friedman (1969) has found that people interested in close interpersonal relationships tend to structure smaller, more enclosed spaces, presumably to establish the necessary propinquity.

In a typical propinquity study (Festinger, Schachter, and Back, 1950), the subjects, married students, were asked to list the three couples they saw most often socially. Forty-one percent chose the couple in the apartment next door; 23 percent chose the couple two units away; 16 percent chose the couple three units away; and 10 percent chose the couple four units away. The position of an apartment, or functional distance, is also important. For example, people who lived at the bottom of stairways generally had more friends on the upper floors, since they would be more likely to meet going up and down the stairs. Why is it that physical closeness has such a strong impact on attraction patterns? It is easy to see that in order for attraction to take place, the possibility of some sort of interaction must exist—for example, the chances of a person from Des Moines, Iowa, establishing a friendship with someone from Afghanistan are quite slim if neither of them ever leaves home. But why should a matter of a few feet, as in the Festinger study cited above, make a difference?

According to Thibaut and Kelley's social exchange theory (1959), a relationship between two people continues if the rewards from the relationship are greater than the costs. Furthermore, they say, individuals compare the cost/reward ratio of one interaction with the cost/reward ratio of other available alternative behaviors and then choose accordingly, a concept these authors call the *comparison level of alternatives*. Exchange theory, as interpreted by these two authors, then, offers a number of ways in which proximity may be related to attraction. First, proximity lowers the cost of initiating such interactions. This low cost, in turn, lowers the necessity for high rewards: the relationship does not have to be so special to be worthwhile. Sustaining interaction with those who live close by also costs less in time and effort. In addition, persons who are physically close are more likely to be similar to each other, which has an effect on the cost/reward ratio. Finally, with continued interaction, each person is better able to predict the behavior of the other and again the result is a more favorable cost/reward outcome.

Proximity effects, such as those cited above, are strongest when the populations involved are homogeneous. Furthermore, values and lifestyles strongly influence the relationship between proximity and the attraction pattern (Kuper, 1953). And it is also true, as we will see, that for many individuals, attraction is based on similarities of interest and lifestyle. Thus, proximity, attraction, and similarities of lifestyle and personal characteristics all work together to promote social interaction and the bonds of friendship. However, as Webber (1963) and others have pointed out, the attraction patterns of some people, particularly middle-class professionals, are not based directly on propinquity, but rather on common interests and values. Access to an advanced technology—phones, planes, automobiles—allows these individuals to, in a sense, transcend space and time and live in what McLuhan has called a "global village." It is now possible, for example, to fly to Paris from the East Coast of the United States in less than four hours. Almost any place on the globe is quickly accessible by phone. Because of this, many "global villagers" become insensitive to the idea of attraction patterns which are strongly influenced by proximity and spatial accessibility.

Friedman and Juhasz (1974, p. 236), for example, have noted the social and psychological havoc which often results when middle-class planners, who may not be oriented toward considerations of the impact of proximity on attraction, displace individuals from neighborhoods that they have occupied for many years. A number of studies (Young and Willmott, 1957; Fried, 1963) are consistent in showing that people react negatively when, in their new settings, it becomes impossible to sustain attraction patterns and lifestyles that were based on spatial proximity.

Similarity. "Birds of a feather flock together," says the old adage, and there is considerable social psychological evidence that this is so. Byrne (1961) found that subjects liked another person the most when that person answered twenty-six attitude items exactly as the ubject had. In a later study (Byrne and Nelson, 1965), it was found that it was not merely the number of agreements, but rather the proportion of agreements to disagreements that was crucial. Couples who were matched for similarity before a date showed greater attraction (Byrne, Ervin, and Lambreth, 1970) toward each other than did couples who were matched for dissimilarity. A number of studies (Stein, Hardyck, and Smith, 1965; Rokeach, 1968) have shown that whites prefer associating with blacks who have attitudes similar to their own, rather than with other whites who have differing attitudes.

In a naturalistic study, Newcomb (1961) obtained a house at the University of Michigan and allowed students to live there rent-free if they provided him with social psychological data. Newcomb took a variety of attitude and personality measures for each student and also had them fill out several attraction ratings throughout the year. He found that students with similar attitudes and values were not more likely to be attracted to each other at the start of the semester, but that these factors did influence attraction patterns by the end of the semester. Berscheid and Walster (1969) have found that married couples are more similar in height than would be expected by chance, and Berkowitz, Nebel, and Reitman (1971) presented evidence that in the 1971 New York mayoralty election, people preferring the taller candidate (Lindsay) were taller than those preferring the shorter candidate (Procaccino).

Physical beauty. The words "attractive" and "attraction" are related in ways other than linguistically. Thus, it is not surprising that social psychologists

Figure 11–2. Are middle-class high school girls more attractive than their working-class counterparts? Senior high school staff members in several California schools thought so. They rated working-class girls nearly ten points lower than middle-class girls in general appearance.

**Social-Class Variations in the
Appearance of Girls in High School (mean ratings)**

Senior High Staff Ratings	Middle Class	Working Class
Appearance		
Good Physique	56.6	48.6
Well-groomed	57.8	49.0
Sex Appeal	56.2	48.9
Appearance		
General Rating	55.8	46.3

SOURCE: Adapted from Elder, G. Appearance and education in marriage mobility. *American Sociological Review,* 1969, **34,** 519–533.

have found that physical beauty is an important determinant of attraction. Walster, Aronson, Abrahams, and Rottman (1966) set up a dance for freshmen during "welcome week" at the University of Minnesota. Subjects were told that they would be matched with dates on the basis of personality similarity, but actually men were assigned to women at random. Partners rated their dates for attractiveness, and the four experimenters also rated each subject's personal attractiveness. In a follow-up study done several months later, it was found that the best predictor of whether the men liked their dates and asked them out again was the attractiveness of the women.

Physical beauty has been shown to correlate with many factors that can be construed as social rewards. Attractive subjects as young as ages four to six are more popular than their peers (Dion and Berscheid, 1974), and research (Huston, 1973) has shown that attractive subjects have a greater degree of self-confidence and social orientation. Transgressions committed by attractive children are treated as less severe (Dion, 1972), and there is evidence (Landy and Sigall, 1974) that physical attractiveness affects rating of intellectual ability. Sigall and Landy (1973) have demonstrated that a male is evaluated more positively when he is with an attractive female and that males feel that they will be evaluated more favorably when seen with an attractive woman. Elder (1969) reports that women who marry into a higher social class are prettier than those who do not. Although issues of causality are difficult to investigate, physical beauty has been found to be an important factor in attraction.

Altruism

Do people help each other, and if so, how? What do investigations of altruism reveal about the processes involved in helping others? Can psychologists be of assistance in training others to help in crisis situations? Altruistic, or prosocial, behavior, is being increasingly investigated in attempts both to understand the more positive aspects of social interaction and to generate useful information to enhance contemporary life.

Helping behavior in emergencies. "On a March night in 1964, Kitty Genovese was set upon by a maniac as she came home from work at 3:00 A.M. Thirty-eight of her Kew Gardens neighbors came to their windows when she cried out in terror—none came to her assistance. Even though her assailant took over half an hour to murder her, no one so much as called the police" (Latané and Darley, 1970). The above incident prompted a host of experiments on helping behavior. As a description of contemporary behavior, it seemed to confirm the darkest suspicions of both those who talked of human aggressiveness and those who talked of the dehumanizing effects of living in cities.

Latané and Darley (1970) were prompted by the Genovese murder to undertake a series of investigations on the nature of intervention in emergencies. They point out that the very nature of an emergency would seem to predispose against intervention. At least four factors make this so: (1) the possibility of harm befalling the helper; (2) the fact that an emergency is an unusual and rare event; (3) the fact that emergencies differ from each other; and (4) the fact that emergencies occur suddenly. Should a person choose to intervene, the choice is made at the end of a series of acts which include noticing that an event out of the ordinary is happening; interpreting the event as an emergency; deciding that he or she has responsibility for helping; and lastly, deciding on the form of assistance. Latané and Darley do not assume that each individual is always cool and reasonable, systematically making each of the above decisions, but they do believe that anyone who chooses to intervene must confront each of the above issues.

By means of a series of rather ingenious experiments, Latané and Darley demonstrated that the presence of other individuals frequently mediated against intervention. With other people present, two processes, *social influence* and *diffusion of responsibility*, are activated. By social influence (see social comparison in chapter 10) the authors refer to a situation in which an individual cannot obtain the information needed to make a decision to intervene in an emergency, and as a consequence, observes others to see how they are reacting. Unfortunately, these others are probably doing the same thing, and an atmosphere of "pluralistic ignorance" can quickly develop. For example, a person may be walking down the street and may notice a man lying near a door. Has he just suffered a heart attack? Is he drunk? If the street is deserted, the individual may investigate, but if others are present, clues to appropriate

*It is surprising
how often people
will stop to
offer assistance
on the highway.
Would you
help this woman?*

behavior can be obtained by watching them: "They're not stopping, so it must be okay." The presence of others can also lead to a diffusion of responsibility—a feeling that "I'm not the only one responsible, because there are other people here, and surely someone's doing something" (Latané and Darley, 1970).

Although the Latané and Darley studies do not absolve those who refuse to come to the aid of people in distress, the studies do point out that the complexities of the situation itself are a contributing cause for nonintervention. People are not necessarily acting in an evil or apathetic fashion when they refuse to help; they may fail to feel personally responsible. Other studies have demonstrated that if a person has just observed another perform a helpful act, he is more likely to help (Bryan and Test, 1967). Piliavin, Rodin, and Piliavin (1969) found that helping in New York City subway cars was quite common, and helping responses were more frequent when the victim was perceived as being sick rather than drunk.

Action research and family intervention. Morton Bard and his colleagues (Bard and Berkowitz, 1967; Bard, 1972) have been involved in a helping project with New York police for many years. They note that although "80 to 90 percent of police man-hours are devoted to order maintenance and service functions," police organizations continue to be structured along "crime-combat" lines (Bard, 1972, p. 20). However, for many poor urban families, the police are the primary helping agency available and in cases of family fights, they are called regularly. These disturbances are potentially dangerous and each year the ordinary family fight is responsible for a significant number of police injuries and deaths. What makes the situation dangerous is the lack of knowledge about the potential for violence and catastrophe in a family fight. Indeed, most individuals, and until recently, many police officers, would not classify a family fight as a dangerous situation.

Bard and his colleagues have trained police officers to intervene in these situations, and preliminary data are most encouraging: "There was . . . an absence of family homicide in families known to the family unit, a decrease in family assault arrests, a total absence of injuries to police officers, and a significant increase in police utilization of social and mental health agencies" (Bard, 1972, p. 23).

In describing his action research, Bard points out that in addition to the benefits derived from applied social science, there is also an opportunity to gather data in natural settings. This data cannot help but be useful in supplementing information gathered about aggression and altruism in more controlled, experimental settings. Indeed, the dialogue between pure and applied research, intervention, and data gathering seems to be a useful strategy to understand social motivation and interpersonal behavior in their full complexity.

Power

There has always been resistance among social scientists to the explicit recognition of power, conflict, and coercion. Power is not a nice word for the liberal or the humanitarian. Even people wanting and using power have difficulty in justifying this motive. Sometimes people in power or seeking power will justify their motivation for control by representing themselves as fulfilling the will of God or acting as the instrument of the people. If our reactions to aggression are ambivalent, our attitude toward power is even more so.

Power becomes salient when there is a conflict of interests. The capability of one faction to achieve its own ends at the expense of the others is the essence of power. Thus, power contains a coercive element. Power may involve the ability to use physical coercion, but the coercion is not necessarily one of force and violence. Short of direct coercion, power is associated with the command of resources: economic assets, manpower, communication networks, or a monopoly of information. The closer a group comes to monopolistic control of such resources, the closer it approaches a position of absolute power. Differential possession and access to resources then become critical in any consideration of power. Of the concepts that have been dealt with in this chapter—aggression, affiliation, attraction, altruism, and power—the last is by far the most intimately intertwined with the larger social context.

Power may be defined as the exercise of coercive control in a situation of conflict of interests or values between two or more parties, either individuals or groups. Thus, discussion and persuasion would not be considered an aspect of the exercise of power. In a *kibbutz*, for example, ideally, individuals influence one another through their knowledge of the problem, their ability to formulate and analyze the issues, their credibility. They have no economic or coercive sanctions which can be employed against one another. Even the formal leaders cannot fall back upon the authority of their positions to control others. In an American factory, in contrast, members of management can issue orders and can implement these orders with sanctions of fines, demotion, and even dismissal. The authority structure of the organization gives them control over rewards and punishments. They operate from a position of power. They are held in check only by the opposing power of a labor union, if there is one.

Forms of coercion vary from the use of physical force at the one extreme to control through a monopoly of information at the other—from violence to propaganda. Between these extremes lie other power bases such as economic resources, access to the symbols of legitimacy, and the capability of mobilizing social support in the form of public opinion. In the exercise of power at the national level, these forms are intertwined. In international affairs there is a greater reliance upon economic sanctions and military force than upon ideological legitimation.

The compelling nature of physical force is recognized from early childhood on, first by the physical superiority of parents over the child, and second by the prowess of older children in the school playground or the street corner. As the socialization process proceeds, the child finds that the use of force is sanctioned for the individual only within a very restricted framework, as in self-defense. At the group level, however, physical force is used as a means of social control and the protection of group interests; the state uses police power against citizens and military power against external enemies.

Economic power

The control of economic resources is the most general form of power, in that it can be converted to military power, information control, and to a great extent, political influence. Gabriel Kolko (1969), who sees political power as an aspect of economic power, maintains that business runs the military, not military the business corporations. He points out that between 1944 and 1960 some 678 key posts in the Departments of State, Defense, the Treasury, and Commerce and related executive agencies were held by 234 individuals who rotated through these positions. In the aggregate, some 60 percent of these key jobs was held by men from the larger corporations, corporate law firms, the large banks, and investment firms. Thirty-two percent was held by government career officials. These career people, moreover, often retired to accept positions in business. Some 30 men from the American corporate structure held 22 percent of all the key posts. Business careers, Kolko holds, are the inspired goals of many military officers. In fact, in 1959 the 72 largest arms suppliers alone employed 1,426 retired officers—251 of the rank of general or higher.

In the field of the mass media, the trend toward organizational bigness is indicated by the tie between economic resources and the control of information. The small independent newspaper is becoming a thing of the past. Though the population of the country has been increasing steadily, the number of daily newspapers reached its peak some sixty years ago and has been declining since. Only one city in twelve, in the United States, has more than one daily independent newspaper (Presthus, 1962). Newspaper publishing is big business and many newspapers also run radio stations. The three major television networks, which control the viewing of some 200 million people, are big business enterprises with other holdings in radio, book publishing, and allied fields. The issue is not that corporate interests necessarily dictate the content and viewpoint of the media, but that there has come to be a fusion between the economic and news aspects of the system.

Restricted sources of information and the lack of competition in the news field do not in themselves constitute the exercise of power. It is only when individuals and groups can utilize these agencies to restrict and distort information to impose their wishes upon others that power is exercised. In a community in which the same interests own the only town newspaper and the only local radio station, these interests, for example, may, through the use of their monopolistic position, be able to defeat an urban development plan which most citizens want. Thus, through lack of information, people may be coerced into following a course running counter to their own interests. It is as if motorists seeking a direct route to a major city were deprived of maps and compass and made to rely on signposts—signposts which deliberately led them on a circuitous route to insure their patronage of commercial attractions. Information, then, can be coercive when one group has disproportionate control of it so that they can manipulate others to do things they do not want to do. As G. Almond and S. Verba wrote: "One might even argue that the crucial control in the totalitarian political system is not coercion—although it is essential—but the monopoly of the media of communication" (1965, p. 47).

Control of the symbols of legitimacy

The bases of power indispensable for the control of a territory are, as we have argued, possession of, or access to, economic resources and military and police force. But the possession of, and access to, such forms of power also involve the acceptance by the populace of the arrangements by which certain individuals or groups control these resources. The institution of private property, for example, allows some people to acquire economic assets through which they can exert power. However, private property as an institution rests upon shared

*The motive to obtain
money is closely connected
with the motive for power.
With one, a person
can command the other.*

attitudes. Similarly, the use of physical force by the police and the military is a significant means of control in itself, but it also depends for its long-term effectiveness upon the consent of people to such coercive arrangements. In brief, authority is legitimated power.

Legitimacy refers to the acceptance of institutional arrangements because they are perceived by members of the system as normative and binding upon members. In a traditional society, legitimate norms are based upon an absolute and unchanging morality, not a relative morality, which shifts the concepts of right and wrong. In a traditional society, to disobey one's parents is morally wrong under any set of circumstances, as is disobedience by an adult of any authority figure. In present-day bureaucratic society, there is some survival of traditional authority, but the more stable basis of compliance is a legitimacy which rests upon two sets of beliefs. In the first place, the people must believe that the rules and regulations of the system operate equitably; it must appear to treat all members as equal before the law in a consistent fashion. Without a perception of equity, the legitimate basis of bureaucratic authority crumbles. In the second place, the people must perceive that the system is in working order—getting results—to justify the compliance of its members. The organization, the institution, and the social order in modern society are all social tools for accomplishing given ends. To the extent that these arrangements work, they retain their legitimacy, and those who control these societal arrangements may use coercive power.

The authorities in power have two sources of coercion to secure obedience: (1) they can invoke sanctions or the threat of sanctions, and (2) they can manipulate the symbols of legitimacy to which they have special access to prevent the mobilization of an effective dissent. There is little need to resort to coercion, however, under two conditions: (1) if there is strong internalization of law as a principle of high priority, and (2) if the laws and their enforcement meet the specific expectations of the people about what is just and proper. The German people of the 1930s, for example, conformed to the first condition because of the respect in which they held the law. The Nazis took advantage of this respect for the law by legitimizing their totalitarian regime and met with surprisingly little resistance. Thus, Hitler did not seize power directly, but became chancellor legally and then tried to cover most of his actions with the cloak of legitimacy. Nonetheless, there were limits to compliance as specific Nazi decrees came into conflict with traditional concepts of justice and legality. When both internalized compliance to law and the thin veils of legitimacy failed, the Nazis resorted to violence, which was a conspicuous feature of their rule.

The experiments of Milgram (1965) are of relevance in examining the coercive aspects of obedience. (See box in chapter 1 describing this experiment.) Milgram told subjects that they were to act as trainers in a learning experiment and to administer shocks to other subjects when they made errors. The experimenters wanted to see how long the subjects as experimental trainers would keep increasing the intensity of what the subjects thought to be painful shocks. In about 65 percent of the cases, they did keep moving up the dial to the maximum values. These people did so under considerable discomfort to themselves. They tried very hard to avoid their disagreeable roles, which were causing them considerable mental anguish.

The major reason for their compliance was their acceptance of the legitimacy of the role of experimenter, who claimed he was carrying on important work for science. The experimenter on this basis, then, forced them to act in a manner contrary to their own wishes. Although physically it was possible for them to have walked out of the distressing situation, psychologically they were coerced into remaining. We would regard this as an exertion of power rather than of persuasion because of the internal conflict involved. In fact, Milgram has captured in his experimental setting the way in which a generalized legitimacy is employed in the larger society to exact obedience.

Personality factors in the exercise of power

Too often psychologists as well as laymen have looked at the use of power and the exertion of influence within an individual framework. This leads to an equation of personal domination with institutionalized power and ignores the requirements of different roles. The case of the matching of personality to role is an interesting interaction between individual variables and the larger social context. It seems reasonable that a power-driven person would reach a top power position and attempt to gain a complete and arbitrary control. But even when observing a person in a position of authority who was not originally hungry for power, one is confronted by the doctrine of Lord Acton that "power tends to corrupt and absolute power corrupts absolutely."

An experiment by Kipnis (1972a) showed that subjects assigned to a power role with control of rewards and punishment over their workers did differ in their interpersonal perceptions from the control subjects assigned to a role of legitimate authority without control of rewards or punishment. The subjects in the more powerful positions devalued the worth of those under them more than did the control subjects (leaders without reward or punishment power). The powerful leaders also took credit for the efforts of their subordinates; they expressed preferences for maintaining social distance between themselves and their workers; and they saw subordinates as objects to be manipulated.

These findings have to do with the effects of occupying a position of power and not with original personality differences. The subjects were randomly assigned to the types of leadership roles and hence the differences reported above were due to the different experimental conditions and not to differences

POWER AND MANIPULATION

"All life is a game of power. The object of the game is simple enough: to know what you want and get it. . . . The trick is to make people do what you want them to and *like* it, to persuade them that they want what *you* want," writes Michael Korda in *Power! How to Get It, How to Use It* (1975). According to Korda, power is the key to success in finances, business, and sex, but most people, particularly women, don't know how to recognize it or how to use it. "Power people tend to be father figures."

Korda suggests that there is a power structure underlying the everday objects and interactions that most of us take for granted. He describes the power relationships that are revealed by the tightly knit group of men who cluster around the bar at office parties, by the size and design of offices, and by the location of seats in the conference room. Areas in which a great many people congregate are seldom areas of power, since people gather together for safety.

He also describes power as the result of carefully cultivated personal habits that act as signals which tip off others—particularly subordinates, clients, or women—that the person in charge is indeed a powerful man. "The trick is to develop a style of power based on one's character and desires," writes Korda. For example, the executive who sits behind a big desk staring impassively at a yellow legal pad is deliberately trying to make his clients feel uncomfortable. He may speak in a hushed whisper, feign indifference, or tap a pencil against the desk. All these moves are calculated to establish who is in control.

Once Korda has mapped the spots of power, he begins to discuss tactics. If a person wants to get ahead in a corporation, he or she must know how things work and who is in control. Office gossip is part of the office power structure, and the power-hungry would be wise to study where it originates and what it means. As Korda writes, "If you don't know the geography of the system, then all gossip is meaningless. By observing who talks to whom in coffee breaks and at lunch, which people commute together, or ride in the same car pool, you can fairly easily map the system."

When employees have mastered the power structure and are aware of the power tricks employed by their superiors, they are ready to manipulate the system for their own advantage. Korda recommends gaining access to the control of information, which will make your actions seem brilliant or incomprehensible, depending upon which is more advantageous at that moment. He tells how learning to say "no" consistently can make an executive stand out. He counsels the power-seeker to occupy the most important seat at a meeting and to make a ritual of meetings that are under his control by scheduling them regularly.

The most powerful people understand the system so thoroughly that they rule seemingly without being in control. Presidents and kings learn the tricks from practice or childhood experience, and according to Korda, so can we. Power never shouts its control over others but, like the silent nuances of body language, insinuates its meanings. People would feel less manipulated and less tormented, says Korda, if they were capable of recognizing who was in control and why. For once a person is made aware of a power network, he or she can resist becoming a pawn in someone else's game (Korda, 1975).

in personality types. The experimental manipulations were very weak compared to real-life settings, and they also were of brief duration. Hence one could expect that the corrupting influences of positions of power would be much stronger outside the laboratory. It should be noted, too, that in real-life situations people do not move into power positions at random, but that the more power-oriented are selected and select themselves for such roles. The chances are that their exercise of power will whet rather than satiate their appetite. There is practically no research on this problem, however, and there is even a surprising dearth of research data on the motivational patterns of people entering political, business, and other occupations (Winter, 1973). In some cases, the exertion of power can satisfy the individual's own needs to assert his mastery. The officious or despotic leader who abuses his authority in controlling others is an instance of the power-hungry person.

One source of much of the confusion in the literature on power is the failure to distinguish between power as a form of behavior and power as a motive. It is similar to the confusion of the exercise of authority and expression of authoritarian personalities. Undoubtedly the power motive is a significant factor in human competition and conflict, but how significant will depend upon socialization practices and contemporary social conditions. Rudin (1965), in his content analysis of elementary textbooks in the United States since 1860, found that power imagery indicative of the power motive reached a peak in 1910, declined to a low point in 1930, and has been increasing since that time. It is possible to interpret this rise as reflecting a greater concern with managerial and political issues, as the technological development of an achieving society aggravates rather than alleviates social problems. At any rate, systematic study of trends in basic motivational patterns is an important, though neglected, area of research in the behavioral sciences.

Whether the need for power is a native or a derived drive is disputed, but the significant fact is that it appears early in development as the child strives to assert his independence and to protect himself from physical and psychological collisions with others. Veroff (1957) constructed a measure of power motivation by comparing the responses of a group of candidates for campus office on the eve of election with a group of noninvolved students. The responses were stories written to standard Thematic Apperception Test (TAT) pictures. This projective test, based upon the comparison of arousal and nonarousal conditions, was further validated by examining high scorers and low scorers on other characteristics. The high power scorers were students more argumentative in class who attempted to persuade others to their point of view. They preferred occupations in which they could be in leadership positions. They were lower in social values or humanitarian concerns.

In a nationwide survey in the United States, Veroff, Atkinson, Feld, and Gurin (1960) found that the highest and lowest levels of the occupational hierarchy showed the greatest power motivation. Both managers and unskilled workers made higher scores than professional people. The people at the bottom of the ladder may be more power-oriented for defensive reasons. The same defensive origins for the power motive are suggested by findings that show that persons from broken homes tend to be more power-driven than persons from normal homes. Richard Mann, in his study of small groups (1959), reported that leaders tend to be higher in dominance than nonleaders. The relationship is not monotonic, however, in that there is some evidence that politicians who are moderately high in their power needs are more effective than those who are either very high or very low.

Relationship between Motivation, Sex, and Age

Motive and Age	Percentage of High Scores	
	Men	Women
Achievement		
21–24	66	47
25–34	50	50
35–44	57	50
45–54	54	45
55–64	42	52
65 plus	47	35
Affiliation		
21–24	47	53
25–34	48	53
35–44	44	55
45–54	49	53
55–64	53	36
65 plus	49	38
Power		
21–24	44	55
25–34	45	52
35–44	52	47
45–54	51	49
55–64	49	45
65 plus	54	47

Figure 11–3. Thematic apperception tests reveal that men and women of different ages have different degrees of motivation toward achievement, affiliation, and power. In the table, for example, the motivation for power is strongest in the oldest men and the youngest women.

SOURCE: Adapted from Veroff, J., Atkinson, J. W., Feld, S., and Gurin, G. The use of thematic apperception to assess motivation in a nationwide interview study. *Psychological Monographs*, 1960, **74** (12, Whole No. 449), 24.

Studies of local political leaders in an American city and in a Norwegian community (Valen and Katz, 1964) reported more complex and pluralistic patterns of motivation than would be predicted from a power-drive hypothesis. Precinct captains and other local party officials were interviewed at length about their experiences in party activity, their social and political beliefs, and their gratifications from their roles in the party. In both Norway and the United States, Valen and Katz found that the major sources of satisfaction reported by these local politicians were derived from working with like-minded colleagues, from useful activity, and especially from working for what one believes in. In the United States, Eldersveld (1964) found some suggestion that as one moved up the party hierarchy from local to district leaders, power motives assumed greater importance. However, even at higher levels of party leadership, the same complexity of motivation appears.

The relationship between social structure and personal motives was strikingly demonstrated in a study by Andrews (1967) of two industrial firms in Mexico. One firm was relatively modern and progressive and emphasized accomplishment. The second firm was more traditionally oriented and reflected more of the feudal values of an earlier period. The executives in the two enterprises had been tested for their motives for power and achievement two to four years before Andrews examined their rate of advancement in their respective companies. He found significant positive correlations between the strength of the power motive and advancement in the traditional firm, and negative correlations in the more progressive company. The motive for achievement, moreover, showed high positive correlations with job level and promotion in the progressive company. But for those at the traditional company, there was no correlation between promotion and the need to achieve. This accords with the thesis that the significant motivational syndrome for leadership in technological society is the need for achievement rather than for power. The men moving up the ladder in the Mexican firm with more modern concerns about productivity were not power-driven but achievement-oriented.

Summary

A motive is an impulse to act, especially in regard to moving toward or away from others. The study of motives can be approached by an analysis of aggression, affiliation, attraction, altruism, and power.

Aggression can be defined as a response which has as its goal the injury of a living organism. Explanations for aggression have been attempted by theorists of three different perspectives. In the classical psychoanalytic tradition of Freud, aggression is viewed as self-destruction turned outward against substitute objects. Some neo-Freudians view aggression as one of the principal causes of prejudice. For these investigators, aggression results when aggressive impulses, suppressed during childhood and adolescence, become displaced onto minority groups later in life. Some psychoanalysts feel that aggression can be explained by the frustration–aggression hypothesis. These investigators believe that frustration creates the readiness in the individual for aggressive acts. Then, environmental stimuli play a key role in eliciting the aggressive behavior.

The second group of theorists seeks to explain aggression in light of ethological principles. Chief among these researchers is Konrad Lorenz, who holds that aggression is instinctive and that it helps individuals to survive by enabling adults to protect the young and to safeguard their territory. Finally, the social learning theorists believe that aggression is learned behavior. People learn aggression chiefly by observing and imitating the behavior of others.

Aggression is a social problem because aggressive acts hurt other people. One form of aggression, civil disorder in the urban ghetto, is seen as a protest by blacks against racism. The graffiti on trains and buildings in New York City has been interpreted as an example of an attempt by city inhabitants to humanize harsh and ugly surroundings.

People come together through three processes: affiliation, attraction, and altruism. Anxiety, birth order, fear reduction, and social comparison are four factors that influence affiliation. There are a number of reasons why people are attracted to, and like, each other. One of these is proximity—people who live close together are more likely to be attracted to one another than are people who live far apart. Another factor is similarity: individuals like others who have similar attitudes and values. Not surprisingly, physical beauty is a third important determinant of attraction. People also come together to help one another. Individuals will not help others in an emergency if there are other people present because the operation of two factors—social influence and the diffusion of responsibility—may prevent them from doing so.

Power is a motive which is defined as the exercise of coercive control in a situation of conflicting interests between two or more parties. Forms of coercion vary—from the use of physical force to control through a monopoly of information. The most general form of power is control of economic resources because it can be converted to military power, information control, and political influence.

Some theorists hold that individuals who wield power do not move into power positions at random; rather, those who are power-oriented are selected or select themselves for such roles. However, the power-motive hypothesis fails to explain why some people seek power. One study, for example, showed that politicians derived satisfaction not from their power over others, but from working with like-minded colleagues, from engaging in useful activity, and from working for what they believed in.

Bibliography

ADORNO, T. W., FRENKEL-BRUNSWIK, E., LEVINSON, D. J., AND SANFORD, R. N. *The authoritarian personality.* New York: Harper, 1950.

ALLEN, V. Toward understanding riots: Some perspectives. *Journal of Social Issues,* Winter 1970, **26**(1), 1–18.

ALMOND, G. A., AND VERBA, S. *The civic culture.* Boston: Little, Brown, 1965.

ANDREWS, J. D. W. The achievement motive and advancement in two types of organizations. *Journal of Personality and Social Psychology,* 1967, **6**, 163–169.

ALVAREZ, A. *The savage god: A study of suicide.* London: Weidenfeld and Nicolson, 1971.

BANDURA, A. Influence of model's reinforcement contingencies on the acquisition of imitative responses. *Journal of Personality and Social Psychology,* 1965, **1**, 589–595.

BANDURA, A. ROSS, D., AND ROSS, S. A. Transmission of aggression through imitation of aggressive models. *Journal of Abnormal and Social Psychology,* 1961, **63**, 575–582.

BANDURA, A., ROSS, D., AND ROSS, S. A. A comparative test of status envy, social power, and secondary reinforcement theories of identificatory learning. *Journal of Abnormal and Social Psychology,* 1963, **67**, 527–534.

BANDURA, A., AND WALTERS, R. *Social learning and personality development.* New York: Holt, Rinehart and Winston, 1963.

BARD, M. A model for action research. In D. Adelson (Ed.), *Man as the measure: The crossroads.* New York: Behavioral Publications, 1972.

BARD, M., AND BERKOWITZ, B. Training police as specialists in family crisis intervention: A community psychology action program. *Community Mental Health Journal,* 1967, **3**, 315–317.

BARKER, R. G., DEMBO, T., AND LEWIN, K. Frustration and regression: A study of young children. *University of Iowa Studies in Child Welfare,* 1941, **18**(1).

BECKER, S. W., AND CARROLL, J. Ordinal position and conformity. *Journal of Abnormal and Social Psychology,* 1962, **65**, 129–131.

BERKOWITZ, L. Control of aggression. In P. M. Caldwell and H. Ricciuti (Eds.), *Review of child development.* Vol. 3. New York: Russell Sage, 1969. (a)

BERKOWITZ, L. *Roots of aggression.* New York: Atherton, 1969. (b)

BERKOWITZ, W. R., NEBEL, J. C., AND REITMAN, J. W. Height and interpersonal attraction: The 1969 mayoral election in New York City. *Proceedings of the 79th Annual Convention of the American Psychological Association,* 1971, **6**, 281–282.

BERSCHEID, E., AND WALSTER, E. H. *Interpersonal attraction.* Reading, Mass.: Addison-Wesley, 1969.

BOSSARD, J. H. S. Residential propinquity as a factor in mate selection. *American Journal of Sociology,* 1932, **38**, 219–224.

BROWN, N. O. *Life against death: The psychoanalytic meaning of history.* New York: Random House, Vintage Books, 1959.

BROWN, N. O. *Love's body.* New York: Random House, Vintage Books, 1968.

BROWN, R. *Social psychology.* New York: Free Press, 1965.

BRYAN, J. H., AND TEST, M. A. Models and helping: Naturalistic studies in aiding behavior. *Journal of Personality and Social Psychology*, 1967, **6**, 400–407.

BUSS, A. *The psychology of aggression.* New York: John Wiley, 1961.

BYRNE, D. Interpersonal attraction and attitude similarity. *Journal of Abnormal and Social Psychology*, 1961, **62**, 713–715.

BYRNE, D., ERVIN, C. R., AND LAMBRETH, J. Continuity between the experimental study of attraction and real-life computer dating. *Journal of Personality and Social Psychology*, 1970, **16**, 157–165.

BYRNE, D., AND NELSON, D. Attraction as a linear function of proportion of positive reinforcements. *Journal of Personality and Social Psychology*, 1965, **1**, 659–663.

CAPLAN, N. The new ghetto man: A review of recent empirical strides. *Journal of Social Issues*, Winter 1970, **26**(1), 59–74.

CHRISTIE, R., AND COOK, P. A guide to the published literature relating to the authoritarian personality, through 1956. *Journal of Psychology*, 1958, **45**, 171–199.

DION, K. K. Physical attractiveness and evaluation of children's transgressions. *Journal of Personality and Social Psychology*, 1972, **24**, 207–213.

DION, K. K., AND BERSCHEID, E. Physical attraction and peer perception among children. *Sociometry*, 1974, **37**, 1–12.

DOLLARD, J., DOOB, L. W., MILLER, N. E., MOWRER, O. H., AND SEARS, R. R. *Frustration and aggression.* New Haven, Conn.: Yale University Press, 1939.

DOWNES, B. T. Social and political characteristics of riot cities: A comparative study. *Social Science Quarterly*, 1968, **49**, 504–520.

ELDER, G. Appearance and education in marriage mobility. *American Sociological Review*, 1969, **34**, 519–533.

ELDERSVELD, S. J. *Political parties.* Chicago: Rand McNally, 1964.

FESHBACH, S., AND SINGER, R. D. *Television and aggression.* San Francisco: Jossey-Bass, 1970.

FESTINGER, L., SCHACHTER, S., AND BACK, K. *Social pressures in informal groups: A study of human factors in housing.* New York: Harper, 1950.

FOA, U. G. Convergences in the analysis of the structure of interpersonal behavior. *Psychological Review*, 1961, **69**, 341–353.

FREUD, S. *Beyond the pleasure principle.* (First published in 1920.) New York: W. W. Norton, 1975.

FRIED, M. Grieving for a lost home. In L. Duhl (Ed.), *The urban condition.* New York: Basic Books, 1963.

FRIEDMAN, S. Relationships among cognitive complexity, interpersonal dimensions and spatial preferences and propensities. (Doctoral dissertation, University of California) Ann Arbor, Mich.: University Microfilms, 1969.

FRIEDMAN, S., AND JUHASZ, J. *Environments: Notes and selections on objects, spaces and behavior.* Monterey, Calif.: Brooks/Cole, 1974.

FRIEDMAN, S., AND THOMPSON, S. Color, competence and cognition: Notes toward a psychology of environmental color. In T. Porter and B. Mihellides (Eds.), *Color for architecture.* New York: Van Nostrand Reinhold, 1976.

HALL, C. S., AND LINDZEY, G. *Theories of personality.* New York: Wiley, 1957.

HARTMANN, H., KRIS, E., AND LOWENSTEIN, R. N. Notes on a theory of aggression. *Psychoanalytic Study of the Child*, 1949, **3–4**, 9–36.

HORNER, M. Fail: Bright women. *Psychology Today*, 1969, **3**, 36–38.

HOVLAND, C. I., AND SEARS, R. R. Minor studies in aggression: VI. Correlation of lynchings with economic indices. *Journal of Psychology*, 1940, **9**, 301–310.

HUSTON, T. Ambiguity of acceptance, social desirability and dating choice. *Journal of Experimental Social Psychology*, 1973, **9**, 32–42.

HYMAN, H. H., AND SHEATSLEY, P. B. "The authoritarian personality": A methodological critique. In R. Christie and M. Jahoda (Eds.), *Studies in the scope and method of "The authoritarian personality."* New York: Free Press, 1954.

JOHNSON, R. *Aggression in man and animals.* Philadelphia: Saunders, 1972.

KAUFMANN, H. *Aggression and altruism.* New York: Holt, Rinehart and Winston, 1970.

KENISTON, K. The other side of the Oedipus complex. *Radical Therapist*, 1970, **1**(1), 6–7.

KIPNIS, D. Does power corrupt? *Journal of Personality and Social Psychology*, 1972, **24**, 33–41. (a)

KIPNIS, D. Interaction between members of bomber crews as a determinant of sociometric choice. *Human Relations*, 1972, **10**, 263–270. (b)

KOLKO, G. *Roots of American foreign policy.* Boston: Beacon Press, 1969.

KORDA, M. *Power! How to get it, how to use it.* New York: Ballantine, 1975.

KUPER, L. *Living in towns.* London: Cresset Press, 1953.

LANDY, D., AND SIGALL, H. Beauty is talent: Task evaluation as a function of the performer's physical attractiveness. *Journal of Personality and Social Psychology*, 1974, **29**, 299–304.

LATANÉ, B., AND DARLEY, J. M. *The unresponsive bystander: Why doesn't he help?* New York: Appleton-Century-Crofts, 1970.

LORENZ, K. *On aggression.* New York: Harcourt Brace Jovanovich, 1966.

MANN, R. D. A review of the relationships between personality and performance in small groups. *Psychological Bulletin*, 1959, **56**, 241–270.

MARX, G. T. Civil disorder and the agents of social control. *Journal of Social Issues*, Winter 1970, **26**(1), 19–58.

MILGRAM, S. Some conditions of obedience and disobedience to authority. *Human Relations*, 1965, **18**, 57–76.

MILLER, N. The frustration–aggression hypothesis. *Psychological Review*, 1941, **48**, 337–342.

MONTAGUE, A. *Man and aggression.* London: Oxford University Press, 1968.

NATIONAL ADVISORY COMMISSION ON CIVIL DISORDERS. *Report of the National Advisory Commission on Civil Disorders.* New York: Bantam Books, 1968.

NEWMAN, O. *Defensible space.* New York: Macmillan, 1972.

PILIAVIN, I. M., RODIN, J., AND PILIAVIN, J. A. Good Samaritanism: An underground phenomenon? *Journal of Personality and Social Psychology*, 1969, **13**, 289–299.

PRESTHUS, R. *The organizational society.* New York: Alfred A. Knopf, 1962.

ROKEACH, M. *Beliefs, attitudes and values.* San Francisco: Jossey-Bass, 1968.

RUDIN, S. A. The personal price of national glory. *Trans-action*, 1965, **2**(5), 4–9.

RYAN, W. *Blaming the victim.* New York: Pantheon, 1971.

SAMPSON, E. E. Birth order, need achievement and conformity. *Journal of Abnormal and Social Psychology,* 1962, **64,** 155–159.

SAMPSON, E. E. The study of ordinal position: Antecedents and outcomes. In B. Maher (Ed.), *Progress in experimental personality research.* Vol. 2. New York: Academic Press, 1965.

SARNOFF, I., AND ZIMBARDO, P. G. Anxiety, fear, and social affiliation. *Journal of Abnormal and Social Psychology,* 1961, **62,** 356–363.

SARTRE, J.-P. *Anti-Semite and Jew.* (First published in 1946.) New York: Schocken Books, 1948.

SCHACHTER, S. *The psychology of affiliation.* Stanford, Calif.: Stanford University Press, 1959.

SCHUTZ, W. C. *FIRO: A three-dimensional theory of interpersonal behavior.* New York: Holt, Rinehart and Winston, 1958.

SCOTT, J. P. *Aggression.* Chicago: University of Chicago Press, 1958.

SEARS, D. O., AND MCCONAHAY, J. B. Racial socialization, comparison levels, and the Watts riots. *Journal of Social Issues,* Winter 1970, **26**(1), 121–140.

SEARS, R. R., MACCOBY, E., AND LEVIN, H. *Patterns in child rearing.* Evanston, Ill.: Row, Peterson, 1957.

SIGALL, H., AND LANDY, D. Radiating beauty: Effects of having a physically attractive partner on person perception. *Journal of Personality and Social Psychology,* 1973, **28,** 218–224.

SOMMER, R. *Tight spaces: Hard architecture and how to use it.* Englewood Cliffs, N.J.: Prentice-Hall, 1974.

STEIN, D. D., HARDYCK, J., AND SMITH, M. B. Race and belief: An open-and-shut case. *Journal of Personality and Social Psychology,* 1965, **1,** 281–290.

STRACHEY, A. *The unconscious motives of war.* London: George Allen and Unwin, 1957.

THIBAUT, J. W., AND KELLEY, H. H. *The social psychology of groups.* New York: John Wiley, 1959.

VALEN, H., AND KATZ, D. *Political parties in Norway.* London: Tavistock Publications, 1964.

VEROFF, J. Development and validation of a projective measure of power motivation. *Journal of Abnormal and Social Psychology,* 1957, **54,** 1–8.

VEROFF, J., ATKINSON, J. W., FELD, S., AND GURIN, G. The use of thematic apperception to assess motivation in a nationwide interview study. *Psychological Monographs,* 1960, **74** (12, Whole No. 449).

WALSTER, E., ARONSON, E., ABRAHAMS, D., AND ROTTMAN, L. Importance of physical attractiveness in dating behavior. *Journal of Personality and Social Psychology,* 1966, **4,** 508–516.

WALTERS, R., AND WILLOWS, D. Imitation of disturbed children following exposure to aggressive and non-aggressive models. *Child Development,* 1968, **39.**

WEBBER, M. Order in diversity: Community without propinquity. In L. Wingor (Ed.), *Cities and space.* Baltimore: Johns Hopkins University Press, 1963.

WINTER, D. G. *The power motive.* New York: Free Press, 1973.

YOUNG, M., AND WILLMOTT, P. *Family and kinship in East London.* New York: Humanities Press, 1957.

12

Stress

Allen's parents have finally decided to divorce after several years of struggling to hold their faltering marriage together. Since he is only ten, he doesn't understand why his parents can't live together anymore. Yesterday his father moved out of the house, taking the stereo, most of Allen's favorite records, and the dining room furniture with him.

The midterm exam schedule was posted this afternoon, and Elizabeth has just discovered that she has all of her exams in the first week. Three of her exams are on the same day. She has two term papers to write and 500 pages of poli-sci reading to finish before exams start.

Bill has just been promoted after only six months in his present position as manager of the computer division of a large automobile plant. He is being transferred to the main office to take charge of nationwide computer operations. His co-workers are delighted for him, but he has to go home and tell his wife and kids that they'll be packing up to move again.

David's mother is dying. Six months ago she had a radical mastectomy after she discovered a lump in her right breast. At first the surgeon thought he had successfully arrested the growth of her cancer, but later the disease was found in several other sites in her body. David visits his mother in the hospital every day, but he is finding it harder and harder to see her without crying.

431

Each of these people is suffering from what social psychologists call *stress*. Stress has been defined as "the failure of routine methods for managing threats" (Gross, 1970), a description that points out one of the many complicating factors in stress research. The experience of stress is a very personal matter. Each person has developed his or her own characteristic ways of handling threats, his or her own routines for getting through life successfully, and it is the breakdown of these individual patterns of coping with threat that produces stress in that person.

In addition, what is threatening for one person may not be threatening for another. Thus, a student who has completed all of her papers and reading and who is planning to begin an extended vacation as soon as her exams are finished might respond quite differently to Elizabeth's exam schedule. At the same time, there are events, such as the death of a close family member, that are threatening to almost every individual. It is difficult to imagine anyone who would not be stressed by David's situation.

These personal responses are also complex, involving an interweaving of biological, psychological, and social factors. In a comprehensive model of the variables included in stress research, one study (House, 1974) proposes five groups of variables: the objective social conditions that may precipitate the stress; the perception of the stress by the person who is threatened; the biological, emotional, and behavioral reactions of that person to the perceived stress; the long-range outcomes for the stressed person that result from his perception of, and reaction to the stress; and the personal and situational conditions that determine the relationship among the first four variables.

In the case of little Allen and his estranged parents, for example, the precipitating social condition is the divorce and his resulting separation from his father. His perception of that event as confusing and threatening may cause a whole range of stressful reactions in the boy: he may become sad and withdrawn, or, conversely, he may become angry and misbehave as spectacularly as he can. He may suffer physiological reactions such as vomiting, asthma, or headaches. His long-range reaction to the divorce might include poor performance in school and difficulty in relating to one or both of his parents; on the other hand, the divorce might enable him to get along better with his parents, especially if their separation is positive for them. All of these reactions will be influenced by conditioning variables: his previous experience with divorce in other families, his early childhood relationships with his parents, his characteristic ways of coping with problems, and so on.

It is commonly recognized that stress can be harmful and that the effects of stress may be seen in physical and emotional reactions. Many people believe, for example, that worry can quite literally make you sick. Among our descriptive terms for the psychological effects of stress is the term "uptight," which

RANK	LIFE EVENT	MEAN VALUE
1	Death of spouse	100
2	Divorce	73
3	Marital separation	65
4	Jail term	63
5	Death of close family member	63
6	Personal injury or illness	53
7	Marriage	50
8	Fired at work	47
9	Marital reconciliation	45
10	Retirement	45
11	Change in health of family member	44
12	Pregnancy	40
13	Sex difficulties	39
14	Gain of new family member	39
15	Business readjustment	39
16	Change in financial state	38
17	Death of close friend	37
18	Change to different line of work	36
19	Change in number of arguments with spouse	35
20	Mortgage over $10,000	31
21	Foreclosure of mortgage or loan	30
22	Change in responsibilities at work	29
23	Son or daughter leaving home	29
24	Trouble with in-laws	29
25	Outstanding personal achievement	28
26	Wife begin or stop work	26
27	Begin or end school	26
28	Change in living conditions	25
29	Revision of personal habits	24
30	Trouble with boss	23
31	Change in work hours or conditions	20
32	Change in residence	20
33	Change in schools	20
34	Change in recreation	19
35	Change in church activities	19
36	Change in social activities	18
37	Mortgage or loan less than $10,000	17
38	Change in sleeping habits	16
39	Change in number of family get-togethers	15
40	Change in eating habits	15
41	Vacation	13
42	Christmas	12
43	Minor violations of the law	11

Figure 12–1. Social Readjustment Rating Scale ranks life events in descending order; highest values require greatest adaptation and are most likely to trigger disease.

SOURCE: Solomon, J. The price of change. *The Sciences,* November 1971, **11**(9), 29.

conveys a strong graphic image of the emotionally threatened person. This cause-and-effect relationship between stress and its negative effects is recognized in such colloquial expressions as "Take it easy" and "Roll with the punches." The sense of these expressions encompasses a kind of folk wisdom about stress. They acknowledge that stress is a part of life, that stress can be harmful, and they offer a solution: a good way to handle stress is not to take a stressful situation too seriously, to be flexible.

At the same time, it is sometimes impossible to be relaxed about the effects of stressful events in our lives. Indeed, the whole notion of stress includes the demand for coping in a situation in which we feel we cannot cope. Stress is related to change—the routines that no longer work—and change is a part of everyone's life. Research has shown that significant changes in a person's life—beginning a new job or being fired from the old one, falling in or out of love, getting your degree or flunking out of school—require social adjustment and will be physically and emotionally stressful. The number and magnitude of such changes in a person's life in a given period of time have been correlated with his or her susceptibility to accident and to physical and emotional disorders (Solomon, 1971). There are, then, times in your life when you cannot take it easy, and you are more likely to suffer physical and/or emotional difficulties during those times (see Figure 12–1).

Stress and Coronary Heart Disease

One of the most comprehensive and interesting examples of research in the relationships between stress and physical disorder can be found in studies of coronary heart disease and stress. Coronary heart disease (commonly called "heart attack") is the leading cause of death among Americans. It is responsible for about one-third of all deaths annually (Moriyama et al., 1971). Men between the ages of 35 and 65 are particularly likely to suffer from the disease, and their personal loss is compounded by its effects on their families. Add to this the economic loss sustained when a substantial portion of the most productive working force is stricken; the estimated costs are enormous (Felton and Cole, 1963). It is small wonder, then, that in the past two decades medical researchers and social psychologists have focused on the reasons for the high incidence of the disease.

Who are the victims of coronary heart disease? Its distribution cannot be accounted for by referring to broad demographic variables or standard socioeconomic indicators (Marks, 1967). The risk for men is much greater than for women, but this relationship is complicated by the effects of race and social status. Women who are black or of lower social class have a significantly higher risk of death from heart attack than do white women and women of higher social class (House, 1974). Moreover, since 1950 the rate of coronary heart disease among men has leveled off, or even declined, while that of women is increasing. Thus, we must rule out explanations based solely on the biologic makeup of men and women, such as differences in their hormones.

Correlations between occupational groupings and heart attack rates have been drawn in many studies (House, 1974). An analysis of deaths occurring in 1950 among American men, tabulated separately by occupational group and by cause of death (National Center for Health Statistics, 1963), showed wide differences between groups in the mortality rate for coronary heart disease. Physicians and surgeons, for example, had, as a group, a disproportionate number of deaths from coronary heart disease. Medical technicians, on the other hand, did not show a high incidence of heart attack deaths. Cabinetmakers had a significantly higher mortality rate for coronary heart disease, but carpenters did not. Disproportionate numbers of heart attack deaths were found among locomotive engineers, lawyers, judges, cab drivers, and power station operators, but not among railroad brakemen, clergymen, truck drivers, or power linemen. These examples illustrate a striking feature of the current heart attack epidemic: not only do heart attacks occur selectively within the population, but we cannot rely on such variables as income or availability of health care in predicting the distribution of the disease among demographic groups, as we often can with other diseases.

Heart attack and occupational stress

The characteristic occupations of those with a high risk of heart attack offer some clues about job-related stress. Many studies suggest that the jobs of high-risk people generally entail a high degree of responsibility for others, comparatively high work overloads, and role conflicts, among other stresses (cf. Jenkins, 1971a). The impact of a person's occupational life has also been measured in terms of individual attitudes, such as job dissatisfaction (House, 1974), and ratings of job tediousness and job difficulties (Jenkins, 1971b). These stresses correlate with coronary heart disease, independent of specific occupational categories.

The differences in the pattern of heart attack incidence between men and women has also been explained in terms of *occupational stress* (House, 1974). Black and lower-class women are more likely than white middle-class women to suffer from work stresses, and the increase in employment among women over the past decade parallels increases in heart attack rates among women. Apparently it is the stressful situation, rather than the sex, of the victim that matters.

Studies linking stress on the job with a greater risk of coronary heart disease have been so numerous that it has become commonplace to assume that certain aspects of corporate working life, for example, will inevitably increase a person's risk of having a heart attack. Among the stresses often cited are rapid promotion, a large number of transfers from one geographic location to another, and a high level of corporate responsibility. But the correlation between these factors and a greater incidence of heart disease has been disputed in at least one study (Hinkle et al., 1968). Two hundred seventy thousand men employed by the Bell Systems Operating Company in the United States were followed in this longitudinal study of workers in a typical large corporation. No significant relationship was found between job mobility and increased heart attack risk, or between such risk and heavy responsibility on the job. These results suggest that the factors that increase the risk of coronary heart disease are already in existence before adult life and are not greatly influenced by stressful experiences on the job.

The psychology of heart disease

Groups, of course, do not have heart attacks; individuals do. What impact do stressful life situations have on individual behavior and physiology? And, conversely, what predispositions in behavior and biology will mediate the individual's stress response? Questions about the cause of coronary heart disease and the psychosocial forces that influence its development have also been studied on an individual level.

Today, as more women enter the upper echelons of corporate management, they become just as prone to heart attacks as their male counterparts.

A whole complex of physiological and behavioral characteristics of the heart attack-prone individual has been identified. Important among these are *precursor conditions*, including hypertension, heavy smoking, and high levels of cholesterol and other fats in the blood. These characteristics, along with a family history of cardiovascular disease, rather consistently predispose individuals to develop coronary heart disease (Dawber and Kennel, 1961). The exact mechanisms by which hypertension, smoking, and high blood cholesterol ultimately contribute to the risk of heart attack are still being worked out on the physiological level. The accumulation of fatty deposits in arterial walls (atherosclerosis) is seen as a fundamental process in the development of the disease.

What is the connection between these precursors of heart disease and social and occupational stress? One fascinating relationship has been discovered: the same kinds of stress linked in group studies with increased incidence of heart attack risk have been found, on the individual level, to elevate levels of blood cholesterol (Friedman et al., 1958), to raise blood pressure (Cochrane, 1971), and to cause people to smoke more. One group of studies related the physiological symptoms of stress to particular stressful periods in the lives of tax accountants and medical students (House, 1974). Marked increases in blood cholesterol were found in the accountants as the April 15 deadline for filing federal tax returns approached, and significantly higher levels of cholesterol were found in the students on the day before their examinations. These studies suggest that increased work load under the pressure of a deadline may account for the physiological changes found.

Apparently it is the combination of certain precursor conditions with certain individual behavior patterns and life experiences that produces a person's vulnerability to stress. The most-studied and perhaps best-documented behavior pattern is the *Type A* pattern described by Rosenman and his colleagues (1966). The heart attack-prone Type A individual is described as excessively driven, ambitious and aggressive, preoccupied with competition and vocational deadlines, and distinguished by an aggravated sense of time urgency. One of the most telling means of identifying a fully developed Type A individual is that he invariably reports that he is unable to relax and that he feels guilty if he takes a few days, or even a few hours, off from work. Opposed to this is the *Type B* individual who lacks these coronary-prone characteristics.

Large-scale longitudinal studies have established the usefulness of the Type A behavior pattern as a predictor of coronary heart disease. Other investigations (e.g. Jenkins, 1971b) have indicated that long-term anxiety and depression, family conflict, deeply felt losses, and instability in interpersonal relationships may also characterize the heart attack-prone individual.

The social psychology of heart disease

David Glass (1977) has been engaged in an extensive program that is exploring the relationship between stress, Type A behavior, and coronary disease. In one series of experiments, Glass and his associates set out to document three of the alleged characteristics of the Type A behavior pattern: competitive achievement-striving, a sense of urgency, and hostility and aggression.

In examining the competitive aspect of Type A behavior, for example, Burnam, Pennebaker, and Glass (1973) found that college-age Type A individuals attempted more complex arithmetic problems than did Type B individuals in a test in which all subjects were told that there was no time limit for completion of the test. However, when the arithmetic test was administered with a five-minute deadline, there were essentially no differences between Type A individuals and Type B individuals. This discrepancy between the two conditions was due largely to the increased performance of the Type B subjects, since Type A subjects worked at about the same level irrespective of the presence or absence of a deadline.

In another study investigating the competitive aspect, Carver, Coleman, and Glass (1976) devised an experiment which predicted that Type A individuals might suppress feelings of fatigue to a greater degree than Type B individuals and persist at a tiring but challenging task, in order to master it. The task chosen to test this hypothesis was designed to produce feelings of fatigue—subjects were required to walk continuously on a motorized treadmill.

The results bore out the prediction: the Type A subjects worked at a level closer to the limits of their endurance, even expressing less overall fatigue than Type B subjects. The tendency toward fatigue suppression—or at least public denial of fatigue—may be understood in terms of the achievement-oriented character of the Type A individual. Thus, denial of fatigue has value for Type A subjects because it aids in their struggle to attain their goals—in this case superior treadmill performance. The acknowledgment of fatigue, on the other hand, might interfere with mastering the task—a situation which Type A subjects could not easily tolerate.

In the experiment that tested the sense of time urgency in Type A and Type B subjects, Glass, Snyder, and Hollis (1974) predicted that Type A individuals would become impatient with delay and judge a time interval of one minute to have elapsed sooner than would Type B individuals. Again, the expectation was fulfilled: Glass and his associates found that Type A subjects did more poorly than Type B subjects on tasks requiring a delayed response—they responded prematurely on many trials, which necessitated beginning the trial over again.

In testing the third major facet of the Type A behavior pattern—hostility and aggression—Glass (1977) examined the hypothesis that, relative to Type B subjects, Type A subjects would react with aggressiveness toward another person who impeded and denigrated their efforts to perform a difficult task. To test this hypothesis, Glass divided his subjects into two groups, placing them in one of two situations: the "instigator condition" or the "no-instigator condition." In the first condition, Type A individuals and Type B individuals were exposed to a confederate of the experimenter who harassed them in their efforts to solve a difficult perceptual–motor task. These subjects were then given the opportunity to administer ostensible electric shocks to the confederate.

In the "no-instigator" condition, Type A subjects and Type B subjects participated only in the shock phase of the study. The results showed that in the instigator condition, the Type A subjects expressed a substantial amount of aggression, whereas the Type B subjects expressed little or no aggression. In the no-instigator condition, by contrast, there were virtually no differences between Type A and Type B subjects in the amount of shock delivered to the confederate. It would thus appear that Type A subjects are not uniformly more aggressive than Type B subjects; they become so in response to arousing circumstances.

In summary, then, Glass and his associates provided experimental evidence that, in contrast to Type B individuals, Type A individuals work to succeed; suppress subjective states (fatigue, for example) that might interfere with task performance; exhibit rapid pacing of their activities; and express hostility after being harassed in their efforts at task completion—all, Glass and his associates

Fatigue Ratings for Four Trials on Treadmill Test

Subject classification	Fourth to last rating	Third to last rating	Second to last rating	Last rating
Type A	5.30	4.10	3.10	2.20
Type B	3.40	2.80	2.20	1.50

Figure 12–2. When walking continuously on a treadmill, Type A individuals suppressed feelings of fatigue to a greater degree than Type B people. (A smaller number indicates greater fatigue.) For each of the four trials, Type A subjects consistently expressed less overall fatigue than Type B subjects.

SOURCE: Adapted from Carver, C. S., Coleman, A. E., and Glass, D. C. The coronary-prone behavior pattern and the suppression of fatigue on a treadmill test. *Journal of Personality and Social Psychology*, 1976, **33**, 464.

say, in the interests of asserting control over environmental demands and requirements. Glass and his colleagues also suggest that these demands must be at least minimally stressful, for the possibility of failure was inherent in most of the experimental situations used in the studies. The coronary-prone (Type A) behavior pattern might thus be described as a style of responding to environmental stressors that threaten the individual's sense of control. Type A individuals are engaged in a struggle for control, whereas Type B individuals are relatively free of such concerns, and hence, free of characteristic Type A responses.

Glass went on to study the sense of control and defined the concept of controllability as involving the subject's perception that his response will get him what he wants. In contrast, uncontrollability is that which results when an individual perceives that his responses cannot determine what he gets. An *uncontrollable stressor*, then, is a potentially harmful stimulus which the individual can neither avoid nor escape. A *controllable stressor* is a harmful stimulus which can be avoided.

Glass explored the relationship between the Type A behavior pattern and uncontrollable stress in an experiment with Krantz (Glass, 1977). These investigators predicted that Type A individuals will try harder than Type B individuals to master an experimental task administered after a few trials of inescapable noise stimulation. Having been exposed to a brief experience with uncontrollable stress, Type A individuals, the investigators believed, would exert greater efforts to reestablish a sense of mastery and control on a subsequent task. The results of this study showed that the performance of Type A individuals was better than that of Type B individuals after exposure to uncontrollable stress. Thus, says Glass, Type A behavior arises under a special condition—perceived threat to the individual's control over the environment. Apparently, Type A behavior is a strategy for coping with uncontrollable stress: enhanced performance reflects an attempt to assert and maintain control after its loss has been threatened.

In a related experiment, Krantz, Glass, and Snyder (1974) examined the relationship between helplessness, stress level, and the Type A behavior pattern. *Helplessness* is defined by Glass as the state of mind of subjects who are exposed to uncontrollable stress and learn that their responses have no effect. Such learning causes the individual to give up efforts at control and to exhibit helplessness. In such a situation, all individuals experience some degree of helplessness. However, Glass and his colleagues found that in uncontrollable stress situations, Type A people tend to experience greater feelings of helplessness than others because of their tendency to perceive loss of control as more threatening to them. Moreover, they had greater difficulty learning how to avoid subsequent uncontrollable stress situations than did Type B subjects.

How are these findings related to situations outside the laboratory, specifically to coronary heart disease? Glass suggests that the Type A, or coronary-prone, behavior pattern may be the predisposing condition in the relationship between helplessness and coronary heart disease. As we saw in the studies above, a Type A individual who is continuously exposed to uncontrollable stress experiences a high degree of helplessness. It may be, says Glass, that the combination of the Type A behavior pattern with some life event, such as the death of a spouse, divorce, or imprisonment (see Figure 12–1), that is perceived as uncontrollable stress, may be the precursor of coronary heart disease.

Glass tested this hypothesis by examining patients at the Veterans' Administration Hospital in Houston, Texas. Three classes of individuals were compared in terms of their behavior patterns (Type A or Type B), as well as their recall of life events prior to disease onset. The subjects were 45 patients in the coronary care unit; 77 patients in the general medical and psychiatric wards—the hospitalized control group; and 50 building maintenance employees—the healthy unhospitalized control group. Results showed that coronary patients were more apt to exhibit the Type A behavior pattern than either of the other two groups. Furthermore, relative to the healthy control group, a higher percentage of both patient groups (coronaries and hospitalized noncoronaries) had experienced at least one serious life event in the year prior to their hospitalization.

Thus, concludes Glass, individuals with illness appear to have more helplessness-inducing life events than healthy individuals. And since coronary patients are more likely than hospitalized or nonhospitalized controls to have Pattern A behavior, then coronary heart disease seems more likely among Type A individuals than among Type B. However, these findings are only preliminary; more research is needed to corroborate them. Some of the same relationships, such as control over stress-inducing stimuli rather than helplessness in the face of such stimuli, will appear in other aspects of social psychological research on stress. Before examining this body of work we must decide what we mean by the term stress.

Stress

The term *stress* is commonly used in ordinary conversation to refer to all sorts of difficulties: the popular notion of stress seems to be rather vague and intuitive—it is something that everyone feels from time to time, a problem that can be recognized from experience and need not be defined in precise terms. The working definition of stress offered at the beginning of this chapter is only one of many conceptualizations proposed by various studies: there is no agreement among researchers about the best scientifically useful definition (House, 1974). Stress has been identified with a variety of feelings and reactions: anxiety, intense emotional, physiological arousal, and frustration. While stress may involve any or all of these things, it is possible to set stress apart as a concept in its own right, as something different from any of them. Stress is a broader concept. It may be brought on by a wide range of conditions—including conflict or frustration.

A state of stress, then, is composed of the threat, called a *stressor*, and a response which consists of a measurable alteration of the physiology and/or the behavior of an individual. In the beginning of the chapter the example was presented of the ten-year-old Allen whose parents are getting a divorce. However unlikely it might be that Allen is not under stress, we cannot say, scientifically, that stress is present until we can collect some evidence that Allen has responded physically or behaviorally to the divorce. At the moment of his father's departure, for example, he might show an increased heart rate, sweating, and nausea. Later he might report nightmares, wet his bed, or catch a cold more easily than usual.

Systemic stress and the GAS

Several types of stress have been described in the literature, the definitions of which are drawn either from events that produce stress or from the characteristic responses to stress. *Systemic stress* is the physiological reaction outlined by Selye (1956). In his research, Selye subjected rats to a whole range of stresses: fatigue was induced in a motor-driven cage; high noise levels were produced with an unremitting siren; frustration was created by tying the rats to a board; poison, injections of various substances, and cold were also used (Ratcliff, 1970). He found that each of these stresses produced the same physiological reaction, which he termed the *General Adaptive Syndrome* (GAS) (Levi, 1967). GAS occurs in three successive phases: the alarm reaction, the stage of resistance, and the exhaustion stage.

During the alarm reaction, the body's resistance is initially lowered before defensive responses go into operation. After a series of disturbances, signaling that the body is registering the stress, the endocrine glands, which are the body's prime stress reactors, go into action. The adrenal glands increase adrenalin production, and this hormone, along with impulses from the hypothalamus, stimulates an increase in the output of the pituitary gland. Hormones pour into the bloodstream; blood sugar soars, blood pressure rises, stomach acid increases, and arteries constrict as the body prepares for "fight or flight," the classic reaction to threat. The person experiencing GAS feels a faster heartbeat, shortness of breath, a dry mouth, and an outbreak of sweating. Such symptons of stress are particularly disadvantageous for actors, singers, and musicians who play wind instruments. Nervousness before a performance makes them short of breath and dry in the mouth, both of which states make it difficult for them to perform at the top of their capabilities.

In the second, or resistance, stage, these adaptations reach their optimal level and another wave of hormones is released to restore the body's balance: ACTH from the pituitary and cortisone from the adrenals. These hormones prevent the body from reacting so strongly that it hurts itself. But if the stressor continues to threaten the body, the third stage—exhaustion—eventually sets in. The adaptive responses collapse, and the organism is left vulnerable to injury, disease, or even death as the defensive system gradually wears down.

The end result of continuous stress in Selye's rats was always the same: they died after suffering from a whole range of diseases such as peptic ulcers, diabetes, arthritis, and coronary artery disease. Selye believes that an organism has only so much adaptive energy available in its lifetime; once it is expended through the GAS over time, there is no way to replace it (McQuade and Aikman, 1974). If a person lives under conditions of great stress—if she suffers from a boring, unrewarding job, or he is a fully developed Type A—his or her personal supply of adaptive energy may run out, and then the person will age fast and eventually die.

The stress reaction is assumed to be nonspecific; that is, a great number of different stressful conditions from environmental stressors, such as extreme heat and electric shock, to biological stressors, such as fasting or hemorrhaging, will produce the same physiological stress syndrome. Therefore, the formulation of systemic stress has served as the basis for extensions and generalizations of the stress concept in response to psychological and social stressors. The physiological reactions of arousal that characterize systemic stress also become evident when the stressor is purely cognitive or emotional (Levi, 1967). The GAS can be equally aroused by actual physical danger, symbolic danger, and even memories of past dangers.

Stressors

Stress may be caused by any unpleasant, painful, dangerous, embarrassing, or otherwise aversive event. Stressful stimuli range from extreme cold to sudden loss of love, from painful electric shock to a confrontation with an angry person. Two kinds of stressors have been distinguished: physical or environmental stressors, which confront the organism with physical danger of discomfort, and psychosocial stressors, which threaten a person's psychological integrity or well-being.

Physical stressors include such stimuli as high-intensity noise, electric shock, and extremes of temperature. Since these stimuli can be quantified, it is often possible to specify the parameters of physical stressors by measuring their intensity or their duration. However, as we shall see later, a person's response to even so unequivocal a stressor as painful electric shock can be drastically modified by his perception of the shock.

Threats to self-esteem, failure in an intellectual task, interaction with a hostile person, and frustration of personal goals are among the many events that have been used in studies of *psychosocial stress.* Other people may, in fact, be the causes of a stressful situation. A factor such as the social status of a person who creates stress for another may alter the other's response and adaptation. For example, in one study, Hokanson and Burgess (1962) varied the social status of the experimenter who created a stressful situation, to see what effects this would have on emotional and physical responses.

In one condition the experimenter was introduced as a new member of the faculty, a high-status position to the students who served as subjects; in the low-status condition, the same person was represented to the subjects as a student research assistant. During performance of the experimental tasks, the experimenter arbitrarily frustrated the subjects, either by not allowing them to complete the task or by denying them a promised cash award for efficient performance. The subjects were then given an anonymous questionnaire in which they were asked to rate the experimenter on the basis of his work with them. The researchers offered the questionnaire as an opportunity for the subjects to retaliate covertly against the experimenter for his treatment of them. Throughout the experiment, heart rate and systolic blood pressure measures were recorded for each subject. These physiological results showed a marked arousal effect due to the perceived status of the experimenter; interacting with a high-status experimenter was shown to be more arousing, and his high status apparently did not allow for the opportunity to retaliate against him, since there was no subsequent drop in arousal, as there was against the perceived low-status experimenter. This study demonstrates that "a person is an effective stimulus for autonomic response in the light of certain socially defined attributes with which he is endowed" (Shapiro and Crider, 1969).

The distinction between physical and psychosocial stressors admittedly applies only to those situations in which one or the other kind of stressor clearly predominates. When a person must endure pain in an experimental situation, she may be stressed not only by the threat to her bodily comfort and safety, but also by a threat to her self-esteem. She wants to avoid appearing cowardly or weak both to herself and to others, and this important goal may also be threatened by the situation. Often, both sources of stress arousal must be taken into consideration in order to account for the individual's experience and her response.

Stress Responses

A great variety of responses have been studied in relation to stress with two major objectives in mind: first, to obtain information about what is happening within the body (whether it is indeed experiencing stress), and second, to use this information to predict subsequent behavior (for instance, whether task performance will be impaired). These responses are classified in the first case as *psychophysiological* and in the second as *behavioral.* Psychophysiological responses, such as heart rate, blood pressure, and hormonal secretions in the blood or urine (the GAS responses), have most often been measured in order to discover the nature of the organism's *somatic* or bodily state. All sorts of behavioral responses are measured. Performance on verbal, motor, and perceptual tasks has been studied extensively in relation to stress, as have social interaction and emotional behavior. Self-reports of overall tension and mood are also included in the category of behavioral response, and have been employed as direct indicators of response to stress.

Psychophysiological measures

Psychophysiological responses include a great many somatic reactions. Some are sufficiently visible to fall almost within the category of behavior (blushing or muscular tremors, for example); others are so subtle that highly sophisticated equipment and techniques are needed to measure them. In most studies of stress the responses that are measured are caused by an excitation of the *sympathetic nervous system* and the closely allied *pituitary–adrenal endocrine system.* This sympathetic–adrenal system is responsible for such commonly observed stress reactions as increases in breathing rate, sweating of the palms, and dilation of the pupils, as well as less noticeable changes in heart rate, galvanic skin response (GSR), and blood chemistry. Some of these changes are extremely sensitive to social–psychological stimuli (Mason and Brady, 1964; Back and Bogdonoff, 1967).

The emotions and physiological response. Interest in physiological correlates of stress developed in large part from conflicting findings and theories about emotion. Some theorists (Cannon, 1936; Duffy, 1962) contend that emotional experience corresponds to a general state of arousal, characterized by excitation of the sympathetic nervous system, and that particular levels of diffuse arousal are associated with behavioral change. Accordingly, the level of physiological arousal has come to be widely used as an index of the emotional impact of a provocative situation. Schachter and Singer (1962) quote William James, who was among the first to make the connection between physical and emotional states: "Bodily changes follow directly the perception of the exciting fact, and our feeling of the same changes as they occur *is* the emotion."

Many researchers (Ax, 1953) have looked for specific patterns of physiological reactions in response to such emotional states as fear, anger, and anxiety. Schachter and Singer sought an explanation for the emotions which emphasized the thought processes (cognitions) of the physiologically aroused individual. Suppose, they hypothesized, an individual is in an aroused state for which he has no ready explanation: "He will 'label' this state and describe his feelings in terms of the cognitions available to him" (p. 381). If such were the case, the same state of physiological arousal could be labeled "joy" or "anger" or "love," depending on the cognitive aspects of the situation.

The researchers were able to demonstrate this proposition experimentally. By means of the drug epinephrine, they induced in their subjects an arousal of the sympathetic nervous system. One group of subjects was told exactly what effects to expect from the drug; another group was given a false explanation. All subjects were manipulated by a student confederate who pretended to be another subject. With half the subjects he doodled, threw paper balls into a wastebasket, flew paper airplanes, and twirled a hula hoop. Each subject was manipulated individually in the same fashion. The other half of the subjects was given an outrageous questionnaire designed to make them angry.

The results showed that those subjects who were not told about the effects of the drug, for the most part, felt themselves to be in the emotional state designed for them—either angry or euphoric. Those who were told about the effects of the drug were neither angry nor amused, depending on the manipulation; they had the available explanation of the knowledge of the drug effects to account for their physiological state of arousal. From these findings Schachter and Singer concluded that "cognitive factors appear to be indispensable elements in any formulation of emotion" (p. 398).

Stress is the same as emotion in terms of the physiological arousal involved. The difference lies in the cognitions of the aroused individual. If the sudden appearance of a lover causes an arousal of the sympathetic nervous system, an individual would probably label the internal state "love." The sudden appearance of a rattlesnake would be labeled "fear." Thus, it might be said that stress conforms to the emotional states of fear or anxiety as demonstrated in the above study, since the cognition involves a sense of threat to the well-being of the individual involved, our working definition of stress.

Stimulus-response stereotypy. The search for stimulus events which determine physiological response patterns has included other kinds of situations besides those classified as emotional. The term *situational-response,* or *stimulus-response, stereotypy* has been applied to the association of a particular kind of stimulus with a particular kind of response. Lacey, Kagan, Lacey, and Moss (1963) conducted a series of experiments in which subjects performed many different tasks; some of them might be considered stressful, such as a painful cold presser test in which the subject's arm was immersed in ice-cold water; others involved tasks in which stress was minimal, such as having the subject watch different-colored flashing lights. Heart rate and galvanic skin response (GSR) were among the physiological responses recorded. The greatest increases in GSR were produced by loud noises and cognitive tasks such as mental arithmetic. Heart-rate changes showed a different and consistent pattern among eight tasks: when subjects attended to external events, such as the task of tape-recording the rules of an imaginary card game, listening to loud noises, or watching flashing lights, their heart rates characteristically decreased; when internal, cognitive work was required, such as making up sentences or performing simple addition, or when there seemed to be some adaptive advantage to blocking out intense external stimuli, such as the painful cold of the cold presser test, heart rate generally increased.

These studies demonstrate that people do not always respond physiologically in just one characteristic pattern to stressful or arousing events; indeed, many typical ways of responding are to be expected, depending on a multitude of factors including the nature of the stressful task itself. Recent research has shown that these relationships are more complicated, and one could say more specific, than was first thought. The actual demands of a threatening environment on an individual may transcend the emotional arousal of the individual in determining the physiological response. And, conversely, emotional states and/or social factors in the situation may transcend the threat from the environment. Thus, psychophysiological measurements do not constitute a magical shortcut to the internal state of the organism. Psychophysiological measures must be read in the context of observations of behavioral responses in order to get a more complete picture of the organism's stress experience.

Behavioral measures

So far we have considered only those responses to stress which arise from the arousal of the sympathetic nervous system. Stress research has also focused on behavioral responses which are not only more overt but voluntary. Many social psychologists have used *task performance* as a measure of response to stress because it is convenient to measure and to manipulate.

How much stress can an organism endure and continue to perform essential tasks? One hypothesis concerning stress and task performance suggests that a curvilinear relation obtains between physiological arousal and task performance: that is, as arousal increases, task performance also improves, but after reaching an optimal level, performance efficiency levels off and then begins to decline with increased arousal (cf. Cofer and Appley, 1962). This function is often called the *inverted-U hypothesis*, because its graphic representation resembles the letter U turned upside down. Many students, for example, will do very well on an examination for which they are prepared if they are nervous and frightened enough to be in a state of physiological arousal; the mind and the body are both in a state of readiness to fight, so to speak. However, if they read the exam through and encounter some terms or questions they cannot deal with, they may become too frightened to write at a level consistent with their ability. The extra dose of fear causes their performance to drop off.

Task complexity is one of the more important variables in which the inverted-U hypothesis has been applied. Schlosberg and Stanley (1953) used GSR as a measure of activation level and reported a curvilinear relationship between activation and task efficiency. They found that the optimal GSR level for efficiency on a steadiness task was lower than that for a more complex reaction-time task. With both tasks, efficiency decreased when arousal levels were higher than the optimum. Easterbrook (1959) has suggested that the reason for such a relationship may have to do with the number of cues necessary to perform a task. Difficult tasks, which involve large numbers of cues, cannot be performed well under high arousal because attention to the cues is impaired. Easy tasks, by contrast, are performed more efficiently because high arousal narrows the range of available cues, and seems to facilitate performance. Since complex task performance deteriorates under high levels of arousal, experimenters have used task efficiency as a behavioral index of stress.

Cognitive factors in altering the perception of stress

Our habit of thinking and talking about the mind and the body as if they were two separate and distinct entities may lead us to assume that the physical responses of our bodies come from cues that are independent of our state of mind. Indeed, physical functions were once thought to be automatic, adaptive, and not particularly amenable to modification by cognitive processes. However, stressful stimuli do occur in a context of cognitive and social circumstances, as we have seen in Schachter and Singer's study of emotion. There may be unusual circumstances, such as the stress of the surgeon's knife on a totally anesthetized patient, but it is rare for a stimulus to have only a physical effect.

Integral to a person's response to stress is her evaluation of the stressor: how she perceives the threat, to what sources she attributes her feelings of being threatened, and what she sees as the best way to deal with the situation. It is not surprising, therefore, to find that cognitive factors influence responses to both physical and psychological stressors.

Davison and Valins (1969) were interested in a person's attributions of the causes of a change in his behavior. If, for example, a person behaves in a certain fashion, will he think and behave differently if he believes he is in complete control of his own behavior rather than that his behavior can be attributed to an outside source, such as a drug? We have seen in the Schachter and Singer experiment that if one's internal behavior is attributed to oneself, the behavior is different than if one knows that one's reactions are caused by a drug.

Davison and Valins turned the situation around. They told their subjects that they were being given a drug which would give them some immunity to severe shock, when, in fact, they had been given a placebo. They then retested the subject's ability to withstand increasing doses of shock. This second test was made to seem to the subject to be exactly the same as the first one. Actually the shocks were reduced by one-half, thereby allowing the subject to think he was withstanding far more severe shock while under the influence of the "drug."

In the next stage of the experiment, the experimental subjects were told that the drug was a placebo but were not told that they had received a schedule of shocks that was half as strong as the first time. (See Figure 12–3 for a summary of the design of this experiment.) In the third and final round of testing, the subjects who had been told that it was only a placebo that made them able to withstand shock the second time around and thought their improved performance was due to their own endurance rather than a drug were, in fact, able to withstand a greater amount of shock than they were the first time. The control group, on the other hand, did approximately the same on the first and third tests.

Despite the complications of the double deception involved in the design of this experiment, it demonstrates the importance of attribution of the cause of a given behavior; an improvement may become permanent if an individual is able to give credit for it to himself rather than having to attribute it to an outside source. Davison and Valins were interested in a particular application of this principle. They pointed to the use of tranquilizers in the care of patients being treated for mental illness, which makes it possible to release so many people from institutions. However, when the use of tranquilizers is stopped,

Summary of Experimental Design

Group	1	2	3	4
Placebo	Threshold	Threshold II (half the intensity) with pill	Disabuse: "It was a placebo"	Threshold III
Drug	same as above	same as above	No disabuse: "Now the drug has worn off"	same as above

Figure 12–3. 1. All subjects are tested for sensitivity to electric shock. 2. The experimental subjects are given a placebo; the control subjects, a drug. The second shock administered is half the intensity—the double deception. 3. The experimental subjects discover they have been given the placebo. 4. On the third round they are able to withstand more shock.

SOURCE: Adapted from Davison, G. C., and Valins, S. Maintenance of self-attributed and drug-attributed behavior change. *Journal of Personality and Social Psychology*, 1969, **11**(1), 27.

many patients revert to their former behavior. These researchers are suggesting that it might be possible to induce patients to maintain their improved, "tranquilized" behavior if they are led to believe they are using tranquilizers when, in fact, they have been taking sugar pills. Such might be the power of the mind over response to stress.

Cognitive factors in response to psychological stressors. The impact of psychological stressors, dependent as they are on perception and cognition for their threatening quality, can also be manipulated by cognitive means. Aversive or tension-arousing motion picture films are frequently used in research for inducing psychological stress (Lazarus, 1964; Goldstein et al., 1965). Lazarus and his colleagues (Speisman et al., 1964) have used a film entitled "Subincison," which shows crude surgical operations performed in the puberty rites of a tribe of Australian aborigines, as a stressor in a series of experiments seeking to influence the individual's method of coping with stress. The film has been presented to subjects with one of three soundtracks: a *denial* soundtrack, in which the narrator speaks of the joy and anticipation of the boys participating in the rites but ignores the evident pain they experience; an *intellectualization* soundtrack, in which the narrator objectively points out the pain and other aspects of the operations and discusses them from an anthropological viewpoint; and a *trauma* track, in which the narrator emphasizes the pain, the unsanitary conditions, and the potential danger of the operations.

Subjects had beforehand filled out personality questionnaires aimed at discovering their characteristic styles of coping with stress. It was expected that subjects who generally used denial of stressful stimuli as a defensive response would show fewer stress reactions to the film when it was accompanied by the denial soundtrack. Similarly, intellectualizers were expected to show less stress when the film was presented with the intellectualization soundtrack. On the other hand, the denial track was not expected to be very effective for intellectualizers, nor would the intellectualization track be of much help to deniers. The trauma track and a showing of the film without sound were used as controls. Subjective reports of stress and measures of mood were taken immediately after the film was shown; heart rate and galvanic skin response (GSR) were recorded throughout the film session.

The mood measures did not show the expected differences, but subjective ratings of stress and the physiological measures showed reliable differences in the predicted direction; subjects who listened to the intellectualization and denial soundtracks showed less severe stress reactions. In a related study, Lazarus and Alfert (1964) found that giving a brief orienting talk before showing the film was at least as effective in short-circuiting the threat as was a soundtrack. Similar results have been obtained using electric shock as the stressor (Holmes and Houston, 1974); instructions which redefined the stressful nature of the shock (suggesting, for example, that the subject look at the shock as a new physical sensation) were effective in reducing both self-reports of stress and such physiological reactions as pulse rate and skin resistance.

Adapting to Stress

Lazarus's study attempted to manipulate the subject's defensive response, one of the ways that individuals use to reduce the impact of stressful events. The term *coping process* (Lazarus, 1966) has been applied to the various mechanisms a person can use to escape, modify, or learn to live with a threat. Many of the cognitive factors mentioned so far appear to be central to the coping process, particularly evaluations of the stressful stimuli, expectations of their effects, and the individual's more or less enduring predispositions to act in the situation. When a person is placed in a situation most people would judge to be stressful, she cannot be said to be stressed unless the situation has the impact of stress for her. This requires that she evaluate the situation as threatening. Lazarus calls this cognitive process *primary appraisal.*

Secondary appraisal follows: the stressed person considers ways and means of escaping or ending the threatening event; she may seek to discover the source of her stressful state; or she may resort to such coping mechanisms as denial or intellectualization, as in the Lazarus experiments. Further interaction with the environment can lead her to reappraise the threat. The expected harm may not come to pass, for example, or the coping mechanisms may have blunted the effects of her primary appraisal. The situation then comes to be seen as less threatening than before, and this reevaluation may continue until the formerly stressful events are perceived as part of the normal routine. In turn, there are corresponding reductions in the physiological reactions to the stressor as well as changes in coping behavior. The whole process can be called an adaptive response to the stressor.

Cognitive factors in adapting to stress

A series of studies designed to investigate cognitive factors in the adaptation to stress and, particularly, its immediate aftereffects (Glass, Singer, and Friedman, 1969) used high-intensity noise as a stressor. Subjects were presented with bursts of noise while working on several verbal and numerical tasks. The twenty-three noise bursts occurred at random intervals with one group and at fixed interval with the other. It was expected that the aftereffects of adapting to the random noise bursts would be more severe than those following the predictable fixed-interval noise. Both groups of subjects showed significant adaptation by the time of the twenty-third noise burst, as measured by decreases in

GSR and by decreases in the number of task errors throughout the session. On tasks performed after the noise was over, however, the two groups were very different; a test of tolerance for frustration, in which subjects were asked to solve puzzles that were actually insoluble, showed that those subjects who had been exposed to unpredictable noise were more easily frustrated (they were less persistent in trying to solve the puzzles) than those who had heard predictable noise.

Further experiments showed that the aftereffects of adaptation were substantially reduced when the subject believed he had potential control over unpredictable noise (Glass, Singer, and Friedman, 1969; Glass, Reim, and Singer, 1971). For example, subjects were given the option of pressing a button to end the noise. Although few actually pressed the button, the subjects who were given the option showed, on the whole, less severe aftereffects of adaptation to stress. Thus, control over a stressful situation is one cognitive factor in the amelioration of undesirable responses. Or, to put it another way, feeling helpless in the face of stressful events may exacerbate their harmful effects.

In another study, Glass and his colleagues (1973) have shown that reductions in the subjective painfulness of a controllable electric shock, as well as less detrimental aftereffects, are dependent on the subjects' actually experiencing a reduction in shock after their attempts to control it. If one can demonstrate that he or she is not helpless in the face of stress, the detrimental effects may be lessened. Thus it may be that effective control over the stress, perceived through ongoing transactions between subject and environment, is of particular importance in determining both the immediate and the long-term stress reactions.

To sum up, when a person is confronted with threatening events, the behavior he exhibits and the physiological changes he undergoes generally cannot be predicted or explained simply by measuring the intensity of the stressor, whether physical or psychological. All aspects of the stress response, from first anticipation of harm to aftereffects of adaptation, are mediated by cognitive variables. The experience of stress depends on evaluation of the threat; coping behavior is determined by appraisal processes; psychophysiological response patterns are influenced by interpretations of the stressful event; and the aftereffects of stress may be altered by beliefs and expectations about the threat and effective ways to deal with it. In short, if you are able to explain away, control, or normalize stressful events, you may very well ease the effects of that stress.

Social factors

In the preceding section we have discussed research which demonstrates that cognitions play a significant role in determining both the experience of stress and the nature of stress responses. The relationship between social factors and stress response has also been studied by many researchers. That is, they have sought experimental evidence to show that other people not only act as social stressors, as we have seen, but they also play an important role in one's ability to adapt to stress. The first question that might be asked is: Do people under duress tend to seek the company of others in the same predicament? One classic approach to this problem is the theory of emotional comparison derived from Stanley Schachter's affiliation studies (1959). Briefly, Schachter's reasoning is as follows: When a person is significantly aroused by an ambiguous and stressful situation, he seeks out other people to assist him in evaluating the situation. He needs to know the meaning of the ambiguous stimuli and of his own aroused state; he wants to label his emotions, to determine their relative intensity and social appropriateness; and he wants to know if he is reacting adaptively to the situation. All this information must be obtained through interaction with other people. That is, you can get information about the meaning and appropriateness of your stress reaction by comparing it with the reactions of other people. But since stress is an internal state, the only way you can get that information is by communicating with others so that they will tell you about their reactions to both the stressful event and your own reaction to the event.

This emotional comparison hypothesis was subsequently supported in a study by Darley and Aronson (1966), who found that highly fearful subjects chose to wait for the shock with another subject who had rated herself slightly more anxious rather than with one who was somewhat calmer. Presumably the calmer other person would have provided more reassurance to the subject; choosing the more anxious other person indicates that social comparison motives largely determine the tendency to affiliate in fear situations.

Another example of the relationship between affiliation and stress is provided by studies of the development and significance of rumors in social interaction. In an extensive discussion of the sociological meaning of rumor, Shibutani (1966) defined rumor as "a recurrent form of communication through which [people] caught together in an ambiguous situation attempt to construct a meaningful interpretation of it by pooling their intellectual resources." Rumor is seen, in this hypothesis, as a social means of coping with an ambiguous environment, a kind of collective problem-solving. The importance of affiliation here is central. According to Shibutani, one person alone cannot create a rumor and keep it going; rumor-making and rumor development are group activities whose purpose is to allow people caught in a threatening situation to understand what is happening. Each person involved in this communication may play various roles: he may be a messenger, who brings information to the others; an interpreter, who relates one piece of information to other pieces and evaluates its importance in the situation as a whole; a skeptic, who points out the need for additional information and expresses the wisdom of caution; a decision-maker, who leads the others in choosing a course of action; and so on. Rumor is thus seen as a social response to an ill-defined situation whose purpose is to define the situation and to achieve a group consensus about its meaning, thereby alleviating stress.

A person's reaction to a stressful event may depend on whom he happens to be with at the time of stress. Research has demonstrated that friendship or previous acquaintance influences stress response. Kissel (1965) reports that GSR scores during a stressful task situation were lower in the presence of another person than when the subject worked alone, providing that the other person was a friend. Strangers had no appreciable effect on response. Back and Bogdonoff (1964) found a higher level of arousal among groups of strangers tested together than among friends tested as a group: those who were thrust into a position of leadership in a group of strangers were more aroused than those who were given the leadership role in a group of friends. In the latter situation, however, the leaders reacted more strongly when their friends in the group disagreed with them. The authors conclude that the degree of physiological arousal can be modified by conditions of interaction, particularly those of leadership and conformity, among members of a group.

Behavioral responses to a threatening situation may also be altered by the presence of others in the same situation. A number of studies of social modeling, for instance, have shown that watching another person deal calmly with a

Effect of Task Importance and Ease on Group Mean FFA Level

Free fatty acid level in 5 blood samples

Condition	Sample 1	Sample 2	Sample 3	Sample 4	Sample 5
Important, difficult	949	698	777	869	987
Important, easy	814	723	673	876	932
Unimportant, difficult	604	527	619	611	613
Unimportant, easy	716	584	621	667	710

Figure 12–4. The level of free fatty acids (FFA) in the blood is an indicator of stress. Subjects instructed to perform both difficult and easy perceptual tasks that were important to them had the highest levels of FFA in their blood samples.

SOURCE: Adapted from Back, K. W., and Bogdonoff, M. D. Plasma lipid responses to leadership, conformity, and deviation. In P. H. Leiderman and D. Shapiro (Eds.), *Psychobiological approaches to social behavior.* Stanford, Calif.: Stanford University Press, 1964. P. 34.

frightening object (Bandura, Grusec, and Menlove, 1967; Bandura and Menlove, 1968; Geer and Turtletaub, 1967) or with a threatening event (Vernon, 1973) can produce fewer behavioral manifestations of fear than when no appropriate model is made available. It is possible that such social interactions intervene in the appraisal process itself, with the calm behavior of the other person making the situation appear less threatening.

Stress and Life Events

Many stress researchers have included a caveat in discussions of their work to the effect that stress is an inevitable part of every person's life. Hinkle (1973), for example, notes that "to be alive is to be under stress." This is surely so, and yet to say that life is stressful simply raises a host of other questions. Chief among these are two: What makes some life experiences more stressful than others, and what are the damaging effects of stressful life events? (Dohrenwend and Dohrenwend, 1974).

Most studies of the relationships between life experience and stress have focused on events that change a person's life. Habitual activities, the routines of our day-to-day living, are assumed to be relatively benign, but a potential threat arises with any change that interrupts daily routines. Thus, getting married is seen as stressful, and so is getting a divorce, but the ordinary settled sequence of married life is not. Researchers disagree about the extent to which a given life event can be defined objectively as stressful (Dohrenwend and Dohrenwend, 1974). Some studies hold that individual differences are central to the determination of what is stressful; others provide rating scales against which to measure everyone's life events in the same way. It has also been suggested that a good addition to the definition of possible stressors in life would be a nonevent—something that is anticipated or desired but that does not happen. Most research, however, begins with the premise that both negative and positive changes in life events are the places to look for stressors. A further question, then, could be: What can a person do to lessen the potential of such changes for inducing stress?

Research aimed at the relations between life events and stress has, by and large, focused on the broader social context of these events rather than on individual characteristics that may or may not be alterable. In discussing the stresses related to occupation, for example, Gross (1970) attributed many job-related stresses to sociocultural factors, rather than to, for example, physiological or psychological factors. Thus the large-scale organization has been developed in Western society to handle such diverse activities as producing goods, educating the young, and protecting society from criminals. "The net result," according to Gross, "is that the individual finds that in order to earn a living, or to obtain any long-range goal, he must associate himself with some large organization, and usually quite a number of them, for all of his life in order to survive." These organizations then become the source of stress, through such threats as the fear of losing one's job or of failure to meet the demands of one's boss.

Gross suggests several kinds of remedies in his discussion. He proposes that much more attention be paid to teaching the young to cope with organizational stress; if an individual can learn to deal effectively with and within organizations, he or she will be in a much better position to avoid the stresses that organizations may induce. Avoiding being fired, for example, is probably a learnable skill in most organizational structures since some people are fired and others are not. Another strategy for avoiding this kind of occupational stress is to keep your distance from the organization by maintaining alternate means to achieve your own personal goals and establishing important parts of your life outside of organizational structures. A third important factor, in Gross's estimation, is the working conditions that exist within the organization itself. Stressful working conditions can be mediated by strong group attachments, so that affiliation within the working group effectively ameliorates the stress. The importance of the affiliation factor has also been found in various studies of groups under stress, as we have seen.

Class and race as factors in stress

Another source of social stress may be the class and/or racial group with which an individual is identified (Dohrenwend and Dohrenwend, 1970). No firm evidence has been found of a relationship between social class and the number of stressors in a person's life; class has not been demonstrated to affect the number of events in one's life that will be stressful. This is partly because a stressor is defined as any change in habitual living patterns, including positive change; middle-class people are more likely to be stressed by job promotion, for example, than lower-class people. In terms of race, the evidence suggests that both lower-class and middle-class blacks experience stressors more often than their white counterparts. Thus, lower-class blacks have higher rates of unemployment, illness, and divorce than lower-class whites; and middle-class blacks have a higher divorce rate than middle-class whites.

Lower-class persons of both races have been shown, however, to be less well equipped by their life situations to deal effectively with the stress they encounter in their lives than middle-class people. Because lower-class people have less money than middle-class people, they are less able to buy needed goods and services to ameliorate the effects of stress. If a lower-class person is stressed by serious illness, for example, he has fewer resources on which to draw to relieve the stress. In terms of variables other than money which are

CITY NOISE THWARTS BRAINWORK

People who live in dense urban environments are constantly barraged by a host of stimuli that adversely affect their well-being. Polluting chemicals, dirt, and a criminal underworld are just a few of the irritants. Then, of course, there is the assault of noise. Most residents learn to tolerate city noises, and some are able to shut noise out of their consciousness completely. Recent research has confirmed that noise has deleterious effects on learning, concentration, and the ability to cope with frustration.

A series of interesting experiments by David Glass, Sheldon Cohen, and Jerome Singer (1973) has turned up some intriguing information about the effect of noise on the ability to perform certain mental tasks. In one experiment, forty-eight female undergraduates were asked to trace over the lines of a diagram. The subjects were not to go over any line more than once, and were not to lift their pencils from the diagrams. Since two of the problems were insoluble, a subject's continued attempts to solve the problems were interpreted as indications of her ability to put up with frustration.

The researchers found that individuals who were exposed to unpredictable noise—whether loud or soft—abandoned their attempts to solve the insoluble puzzles sooner than subjects who worked in relatively quiet conditions. In a similar experiment involving proofreading, the investigators obtained the same results: subjects who tried to proofread a seven-page manuscript while being assaulted by unpredictable noise overlooked more errors.

High noise levels also seem to have a detrimental effect on reading ability. In another experiment, Glass, Cohen, and Singer found that the reading ability of elementary-school children living in a Manhattan apartment complex differed according to the amount of traffic noise to which they were exposed. These investigators studied fifty-four grade-school children who lived in one of four thirty-two-story apartment buildings that straddle a heavily traveled expressway. Because of the onrushing traffic, the noise in each building is moderately loud at ground level, but decreases as one moves toward the upper floors.

Based on the results of the problem-solving and proofreading experiments, the researchers predicted that children living on lower floors would do more poorly on auditory discrimination and reading tests than would those living on higher floors. Their prediction was borne out: the experimenters found that children who had lived on the lower floors for four years or more scored lower in auditory discrimination and reading than those who lived on the upper floors. (These relationships, however, were not true for those who had lived in the apartments for less than four years.) For example, children living on the fifth to the eleventh floors of the apartment complex ranked, on the average, in the fifty-first percentile on reading achievement tests. By contrast, those living on the twenty-sixth to the thirty-second floors ranked in the eighty-fifth percentile in the same tests.

So it seems that living in today's large cities takes its toll on the individual. Glass and his colleagues conclude their report with this observation: "Our evidence warns that decreased tolerance for frustration, loss of efficiency, deficits in auditory discrimination, and lowered reading achievement may be the price for living in modern cities" (Glass et al., 1973, p. 99).

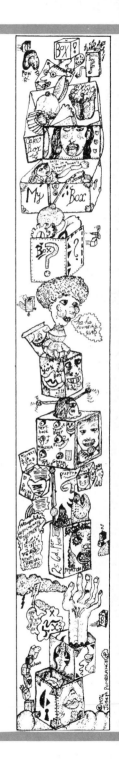

important factors in the ability to cope with stress, there is some evidence that lower-class persons have fewer emotional resources as well. It has been found, for example, that lower-class husbands and wives provide each other with relatively less psychological support and that, with important exceptions, lower-class people have fewer support relationships outside of the family.

Lower-class blacks earn even less than most of their white counterparts, and, even given comparable income, blacks cannot, for example, buy housing in many areas comparable to the housing of whites at their income level. Thus, when a black family moves, they will be more likely to be stressed by barriers to their living in the most desirable neighborhoods in addition to the stress of moving. These factors, among others, lead Dohrenwend and Dohrenwend to conclude that blacks as a racial group are less likely than whites to have the external resources needed to ameliorate the effects of the stressors they experience.

A third factor considered in this study was the severity of the stress encountered by different social classes and races, measured by the duration and intensity of the stress. The researchers attempted to find evidence to confirm or disconfirm the popular belief that stress is more severe among lower-class and black people. Their overall finding was that severity of stress is greatest for lower-class blacks and least for middle-class whites.

Remedies for such inequities depend upon far-reaching changes in the social and economic systems of our culture. William Ryan (1971) has suggested that one reason more progress has not been made in relieving the stresses on blacks and lower-class people is that we prefer to blame the victims of these inequities rather than the society which perpetuates them. Instead of acknowledging, for example, that ghetto schools are institutions in which it is often impossible to learn anything useful, we attribute the learning difficulties of the ghetto child to his being "culturally deprived." Similarly, Teele (1970) notes that what he calls "the disease model" of crime is often chosen by society to explain social pathology because it is comfortable and easy to view criminals as sick and different from themselves (see chapter 6).

Stress and the physical environment

The influence on social behavior of such environmental factors as the deterioration of urban centers, crowding, and noise has been explored in many research studies (Geen and Powers, 1971; Baron and Bell, 1976). These studies have found that environmental stressors such as extreme heat, crowding, and high noise levels have various negative effects on task efficiency and social behavior. Thus, as we saw earlier in the chapter, Glass, Singer, and Friedman (1969) found that individuals exposed to high noise levels do poorer on certain tasks that require concentration (for example, proofreading and problem-solving) than those who work in relatively quiet conditions.

In another study, Mathews and Canon (1975) conducted two experiments designed to measure the effects of various noise levels on helping behavior. In the laboratory experiment, subjects were asked to wait in a room where a confederate of the experimenter was already sitting with a pile of books, journals, and papers in his lap. As soon as the subject was seated, the experimenter called the confederate to take his turn in the experiment, whereupon he rose and dropped his books and papers all over the floor. The dependent variable was the presence or absence of helping behavior on the part of the subject in the face of this difficulty. The independent variable was the noise level in the room. Three different levels were used: natural noise level (no noise); a broadband white noise at 65 decibels (low noise); and a broadband white noise at 85 decibels (high noise).

A similar situation in a field study experiment was devised which allowed the subject to assist or not assist a confederate who needed help. The confederate carried two heavy boxes full of books across a sidewalk in front of the subject. As the subject passed by, two of the books on top of the box dropped out, requiring the confederate to put down the boxes in order to retrieve them. Again, the subject was rated on whether or not he offered help. In this second experiment an additional variable was added. The confederate in one condition wore an arm cast from his wrist to his shoulder to provide an additional cue

Several vest-pocket parks located in the busy midtown area have been donated to New York City. The sound of the fall of water on the fountain wall offers a buffer against the noise of the city.

that he needed assistance; in the other condition, he wore no cast. The high noise condition was supplied in the field study by a second confederate who ran a lawn mower without a muffler nearby, creating a noise level of approximately 85 decibels. Regular street noise created the low-noise condition.

It was predicted that high noise level would be inversely related to helping behavior and that the added visual cue (the cast) would increase the likelihood of helping behavior. The basic findings were consistent for both experiments and confirmed the predictions: when the noise level was high, helping behavior decreased. The visual cue increased helping in the low-noise condition but not in the high-noise condition. The authors related their results to the findings in other studies that high noise levels reduce attention to peripheral cues. They also advanced several other possible explanations: that the subjects simply wanted to escape the loud noise as soon as possible, although this explanation is less plausible in the laboratory study than in the field study; and that the stress of the noise made the subjects irritable and therefore less likely to be helpful. The authors concluded that "high levels of noise may be an important factor not only in helping behavior but in other social interaction situations as well" (Mathews and Canon, 1975).

The implications of this kind of research for living and working conditions in which there is a high level of environmental stress are great. Stanley Milgram (1970) has suggested that the experience of living in cities involves continuous overload, requiring continuous adaptation. His notion of overload comes from systems analysis and refers to the inability of a system to process a great many inputs at once. In the Mathews and Canon experiment, for example, the subject might be said to have been overloaded by the stress of the high noise so that he was unable to perceive or react to the need for help. Milgram accounts for a number of the difficulties in social interaction among city dwellers by explaining that these people are constantly stressed by overload. He maintains, for example, that moral and social involvement with other people is restricted because people who live in cities have to tune out most social phenomena in order to function at all. They become less courteous, less willing to help strangers, more isolated and alienated from others, and more fragmented in their roles as a result. Indeed, many critics have suggested that living in cities is so destructive that we would be better off if the urban centers were dismantled entirely.

There are some psychologists, however, who believe that the benefits of city living outweigh the disadvantages. One of these is Jonathan Freedman, who has done extensive research in the area of crowding and behavior (Freedman, 1975). He and his colleagues have found that high density does not generally have negative effects on people. They base this conclusion on evidence that there is no relation between crowding and pathology in real-life situations (when income and such factors are controlled, for example, highly dense cities have no more crime than less dense areas). Experimental situations in which people have been confined in very small spaces for periods of up to twenty days have not produced dysfunctioning due to the stress of being closed in. Furthermore, there is no evidence that crowding, as such, causes either stress or arousal; and neighborhoods in which people have relatively small spaces in which to live have no more pathology than neighborhoods in which people live in larger spaces. Freedman is convinced that high-density population is a given in our world and that low crime rates, the absence of violence, and a high quality of life are not incompatible with this high density.

He acknowledges that the rise in the world's population has produced a number of real problems, among them pollution, energy depletion, and the scarcity of food, housing, and social services. But he points out that all of these problems would still be as great if the existing population were distributed over the world's land area evenly—and some of them would be worse, since it is easier to supply high-density areas with food and services.

In addition, Freedman argues that the aesthetic and economic advantages of cities make them extremely worthwhile places for people to live in. Cities are stimulating and exciting. They provide more varied experiences than either country or suburban living, although Freedman believes that the best situation is to have a mixture of all of these possibilities so that people can choose among them. Economically, cities provide the necessary concentration of consumers to support all kinds of desirable enterprises—from successful theater to fine restaurants and shops that specialize in unusual items of all kinds. Thus, the city is an enriching atmosphere as a direct result of the high density that is found there.

One of the most important suggestions advanced by Freedman for making cities more habitable echoes some of the observations of the Milgram study. He suggests that cities cannot be made less crowded, since they are, by definition, areas in which the population density is high, but that they can be made much more humane and safe if efforts are made to encourage social interaction and a sense of community among those who live there. While city housing cannot be designed to provide spacious private outdoor areas for each family, for example, it can be designed so that people can see and use the public spaces within and outside of buildings as part of their own living space. When this happens, the public spaces become more safe because there are more people in them, and living in the city becomes more pleasant. We have seen that stressors introduced by the physical environment can have a negative effect on social and interpersonal behavior. Many of the remedies for these kinds of stress are within the competence of our current technology. We need to remember that some aspects of life in industrial society in the last quarter of the twentieth century are givens: there are more people on our planet now than there have ever been before, for example. But the quality of our lives can be enhanced rather than lowered if we focus our resources on planning for human needs.

Stress and growth

Hans Selye, the researcher whose admonition on the destructive effects of stress we quoted earlier, said in the same interview that "stress is the salt of life. . . . Stress wakes us up, makes us live" (Ratcliff, 1970). Any balanced consideration of the effects of stress must also include this view. There is ample support for the view that an intense stimulation such as stress is not invariably aversive, although it may often be so, and that a nearly complete lack of stimulation is also stressful and may lead to long-term adverse effects. Bexton, Heron, and Scott (1954) have demonstrated that deprivation of nearly all sensory input is experienced as an extremely stressful situation. Others (e.g. Reisen, 1966) have shown that sensory deprivation in young animals leads to abnormal development of sensory receptors. It may well be, in fact, that animals tend to seek out stimulation somewhat more intense than that to which they have been adapted. Butler (1953), for example, has found that a monkey confined in a cage covered by an opaque box will readily learn a discrimination response when the only reinforcement is the opportunity to look through a window in the box for thirty seconds. Other studies (Berlyne, 1957) have shown that both people and other animals tend to respond more to stimuli that are complex, novel, or surprising. The so-called enhancement drives, which result in curiosity and exploratory behavior (Berlyne, 1960), have been postulated to account for this observed seeking of stimulation.

Even stress as we have defined it here (the state of the organism when faced with a threat to its well-being) may have beneficial as well as adverse effects in the long run. The concept of *inoculation,* whereby experiencing moderate levels of stress will lead to more competence in handling subsequent severe stress, provides an explanation. Developmental studies (Lindzey, Lykken, and Winston, 1960) have shown that young animals who are subjected to handling, electric shock, or toe-pinching seem better able, as adults, to cope with stressful situations than their littermates who were not stressed earlier. In a study of human response to stress, Janis (1958) found that surgical patients who experienced mild stress prior to their operations were better able to cope with the severe stresses of postoperative recovery than those patients who reported either very high or very low levels of postoperative stress.

It would seem, then, that stress, while aversive, is also beneficial. The organism grows in adaptive capacity through its encounters with stress, and faced with a bland, safe environment, may even generate its own stimulation or direct its energies toward creating a more stimulating environment. This can be seen in every phase of the development of a child from infancy through adolescence. From the struggle to learn to walk to the struggle to earn one's living, stress is invariably involved in all personal growth.

In considering stress from a long-term view, we find that stress seems to be an essential condition for coping with life. And again, cognitive variables seem to play as important a role in determining the long-term stress responses as they do in immediate stress reactions. When a person finds that the anticipated harm has not occurred, or that he has been able to deal with the harm, he comes to view the situation as more or less harmless. He is less vigilant and defensive, he may recover most of his task efficiency, and his physiological reactions become less and less marked and may disappear altogether. Adaptation seems to be responsible for the ability of most people to continue functioning even under extreme conditions of duress, as in war and natural disasters.

Since stress is so much a part of human life, we need to be able to adapt to it if we are to continue to function, and people are known to be able to adjust to all but the most severe stressors. However, a variety of harmful consequences of stress may follow even after adaptation has occurred. Psychosomatic diseases, a decreased tolerance for frustration, and debilitated task performance may be the eventual price people pay for successful adaptation to a stressful environment. Some of the effects, in fact, may be seen in the immediate aftermath of a stressful experience. Basowitz and his colleagues (1955), for instance, found that paratroop trainees who performed a stressful jump with a minimum of stress reaction before and during the task often were overwhelmed with anxiety immediately afterwards. Their adaptive responses were effective, but the cumulative effects of the stress could not be completely eliminated.

The search for stressful situations may be seen in many behaviors in ordinary life. Riding a roller coaster can be a threatening experience, and it could certainly be felt as an aversive event. Yet many people will seek it out, even paying money for the privilege of being stressed. Similar arguments may be made for gambling, using stimulating or exciting drugs (Louria, 1968), and other instances in which people deliberately seek out situations of stress or danger (Klausner, 1968). Even more persuasive is the drive in many people to challenge themselves by pushing to the limits of their capabilities. Enrolling in a difficult course in school or accepting the discipline of marathon running are only two of many examples. Stress-seeking, then, may be regarded as a complement to stress-avoidance, and as a process just as basic to life. The goal, in both cases, is not merely the maintenance of a set equilibrium level, but, instead, the achievement of a higher level of adaptiveness. These considerations suggest that stress-seeking behavior, as well as stress-avoidance behavior, should properly be included in the mainstream of stress research.

Summary

Stress, the failure of routine methods for managing threats, is experienced in a different fashion from one person to the next. Stress is usually considered harmful, but since it is caused by change, it should also be included as a stimulus to the coping process, and as such, a positive force.

Stress can cause physical disorders, and there is a high correlation between stress and heart disease. People in certain occupations, such as doctors, lawyers, judges, and cab drivers, have been found to be particularly prone to heart disease. In addition, a particular syndrome of personality traits, a Type A personality, renders such individuals more prone to heart disease. A Type A individual is ambitious and aggressive, and has a strong sense of time urgency.

Stress is defined as an internal state of the organism when it is faced with threats to its well-being. The threat is called the stressor. The physiological reaction aroused by stress has been called the General Adaptive Syndrome (GAS) by Hans Selye, who used many different stressors with animal subjects. GAS consists of three successive stages: the arousal stage (basically an arousal of the sympathetic nervous system), the alarm reaction (a release of hormones to restore the body's balance), and the exhaustion stage, which, if the stressor continues to threaten the organism, can lead to collapse and death. Stressors can consist of any unpleasant or aversive events and are classified as either physical (for example, electric shock) or psychosocial (for example, an individual is laid off from her job).

Responses to stress may be psychophysiological or behavioral. The same physiological state of response may be defined by the individual as any one of a variety of emotions. Behavioral stress can be measured by the ability to perform a task. Cognitive factors are most important in the perception of stress, particularly in the way in which the individual perceives the threat. In addition, cognitive factors are important in the process of adapting to stress. Research shows that control over the stressful situation reduces stress. Other people also are important in adaptation to stress, particularly other people who are similar to oneself in suffering from the stressor. Other people also help in an interpretation of the stressful event.

Certain life events, particularly those that change the daily routine, are perceived as stressful. In terms of class and race, lower-class and nonwhite people are at a disadvantage in having fewer resources to cope with stress.

It has been found that such stressors in the physical environment as crowding and noise have a negative effect on task efficiency and social behavior. Some researchers, however, claim that the stimulation and excitement of city life outweigh its stressful disadvantages and that, furthermore, no correlation between high density, crime, and other antisocial influences has been established. Some investigators of stress have been quick to point out that "stress is the salt of life." A lack of stress is in itself an occasion for stress, whereas successful coping leads to a higher level of achievement and confidence.

Bibliography

Ax, A. F. The physiological differentiation between fear and anger in humans. *Psychosomatic Medicine*, 1953, **15**, 433–442.

Back, K. W., and Bogdonoff, M. D. Plasma lipid responses to leadership, conformity, and deviation. In P. H. Leiderman and D. Shapiro (Eds.), *Psychobiological approaches to social behavior*. Stanford, Calif.: Stanford University Press, 1964.

Back, K. W., and Bogdonoff, M. D. Buffer conditions in experimental stress. *Behavioral Science*, 1967, **12**, 384–390.

Bandura, A., Grusec, J. E., and Menlove, F. L. Vicarious extinction of avoidance behavior. *Journal of Personality and Social Psychology*, 1967, **5**, 16–23.

Bandura, A., and Menlove, F. L. Factors determining vicarious extinction of avoidance behavior through symbolic modeling. *Journal of Personality and Social Psychology*, 1968, **8**, 99–108.

Baron, R. A., and Bell, P. A. Aggression and heat: The influence of ambient temperature, negative affect, and a cooling drink on physical aggression. *Journal of Personality and Social Psychology*, 1976, **33**(3), 245–255.

Basowitz, H., Persky, H., Korchin, S. J., and Grinker, R. R. *Anxiety and stress*. New York: McGraw-Hill, 1955.

BERLYNE, D. E. Conflict and information-theory variables as determinants of human perceptual curiosity. *Journal of Experimental Psychology*, 1957, **53**, 399–404.

BERLYNE, D. E. *Conflict, arousal and curiosity.* New York: McGraw-Hill, 1960.

BEXTON, W. H., HERON, W., AND SCOTT, T. H. Effects of decreased variation in the sensory environment. *Canadian Journal of Psychology*, 1954, **8**, 70–76.

BURNAM, M. A., PENNEBAKER, J. W., AND GLASS, D. C. Time consciousness, achievement striving, and the Type A coronary-prone behavior pattern. *Journal of Abnormal Psychology*, 1973, **84**, 76–79.

BUTLER, R. A. Discrimination learning by rhesus monkeys to visual-exploration motivation. *Journal of Comparative Physiology and Psychology*, 1953, **46**, 95–98.

CANNON, W. B. *Bodily changes in pain, fear, and rage.* (2nd ed.) New York: Appleton-Century-Crofts, 1936.

CARVER, C. S., COLEMAN, A. E., AND GLASS, D. C. The coronary-prone behavior pattern and the suppression of fatigue on a treadmill test. *Journal of Personality and Social Psychology*, 1976, **33**, 460–466.

COCHRANE, R. High blood pressure as a psychosomatic disorder: A selective review. *British Journal of Social and Clinical Psychology*, 1971, **10**, 61–72.

COFER, C. N., AND APPLEY, M. H. *Motivation: Theory and research.* New York: John Wiley, 1964.

DARLEY, J. M., AND ARONSON, E. Self-evaluation vs. direct anxiety reduction as determinants of the fear–affiliation relationship. *Journal of Experimental Social Psychology*, 1966, **41** (Supplement 1).

DAVISON, G. C., AND VALINS, S. Maintenance of self-attributed and drug-attributed behavior change. *Journal of Personality and Social Psychology*, 1969, **11**(1), 25–33.

DAWBER, T. R., AND KENNEL, W. B. Susceptibility to coronary heart disease. *Modern Concepts of Cardiovascular Disease*, 1961, **30**, 671–676.

DOHRENWEND, B. S., AND DOHRENWEND, B. P. Class and race as status-related sources of stress. In S. Levine and N. Scotch (Eds.), *Social stress.* Chicago: Aldine, 1970.

DOHRENWEND, B. S., AND DOHRENWEND, B. P. (Eds.) *Stressful life events: Their nature and effects.* New York: John Wiley, 1974.

DUFFY, E. *Activation and behavior.* New York: John Wiley, 1962.

EASTERBROOK, J. A. The effect of emotion on cue utilization and the organization of behavior. *Psychological Review*, 1959, **66**, 183–201.

FELTON, J. S., AND COLE, R. The high cost of heart disease. *Circulation*, 1963, **27**, 957–962.

FREEDMAN, J. L. *Crowding and behavior: The psychology of high-density living.* New York: Viking Press, 1975.

FRIEDMAN, M., ROSENMAN, R. H., AND CARROLL, U. Changes in the serum cholesterol and blood clotting time in men subjected to cyclic variation of occupational stress. *Circulation*, 1958, **17**, 852–861.

GEEN, R. G., AND POWERS, P. C. Shock and noise as instigating stimuli in human aggression. *Psychological Reports*, 1971, **28**, 983–985.

GEER, J. H., AND TURTLETAUB, A. Fear reduction following observation of a model. *Journal of Personality and Social Psychology,* 1967, **6,** 327–331.

GLASS, D. C. *Stress and coronary-prone behavior.* Hillsdale, N.J.: Lawrence Erlbaum Associates, 1977.

GLASS, D. C., COHEN, S., AND SINGER, J. Urban din fogs the brain. *Psychology Today,* 1973, **6**(12), 94–99.

GLASS, D. C., REIM, B., AND SINGER, J. E. Behavioral consequences of adaptation to controllable and uncontrollable noise. *Journal of Experimental Social Psychology,* 1971, **7,** 244–257.

GLASS, D. C., SINGER, J. E., AND FRIEDMAN, L. N. Psychic cost of adaptation to an environmental stressor. *Journal of Personality and Social Psychology,* 1969, **12,** 200–210.

GLASS, D. C., SINGER, J. E., LEONARD, H. S., KRANTZ, D., COHEN, S., AND CUMMINGS, H. Perceived control of aversive stimulation and the reduction of stress responses. *Journal of Personality,* 1973, **41,** 577–595.

GLASS, D. C., SNYDER, M. L., AND HOLLIS, J. F. Time urgency and the Type A coronary-prone behavior pattern. *Journal of Applied Social Psychology,* 1974, **4,** 125–140.

GOLDSTEIN, M. J., JONES, R. B., CLEMENS, T. L., FLAGG, G. W., AND ALEXANDER, F. G. Coping style as a factor in psychophysiological response to a tension-arousing film. *Journal of Personality and Social Psychology,* 1965, **1,** 290–302.

GROSS, E. Work, organization, and stress. In S. Levine and N. A. Scotch (Eds.), *Social stress.* Chicago: Aldine, 1970.

HALLECK, S. L. *The politics of therapy.* New York: Science House, 1971.

HENRY, J. P., ELY, D. L., AND STEPHENS, P. M. Mental factors and cardiovascular disease: Psychosocial factors facilitating and inhibiting the influence of neuroendocrine alarm responses upon the course of cardiovascular disease. *Psychiatric Annals,* 1972, **2,** 25–71.

HINKLE, L. E., JR. The concept of "stress" in the biological and social sciences. *Science, Medicine, and Man,* 1973, **1,** 31–48.

HINKLE, L. E., JR., WHITNEY, L. H., LEHMAN, E. W., DUNN, J., BENJAMIN, B., KING, R., PLAKUN, A., AND FLEHINGER, B. Occupation, education, and coronary heart disease. *Science,* July 19, 1968, **161**(3839), 238–246.

HOKANSON, J. E., AND BURGESS, M. The effects of status, type of frustration, and aggression on vascular processes. *Journal of Abnormal and Social Psychology,* 1962, **65,** 232–237.

HOLMES, D. S., AND HOUSTON, B. K. Effectiveness of situation redefinition and affective isolation in coping with stress. *Journal of Personality and Social Psychology,* 1974, **29,** 212–218.

HOUSE, J. S. Occupation stress and coronary heart disease: A review and theoretical integration. *Journal of Health and Social Behavior,* March 1974, **15**(1), 12–27.

JACO, E. G. Mental illness in response to stress. In S. Levine and N. A. Scotch (Eds.), *Social stress.* Chicago: Aldine, 1970.

JANIS, I. L. *Psychological stress.* New York: John Wiley and Sons, 1958.

JENKINS, C. D. Psychologic and social precursors of coronary disease: I. *New England Journal of Medicine*, 1971, **284**(6), 244–255. (a)

JENKINS, C. D. Psychologic and social precursors of coronary disease: II. *New England Journal of Medicine*, 1971, **284**, 307–317. (b)

KISSEL, S. Stress-reducing properties of social stimuli. *Journal of Personality and Social Psychology*, 1965, **2**, 378–384.

KLAUSNER, S. N. (Ed.) *Why men take chances.* Garden City, N.Y.: Doubleday, Anchor, 1968.

KRANTZ, D. S., GLASS, D. C., AND SNYDER, M. L. Helplessness, stress level, and the coronary-prone behavior pattern. *Journal of Experimental Social Psychology*, 1974, **10**, 284–300.

LACEY, J. I., KAGAN, J., LACEY, B. C., AND MOSS, H. A. The visceral level: Situational determinants and behavioral correlates of autonomic response patterns. In P. H. Knapp (Ed.), *Expression of the emotions in man.* New York: International Universities Press, 1963.

LAZARUS, R. S. A laboratory approach to the dynamics of psychological stress. *American Psychologist*, 1964, **19**, 400–411.

LAZARUS, R. S. *Psychological stress and the coping process.* New York: McGraw-Hill, 1966.

LAZARUS, R. S., AND ALFERT, E. Short-circuiting of threat by experimentally altering cognitive appraisal. *Journal of Abnormal and Social Psychology*, 1964, **6 9**, 195–205.

LEVI, L. *Stress: Sources, management, & prevention.* New York: Liveright Publishing, 1967.

LINDZEY, G., LYKKEN, D. T., AND WINSTON, H. D. Infantile trauma, genetic factors, and adult temperament. *Journal of Abnormal and Social Psychology*, 1960, **6 1**, 7–14.

LOURIA, D. B. *The drug scene.* New York: McGraw-Hill, 1968.

McQUADE, W., AND AIKMAN, A. *Stress: What it is, what it can do to your health, how to fight back.* New York: E. P. Dutton, 1974.

MARKS, R. Factors involving social and demographic characteristics: A review of empirical findings. *Milbank Memorial Fund Quarterly*, 1967, **45** (part 2), 51–108.

MATHEWS, K. E., JR., AND CANON, L. K. Environmental noise level as a determinant of helping behavior. *Journal of Personality and Social Psychology*, 1975, **32**(4), 571–577.

MILGRAM, S. The experience of living in cities. *Science*, March 1970, **167**, 1461–1468.

MORIYAMA, I. M., KRUEGER, D. E., AND STAMLER, J. *Cardiovascular disease in the United States.* Cambridge, Mass.: Harvard University Press, 1971.

NATIONAL CENTER FOR HEALTH STATISTICS. U.S. National Vital Statistics Division. Mortality by occupation and cause of death among men 20 to 64. *Vital Statistics Special Reports*, 1963, **53**(3).

RATCLIFF, J. D. How to avoid harmful stress. *Today's Health*, July 1970, **48**(7), 42–44.

REISEN, A. H. Sensory deprivation. In E. Stellar and J. M. Sprague (Eds.), *Progress in physiological psychology.* Vol. 1. New York: Academic Press, 1966.

ROSENMAN, R. H., FRIEDMAN, M., STRAUS, R., WURM, M., JENKINS, C. D., AND MESSINGER, H. B. Coronary heart disease in the Western collaborative group study. *Journal of the American Medical Association*, 1966, **195**, 130–136.

RYAN, W. *Blaming the victim.* New York: Random House, Pantheon Books, 1971.

SCHACHTER, S. *The psychology of affiliation.* Stanford, Calif.: Stanford University Press, 1959.

SCHACHTER, S., AND SINGER, J. E. Cognitive, social, and physiological determinants of emotional state. *Psychological Review,* 1962, **6 9,** 379–399.

SCHLOSBERG, H., AND STANLEY, W. C. A simple test of the normality of twenty-four distributions of electrical skin conductance. *Science,* 1953, **117,** 35–37.

SELYE, H. *The stress of life.* New York: McGraw-Hill, 1956.

SHAPIRO, D., AND CRIDER, A. Psychophysiological approaches in social psychology. In G. Lindzey and E. Aronson (Eds.), *Handbook of social psychology.* (2nd ed.) Vol. 3. Reading, Mass.: Addison-Wesley, 1968.

SHIBUTANI, T. *Improvised news: A sociological study of rumor.* Indianapolis: Bobbs-Merrill, 1966.

SOLOMON, J. The price of change. *The Sciences,* November 1971, **11**(9), 28–31.

SPEISMAN, J. C., LAZARUS, R. S., MORDKOFF, A., AND DAVISON, L. Experimental reduction of stress based on ego defense theory. *Journal of Abnormal and Social Psychology,* 1964, **6 7,** 368–386.

TEELE, J. E. Social pathology and stress. In S. Levine and N. A. Scotch (Eds.), *Social stress.* Chicago: Aldine, 1970.

VERNON, D. T. Use of modeling to modify children's responses to a natural, potentially stressful situation. *Journal of Applied Psychology,* 1973, **58,** 351–356.

Acknowledgments

Figure 1–4 adapted from S. Milgram. Interpreting obedience: Error and evidence. A reply to Orne and Holland. Copyright by Stanley Milgram, 1970. Reprinted by permission of the author.

Figure 2–1 adapted from E. E. Maccoby and C. N. Jacklin. *The psychology of sex differences.* Copyright 1974 Stanford University Press. Reprinted by permission.

Figures 2–2, 2–3, and 2–4 from B. Inhelder. Criteria of the stages of mental development. Copyright Tavistock Publications. Reprinted by permission.

Figure 3–1 adapted from R. Christie and F. Geis. *Studies in Machiavellianism.* Pp. 17–18. Copyright 1970 by Academic Press, Inc. Reprinted by permission.

Figure 3–2 from M. Deutsch and R. M. Krauss. The effect of threat upon interpersonal bargaining. *Journal of Abnormal and Social Psychology,* 1960, **61**(2), 183. Copyright 1960 by the American Psychological Association. Reprinted by permission.

Extract from R. D. Mann, *Interpersonal styles and group development,* pp. 22–25. Copyright 1967. Reprinted by permission of John Wiley & Sons, Inc.

Extract from Harold Garfinkel, *Studies in ethnomethodology,* 1967, pp. 25–26 and 43. Reprinted by permission of Prentice-Hall, Inc., Englewood Cliffs, New Jersey.

Figure 4–3 from H. J. Leavitt. Some effects of certain communication patterns on group performance. *Journal of Abnormal and Social Psychology,* 1951, **46**, 42. Copyright 1951 by the American Psychological Association. Reprinted by permission.

Figure 4–4 adapted from N. Kogan and M. A. Wallach. Risk taking as a function of the situation, the person, and group. Copyright 1967 by Holt, Rinehart and Winston, Inc. Reprinted by permission.

Extract from *Kinflicks,* by Lisa Alther, copyright 1975 by Lisa Alther. Reprinted by permission of Alfred A. Knopf, Inc.

Extracts from R. B. Zajonc, Social facilitation. *Science,* 1965, **149**(3681), 270 and 274. Copyright 1965 by the American Association for the Advancement of Science. Reprinted by permission.

Figure 5–1 adapted from R. Martens. Palmar sweating and the presence of an audience. *Journal of Experimental Social Psychology,* 1969, **5**, 373. Copyright 1969 by Academic Press, Inc. Reprinted by permission.

Figure 5–2 from R. Martens and D. Landers. Evaluation potential as a determinant of coaction effects. *Journal of Experimental Social Psychology,* 1972, **8**, 350. Copyright 1972 by Academic Press, Inc. Reprinted by permission.

Figure 5–3 from L. Festinger, A. Pepitone, and T. Newcomb. Some consequences of de-individuation in a group. *Journal of Abnormal and Social Psychology,* 1952, **47**, 386. Copyright 1952 by the American Psychological Association. Reprinted by permission.

Figure 6–1 adapted and reprinted with permission of Macmillan Publishing Co., Inc. from R. K. Merton. *Social theory and social structure.* P. 194. Free Press, 1968. Copyright 1967, 1968 by Robert K. Merton.

Acknowledgments

472

Figure 7–3 adapted from E. S. Bogardus. Measuring social distances. *Journal of Applied Sociology*, 1925, **9.** Copyright *Sociology and Social Research.* Reprinted by permission.

Figure 7–4 adapted from C. E. Osgood, G. J. Suci, and P. H. Tannenbaum. *The measurement of meaning.* Copyright 1957 University of Illinois Press. Reprinted by permission.

Figure 8–1 adapted from C. Hovland and W. Weiss. The influence of source credibility on communication effectiveness. *Public Opinion Quarterly*, 1951, **15**, 635–650. Copyright Columbia University Press. Reprinted by permission.

Figure 8–3 adapted from E. Efron. *The news twisters.* Copyright 1971 by Manor Books. Reprinted by permission.

Figure 9–1 adapted from P. Ekman, E. R. Sorenson, and W. Friesen. Pan-cultural elements in facial displays of emotion. *Science*, 1969, **164,** 87. Copyright 1969 by the American Association for the Advancement of Science. Reprinted by permission.

Figure 10–1 adapted from S. E. Asch. Forming impressions of personality. *Journal of Abnormal and Social Psychology*, 1946, **41**, 263. Copyright 1946 by the American Psychological Association. Reprinted by permission.

Figure 10–2 adapted from J. E. Williams, J. K. Moreland, and W. L. Underwood. Connotations of color names in the United States, Europe, and Asia. *Journal of Social Psychology*, 1970, **82**(1), 7. Copyright 1970 by the Journal of Social Psychology. Reprinted by permission.

Figure 10–3 from J. A. Bayton, L. B. McAlister, and J. Hamer. Race–class stereotypes. *Journal of Negro Education*, 1956, 75–78, Table 2. Reprinted by permission.

Extract from K. Keniston. The other side of the Oedipus complex. *Radical Therapist*, 1970, **1**(1), 6–7. Reprinted by permission of the author.

Figure 11–1 adapted from D. Byrne, C. R. Ervin, and J. Lambreth. Continuity between the experimental study of attraction and real-life computer dating. *Journal of Personality and Social Psychology*, 1970, **16**, 157–165. Copyright 1970 by the American Psychological Association. Reprinted by permission.

Figure 11–2 adapted from G. Elder. Appearance and education in marriage mobility. *American Sociological Review*, 1969, **34**, 519–533. Copyright 1969 by American Sociological Association. Reprinted by permission.

Figure 11–3 adapted from J. Veroff, J. W. Atkinson, S. Feld, and G. Gurin. The use of thematic apperception to assess motivation in a nationwide interview study. *Psychological Monographs*, 1960, **74** (12, Whole No. 449), 24. Copyright 1960 by the American Psychological Association. Reprinted by permission.

Figure 12–1 from J. Solomon. The price of change. *The Sciences*, November 1971, **11**(9), 29. Copyright by The New York Academy of Sciences. Reprinted by permission.

Figure 12–2 adapted from C. S. Carver, A. E. Coleman, and D. C. Glass. The coronary-prone behavior pattern and the suppression of fatigue on a treadmill test. *Journal of Personality and Social Psychology*, 1976, **33**, 464. Copyright 1976 by the American Psychological Association. Reprinted by permission.

Figure 12–3 adapted from G. C. Davison and S. Valins. Maintenance of self-attributed and drug-attributed behavior change. *Journal of Personality and Social Psychology*, 1969, **11**(1), 27. Copyright 1969 by the American Psychological Association. Reprinted by permission.

Figure 12–4 adapted from K. W. Back and M. D. Bogdonoff. Plasma lipid responses to leadership, conformity, and deviation. In P. H. Leiderman and D. Shapiro (Eds.), *Psychobiological approaches to social behavior.* Copyright 1964 by Stanford University Press. Reprinted by permission.

Glossary

ACTH   Adrenocorticotropic hormone, a pituitary hormone which prepares the organism to respond to stress.

Affect   Feeling, mood, temperament, emotion.

Affiliation   The seeking out of, and the association with, other persons.

Aggression   Any harmful act directed toward another person. This can take the form of physical aggression against his person or property, or it can take a more subtle form such as verbal aggression.

Altruism   Acting on behalf of others without regard to personal reward.

Anxiety   A state of agitated arousal in response to a generalized fear.

Approach–approach conflict   A situation in which there are two stimuli that are both attractive and incompatible.

Approach–avoidance conflict   A situation in which the stimulus to approach and the stimulus to avoid are simultaneous.

A priori   That which is presupposed or self-evident; that which is a necessary given before knowing.

Attitude   An enduring, learned predisposition to conceptualize in a consistent way a given class of objects, persons, or abstract ideas.

Attraction   A characteristic attributed to a person or group, such that a person tends to approach and interact.

Attribution theory   A theory which postulates that we make evaluative attributions concerning the reasons for the behavior of others, in order to determine whether another person's words or behavior reflect his true feelings or are elicited by the situation.

Authoritarian personality   A personality characterized by a high need for unquestioning obedience and subordination; frequently associated with acceptance of strong leaders, scorn of weakness and nonconformity, and hostility to out-groups.

Autokinetic effect   A perceptual illusion in which a stationary point of light, as seen by an observer in a dark room, seems to move.

Balance theory   A hypothesis, developed by Heider, in which it is suggested that people prefer to hold a belief consistent with that of another person whom they respect, and therefore will either change their belief or discredit the other person, in order to achieve a balance.

473

Belief The attribution of a cognition to an object. The statement, "Breast-feeding makes for happier babies" attributes happy babies to the object, breast-feeding. A belief is based more on fact or presumed fact than an attitude, but several beliefs are usually associated with a given attitude.

Bias Any factor in an experiment or study which systematically introduces error.

Catharsis The release of tension or anxiety by any kind of expressive reaction.

Causal relationship A relationship in which one event is not only antecedent to, but the cause of, the occurrence of a second event.

Central traits According to Asch, traits such as "warm" or "cold," which assume the role of essentializing labels and influence the way other traits are interpreted, are central.

Circular reaction A process whereby the emotions of others elicit the same emotions in oneself. This reaction, in turn, serves to intensify the emotions of others.

Classical conditioning A procedure by which a neutral stimulus (such as a bell) becomes strongly associated with a stimulus which can elicit a response (such as food, which will elicit salivation from an animal). By pairing the two stimuli for a period of time, it is possible to condition the organism so that the originally neutral stimulus (the bell) will elicit the same response as the unconditioned stimulus (the food).

Cognition Any mental or thinking process.

Cognitive dissonance An unbalanced and uncomfortable state in which a person holds two conflicting or mutually exclusive ideas. According to Festinger, the person will relieve the dissonance by changing one of the beliefs to make it consistent with the other, or by adding other beliefs which lessen the dissonance.

Competition A contest in which one individual or group is rewarded at the expense of other individuals or groups.

Conformity Behavior and/or attitudes which correspond to the norms, standards, or laws of the larger group or society by acceding to social pressure.

Control group The group in an experiment which is treated in every way the same as the experimental group, except that it is not exposed to the independent variable that is manipulated by the experimenter.

Cooperation An association of people harmoniously working for mutual benefit.

Correctionalist perspective In the study of deviance, the view that people who are deviants are somehow different from "normal" people in their physical, psychological, or moral makeup.

Correlation The corelationship of two variables such that a change in one is associated with a change in the other. Correlations are descriptive statements of relationships; they do not imply a causal direction between variables.

Crowd contagion   Mass imitation in which feelings and/or behavior are spread from one participant in a crowd to another.

Deindividuation   Behavior performed in or with a group in which an individual's identity is overpowered by identification with the group and the sense of individuality is lost.

Dependent variable   The variable in an experiment that is presumed to vary in accordance with the manipulation of the independent variable.

Deviance   Deviance, according to the labeling perspective, is a situation created by groups within a society who make the rules, in which negative sanctions are imposed on some forms of behavior.

Diglossic society   A society in which two or more languages are used.

Distributive justice   The notion, developed by Homans, that people expect rewards to be proportional to their costs and investments in a social exchange.

Ego   According to Freud, that part of the psyche which arbitrates between the demands of the id for gratification and the reality of the external universe; the "I" or self, as distinguished from the id and the superego.

Emergent norm theory   The hypothesis that when a number of unrelated people are faced with an ambiguous situation they become a purposeful crowd when they perceive the emergence of a norm to guide their behavior. For example, one person throws a rock, or shouts epithets at a policeman.

Essentializing label   A label which makes a global statement about a person's entire character. To say someone is shy is not to give him an essentializing label; to say someone is a thief is.

Ethnomethodology   The investigation of the hidden meanings or the "unwritten social script" used in everyday life. The methodology used by ethnomethodologists, in which unwritten social norms are violated, may be described as a demonstration of the ordinary by use of the absurd.

Expectancies   A person's anticipation of future events. This anticipation may be a powerful determinant of present behavior.

Experimental group   In an experiment, the group which is treated in every way the same as the control group except that it is exposed to the independent variable which is manipulated by the experimenter.

Experimental method   A scientific method demonstrating a causal relationship between two variables, in which a control group and an experimental group, random assignment to groups, and a pretest and posttest are integrated into the experiment.

Fear   The emotion of strong agitation in the presence of actual or anticipated pain or danger.

Frustration   The blocking of, or interference with, ongoing goal-directed behavior, or the threat to do so.

Frustration–aggression hypothesis   A hypothesis developed in the late 1930s which holds that frustration is the only cause of aggression. Although current research indicates that there may be other causes of aggression, and that frustration may lead to behavior other than aggression, the theory has generally held up well in research spanning more than thirty-five years.

Group cohesion   A pattern of strong relationships and identification among individuals in a group.

Halo effect   Refers to the phenomenon that if one highly desirable trait is noted in an individual, others are likely to be inferred. Thus, if someone is physically attractive, it is quite likely that other desirable characteristics, such as friendliness or intelligence, will be attributed to the person.

Hypothesis   A proposition that accounts for a set of facts that is subject to verification or proof.

Id   According to Freud, that part of the psyche responsible for the seeking of gratification of pleasurable, instinctive impulses such as sexual release.

Identification   The acceptance of the purposes and values of another as one's own.

Independent variable   The variable manipulated by the experimenter in order to produce a change in another variable (the dependent variable).

Instinct   A behavior said to be caused by a biological predisposition which is innate, unlearned, and complex.

Instrumental conditioning   A procedure in which the organism is trained to respond in a specific way in order to obtain a reward or to terminate or prevent the occurrence of an adversive stimulus.

Interaction   The mutual influence between two or more persons or groups in which the behavior of either one is the stimulus for the behavior of the other.

Internalization   The incorporation as part of oneself of the ideas, practices, and values of others, such that they are seen as internally rather than externally imposed. According to Freud, the superego is formed by internalizing the values of one's parents.

Kinesics   The study of gestures.

Labeling perspective   In the study of deviance, the concept that what is deviant is that which is labeled as deviant by the larger group. (See **Deviance.**)

Legitimacy   The social perception of actions and attitudes as being in accordance with socially recognized principles, laws, or social norms.

Locus of control   In attribution theory, the locus of control is either external, in which the cause of an action is attributed to outside forces and beyond the control of the individual, or internal—willed by the individual and under his control.

Modeling   Imitation of another. This can take the form of imitation of another's behavior, or it may go deeper when the values and beliefs of the person serving as the model are internalized.

Motivation   The impulse in people that stimulates them to act, especially in regard to moving toward or away from other people.

Motive   See **Motivation**.

Oedipal complex   The repressed desire of a male child to have sexual union with his mother. In Freudian theory, this takes the form of a triadic drama between both parents and the child, who overcomes this complex by identifying with and imitating the father (and the male sex role), since this is the only way he can resolve the sexual rivalry with his seemingly omnipotent father.

Operant conditioning The reinforcement or nonreinforcement of an already occurring behavior in order to increase or decrease its occurrence.

Paralanguage Nonverbal vocalizations. These include the inflection and emphasis of verbal statements as well as other nonverbal vocalizations such as a laugh, a sign, or a moan, all of which frequently convey meaning.

Population In statistics, a population is the statistical universe of any group, from whom a sample can be drawn and analyzed in order to generalize to the entire group.

Prejudice Literally, a prejudgment; a negative attitude toward a socially defined group and toward any person who can be identified as a member of that group.

Pretests and posttests An integral part of the strategy of the experimental method, in which a group is tested, exposed to the independent variable, and then retested. If the independent variable has had an effect, there will be a change in score on the posttest.

Primacy effect The phenomenon which is manifested when people attach greater importance to, or greater belief in, information presented first rather than last.

Propinquity Nearness; closeness in regard to space.

Proxemics The study of the use and perception of personal and social space.

Racism According to the U.S. Commission on Civil Rights, "an attitude, action, or institutional structure which subordinates a person because of his or her color." Racism not only has the component of antagonism within it, but also is an attempt to relegate the group to a lower status.

Randomization In the experimental method, the assigning of subjects to the experimental or the control group on the basis of chance to insure the elimination of any selective factor that would introduce bias.

Recency effect The phenomenon which is manifested when people attach greater importance to, or greater belief in, information presented last (most recently) rather than first.

Reliability If an experiment shows the same results run at different times and with different subjects, it is said to be reliable.

Risky shift The tendency of an individual within a group to make decisions which are riskier than the decisions the same individual would make alone.

Sample A number of units selected from a population to represent the whole. If the sample is randomly drawn, its characteristics may be generalized to the population.

Scapegoating The practice of displacing aggression on an out-group that is held responsible for the problems facing the larger group.

Self-awareness The state of being an observer of the self as actor.

Self-concept A person's view of himself and his relative worth.

Self-fulfilling prophecy Descriptive of a process in which a person's belief about what he expects to happen can cause him to act in such a way as to create the conditions by which his expectations may come about.

Semantic differential A scale developed by Osgood, based on the finding that people describe most personality traits along three dimensions: evaluative (good–bad), potency (strong–weak), and activity (active–passive).

Sexism Similar to racism except that the target is women. In both sexism and racism the targets are treated not only as inferior but as children in need of guidance.

Sleeper effect The phenomenon in which the negative source of a message is forgotten over time but the actual message is remembered.

Social facilitation The effect of the presence of others, such that task performance is improved when compared to performance on the same task when alone.

Social learning theory Learning not only by reinforcement but by observation, imitation, and modeling. An individual can learn a new response by watching it being performed by another person.

Socialization The process by which a child learns the "script" of his or her culture. The child gradually becomes sensitive to the pressures and obligations which the social order will impose upon him or her.

Sociometry A measure of group cohesion developed by Moreno. Each individual indicates which members of the group he likes best. By comparing the frequencies, it is possible to construct a sociogram, a diagram that shows one form of group structure.

Status The social position of an individual, indicating his relative standing compared to that of others in the same group.

Stereotype Overgeneralized judgment of an individual or a group, frequently inaccurate and often negative. Stereotypes serve as essentializing labels which serve to denote a trait or traits which members of a group are presumed to share.

Stress Any force which physically and/or psychologically strains the coping mechanisms of an organism.

Subconscious That which is beyond the border of conscious attention, conceived by Freud as influencing, but not apprehended by, personal consciousness.

Superego According to Freud, that part of the psyche which incorporates the moral standards of parents and society. Whereas the id deals with gratification and the ego with rational choice, the superego contains the larger moral code.

Symbolic universe The perception of a moral framework which exists as a reality independent of the individual.

Thanatos From Freudian theory, a death instinct.

Transactional analysis The model developed by Berne for interpreting interpersonal interactions as exchanges which can be categorized as belonging to the ego state of the child, the parent, or the adult.

Type A behavior   A behavior pattern highly correlated with the occurrence of coronary heart disease.

Unconscious   A collective name for any mental activity which is thought to occur and to influence behavior but which is not consciously experienced by the individual.

Validity   Validity exists when a test can be shown to measure that which it is claimed it measures.

Value   A basic principle on which to base moral judgments.

Variable   Any concept which is amenable to measurement.

Zero sum game   Any game (or interaction) in which the gains and losses of the players sum to zero.

Index

481